WITHDRAWN

BURT FRANKLIN: RESEARCH & SOURCE WORKS SERIES
American Classics in History and Social Science 241

MEMOIRS

OF

MARGARET FULLER OSSOLI

Dag^{rtd} by Plumbe   R.Babson & J.Andrews Sc

Margaret Fuller

(MARCHIONESS OSSOLI)

Print^d by Wilson & Daniels

MEMOIRS

OF

MARGARET FULLER OSSOLI

BY

R. W. EMERSON, W. H. CHANNING, AND
J. F. CLARKE

𝔚ith a 𝔓ortrait and an 𝔄ppendix

Only a learned and a manly soul
    I purposed her, that should with even powers
The rock, the spindle, and the shears control
    Of Destiny, and spin her own free hours.
                                BEN JONSON.

Però che ogni diletto nostro e doglia
Sta in sì e nò saper, voler, potere ;
Adunque quel sol può, che col dovere
Ne trae la ragion fuor di sua soglia.

Adunque tu, lettor di queste note,
S' a te vuoi esser buono, e agli altri caro,
Vogli sempre poter quel che tu debbi.
                        LEONARDO DA VINCI.

VOL. I.

BURT FRANKLIN
NEW YORK

PS
2506
A6
1972

Published by LENOX HILL Pub. & Dist. Co. (Burt Franklin)
235 East 44th St., New York, N.Y. 10017
Reprinted: 1972
Printed in the U.S.A.

Burt Franklin: Research and Source Works Series
American Classics in History and Social Science: 241

Library of Congress Cataloging in Publication Data

Ossoli, Sarah Margaret (Fuller) marchesa d', 1810-1850.
  Memoirs of Margaret Fuller Ossoli.

  Reprint of the 1884 ed.
    I. Emerson, Ralph Waldo, 1803-1882. II. Channing, William Henry, 1810-
1884. III. Clarke, James Freeman, 1810-1888.
PS2506.A6 1972   818'.3'09 [B]   72-82356
ISBN 0-8337-1250-0

PREFACE.

THE present edition of my sister's Memoirs appears without change, as it came from the hands of the accomplished editors whose names appear on the title-page. Theirs was a work of love, to diffuse wide a knowledge of my sister's eventful life and noble character; and most lovingly and well has their work been done.

I have, however, while refraining from changes, made some additions to this volume, on my own responsibility, which I trust will enhance its value to the reader. As a frontispiece appears the beautiful engraving of Hicks's portrait of Margaret Fuller, which was painted by him from life during her residence in Rome, only a year or two before her death. It is the only painting in existence which serves to perpetuate her likeness. No daguerreotype, engraving, or portrait, seems, to many of her friends, to present her to the eye just as she remains in their memories; but this is doubtless the most authentic likeness which the public can ever now possess, and will " grow upon " the love and favor of those who attentively study it.

The Appendix contains two articles, published, the one in the New England Historical and Genealogical Register for October, 1859, where a " Genealogy of the Fuller Family " also appears, and the other in the Quarterly Journal of the American Unitarian Association for October, 1859 ; and also some poetical tributes. The historical article first named is inserted as giving some information in reference to the various members of my sister's family, to whom many of the letters in these volumes are addressed. Several of these loved ones — a brother, a sister, a mother — have entered the " spirit land " since these Memoirs first appeared ; and in how few years will all have gone there to rejoin that " great and noble soul," who, reaching first those eternal shores, has by none of us been, or ever can be, forgotten ! I would fain twine their memories, as were their lives, in one wreath together.

This sketch, however, finds its place here chiefly as serving to remove, in some degree, a most unintentional injustice to my father's memory, which has been done by the autobiographical sketch in the first pages of these Memoirs. This conveys an impression that he was stern and exacting, and utterly overlooked the physical health of his daughter by tasking to the utmost her extraordinary powers. My sister never would have published this sketch — which she herself entitled an autobiographical romance — without such modifications as would have shown our father to have been a most judicious and tender one, erring, perhaps, in stimulating too much the rare intellect of his first child, but erring through no lack of love or general good judgment, but as all the educators of his time erred, and as would have harmed none but one possessing a mind so precocious and unusual. This error, too, he saw, and avoided in the education of his other children. He was a man whose memory deserves to be entirely honored, and to perpetuate which Margaret desired to write a memoir of one whom she, each year of life, saw more and more was a person to be deeply loved and respected. I feel that the insertion of this brief record in part accomplishes an object she herself once had in view, and would be entirely in harmony with her own wishes.

The memorial of my sainted mother deserves also a place here. Bearing the same name, this mother and daughter shared also the same pure, noble spirit, and in their separate spheres were alike remarkable and excellent. This brief sketch of the mother's history finds fitting place in her daughter's Memoirs, since both " were lovely and pleasant in their lives," and now are " not divided."

One word only remains to be said. The reader of these Memoirs who desires a thorough knowledge of Margaret Fuller's intellectual life and spiritual character must read, not them alone, but also the volumes of her works which are now, for the first time, published in complete form, and whose ideas deserve, not only to be studied, but embodied in the lives of those who would themselves be true and noble.

ARTHUR B. FULLER.

WATERTOWN, MASS.

TABLE OF CONTENTS

FOR

VOLUME FIRST.

APPENDIX.

YOUTH.

AUTOBIOGRAPHY.

——————

' Aus Morgenduft gewebt und Sonnenklarheit
Der Dichtung Schleir aus der Hand der Wahrheit.'

GOETHE

" The million stars which tremble
O'er the deep mind of dauntless infancy."

TENNYSON.

" Wie leicht ward er dahin getragen,
Was war dem Glücklichen zu schwer !
Wie tanzte vor des Lebens Wagen
Die luftige Begleitung her !
Die Liebe mit dem süssen Lohne,
Das Glück mit seinem gold'nen Kranz,
Der Ruhm mit seiner Sternenkrone,
Die Wahrheit in der Sonne Glanz."

SCHILLER

"What wert thou then? A child most infantine,
  Yet wandering far beyond that innocent age,
  In all but its sweet looks and mien divine ;
  Even then, methought, with the world's tyrant rage
  A patient warfare thy young heart did wage,
  When those soft eyes of scarcely conscious thought
  Some tale, or thine own fancies, would engage
  To overflow with tears, or converse fraught
  With passion o'er their depths its fleeting light had wrought."
                                                    SHELLEY.

  "And I smiled, as one never smiles but once ;
    Then first discovering my own aim's extent,
    Which sought to comprehend the works of God,
    And God himself, and all God's intercourse
    With the human mind."
                                    BROWNING.

1.

YOUTH.

'TIECK, who has embodied so many Runic secrets,
'explained to me what I have often felt toward myself,
'when he tells of the poor changeling, who, turned from
'the door of her adopted home, sat down on a stone and
'so pitied herself that she wept. Yet me also, the wonder-
'ful bird, singing in the wild forest, has tempted on, and
'not in vain.'

Thus wrote Margaret in the noon of life, when looking back through youth to the "dewy dawn of memory." She was the eldest child of Timothy Fuller* and
Margaret Crane,† and was born in Cambridge-Port, Massachusetts, on the 23d of May, 1810.

Among her papers fortunately remains this unfinished
sketch of youth, prepared by her own hand, in 1840, as
the introductory chapter to an autobiographical romance.

PARENTS.

'My father was a lawyer and a politician. He was
'a man largely endowed with that sagacious energy,
'which the state of New England society, for the last half

* See Appendix A.   † See Appendix B.

'century, has been so well fitted to develop. His father
' was a clergyman, settled as pastor in Princeton, Mas-
' sachusetts, within the bounds of whose parish-farm was
' Wachuset.   His means were small, and the great object
' of his ambition was to send his sons to college.   As a
' boy, my father was taught to think only of preparing
' himself for Harvard University, and when there of
' preparing himself for the profession of Law.   As a
' Lawyer, again, the ends constantly presented were to
' work for distinction in the community, and for the
' means of supporting a family.   To be an honored cit-
' izen, and to have a home on earth, were made the great
' aims of existence.   To open the deeper fountains of the
' soul, to regard life here as the prophetic entrance to
' immortality, to develop his spirit to perfection, — mo-
' tives like these had never been suggested to him, either
' by fellow-beings or by outward circumstances.   The
' result was a character, in its social aspect, of quite the
' common sort.   A good son and brother, a kind neigh-
' bor, an active man of business — in all these outward
' relations he was but one of a class, which surrounding
' conditions have made the majority among us.   In the
' more delicate and individual relations, he never ap-
' proached but two mortals, my mother and myself.

   ' His love for my mother was the green spot on
' which he stood apart from the common-places of a
' mere bread-winning, bread-bestowing existence.   She
' was one of those fair and flower-like natures, which
' sometimes spring up even beside the most dusty high-
' ways of life — a creature not to be shaped into a merely
' useful instrument, but bound by one law with the blue
' sky, the dew, and the frolic birds.   Of all persons
' whom I have known, she had in her most of the angelic,

'— of that spontaneous love for every living thing,
'for man, and beast, and tree, which restores the golden
' age.'

DEATH IN THE HOUSE.

'My earliest recollection is of a death, — the death of
'a sister, two years younger than myself. Probably there
'is a sense of childish endearments, such as belong to this
'tie, mingled with that of loss, of wonder, and mystery;
'but these last are prominent in memory. I remember
'coming home and meeting our nursery-maid, her face
'streaming with tears. That strange sight of tears made
'an indelible impression. I realize how little I was of
'stature, in that I looked up to this weeping face; — and
'it has often seemed since, that — full-grown for the life
'of this earth, I have looked up just so, at times of threat-
'ening, of doubt, and distress, and that just so has some
'being of the next higher order of existences looked
'down, aware of a law unknown to me, and tenderly
'commiserating the pain I must endure in emerging from
'my ignorance.

'She took me by the hand and led me into a still and
'dark chamber, — then drew aside the curtain and showed
'me my sister. I see yet that beauty of death! The
'highest achievements of sculpture are only the reminder
'of its severe sweetness. Then I remember the house all
'still and dark, — the people in their black clothes and
'dreary faces, — the scent of the newly-made coffin, —
'my being set up in a chair and detained by a gentle hand
'to hear the clergyman, — the carriages slowly going,
'the procession slowly doling out their steps to the grave.
'But I have no remembrance of what I have since been
'told I did, — insisting, with loud cries, that they should

'not put the body in the ground. I suppose that my emo-
' tion was spent at the time, and so there was nothing to
' fix that moment in my memory.

   ' I did not then, nor do I now, find any beauty in these
' ceremonies.   What had they to do with the sweet play-
' ful child ? Her life and death were alike beautiful, but
' all this sad parade was not.   Thus my first experience
' of life was one of death. She who would have been the
' companion of my life was severed from me, and I was
' left alone.   This has made a vast difference in my lot.
' Her character, if that fair face promised right, would
' have been soft, graceful and lively ; it would have tem-
' pered mine to a gentler and more gradual course.

OVERWORK.

   ' My father, — all whose feelings were now concentred
' on me, — instructed me himself. The effect of this
' was so far good that, not passing through the hands of
' many ignorant and weak persons as so many do at pre-
' paratory schools, I was put at once under discipline of
' considerable severity, and, at the same time, had a more
' than ordinarily high standard presented to me.   My
' father was a man of business, even in literature ; he had
' been a high scholar at college, and was warmly attached
' to all he had learned there, both from the pleasure he
' had derived in the exercise of his faculties and the asso-
' ciated memories of success and good repute.   He was,
' beside, well read in French literature, and in English, a
' Queen Anne's man.   He hoped to make me the heir of
' all he knew, and of as much more as the income of his
' profession enabled him to give me means of acquir-
' ing.   At the very beginning, he made one great mistake,

'more common, it is to be hoped, in the last generation,
'than the warnings of physiologists will permit it to be
'with the next.   He thought to gain time, by bringing
'forward the intellect as early as possible.   Thus I had
'tasks given me, as many and various as the hours would
'allow, and on subjects beyond my age; with the addi-
'tional disadvantage of reciting to him in the evening,
'after he returned from his office.   As he was subject to
'many interruptions, I was often kept up till very late;
'and as he was a severe teacher, both from his habits of
 mind and his ambition for me, my feelings were kept on
'the stretch till the recitations were over.   Thus fre-
'quently, I was sent to bed several hours too late, with
'nerves unnaturally stimulated.   The consequence was a
'premature development of the brain, that made me a
'"youthful prodigy" by day, and by night a victim of
'spectral illusions, nightmare, and somnambulism, which
'at the time prevented the harmonious development of
'my bodily powers and checked my growth, while, later,
'they induced continual headache, weakness and nervous
'affections, of all kinds.   As these again re-acted on the
'brain, giving undue force to every thought and every
'feeling, there was finally produced a state of being both
'too active and too intense, which wasted my constitution,
'and will bring me, — even although I have learned to
'understand and regulate my now morbid temperament,
'— to a premature grave.

   'No one understood this subject of health then.   No
'one knew why this child, already kept up so late, was
 still unwilling to retire.   My aunts cried out upon the
'"spoiled child, the most unreasonable child that ever
'was, — if brother could but open his eyes to see it, — who
'was never willing to go to bed."   They did not know

'that, so soon as the light was taken away, she seemed to
'see colossal faces advancing slowly towards her, the eyes
'dilating, and each feature swelling loathsomely as they
'came, till at last, when they were about to close upon
'her, she started up with a shriek which drove them
'away, but only to return when she lay down again.
'They did not know that, when at last she went to
'sleep, it was to dream of horses trampling over her, and
'to awake once more in fright; or, as she had just read
'in her Virgil, of being among trees that dripped with
'blood, where she walked and walked and could not get
'out, while the blood became a pool and plashed over
'her feet, and rose higher and higher, till soon she
'dreamed it would reach her lips. No wonder the child
'arose and walked in her sleep, moaning all over the
'house, till once, when they heard her, and came and
'waked her, and she told what she had dreamed, her
'father sharply bid her " leave off thinking of such non-
'" sense, or she would be crazy,"— never knowing that
'he was himself the cause of all these horrors of the
'night. Often she dreamed of following to the grave
'the body of her mother, as she had done that of her
'sister, and woke to find the pillow drenched in tears.
'These dreams softened her heart too much, and cast a
'deep shadow over her young days ; for then, and later,
'the life of dreams,— probably because there was in it
'less to distract the mind from its own earnestness,— has
'often seemed to her more real, and been remembered
'with more interest, than that of waking hours.

    'Poor child ! Far remote in time, in thought, from
'that period, I look back on these glooms and terrors,
'wherein I was enveloped, and perceive that I had no
'natural childhood.'

BOOKS.

'Thus passed my first years. My mother was in deli-
'cate health, and much absorbed in the care of her
'younger children. In the house was neither dog nor
'bird, nor any graceful animated form of existence. I
'saw no persons who took my fancy, and real life offered
'no attraction. Thus my already over-excited mind
'found no relief from without, and was driven for refuge
'from itself to the world of books. I was taught Latin
'and English grammar at the same time, and began to
'read Latin at six years old, after which, for some years,
'I read it daily. In this branch of study, first by my
'father, and afterwards by a tutor, I was trained to quite
'a high degree of precision. I was expected to under-
'stand the mechanism of the language thoroughly, and in
'translating to give the thoughts in as few well-arranged
'words as possible, and without breaks or hesitation,—
'for with these my father had absolutely no patience.

'Indeed, he demanded accuracy and clearness in every-
'thing: you must not speak, unless you can make your
'meaning perfectly intelligible to the person addressed;
'must not express a thought, unless you can give a reason
'for it, if required; must not make a statement, unless
'sure of all particulars — such were his rules. "But,"
'"if," "unless," "I am mistaken," and "it may be
'"so," were words and phrases excluded from the prov-
'ince where he held sway. Trained to great dexterity in
'artificial methods, accurate, ready, with entire com-
'mand of his resources, he had no belief in minds that
'listen, wait, and receive. He had no conception of the
'subtle and indirect motions of imagination and feeling.
'His influence on me was great, and opposed to the nat-

'ural unfolding of my character, which was fervent, of
'strong grasp, and disposed to infatuation, and self-forget-
'fulness. He made the common prose world so present
'to me, that my natural bias was controlled. I did not
'go mad, as many would do, at being continually roused
'from my dreams. I had too much strength to be
'crushed,— and since I must put on the fetters, could not
'submit to let them impede my motions. My own world
'sank deep within, away from the surface of my life;
'in what I did and said I learned to have reference to
'other minds. But my true life was only the dearer
'that it was secluded and veiled over by a thick curtain
'of available intellect, and that coarse, but wearable
stuff woven by the ages,— Common Sense.

'In accordance with this discipline in heroic common
sense, was the influence of those great Romans, whose
'thoughts and lives were my daily food during those plas-
'tic years. The genius of Rome displayed itself in Char-
'acter, and scarcely needed an occasional wave of the
'torch of thought to show its lineaments, so marble strong
'they gleamed in every light. Who, that has lived with
'those men, but admires the plain force of fact, of
'thought passed into action? They take up things
'with their naked hands. There is just the man,
'and the block he casts before you, — no divinity, no
'demon, no unfulfilled aim, but just the man and Rome,
'and what he did for Rome. Everything turns your
'attention to what a man can become, not by yielding
'himself freely to impressions, not by letting nature play
'freely through him, but by a single thought, an earnest
'purpose, an indomitable will, by hardihood, self-com-
'mand, and force of expression. Architecture was the art
'in which Rome excelled, and this corresponds with the

feeling these men of Rome excite. They did not grow,
'—-they built themselves up, or were built up by the
'fate of Rome, as a temple for Jupiter Stator. The
' ruined Roman sits among the ruins; he flies to no green
' garden; he does not look to heaven; if his intent is
' defeated, if he is less than he meant to be, he lives no
' more. The names which end in "*us*," seem to speak
' with lyric cadence. That measured cadence,— that
' tramp and march,— which are not stilted, because they
' indicate real force, yet which seem so when compared
' with any other language,— make Latin a study in itself
' of mighty influence. The language alone, without the
' literature, would give one the *thought* of Rome. Man
' present in nature, commanding nature too sternly to be
' inspired by it, standing like the rock amid the sea, or
' moving like the fire over the land, either impassive, or
' irresistible; knowing not the soft mediums or fine flights
' of life, but by the force which he expresses, piercing to
' the centre.

' We are never better understood than when we speak
' of a " Roman virtue," a " Roman outline." There is
' somewhat indefinite, somewhat yet unfulfilled in the
' thought of Greece, of Spain, of modern Italy; but
' ROME ! it stands by itself, a clear Word. The power of
' will, the dignity of a fixed purpose is what it utters.
' Every Roman was an emperor. It is well that the
' infallible church should have been founded on this rock,
' that the presumptuous Peter should hold the keys, as
' the conquering Jove did before his thunderbolts, to be
' seen of all the world. The Apollo tends flocks with
· Admetus; Christ teaches by the lonely lake, or plucks
' wheat as he wanders through the fields some Sabbath
' morning. They never come to this stronghold; they

'could not have breathed freely where all became stone
'as soon as spoken, where divine youth found no horizon
'for its all-promising glance, but every thought put on,
'before it dared issue to the day in action, its *toga*
'*virilis.*

'Suckled by this wolf, man gains a different complex-
'ion from that which is fed by the Greek honey.   He
'takes a noble bronze in camps and battle-fields; the
'wrinkles of council well beseem his brow, and the eye
'cuts its way like the sword.   The Eagle should never
'have been used as a symbol by any other nation: it
'belonged to Rome.

'The history of Rome abides in mind, of course, more
'than the literature.   It was degeneracy for a Roman to
'use the pen; his life was in the day.   The "vaunting"
'of Rome, like that of the North American Indians, is her
'proper literature.   A man rises; he tells who he is, and
'what he has done; he speaks of his country and her
'brave men; he knows that a conquering god is there,
'whose agent is his own right hand; and he should end
'like the Indian, "I have no more to say."

'It never shocks us that the Roman is self-conscious.
'One wants no universal truths from him, no philosophy,
'no creation, but only his life, his Roman life felt in every
'pulse, realized in every gesture.   The universal heaven
'takes in the Roman only to make us feel his individual-
'ity the more.   The Will, the Resolve of Man ! — it has
'been expressed, — fully expressed !

'I steadily loved this ideal in my childhood, and this
'is the cause, probably, why I have always felt that
'man must know how to stand firm on the ground,
'before he can fly.   In vain for me are men more, if
they are less, than Romans.   Dante was far greater

'than any Roman, yet I feel he was right to take the
'Mantuan as his guide through hell, and to heaven.

'Horace was a great deal to me then, and is so still.
'Though his words do not abide in memory, his pres-
'ence does : serene, courtly, of darting hazel eye, a self-
'sufficient grace, and an appreciation of the world of
'stern realities, sometimes pathetic, never tragic.   He is
'the natural man of the world; he is what he ought to
'be, and his darts never fail of their aim.   There is a
'perfume and raciness, too, which makes life a banquet,
'where the wit sparkles no less that the viands were
'bought with blood.

'Ovid gave me not Rome, nor himself, but a view into
'the enchanted gardens of the Greek mythology.   This
'path I followed, have been following ever since; and
'now, life half over, it seems to me, as in my child-
'hood, that every thought of which man is suscep-
'tible, is intimated there.   In those young years, indeed,
'I did not see what I now see, but loved to creep from
'amid the Roman pikes to lie beneath this great vine,
'and see the smiling and serene shapes go by, woven
'from the finest fibres of all the elements.   I knew not
'why, at that time,— but I loved to get away from the
'hum of the forum, and the mailed clang of Roman
'speech, to these shifting shows of nature, these Gods
'and Nymphs born of the sunbeam, the wave, the
'shadows on the hill.

'As with Rome I antedated the world of deeds, so I
'lived in those Greek forms the true faith of a refined
'and intense childhood.   So great was the force of real-
'ity with which these forms impressed me, that I prayed
'earnestly for a sign,— that it would lighten in some
particular region of the heavens, or that I might find a

'bunch of grapes in the path, when I went forth in the
'morning. But no sign was given, and I was left a
'waif stranded upon the shores of modern life!

'Of the Greek language, I knew only enough to feel
'that the sounds told the same story as the mythology; —
'that the law of life in that land was beauty, as in
'Rome it was a stern composure. I wish I had learned
'as much of Greece as of Rome,— so freely does the
'mind play in her sunny waters, where there is no chill,
'and the restraint is from within out; for these Greeks,
'in an atmosphere of ample grace, could not be impetu-
'ous, or stern, but loved moderation as equable life
'always must, for it is the law of beauty.

'With these books I passed my days. The great
'amount of study exacted of me soon ceased to be a
'burden, and reading became a habit and a passion.
'The force of feeling, which, under other circumstances,
'might have ripened thought, was turned to learn the
'thoughts of others. This was not a tame state, for the
'energies brought out by rapid acquisition gave glow
'enough. I thought with rapture of the all-accom-
'plished man, him of the many talents, wide resources,
'clear sight, and omnipotent will. A Cæsar seemed
'great enough. I did not then know that such men
'impoverish the treasury to build the palace. I kept
'their statues as belonging to the hall of my ancestors,
'and loved to conquer obstacles, and fed my youth and
'strength for their sake.

'Still, though this bias was so great that in earliest
'years I learned, in these ways, how the world takes hold
'of a powerful nature, I had yet other experiences. None
'of these were deeper than what I found in the happiest

haunt of my childish years,— our little garden. Our
'house, though comfortable, was very ugly, and in a
'neighborhood which I detested,— every dwelling and its
'appurtenances having a *mesquin* and huddled look. I
'liked nothing about us except the tall graceful elms
'before the house, and the dear little garden behind.
'Our back door opened on a high flight of steps, by
'which I went down to a green plot, much injured in
'my ambitious eyes by the presence of the pump and
'tool-house. This opened into a little garden, full of
'choice flowers and fruit-trees, which was my mother's
'delight, and was carefully kept. Here I felt at home.
'A gate opened thence into the fields,— a wooden gate
'made of boards, in a high, unpainted board wall, and
embowered in the clematis creeper. This gate I used
'to open to see the sunset heaven; beyond this black
'frame I did not step, for I liked to look at the deep gold
'behind it. How exquisitely happy I was in its beauty,
'and how I loved the silvery wreaths of my protecting
'vine! I never would pluck one of its flowers at that
'time, I was so jealous of its beauty, but often since I
'carry off wreaths of it from the wild-wood, and it
'stands in nature to my mind as the emblem of domestic
'love.

'Of late I have thankfully felt what I owe to that
'garden, where the best hours of my lonely childhood
'were spent. Within the house everything was socially
'utilitarian; my books told of a proud world, but in
'another temper were the teachings of the little garden.
'There my thoughts could lie callow in the nest, and
'only be fed and kept warm, not called to fly or sing
'before the time. I loved to gaze on the roses, the vio-
'lets, the lilies, the pinks; my mother's hand had planted

'them, and they bloomed for me. I culled the most
'beautiful. I looked at them on every side. I kissed
'them, I pressed them to my bosom with passionate
'emotions, such as I have never dared express to any
'human being. An ambition swelled my heart to be as
'beautiful, as perfect as they. I have not kept my
'vow. Yet, forgive, ye wild asters, which gleam so
'sadly amid the fading grass; forgive me, ye golden
'autumn flowers, which so strive to reflect the glories
'of the departing distant sun; and ye silvery flowers,
'whose moonlight eyes I knew so well, forgive! Living
'and blooming in your unchecked law, ye know noth-
'ing of the blights, the distortions, which beset the
'human being; and which at such hours it would seem
'that no glories of free agency could ever repay!

'There was, in the house, no apartment appropriated
'to the purpose of a library, but there was in my father's
'room a large closet filled with books, and to these I had
'free access when the task-work of the day was done.
'Its window overlooked wide fields, gentle slopes, a rich
'and smiling country, whose aspect pleased without
'much occupying the eye, while a range of blue hills,
'rising at about twelve miles distance, allured to reverie.
'"Distant mountains," says Tieck, "excite the fancy, for
'"beyond them we place the scene of our Paradise."
'Thus, in the poems of fairy adventure, we climb the
'rocky barrier, pass fearless its dragon caves, and dark
'pine forests, and find the scene of enchantment in the
'vale behind. My hopes were never so definite, but my
'eye was constantly allured to that distant blue range,
'and I would sit, lost in fancies, till tears fell on my
cheek. I loved this sadness; but only in later years,

'when the realities of life had taught me moderation,
'did the passionate emotions excited by seeing them
'again teach how glorious were the hopes that swelled
'my heart while gazing on them in those early days.

'Melancholy attends on the best joys of a merely ideal
'life, else I should call most happy the hours in the gar-
'den, the hours in the book closet. Here were the best
'French writers of the last century; for my father had
'been more than half a Jacobin, in the time when the
'French Republic cast its glare of promise over the
'world. Here, too, were the Queen Anne authors, his
'models, and the English novelists; but among them
'I found none that charmed me. Smollett, Fielding,
'and the like, deal too broadly with the coarse actuali-
'ties of life. The best of their men and women — so
'merely natural, with the nature found every day — dc
'not meet our hopes. Sometimes the simple picture
'warm with life and the light of the common sun, can-
'not fail to charm, — as in the wedded love of Fielding's
'Amelia, — but it is at a later day, when the mind is
'trained to comparison, that we learn to prize excellence
'like this as it deserves. Early youth is prince-like:
'it will bend only to "the king, my father." Various
'kinds of excellence please, and leave their impression,
'but the most commanding, alone, is duly acknowledged
'at that all-exacting age.

'Three great authors it was my fortune to meet at
'this important period, — all, though of unequal, yet
'congenial powers, — all of rich and wide, rather than
'aspiring genius, — all free to the extent of the horizon
'their eye took in, — all fresh with impulse, racy with
'experience; never to be lost sight of, or superseded, but
'always to be apprehended more and more.

' Ever memorable is the day on which I first took ?
' volume of SHAKSPEARE in my hand to read.   It was on
' a Sunday.

'— This day was punctiliously set apart in our house
' We had family prayers, for which there was no time or
' other days.   Our dinners were different, and our clothes
' We went to church.   My father put some limitations
' on my reading, but — bless him for the gentleness which
' has left me a pleasant feeling for the day ! — he did not
' prescribe what was, but only what was *not*, to be done.
' And the liberty this left was a large one.   " You must
' "not read a novel, or a play;" but all other · books,
' the worst, or the best, were open to me.   The distinc-
' tion was merely technical.   The day was pleasing to
' me, as relieving me from the routine of tasks and reci-
' tations; it gave me freer play than usual, and there
' were fewer things occurred in its course, which
' reminded me of the divisions of time; still the church-
' going, where I heard nothing that had any connection
' with my inward life, and these rules, gave me asso-
' ciations with the day of empty formalities, and arbi-
' trary restrictions; but though the forbidden book or
' walk always seemed more charming then, I was sel-
' dom tempted to disobey. —

' This Sunday — I was only eight years old — I took
' from the book-shelf a volume lettered SHAKSPEARE.   It
' was not the first time I had looked at it, but before I
' had been deterred from attempting to read, by the
' broken appearance along the page, and preferred
' smooth narrative.   But this time I held in my hand
' " Romeo and Juliet" long enough to get my eye fast-
' ened to the page.   It was a cold winter afternoon.   I
' took the book to the parlor fire, and had there been

seated an hour or two, when my father looked up and
'asked what I was reading so intently. "Shakspeare,"
'replied the child, merely raising her eye from the page.
'"Shakspeare,— that won't do; that's no book for Sun-
'"day; go put it away and take another." I went as
'I was bid, but took no other. Returning to my seat,
'the unfinished story, the personages to whom I was but
'just introduced, thronged and burnt my brain. I could
'not bear it long; such a lure it was impossible to resist.
'I went and brought the book again. There were sev-
'eral guests present, and I had got half through the
'play before I again attracted attention. "What is that
'"child about that she don't hear a word that's said
'"to her?" quoth my aunt. "What are you read-
'"ing?" said my father. "Shakspeare" was again
'the reply, in a clear, though somewhat impatient, tone.
'"How?" said my father angrily, — then restraining
'himself before his guests, — "Give me the book and
'"go directly to bed."

' Into my little room no care of his anger followed me.
'Alone, in the dark, I thought only of the scene placed
'by the poet before my eye, where the free flow of life,
'sudden and graceful dialogue, and forms, whether gro-
'tesque or fair, seen in the broad lustre of his imagina-
'tion, gave just what I wanted, and brought home the
'life I seemed born to live. My fancies swarmed like
'bees, as I contrived the rest of the story; — what all
'would do, what say, where go. My confinement tor-
'tured me. I could not go forth from this prison to ask
'after these friends; I could not make my pillow of the
'dreams about them which yet I could not forbear to
'frame. Thus was I absorbed when my father entered.
He felt it right, before going to rest, to reason with me

'about my disobedience, shown in a way, as he consid<
'ered, so insolent. I listened, but could not feel inter-
'ested in what he said, nor turn my mind from what
'engaged it. He went away really grieved at my im-
'penitence, and quite at a loss to understand conduct
'in me so unusual.

   '— Often since I have seen the same misunderstand-
'ing between parent and child, — the parent thrusting
'the morale, the discipline, of life upon the child, when
'just engrossed by some game of real importance and
'great leadings to it. That is only a wooden horse
'to the father, — the child was careering to distant
'scenes of conquest and crusade, through a country of
'elsewhere unimagined beauty. None but poets remem-
'ber their youth; but the father who does not retain
'poetical apprehension of the world, free and splendid
'as it stretches out before the child, who cannot read
'his natural history, and follow out its intimations with
'reverence, must be a tyrant in his home, and the purest
'intentions will not prevent his doing much to cramp
'him. Each new child is a new Thought, and has
'bearings and discernings, which the Thoughts older in
'date know not yet, but must learn. —

   'My attention thus fixed on Shakspeare, I returned
'to him at every hour I could command. Here was a
'counterpoise to my Romans, still more forcible than
'the little garden. My author could read the Roman
'nature too, — read it in the sternness of Coriolanus,
'and in the varied wealth of Cæsar. But he viewed
'these men of will as only one kind of men; he kept
'them in their place, and I found that he, who could
'understand the Roman, yet expressed in Hamlet a
deeper thought.

'In CERVANTES, I found far less productive talent, —
'indeed, a far less powerful genius, — but the same wide
'wisdom, a discernment piercing the shows and sym-
'bols of existence, yet rejoicing in them all, both for
'their own life, and as signs of the unseen reality. Not
'that Cervantes philosophized, — his genius was too
'deeply philosophical for that; he took things as they
'came before him, and saw their actual relations and
'bearings. Thus the work he produced was of deep
'meaning, though he might never have expressed that
'meaning to himself. It was left implied in the whole.
'A Coleridge comes and calls Don Quixote the pure
'Reason, and Sancho the Understanding. Cervantes
'made no such distinctions in his own mind; but he
'had seen and suffered enough to bring out all his
'faculties, and to make him comprehend the higher as
'well as the lower part of our nature. Sancho is too
'amusing and sagacious to be contemptible; the Don
'too noble and clear-sighted towards absolute truth, to
'be ridiculous. And we are pleased to see manifested
'in this way, how the lower must follow and serve the
'higher, despite its jeering mistrust and the stubborn
'realities which break up the plans of this pure-minded
'champion.

    'The effect produced on the mind is nowise that
'described by Byron : —

      " Cervantes smiled Spain's chivalry away," &c.

'On the contrary, who is not conscious of a sincere rev-
'erence for the Don, prancing forth on his gaunt steed?
'Who would not rather be he than any of the persons
'who laugh at him? — Yet the one we would wish to

'be is thyself, Cervantes, unconquerable spirit! gaining
'flavor and color like wine from every change, while
'being carried round the world; in whose eye the serene
'sagacious laughter could not be dimmed by poverty,
'slavery, or unsuccessful authorship. Thou art to us
'still more the Man, though less the Genius, than Shak-
'speare; thou dost not evade our sight, but, holding the
'lamp to thine own magic shows, dost enjoy them with
'us.

  · 'My third friend was MOLIÉRE, one very much lower,
'both in range and depth, than the others, but, as far as
'he goes, or the same character. Nothing secluded or par-
'tial is there about his genius,— a man of the world, and
'a man by himself, as he is. It was, indeed, only the
'poor social world of Paris that he saw, but he viewed
'it from the firm foundations of his manhood, and every
'lightest laugh rings from a clear perception, and teaches
'life anew.

  'These men were all alike in this,— they loved the
'*natural history* of man. Not what he should be, but
'what he is, was the favorite subject of their thought.
'Whenever a noble leading opened to the eye new paths
'of light, they rejoiced; but it was never fancy, but
'always fact, that inspired them. They loved a thorough
'penetration of the murkiest dens, and most tangled paths
'of nature; they did not spin from the desires of their
'own special natures, but reconstructed the world from
'materials which they collected on every side. Thus
'their influence upon me was not to prompt me to follow
out thought in myself so much as to detect it every-
'where, for each of these men is not only a nature, but
'a happy interpreter of many natures. They taught me
to distrust all invention which is not based on a wide

'experience. Perhaps, too, they taught me to overvalue
'an outward experience at the expense of inward
'growth; but all this I did not appreciate till later.

'It will be seen that my youth was not unfriended,
'since those great minds came to me in kindness. A
'moment of action in one's self, however, is worth an
'age of apprehension through others; not that our deeds
'are better, but that they produce a renewal of our being.
'I have had more productive moments and of deeper joy,
'but never hours of more tranquil pleasure than those in
'which these demi-gods visited me,— and with a smile
'so familiar, that I imagined the world to be full of such.
'They did me good, for by them a standard was early
'given of sight and thought, from which I could never
'go back, and beneath which I cannot suffer patiently
'my own life or that of any friend to fall. They did me
'harm, too, for the child fed with meat instead of milk
'becomes too soon mature. Expectations and desires
'were thus early raised, after which I must long toil
'before they can be realized. How poor the scene
'around, how tame one's own existence, how meagre and
'faint every power, with these beings in my mind!
'Often I must cast them quite aside in order to grow in
'my small way, and not sink into despair. Certainly I
'do not wish that instead of these masters I had read
'baby books, written down to children, and with such
'ignorant dulness that they blunt the senses and corrupt
the tastes of the still plastic human being. But I do wish
that I had read no books at all till later,— that I had
lived with toys, and played in the open air. Children
should not cull the fruits of reflection and observation
'early, but expand in the sun, and let thoughts come to
'them. They should not through books antedate their

'actual experiences, but should take them gradually, as
'sympathy and interpretation are needed.   With me,
'much of life was devoured in the bud.

FIRST FRIEND.

'For a few months, this bookish and solitary life was
'invaded by interest in a living, breathing figure.   At
'church, I used to look around with a feeling of coldness
'and disdain, which, though I now well understand its
'causes, seems to my wiser mind as odious as it was
'unnatural.   The puny child sought everywhere for
'the Roman or Shakspeare figures, and she was met
'by the shrewd, honest eye, the homely decency, or the
'smartness of a New England village on Sunday.   There
'was beauty, but I could not see it then; it was not of
'the kind I longed for.   In the next pew sat a family
'who were my especial aversion.   There were five
'daughters, the eldest not above four-and-twenty,— yet
'they had the old fairy, knowing look, hard, dry, dwarfed,
'strangers to the All-Fair,— were working-day residents
'in this beautiful planet.   They looked as if their
'thoughts had never strayed beyond the jobs of the day,
'and they were glad of it.   Their mother was one of
'those shrunken, faded patterns of woman who have
'never done anything to keep smooth the cheek and
'dignify the brow.   The father had a Scotch look of
'shrewd narrowness, and entire self-complacency.   I
'could not endure this family, whose existence contra-
'dicted all my visions; yet I could not forbear looking
'at them.

'As my eye one day was ranging about with its
accustomed coldness, and the proudly foolish sense of
being in a shroud of thoughts that were not their

thoughts, it was arrested by a face most fair, and well-
'known as it seemed at first glance,— for surely I had
'met her before and waited for her long. But soon I
'saw that she was a new apparition foreign to that scene,
'if not to me. Her dress,— the arrangement of her hair,
'which had the graceful pliancy of races highly cultiva-
'ted for long,— the intelligent and full picture of her eye,
'whose reserve was in its self-possession, not in timidity,
'— all combined to make up a whole impression, which,
'though too young to understand, I was well prepared
'to feel.

'How wearisome now appears that thorough-bred
'*millefleur* beauty, the distilled result of ages of Euro-
'pean culture! Give me rather the wild heath on the
'lonely hill-side, than such a rose-tree from the daintily
'clipped garden. But, then, I had but tasted the cup,
'and knew not how little it could satisfy; more, more,
'was all my cry; continued through years, till I had
'been at the very fountain. Indeed, it was a ruby-red,
'a perfumed draught, and I need not abuse the wine
'because I prefer water, but merely say I have had
'enough of it. Then, the first sight, the first knowledge
'of such a person was intoxication.

'She was an English lady, who, by a singular chance,
'was cast upon this region for a few months. Elegant
'and captivating, her every look and gesture was tuned
'to a different pitch from anything I had ever known.
'She was in various ways "accomplished," as it is
'called, though to what degree I cannot now judge.
'She painted in oils; — I had never before seen any one
'use the brush, and days would not have been too long
'for me to watch the pictures growing beneath her hand.
'She played the harp; and its tones are still to me the

'heralds of the promised land I saw before me then.
She rose, she looked, she spoke ; and the gentle sway-
'ing motion she made all through life has gladdened
'memory, as the stream does the woods and meadows.

   ' As she was often at the house of one of our neighbors,
'and afterwards at our own, my thoughts were fixed on
'her with all the force of my nature. It was my first real
'interest in my kind, and it engrossed me wholly. I had
'seen her,— I should see her,— and my mind lay steeped
'in the visions that flowed from this source. My task-
'work I went through with, as I have done on similar
'occasions all my life, aided by pride that could not bear
'to fail, or be questioned. Could I cease from doing
'the work of the day, and hear the reason sneeringly
'given,—" Her head is so completely taken up with ——
'"that she can do nothing"? Impossible.

   ' Should the first love be blighted, they say, the mind
'loses its sense of eternity. All forms of existence seem
'fragile, the prison of time real, for a god is dead.
'Equally true is this of friendship. I thank Heaven that
'this first feeling was permitted its free flow. The years
'that lay between the woman and the girl only brought
'her beauty into perspective, and enabled me to see her
'as I did the mountains from my window, and made her
'presence to me a gate of Paradise. That which she
'was, that which she brought, that which she might
'have brought, were mine, and over a whole region of
'new life I ruled proprietor of the soil in my own right.

   ' Her mind was sufficiently unoccupied to delight in
'my warm devotion. She could not know what it was
'to me, but the light cast by the flame through so delicate
a vase cheered and charmed her   All who saw admired
her in their way ; but she would lightly turn her head

'from their hard or oppressive looks, and fix a glance
'of full-eyed sweetness on the child, who, from a dis-
'tance, watched all her looks and motions. She did not
'say much to me — not much to any one; she spoke in
'her whole being rather than by chosen words. Indeed,
'her proper speech was dance or song, and what was less
'expressive did not greatly interest her. But she saw
'much, having in its perfection the woman's delicate
'sense for sympathies and attractions. We walked in
'the fields, alone. Though others were present, her eyes
'were gliding over all the field and plain for the objects
'of beauty to which she was of kin. She was not cold
'to her seeming companions; a sweet courtesy satisfied
'them, but it hung about her like her mantle that she
'wore without thinking of it; her thoughts were free, for
'these civilized beings can really live two lives at the
'same moment. With them she seemed to be, but her
'hand was given to the child at her side; others did not
'observe me, but to her I was the only human presence.
'Like a guardian spirit she led me through the fields and
'groves, and every tree, every bird greeted me, and said,
'what I felt, "She is the first angel of your life."

'One time I had been passing the afternoon with her.
'She had been playing to me on the harp, and I sat lis-
'tening in happiness almost unbearable. Some guests
'were announced. She went into another room to
'receive them, and I took up her book. It was Guy
'Mannering, then lately published, and the first of
'Scott's novels I had ever seen. I opened where her
'mark lay, and read merely with the feeling of continu-
'ing our mutual existence by passing my eyes over the
same page where hers had been. It was the description
of the rocks on the sea-coast where the little Harry

'Bertram was lost. I had never seen such places, and
'my mind was vividly stirred to imagine them. The
'scene rose before me, very unlike reality, doubtless, but
'majestic and wild. I was the little Harry Bertram, and
'had lost her,— all I had to lose,— and sought her
'vainly in long dark caves that had no end, plashing
'through the water; while the crags beetled above,
'threatening to fall and crush the poor child. Absorbed
'in the painful vision, tears rolled down my cheeks.
'Just then she entered with light step, and full-beaming
'eye. When she saw me thus, a soft cloud stole over
'her face, and clothed every feature with a lovelier ten-
'derness than I had seen there before. She did not ques-
'tion, but fixed on me inquiring looks of beautiful love.
'I laid my head against her shoulder and wept,— dimly
'feeling that I must lose her and all,— all who spoke to
'me of the same things,— that the cold wave must rush
over me. She waited till my tears were spent, then
'rising, took from a little box a bunch of golden ama-
'ranths or everlasting flowers, and gave them to me.
'They were very fragrant. "They came," she said,
'" from Madeira." These flowers stayed with me seven-
'teen years. " Madeira " seemed to me the fortunate isle,
'apart in the blue ocean from all of ill or dread. When-
'ever I saw a sail passing in the distance,— if it bore
'itself with fulness of beautiful certainty, — I felt that it
'was going to Madeira. Those thoughts are all gone
'now. No Madeira exists for me now,— no fortunate
'purple isle,— and all these hopes and fancies are lifted
'from the sea into the sky. Yet I thank the charms that
'fixed them here so long,— fixed them till perfumes like
'those of the golden flowers were drawn from the earth,
teaching me to know my birth-place.

'I can tell little else of this time, — indeed, I remember
'little, except the state of feeling in which I lived.　For
'I *lived*, and when this is the case, there is little to tell in
'the form of thought.　We meet — at least those who
'are true to their instincts meet — a succession of per-
'sons through our lives, all of whom have some pecu-
'liar errand to us.　There is an outer circle, whose exist-
'ence we perceive, but with whom we stand in no real
'relation.　They tell us the news, they act on us in the
'offices of society, they show us kindness and aversion;
'but their influence does not penetrate; we are nothing
'to them, nor they to us, except as a part of the world's
'furniture.　Another circle, within this, are dear and near
'to us.　We know them and of what kind they are.
'They are to us not mere facts, but intelligible thoughts
'of the divine mind.　We like to see how they are
'unfolded; we like to meet them and part from them; we
'like their action upon us and the pause that succeeds
'and enables us to appreciate its quality.　Often we
'leave them on our path, and return no more, but we
'bear them in our memory, tales which have been told,
'and whose meaning has been felt.

'But yet a nearer group there are, beings born under
'the same star, and bound with us in a common destiny.
'These are not mere acquaintances, mere friends, but,
'when we meet, are sharers of our very existence.　There
'is no separation ; the same thought is given at the same
'moment to both, — indeed, it is born of the meeting, and
'would not otherwise have been called into existence at
'all.　These not only know themselves more, but *are*
'more for having met, and regions of their being, which
'would else have laid sealed in cold obstruction, burst into
'leaf and bloom and song.

'The times of these meetings are fated, nor will either
'party be able ever to meet any other person in the same
'way. Both seem to rise at a glance into that part of
'the heavens where the word can be spoken, by which
'they are revealed to one another and to themselves.
'The step in being thus gained, can never be lost, nor can
'it be re-trod; for neither party will be again what the
'other wants. They are no longer fit to interchange
'mutual influence, for they do not really need it, and if
'they think they do, it is because they weakly pine after
'a past pleasure.

'To this inmost circle of relations but few are admit-
'ted, because some prejudice or lack of courage has pre-
'vented the many from listening to their instincts the
'first time they manifested themselves. If the voice is
'once disregarded it becomes fainter each time, till, at
'last, it is wholly silenced, and the man lives in this
'world, a stranger to its real life, deluded like the maniac
'who fancies he has attained his throne, while in real-
'ity he is on a bed of musty straw. Yet, if the voice
'finds a listener and servant the first time of speaking, it
'is encouraged to more and more clearness. Thus it
'was with me,— from no merit of mine, but because I
'had the good fortune to be free enough to yield to my
'impressions. Common ties had not bound me; there
'were no traditionary notions in my mind; I believed in
'nothing merely because others believed in it; I had
'taken no feelings on trust. Thus my mind was open to
'their sway.

'This woman came to me, a star from the east, a
'morning star, and I worshipped her. She too was
'elevated by that worship, and her fairest self called out.
To the mind she brought assurance that there was a

region congenial with its tendencies and tastes, a region
of elegant culture and intercourse, whose object, fulfilled
'or not, was to gratify the sense of beauty, not the mere
'utilities of life. In our relation she was lifted to the top
'of her being. She had known many celebrities, had
'roused to passionate desire many hearts, and became
'afterwards a wife; but I do not believe she ever more
'truly realized her best self than towards the lonely child
'whose heaven she was, whose eye she met, and whose
'possibilities she predicted. "He raised me," said a
'woman inspired by love, "upon the pedestal of his own
'"high thoughts, and wings came at once, but I did not
'"fly away. I stood there with downcast eyes worthy
'"of his love, for he had made me so."

'Thus we do always for those who inspire us to ex-
'pect from them the best. That which they are able to
'be, they become, because we demand it of them. "We
'"expect the impossible — and find it."

'My English friend went across the sea. She passed
'into her former life, and into ties that engrossed her
'days. But she has never ceased to think of me. Her
'thoughts turn forcibly back to the child who was to her
'all she saw of the really New World. On the promised
'coasts she had found only cities, careful men and women,
'the aims and habits of ordinary life in her own land,
'without that elegant culture which she, probably, over-
'estimated, because it was her home. But in the mind of
'the child she found the fresh prairie, the untrodden for-
'ests for which she had longed. I saw in her the storied
'castles, the fair stately parks and the wind laden with
'tones from the past, which I desired to know. We wrote
'to one another for many years; — her shallow and delicate epistles did not disenchant me, nor did she fail to

' see something of the old poetry in my rude characters
' and stammering speech. But we must never meet again.

  ' When this friend was withdrawn I fell into a pro-
' found depression. I knew not how to exert myself, but
' lay bound hand and foot. Melancholy enfolded me in
' an atmosphere, as joy had done. This suffering, too,
' was out of the gradual and natural course. Those who
' are really children could not know such love, or feel
' such sorrow. "I am to blame," said my father, "in
' " keeping her at home so long merely to please myself.
' " She needs to be with other girls, needs play and vari-
' " ety. She does not seem to me really sick, but dull
' " rather. She eats nothing, you say. I see she grows
' " thin. She ought to change the scene."

  ' I was indeed *dull*. The books, the garden, had lost
' all charm. I had the excuse of headache, constantly,
' for not attending to my lessons. The light of life was
' set, and every leaf was withered. At such an early age
' there are no back or side scenes where the mind, wea-
' ry and sorrowful, may retreat. Older, we realize the
' width of the world more, and it is not easy to despair
' on any point. The effort at thought to which we are
' compelled relieves and affords a dreary retreat, like
' hiding in a brick-kiln till the shower be over. But then all
' joy seemed to have departed with my friend, and the
' emptiness of our house stood revealed. This I had not felt
' while I every day expected to see or had seen her, or
' annoyance and dulness were unnoticed or swallowed
' up in the one thought that clothed my days with beauty.
' But now she was gone, and I was roused from habits
' of reading or reverie to feel the fiery temper of the
' soul, and to learn that it must have vent, that it would
' not be pacified by shadows, neither meet without con-

'suming what lay around it. I avoided the table as much
'as possible, took long walks and lay in bed, or on the
'floor of my room. I complained of my head, and it was
'not wrong to do so, for a sense of dulness and suffoca-
'tion, if not pain, was there constantly.

   'But when it was proposed that I should go to school,
'that was a remedy I could not listen to with patience
'for a moment. The peculiarity of my education had
'separated me entirely from the girls around, except that
'when they were playing at active games, I would some-
'times go out and join them. I liked violent bodily exer-
'cise, which always relieved my nerves. But I had no
'success in associating with them beyond the mere play.
'Not only I was not their school-mate, but my book-life
'and lonely habits had given a cold aloofness to my
'whole expression, and veiled my manner with a hau-
'teur which turned all hearts away. Yet, as this reserve
'was superficial, and rather ignorance than arrogance,
'it produced no deep dislike. Besides, the girls supposed
'me really superior to themselves, and did not hate me
'for feeling it, but neither did they like me, nor wish
'to have me with them. Indeed, I had gradually given
'up all such wishes myself; for they seemed to me rude,
'tiresome, and childish, as I did to them dull and strange.
'This experience had been earlier, before I was admitted
'to any real friendship; but now that I had been lifted
'into the life of mature years, and into just that atmos-
'phere of European life to which I had before been tend-
'ing, the thought of sending me to school filled me with
'disgust.

   'Yet what could I tell my father of such feelings?
'I resisted all I could, but in vain. He had no faith in
'medical aid generally, and justly saw that this was nc

'occasion for its use. He thought I needed change of
'scene, and to be roused to activity by other children.
' "I have kept you at home," he said, "because I took
' " such pleasure in teaching you myself, and besides I
' " knew that you would learn faster with one who is so
' " desirous to aid you. But you will learn fast enough
' " wherever you are, and you ought to be more with
' "others of your own age. I shall soon hear that you
' "are better, I trust." '

SCHOOL-LIFE.

The school to which Margaret was sent was that of
the Misses Prescott, in Groton, Massachusetts. And her
experience there has been described with touching truthfulness by herself, in the story of " Mariana."*

'At first her school-mates were captivated with her
' ways; her love of wild dances and sudden song, her
' freaks of passion and of wit. She was always new,
' always surprising, and, for a time, charming.

'But after a while, they tired of her. She could never
'be depended on to join in their plans, yet she expected
'them to follow out hers with their whole strength. She
'was very loving, even infatuated in her own affections,
'and exacted from those who had professed any love for
'her the devotion she was willing to bestow.

'Yet there was a vein of haughty caprice in her char-
'acter, and a love of solitude, which made her at times
'wish to retire apart, and at these times she would ex-
'pect to be entirely understood, and let alone, yet to be
'welcomed back when she returned. She did not thwart

* Summer on the Lakes, p. 81.

'others in their humors, but she never doubted of great
'indulgence from them.

'Some singular habits she had, which, when new,
'charmed, but, after acquaintance, displeased her com-
'panions. She had by nature the same habit and power
'of excitement that is described in the spinning der-
'vishes of the East. Like them she would spin until all
'around her were giddy, while her own brain, instead of
'being disturbed, was excited to great action. Pausing,
'she would declaim verses of others, or her own, or act
'many parts, with strange catchwords and burdens, that
'seemed to act with mystical power on her own fancy,
'sometimes stimulating her to convulse the hearers with
'laughter, sometimes to melt them to tears. When her
'power began to languish, she would spin again till fired
'to re-commence her singular drama, into which she wove
'figures from the scenes of her earlier childhood, her com-
'panions, and the dignitaries she sometimes saw, with
'fantasies unknown to life, unknown to heaven or earth.

'This excitement, as may be supposed, was not good
'for her. It usually came on in the evening, and often
'spoiled her sleep. She would wake in the night, and
'cheat her restlessness by inventions that teased, while
'they sometimes diverted her companions.

'She was also a sleep-walker; and this one trait of
'her case did somewhat alarm her guardians, who, oth-
'erwise, showed the profound ignorance as to this pecu-
'liar being, usual in the overseeing of the young. They
'consulted a physician, who said she would outgrow it,
'and prescribed a milk diet.

'Meantime, the fever of this ardent and too early stimulated nature was constantly increased by the restraints
'and narrow routine of the boarding-school. She was

'always devising means to break in upon it. She had a
'taste — which would have seemed ludicrous to her mates,
'if they had not felt some awe of her, from the touch of
'genius and power that never left her — for costume and
'fancy dresses. There was always some sash twisted
'about her, some drapery, something odd in the arrange-
'ment of her hair and dress; so that the methodical pre-
'ceptress dared not let her go out without a careful
'scrutiny and remodelling, whose soberizing effects gen-
'erally disappeared the moment she was in the free air.

'At last a vent was assured for her in private theatri-
'cals. Play followed play, and in these and the rehear-
'sals, she found entertainment congenial with her. The
'principal parts, as a matter of course, fell to her lot:
'most of the good suggestions and arrangements came
'from her; and, for a time, she ruled mostly, and shone
'triumphant.

'During these performances, the girls had heightened
'their bloom with artificial red; this was delightful to
'them, it was something so out of the way. But Ma-
'riana, after the plays were over, kept her carmine
'saucer on the dressing-table, and put on her blushes,
'regularly as the morning. When stared and jeered at,
'she at first said she did it because she thought it made
'her look pretty; but, after a while, she became petulant
'about it, — would make no reply to any joke, but merely
'kept up the habit.

'This irritated the girls, as all eccentricity does the
'world in general, more than vice or malignity. They
'talked it over among themselves till they were wrought
'up to a desire of punishing, once for all, this sometimes
'amusing, but so often provoking non-conformist. And
'having obtained leave of the mistress, they laid with

'great glee, a plan, one evening, which was to be carried
'into execution next day at dinner.

'Among Mariana's irregularities was a great aversion
'to the meal-time ceremonial,— so long, so tiresome, she
'found it, to be seated at a certain moment, and to wait
'while each one was served, at so large a table, where
'there was scarcely any conversation; and from day to
'day it became more heavy to sit there, or go there at
'all; often as possible she excused herself on the ever-
'convenient plea of headache, and was hardly ever
'ready when the dinner-bell rang.

'To-day the summons found her on the balcony, but
'gazing on the beautiful prospect. I have heard her say
'afterwards, that she had scarcely in her life been so
'happy, — and she was one with whom happiness was a
'still rapture. It was one of the most blessed summer
'days; the shadows of great white clouds empurpled the
'distant hills for a few moments, only to leave them
'more golden; the tall grass of the wide fields waved in
'the softest breeze. Pure blue were the heavens, and
'the same hue of pure contentment was in the heart of
'Mariana.

'Suddenly on her bright mood jarred the dinner-bell.
'At first rose her usual thought, I will not, cannot go;
'and then the *must*, which daily life can always enforce,
'even upon the butterflies and birds, came, and she
'walked reluctantly to her room. She merely changed
'her dress, and never thought of adding the artificial
'rose to her cheek.

'When she took her seat in the dining-hall, and was
'asked if she would be helped, raising her eyes, she saw
'the person who asked her was deeply rouged, with a
'bright glaring spot, perfectly round, on either cheek

'She looked at the next,— same apparition ! She then
'slowly passed her eyes down the whole line, and saw
'the same, with a suppressed smile distorting every
'countenance. Catching the design at once, she deliber-
'ately looked along her own side of the table, at every
'schoolmate in turn ; every one had joined in the trick.
'The teachers strove to be grave, but she saw they
enjoyed the joke. The servants could not suppress a
'titter.

'When Warren Hastings stood at the bar of West-
'minster Hall, — when the Methodist preacher walked
'through a line of men, each of whom greeted him with
'a brickbat or rotten egg, — they had some preparation for
'the crisis, though it might be very difficult to meet it
'with an impassible brow. Our little girl was quite
'unprepared to find herself in the midst of a world
'which despised her, and triumphed in her disgrace.

'She had ruled like a queen, in the midst of her com-
'panions; she had shed her animation through their
'lives, and loaded them with prodigal favors, nor once
'suspected that a popular favorite might not be loved.
'Now she felt that she had been but a dangerous play-
'thing in the hands of those whose hearts she never had
'doubted.

'Yet the occasion found her equal to it, for Mariana
'had the kind of spirit which, in a better cause, had
'made the Roman matron truly say of her death-wound,
'"It is not painful, Pœtus." She did not blench, — she
'did not change countenance. She swallowed her din-
'ner with apparent composure. She made remarks to
'those near her, as if she had no eyes.

'The wrath of the foe, of course, rose higher, and the
moment they were freed from the restraints of the din-

'ing room, they all ran off, gayly calling, and sarcasti-
'cally laughing, with backward glances, at Mariana, left
'alone.

'Alone she went to her room, locked the door, and
'threw herself on the floor in strong convulsions. These
'had sometimes threatened her life, in earlier childhood,
'but of later years she had outgrown them. School-
'hours came, and she was not there. A little girl, sent
'to her door, could get no answer. The teachers became
'alarmed, and broke it open. Bitter was their penitence,
'and that of her companions, at the state in which they
'found her. For some hours terrible anxiety was felt,
'but at last nature, exhausted, relieved herself by a deep
'slumber.

'From this Mariana arose an altered being. She
'made no reply to the expressions of sorrow from her
'companions, none to the grave and kind, but undiscern-
'ing, comments of her teacher. She did not name the
'source of her anguish, and its poisoned dart sank deeply
'in. This was the thought which stung her so: —
' "What, not one, not a single one, in the hour of trial,
' "to take my part? not one who refused to take part
' "against me?" Past words of love, and caresses, little
'heeded at the time, rose to her memory, and gave fuel to
'her distempered heart. Beyond the sense of burning re-
'sentment at universal perfidy, she could not get. And
'Mariana, born for love, now hated all the world.

'The change, however, which these feelings made in
'her conduct and appearance, bore no such construction
'to the careless observer. Her gay freaks were quite
'gone, her wildness, her invention. Her dress was uni-
'form, her manner much subdued. Her chief interest
seemed to be now in her studies, and in music Her

'companions she never sought; but they, partly from
' uneasy, remorseful feelings, partly that they really liked
'her much better now that she did not puzzle and
'oppress them, sought her continually. And here the
'black shadow comes upon her life, the only stain upon
'the history of Mariana.

' They talked to her, as girls having few topics natur-
'ally do, of one another. Then the demon rose within
'her, and spontaneously, without design, generally with-
'out words of positive falsehood, she became a genius of
'discord amongst them. She fanned those flames of
'envy and jealousy which a wise, true word from a third
'person will often quench forever; and by a glance, or
'seemingly light reply, she planted the seeds of dissen-
'sion, till there was scarcely a peaceful affection, or sin-
'cere intimacy, in the circle where she lived, and could
'not but rule, for she was one whose nature was to that
'of the others as fire to clay.

'It was at this time that I came to the school, and
'first saw Mariana. Me she charmed at once, for I was
'a sentimental child, who, in my early ill health, had
'been indulged in reading novels, till I had no eyes for
'the common. It was not, however, easy to approach
'her. Did I offer to run and fetch her handkerchief, she
'was obliged to go to her room, and would rather do it
'herself. She did not like to have people turn over for
'her the leaves of the music-book as she played. Did I
'approach my stool to her feet, she moved away as if to
'give me room. The bunch of wild flowers, which I
'timidly laid beside her plate, was left untouched.
After some weeks, my desire to attract her notice really
'preyed upon me; and one day, meeting her alone in the
'entry, I fell upon my knees, and, kissing her hand, cried,

' "O, Mariana, do let me love you, and try to love me a
' "little!" But my idol snatched away her hand, and
' laughing wildly, ran into her room. After that day,
' her manner to me was not only cold, but repulsive, and
' I felt myself scorned.

'Perhaps four months had passed thus, when, one
' afternoon, it became obvious that something more than
' common was brewing. Dismay and mystery were
' written in many faces of the older girls; much whisper-
' ing was going on in corners.

'In the evening, after prayers, the principal bade us
' stay; and, in a grave, sad voice, summoned forth
' Mariana to answer charges to be made against her.

'Mariana stood up and leaned against the chimney-
' piece. Then eight of the older girls came forward, and
' preferred against her charges,— alas! too well founded,
' of calumny and falsehood.

'At first, she defended herself with self-possession and
' eloquence. But when she found she could no more
' resist the truth, she suddenly threw herself down,
' dashing her head with all her force against the iron
' hearth, on which a fire was burning, and was taken up
' senseless.

'The affright of those present was great. Now that
' they had perhaps killed her, they reflected it would
' have been as well if they had taken warning from the
' former occasion, and approached very carefully a
' nature so capable of any extreme. After a while she
' revived, with a faint groan, amid the sobs of her com-
' panions. I was on my knees by the bed, and held her
' cold hand. One of those most aggrieved took it from
' me, to beg her pardon, and say, it was impossible not to
' love her. She made no reply.

' Neither that night, nor for several days, could a word
' be obtained from her, nor would she touch food; but,
' when it was presented to her, or any one drew near
' from any cause, she merely turned away her head, and
' gave no sign. The teacher saw that some terrible ner-
' vous affection had fallen upon her — that she grew
' more and more feverish. She knew not what to do.

' Meanwhile, a new revolution had taken place in the
' mind of the passionate but nobly-tempered child. All
' these months nothing but the sense of injury had
' rankled in her heart. She had gone on in one
' mood, doing what the demon prompted, without
' scruple, and without fear.

' But at the moment of detection, the tide ebbed, and
' the bottom of her soul lay revealed to her eye. How
' black, how stained, and sad! Strange, strange,
' that she had not seen before the baseness and cruelty
' of falsehood, the loveliness of truth! Now, amid the
' wreck, uprose the moral nature, which never before
' had attained the ascendant. "But," she thought,
' " too late sin is revealed to me in all its deformity, and
' " sin-defiled, I will not, cannot live. The main-spring
' " of life is broken."

' The lady who took charge of this sad child had
' never well understood her before, but had always
' looked on her with great tenderness. And now love
' seemed, — when all around were in the greatest dis-
' tress, fearing to call in medical aid, fearing to do with-
' out it, — to teach her where the only balm was to be
' found that could heal the wounded spirit.

' One night she came in, bringing a calming draught.
' Mariana was sitting as usual, her hair loose, her dress
' the same robe they had put on her at first, her eyes

'fixed vacantly upon the whited wall. To the proffers
'and entreaties of her nurse, she made no reply.

'The lady burst into tears, but Mariana did not seem
'even to observe it.

'The lady then said, "O, my child, do not despair; do
'"not think that one great fault can mar a whole life!
'"Let me trust you; let me tell you the griefs of my sad
'"life. I will tell you, Mariana, what I never expected
'"to impart to any one."

'And so she told her tale. It was one of pain, of
'shame, borne not for herself, but for one near and dear
'as herself. Mariana knew the dignity and reserve of
'this lady's nature. She had often admired to see how
'the cheek, lovely, but no longer young, mantled with
'the deepest blush of youth, and the blue eyes were
'cast down at any little emotion. She had understood
'the proud sensibility of her character. She fixed her
'eyes on those now raised to hers, bright with fast-fall-
'ing tears. She heard the story to the end, and then,
'without saying a word, stretched out her hand for the
'cup.

'She returned to life, but it was as one who had
'passed through the valley of death. The heart of
'stone was quite broken in her, — the fiery will fallen
'from flame to coal. When her strength was a little
'restored, she had all her companions summoned, and
'said to them, — "I deserved to die, but a generous
'"trust has called me back to life. I will be worthy
'"of it, nor ever betray the trust, or resent injury more.
'"Can you forgive the past?"

'And they not only forgave, but, with love and ear-
'nest tears, clasped in their arms the returning sister.
'They vied with one another in offices of humble love

'to the humbled one; and let it be recorded, as an
'instance of the pure honor of which young hearts are
'capable, that these facts, known to some forty persons,
'never, so far as I know, transpired beyond those walls.

'It was not long after this that Mariana was
'summoned home. She went thither a wonderfully
'instructed being, though in ways those who had sent
'her forth to learn little dreamed of.

'Never was forgotten the vow of the returning prodi-
'gal. Mariana could not *resent*, could not *play false*.
'The terrible crisis, which she so early passed through,
probably prevented the world from hearing much of
'her. A wild fire was tamed in that hour of penitence
'at the boarding-school, such as has oftentimes wrapped
'court and camp in a destructive glow.'

SELF-CULTURE.

Letters written to the beloved teacher, who so wisely
befriended Margaret in her trial-hour, will best show
how this high-spirited girl sought to enlarge and harmonize her powers.

'*Cambridge, July* 11, 1825. — Having excused myself
'from accompanying my honored father to church, which
'I always do in the afternoon, when possible, I devote
'to you the hours which Ariosto and Helvetius ask of
'my eyes, — as, lying on my writing-desk, they put me
'in mind that they must return this week to their
'owner.

'You keep me to my promise of giving you some
'sketch of my pursuits. I rise a little before five, walk
'an hour, and then practise on the piano, till seven,
'when we breakfast. Next I read French, — Sismondi's

'Literature of the South of Europe,— till eight, then two
'or three lectures in Brown's Philosophy. About half-
'past nine I go to Mr. Perkins's school and study Greek
'till twelve, when, the school being dismissed, I recite, go
'home, and practise again till dinner, at two. Some-
'times, if the conversation is very agreeable, I lounge
'for half an hour over the dessert, though rarely so lav-
'ish of time. Then, when I can, I read two hours in
'Italian, but I am often interrupted. At six, I walk, or
'take a drive. Before going to bed, I play or sing, for
'half an hour or so, to make all sleepy, and, about
'eleven, retire to write a little while in my journal, exer-
'cises on what I have read, or a series of characteristics
'which I am filling up according to advice. Thus, you
'see, I am learning Greek, and making acquaintance
'with metaphysics, and French and Italian literature.

'"How," you will say, "can I believe that my indo-
'"lent, fanciful, pleasure-loving pupil, perseveres in such
'"a course?" I feel the power of industry growing
'every day, and, besides the all-powerful motive of
'ambition, and a new stimulus lately given through a
'friend, I have learned to believe that nothing, no! not
'perfection, is unattainable. I am determined on dis-
'tinction, which formerly I thought to win at an easy
'rate; but now I see that long years of labor must be
'given to secure even the "succès de societé,"—which,
'however, shall never content me. I see multitudes of
'examples of persons of genius, utterly deficient in
'grace and the power of pleasurable excitement. I
'wish to combine both. I know the obstacles in my
'way. I am wanting in that intuitive tact and polish,
'which nature has bestowed upon some, but which I
'must acquire. And, on the other hand, my powers of

'intellect, though sufficient, I suppose, are not well disci-
'plined. Yet all such hindrances may be overcome by
'an ardent spirit. If I fail, my consolation shall be
'found in active employment.'

'*Cambridge, March* 5, 1826.—Duke Nicholas is to suc-
'ceed the Emperor Alexander, thus relieving Europe from
'the sad apprehension of evil to be inflicted by the bru-
'tal Constantine, and yet depriving the Holy Alliance of
'its very soul. We may now hope more strongly for the
'liberties of unchained Europe; we look in anxious sus-
'pense for the issue of the struggle of Greece, the result
'of which seems to depend on the new autocrat. I have
'lately been reading Anastasius, the Greek Gil Blas,
'which has excited and delighted me; but I do not think
'you like works of this cast. You did not like my sombre
'and powerful Ormond, — though this is superior to Or-
'mond in every respect; it translates you to another scene,
'hurls you into the midst of the burning passions of the
'East, whose vicissitudes are, however, interspersed by
'deep pauses of shadowy reflective scenes, which open
'upon you like the green watered little vales occasion-
'ally to be met with in the burning desert. There is
'enough of history to fix profoundly the attention, and
'prevent you from revolting from scenes profligate and
'terrific, and such characters as are never to be met
'with in our paler climes. How delighted am I to
'read a book which can absorb me to tears and shud-
'dering, — not by individual traits of beauty, but by
'the spirit of adventure,—happiness which one seldom
'enjoys after childhood in this blest age, so philosophic,
'free, and enlightened to a miracle, but far removed from
'the ardent dreams and soft credulity of the world's

'youth. Sometimes I think I would give all our gains
'for those times when young and old gathered in the
'feudal hall, listening with soul-absorbing transport to
'the romance of the minstrel, unrestrained and regard-
'less of criticism, and when they worshipped nature,
'not as high-dressed and pampered, but as just risen
'from the bath.'

' *Cambridge, May* 14, 1826. — I am studying Madame
'de Stael, Epictetus, Milton, Racine, and Castilian bal-
'lads, with great delight. There's an assemblage for you.
'Now tell me, had you rather be the brilliant De Stael or
'the useful Edgeworth? — though De Stael is useful too,
'but it is on the grand scale, on liberalizing, regenerating
' principles, and has not the immediate practical success
'that Edgeworth has. I met with a parallel the other
' day between Byron and Rousseau, and had a mind to
'send it to you, it was so excellent.'

' *Cambridge, Jan.* 10, 1827. — As to my studies, I am
'engrossed in reading the elder Italian poets, beginning
' with Berni, from whom I shall proceed to Pulci and Poli-
'tian. I read very critically. Miss Francis * and I think
'of reading Locke, as introductory to a course of English
'metaphysics, and then De Stael on Locke's system.
'Allow me to introduce this lady to you as a most inter-
'esting woman, in my opinion. She is a natural person,
'— a most rare thing in this age of cant and pretension.
' Her conversation is charming,—she brings all her pow-
'ers to bear upon it; her style is varied, and she has a
very pleasant and spirited way of thinking. I should
judge, too, that she possesses peculiar purity of mind. I

* Lydia Maria Child.

'am going to spend this evening with her, and wish you
'were to be with us.'

'*Cambridge, Jan.* 3, 1828. — I am reading Sir William
'Temple's works, with great pleasure. Such enlarged
'views are rarely to be found combined with such acute-
'ness and discrimination. His style, though diffuse, is
'never verbose or overloaded, but beautifully expressive;
''t is English, too, though he was an accomplished linguist,
'and wrote much and well in French, Spanish, and Latin.
'The latter he used, as he says of the Bishop of Mun-
'ster, (with whom he corresponded in that tongue,)
' " more like a man of the court and of business than a
' " scholar." He affected not Augustan niceties, but his
'expressions are free and appropriate. I have also read
'a most entertaining book, which I advise you to read,
'(if you have not done so already,) Russell's Tour in Ger-
'many. There you will find more intelligent and detailed
'accounts than I have seen anywhere of the state of the
'German universities, Viennese court, secret associations,
'Plica Polonica, and other very interesting matters.
'There is a minute account of the representative gov-
'ernment given to his subjects by the Duke of 'Wei-
'mar. I have passed a luxurious afternoon, having
'been in bed from dinner till tea, reading Rammohun
'Roy's book, and framing dialogues aloud on every
'argument beneath the sun. Really, I have not had my
'mind so exercised for months; and I have felt a gladi-
'atorial disposition lately, and don't enjoy mere light con-
'versation. The love of knowledge is prodigiously kin-
'dled within my soul of late; I study much and reflect
'more, and feel an aching wish for some person with
'whom I might talk fully and openly.

'Did you ever read the letters and reflections of Prince
'de Ligne, the most agreeable man of his day? I have
'just had it, and if it is new to you, I recommend it as
'an agreeable book to read at night just before you go to
'bed. There is much curious matter concerning Catha-
'rine II.'s famous expedition into Taurida, which puts
'down some of the romantic stories prevalent on that
'score, but relates more surprising realities. Also it
'gives much interesting information about that noble
'philosopher, Joseph II., and about the Turkish tactics
'and national character.'

'*Cambridge, Jan.* 1830. — You need not fear to revive
'painful recollections. I often think of those sad experi-
'ences. True, they agitate me deeply. But it was best
'so. They have had a most powerful effect on my char-
'acter. I tremble at whatever looks like dissimulation.
'The remembrance of that evening subdues every proud,
'passionate impulse. My beloved supporter in those sor-
'rowful hours, your image shines as fair to my mind's eye
'as it did in 1825, when I left you with my heart over-
'flowing with gratitude for your singular and judicious
'tenderness. Can I ever forget that to your treatment in
'that crisis of youth I owe the true life, — the love of
'Truth and Honor?'

LIFE IN CAMBRIDGE.

BY JAMES FREEMAN CLARKE.

"Extraordinary, generous seeking."

GOETHE.

"Through, brothers, through, — this be
Our watchword in danger or sorrow,
Common clay to its mother dust,
All nobleness heavenward!"

THEODORE KOERNER.

"Thou friend whose presence on my youthful heart
Fell, like bright Spring upon some herbless plain;
How beautiful and calm and free thou wert
In thy young wisdom, when the mortal chain
Of custom thou didst burst and rend in twain,
And walk as free as light the clouds among!"

SHELLEY.

"THERE are not a few instances of that conflict, known also to the fathers, of the spirit with the flesh, the inner with the outer man, of the freedom of the will with the necessity of nature, the pleasure of the individual with the conventions of society, of the emergency of the case with the despotism of the rule. It is this, which, while it makes the interest of life, makes the difficulty of living. It is a struggle, indeed, between unequal powers, — between the man, who is a conscious moral person, and nature, or events, or bodies of men, which either want personality or unity ; and hence the man, after fearful and desolating war, sometimes rises on the ruins of all the necessities of nature and all the prescriptions of society. But what these want in personality they possess in number, in recurrency, in invulnerability. The spirit of man, an agent indeed of curious power and boundless resource, but trembling with sensibilities, tender and irritable, goes out against the inexorable conditions of destiny, the lifeless forces of nature, or the ferocious cruelty of the multitude, and long before the hands are weary or the invention exhausted, the heart may be broken in the warfare."

N. A. REVIEW, Jan., 1817, article " *Dichtung und Wahrheit* "

II.

CAMBRIDGE.

THE difficulty which we all feel in describing our past intercourse and friendship with Margaret Fuller, is, that the intercourse was so intimate, and the friendship so personal, that it is like making a confession to the public of our most interior selves. For this noble person, by her keen insight and her generous interest, entered into the depth of every soul with which she stood in any real relation. To print one of her letters, is like giving an extract from our own private journal. To relate what she was to us, is to tell how she discerned elements of worth and beauty where others could only have seen what was common-place and poor; it is to say what high hopes, what generous assurance, what a pure ambition, she entertained on our behalf, — a hope and confidence which may well be felt as a rebuke to our low attainments and poor accomplishments.

Nevertheless, it seems due to this great soul that those of us who have been blessed and benefited by her friendship should be willing to say what she has done for us, — undeterred by the thought that to reveal her is to expose ourselves.

My acquaintance with Sarah Margaret Fuller began in 1829. We both lived in Cambridge, and from that time until she went to Groton to reside, in 1833, I saw her, or heard from her, almost every day. There was a family connection, and we called each other cousin.* During this period, her intellect was intensely active. With what eagerness did she seek for knowledge! What fire, what exuberance, what reach, grasp, overflow of thought, shone in her conversation! She needed a friend to whom to speak of her studies, to whom to express the ideas which were dawning and taking shape in her mind. She accepted me for this friend, and to me it was a gift of the gods, an influence like no other.

For the first few months of our acquaintance, our intercourse was simply that of two young persons seeking entertainment in each other's society. Perhaps a note written at this time will illustrate the easy and graceful movement of her mind in this superficial kind of intercourse.

'*March* 16*th*, 1830. *Half-past six, morning.* — I have 'encountered that most common-place of glories, sunrise, '(to say naught of being praised and wondered at by 'every member of the family in succession,) that I 'might have leisure to answer your note even as you 'requested. I thank you a thousand times for " The

---

* I had once before seen Margaret, when we were both children about five years of age. She made an impression on my mind which was never effaced, and I distinctly recollect the joyful child, with light flowing locks and bright face, who led me by the hand down the back-steps of her house into the garden. This was when her father lived in Cambridgeport, in a house on Cherry street, in front of which still stand some handsome trees, planted by him in the year of Margaret's birth.

'Rivals." * Alas!! I must leave my heart in the
'book, and spend the livelong morning in reading to a
'sick lady from some amusing story-book. I tell you
'of this act of (in my professedly unamiable self) most
'unwonted charity, for three several reasons. Firstly,
'and foremostly, because I think that you, being a social-
'ist by vocation, a sentimentalist by nature, and a Chan-
'ningite from force of circumstances and fashion, will
'peculiarly admire this little self-sacrifice exploit. Sec-
'ondly, because 't is neither conformable to the spirit of
'the nineteenth century, nor the march of mind, that
'those churlish reserves should be kept up between *the*
'*right and left hands*, which belonged to ages of barba-
'rism and prejudice, and could only have been inculcated
'for their use. Thirdly, and lastly, the true lady-like
'reason, — because I would fain have my correspondent
'enter into and sympathize with my feelings of the
'moment.

  'As to the relationship; 't is, I find, on inquiry, by no
'means to be compared with that between myself and
' —; of course, the intimacy cannot be so great. But no
'matter; it will enable me to answer your notes, and you
'will interest my imagination much more than if I knew
'you better. But I am exceeding legitimate note-writing
'limits. With a hope that this epistle may be legible to
'your undiscerning eyes, I conclude,

  'Your cousin only thirty-seven degrees removed,

                                                      'M.'

The next note which I shall give was written not
many days after, and is in quite a different vein. It is

---

* "The Rivals" was a novel I had lent her, — if I remember right, by
the author of "The Collegians;" a writer who in those days interested us
not a little.

memorable to me as laying the foundation of a friendship which brought light to my mind, which enlarged my heart, and gave elevation and energy to my aims and purposes. For nearly twenty years, Margaret remained true to the pledges of this note. In a few years we were separated, but our friendship remained firm. Living in different parts of the country, occupied with different thoughts and duties, making other friends,— sometimes not seeing nor hearing from each other for months,— we never met without my feeling that she was ready to be interested in all my thoughts, to love those whom I loved, to watch my progress, to rebuke my faults and follies, to encourage within me every generous and pure aspiration, to demand of me, always, the best that I could be or do, and to be satisfied with no mediocrity, no conformity to any low standard.

And what she thus was to me, she was to many others. Inexhaustible in power of insight, and with a good-will "broad as ether," she could enter into the needs, and sympathize with the various excellences, of the greatest variety of characters. One thing only she demanded of all her friends,— that they should have some "extraordinary generous seeking,"* that they should not be satisfied with the common routine of life,— that they should aspire to something higher, better, holier, than they had now attained. Where this element of aspiration existed, she demanded no originality of intellect, no greatness of soul. If these were found, well; but she could love,

---

* These words of Goethe, which I have placed among the mottoes at the beginning of this chapter, were written by Margaret on the first page of a richly gilt and bound blank book, which she gave to me, in 1832, for a private journal. The words of Körner are also translated by herself, and were given to me about the same time

tenderly and truly, where they were not. But for a worldly character, however gifted, she felt and expressed something very like contempt. At this period, she had no patience with self-satisfied mediocrity. She afterwards learned patience and unlearned contempt; but at the time of which I write, she seemed, and was to the multitude, a haughty and supercilious person, — while to those whom she loved, she was all the more gentle, tender and true.

Margaret possessed, in a greater degree than any person I ever knew, the power of so magnetizing others, when she wished, by the power of her mind, that they would lay open to her all the secrets of their nature. She had an infinite curiosity to know individuals,— not the vulgar curiosity which seeks to find out the circumstances of their outward lives, but that which longs to understand the inward springs of thought and action in their souls. This desire and power both rested on a profound conviction of her mind in the individuality of every human being. A human being, according to her faith, was not the result of the presence and stamp of outward circumstances, but an original *monad*, with a certain special faculty, capable of a certain fixed development, and having a profound personal unity, which the ages of eternity might develop, but could not exhaust. I know not if she would have stated her faith in these terms, but some such conviction appeared in her constant endeavor to see and understand the germinal principle, the special characteristic, of every person whom she deemed worthy of knowing at all. Therefore, while some persons study human nature in its universal laws, and become great philosophers, moralists and teachers of the race, — while others study mankind in action, and, seeing the motives

and feelings by which masses are swayed, become eminent politicians, sagacious leaders, and eminent in all
political affairs,— a few, like Margaret, study character,
and acquire the power of exerting profoundest influence
on individual souls.

I had expressed to her my desire to know something
of the history of her mind,— to understand her aims, her
hopes, her views of life. In a note written in reply, she
answered me thus :—

'I cannot bring myself to write you what you wished.
'You would be disappointed, at any rate, after all the
'solemn note of preparation; the consciousness of this
'would chill me now. Besides, I cannot be willing to
'leave with you such absolute *vagaries* in a tangible,
'examinable shape. I think of your after-smiles, of
'your colder moods. But I will tell you, when a fitting
'opportunity presents, all that can interest you, and per-
'haps more. And excuse my caution. I do not profess,
'I may not dare, to be generous in these matters.'

To this I replied to the effect that, "in my coldest
mood I could not criticize words written in a confiding
spirit;" and that, at all events, she must not expect of
me a confidence which she dared not return. This was
the substance of a note to which Margaret thus replied :—

'I thank you for your note. Ten minutes before I
'received it, I scarcely thought that anything again
'would make my stifled heart throb so warm a pulse of
'pleasure. Excuse my cold doubts, my selfish arrogance,
'— you will, when I tell you that this experiment has
'before had such uniform results; those who professed

'to seek my friendship, and whom, indeed, I have often
'truly loved, have always learned to content themselves
'with that inequality in the connection which I have
'never striven to veil. Indeed, I have thought myself
'more valued and better beloved, because the sympathy,
'the interest, were all on my side. True! such regard
'could never flatter my pride, nor gratify my affections,
'since it was paid not to myself, but to the need they
'had of me; still, it was dear and pleasing, as it has
'given me an opportunity of knowing and serving many
'lovely characters; and I cannot see that there is any-
'thing else for me to do on earth. And I should rejoice
'to cultivate generosity, since (see that *since*) affections
'gentler and more sympathetic are denied me.

'I would have been a true friend to you : ever ready
'to solace your pains and partake your joy as far as
'possible. Yet I cannot but rejoice that I have met a
'person who could discriminate and reject a proffer of
'this sort. Two years ago I should have ventured to
'proffer you friendship, indeed, on seeing such an in-
'stance of pride in you; but I have gone through a sad
'process of feeling since, and those emotions, so necessa-
'rily repressed, have lost their simplicity, their ardent
'beauty. *Then*, there was nothing I might not have
'disclosed to a person capable of comprehending, had I
'ever seen such an one ! Now there are many voices of
'the soul which I imperiously silence. This results not
'from any particular circumstance or event, but from a
'gradual ascertaining of realities.

'I cannot promise you any limitless confidence, but I
'*can* promise that no timid caution, no haughty dread
'shall prevent my telling you the truth of my thoughts

'on any subject we may have in common. Will this 'satisfy you? Oh let it! suffer me to know you.'

In a postscript she adds, ' No other cousin or friend of any style is to see this note.' So for twenty years it has lain unseen, but for twenty years did we remain true to the pledges of that period. And now that noble heart sleeps beneath the tossing Atlantic, and I feel no reluctance in showing to the world this expression of pure youthful ardor. It may, perhaps, lead some wise worldlings, who doubt the possibility of such a relation, to reconsider the grounds of their scepticism; or, if not that, it may encourage some youthful souls, as earnest and eager as ours, to trust themselves to their hearts' impulse, and enjoy some such blessing as came to us.

Let me give extracts from other notes and letters, written by Margaret, about the same period.

' *Saturday evening, May* 1*st*, 1830. — The holy 'moon and merry-toned wind of this night woo to a 'vigil at the open window; a half-satisfied interest 'urges me to live, love and perish! in the noble, ' wronged heart of Basil;* my Journal, which lies before ' me, tempts to follow out and interpret the as yet only 'half-understood musings of the past week. Letter-' writing, compared with any of these things, takes the 'ungracious semblance of a duty. I have, nathless, ' after a two hours' reverie, to which this resolve and its 'preliminaries have formed excellent warp, determined ' to sacrifice this hallowed time to you.

' It did not in the least surprise me that you found it impossible at the time to avail yourself of the confiden·

---

* The hero of a novel she was reading.

'tial privileges I had invested you with. On the con-
'trary, I only wonder that we should ever, after such
'gage given and received, (not by a look or tone, but by
'letter,) hold any frank communication. Preparations
'are good in life, prologues ruinous. I felt this even
'before I sent my note, but could not persuade myself to
'consign an impulse so embodied, to oblivion, from any
'consideration of expediency.' * *

' *May 4th*, 1830. — * * I have greatly wished to see
'among us such a person of genius as the nineteenth
'century can afford — *i. e.*, one who has tasted in the
'morning of existence the extremes of good and ill,
'both imaginative and real. I had imagined a person
'endowed by nature with that acute sense of Beauty,
'(*i. e.*, Harmony or Truth,) and that vast capacity
'of desire, which give soul to love and ambition. I
'had wished this person might grow up to manhood
'alone (but not alone in crowds); I would have placed
'him in a situation so retired, so obscure, that he
'would quietly, but without bitter sense of isolation,
'stand apart from all surrounding him. I would have
'had him go on steadily, feeding his mind with con-
'genial love, hopefully confident that if he only nour-
'ished his existence into perfect life, Fate would, at
'fitting season, furnish an atmosphere and orbit meet for
'his breathing and exercise. I wished he might adore,
'not fever for, the bright phantoms of his mind's crea-
'tion, and believe them but the shadows of external
'things to be met with hereafter. After this steady
'intellectual growth had brought his powers to manhood,
'so far as the ideal can do it, I wished this being might
'be launched into the world of realities, his heart glow-
'ing with the ardor of an immortal toward perfection,

'his eyes searching everywhere to behold it; I wished
'he might collect into one burning point those withering,
'palsying convictions, which, in the ordinary routine of
'things, so gradually pervade the soul; that he might
'suffer, in brief space, agonies of disappointment com-
'mensurate with his unpreparedness and confidence.
'And I thought, thus thrown back on the representing
'pictorial resources I supposed him originally to possess,
'with such material, and the need he must feel of using
'it, such a man would suddenly dilate into a form of
'Pride, Power, and Glory, — a centre, round which ask-
'ing, aimless hearts might rally, — a man fitted to act as
'interpreter to the one tale of many-languaged eyes!

   'What words are these! Perhaps you will feel as if
'I sought but for the longest and strongest. Yet to my
'ear they do but faintly describe the imagined powers of
'such a being.'

   Margaret's home at this time was in the mansion-
house formerly belonging to Judge Dana,— a large, old-
fashioned building, since taken down, standing about a
quarter of a mile from the Cambridge Colleges, on the
main road to Boston. The house stood back from the
road, on rising ground, which overlooked an extensive
landscape. It was always a pleasure to Margaret to
look at the outlines of the distant hills beyond the river,
and to have before her this extent of horizon and sky.
In the last year of her residence in Cambridge, her father
moved to the old Brattle place, — a still more ancient
edifice, with large, old-fashioned garden, and stately
rows of Linden trees. Here Margaret enjoyed the garden
walks, which took the place of the extensive view.

   During these five years her life was not diversified
by events, but was marked by an inward history

Study, conversation, society, friendship, and reflection on the aim and law 'of life, made up her biography. Accordingly, these topics will constitute the substance of this chapter, though sometimes, in order to give completeness to a subject, we may anticipate a little, and insert passages from the letters and journals of her Groton life.

I.

FRIENDSHIP.

"Friendly love perfecteth mankind.'
BACON.

"To have found favor in thy sight
    Will still remain
A river of thought, that full of light
    Divides the plain."
MILNES.

"Cui potest vita esse vitalis, (ut ait Ennius,) quæ non in amici mutatâ benevolentiâ requiescat?" — CICERO.

———

IT was while living at Cambridge that Margaret commenced several of those friendships which lasted through her life, and which were the channels for so large a part of her spiritual activity. In giving some account of her in these relations, there is only the alternative of a prudent reserve which omits whatever is liable to be misunderstood, or a frank utterance which confides in the good sense and right feeling of the reader. By the last course, we run the risk of allowing our friend to be misunderstood; but by the first we make it certain that the most important part of her character shall not be understood at all. I have, therefore, thought it best to follow, as far as I can, her own ideas on this subject, which I find in two of her letters to myself. The first is dated, Groton, Jan. 8th, 1839. I was at that time editing a theological and literary magazine, in the West, and this letter was occasioned by my asking her to allow me to publish therein certain poems, and articles of hers, which she had given me to read.

'And I wish now, as far as I can, to give my reasons 'for what you consider absurd squeamishness in me. 'You may not acquiesce in my view, but I think you 'will respect it *as* mine, and be willing to act upon it so 'far as I am concerned.

'Genius seems to me excusable in taking the public 'for a confidant. Genius is universal, and can appeal 'to the common heart of man. But even here I would 'not have it too direct. I prefer to see the thought or 'feeling made universal. How different the confidence 'of Goethe, for instance, from that of Byron!

'But for us lesser people, who write verses merely as 'vents for the overflowings of a personal experience, 'which in every life of any value craves occasionally 'the accompaniment of the lyre, it seems to me that all 'the value of this utterance is destroyed by a hasty or 'indiscriminate publicity. The moment I lay open my 'heart, and tell the fresh feeling to any one who chooses 'to hear, I feel profaned.

'When it has passed into experience, when the flower 'has gone to seed, I don't care who knows it, or whither 'they wander. I am no longer it, — I stand on it. I do 'not know whether this is peculiar to me, or not, but I 'am sure the moment I cease to have any reserve or 'delicacy about a feeling, it is on the wane.

'About putting beautiful verses in your Magazine, I 'have no feeling except what I should have about fur- 'nishing a room. I should not put a dressing-case into 'a parlor, or a book-case into a dressing-room, because,

'however good things in their place, they were not in
'place there. And this, not in consideration of the
'public, but of my own sense of fitness and harmony.'

The next extract is from a letter written to me in
1842, after a journey which we had taken to the White
Mountains, in the company of my sister, and Mr. and
Mrs. Farrar. During this journey Margaret had conversed with me concerning some passages of her private
history and experience, and in this letter she asks me to
be prudent in speaking of it, giving her reasons as follows : —

'*Cambridge, July* 31, 1842.— * * I said I was happy
'in having no secret. It is my nature, and has been
'the tendency of my life, to wish that all my thoughts
'and deeds might lie, as the "open secrets" of Nature,
'free to all who are able to understand them. I have no
'reserves, except intellectual reserves; for to speak of
'things to those who cannot receive them is stupidity,
'rather than frankness. But in this case, I alone am
'not concerned. Therefore, dear James, give heed to
'the subject. You have received a key to what was
'before unknown of your friend; you have made use
'of it, now let it be buried with the past, over whose
'passages profound and sad, yet touched with heaven-
'born beauty, "let silence stand sentinel."'

I shall endeavor to keep true to the spirit of these sentences in speaking of Margaret's friendships. Yet not
to speak of them in her biography would be omitting
the most striking feature of her character. It would
be worse than the play of Hamlet with Hamlet omitted. Henry the Fourth without Sully, Gustavus

Adolphus without Oxenstiern, Napoleon without his marshals, Socrates without his scholars, would be more complete than Margaret without her friends. So that, in touching on these private relations, we must be everywhere "bold," yet not "too bold." The extracts will be taken indiscriminately from letters written to many friends.

The insight which Margaret displayed in finding her friends, the magnetism by which she drew them toward herself, the catholic range of her intimacies, the influence which she exercised to develop the latent germ of every character, the constancy with which she clung to each when she had once given and received confidence, the delicate justice which kept every intimacy separate, and the process of transfiguration which took place when she met any one on this mountain of Friendship, giving a dazzling lustre to the details of common life, — all these should be at least touched upon and illustrated, to give any adequate view of her in these relations.

Such a prejudice against her had been created by her faults of manner, that the persons she might most wish to know often retired from her and avoided her. But she was "sagacious of her quarry," and never suffered herself to be repelled by this. She saw when any one belonged to her, and never rested till she came into possession of her property. I recollect a lady who thus fled from her for several years, yet, at last, became most nearly attached to her. This "wise sweet" friend, as Margaret characterized her in two words, a flower hidden in the solitude of deep woods, Margaret saw and appreciated from the first.

See how, in the following passage, she describes to

one of her friends her perception of character. and her power of attracting it, when only fifteen years old.

'*Jamaica Plains, July*, 1840. — Do you remember my
'telling you, at Cohasset, of a Mr. ——— staying with
'us, when I was fifteen, and all that passed? Well, I
'have not seen him since, till, yesterday, he came here.
'I was pleased to find, that, even at so early an age, I
'did not overrate those I valued. He was the same as
'in memory; the powerful eye dignifying an otherwise
'ugly face; the calm wisdom, and refined observation,
'the imposing *manière d'être*, which anywhere would
'give him an influence among men, without his taking
'any trouble, or making any sacrifice, and the great
'waves of feeling that seemed to rise as an attractive
'influence, and overspread his being. He said, nothing
'since his childhood had been so marked as his visit
'to our house; that it had dwelt in his thoughts
'unchanged amid all changes. I could have wished
'he had never returned to change the picture. He
'looked at me continually, and said, again and again,
'he should have known me anywhere; but O how
'changed I must be since that epoch of pride and ful-
'ness! He had with him his son, a wild boy of five
'years old, all brilliant with health and energy, and
'with the same powerful eye. He said, — You know
'I am not one to confound acuteness and rapidity of
'intellect with real genius; but he is for those an ex-
'traordinary child. He would astonish you, but I look
'deep enough into the prodigy to see the work of an
'extremely nervous temperament, and I shall make him
'as dull as I can. "*Margaret*," (pronouncing the name
'in the same deliberate searching way he used to do,)

' " I love him so well, I will try to teach him moderation.
' " If I can help it, he shall not feed on bitter ashes, nor
' " try these paths of avarice and ambition." It made me
' feel very strangely to hear .him talk so to my old self.
' What a gulf between ! There is scarce a fibre left of
' the haughty, passionate, ambitious child he remembered
' and loved. I felt affection for him still; for his charac-
' ter was formed then, and had not altered, except by
' ripening and expanding! But thus, in other worlds,
' we shall remember our present selves.'

Margaret's constancy to any genuine relation, once
established, was surprising. If her friends' *aim* changed,
so as to take them out of her sphere, she was saddened
by it, and did not let them go without a struggle. But
wherever they continued " true to the original standard,"
(as she loved to phrase it) her affectionate interest would
follow them unimpaired through all the changes of life.
The principle of this constancy she thus expresses in a
letter to one of her brothers: —

' Great and even *fatal* errors (so far as this life is con-
' cerned) could not destroy my friendship for one in
' whom I am sure of the kernel of nobleness.'

She never formed a friendship until she had seen and
known this germ of good ; and afterwards judged conduct by this. To this germ of good, to this highest law
of each individual, she held them true. But never did
she act like those who so often judge of their friend from
some report of his conduct, as if they had never known
him, and allow the inference from a single act to alter
the opinion formed by an induction from years of inter-

course. From all such weakness Margaret stood wholly free.

I have referred to the wide range of Margaret's friendships. Even at this period this variety was very apparent. She was the centre of a group very different from each other, and whose only affinity consisted in their all being polarized by the strong attraction of her mind,— all drawn toward herself. Some of her friends were young, gay and beautiful; some old, sick or studious. Some were children of the world, others pale scholars. Some were witty, others slightly dull. But all, in order to be Margaret's friends, must be capable of seeking something,— capable of some aspiration for the better. And how did she glorify life to all! all that was tame and common vanishing away in the picturesque light thrown over the most familiar things by her rapid fancy, her brilliant wit, her sharp insight, her creative imagination, by the inexhaustible resources of her knowledge, and the copious rhetoric which found words and images always apt and always ready. Even then she displayed almost the same marvellous gift of conversation which afterwards dazzled all who knew her,— with more perhaps of freedom, since she floated on the flood of our warm sympathies. Those who know Margaret only by her published writings know her least; her notes and letters contain more of her mind; but it was only in conversation that she was perfectly free and at home.

Margaret's constancy in friendship caused her to demand it in others, and thus she was sometimes exacting. But the pure Truth of her character caused her to express all such feelings with that freedom and simplicity that they became only as slight clouds on a serene

sky, giving it a tenderer beauty, and casting picturesque
shades over the landscape below. From her letters to
different friends I select a few examples of these feelings.

'The world turns round and round, and you too must
'needs be negligent and capricious. You have not
'answered my note; you have not given me what I
'asked. You do not come here. Do not you act so,— it
'is the drop too much. The world seems not only turning
'but tottering, when my kind friend plays such a part.'

'You need not have delayed your answer so long;
'why not at once answer the question I asked? Faith is
'not natural to me; for the love I feel to others is not in
'the idleness of poverty, nor can I persist in believing
'the best, merely to save myself pain, or keep a leaning
'place for the weary heart. But I should believe you,
'because I have seen that your feelings are strong and
'constant; they have never 'disappointed me, when
'closely scanned.'

'*July* 6, 1832. — I believe I behaved very badly the
'other evening. I did not think so yesterday. I had
'been too surprised and vexed to recover very easily,
'but to-day my sophistries have all taken wing, and I
'feel that nothing good could have made me act with
'such childish petulance and bluntness towards one
'who spoke from friendly emotions. Be at peace; I
'will astonish you by my repose, mildness, and self-pos-
'session. No, that is silly; but I believe it cannot be
'right to be on such terms with any one, that, on the
'least vexation, I indulge my feelings at his or her
'expense. We will talk less, but we shall be very good
'friends still, I hope. Shall not we?'

In the last extract, we have an example of that genuine humility, which, being a love of truth, underlaid her
whole character, notwithstanding its seeming pride
She could not have been great as she was, without it.*

'*December* 19*th*, 1829. — I shall always be glad to
'have you come to me when saddened. The melan-
'cholic does not misbecome you. The lights of your
'character are *wintry*. They are generally inspiriting,
'life-giving, but, if perpetual, would glare too much on
'the tired sense; one likes sometimes a cloudy day, with
'its damp and warmer breath,— its gentle, down-look-
'ing shades. Sadness in some is intolerably ungraceful
'and oppressive; it affects one like a cold rainy day in
'June or September, when all pleasure departs with the
'sun; everything seems out of place and irrelative to
'the time ; the clouds are fog, the atmosphere leaden, —
'but 'tis not so with you.'

Of her own truthfulness to her friends, which led her
frankly to speak to them of their faults or dangers, her
correspondence gives constant examples.

The first is from a letter of later date than properly
belongs to this chapter, but is so wholly in her spirit of
candor that I insert it here. It is from a letter written in
1843.

---

* According to Dryden's beautiful statement—

        For as high turrets, in their airy sweep
        Require foundations, in proportion deep.
        And lofty cedars as far upward shoot
        As to the nether heavens they drive the root;
        So low did her secure foundation lie,
        She was not humble, but humility.'

'I have been happy in the sight of your pure design,
'of the sweetness and serenity of your mind. In the
'inner sanctuary we met. But I shall say a few blunt
'words, such as were frequent in the days of intimacy,
'and, if they are needless, you will let them fall to the
'ground. Youth is past, with its passionate joys and
'griefs, its restlessness, its vague desires. You have
'chosen your path, you have rounded out your lot, your
'duties are before you. *Now* beware the mediocrity
'that threatens middle age, its limitation of thought and
'interest, its dulness of fancy, its too external life, and
'mental thinness. Remember the limitations that
'threaten every professional man, only to be guarded
'against by great earnestness and watchfulness. So
'take care of yourself, and let not the intellect more
'than the spirit be quenched.

'It is such a relief to me to be able to speak to you
'upon a subject which I thought would never lie open
'between us. Now there will be no place which does
'not lie open to the light. I can always say what I feel.
'And the way in which you took it, so like yourself, so
'manly and noble, gives me the assurance that I shall
'have the happiness of seeing in you that symmetry, that
'conformity in the details of life with the highest aims,
'of which I have sometimes despaired. How much
'higher, dear friend, is " the mind, the music breathing
'" from the " *life*, than anything we can say! Character
'is higher than intellect; this I have long felt to be true;
'may we both live as if we knew it.

* * 'I hope and believe we may be yet very much
'to each other. Imperfect as I am, I feel myself not
unworthy to be a true friend. Neither of us is

'unworthy. In few natures does such love for the
'good and beautiful survive the ruin of all youthful
'hopes, the wreck of all illusions.'

"I supposed our intimacy would terminate when I
'left Cambridge. Its continuing to subsist is a matter
'of surprise to me. And I expected, ere this, you would
'have found some Hersilia, or such-like, to console you
'for losing your Natalia. See, my friend, I am three
'and twenty. I believe in love and friendship, but I
'cannot but notice that circumstances have appalling
'power, and that those links which are not riveted by
'situation, by *interest*, (I mean, not mere worldly inter-
'est, but the instinct of self-preservation,) may be lightly
'broken by a chance touch. I speak not in misan-
'thropy, I believe

"Die Zeit ist schlecht, doch giebts noch grosse Herzen."

'Surely I may be pardoned for aiming at the same
'results with the chivalrous "gift of the Gods." I can-
'not endure to be one of those shallow beings who can
'never get beyond the primer of experience, — who are
'ever saying, —

"Ich habe geglaubt, *nun glaube ich erst recht,*
Und geht es auch wunderlich, geht es auch schlecht,
Ich bleibe in glaubigen Orden."

'Yet, when you write, write freely, and if I don't like
'what you say, let me say so. I have ever been frank,
'as if I expected to be intimate with you good three-
'score years and ten. I am sure we shall always esteem
'each other. I have that much faith.'

'*Jan.* 1832. — All that relates to · —— must be inter-
'esting to me, though I never voluntarily think of him
'now. The apparent caprice of his conduct has shaken
'my faith, but not destroyed my hope. That hope, if I,
'who have so mistaken others, may dare to think I know
'myself, was never selfish. It is painful to lose a friend
'whose knowledge and converse mingled so intimately
'with the growth of my mind,—an early friend to whom
'I was all truth and frankness, seeking nothing but
'equal truth and frankness in return. But this evil may
'be borne; the hard, the lasting evil was to learn to
'distrust my own heart, and lose all faith in my power
'of knowing others. In this letter I see again that pecu-
'liar pride, that contempt of the forms and shows of
'goodness, that fixed resolve to be anything but "like
'"unto the Pharisees," which were to my eye such
'happy omens. Yet how strangely distorted are all his
'views! The daily influence of his intercourse with
'me was like the breath he drew; it has become a part
'of him. Can he escape from himself? Would he be
'unlike all other mortals? His feelings are as false as
'those of Alcibiades. He influenced me, and helped
'form me to what I am. Others shall succeed him.
'Shall I be ashamed to owe anything to friendship?
'But why do I talk?—a child might confute him
'by defining the term *human being*. He will gradually
'work his way into light; if too late for our friendship,
'not, I trust, too late for his own peace and honorable
'well-being. I never insisted on being the instrument
'of good to him. I practised no little arts, no! not to
'effect the good of the friend I loved. I have prayed to
'Heaven, (surely we are sincere when doing that,) to
'guide him in the best path for him, however far from

'me that path might lead. The lesson I have learned
'may make me a more useful friend, a more efficient aid
'to others than I could be to him; yet I hope I shall
'not be denied the consolation of knowing surely, one
'day, that all which appeared evil in the companion of
'happy years was but error.'

  * * * * *

 'I think, since you have seen so much of my char-
'acter, that you must be sensible that any reserves with
'those whom I call my friends, do not arise from duplic-
'ity, but an instinctive feeling that I could not be under-
'stood. I can truly say that I wish no one to overrate
'me; undeserved regard could give me no pleasure; nor
'will I consent to practise charlatanism, either in friend-
'ship or anything else.'

  * * * * *

 'You ought not to think I show a want of generous
'confidence, if I sometimes try the ground on which I
'tread, to see if perchance it may return the echoes of
'hollowness.'

  * * * * *

 'Do not cease to respect me as formerly. It seems to
'me that I have reached the "parting of the ways" in
'my life, and all the knowledge which I have toiled to
'gain only serves to show me the disadvantages of each.
'None of those who think themselves my friends can
'aid me; each, careless, takes the path to which present
'convenience impels; and all would smile or stare, could
'they know the aching and measureless wishes, the sad
'apprehensiveness, which make me pause and strain
'my almost hopeless gaze to the distance. What won-
'der if my present conduct should be mottled by self-
'ishness and incertitude? Perhaps you, who *can* make

your views certain, cannot comprehend me; though
'you showed me last night a penetration which did not
'flow from sympathy. But this I may say — though
'the glad light of hope and ambitious confidence, which
'has vitalized my mind, should be extinguished forever,
'I will not in life act a mean, ungenerous, or useless
'part. Therefore, let not a slight thing lessen your
'respect for me. If you feel as much pain as I do, when
'obliged to diminish my respect for any person, you will
'be glad of this assurance. I hope you will not think
'this note in the style of a French novel.'

POWER OF CIRCUMSTANCES.

'Do you remember a conversation we had in the gar-
'den, one starlight evening, last summer, about the
'incalculable power which outward circumstances have
'over the character? You would not sympathize with
'the regrets I expressed, that mine had not been formed
'amid scenes and persons of nobleness and beauty,
'eager passions and dignified events, instead of those
'secret trials and petty conflicts which make my trans-
'ition state so hateful to my memory and my tastes.
'You then professed the faith which I resigned with
'such anguish, — the faith which a Schiller could never
'attain, — a faith in the power of the human will. Yet
'now, in every letter, you talk to me of the power of
'circumstances. You tell me how changed you are.
'Every one of your letters is different from the one pre-
'ceding, and all so altered from your former self. For
'are you not leaving all our old ground, and do you not
'apologize to me for all your letters? Why do you
'apologize? I think I know you very, very well; con-

' sidering that we are both human, and have the gift of
'concealing our thoughts with words.   Nay, further —
'I do not believe you will be able to become anything
' which I cannot understand.   I know I can sympathize
' with all who feel and think, from a Dryfesdale up to
'a Max Piccolomini.   You say, you have become a
'machine.   If so, I shall expect to find you a grand,
'high-pressure, wave-compelling one — requiring plenty
'of fuel.   You must be a steam-engine, and move some
'majestic fabric at the rate of thirty miles an hour along
'the broad waters of the nineteenth century.   None of
'your pendulum machines for me!   I should, to be sure,
'turn away my head if I should hear you tick, and mark
'the quarters of hours; but the buzz and whiz of a good
'large life-endangerer would be music to mine ears.
'Oh, no! sure there is no danger of your requiring to be
'set down quite on a level, kept in a still place, and
'wound up every eight days.   Oh no, no! you are not
'one of that numerous company, who

> —— " live and die,
> Eat, drink, wake, sleep between,
> Walk, talk like clock-work too,
> So pass in order due,
>   Over the scene,
> To where the past — *is* past,
> The future — nothing yet," &c. &c.

' But we must all be machines : you shall be a steam-
'engine ; — shall be a mill, with extensive water-privi-
'leges, — and I will be a spinning jenny.   No! upon
'second thoughts, I will not be a machine.   I will
'be an instrument, not to be confided to vulgar hands, —
'for instance, a chisel to polish marble, or a whetstone
'to sharpen steel!'

In an unfinished tale, Margaret has given the following studies of character. She is describing two of the friends of the hero of her story. Unquestionably the traits here given were taken from life, though it might not be easy to recognize the portrait of any individual in either sketch. Yet we insert it here to show her own idea of this relation, and her fine feeling of the action and reaction of these subtle intimacies.

'Now, however, I found companions, in thought, at 'least. One, who had great effect on my mind, I may call 'Lytton. He was as premature as myself; at thirteen a 'man in the range of his thoughts, analyzing motives, 'and explaining principles, when he ought to have been 'playing cricket, or hunting in the woods. The young 'Arab, or Indian, may dispense with mere play, and 'enter betimes into the histories and practices of man-'hood, for all these are, in their modes of life, closely 'connected with simple nature, and educate the body 'no less than the mind; but the same good cannot be said of lounging lazily under a tree, while mentally accompanying Gil Blas through his course of intrigue 'and adventure, and visiting with him the impure 'atmosphere of courtiers, picaroons, and actresses. This 'was Lytton's favorite reading; his mind, by nature 'subtle rather than daring, would in any case have 'found its food in the now hidden workings of char-'acter and passion, the by-play of life, the unexpected 'and seemingly incongruous relations to be found there. 'He loved the natural history of man, not religiously, 'but for entertainment. What he sought, he found, but 'paid the heaviest price. All his later days were poi-'soned by his subtlety, which made it impossible for him

'to look at any action with a single and satisfied eye.
'He tore the buds open to see if there were no worm
'sheathed in the blushful heart, and was so afraid of
'overlooking some mean possibility, that he lost sight
'of virtue. Grubbing like a mole beneath the surface
'of earth, rather than reading its living language above,
'he had not faith enough to believe in the flower, neither
'faith enough to mine for the gem, and remains at pen-
'ance in the limbo of halfnesses, I trust not forever.
'Then all his characteristics wore brilliant hues. He
'was very witty, and I owe to him the great obligation
'of being the first and only person who has excited me
'to frequent and boundless gayety. The sparks of his
'wit were frequent, slight surprises; his was a slender
'dart, and rebounded easily to the hand. I like the
'scintillating, arrowy wit far better than broad, genial
'humor. The light metallic touch pleases me. When
'wit appears as fun and jollity, she wears a little of the
'Silenus air; — the Mercurial is what I like.

   'In later days, — for my intimacy with him lasted
'many years, — he became the feeder of my intellect. He
'delighted to ransack the history of a nation, of an art
'or a science, and bring to me all the particulars. Tel-
'ling them fixed them in his own memory, which was
'the most tenacious and ready I have ever known; he
'enjoyed my clear perception as to their relative value,
'and I classified them in my own way. As he was
'omnivorous, and of great mental activity, while my
'mind was intense, though rapid in its movements, and
'could only give itself to a few things of its own accord,
'I traversed on the wings of his effort large demesnes
'that would otherwise have remained quite unknown
'to me. They were not, indeed, seen to the same profit

'as my own province, whose tillage I knew, and whose
'fruits were the answer to. my desire; but the fact of
'seeing them at all gave a largeness to my view, and a
'candor to my judgment. I could not be ignorant how
'much there was I did not know, nor leave out of
'sight the many sides to every question, while, by the
'law of affinity, I chose my own.

'Lytton was not loved by any one. He was not
'positively hated, or disliked; for there was nothing
'which the general mind could take firm hold of enough
'for such feelings. Cold, intangible, he was to play across
'the life of others. A momentary resentment was some-
'times felt at a presence which would not mingle with
'theirs; his scrutiny, though not hostile, was recog-
'nized as unfeeling and impertinent, and his mirth
'unsettled all objects from their foundations. But he
'was soon forgiven and forgotten. Hearts went not
'forth to war against or to seek one who was a mere
'experimentalist and observer in existence. For myself,
'I did not love, perhaps, but was attached to him, and
'the attachment grew steadily, for it was founded, not
'on what I wanted of him, but on his truth to himself.
'His existence was a real one; he was not without a
'pathetic feeling of his wants, but was never tempted
'to supply them by imitating the properties of any other
·character. He accepted the law of his being, and never
'violated it. This is next best to the nobleness which
'transcends it. I did not disapprove, even when I dis-
'liked, his acts.

'Amadin, my other companion, was as slow and deep
'of feeling, as Lytton was brilliant, versatile, and cold.
'His temperament was generally grave, even to appa-
'rent dulness; his eye gave little light, but a slow fire

'burned in its depths. His was a character not to be
'revealed to himself, or others, except by the important
'occasions of life. Though every day, no doubt, deep-
'ened and enriched him, it brought little that he could
'show or recall. But when his soul, capable of religion,
'capable of love, was moved, all his senses were united
'in the word or action that followed, and the impression
'made on you was entire. I have scarcely known any
'capable of such true manliness as he. His poetry,
'written, or unwritten, was the experience of life. It
'lies in few lines, as yet, but not one of them will ever
'need to be effaced.

'Early that serious eye inspired in me a trust that has
'never been deceived. There was no magnetism in
'him, no lights and shades that could stir the imagina-
'tion; no bright ideal suggested by him stood between
'the friend and his self. As the years matured that
'self, I loved him more, and knew him as he knew him-
'self, always in the present moment; he could never
'occupy my mind in absence.'

Another of her early friends, Rev. F. H. Hedge, has
sketched his acquaintance with her in the following
paper, communicated by him for these memoirs. Somewhat older than Margaret, and having enjoyed an education at a German university, his conversation was full
of interest and excitement to her. He opened to her a
whole world of thoughts and speculations which gave
movement to her mind in a congenial direction.

———

"My acquaintance with Margaret commenced in the
year 1823, at Cambridge, my native place and hers. I
was then a member of Harvard College, in which my

father held one of the offices of instruction, and I used frequently to meet her in the social circles of which the families connected with the college formed the nucleus. Her father, at this time, represented the county of Middlesex in the Congress of the United States.

"Margaret was then about thirteen, — a child in years, but so precocious in her mental and physical developments, that she passed for eighteen or twenty. Agreeably to this estimate, she had her place in society, as a lady full-grown.

"When I recall her personal appearance, as it was then and for ten or twelve years subsequent to this, I have the idea of a blooming girl of a florid complexion and vigorous health, with a tendency to robustness, of which she was painfully conscious, and which, with little regard to hygienic principles, she endeavored to suppress or conceal, thereby preparing for herself much future suffering. With no pretensions to beauty then, or at any time, her face was one that attracted, that awakened a lively interest, that made one desirous of a nearer acquaintance. It was a face that fascinated, without satisfying. Never seen in repose, never allowing a steady perusal of its features, it baffled every attempt to judge the character by physiognomical induction. You saw the evidence of a mighty force, but what direction that force would assume, — whether it would determine itself to social triumphs, or to triumphs of art, — it was impossible to divine. Her moral tendencies, her sentiments, her true and prevailing character, did not appear in the lines of her face. She seemed equal to anything, but might not choose to put forth her strength. You felt that a great possibility lay behind that brow but you felt, also, that the talent that was in her might miscarry through indifference or caprice.

"I said she had no pretensions to beauty. Yet she was not plain. She escaped the reproach of positive plainness, by her blond and abundant hair, by her excellent teeth, by her sparkling, dancing, busy eyes, which, though usually half closed from near-sightedness, shot piercing glances at those with whom she conversed, and, most of all, by the very peculiar and graceful carriage of her head and neck, which all who knew her will remember as the most characteristic trait in her personal appearance.

"In conversation she had already, at that early age, begun to distinguish herself, and made much the same impression in society that she did in after years, with the exception, that, as she advanced in life, she learned to control that tendency to sarcasm, — that disposition to 'quiz,' — which was then somewhat excessive. It frightened shy young people from her presence, and made her, for a while, notoriously unpopular with the ladies of her circle.

"This propensity seems to have been aggravated by unpleasant encounters in her school-girl experience. She was a pupil of Dr. Park, of Boston, whose seminary for young ladies was then at the height of a well-earned reputation, and whose faithful and successful endeavors in this department have done much to raise the standard of female education among us. Here the inexperienced country girl was exposed to petty persecutions from the dashing misses of the city, who pleased themselves with giggling criticisms not inaudible, nor meant to be inaudible to their subject, on whatsoever in dress and manner fell short of the city mark.

Then it was first revealed to her young heart, and laid up for•future reflection, how large a place in woman's world is given to fashion and frivolity. Her mind reacted on these attacks with indiscriminate sarcasms. She made herself formidable by her wit, and, of course, unpopular. A root of bitterness sprung up in her which vears of moral culture were needed to eradicate.

"Partly to evade the temporary unpopularity into which she had fallen, and partly to pursue her studies secure from those social avocations which were found unavoidable in the vicinity of Cambridge and Boston, in 1824 or 5 she was sent to Groton, where she remained two years in quiet seclusion.

"On her return to Cambridge, in 1826, I renewed my acquaintance, and an intimacy was then formed, which continued until her death. The next seven years, which were spent in Cambridge, were years of steady growth, with little variety of incident, and little that was note-worthy of outward experience, but with great intensity of the inner life. It was with her, as with most young women, and with most young men, too, between the ages of sixteen and twenty-five, a period of prepon-derating sentimentality, a period of romance and of dreams, of yearning and of passion. She pursued at this time, I think, no systematic study, but she read with the heart, and was learning more from social expe-rience than from books.

"I remember noting at this time a trait which contin-ued to be a prominent one through life, — I mean a pas-sionate love for the beautiful, which comprehended all the kingdoms of nature and art. I have never known one who seemed to derive such satisfaction from the contemplation of lovely forms.

"Her intercourse with girls of her own age and standing was frank and excellent. Personal ˙attractions, and the homage which they received, awakened in her no jealousy. She envied not their success, though vividly aware of the worth of beauty, and inclined to exaggerate her own deficiencies in that kind. On the contrary, she loved to draw these fair girls to herself, and to make them her guests, and was never so happy as when surrounded, in company, with such a bevy. This attraction was mutual, as, according to Goethe, every attraction is. Where she felt an interest, she awakened an interest. Without flattery or art, by the truth and nobleness of her nature, she won the confidence, and made herself the friend and intimate, of a large number of young ladies, — the belles of their day, — with most of whom she remained in correspondence during the greater part of her life.

"In our evening reünions she was always conspicuous by the brilliancy of her wit, which needed but little provocation to break forth in exuberant sallies, that drew around her a knot of listeners, and made her the central attraction of the hour. Rarely did she enter a company in which she was not a prominent object.

"I have spoken of her conversational talent. It continued to develop itself in these years, and was certainly her most decided gift. One could form no adequate idea of her ability without hearing her converse. She did many things well, but nothing so well as she talked. It is the opinion of all her friends, that her writings do her very imperfect justice. For some reason or other, she could never deliver herself in print as she did with her lips. She required the stimulus of attentive ears

and answering eyes, to bring out all her power. She must have her auditory about her.

" Her conversation, as it was then, I have seldom heard equalled. It was not so much attractive as commanding. Though remarkably fluent and select, it was neither fluency, nor choice diction, nor wit, nor sentiment, that gave it its peculiar power, but accuracy of statement, keen discrimination, and a certain weight of judgment, which contrasted strongly and charmingly with the youth and sex of the speaker. I do not remember that the vulgar charge of talking ' like a book ' was ever fastened upon her, although, by her precision, she might seem to have incurred it. The fact was, her speech, though finished and true as the most deliberate rhetoric of the pen, had always an air of spontaneity which made it seem the grace of the moment,— the result of some organic provision that made finished sentences as natural to her as blundering and hesitation are to most of us. With a little more imagination, she would have made an excellent improvisatrice.

" Here let me say a word respecting the character of Margaret's mind. It was what in woman is generally called a masculine mind; that is, its action was determined by ideas rather than by sentiments. And yet, with this masculine trait, she combined a woman's appreciation of the beautiful in sentiment and the beautiful in action. Her intellect was rather solid than graceful, yet no one was more alive to grace. She was no artist, — she would never have written an epic, or romance, or drama,— yet no one knew better the qualities which go to the making of these; and though catholic as to kind, no one was more rigorously exacting as to quality. Nothing short of the best in each kind would content her.

" She wanted imagination, and she wanted productiveness. She wrote with difficulty. Without external pressure, perhaps, she would never have written at all. She was dogmatic, and not creative. Her strength was in characterization and in criticism. Her *critique* on Goethe, in the second volume of the Dial, is, in my estimation, one of the best things she has written. And, as far as it goes, it is one of the best criticisms extant of Goethe.

" What I especially admired in her was her intellectual sincerity. Her judgments took no bribe from her sex or her sphere, nor from custom nor tradition, nor caprice. She valued truth supremely, both for herself and others. The question with her was not what should be believed, or what ought to be true, but what *is* true. Her yes and no were never conventional ; and she often amazed people by a cool and unexpected dissent from the commonplaces of popular acceptation."

Margaret, we have said, saw in each of her friends the secret interior capability, which might become hereafter developed into some special beauty or power. By means of this penetrating, this prophetic insight, she gave each to himself, acted on each to draw out his best nature, gave him an ideal out of which he could draw strength and liberty hour by hour. Thus her influence was ever ennobling, and each felt that in her society he was truer, wiser, better, and yet more free and happy, than elsewhere. The " dry light" which Lord Bacon loved, she never knew ; her light was life, was love, was warm with sympathy and a boundless energy of affection and hope. Though her love flattered and charmed her friends, it did not spoil them, for they knew her perfect truth. They knew that she loved them, not for what she imagined, but for what she saw, though she saw it only in the germ. But as the Greeks beheld a Persephone and Athene in the passing stranger, and ennobled humanity into ideal beauty, Margaret saw all her friends thus idealized. She was a balloon of sufficient power to take us all up with her into the serene depth of heaven, where she loved to float, far above the low details of earthly life. Earth lay beneath us as a lovely picture, — its sounds came up mellowed into music.

Margaret was, to persons younger than herself, a Makaria and Natalia. She was wisdom and intellectual beauty, filling life with a charm and glory "known to neither sea nor land." To those of her own age she was sibyl and seer, — a prophetess, revealing the future, pointing the path, opening their eyes to the great aims only worthy of pursuit in life. To those older than herself she was like the Euphorion in Goethe's drama, child of Faust and Helen, — a wonderful union of exuberance and judgment, born of romantic fulness and classic limitation. They saw with surprise her clear good-sense balancing her flow of sentiment and ardent courage. They saw her comprehension of both sides of every question, and gave her their confidence, as to one of equal age, because of so ripe a judgment.

But it was curious to see with what care and conscience she kept her friendships distinct. Her fine practical understanding, teaching her always the value of limits, enabled her to hold apart all her intimacies, nor did one ever encroach on the province of the other. Like a moral Paganini, she played always on a single string, drawing from each its peculiar music,— bringing wild beauty from the slen-

der wire, no less than from the deep-sounding harp-string.
Some of her friends had little to give her when compared
with others ; but I never noticed that she sacrificed in
any respect the smaller faculty to the greater. She fully
realized that the Divine Being makes each part of this
creation divine, and that He dwells in the blade of grass
as really if not as fully as in the majestic oak which has
braved the storm for a hundred years. She felt in full
the thought of a poem which she once copied for me from
Barry Cornwall, which begins thus :—

> " She was not fair, nor full of grace,
>   Nor crowned with thought, nor aught beside
>   No wealth had she of mind or face,
>   To win our love, or gain our pride,—
>   No lover's thought her heart could touch,—
>   No poet's dream was round her thrown ;
>   And yet we miss her — ah, so much !
>   Now — she has flown."

I will close this section of Cambridge Friendship with
the two following .passages, the second of which was
written to some one unknown to me :

'Your letter was of cordial sweetness to me, as is
'ever the thought of our friendship, — that sober-suited
'friendship, of which the web was so deliberately and
'well woven, and which wears so well.

*   *   *   *   *   *

'I want words to express the singularity of all my
'past relations; yet let me try.

'From a very early age I have felt that I was not
'born to the common womanly lot.   I knew I should
'never find a being who could keep the key of my char-
'acter; that there would be none on whom I could

'always lean, from whom I could always learn; that
'I should be a pilgrim and sojourner on earth, and
'that the birds and foxes would be surer of a place to
'lay the head than I. You understand me, of course;
'such beings can only find their homes in hearts. All
'material luxuries, all the arrangements of society, are
'mere conveniences to them.

'This thought, all whose bearings I did not, indeed,
'understand, affected me sometimes with sadness, some-
'times with pride. I mourned that I never should have
'a thorough experience of life, never know the full riches
'of my being; I was proud that I was to test myself in
'the sternest way, that I was always to return to myself,
'to be my own priest, pupil, parent, child, husband, and
'wife. All this I did not understand as I do now; but
'this destiny of the thinker, and (shall I dare to say it?)
'of the poetic priestess, sibylline, dwelling in the cave,
'or amid the Lybian sands, lay yet enfolded in my
'mind. Accordingly, I did not look on any of the per-
'sons, brought into relation with me, with common
'womanly eyes.

'Yet, as my character is, after all, still more feminine
'than masculine, it would sometimes happen that I put
'more emotion into a state than I myself knew. I
'really was capable of attachment, though it never
seemed so till the hour of separation. And if a con-
nexion was torn up by the roots, the soil of my exist-
'ence showed an unsightly wound, which long refused
'to clothe itself in verdure.

'With regard to yourself, I was to you all that I
'wished to be. I knew that I reigned in your thoughts
'in my own way. And I also lived with you more
truly and freely than with any other person. We were

'truly friends, but it was not friends as men are friends to
'one another, or as brother and sister. There was, also,
'that pleasure, which may, perhaps, be termed conjugal,
'of finding oneself in an alien nature. Is there any
'tinge of love in this? Possibly! At least, in compar-
'ing it with my relation to ——, I find *that* was strictly
'fraternal. I valued him for himself. I did not care
'for an influence over him, and was perfectly willing to
'have one or fifty rivals in his heart. * *

* * 'I think I may say, I never loved. I but see
'my possible life reflected on the clouds. As in a glass
'darkly, I have seen what I might feel as child, wife,
'mother, but I have never really approached the close
'relations of life. A sister I have truly been to many, —
'a brother to more, — a fostering nurse to, oh how
'many! The bridal hour of many a spirit, when first
'it was wed, I have shared, but said adieu before the
'wine was poured out at the banquet. And there is one
'I always love in my poetic hour, as the lily looks up to
'the star from amid the waters; and another whom I
'visit as the bee visits the flower, when I crave sympa-
'thy. Yet those who live would scarcely consider that
'I am among the living,—and I am isolated, as you say.

'My dear ——, all is well; all has helped me to deci-
'pher the great poem of the universe. I can hardly
'describe to you the happiness which floods my solitary
'hours. My actual life is yet much clogged and im-
'peded, but I have at last got me an oratory, where I
'can retire and pray. With your letter, vanished a last
'regret. · You did not act or think unworthily. It is
'enough. As to the cessation of our confidential inter-
'course, circumstances must have accomplished that
'long ago; my only grief was that you should do it

'with your own free will, and for reasons that I thought
'unworthy. I long to honor you, to be honored by you.
'Now we will have free and noble thoughts of one
'another, and all that is best of our friendship shall
'remain.'

II.

CONVERSATION. — SOCIAL INTERCOURSE.

" Be thou what thou singly art, and personate only thyself. Swim
smoothly in the stream of thy nature, and live but one man."

SIR THOMAS BROWNE.

" Ah, how mournful look in letters
    Black on white, the words to me,
    Which from lips of thine cast fetters
    Round the heart, or set it free."

GOETHE, *translated by J. S. Dwight.*

" Zu erfinden, zu beschliessen,
    Bleibe, Kunstler, oft allein ;
    Deines Wirkes zu geniessen
    Eile freudig zum Verein,
    Hier im Ganzen schau erfahre
    Deines eignes Lebenslauf,
    Und die Thaten mancher Jahre
    Gehn dir in dem Nachbar auf."

GOETHE, *Artist's Song.*

—

WHEN I first knew Margaret, she was much in society, but in a circle of her own, — of friends whom she
had drawn around her, and whom she entertained and
delighted by her exuberant talent. Of those belonging
to this circle, let me recall a few characters.

The young girls whom Margaret had attracted were
very different from herself, and from each other. From
Boston, Charlestown, Roxbury, Brookline, they came to
her, and the little circle of companions would meet now

in one house, and now in another, of these pleasant towns. There was A——, a dark-haired, black-eyed beauty, with clear olive complexion, through which the rich blood flowed. She was bright, beauteous, and cold as a gem, — with clear perceptions of character within a narrow limit, — enjoying society, and always surrounded with admirers, of whose feelings she seemed quite unconscious. While they were just ready to die of unrequited love, she stood untouched as Artemis, scarcely aware of the deadly arrows which had flown from her silver bow. I remember that Margaret said, that Tennyson's little poem of the skipping-rope must have been written for her, — where the lover expressing his admiration of the fairy-like motion and the light grace of the lady, is told —

> " Get off, or else my skipping-rope
> Will hit you in the eye."

Then there was B——, the reverse of all this,— tender, susceptible, with soft blue eyes, and mouth of trembling sensibility. How sweet were her songs, in which a single strain of pure feeling ever reminded me of those angel symphonies, —

> " In all whose music, the pathetic minor
> Our ears will cross — "

and when she sang or spoke, her eyes had often the expression of one looking *in* at her thought, not *out* at her companion.

Then there was C——, all animated and radiant with joyful interest in life, — seeing with ready eye the beauty of Nature and of Thought, — entering with quick sympathy into all human interest, taking readily everything which belonged to her, and dropping with sure instinct whatever suited her not. Unknown to her was struggle, conflict, crisis; she grew up harmonious as the flower, drawing nutriment from earth and air, — from " common things which round us lie," and equally from the highest thoughts and inspirations.

Shall I also speak of D——, whose beauty had a half-voluptuous character, from those ripe red lips, those ringlets overflowing the well-rounded shoulders, and the hazy softness of those large eyes? Or of E——, her companion, beautiful too, but in a calmer, purer style, — with eye from which looked forth self-posses-sion, truth and fortitude? Others, well worth notice, I must not notice now.

But among the young men who surrounded Margaret, a like variety prevailed. One was to her interesting, on account of his quick, active intellect, and his contempt for shows and pretences; for his inexhaustible wit, his exquisite taste, his infinitely varied stores of information, and the poetic view which he took of life, painting it with Rembrandt depths of shadow and bursts of light. Another she gladly went to for his compact, thoroughly considered views of God and the world, — for his culture, so much more deep and rich than any other we could find here, — for his conversation, opening in systematic form new fields of thought. Yet men of strong native talent, and rich character, she also liked well to know, however deficient in culture, knowledge, or power of utterance. Each was to her a study, and she never rested till she had found the bottom of every mind, — till she had satisfied herself of its capacity and currents, — measuring it with her sure line, as

— " All human wits
Are measured, but a few."

It was by her singular gift of speech that she cast her
spells and worked her wonders in this little circle. Full
of thoughts and full of words; capable of poetic impro-
visation, had there not been a slight overweight of a
tendency to the tangible and real; capable of clear,
complete, philosophic statement, but for the strong tendency to life which melted down evermore in its lava-
current the solid blocks of thought; she was yet, by
these excesses, better fitted for the arena of conversation.
Here she found none adequate for the equal encounter;
when she laid her lance in rest, every champion must
go down before it. How fluent her wit, which, for hour
after hour, would furnish best entertainment, as she described scenes where she had lately been, or persons she
had lately seen! Yet she readily changed from gay to
grave, and loved better the serious talk which opened
the depths of life. Describing a conversation in relation
to Christianity, with a friend of strong mind, who told
her he had found, in this religion, a home for his best
and deepest thoughts, she says — ' Ah! what a pleasure
' to meet with such a daring, yet realizing, mind as his!'
But her catholic taste found satisfaction in intercourse
with persons quite different from herself in opinions and
tendencies, as the following letter, written in her twen-
tieth year, will indicate:

*   *   *   *   *

' I was very happy, although greatly restrained by
' the apprehension of going a little too far with these
' persons of singular refinement and settled opinions

'However, I believe I did pretty well, though I did make
'one or two little mistakes, when most interested; but I
'was not so foolish as to try to retrieve them.   One occa-
'sion more particularly, when Mr. G——, after going
'more fully into his poetical opinions than I could have
'expected, stated his sentiments: first, that Wordsworth
'had, in truth, guided, or, rather, completely vivified the
'poetry of this age; secondly, that 't was his influence
'which had, in reality, given all his better individuality
'to Byron.   He recurred again and again to this opinion,
'*con amore*, and seemed to wish much for an answer; but
'I would not venture, though 't was hard for me to for-
'bear, I knew so well what I thought.   Mr. G——'s
'Wordsworthianism, however, is excellent; his beauti-
'ful simplicity of taste, and love of truth, have preserved
'him from any touch of that vague and imbecile enthu-
'siasm, which has enervated almost all the exclusive and
'determined admirers of the great poet whom I have
'known in these parts.   His reverence, his feeling, are
'thoroughly intelligent.   Everything in his mind is well
'defined; and his horror of the vague, and false, nay, even
'(suppose another horror here, for grammar's sake)
'of the startling and paradoxical, have their beauty.   I
'think I could know Mr. G—— long, and see him per-
'petually, without any touch of satiety; such variety is
'made by the very absence of pretension, and the love
'of truth.   I found much amusement in leading him to
'sketch the scenes and persons which Lockhart portrays
'in such glowing colors, and which he, too, has seen
'with the *eye of taste*, but how different !'

   * * * * *

Our friend was well aware that her *forte* was in conversation.   Here she felt at home. here she felt her

power, and the excitement which the presence of living persons brought, gave all her faculties full activity 'After all,' she says, in a letter, ' this writing is mighty 'dead. Oh, for my dear old Greeks, who talked every-'thing — not to shine as in the Parisian saloons, but to 'learn, to teach, to vent the heart, to clear the mind ! '

Again, in 1832 : —

'Conversation is my natural element. I need to be 'called out, and never think alone, without imagining 'some companion. Whether this be nature or the force 'of circumstances, I know not ; it is my habit, and be-'speaks a second-rate mind.'

I am disposed to think, much as she excelled in general conversation, that her greatest mental efforts were made in intercourse with individuals. All her friends will unite in the testimony, that whatever they may have known of wit and eloquence in others, they have never seen one who, like her, by the conversation of an hour or two, could not merely entertain and inform, but make an epoch in one's life. We all dated back to this or that conversation with Margaret, in which we took a complete survey of great subjects, came to some clear view of a difficult question, saw our way open before us to a higher plane of life, and were led to some definite reso-lution or purpose which has had a bearing on all our subsequent career. For Margaret's conversation turned, at such times, to life, — its destiny, its duty, its prospect. With comprehensive glance she would survey the past, and sum up, in a few brief words, its results ; she would then turn to the future, and by a natural order, sweep through its chances and alternatives, — passing ever into a more earnest tone, into a more serious view, — and then bring all to bear on the present, till its duties grew plain, and its opportunities attractive. Happy he who can lift conversation, without loss of its cheer, to the highest uses!   Happy he who has such a gift as this, an original faculty thus accomplished by culture, by which he can make our common life rich, significant and fair, — can give to the hour a beauty and brilliancy which shall make it eminent long after, amid dreary years of level routine!

I recall many such conversations. I remember one summer's day, in which we rode together, on horseback, from Cambridge to Newton, — a day all of a piece, in which my eloquent companion helped me to understand my past life, and her own, — a day which left me in that calm repose which comes to us, when we clearly apprehend what we ought to do, and are ready to attempt it. I recall other mornings when, not having seen her for a week or two, I would walk with her for hours, beneath the lindens or in the garden, while we related to each other what we had read in our German studies.   And I always left her astonished at the progress of her mind, at the amount of new thoughts she had garnered, and filled with a new sense of the worth of knowledge, and the value of life.

There were other conversations, in which, impelled by the strong instinct of utterance, she would state, in words of tragical pathos, her own needs and longings, — her demands on life, — the struggles of mind, and of heart, — her conflicts with self, with nature, with the limitations of circumstances, with insoluble prob-iems, with an unattainable desire.   She seemed to

feel relief from the expression of these thoughts, though
she gained no light from her companion. Many such
conversations I remember, while she lived in Cambridge,
and one such in Groton; but afterwards, when I met
her, I found her mind risen above these struggles, and in
a self-possessed state which needed no such outlet for its
ferment.

It is impossible to give any account of *these* conversations; but I add a few scraps, to indicate, however
slightly, something of her ordinary manner.

'Rev. Mr. —— preached a sermon on TIME. But
'what business had he to talk about time? We should
'like well to hear the opinions of a great man, who had
'made good use of time; but not of a little man, who
'had not used it to any purpose. I wished to get up and
'tell him to speak of something which he knew and felt.'

'The best criticism on those sermons which proclaim
'so loudly the dignity of human nature was from our
'friend E. S. She said, coming out from Dr. Chan-
'ning's church, that she felt fatigued by the demands
'the sermon made on her, and would go home and read
'what Jesus said, — "*Ye are of more value than many*
'"*sparrows.*" *That* she could bear; it did not seem
'exaggerated praise.'

'The Swedenborgians say, "that is *Correspondence*,"
'and the phrenologists, "that it is *Approbativeness*," and
'so think they know all about it. It would not be so, if
'we could be like the birds, — make one method, and
'then desert it, and make a new one, — as they build
'their nests.'

'As regards crime, we cannot understand what we
'have not *already* felt; — thus, all crimes have formed
'part of our minds. We do but recognize one part of
'ourselves in the worst actions of others. When you
'take the subject in this light, do you not incline to
'consider the capacity for action as something widely
'differing from the experience of a feeling?'

'How beautiful the life of Benvenuto Cellini! How
'his occupations perpetually impelled to thought, — to
'gushings of thought naturally excited!'

'Father lectured me for looking satirical when the
'man of Words spake, and so attentive to the man of
'Truth,— that is, of God.'

Margaret used often to talk about the books which she
and I were reading.

GODWIN. 'I think you will be more and more satisfied
'with Godwin. He has fully lived the double existence
'of man, and he casts the reflexes on his magic mirror
'from a height where no object in life's panorama can
'cause one throb of delirious hope or grasping ambition.
'At any rate, if you study him, you may know all he
'has to tell. He is quite free from vanity, and conceals
'not miserly any of his treasures from the knowledge of
'posterity.

M'LLE. D'ESPINASSE. 'I am swallowing by gasps
'that *cauldrony* beverage of selfish passion and mor-
'bid taste, the letters of M'lle D'Espinasse. It is
'good for me. How odious is the abandonment of pas-
'sion, such as this, unshaded by pride or delicacy, unha.·

'lowed by religion,—a selfish craving only; every 'source of enjoyment stifled to cherish this burning 'thirst. Yet the picture, so minute in its touches, is true 'as death. I should not like Delphine now.'

Events in life, apparently trivial, often seemed to her full of mystic significance, and it was her pleasure to turn such to poetry. On one occasion, the sight of a passion-flower, given by one lady to another, and then lost, appeared to her so significant of the character, relation, and destiny of the two, that it drew from her lines of which two or three seem worth preserving, as indicating her feeling of social relations.

> 'Dear friend, my heart grew pensive when I saw
> 'The flower, for thee so sweetly set apart,
> 'By one whose passionless though tender heart
> 'Is worthy to bestow, as angels are,
> 'By an unheeding hand conveyed away,
> 'To close, in unsoothed night, the promise of its day.
>
>   *   *   *   *   *
>
> 'The mystic flower read in thy soul-filled eye
> 'To its life's question the desired reply,
> 'But came no nearer. On thy gentle breast
> 'It hoped to find the haven of its rest ;
> 'But in cold night, hurried afar from thee,
> 'It closed its once half-smiling destiny.
>
> 'Yet thus, methinks, it utters as it dies, —
> ' " By the pure truth of those calm, gentle eyes
> ' " Which saw my life should find its aim in thine,
> ' " I see a clime where no strait laws confine.
> ' " In that blest land where *twos* ne'er know a *three*,
> ' " Save as the accord of their fine sympathy,
> ' " O, best-loved, I will wait for thee ! " ' '

III.

STUDIES.

'Nur durch das Morgenthor des Schönen
Drangst du in der Erkenntniss Land ;
An höhen Glanz sich zu gewöhnen
Uebt sich am Reize der Verstand.
Was bei dem Saitenklang der Musen
Mit süssem Beben dich durchdrang,
Erzog die Kraft in deinem Busen,
Die sich dereinst zum Weltgeist schwang.''

SCHILLER.

'To work, with heart resigned and spirit strong ;
Subdue, with patient toil, life's bitter wrong,
Through Nature's dullest, as her brightest ways,
We will march onward, singing to thy praise.''

E. S., *in the Dial.*

'The peculiar nature of the scholar's occupation consists in this, — that science, and especially that side of it from which he conceives of the whole, shall continually burst forth before him in new and fairer forms. Let this fresh spiritual youth never grow old within him ; let no form become fixed and rigid ; let each sunrise bring him new joy and love in his vocation, and larger views of its significance.''

FICHTE.

———

OF Margaret's studies while at Cambridge, I knew personally only of the German. She already, when I first became acquainted with her, had become familiar with the masterpieces of French, Italian and Spanish literature. But all this amount of reading had not made her "deep-learned in books and shallow in herself;"

for she brought to the study of most writers "a spirit and genius equal or superior,"— so far, at least, as the analytic understanding was concerned. Every writer whom she studied, as every person whom she knew, she placed in his own class, knew his relation to other writers, to the world, to life, to nature, to herself. Much as they might delight her, they never swept her away. She breasted the current of their genius, as a stately swan moves up a stream, enjoying the rushing water the more because she resists it. In a passionate love-struggle she wrestled thus with the genius of De Staël, of Rousseau, of Alfieri, of Petrarch.

The first and most striking element in the genius of Margaret was the clear, sharp understanding, which keenly distinguished between things different, and kept every thought, opinion, person, character, in its own place, not to be confounded with any other. The god Terminus presided over her intellect. She knew her thoughts as we know each other's faces; and opinions, with most of us so vague, shadowy, and shifting, were in her mind substantial and distinct realities. Some persons see distinctions, others resemblances; but she saw both. No sophist could pass on her a counterfeit piece of intellectual money; but also she recognized the one pure metallic basis in coins of different epochs, and when mixed with a very ruinous alloy. This gave a comprehensive quality to her mind most imposing and convincing, as it enabled her to show the one Truth, or the one Law, manifesting itself in such various phenomena. Add to this her profound faith in truth, which made her a Realist of that order that thoughts to her were things. The world of her thoughts rose around her mind as a panorama, — the sun in the sky, the flowers distinct in the foreground, the pale mountain sharply, though faintly, cutting the sky with its outline in the distance, — and all in pure light and shade, all in perfect perspective.

Margaret began to study German early in 1832. Both she and I were attracted towards this literature, at the same time, by the wild bugle-call of Thomas Carlyle, in his romantic articles on Richter, Schiller, and Goethe, which appeared in the old Foreign Review, the Edinburgh Review, and afterwards in the Foreign Quarterly.

I believe that in about three months from the time that Margaret commenced German, she was reading with ease the masterpieces of its literature. Within the year, she had read Goethe's Faust, Tasso, Iphigenia, Hermann and Dorothea, Elective Affinities, and Memoirs; Tieck's William Lovel, Prince Zerbino, and other works; Körner, Novalis, and something of Richter; all of Schiller's principal dramas, and his lyric poetry. Almost every evening I saw her, and heard an account of her studies. Her mind opened under this influence, as the apple-blossom at the end of a warm week in May. The thought and the beauty of this rich literature equally filled her mind and fascinated her imagination.

But if she studied books thus earnestly, still more frequently did she turn to the study of men. Authors and their personages were not ideal beings merely, but full of human blood and life. So living men and women were idealized again, and transfigured by her rapid fancy, — every trait intensified, developed, ennobled. Lessing says that " The true portrait painter will paint his subject, flattering him as art ought to flatter, — painting the face not as it actually is, but as creation designed, omitting the imperfections arising from the resistance of the material worked in." Margaret's portrait-painting intellect treated persons in this way. She saw them as God designed them, — omitting the loss from wear and tear, from false position, from friction of untoward circumstances. If we may be permitted to take a somewhat transcendental distinction, she saw them not as they *actually* were, but as they *really* were. This accounts for her high estimate of her friends, — too high, too flattering, indeed, but justified to her mind by her knowledge of their interior capabilities.

The following extract illustrates her power, even at the age of nineteen, of comprehending the relations of two things lying far apart from each other, and of rising to a point of view which could overlook both : —

'I have had, — while staying a day or two in Bos-
'ton, — some of Shirley's, Ford's, and Heywood's plays
'from the Athenæum. There are some noble strains
'of proud rage, and intellectual, but most poetical, all-
'absorbing, passion. One of the finest fictions I recol-
'lect in those specimens of the Italian novelists, —
'which you, I think, read when I did, — noble, where it
'illustrated the Italian national spirit, is ruined by the
'English novelist, who has transplanted it to an uncon-
'genial soil; yet he has given it beauties which an
'Italian eye could not see, by investing the actors with
'deep, continuing, truly English affections.'

  *   *   *   *   *

The following criticism on some of the dialogues of Plato, (dated June 3d, 1833,) in a letter returning the book, illustrates her downright way of asking world-

revered authors to accept the test of plain common
sense. As a finished or deliberate opinion, it ought not
to be read; for it was not intended as such, but as a
first impression hastily sketched. But read it as an
illustration of the method in which her mind worked,
and you will see that she meets the great Plato modestly, but boldly, on human ground, asking him for satisfactory proof of all that he says, and treating him as a
human being, speaking to human beings.

   '*June* 3, 1833. — I part with Plato with regret. I
'could have wished to "enchant myself," as Socrates
'would say, with him some days longer. Eutyphron is
'excellent. 'Tis the best specimen I have ever seen of
'that mode of convincing. There is one passage in
'which Socrates, as if it were *aside*, — since the remark
'is quite away from the consciousness of Eutyphron, —
'declares, "qu'il aimerait incomparablement mieux des
' "principes fixes et inébranlables à l'habilité de Dédale
' "avec les tresors de Tantale." I delight to hear such
'things from those whose lives have given the right to
'say them. For 't is not always true what Lessing says,
and I, myself, once thought, —

> " F. — Von was fur Tugenden spricht er denn ?
> Minna. — Er spricht von keiner ; denn ihn fehlt keine."

For the mouth sometimes talketh virtue from the
'overflowing of the heart, as well as love, anger, &c.

   '"Crito" I have read only once, but like it. I have
'not got it in my heart though, so clearly as the others.
   'The "Apology" I deem only remarkable for the

'noble tone of sentiment, and beautiful calmness. I
'was much affected by Phædo, but think the argu-
'ment weak in many respects. The nature of abstract
'ideas is clearly set forth; but there is no justice in rea-
'soning, from their existence, that our souls have lived
'previous to ·our present state, since it was as easy for
'the Deity to create at once the idea of beauty within
'us, as the sense which brings to the soul intelligence
'that it exists in some outward ·shape. He does not
'clearly show his opinion of what the soul is; whether
'eternal *as* the Deity, created *by* the Deity, or how.   In
'his answer to Simmias, he takes advantage of the gen-
'eral meaning of the words harmony, discord, &c. The
'souLmight be a result, without being a harmony. But
'I think too many things to write, and some I have not
'had time to examine. Meanwhile I can think over
'parts, and say to myself, "beautiful," "noble," and use
'this as one of my enchantments.'

   'I send two of your German books. It pains me to
'part with Ottilia. I wish we could learn books, as we
'do pieces of music, and repeat them, in the author's
'order, when taking a solitary walk. But, now, if I
'set out with an Ottilia, this wicked fairy associa-
'tion conjures up such crowds of less lovely compan-
'ions, that I often cease to feel the influence of the elect
'one. I don't like Goethe so well as Schiller now. I
'mean, I am not so happy in reading him. That per-
'fect wisdom and *merciless* nature seems cold, after
'those seducing pictures of forms more beautiful than
'truth. Nathless, I should like to read the second part
'of Goethe's Memoirs, if you do not use it now

'1832 — I am thinking how I omitted to talk a vol-
'ume to you about the "Elective Affinities." Now I
'shall never say half of it, for which I, on my own
'account, am sorry. But two or three things I would
'ask : —

'What do you think of Charlotte's proposition, that
'the accomplished pedagogue must be tiresome in soci-
'ety?

'Of Ottilia's, that the afflicted, and ill-educated, are
'oftentimes singled out by fate to instruct others, and
'her beautiful reasons why?

'And what have you thought of the discussion touch-
'ing graves and monuments?

'I am now going to dream of your sermon, and of
'Ottilia's china-asters. Both shall be driven from my
'head to-morrow, for I go to town, allured by de-
'spatches from thence, promising much entertainment.
'Woe unto them if they disappoint me!

'Consider it, I pray you, as the "nearest duty" to
'answer my questions, and not act as you did about the
'sphinx-song.'

'I have not anybody to speak to, that does not
'talk common-place, and I wish to talk about such an
'uncommon person, — about Novalis! a wondrous youth,
'and who has only written one volume. That is pleas-
'ant! I feel as though I could pursue my natural
'mode with him, get acquainted, then make my mind
'easy in the belief that I know all that is to be known.
'And he died at twenty-nine, and, as with Körner, your
'feelings may be single; you will never be called upon
'to share his experience, and compare his future feelings
'with his present. And his life was so full and so still.

'Then it is a relief, after feeling the immense superiority
'of Goethe. It seems to me as if the mind of Goethe
'had embraced the universe. I have felt this lately, in
'reading his lyric poems. I am enchanted while I read.
'He comprehends every feeling I have ever had so per-
'fectly, expresses it so beautifully; but when I shut the
'book, it seems as if I had lost my personal identity;
'all my feelings linked with such an immense variety
'that belong to beings I had thought so different. What
'can I bring? There is no answer in my mind, except
'"It is so," or "It will be so," or "No doubt such and
'"such feel so." Yet, while my judgment becomes
'daily more tolerant towards others, the same attracting
'and repelling work is going on in my feelings. But I
persevere in reading the great sage, some part of every
day, hoping the time will come, when I shall not feel
'so overwhelmed, and leave off this habit of wishing to
'grasp the whole, and be contented to learn a little every
'day, as becomes a pupil.

'But now the one-sidedness, imperfection, and glow,
'of a mind like that of Novalis, seem refreshingly human
'to me. I have wished fifty times to write some letters
'giving an account, first, of his very pretty life, and
'then of his one volume, as I re-read it, chapter by
'chapter. If you will pretend to be very much inter-
'ested, perhaps I will get a better pen, and write them
'to you.' * *

NEED OF COMMUNION.

'*Aug.* 7, 1832. — I feel quite lost; it is so long since I
'have talked myself. To see so many acquaintances, to
'talk so many words, and never tell my mind completely

' on any subject — to say so many things which do not
' seem called out, makes me feel strangely vague and
' movable.

'"Tis true, the time is probably near when I must live
' alone, to all intents and purposes, — separate entirely
' my acting from my thinking world, take care of my
' ideas without aid, — except from the illustrious dead,
' — answer my own questions, correct my own feelings,
' and do all that hard work for myself. How tiresome
'"tis to find out all one's self-delusion! I thought
' myself so very independent, because I could conceal
' some feelings at will, and did not need the same
' excitement as other young characters did. And I am
' not independent, nor never shall be, while I can get
' anybody to minister to me. But I shall go where
' there is never a spirit to come, if I call ever so loudly.

' Perhaps I shall talk to you about Körner, but
' need not write. He charms me, and has become
' a fixed star in the heaven of my thought; but I
' understand all that he excites perfectly. I felt very
· *new* about Novalis, — "the good Novalis," as you call
' him after Mr. Carlyle. He is, indeed, *good*, most
' enlightened, yet most pure; every link of his experi-
' ence framed — no, *beaten* — from the tried gold.

· I have read, thoroughly, only two of his pieces, " Die
' " Lehrlinge zu Sais," and " Heinrich von Ofterdingen."
' From the former I have only brought away piecemeal
' impressions, but the plan and treatment of the latter,
' I believe, I understand. It describes the development
' of poetry in a mind; and with this several other devel-
' opments are connected. I think I shall tell you all I
· know about it, some quiet time after your return, but,

'if not, will certainly keep a Novalis-journal for you
' some favorable season, when I live regularly for a fort-
' night.'

' *June*, 1833. — I return Lessing. I could hardly get
' through Miss Sampson. E. Galeotti is good in the
' same way as Minna. Well-conceived and sustained
' characters, interesting situations, but never that pro-
' found knowledge of human nature, those minute
' beauties, and delicate vivifying traits, which lead on
' so in the writings of some authors, who may be name-
' less. I think him easily followed; strong, but not
' deep.'

' *May*, 1833. — *Groton.* — I think you are wrong in
' applying your artistical ideas to occasional poetry. An
' epic, a drama, must have a fixed form in the mind of
' the poet from the first; and copious draughts of ambro-
' sia quaffed in the heaven of thought, soft fanning gales
' and bright light from the outward world, give muscle
' and bloom, — that is, give life, — to this skeleton. But
' all occasional poems must be moods, and can a mood
' have a form fixed and perfect, more than a wave of
' the sea?'

' Three or four afternoons I have passed very happily
' at my beloved haunt in the wood, reading Goethe's
' "Second Residence in Rome." Your pencil-marks
' show that you have been before me. I shut the
' book each time with an earnest desire to live as he
' did, — always to have some engrossing object of pur-
' suit. I sympathize deeply with a mind in that
' state. While mine is being used up by ounces, I wish

'pailfuls might be poured into it. I am dejected and
'uneasy when I see no results from my daily existence,
'but I am suffocated and lost when I have not the bright
'feeling of progression.' * *

'I think I am less happy, in many respects, than you,
'but particularly in this. You can speak freely to me
'of all your circumstances and feelings, can you not?
'It is not possible for me to be so profoundly frank with
'any earthly friend. Thus my heart has no proper
'home; it only can prefer some of its visiting-places to
'others; and with deep regret I realize that I have, at
'length, entered on the concentrating stage of life. It
'was not time. I had been too sadly cramped. I had
'not learned enough, and must always remain imper-
'fect. Enough! I am glad I have been able to say so
'much.'

'I have read nothing, — to signify, — except Goethe's
'"Campagne in Frankreich." Have you looked through
'it, and do you remember his intercourse with the Wer-
'therian Plessing? That tale pained me exceedingly.
'We cry, "help, help," and there is no help — in man
'at least. How often I have thought, if I could see
'Goethe, and tell him my state of mind, he would sup-
'port and guide me! He would be able to understand;
'he would show me how to rule circumstances, instead
'of being ruled by them; and, above all, he would not
'have been so sure that all would be for the best, with-
'out our making an effort to act out the oracles; he
'would have wished to see me what Nature intended.
'But his conduct to Plessing and Ohlenschlager shows
'that to him, also, an appeal would have been vain.'

'Do you really believe there is anything "all-compre-
'"hending" but religion? Are not these distinctions
'imaginary? Must not the philosophy of every mind,
'or set of minds, be a system suited to guide them, and
'give a home where they can bring materials among
'which to accept, reject, and shape at pleasure? Nova-
'lis calls those, who harbor these ideas, "unbelievers;"
'but hard names make no difference. He says with
'disdain, "To *such*, philosophy is only a system which
'"will spare them the trouble of reflecting." Now this
'is just my case. I *do* want a system which shall suf-
'fice to my character, and in whose applications I shall
'have faith. I do not wish to *reflect* always, if reflect-
'ing must be always about one's identity, whether
'"*ich*" am the true "*ich*," &c. I wish to arrive at
'that point where I can trust myself, and leave off say-
'ing, "It seems to me," and boldly feel, It *is* so TO ME.
'My character has got its natural regulator, my heart
'beats, my lips speak truth, I can walk alone, or offer
'my arm to a friend, or if I lean on another, it is not
'the debility of sickness, but only wayside weariness.
'This is the philosophy *I* want; this much would sat-
'isfy *me*.

'Then Novalis says, "Philosophy is the art of dis-
'"covering the place of truth in every encountered
'"event and circumstance, to attune all relations to
'"truth."

'Philosophy is peculiarly home-sickness; an over-
'mastering desire to be at home.

'I think so; but what is there *all-comprehending*,
eternally-conscious, about that?'

'*Sept.*, 1832. — "Not see the use of metaphysics?'

'A moderate portion, taken at stated intervals, I hold to
'be of much use as discipline of the faculties. I only
object to them as having an absorbing and anti-produc-
'tive tendency. But 't is not always so; may not be so
'with you. Wait till you are two years older, before you
'decide that 't is your vocation. Time enough at six-
'and-twenty to form yourself into a metaphysical phi-
'losopher. The brain does not easily get too dry for *that*.
'Happy you, in these ideas which give you a tendency to
'optimism. May you become a proselyte to that con-
'soling faith. I shall never be able to follow you, but
'shall look after you with longing eyes.'

'*Groton.* — Spring has come, and I shall see you soon.
'If I could pour into your mind all the ideas which
'have passed through mine, you would be well enter-
'tained, I think, for three or four days. But no hour
'will receive aught beyond its own appropriate wealth.
'I am at present engaged in surveying the level on
'which the public mind is poised. I no longer lie in
'wait for the tragedy and comedy of life; the rules of
'its *prose* engage my attention. I talk incessantly with
'common-place people, full of curiosity to ascertain the
'process by which materials, apparently so jarring and
'incapable of classification, get united into that strange
'whole, the American public. I have read all Jefferson's
'letters, the North American, the daily papers, &c.,
'without end. H. seems to be weaving his Kantisms
'into the American system in a tolerably happy manner.'

* * 'George Thompson has a voice of uncommon
'compass and beauty; never sharp in its highest, or
'rough and husky in its·lowest, tones. A perfect enun-

' ciation, every syllable round and energetic; though his
' manner was the one I love best, very rapid, and full of
' eager climaxes. Earnestness in every part. — sometimes
' impassioned earnestness, — a sort of " Dear friends, be-
' " lieve, *pray* believe, I love you, and you MUST believe as
' " I do " expression, even in the argumentative parts. I
' felt, as I have so often done before, if I were a man,
' the gift I would choose should be that of eloquence.
' That power of forcing the vital currents of thousands
' of human hearts into ONE current, by the constraining
' power of that most delicate instrument, the voice, is so
' intense, — yes, I would prefer it to a more extensive
' fame, a more permanent influence.'

' Did I describe to you my feelings on hearing Mr.
' Everett's eulogy on Lafayette? No; I did not.
' That was exquisite. The old, hackneyed story; not
' a new anecdote, not a single reflection of any value;
' but the manner, the *manner*, the delicate inflections of
' voice, the elegant and appropriate gesture, the sense
' of beauty produced by the whole, which thrilled us all
' to tears, flowing from a deeper and purer source than
' that which answers to pathos. This was fine; but I
' prefer the Thompson manner. Then there is Mr. Web-
' ster's, unlike either; simple grandeur, nobler, more
' impressive, less captivating. I have heard few fine
' speakers; I wish I could hear a thousand.

' Are you vexed by my keeping the six volumes of your
' Goethe? I read him very little either; I have so little
' time, — many things to do at home, — my three children,
' and three pupils besides, whom I instruct.

' By the way, I have always thought all that was
' said about the anti-religious tendency of a classical edu-
' cation to be old wives' tales. But their puzzles abou

' Virgil's notions of heaven and virtue, and his gracefully-
' described gods and goddesses, have led me to alter my
' opinions; and I suspect, from reminiscences of my own
' mental history, that if all governors do not think the
' same 't is from want of that intimate knowledge of their
' pupils' minds which I naturally possess. I really find
' it difficult to keep their *morale* steady, and am inclined
' to think many of my own sceptical sufferings are
' traceable to this source. I well remember what reflec-
' tions arose in my childish mind from a comparison of
' the Hebrew history, where every moral obliquity is
' shown out with such naïveté, and the Greek history,
' full of sparkling deeds and brilliant sayings, and their
' gods and goddesses, the types of beauty and power, with
' the dazzling veil of flowery language and poetical im-
' agery cast over their vices and failings.'

' My own favorite project, since I began seriously to
' entertain any of that sort, is six historical tragedies; of
' which I have the plans of three quite perfect. How-
' over, the attempts I have made on them have served to
' show me the vast difference between conception and
' execution. Yet I am, though abashed, not altogether
' discouraged. My next favorite plan is a series of tales
' illustrative of Hebrew history. The proper junctures
' have occurred to me during my late studies on the his-
' torical books of the Old Testament. This task, how-
' ever, requires a thorough and imbuing knowledge of
' the Hebrew manners and spirit, with a chastened energy
' of imagination, which I am as yet far from possessing.
' But if I should be permitted peace and time to follow
' out my ideas, I have hopes. Perhaps it is a weakness

' to confide to you embryo designs, which never may
' glow into life, or mock me by their failure.'

'I have long had a suspicion that no mind can sys-
' tematize its knowledge, and carry on the concentrating
' processes, without some fixed opinion on the subject of
' metaphysics. But that indisposition, or even dread of
' the study, which you may remember, has kept me
' from meddling with it, till lately, in meditating on the
' life of Goethe, I thought I must get some idea of the
' history of philosophical opinion in Germany, that I
' might be able to judge of the influence it exercised upon
' his mind. I think I can comprehend him every other way,
' and probably interpret him satisfactorily to others,— if I
' can get the proper materials. When I was in Cambridge,
' I got Fichte and Jacobi; I was much interrupted, but
' some time and earnest thought I devoted. Fichte I
' could not understand at all; though the treatise which
' I read was one intended to be popular, and which he
' says must compel (*bezwingen*) to conviction. Jacobi I
' could understand in details, but not in system. It
' seemed to me that his mind must have been moulded
' by some other mind, with which I ought to be ac-
' quainted, in order to know him well,— perhaps Spi-
' noza's. Since I came home, I have been consulting
' Buhle's and Tennemann's histories of philosophy, and
' dipping into Brown, Stewart, and that class of books.'

'After I had cast the burden of my cares upon you, I
' rested, and read Petrarch for a day or two. But that
' could not last. I had begun to "take an account
" of stock," as Coleridge calls it, and was forced to pro-
' ceed He says few persons ever did this faithfully

without being dissatisfied with the result, and lowering
'their estimate of their supposed riches. With me it
'has ended in the most humiliating sense of poverty;
'and only just enough pride is left to keep your poor
'friend off the parish. As it is, I have already asked
'items of several besides yourself; but, though they
'have all given what they had, it has by no means an-
'swered my purpose; and I have laid their gifts aside,
'with my other hoards, which gleamed so fairy bright,
'and are now, in the hour of trial, turned into mere
'slate-stones. I am not sure that even if I do find the
'philosopher's stone, I shall be able to transmute them
'into the gold they looked so like formerly. It will be
'long before I can give a distinct, and at the same time
'concise, account of my present state. I believe it is a
'great era. I am thinking now, — really thinking, I
'believe; certainly it seems as if I had never done
'so before. If it does not kill me, something will come
'of it. Never was my mind so active; and the subjects
'are God, the universe, immortality. But shall I be fit
'for anything till I have absolutely re-educated myself?
'Am I, can I make myself, fit to write an account of
'half a century of the existence of one of the master-
'spirits of this world? It seems as if I had been very
'arrogant to dare to think it; yet will I not shrink back
'from what I have undertaken, — even by failure I shall
'learn much.'

'I am shocked to perceive you think I am *writing* the
'life of Goethe. No, indeed! I shall need a great deal
'of preparation before I shall have it clear in my head.
'I have taken a great many notes; but I shall not begin
'to write it, till it all lies mapped out before me. I have
no materials for ten years of his life, from the time he

'went to Weimar, up to the Italian journey. Besides, I
'wish to see the books that have been written about him
'in Germany, by friend or foe. I wish to look at the
'matter from all sides. New lights are constantly dawn-
'ing on me; and I think it possible I shall come out from
'the Carlyle view, and perhaps from yours, and distaste
'you, which will trouble me.

    * * 'How am I to get the information I want, unless
'I go to Europe? To whom shall I write to choose my
'materials? I have thought of Mr. Carlyle, but still
'more of Goethe's friend, Von Muller. I dare say he
'would be pleased at the idea of a life of G. written
'in this hemisphere, and be very willing to help me.
'If you have anything to tell me, you will, and not
'mince matters. Of course, my impressions of Goethe's
'works cannot be influenced by information I get about
'his *life;* but, as to this latter, I suspect I must have
'been hasty in my inferences. I apply to you without
'scruple. There are subjects on which men and women
'usually talk a great deal, but apart from one another.
'You, however, are well aware that I am very destitute
'of what is commonly *called* modesty. With regard to
'this, how fine the remark of our present subject :
'" Courage and modesty are virtues which every sort of
'" society reveres, because they are virtues which cannot
'" be counterfeited; also, they are known by the *same*
'" *hue.*" When that blush does not come naturally to
'my face, I do not drop a veil to make people think it is
'there. All this may be very unlovely, but it is *I.*'

CHANNING ON SLAVERY.

   'This is a noble work. So refreshing its calm, benign
'atmosphere, after the pestilence-bringing gales of the

'day. It comes like a breath borne over some solemn
'sea which separates us from an island of righteousness.
'How valuable is it to have among us a man who,
'standing apart from the conflicts of the herd, watches
'the principles that are at work, with a truly paternal
'love for what is human, and may be permanent; ready
'at the proper point to give his casting-vote to the cause
'of Right! The author has amplified on the grounds of
'his faith, to a degree that might seem superfluous, if the
'question had not become so utterly bemazed and be-
'darkened of late. After all, it is probable that, in
'addressing the public at large, it is *not* best to express a
'thought in as few words as possible; there is much
'classic authority for diffuseness.'

RICHTER.

Groton.—'Ritcher says, the childish heart vies in the
'height of its surges with the manly, only is not furnished
'with *lead* for sounding them.

'How thoroughly am I converted to the love of Jean
'Paul, and wonder at the indolence or shallowness
'which could resist so long, and call his profuse riches
'want of system! What a mistake! System, plan,
'there is, but on so broad a basis that I did not at first
'comprehend it. In every page I am forced to pencil. I
'will make me a book, or, as he would say, bind me a
'bouquet from his pages, and wear it on my heart of
'hearts, and be ever refreshing my wearied inward sense
 with its exquisite fragrance. I must have improved, tc
'love him as I do.'

CHARACTER. — AIMS AND IDEAS OF LIFE.

> " O friend, how flat and tasteless such a life !
>   Impulse gives birth to impulse, deed to deed,
>   Still toilsomely ascending step by step,
>   Into an unknown realm of dark blue clouds.
>   What crowns the ascent ?   Speak, or I go no further.
>   I need a goal, an aim.   I cannot toil,
>   *Because the steps are here ;* in their ascent
>   Tell me THE END, or I sit still and weep."
> > " NATURLICHE TOCHTER,"
> > > *Translated by Margaret.*
>
> ' And so he went onward, ever onward, for twenty-seven years —
> then, indeed, he had gone far enough."
> > GOETHE'S *words concerning Schiller*

——

I WOULD say something of Margaret's inward condition, of her aims and views in life, while in Cambridge, before closing this chapter of her story.   Her powers, whether of mind, heart, or will, have been sufficiently indicated in what has preceded.   In the sketch of her friendships and of her studies, we have seen the affluence of her intellect, and the deep tenderness of her woman's nature.   We have seen the energy which she displayed in study and labor.

But to what *aim* were these powers directed ?   Had she any clear view of the demands and opportunities of life, any definite plan, any high, pure purpose ?   This is, after all, the test question, which detects the low-born and low-minded wearer of the robe of gold, —

"Touch them inwardly. they smell of copper."

Margaret's life *had an aim*, and she was, therefore, essentially a moral person, and not merely an overflowing genius, in whom "impulse gives birth to impulse, deed to deed." This aim was distinctly apprehended and steadily pursued by her from first to last. It was a high, noble one, wholly religious, almost Christian. It gave dignity to her whole career, and made it heroic.

This aim, from first to last, was SELF-CULTURE. If she ever was ambitious of knowledge and talent, as a means of excelling others, and gaining fame, position, admiration, — this vanity had passed before I knew her, and was replaced by the profound desire for a full development of her whole nature, by means of a full experience of life.

In her description of her own youth, she says, 'VERY 'EARLY I KNEW THAT THE ONLY OBJECT IN LIFE WAS TO 'GROW.' This is the passage : —

'I was now in the hands of teachers, who had not, 'since they came on the earth, put to themselves one 'intelligent question as to their business here. Good 'dispositions and employment for the heart gave a tone 'to all they said, which was pleasing, and not perverting. 'They, no doubt, injured those who accepted the husks 'they proffered for bread, and believed that exercise of 'memory was study, and to know what others knew, 'was the object of study. But to me this was all pene-trable. I had known great living minds, — I had seen

'how they took their food and did their exercise, and
'what their objects were. *Very early I knew that the
' only object in life was to grow.* I was often false to
'this knowledge, in idolatries of particular objects, or
'impatient longings for happiness, but I have never lost
'sight of it, have always been controlled by it, and this
'first gift of thought has never been superseded by a
'later love.'

In this she spoke truth. The good and the evil
which flow from this great idea of self-development
she fully realized. This aim of life, originally self-
chosen, was made much more clear to her mind by the
study of Goethe, the great master of this school, in
whose unequalled eloquence this doctrine acquires an
almost irresistible beauty and charm.

" Wholly religious, and almost Christian," I said, was
this aim. It was religious, because it recognized something divine, infinite, imperishable in the human soul, —
something divine in outward nature and providence, by
which the soul is led along its appointed way. It was
almost Christian in its superiority to all low, worldly,
vulgar thoughts and cares ; in its recognition of a high
standard of duty, and a great destiny for man. In its
strength, Margaret was enabled to do and bear, with
patient fortitude, what would have crushed a soul not
thus supported. Yet it is not the highest aim, for in all
its forms, whether as personal improvement, the salva-
tion of the soul, or ascetic religion, it has at its core a
profound selfishness. Margaret's soul was too generous
for any low form of selfishness. Too noble to become an
Epicurean, too large-minded to become a modern ascetic,
the defective nature of her rule of life, showed itself in

her case, only in a certain supercilious tone toward " the
vulgar herd," in the absence (at this period) of a tender humanity, and in an idolatrous hero-worship of
genius and power.   Afterward, too, she may have suffered from her desire for a universal human experience,
and an unwillingness to see that we must often be content to enter the Kingdom of Heaven halt and maimed,
— that a perfect development here must often be wholly
renounced.

But how much better to pursue with devotion, like
that of Margaret, an imperfect aim, than to worship
with lip-service, as most persons do, even though it be
in a loftier temple, and before a holier shrine !   With
Margaret, the doctrine of self-culture was a devotion to
which she sacrificed all earthly hopes and joys, — everything but manifest duty.   And so her course was "onward, ever onward," like that of Schiller, to her last
hour of life.

> Burned in her cheek with ever deepening fire
> The spirit's YOUTH, which never passes by ; —
> The COURAGE which, though worlds in hate conspire,
> Conquers, at last, their dull hostility ; —
> The lofty FAITH, which, ever mounting higher,
> Now presses on, now waiteth patiently, —
> With which the good tends ever to his goal,
> With which day finds, at last, the earnest soul.

But this high idea which governed our friend's life,
brought her into sharp conflicts, which constituted the
pathos and tragedy of her existence, — first with her circumstances, which seemed so inadequate to the needs of
her nature, — afterwards with duties to relatives and
friends, — and, finally, with the law of the Great Spirit,
whose will she found it so hard to acquiesce in.

The circumstances in which Margaret lived appeared to her life a prison. She had no room for utterance, no sphere adequate; her powers were unemployed. With what eloquence she described this want of a field! Often have I listened with wonder and admiration, satisfied that she exaggerated the evil, and yet unable to combat her rapid statements. Could she have seen in how few years a way would open before her, by which she could emerge into an ample field, — how soon she would find troops of friends, fit society, literary occupation, and the opportunity of studying the great works of art in their own home, — she would have been spared many a sharp pang.

Margaret, like every really earnest and deep nature, felt the necessity of a religious faith as the foundation of character   The first notice which I find of her views on this point is contained in the following letter to one of her youthful friends, when only nineteen : —

*   *   *   *   *

'I have hesitated much whether to tell you what you 'ask about my religion. You are mistaken! I have 'not formed an opinion. I have determined not to form 'settled opinions at present. Loving or feeble natures 'need a positive religion, a visible refuge, a protection, 'as much in the passionate season of youth as in those 'stages nearer to the grave. But mine is not such. My 'pride is superior to any feelings I have yet experienced: 'my affection is strong admiration, not the necessity of 'giving or receiving assistance or sympathy. When dis-'appointed, I do not ask or wish consolation, — I wish to 'know and feel my pain, to investigate its nature and 'its source; I will not have my thoughts diverted, or my

'feelings soothed; 't is therefore that my young life is
'so singularly barren of illusions. I know, I feel the
'time must come when this proud and impatient heart
'shall be stilled, and turn from the ardors of Search and
'Action, to lean on something above. But — shall I say
'it ? — the thought of that calmer era is to me a thought
'of deepest sadness; so remote from my present being is
'that future existence, which still the mind may con-
'ceive. I believe in Eternal Progression. I believe in
'a God, a Beauty and Perfection to which I am to strive
'all my life for assimilation. From these two articles
'of belief, I draw the rules by which I strive to regulate
'my life. But, though I reverence all religions as neces-
'sary to the happiness of man, I am yet ignorant of
'the religion of Revelation. Tangible promises ! well
'defined hopes ! are things of which I do not *now* feel
'the need. At present, my soul is intent on this life, and
'I think of religion as its rule; and, in my opinion, this
'is the natural and proper course from youth to age.
'What I have written is not hastily concocted, it has a
'meaning. I have given you, in this little space, the
'substance of many thoughts, the clues to many cher-
'ished opinions. 'T is, a subject on which I rarely
'speak. I never said so much but once before. I
'have here given you all I know, or think, on the most
'important of subjects — could you but read understand-
'ingly ! '

＊　　　＊　　　＊　　　＊　　　＊

I find, in her journals for 1833, the following passages,
expressing the religious purity of her aspirations at that
time : —

' Blessed Father, nip every foolish wish in blossom,
' Lead me *any way* to truth and goodness ; but if it might
' be, I would not pass from idol to idol. Let no mean
' sculpture deform a mind disorderly, perhaps ill-fur-
' nished, but spacious and life-warm. Remember thy
' child, such as thou madest her, and let her understand
' her little troubles, when possible, oh, beautiful Deity ! '

' *Sunday morning.* — Mr. —— preached on the nature
' of our duties, social and personal. The sweet dew of
' truth penetrated my heart like balm. He pointed out
' the various means of improvement, whereby the hum-
' blest of us may be beneficent at last. How just, how
' nobly true, — how modestly, yet firmly uttered, — his
' opinions of man, — of time, — of God !
' My heart swelled with prayer. I began to feel hope
' that time and toil might strengthen me to despise the
' "vulgar parts of felicity," and live as becomes an
' immortal creature. I am sure, quite sure, that I am
' getting into the right road. Oh, lead me, my Father !
' root out false pride and selfishness from my heart;
' inspire me with virtuous energy, and enable me to im-
' prove every talent for the eternal good of myself and
' others.'

A friend of Margaret, some years older than herself,
gives me the following narrative : —

"I was," says she, in substance, " suffering keenly
from a severe trial, and had secluded myself from all my
friends, when Margaret, a girl of twenty, forced her way
to me. She sat with me, and gave me her sympathy,
and, with most affectionate interest, sought to draw me

away from my gloom.   As far as she was able, she gave
me comfort.   But as my thoughts were then much led
to religious subjects, she sought to learn my religious
experience, and listened to it with great interest.   I told
her how I had sat in darkness for two long years, waiting for the light, and in full faith that it would come;
how I had kept my soul patient and quiet, — had surrendered self-will to God's will, — had watched and waited
till at last His great mercy came in an infinite peace to
my soul.   Margaret was never weary of asking me concerning this state, and said, ' I would gladly give all my
talents and knowledge for such an experience as this.'

   " Several years after," continues this friend, " I was
travelling with her, and we sat, one lovely night, looking at the river, as it rolled beneath the yellow moonlight.   We spoke again of God's light in the soul, and I
said — ' Margaret! has that light dawned on *your* soul?'
She answered, ' I think it has.   But, oh! it is so glorious that I fear it will not be permanent, and so precious
that I dare not speak of it, lest it should be gone.'

   " That was the whole of our conversation, and I did
not speak to her again concerning it."

   Before this time, however, during her residence at
Cambridge, she seemed to reach the period of her existence in which she descended lowest into the depths of
gloom.   She felt keenly, at this time, the want of a
home for her heart.   Full of a profound tendency toward
life, capable of an ardent love, her affections were thrown
back on her heart, to become stagnant, and for a while
to grow bitter there.   Then it was that she felt how
empty and worthless were all the attainments and triumphs of the mere intellect; then it was that " she went

about to cause her heart to despair of all the labor she
had taken under the sun." Had she not emerged from
this valley of the shadow of death, and come on to a
higher plane of conviction and hope, her life would have
been a most painful tragedy. But, when we know how
she passed on and up, ever higher and higher, to the
mountain-top, leaving one by one these dark ravines
and mist-shrouded valleys, and ascending to where a
perpetual sunshine lay, above the region of clouds, and
was able to overlook with eagle glance the widest panorama, — we can read, with sympathy indeed, but without
pain, the following extracts from a journal: —

'It was Thanksgiving day, (Nov., 1831,) and I was
'obliged to go to church, or exceedingly displease my
'father. I almost always suffered much in church from
'a feeling of disunion with the hearers and dissent from
'the preacher; but to-day, more than ever before, the
'services jarred upon me from their grateful and joyful
'tone. I was wearied out with mental conflicts, and in
'a mood of most childish, child-like sadness. I felt
'within myself great power, and generosity, and tender-
'ness; but it seemed to me as if they were all unrecog-
'nized, and as if it was impossible that they should be
'used in life. I was only one-and-twenty; the past
'was worthless, the future hopeless; yet I could not
'remember ever voluntarily to have done a wrong thing,
'and my aspiration seemed very high. I looked round
'the church, and envied all the little children; for I sup-
'posed they had parents who protected them, so that
'they could never know this strange anguish, this dread
'uncertainty. I knew not, then, that none could have
'any father but God. I knew not, that I was not the

'only lonely one, that I was not the selected Œdipus,
'the special victim of an iron law. I was in haste for
'all to be over, that I might get into the free air. * *

'I walked away over the fields as fast as I could walk.
'This was my custom at that time, when I could no
'longer bear the weight of my feelings, and fix my atten-
'tion on any pursuit; for I do believe I never voluntarily
'gave way to these thoughts one moment. The force I
'exerted I think, even now, greater than I ever knew in
'any other character. But when I could bear myself no
'longer, I walked many hours, till the anguish was
'wearied out, and I returned in a state of prayer. To-
'day all seemed to have reached its height. It seemed
'as if I could never return to a world in which I had no
'place, — to the mockery of humanities. I could not act
'a part, nor seem to live any longer. It was a sad and
'sallow day of the late autumn. Slow processions of sad
'clouds were passing over a cold blue sky; the hues of
'earth were dull, and gray, and brown, with sickly strug-
'gles of late green here and there; sometimes a moaning
'gust of wind drove late, reluctant leaves across the
'path; — there was no life else. In the sweetness of my
'present peace, such days seem to me made to tell man
'the worst of his lot; but still that November wind can
'bring a chill of memory.

'I paused beside a little stream, which I had envied in
'the merry fulness of its spring life. It was shrunken,
'voiceless, choked with withered leaves. I marvelled
'that it did not quite lose itself in the earth. There was
'no stay for me, and I went on and on, till I came to
'where the trees were thick about a little pool, dark and
'silent. I sat down there. I did not think; all was
dark, and cold, and still. Suddenly the sun shone out

with that transparent sweetness, like the last smile of a
'dying lover, which it will use when it has been unkind
'all a cold autumn day. And, even then, passed into
'my thought a beam from its true sun, from its native
'sphere, which has never since departed from me. I
'remembered how, a little child, I had stopped myself
'one day on the stairs, and asked, how came I here?
'How is it that I seem to be this Margaret Fuller?
'What does it mean? What shall I do about it? I
'remembered all the times and ways in which the same
'thought had returned. I saw how long it must be be-
'fore the soul can learn to act under these limitations of
'time and space, and human nature; but I saw, also,
'that it MUST do it, — that it must make all this false
'true, — and sow new and immortal plants in the garden
'of God, before it could return again. I saw there was no
'self; that selfishness was all folly, and the result of cir-
'cumstance; that it was only because I thought self real
'that I suffered; that I had only to live in the idea of the
'ALL, and all was mine. This truth came to me, and I
'received it unhesitatingly; so that I was for that hour
'taken up into God. In that true ray most of the rela-
'tions of earth seemed mere films, phenomena. * *

'My earthly pain at not being recognized never went
'deep after this hour. I had passed the extreme of pas-
'sionate sorrow; and all check, all failure, all ignorance,
'have seemed temporary ever since. When I consider
'that this will be nine years ago next November, I am
'astonished that I have not gone on faster since; that I
'am not yet sufficiently purified to be taken back to God.
'Still, I did but touch then on the only haven of Insight.
'You know what I would say. I was dwelling in the ineffable, the unutterable. But the sun of earth set, and

' it grew dark around; the moment came for me to go
' I had never been accustomed to walk alone at night,
' for my father was very strict on that subject, but
' now I had not one fear. When I came back, the moon
' was riding clear above the houses. I went into the
' churchyard, and there offered a prayer as holy, if not
' as deeply true, as any I know now; a prayer, which per-
' haps took form as the guardian angel of my life. If that
' word in the Bible, Selah, means what gray-headed old
' men think it does, when they read aloud, it should be
' written here, — Selah !

  ' Since that day, I have never more been completely
' engaged in self; but the statue has been emerging,
' though slowly, from the block. Others may not see
' the promise even of its pure symmetry, but I do, and
' am learning to be patient. I shall be all human yet;
' and then the hour will come to leave humanity, and
' live always in the pure ray.

  ' This first day I was taken up; but the second time
' the Holy Ghost descended like a dove. I went out
' again for a day, but this time it was spring. I walked
' in the fields of Groton. But I will not describe that
' day; its music still sounds too sweetly near. Suffice it
' to say, I gave it all into our Father's hands, and was no
' stern-weaving Fate more, but one elected to obey, and
' love, and at last know. Since then I have suffered, as
' I must suffer again, till all the complex be made simple,
' but I have never been in discord with the grand har
' mony.'

GROTON AND PROVIDENCE.

LETTERS AND JOURNALS.

" What hath not man sought out and found,
But his dear God? Who yet his glorious love
Embosoms in us, mellowing the ground
   With showers, and frosts, with love and awe.''
                                        HERBERT.

" No one need pride himself upon Genius, for it is the free-gift of God ;
but of honest Industry and true devotion to his destiny any man may
well be proud ; indeed, this thorough integrity of purpose is itself the
Divine Idea in its most common form, and no really honest mind is
without communion with God "
                                        FICHTE.

"God did anoint thee with his odorous oil,
To wrestle, not to reign; and he assigns
All thy tears over, like pure crystallines,
For younger fellow-workers of the soil
To wear for amulets. So others shall
Take patience, labor, to their hearts and hands,
From thy hands, and thy heart, and thy brave cheer,
And God's grace fructify through thee to all."

ELIZABETH B. BARRETT

"While I was restless, nothing satisfied,
Distrustful, most perplexed — yet felt somehow
A mighty power was brooding, taking shape
Within me ; and this lasted till one night
When, as I sat revolving it and more,
A still voice from without said, — 'Seest thou not,
Desponding child, whence came defeat and loss?
Even from thy strength.' "

BROWNING.

III.

GROTON AND PROVIDENCE.

'H AVEN's discipline has been invariable to me.
'The seemingly most pure and noble hopes have
'been blighted; the seemingly most promising con-
'nections broken. The lesson has been endlessly
'repeated : "Be humble, patient, self-sustaining; hope
'"only for occasional aids; love others, but not engross-
'"ingly, for by being much alone your appointed task
'"can best be done!" What a weary work is before me,
'ere that lesson shall be fully learned! Who shall
'wonder at the stiff-necked, and rebellious folly of
'young Israel, bowing down to a brute image, though
'the prophet was bringing messages from the holy
'mountain, while one's own youth is so obstinately
'idolatrous! Yet will I try to keep the heart with
'diligence, nor ever fear that the sun is gone out
'because I shiver in the cold and dark!'

Such was the tone of resignation in which Margaret
wrote from Groton, Massachusetts, whither, much to
her regret, her father removed in the spring of 1833.
Extracts from letters and journals will show how stern

was her schooling there, and yet how constant was her
faith, that

"God keeps a niche
In heaven to hold our idols !   And albeit
He breaks them to our faces, and denies
That our close kisses should impair their white,
I know we shall behold them raised, complete,
The dust shook from their beauty, — glorified,
New Memnons singing in the great God-light."

SAD WELCOME HOME.

' *Groton, April* 25, 1833. — I came hither, summoned
' by the intelligence, that our poor ———— had met with
' a terrible accident.   I found the dear child, — who had
' left me so full of joy and eagerness, that I thought
' with a sigh, not of envy, how happy he, at least, would
' be here, — burning with fever.   He had expected me
' impatiently, and was very faint lest it should not be
' " Margaret " who had driven up.   I confess I greeted
' our new home with a flood of bitter tears.   He behaves
' with great patience, sweetness, and care for the com-
' fort of others.   This has been a severe trial for mother,
' fatigued, too, as she was, and full of care; but her con-
' duct is angelic.   I try to find consolation in all kinds
' of arguments, and to distract my thoughts till the pre-
' cise amount of injury is surely known.   I am not idle
' a moment.   When not with ————, in whose room I
' sit, sewing, and waiting upon him, or reading aloud
' a great part of the day, I solace my soul with Goethe,
' and follow his guidance into realms of the " Wahren
' " Guten, and Schönen." '

OCCUPATIONS.

' *May*, 1833. —- As to German, I have done less than

'I hoped, so much had the time been necessarily broken
'up. I have with me the works of Goethe which I
'have not yet read, and am now engaged upon
'"Kunst and Alterthum," and "Campagne in Frank-
'reich." I still prefer Goethe to any one, and, as I
'proceed, find more and more to learn, and am made
'to feel that my general notion of his mind is most
'imperfect, and needs testing and sifting.

'I brought your beloved Jean Paul with me, too.
'I cannot yet judge well, but think we shall not be
'intimate. His infinitely variegated, and certainly most
'exquisitely colored, web fatigues attention. I prefer,
'too, wit to humor, and daring imagination to the rich-
'est fancy. Besides, his philosophy and religion seem
'to be of the sighing sort, and, having some tendency
'that way myself, I want opposing force in a favorite
'author. Perhaps I have spoken unadvisedly ;• if so, I
'shall recant on further knowledge.'

And thus recant she did, when familiar acquaintance
with the genial and sagacious humorist had won for
him her reverent love.

RICHTER.

'Poet of Nature! Gentlest of the wise,
'Most airy of the fanciful, most keen
'Of satirists! — thy thoughts, like butterflies,
'Still near the sweetest scented flowers have been•
'With Titian's colors thou canst sunset paint,
'With Raphael's dignity, celestial love;
'With Hogarth's pencil, each deceit and feint
'Of meanness and hypocrisy reprove;

'Canst to devotion's highest flight sublime
  'Exalt the mind, by tenderest pathos' art,
  'Dissolve, in purifying tears, the heart,
'Or bid it, shuddering, recoil at crime;
  'The fond illusions of the youth and maid,
'At which so many world-formed sages sneer,
  'When by thy altar-lighted torch displayed,
'Our natural religion must appear.
'All things in thee tend to one polar star,
'Magnetic all thy influences are!'

'Some murmur at the "want of system" in Richter's
'writings.

'A labyrinth! a flowery wilderness!
  'Some in thy "slip-boxes" and "honey-moons"
'Complain of — *want of order*, I confess,
  'But not of *system* in its highest sense.
'Who asks a guiding clue through this wide mind,
'In love of Nature such will surely find.
  'In tropic climes, live like the tropic bird,
'Whene'er a spice-fraught grove may tempt thy stay;
  'Nor be by cares of colder climes disturbed —
'No frost the summer's bloom shall drive away;
'Nature's wide temple and the azure dome
'Have plan enough for the free spirit's home!'

'Your Schiller has already given me great pleas
are. I have been reading the "Revolt in the Neth-
erlands" with intense interest, and have reflected
much upon it. The volumes are numbered in my
little book-case, and as the eye runs over them, I
'thank the friendly heart that put all this genius and
passion within my power.

'I am glad, too, that you thought of lending me
'"Bigelow's Elements." I have studied the Archi-
'tecture attentively, till I feel quite mistress of it all

' But I want more engravings, Vitruvius, Magna Græcia,
' the Ionian Antiquities, &c. Meanwhile, I have got out
' all our tours in Italy. Forsyth, a book I always loved
' much, I have re-read with increased pleasure, by this
' new light. Goethe, too, studied architecture while in
' Italy; so his books are full of interesting information,
' and Madame De Stael, though not deep, is tasteful."

' American History! Seriously, my mind is regener-
' ating as to my country, for I am beginning to appre-
' ciate the United States and its great men. The violent
' antipathies, — the result of an exaggerated love for,
' shall I call it by so big a name as the "poetry of being?"
' — and the natural distrust arising from being forced to
' hear the conversation of half-bred men, all whose petty
' feelings were roused to awkward life by the paltry
' game of local politics, — are yielding to reason and
' calmer knowledge. Had I but been educated in the
' knowledge of such men as Jefferson, Franklin, Rush!
' I have learned now to know them partially. And I
' rejoice, if only because my father and I can have so
' much in common on this topic. All my other pursuits
' have led me away from him; here he has much infor-
' mation and ripe judgment. But, better still, I hope to
' feel no more that sometimes despairing, sometimes
' insolently contemptuous, feeling of incongeniality with
' my time and place. Who knows but some proper and
' attainable object of pursuit may present itself to the
' cleared eye? At any rate, wisdom is good, if it brings
' neither bliss nor glory.'

' *March*, 1834. — Four pupils are a serious and fatiguing charge for one of my somewhat ardent and

'impatient disposition. Five days in the week I have
'given daily lessons in three languages, in Geography
'and History, besides many other exercises on alternate
'days. This has consumed often eight, always five
'hours of my day. There has been, also, a great deal
'of needle-work to do, which is now nearly finished, so
'that 1 shall not be obliged to pass my time about it
'when everything looks beautiful, as I did last summer.
'We have had very poor servants, and, for some time
'past, only one. My mother has been often ill. My
'grandmother, who passed the winter with us, has been
'ill. Thus, you may imagine, as I am the only grown-up
'daughter, that my time has been considerably taxed.

'But as, sad or merry, I must always be learning, I
'laid down a course of study at the beginning of winter,
'comprising certain subjects, about which I had always
'felt deficient. These were the History and Geography
'of modern Europe, beginning the former in the four-
'teenth century ; the Elements of Architecture ; the
'works of Alfieri, with his opinions on them ; the his-
'torical and critical works of Goethe and Schiller, and
'the outlines of history of our own country.

'I chose this time as one when I should have nothing
'to distract or dissipate my mind. I have nearly com-
'pleted this course, in the style I proposed, — not minute
'or thorough, I confess, — though I have had only three
'evenings in the week, and chance hours in the day,
'for it. I am very glad I have undertaken it, and feel
'the good effects already. Occasionally, I try my hand
'at composition, but have not completed anything to my
'own satisfaction. I have sketched a number of plans,
'but if ever accomplished, it must be in a season of more
'joyful energy, when my mind has been renovated, and

refreshed by change of scene or circumstance. My
translation of Tasso cannot be published at present, if
' it ever is.'

'My object is to examine thoroughly, as far as my
'time and abilities will permit, the evidences of the
'Christian Religion. I have endeavored to get rid of
'this task as much and as long as possible; to be con-
'tent with superficial notions, and, if I may so express
'it, to adopt religion as a matter of taste. But I meet
'with infidels very often; two or three of my particular
'friends are deists; and their arguments, with distress-
'ing sceptical notions of my own, are haunting me
'forever. I must satisfy myself; and having once be-
'gun, I shall go on as far as I can.

'My mind often swells with thoughts on these sub-
'jects, which I long to pour out on some person of supe-
'rior calmness and strength, and fortunate in more
'accurate knowledge. I should feel such a quieting
'reaction. But, generally, it seems best that I should go
'through these conflicts alone. The process will be
'slower, more irksome, more distressing, but the results
'will be my own, and I shall feel greater confidence in
'them.'

MISS MARTINEAU.

In the summer of 1835, Margaret found a fresh stimulus to self-culture in the society of Miss Martineau,
whom she met while on a visit at Cambridge, in the
house of her friend, Mrs. Farrar. How animating
this intercourse then was to her, appears from her journals.

'Miss Martineau received me so kindly as to banish
all embarrassment at once. * * We had some talk
'about "Carlyleism," and I was not quite satisfied. with
'the ground she took, but there was no opportunity for
'full discussion. * * I wished to give myself wholly
'up to receive an impression of her. * * What shrewd-
'ness in detecting various shades of character ! Yet,
'what she said of Hannah More and Miss Edgeworth,
'grated upon my feelings.' * *

Again, later : — 'I cannot conceive how we chanced
'upon the subject of our conversation, but never shall I
'forget what she said. It has bound me to her. In
'that hour, most unexpectedly to me, we passed the bar-
'rier that separates acquaintance from friendship, and
'1 saw how greatly her heart is to be valued.'

And again : — 'We sat together close to the pulpit.
'I was deeply moved by Mr. ——'s manner of praying
'for "our friends," and I put up this prayer for my com-
'panion, which I recorded, as it rose in my heart : "Au-
'"thor of good, Source of all beauty and holiness, thanks
'"to Thee for the purifying, elevating communion that
'"I have enjoyed with this beloved and revered being.
'"Grant, that the thoughts she has awakened, and the
'"bright image of her existence, may live in my mem-
'"ory, inciting my earth-bound spirit to higher words
'"and deeds. May her path be guarded and blessed.
'"May her noble mind be kept firmly poised in its
'"native truth, unsullied by prejudice or error, and
'"strong to resist whatever outwardly or inwardly shall
'"war against its high vocation. May each day bring
'"to this generous seeker new riches cf true philosophy

'"and of Divine Love. And, amidst all trials, give her
'"to know and feel that Thou, the All-sufficing, art
'"with her, leading her on through eternity to likeness
'"of Thyself."'

'I sigh for an intellectual guide. Nothing but the
'sense of what God has done for me, in bringing me
'nearer to himself, saves me from despair. With what
'envy I looked at Flaxman's picture of Hesiod sitting
'at the the feet of the Muse! How blest would it be to
'be thus instructed in one's vocation! Anything would
'I do and suffer, to be sure that, when leaving earth,
'I should not be haunted with recollections of "aims
'"unreached, occasions lost." I have hoped some friend
'would do, — what none has ever yet done, — compre-
'hend me wholly, mentally, and morally, and enable me
·better to comprehend myself. I have had some hope
that Miss Martineau might be this friend, but cannot
'yet tell. She has what I want, — vigorous reasoning
'powers, invention, clear views of her objects, — and she
'has been trained to the best means of execution. Add
'to this, that there are no strong intellectual sympathies
'between us, such as would blind her to my defects.'

'A delightful letter from Miss Martineau. I mused
'long upon the noble courage with which she stepped
'forward into life, and the accurate judgment with
'which she has become acquainted with its practical
'details, without letting her fine imagination become
'tamed. I shall be cheered and sustained, amidst all
'fretting and uncongenial circumstances, by remembrance
'of her earnest love of truth and ardent faith.'

ILLNESS.

'A terrible feeling in my head, but kept about my
'usual avocations.' Read Ugo Foscolo's Sepolcri, and
'Pindemonti's answer, but could not relish either, so dis-
'tressing was the weight on the top of the brain; sewed
'awhile, and then went out to get warm, but could not,
'though I walked to the very end of Hazel-grove, and
'the sun was hot upon me. Sat down, and, though
'seemingly able to think with only the lower part of my
'head, meditated literary plans, with full hope that, if I
'could command leisure, I might do something good.
'It seemed as if I should never reach home, as I was
'obliged to sit down incessantly. * *

'For nine long days and nights, without intermission,
'all was agony, — fever and dreadful pain in my head.
'Mother tended me like an angel all that time, scarcely
'ever leaving me, night or day. My father, too, habitu-
'ally so sparing in tokens of affection, was led by his
'anxiety to express what he felt towards me in stronger
'terms than he had ever used in the whole course of my
'life. He thought I might not recover, and one morning,
'coming into my room, after a few moments' conversa-
'tion, he said : " My dear, I have been thinking of you
' " in the night, and I cannot remember that you have
' " any *faults*. You have defects, of course, as all mortals
' " have, but I do not know that you have a single fault."
'These words, — so strange from him, who had scarce
'ever in my presence praised me, and who, as I knew,
'abstained from praise as hurtful to his children, —
'affected me to tears at the time, although I could not
'foresee how dear and consolatory this extravagant
'expression of regard would very soon become. The

·family were deeply moved by the fervency of his
' prayer of thanksgiving, on the Sunday morning when I
' was somewhat recovered ; and to mother he said, "I
' "have no room for a painful thought now that our
' "daughter is restored."

'For myself, I thought I should die; but I was calm,
' and looked to God without fear. When I remem-
' bered how much struggle awaited me if I remained,
' and how improbable it was that any of my cherished
' plans would bear fruit, I felt willing to go. But
' Providence did not so will it. A much darker dispen-
' sation for our family was in store.'

DEATH OF HER FATHER.

'On the evening of the 30th of September, 1835,
' my father was seized with cholera, and on the 2d
' of October, was a corpse. For the first two days, my
' grief, under this calamity, was such as I dare not
' speak of. But since my father's head is laid in the
' dust, I feel an awful calm, and am becoming famil-
' iar with the thoughts of being an orphan. I have
' prayed to God that duty may now be the first object,
' and self set, aside. May I have light and strength
' to do what is right, in the highest sense, for my
' mother, brothers, and sister. * *

'It has been a gloomy week, indeed. The children
' have all been ill, and dearest mother is overpowered
' with sorrow, fatigue, and anxiety. I suppose she must
' be ill too, when the children recover. I shall endeavor
' to keep my mind steady, by remembering that there is
' a God, and that grief is but for a season. Grant, oh
' Father, that neither the joys nor sorrows of this past

'year shall have visited my heart in vain! Make me
'wise and strong for the performance of immediate
'duties, and ripen me, by what means Thou seest best,
'for those which lie beyond. * *

'My father's image follows me constantly. Whenever
'I am in my room, he seems to open the door, and to
'look on me with a complacent, tender smile. What
'would I not give to have it in my power, to make that
'heart once more beat with joy! The saddest feeling
'is the remembrance of little things, in which I have
'fallen short of love and duty. I never sympathized in
'his liking for this farm, and secretly wondered how a
'mind which had, for thirty years, been so widely
'engaged in the affairs of men, could care so much for
'trees and crops. But now, amidst the beautiful autumn
'days, I walk over the grounds, and look with painful
'emotions at every little improvement. He had selected
'a spot to place a seat where I might go to read alone,
'and had asked me to visit it. I contented myself with
'"When you please, father;" but we never went! What
'would I not now give, if I had fixed a time, and shown
'more interest! A day or two since, I went there. The
'tops of the distant blue hills were veiled in delicate
'autumn haze; soft silence brooded over the landscape;
'on one side, a brook gave to the gently sloping meadow
'spring-like verdure; on the other, a grove, — which he
'had named for me, — lay softly glowing in the gor-
'geous hues of October. It was very sad. May this
'sorrow give me a higher sense of duty in the relation-
'ships which remain.

'Dearest mother is worn to a shadow. Sometimes,
'when I look on her pale face, and think of all her grief,
'and the cares and anxieties which now beset her, I am

'appalled by the thought that she may not continue
'with us long. Nothing sustains me now but the
'thought that God, who saw fit to restore me to life
'when I was so very willing to leave it, — more so, per-
'haps, than I shall ever be again, — must have some
'good work for me to do.'

'*Nov.* 3, 1835. — I thought I should be able to write
ere now, how our affairs were settled, but that time has
not come yet. My father left no will, and, in conse-
'quence, our path is hedged in by many petty difficul-
'ties. He has left less property than we had antici-
'pated, for he was not fortunate in his investments in
'real estate. There will, however, be enough to main-
'tain my mother, and educate the children decently. I
'have often had reason to regret being of the softer sex,
'and never more than now. If I were an eldest son, I
'could be guardian to my brothers and sister, adminis-
'ter the estate, and really become the head of my family.
'As it is, I am very ignorant of the management and
'value of property, and of practical details. I always
'hated the din of such affairs, and hoped to find a life-
'long refuge from them in the serene world of litera-
'ture and the arts. But I am now full of desire to learn
'them, that I may be able to advise and act, where it is
'necessary. The same mind which has made other
'attainments, can, in time, compass these, however un-
'congenial to its nature and habits.'

'I shall be obliged to give up selfishness in the end.
'May God enable me to see the way clear, and not to
'let down the intellectual, in raising the moral tone of
'my mind. Difficulties and duties became distinct the

'very night after my father's death, and a solemn
'prayer was offered then, that I might combine what is
'due to others with what is due to myself. The spirit
'of that prayer I shall constantly endeavor to maintain.
'What ought to be done for a few months to come is
'plain, and, as I proceed, the view will open'

TRIAL.

The death of her father brought in its train a disappointment as keen as Margaret could well have been
called on to bear. For two years and more she had
been buoyed up to intense effort by the promise of a visit
to Europe, for the end of completing her culture. And
as the means of equitably remunerating her parents for
the cost of such a tour, she had faithfully devoted herself to the teaching of the younger members of the family Her honored friends, Professor and Mrs. Farrar,
who were about visiting the Old World, had invited
her to be their companion; and, as Miss Martineau was
to return to England in the ship with them, the prospect
before her was as brilliant with generous hopes as her
aspiring imagination could conceive. But now, in her
journal of January 1, 1836, she writes: —

'The New-year opens upon me under circumstances
'inexpressibly sad. I must make the last great sacri-
'fice, and, apparently, for evil to me and mine. Life,
'as I look forward, presents a scene of struggle and pri-
'vation only. Yet "I bate not a jot of heart," though
'much "of hope." My difficulties are not to be com-
'pared with those over which many strong souls have
'triumphed. Shall I then despair? If I do, I am not a
'strong soul.'

Margaret's family treated her, in this exigency, with the grateful consideration due to her love, and urgently besought her to take the necessary means, and fulfil her father's plan. But she could not make up her mind to forsake them, preferring rather to abandon her long-cherished literary designs. Her struggles and her triumph thus appear in her letters : —

'*January* 30, 1836. — I was a great deal with Miss ' Martineau, while in Cambridge, and love her more than ' ever. She is to stay till August, and go to England ' with Mr. and Mrs. Farrar. If I should accompany them ' I shall be with her while in London, and see the best ' literary society. If I should go, you will be with ' mother the while, will not you ? * Oh, dear E——, ' you know not how I fear and tremble to come to a ' decision. My temporal all seems hanging upon it, and ' the prospect is most alluring. A few thousand dollars ' would make all so easy, so safe. As it is, I cannot tell ' what is coming to us, for the estate will not be settled ' when I go. I pray to God ceaselessly that I may decide ' wisely.'

'*April* 17*th*, 1836. — If I am not to go with you I shal ' be obliged to tear my heart, by a violent effort, from its ' present objects and natural desires. But I shall feel the ' necessity, and will do it if the life-blood follows through ' the rent. Probably, I shall not even think it best to ' correspond with you at all while you are in Europe. ' Meanwhile, let us be friends indeed. The generous and ' unfailing love which you have shown me during these ' three years, when I could be so little to you, your indul-

* Her eldest brother.

'gence for my errors and fluctuations, your steady faith
in my intentions, have done more to shield and sustain
'me than any other earthly influence. If I must now
'learn to dispense with feeling them constantly near
'me, at least their remembrance can never, never be
'less dear. I suppose I ought, instead of grieving that
'we are soon to be separated, now to feel grateful for an
'intimacy of extraordinary permanence, and certainly of
'unstained truth and perfect freedom on both sides.

'As to my feelings, I take no pleasure in speaking of
'them; but I know not that I could give you a truer
'impression of them, than by these lines which I trans-
'late from the German of Uhland. They are entitled
'"JUSTIFICATION."

"Our youthful fancies, idly fired,
    The fairest visions would embrace ;
These, with impetuous tears desired,
    Float upward into starry space ;
Heaven, upon the suppliant wild,
    Smiles down a gracious *No !* — In vain
The strife ! Yet be consoled, poor child,
    For the wish passes with the pain.

But when from such idolatry
    The heart has turned, and wiser grown,
In earnestness and purity
    Would make a nobler plan its own, —
Yet, after all its zeal and care,
    Must of its chosen aim despair, —
Some bitter tears may be forgiven
    By *Man*, at least, — *we trust, by Heaven.*"'

BIRTH-DAY.

'*May* 23*d*, 1836. — I have just been reading Goethe's
'Lebensregel. It is easy to say "Do not trouble your-

' " self with useless regrets for the past; enjoy the pres-
' " ent, and leave the future to God." But it is *not* easy
' for characters, which are by nature neither *calm* nor
' *careless*, to act upon these rules. I am rather of the
' opinion of Novalis, that " Wer sich der hochsten Lieb
' "ergeben Genest von ihnen Wunden nie."

' But I will endeavor to profit by the instructions of
' the great philosopher who teaches, I think, what Christ
' did, to use without overvaluing the world.

' Circumstances have decided that I must not go to
' Europe, and shut upon me the door, as I think, forever,
' to the scenes I could have loved. Let me now try to
' forget myself, and act for others' sakes. What I can
' do with my pen, I know not. At present, I feel no con-
' fidence or hope. The expectations so many have been
' led to cherish by my conversational powers, I am dis-
' posed to deem ill-founded. I do not think I can pro-
' duce a valuable work. I do not feel in my bosom that
' confidence necessary to sustain me in such undertakings,
' — the confidence of genius. But I am now but just
' recovered from bodily illness, and still heart-broken by
' sorrow and disappointment. I may be renewed again,
' and feel differently. If I do not soon, I will make up
' my mind to teach. I can thus get money, which I will
' use for the benefit of my dear, gentle, suffering mother,
' — my brothers and sister. This will be the greatest
' consolation to me, at all events.'

DEATH IN LIFE.

' The moon tempted me out, and I set forth for a house
' at no great distance. The beloved south-west was
' blowing; the heavens were flooded with light, which

'could not diminish the tremulously pure radiance of the
'evening star; the air was full of spring sounds, and
'sweet spring odors came up from the earth. I felt that
happy sort of feeling, as if the soul's pinions were
'budding. My mind was full of poetic thoughts, and
'nature's song of promise was chanting in my heart.

'But what a change when I entered that human
dwelling! I will try to give you an impression of what
'you, I fancy, have never come in contact with. The
'little room—they have but one—contains a bed, a
'table, and some old chairs. A single stick of wood
'burns in the fire-place. It is not needed now, but those
'who sit near it have long ceased to know what spring
'is. They are all frost. Everything is old and faded,
'but at the same time as clean and carefully mended as
'possible. For all they know of pleasure is to get
'strength to sweep those few boards, and mend those old
'spreads and curtains. That sort of self-respect they
'have, and it is all of pride their many years of poor-
'tith has left them.

'And there they sit, — mother and daughter! In the
'mother, ninety years have quenched every thought and
'every feeling, except an imbecile interest about her
'daughter, and the sort of self-respect I just spoke of.
'Husband, sons, strength, health, house and lands, all
'are gone. And yet these losses have not had power to
'bow that palsied head to the grave. Morning by morn-
'ing she rises without a hope, night by night she lies
'down vacant or apathetic; and the utmost use she can
'make of the day is to totter three or four times across
'the floor by the assistance of her staff. Yet, though we
wonder that she is still permitted to cumber the ground,
joyless and weary, "the tomb of her dead self," we

'look at this dry leaf, and think how green it once was
'and how the birds sung to it in its summer day.

'But can we think of spring, or summer, or anything
'joyous or really life-like, when we look at the daughter?
'— that bloodless effigy of humanity, whose care is to
'eke out this miserable existence by means of the occa-
'sional doles of those who know how faithful and good
'a child she has been to that decrepit creature; who
'thinks herself happy if she can be well enough, by hours
'of patient toil, to perform those menial services which
'they both require; whose talk is of the price of
'pounds of sugar, and ounces of tea, and yards of flan-
'nel; whose only intellectual resource is hearing five or
'six verses of the Bible read every day, — "my poor
'"head," she says, "cannot bear any more;" and whose
'only hope is the death to which she has been so slowly
'and wearily advancing, through many years like this.

'The saddest part is, that she does *not wish* for death.
'She clings to this sordid existence. Her soul is now so
'habitually enwrapt in the meanest cares, that if she
'were to be lifted two or three steps upward, she would
'not know what to do with life; how, then, shall she
'soar to the celestial heights? Yet she ought; for she
'has ever been good, and her narrow and crushing duties
'have been performed with a self-sacrificing constancy,
'which I, for one, could never hope to equal.

'While I listened to her, — and I often think it good for
·me to listen to her patiently, — the expressions you
'used in your letter, about "drudgery," occurred to me.
'I remember the time when I, too, deified the "soul's
'"impulses." It is a noble worship; but, if we do not
'aid it by a just though limited interpretation of what
'"Ought" means, it will degenerate into idolatry. For

'a time it was so with me, and I am not yet good enough
'to love the *Ought*.

'Then I came again into the open air, and saw those
'resplendent orbs moving so silently, and thought that
'they were perhaps tenanted, not only by beings in whom
'I can see the germ of a possible angel, but by myriads
'like this poor creature, in whom that germ is, so far as
'we can see, blighted entirely, I could not help saying,
'"O my Father! Thou, whom we are told art all Power,
'"and also all Love, how canst Thou suffer such even
'"transient specks on the transparence of Thy creation?
'"These grub-like lives, undignified even by passion,—
'"these life-long quenchings of the spark divine, — why
'"dost Thou suffer them? Is not Thy paternal benevo-
'"lence impatient till such films be dissipated?"

'Such questionings once had power to move my spirit
'deeply; now, they but shade my mind for an instant.
'I have faith in a glorious explanation, that shall make
'manifest perfect justice and perfect wisdom.'

LITERATURE.

Cut off from access to the scholars, libraries, lectures,
galleries of art, museums of science, antiquities, and historic scenes of Europe, Margaret bent her powers to use
such opportunities of culture as she could command in
her solitary country-home. Journals and letters thus
bear witness to her zeal:—

'I am having one of my "intense" times, devouring
'book after book. I never stop a minute, except to talk
'with mother, having laid all little duties on the shelf

' for a few days. Among other things, I have twice read
' through the life of Sir J. Mackintosh; and it has sug-
' gested so much to me, that I am very sorry I did not
' talk it over with you. It is quite gratifying, after my
' late chagrin, to find Sir James, with all his metaphysical
' turn, and ardent desire to penetrate it, puzzling so over
' the German philosophy, and particularly what I was
' myself troubled about, at Cambridge, — Jacobi's letters
' to Fichte.

' Few things have ever been written more discrimi-
' nating or more beautiful than his strictures upon
' the Hindoo character, his portrait of Fox, and his
' second letter to Robert Hall, after his recovery from
' derangement. Do you remember what he says of the
' want of brilliancy in Priestley's moral sentiments?
' Those remarks, though slight, seem to me to show the
' quality of his mind more decidedly than anything in
' the book. That so much learning, benevolence, and
' almost unparalleled fairness of mind, should be in a
' great measure lost to the world, for want of earnestness
' of purpose, might impel us to attach to the latter attri-
' bute as much importance as does the wise uncle in
' Wilhelm Meister.'

' As to what you say of Shelley, it is true that the un-
' happy influences of early education prevented his ever
' attaining clear views of God, life, and the soul. At
' thirty, he was still a seeker, — an experimentalist. But
' then his should not be compared with such a mind as
' ——'s, which, having no such exuberant fancy to
' tame, nor various faculties to develop, naturally comes
' to maturity sooner. Had Shelley lived twenty years
' longer, I have no doubt he would have become a fervent

'Christian, and thus have attained that mental harmony
'which was necessary to him. It is true, too, as you
'say, that we always feel a melancholy imperfection in
'what he writes. But I love to think of those other
'spheres in which so pure and rich a being shall be per-
'fected; and I cannot allow his faults of opinion and
'sentiment to mar my enjoyment of the vast capabilities,
'and exquisite perception of beauty, displayed every-
'where in his poems.'

'*March* 17, 1836.—I think Herschel will be very val-
'uable to me, from the slight glance I have taken of it,
'and I thank Mr. F.; but do not let him expect any-
'thing of me because I have ventured on a book so
'profound as the Novum Organum. I have been ex-
'amining myself with severity, intellectually as well as
'morally, and am shocked to find how vague and super-
'ficial is all my knowledge. I am no longer surprised
'that I should have appeared harsh and arrogant in my
'strictures to one who, having a better-disciplined mind,
'is more sensible of the difficulties in the way of really
'knowing and doing anything, and who, having more
'Wisdom, has more Reverence too. All that passed at
'your house will prove very useful to me; and I trust
'that I am approximating somewhat to that genuine hu-
'mility which is so indispensable to true regeneration.
'But do not speak of this to ——, for I am not yet sure
'of the state of my mind.'

'1836.—I have, for the time, laid aside *De Stael*
'and *Bacon*, for *Martineau* and *Southey*. I find,
'with delight, that the former has written on the very
subjects I wished most to talk out with her, and prob-

'ably I shall receive more from her in this way than by
'personal intercourse, — for I think more of her character
'when with her, and am stimulated through my affections.
'As to Southey, I am steeped to the lips in enjoyment. I
'am glad I did not know this poet earlier; for I am now
'just ready to receive his truly exalting influences in some
'degree. I think, in reading, I shall place him next to
'Wordsworth. I have finished Herschel, and really be-
'lieve I am a little wiser. I have read, too, Heyne's
'letters twice, Sartor Resartus once, some of Goethe's
'late diaries, Coleridge's Literary Remains, and drank a
'great deal from Wordsworth. By the way, do you
'know his "Happy Warrior"? I find my insight of
'this sublime poet perpetually deepening.'

'Mr. —— says the Wanderjahre is "*wise.*" It
'must be presumed so; and yet one is not satisfied.
'I was perfectly so with my manner of interpreting the
'Lehrjahre; but this sequel keeps jerking my clue, and
'threatens to break it. I do not know our Goethe yet.
'I have changed my opinion about his religious views
'many times. Sometimes I am tempted to think that it
'is only his wonderful knowledge of human nature
'which has excited in me such reverence for his philoso-
'phy, and that no worthy fabric has been elevated on
'this broad foundation. Yet often, when suspecting that
'I have found a huge gap, the next turning it appears
'that it was but an air-hole, and there is a brick all ready
'to stop it. On the whole, though my enthusiasm for
'the Goetherian philosophy is checked, my admiration
'for the genius of Goethe is in nowise lessened, and I
'stand in a sceptical attitude, ready to try his philosophy,
'and, if needs must, play the Eclectic.'

'Did I write that a kind-hearted neighbor, fearing
'I might be *dull,* sent to offer me the use of a *book-caseful*
' of Souvenirs, Gems, and such-like glittering ware? I
' took a two or three year old " Token," and chanced on
' a story, called the "Gentle Boy," which I remem-
' bered to have heard was written by somebody in
' Salem. It is marked by so much grace and delicacy
' of feeling, that I am very desirous to know the author,
' whom I take to be a lady.' * *

'With regard to what you say about the American
' Monthly, my answer is, I would gladly sell some part
' of my mind for lucre, to get the command of time; but
' 1 will not sell my soul : that is, I am perfectly willing
' to take the trouble of writing for money to pay the
' seamstress; but I am *not* willing to have what I write
' mutilated, or what I ought to say dictated to suit the
' public taste. You speak of my writing about Tieck.
' It is my earnest wish to interpret the German authors
' of whom I am most fond to such Americans as are
' ready to receive. Perhaps some might sneer at the
' notion of my becoming a teacher; but where I love so
' much, surely I might inspire others to love a little; and
' I think this kind of culture would be precisely the
' counterpoise required by the utilitarian tendencies of
' our day and place. My very imperfections may be of
' value. While enthusiasm is yet fresh, while I am still
' a novice, it may be more easy to communicate with
' those quite uninitiated, than when I shall have attained
' to a higher and calmer state of knowledge. I hope a
' periodical may arise, by and by, which may think me
' worthy to furnish a series of articles on German litera-
' ture, giving room enough and perfect freedom to say
' what I please. In this case, I should wish to devote at

'least eight numbers to Tieck, and should use the Gar-
'den of Poesy, and my other translations.

'I have sometimes thought of translating his Little
'Red Riding Hood, for children. If it could be adorned
'with illustrations, like those in the "Story without an
'End," it would make a beautiful little book; but I do
'not know that this could be done in Boston. There is
'much meaning that children could not take in; but, as
'they would never discover this till able to receive the
'whole, the book corresponds exactly with my notions
'of what a child's book should be.

'I should like to begin the proposed series with a re-
'view of Heyne's letters on German Literature, which
'afford excellent opportunity for some preparatory hints.
'My plans are so undecided for several coming months,
'that I cannot yet tell whether I shall have the time and
'tranquillity needed to write out the whole course, though
'much tempted by the promise of perfect liberty. I
'could engage, however, to furnish at least two articles
'on Novalis and Körner. I trust you will be interested
'in my favorite Körner. Great is my love for both of
'them. But I wish to write something which shall not
'only *be* free from exaggeration, but which shall *seem* so,
'to those unacquainted with their works.

'I have so much reading to go through with this
'month, that I have but few hours for correspondents. I
'have already discussed five volumes in German, two in
'French, three in English, and not without thought and
'examination. * *

'Tell ——— that I read "Titan" by myself, in the after-
'noons and evenings of about three weeks. She need
'not be afraid to undertake it. Difficulties of detail
'may, perhaps, not be entirely conquered without a mas-

'ter or a good commentary, but she could enjoy all that
'is most valuable alone. I should be very unwilling to
'read it with a person of narrow or unrefined mind; for
'it is a noble work, and fit to raise a reader into that
'high serene of thought where pedants cannot enter.'

FAREWELL TO GROTON.

'The place is beautiful, in its way, but its scenery is
'too tamely smiling and sleeping. My associations with
'it are most painful. There darkened round us the
'effects of my father's ill-judged exchange, — ill-judged,
'so far at least as regarded himself, mother, and me, —
'all violently rent from the habits of our former life, and
'cast upon toils for which we were unprepared: there
'my mother's health was impaired, and mine destroyed;
'there my father died; there were undergone the miserable
'perplexities of a family that has lost its head; there I
'passed through the conflicts needed to give up all which
'my heart had for years desired, and to tread a path for
'which I had no skill, and no call, except that it must be
'trodden by some one, and I alone was ready. Wachu-
'set and the Peterboro' hills are blended in my memory
'with hours of anguish as great as I am capable of suf-
'fering. I used to look at them towering to the sky, and
'feel that I, too, from birth, had longed to rise, and,
'though for the moment crushed, was not subdued.

'But if those beautiful hills, and wide, rich fields, saw
'this sad lore well learned, they also saw some precious
'lessons given in faith, fortitude, self-command, and
'unselfish love. There too, in solitude, the mind ac-
'quired more power of concentration, and discerned the
'beauty of strict method; there too, more than all, the

'heart was awakened to sympathize with the ignorant,
'to pity the vulgar, to hope for the seemingly worthless,
'and to commune with the Divine Spirit of Creation,
'which cannot err, which never sleeps, which will not
'permit evil to be permanent, nor its aim of beauty in
'the smallest particular eventually to fail.'

WINTER IN BOSTON.

In the autumn of 1836 Margaret went to Boston, with
the two-fold design of teaching Latin and French in Mr.
Alcott's school, which was then highly prosperous, and
of forming classes of young ladies in French, German,
and Italian.

Her view of Mr. Alcott's plan of education was thus
hinted in a journal, one day, after she had been talking
with him, and trying to place herself in his mental
position : —

Mr. A. 'O for the safe and natural way of Intuition!
'I cannot grope like a mole in the gloomy passages of
'experience. To the attentive spirit, the revelation con-
'tained in books is only so far valuable as it comments
'upon, and corresponds with, the universal revelation.
'Yet to me, a being social and sympathetic by natural im-
'pulse, though recluse and contemplative by training and
'philosophy, the character and life of Jesus have spoken
'more forcibly than any fact recorded in human history.
'This story of incarnate Love has given me the key to
'all mysteries, and showed me what path should be
'taken in returning to the Fountain of Spirit. Seeing
'that other redeemers have imperfectly fulfilled their
'tasks, I have sought a new way. They all, it seemed

'to me, had tried to influence the human being at too
'late a day, and had laid their plans too wide.   They
'began with men; I will begin with babes.   They be-
'gan with the world; I will begin with the family.   So
'I preach the Gospel of the Nineteenth Century.'

   M. 'But, preacher, you make *three* mistakes.

   'You do not understand the nature of Genius or creative power.

   'You do not understand the reäction of matter on
'spirit.

   'You are too impatient of the complex; and, not en-
'joying variety in unity, you become lost in abstractions,
'and cannot illustrate your principles.'

   On the other hand, Mr. Alcott's impressions of Margaret were thus noted in his diaries : —

   "She is clearly a person given to the boldest speculation, and of liberal and varied acquirements.   Not wanting in imaginative power, she has the rarest good sense
and discretion.   She adopts the Spiritual Philosophy, and
has the subtlest perception of its bearings.   She takes
large and generous views of all subjects, and her disposition is singularly catholic.   The blending of sentiment
and of wisdom in her is most remarkable; and her taste
is as fine as her prudence.   I think her the most brilliant
talker of the day.   She has a quick and comprehensive
wit, a firm command of her thoughts, and a speech to
win the ear of the most cultivated."

   In her own classes Margaret was very successful, and
thus in a letter sums up the results : —

   'I am still quite unwell, and all my pursuits and pro-
'pensities have a tendency to make my head worse.   It

'is but a bad head, — as bad as if I were a great man!
'1 am not entitled to so bad a head by anything I have
' done; but I flatter myself it is very interesting to suffer
'so much, and a fair excuse for not writing pretty let-
: ters, and saying to my friends the good things I think
'about them.

'I was so desirous of doing all I could, that I took a
'great deal more upon myself than I was. able to bear.
'Yet now that the twenty-five weeks of incessant toil
'are over, I rejoice in it all, and would not have done
'an iota less. I have fulfilled all my engagements faith-
'fully; have acquired more power of attention, self-
'command, and fortitude; have acted in life as I thought
'I would in my lonely meditations; and have gained
'some knowledge of means. Above all, — blessed be the
'Father of our spirits! — my aims are the same as they
'were in the happiest flight of youthful fancy. I have
'learned too, at last, to rejoice in all past pain, and to see
'that my spirit has been judiciously tempered for its
'work. In future I may sorrow, but can I ever despair?

''The beginning of the winter was forlorn. I was
'always ill; and often thought I might not live, though
'the work was but just begun. The usual disappoint-
'ments, too, were about me. Those from whom aid
' was expected failed, and others who aided did not un-
'derstand my aims. Enthusiasm for the things loved
'best fled when I seemed to be buying and selling them.
'I could not get the proper point of view, and could not
keep a healthful state of mind. Mysteriously a gulf
'seemed to have opened between me and most intimate
'friends, and for the first time for many years I was
'entirely, absolutely, alone. Finally, my own character
' and designs lost all romantic interest, and I felt vulgar-

'ized, profaned, forsaken, — though obliged to smile
'brightly and talk wisely all the while. But these
'clouds at length passed away.

'And now let me try to tell you what has been done.
'To one class I taught the German language, and
'thought it good success, when, at the end of three
'months, they could read twenty pages of German at a
'lesson, and very well. This class, of course, was not
'interesting, except in the way of observation and
'analysis of language.

'With more advanced pupils I read, in twenty-four
'weeks, Schiller's Don Carlos, Artists, and Song of the
'Bell, besides giving a sort of general lecture on Schiller;
'Goethe's Hermann and Dorothea, Goetz von Berlich-
'ingen, Iphigenia, first part of Faust, — three weeks of
'thorough study this, as valuable to me as to them, —
'and Clavigo, — thus comprehending samples of all his
'efforts in poetry, and bringing forward some of his
'prominent opinions; Lessing's Nathan, Minna, Emilia
'Galeotti; parts of Tieck's Phantasus, and nearly the
'whole first volume of Richter's Titan.

'With the Italian class, I read parts of Tasso, Pe-
'trarch, — whom they came to almost adore, — Ariosto,
'Alfieri, and the whole hundred cantos of the Divina
'Commedia, with the aid of the fine Athenæum copy,
'Flaxman's designs, and all the best commentaries.
'This last piece of work was and will be truly valuable
'to myself.

'I had, besides, three private pupils, Mrs. ——, who
'became very attractive to me, ——, and little ——,
'who had not the use of his eyes. I taught him Latin
'orally, and read the History of England and Shakspeare's historical plays in connection. This lesson was

given every day for ten weeks, and was very interesting,
' though very fatiguing. The labor in Mr. Alcott's school
' was also quite exhausting. I, however, loved the
' children, and had many valuable thoughts suggested,
' and Mr. A.'s society was much to me.

'As you may imagine, the Life of Goethe is not yet
' written; but I have studied and thought about it much.
' It grows in my mind with everything that does grow
' there. My friends in Europe have sent me the needed
' books on the subject, and I am now beginning to work
' in good earnest. It is very possible that the task may
' be taken from me by somebody in England, or that in
' doing it I may find myself incompetent; but I go on in
' hope, secure, at all events, that it will be the means of
' the highest culture.'

In addition to other labors, Margaret translated, one
evening every week, German authors into English, for
the gratification of Dr. Channing; their chief reading
being in De Wette and Herder.

'It was not very pleasant,' she writes, ' for Dr. C.
' takes in subjects more deliberately than is conceivable
' to us feminine people, with our habits of ducking,
' diving, or flying for truth. Doubtless, however, he
' makes better use of what he gets, and if his sympathies
' were livelier he would not view certain truths in so
' steady a light. But there is much more talking than
' reading; and I like talking with him. I do not feel that
' constraint which some persons complain of, but am
' perfectly free, though less called out than by other in-
' tellects of inferior power. I get too much food for
' thought from him, and am not bound to any tiresome
' formality of respect on account of his age and rank in

' the world of intellect. He seems desirous to meet even
' one young and obscure as myself on equal terms, and
' trusts to the elevation of his thoughts to keep him in
' his place.'

She found higher satisfaction still in h.s preaching : —

'A discourse from Dr. C. on the spirituality of man's
'nature. This was delightful! I came away in the
'most happy, hopeful, and heroic mood. The tone of
' the discourse was so dignified, his manner was so be-
'nignant and solemnly earnest, in his voice there was
'such a concentration of all his force, physical and
'moral, to give utterance to divine truth, that I felt
'purged as by fire. If some speakers feed intellect more,
'Dr. C. feeds the whole spirit. O for a more calm,
'more pervading faith in the divinity of my own nature!
'I am so far from being thoroughly tempered and
'seasoned, and am sometimes so presumptuous, at others
'so depressed. Why cannot I lay more to heart the text,
' " God is never in a hurry : let man be patient and con-
' " fident " ? '

PROVIDENCE.

In the spring of 1837, Margaret received a very favorable offer to become a principal teacher in the Greene
Street School, at Providence, R. I.

' The proposal is, that I shall teach the elder girls my
'favorite branches, for four hours a day, — choosing my
'own hours, and arranging the course, — for a thousand
'dollars a year, if, upon trial, I am well enough pleased
'to stay. This would be independence, and would

'enable me to do many slight services for my family.
'But, on the other hand, I am not sure that I shall like
'the situation, and am sanguine that, by perseverance,
'the plan of classes in Boston might be carried into full
'effect. Moreover, Mr. Ripley, — who is about publish-
'ing a series of works on Foreign Literature, — has
'invited me to prepare the "Life of Goethe," on very
'advantageous terms. This I should much prefer. Yet
'when the thousand petty difficulties which surround
'us are considered, it seems unwise to relinquish imme-
'diate independence.'

She accepted, therefore, the offer which promised certain means of aiding her family, and reluctantly gave up
the precarious, though congenial, literary project.

SCHOOL EXPERIENCES.

'The new institution of which I am to be "Lady
'"Superior" was dedicated last Saturday. People talk
'to me of the good I am to do; but the last fortnight has
'been so occupied in the task of arranging many scholars
'of various ages and unequal training, that I cannot
'yet realize this new era. * *
'The gulf is vast, wider than I could have conceived
'possible, between me and my pupils; but the sight of
'such deplorable ignorance, such absolute burial of the
'best powers, as I find in some instances, makes me com-
'prehend, better than before, how such a man as Mr.
'Alcott could devote his life to renovate elementary edu-
'cation. I have pleasant feelings when I see that a new
'world has already been opened to them. * *
'Nothing of the vulgar feeling towards teachers, too
'often to be observed in schools, exists towards me.

'The pupils seem to reverence my tastes and opinions
'in all things; they are docile, decorous, and try hard to
'please; they are in awe of my displeasure, but delighted
'whenever permitted to associate with me on familiar
'terms. As I treat them like ladies, they are anxious to
'prove that they deserve to be so treated. * *

'There is room here for a great move in the cause of
'education, and if I could resolve on devoting five or six
'years to this school, a good work might, doubtless, be
'done. Plans are becoming complete in my mind, ways
'and means continually offer, and, so far as I have tried
'them, they succeed. I am left almost as much at lib-
'erty as if no other person was concerned. Some sixty
'scholars are more or less under my care, and many of
'them begin to walk in the new paths pointed out.
'General activity of mind, accuracy in processes, con-
'stant looking for principles, and search after the good
'and the beautiful, are the habits I strive to develop. * *

'I will write a short record of the last day at school.
'For a week past I have given the classes in philosophy,
'rhetoric, history, poetry, and moral science, short lec-
'tures on the true objects of study, with advice as to their
'future course; and to-day, after recitation, I expressed
'my gratification that the minds of so many had been
'opened to the love of good and beauty.

'Then came the time for last words First, I called
'into the recitation room the boys who had been under
'my care. They are nearly all interesting, and have
'showed a chivalric feeling in their treatment of me. Peo-
'ple talk of women not being able to govern boys; but I
'have always found it a very easy task. He must be a
'coarse boy, indeed, who, when addressed in a resolute,
'yet gentle manner, by a lady, will not try to merit her

' esteem. These boys have always rivalled one another
' in respectful behavior. I spoke a few appropriate
' words to each, mentioning his peculiar errors and good
' deeds, mingling some advice with more love, which
' will, I hope, make it remembered. We took a sweet
' farewell. With the younger girls I had a similar inter-
' view.

' Then I summoned the elder girls, who have been my
' especial charge. I reminded them of the ignorance in
' which some of them were found, and showed them
' how all my efforts had necessarily been directed to
' stimulating their minds, — leaving undone much which,
' under other circumstances, would have been deemed
' indispensable. I thanked them for the favorable opin-
' ion of my government which they had so generally
' expressed, but specified three instances in which I had
' been unjust. I thanked them, also, for the moral
' beauty of their conduct, bore witness that an appeal to
' conscience had never failed, and told them of my hap-
' piness in having the faith thus confirmed, that young
' persons can be best guided by addressing their highest
' nature. I declared my consciousness of having com-
' bined, not only in speech but in heart, tolerance and
' delicate regard for the convictions of their parents, with
' fidelity to my own, frankly uttered. I assured them of
' my true friendship, proved by my never having cajoled
' or caressed them into good. Every word of praise had
' been earned; all my influence over them was rooted
' in reality; I had never softened nor palliated their
' faults; I had appealed, not to their weakness, but to
' their strength; I had offered to them, always, the lofti-
' est motives, and had made every other end subordinate
' to that of spiritual growth. With a heartfelt blessing,

'I dismissed them; but none stirred, and we all sat for
'some moments, weeping. Then I went round the circle
'and bade each, separately, farewell.'

PERSONS.

Margaret's Providence journals are made extremely
piquant and entertaining, by her life-like portraiture of
people and events; and every page attests the scrupulous justice with which she sought to penetrate through
surfaces to reality, and, forgetting personal prejudices, to
apply universally the test of truth. A few sketches of
public characters may suffice to show with what sagacious, all-observing eyes, she looked about her.

'At the whig caucus, I heard TRISTAM BURGESS,—"The
'old bald Eagle!" His baldness increases the fine
'effect of his appearance, for it seems as if the locks
'had retreated, that the contour of his very strongly
'marked head might be revealed to every eye. His *per-
'sonnel*, as well as I could see, was fitted to command
'respect rather than admiration. He is a venerable, not
'a beautiful old man.

'He is a rhetorician, — if I could judge from this
'sample; style inwoven and somewhat ornate, matter
'frequently wrought up to a climax, manner rather
'declamatory, though strictly that of a gentleman and a
'scholar. One art in his oratory was, no doubt, very
'effective, before he lost force and distinctness of voice.
'I allude to his way, — after having reasoned a while,
'till he has reached the desired conclusion, — of leaning
'forward, with hands reposing but figure very earnest,
'and communicating, confidentially as it were, the result
'to the audience. The impression produced in former
'days, when those low, emphatic passages could be dis-

'tinctly heard, must have been very strong. Yet there
'is too much apparent trickery in this, to bear frequent
'repetition. His manner is well adapted for argument,
'and for the expression either of satire or of chivalric
'sentiment.'

'Mr. JOHN NEAL addressed my girls on the destiny and
'vocation of Woman in this country. He gave, truly, a
'*manly* view, though not the view of common men, and
'it was pleasing to watch his countenance, where energy
'is animated by genius. He then spoke to the boys, in
'the most noble and liberal spirit, on the exercise of
'political rights. If there is one among them who has
'the germ of a truly independent man, too generous to
'become a party tool, and with soul enough to think, as
'well as feel, for himself, those words were not spoken
'in vain. He was warmed up into giving a sketch of
'his boyhood. It was an eloquent narrative, and is inef-
'faceably impressed on my memory, with every look
'and gesture of the speaker. What gave chief charm to
'this history was its fearless ingenuousness. It was
'delightful to note the impression produced by his mag-
'netic genius and independent character.
'In the evening we had a long conversation upon
'Woman, Whigism, modern English Poets, Shaks-
'peare, — and, in particular, Richard the Third, — about
'which we had actually a fight. Mr. Neal does not
'argue quite fairly, for he uses reason while it lasts, and
'then helps himself out with wit, sentiment and asser-
'tion. I should quarrel with his definitions upon almost
'every subject, but his fervid eloquence, brilliancy, end-
'less resource, and ready tact, give him great advan-
'tage. There was a sort of exaggeration and coxcombry

'in his talk; but his lion-heart, and keen sense of the
'ludicrous, alike in himself as in others, redeem them.
'I should not like to have my motives scrutinized as he
'would scrutinize them, for I prefer rather to disclose
'them myself than to be found out; but I was dis-
'satisfied in parting from this remarkable man before
'having seen him more thoroughly.'

   'Mr. WHIPPLE addressed the meeting at length. His
'presence is not imposing, though his face is intellectual.
'It is difficult to look at him, for you cannot be taken
'prisoner by his eye, while, *en revanche*, he can look
'at you as long as he pleases; and, as usual, with one
'who can get the better of his auditors, he does not call
'out the best in them. His gestures are remarkably
'fine, free, graceful, and expressive. He has no natural
'advantages of voice, — for it is without compass, depth,
'sweetness, — and has none of the winning tones which
'reach the inmost soul, and none of the tones of passion-
'ate energy, which raise you out of your own world into
'the speaker's. But his modulation is smooth, measured,
'dignified, though occasionally injured by too elaborate
'a swell, and his enunciation is admirable.
   'His theme was one which has been so thoroughly
'discussed that novelty was not to be looked for; but
'his method and arrangement were excellent, though
'parts were too much expanded, and the whole might
'well have been condensed. There were many felicitous
'popular hits. The humorous touches were skilful, and
'the illustrations on a broad scale good, though in single
'images he failed. Altogether, there was a pervading
'air of ease and mastery, which showed him fit to be a
leader of the flock. Though not a man of the Webster

'class, he is among the first of the second class of men
'who apply their powers to practical purposes, — and
'that is saying much.'

'I went to hear JOSEPH JOHN GURNEY, one of the most
'distinguished and influential, it is said, of the English
'Quakers. He is a thick-set, beetle-browed man, with a
'well-to-do-in-the-world air of pious stolidity. I was
'grievously disappointed; for Quakerism has at times
'looked lovely to me, and I had expected at least a spir-
'itual exposition of its doctrines from the brother of Mrs.
'Fry. But his manner was as wooden as his matter,
'and had no merit but that of distinct elocution. His
'sermon was a tissue of texts, illy selected, and worse
'patched together, in proof of the assertion that a belief
'in the Trinity is the one thing needful, and that reason,
'unless manacled by a creed, is the one thing dangerous.
'His figures were paltry, his thoughts narrowed down,
'and his very sincerity made corrupt by spiritual pride.
'One could not but pity his notions of the Holy Ghost,
'and his bat-like fear of light. His Man-God seemed to
'be the keeper of a mad-house, rather than the informing
'Spirit of all spirits. •After finishing his discourse, Mr.
'G. sang a prayer, in a tone of mingled shout and whine,
'and then requested his audience to sit a while in devout
'meditation. For one, I passed the interval in praying
'for him, that the thick film of self-complacency might
'be removed from the eyes of his spirit, so that he might
'no more degrade religion.'

'Mr. HAGUE is of the Baptist persuasion, and is very
'popular with his own sect. He is small, and carries
'his head erect; he has a high and intellectual, though

'not majestic, forehead; his brows are lowering
'and, when knit in indignant denunciation, give a thun-
'derous look to the countenance, and beneath them flash,
'sparkle, and flame, — for all that may be said of light
'in rapid motion is true of them, — his dark eyes.   Hazel
'and blue eyes with their purity, steadfastness, subtle
penetration and radiant hope, may persuade and win,
'but black is the color to command.   His mouth has an
'equivocal expression, but as an orator perhaps he gains
'power by the air of mystery this gives.

    'He has a very active intellect, sagacity and elevated
'sentiment; and, feeling strongly that God is love, can
'never preach without earnestness.   His power comes
'first from his glowing vitality of temperament.   While
'speaking, his every muscle is in action, and all his
'action is towards one object.   There is perfect *abandon*.
'He is permeated, overborne, by his thought.   This
'lends a charm above grace, though incessant nervous-
'ness and heat injure his manner.   He is never violent,
'though often vehement; pleading tones in his voice
'redeem him from coarseness, even when most eager;
'and he throws himself into the hearts of his hearers,
'not in weak need of sympathy, but in the confidence of
'generous emotion.   His second attraction is his individ-
'uality.   He speaks direct from the conviction of his
'spirit, without temporizing, or artificial method.   His is
'the "unpremeditated art," and therefore successful. He
'is full of intellectual life; his mind has not been fettered
'by dogmas, and the worship of beauty finds a place
'there.   I am much interested in this truly animated
'being.'

    'Mr. R. H. Dana has been giving us readings in the

'English dramatists, beginning with Shakspeare. The
'introductory was beautiful. After assigning to literature
'its high place in the education of the human soul, he
'announced his own view in giving these readings: that
'he should never pander to a popular love of excitement,
'but quietly, without regard to brilliancy or effect, would
'tell what had struck him in these poets; that he had no
'belief in artificial processes of acquisition or communica-
'tion, and having never learned anything except through
'love, he had no hope of teaching any but loving spirits,
'&c. All this was arrayed in a garb of most delicate
'grace; but a man of such genuine refinement under-
'values the cannon-blasts and rockets which are needed
'to rouse the attention of the vulgar. His naïve gestures,
'the rapt expression of his face, his introverted eye, and
'the almost childlike simplicity of his pathos, carry one
'back into a purer atmosphere, to live over again youth's
'fresh emotions. I greatly enjoyed his readings in
'Hamlet, and have reviewed in connection what Goethe
'and Coleridge have said. Both have successfully
'seized on the main points in the character of Hamlet,
'and Mr. D. took nearly the same range. His views of
'Ophelia, however, are unspeakably more just than are
'those of Serlo in Wilhelm Meister. I regret that the
'whole course is not to be on Shakspeare, for I should
'like to read with him all the plays.
'I never have met with a person of finer perceptions.
'He leaves out nothing; though he over-refines on some
'passages. He has the most exquisite taste, and freshens
'the souls of his hearers with ever new beauty. He is
'greatly indebted to the delicacy of his physical organ-
'ization for the delicacy of his mental appreciation. But
'when he has told you what *he* likes, the pleasure of

'intercourse is over; for he is a man of prejudice more
'than of reason, and though he can make a lively
'*exposé* of his thoughts and feelings, he does not jus-
'tify them. In a word, Mr. Dana has the charms and
'the defects of one whose object in life has been to pre-
'serve his individuality unprofaned.'

ART.

While residing at Providence, and during her visits to
Boston, in her vacations, Margaret's mind was opening
more and more to the charms of art.

'The Ton-Kunst, the Ton-Welt, give me now more
'stimulus than the written Word; for music seems to
'contain everything in nature, unfolded into perfect har-
'mony. In it the *all* and *each* are manifested in most
'rapid transition; the spiral and undulatory movement
'of beautiful creation is felt throughout, and, as we listen,
'thought is most clearly, because most mystically, per-
'ceived. * *
'I have been to hear Neukomm's Oratorio of David.
'It is to music what Barry Cornwall's verses and Tal-
'fourd's Ion are to poetry. It is completely modern,
'and befits an age of consciousness. Nothing can be
'better arranged as a drama; the parts are in excellent
'gradation, the choruses are grand and effective, the
'composition, as a whole, brilliantly imposing. Yet it
'was dictated by taste and science only. Where are
'the enrapturing visions from the celestial world which
'shone down upon Haydn and Mozart; where the
'revelations from the depths of man's nature, which
'impart such passion to the symphonies of Beethoven;
'where, even, the fascinating fairy land, gay with

'delight, of Rossini? O, Genius! none but thee shall
'make our hearts and heads throb, our cheeks crimson,
'our eyes overflow, or fill our whole being with the
'serene joy of faith.' * *

'I went to see Vandenhoff twice, in Brutus and Vir-
'ginius. Another fine specimen of the conscious school;
'no inspiration, yet much taste. Spite of the thread-
'paper Tituses, the chambermaid Virginias, the wash-
'erwoman Tullias, and the people, made up of half a
'dozen chimney-sweeps, in carters' frocks and red night-
'caps, this man had power to recall a thought of the old
'stately Roman, with his unity of will and deed. He
'was an admirable *father*, that fairest, noblest part, —
'with a happy mixture of dignity and tenderness, blend-
'ing the delicate sympathy of the companion with the
'calm wisdom of the teacher, and showing beneath the
'zone of duty a heart that has not forgot to throb with
'youthful love. This character, — which did actual
'fathers know how to be, they would fulfil the order of
'nature, and image Deity to their children, — Vandenhoff
'represented sufficiently, at least, to call up the beauti-
'ful ideal.'

FANNY KEMBLE.

'When in Boston, I saw the Kembles twice, — in
'"Much ado about Nothing," and "The Stranger."
'The first night I felt much disappointed in Miss K.
'In the gay parts a coquettish, courtly manner marred
'the wild mirth and wanton wit of Beatrice. Yet, in
'everything else, I liked her conception of the part; and
'where she urges Benedict to fight with Claudio, and
'where she reads Benedict's sonnet, she was admira-
'ble. But I received no more pleasure from Miss K.'s
acting out the part than I have done in reading it, and

' this disappointed me. Neither did I laugh, but thought
' all the while of Miss K., — how very graceful she was,
' and whether this and that way of rendering the part
' was just. I do not believe she has comic power within
' herself, though tasteful enough to comprehend any
' part. So I went home, vexed because my "heart was
' "not full," and my "brain not on fire" with enthu-
' siasm. I drank my milk, and went to sleep, as on
' other dreary occasions, and dreamed not of Miss
' Kemble.

' Next night, however, I went expectant, and all my
' soul was satisfied. I saw her at a favorable distance,
' and she looked beautiful. And as the scene rose in
' interest, her attitudes, her gestures, had the expres-
' sion which an Angelo could give to sculpture.
' After she tells her story, — and I was almost suffo-
' cated by the effort she made to divulge her sin and
' fall, — she sunk to the earth, her head bowed upon
' her knee, her white drapery falling in large, graceful
' folds about this broken piece of beautiful humanity,
' *crushed* in the very manner so well described by Scott
' when speaking of a far different person, "not as
' "one who intentionally stoops, kneels, or prostrates
' "himself to excite compassion, but like a man borne
' "down on all sides by the pressure of some invisible
' "force, which crushes him to the earth without power
' "of resistance." A movement of abhorrence from me,
' as her insipid confidante turned away, attested the
' triumph of the poet-actress. Had not all been over in
' a moment, I believe I could not have refrained from
' rushing forward to raise the fair frail being, who seemed
' **so** prematurely humbled in her parent dust. I burst
' into tears; and, with the stifled, hopeless feeling of a

'real sorrow, continued to weep till the very end; nor
'could I recover till I left the house.

'That is genius, which could give such life to this
'play; for, if I may judge from other parts, it is defaced
'by inflated sentiments, and verified by few natural
'touches. I wish I had it to read, for I should like to
'recall her every tone and look.'

'I have been studying Flaxman and Retzsch. How
'pure, how immortal, the language of Form! Fools
'cannot fancy they fathom its meaning; witless *dillet-*
'*tanti* cannot degrade it by hackneyed usage; none but
'genius can create or reproduce it. Unlike the colorist,
'he who expresses his thought in form is secure as man
'can be against the ravages of time.'

'I went to the Athenæum in an agonizing conflict of
'mind, when some high influence was needed to rouse
'me from the state of sickly sensitiveness, which, much
'as I despise, I cannot wholly conquer. How soothing
'it was to feel the blessed power of the Ideal world, to
'be surrounded once more with the records of lives
'poured out in embodying thought in beauty! I seemed
'to breathe my native atmosphere, and smoothed my
'ruffled pinions.'

'No wonder God made a world to express his thought
'Who, that has a soul for beauty, does not feel the need
'of creating, and that the power of creation alone can
'satisfy the spirit? When I thus reflect, the Artist seems
'the only fortunate man. Had I but as much creative
genius as I have apprehensiveness!'

'How transcendently lovely was the face of one young
'angel by Raphael! It was the perfection of physical,

'moral, and mental life. Variegated wings, cf pinkish-
'purple touched with green, like the breasts of doves,
'and in perfect harmony with the complexion, spring
'from the shoulders upwards, and against them leans the
'divine head. The eye seems fixed on the centre of
'being, and the lips are gently parted, as if uttering
'strains of celestial melody.'

    'The head of Aspasia · was instinct with the volup-
'tuousness of intellect. From the eyes, the cheek,
'the divine lip, one might hive honey. Both the
'Loves were exquisite: one, that zephyr sentiment
'which visits all the roses of life; the other, the Amore
'Greco, may be fitly described in these words of Landor:
'"There is a gloom in deep love, as in deep water;
'"there is a silence in it which suspends the foot, and
'"the folded arms and the dejected head are the images
'"it reflects. No voice shakes its surface; the Muses
'"themselves approach it with a tardy and a timid step,
'"with a low and tremulous and melancholy song."'

    'The Sibyl I understood. What grace in that beau-
'tiful oval! what apprehensiveness in the eye! Such
'is female Genius; it alone understands the God.
'The Muses only sang the praises of Apollo; the Sibyls
'interpreted his will. Nay, she to whom it was offered,
'refused the divine union, and preferred remaining a
'satellite to being absorbed into the sun. You read
'in the eye of this one, and the observation is
'confirmed by the low forehead, that the secret of her
'inspiration lay in the passionate enthusiasm of her
 nature, rather than in the ideal perfection of any
 faculty.

'A Christ, by Raphael, that I saw the other night,
brought Christianity more home to my heart, made me
'more long to be like Jesus, than ever did sermon. It is
'from one of the Vatican frescoes. The Deity, — a stern,
'strong, wise man, of about forty-five, in a square velvet
'cap, truly the Jewish God, inflexibly just, yet jealous
'and wrathful, — is at the top of the picture, looking with
'a gaze of almost frowning scrutiny down into his world.
'A step below is the Son. Stately angelic shapes kneel
'near him in dignified adoration, — brothers, but not peers.
'A cloud of more ecstatic seraphs floats behind the Father.
'At the feet of the Son is the Holy Ghost, the Heavenly
'Dove. In the description, by a connoisseur, of this pic-
'ture, read to me while I was looking at it, it is spoken
'of as in Raphael's first manner, cold, hard, trammeled.
'But to me how did that face proclaim the Infinite Love!
'His head is bent back, as if seeking to behold the
'Father. His attitude expresses the need of adoring
'something higher, in order to keep him at his highest.
'What sweetness, what purity, in the eyes! I can never
'express it; but I felt, when looking at it, the beauty of
'reverence, of self-sacrifice, to a degree that stripped the
'Apollo of his beams.'

MAGNANIMITY.

Immediately after reading Miss Martineau's book on
America, Margaret felt bound in honor to write her
a letter, the magnanimity of which is brought out in
full relief, by contrast with the expressions already
given of her affectionate regard. Extracts from this
letter, recorded in her journals, come here rightfully in
place: —

'On its first appearance, the book was greeted by a
'volley of coarse and outrageous abuse, and the nine
'days' wonder was followed by a nine days' hue-and-
'cry. It was garbled, misrepresented, scandalously ill-
'treated. This was all of no consequence. The opin-
'ion of the majority you will find expressed in a late
'number of the North American Review. I should think
'the article, though ungenerous, not more so than great
'part of the critiques upon your book.

'The minority may be divided into two classes:
'The one, consisting of those who knew you but slightly,
'either personally, or in your writings. These have now
'read your book; and, seeing in it your high ideal
'standard, genuine independence, noble tone of senti-
'ment, vigor of mind and powers of picturesque descrip-
'tion, they value your book very much, and rate you
'higher for it.

'The other comprises those who were previously aware
'of these high qualities, and who, seeing in a book to
'which they had looked for a lasting monument to your
'fame, a degree of presumptuousness, irreverence, inac-
'curacy, hasty generalization, and ultraism on many
'points, which they did not expect, lament the haste in
'which you have written, and the injustice which you
'have consequently done to so important a task, and to
'your own powers of being and doing. To this class I
'belong.

'I got the book as soon as it came out, — long before I
received the copy endeared by your handwriting, — and
devoted myself to reading it. I gave myself up to my
natural impressions, without seeking to ascertain those of
others. Frequently I felt pleasure and admiration, but

'more frequently disappointment, sometimes positive dis-
'taste.

'There are many topics treated of in this book of
'which I am not a judge; but I do pretend, even where
'I cannot criticize in detail, to have an opinion as to the
'general tone of thought. When Herschel writes his
'Introduction to Natural Philosophy, I cannot test all he
'says, but I cannot err about his fairness, his manliness,
'and wide range of knowledge. When Jouffroy writes
'his lectures, I am not conversant with all his topics of
'thought, but I can appreciate his lucid style and
·admirable method. When Webster speaks on the cur-
'rency, I do not understand the subject, but I do under-
'stand his mode of treating it, and can see what a blaze of
'light streams from his torch. When Harriet Martineau
'writes about America, I often cannot test that rashness
'and inaccuracy of which I hear so much, but I can feel
'that they exist. A want of soundness, of habits of
'patient investigation, of completeness, of arrangement,
'are felt throughout the book; and, for all its fine de-
'scriptions of scenery, breadth of reasoning, and generous
'daring, I cannot be happy in it, because it is not worthy
'of my friend, and I think a few months given to ripen
'it, to balance, compare, and·mellow, would have made
'it so. * *

'Certainly you show no spirit of harshness towards
'this country in general. I think your tone most kindly.
'But many passages are deformed by intemperance of
'epithet. * * Would your heart, could you but investi-
'gate the matter, approve such overstatement, such a
'crude, intemperate tirade as you have been guilty of
'about Mr. Alcott, — a true and noble man, a philan-
'thropist, whom a true and noble woman, also a phi-

'lanthropist, should have delighted to honor; whose
'disinterested and resolute efforts, for the redemption of
'poor humanity, all independent and faithful minds
'should sustain, since the "broadcloth" vulgar will be
'sure to assail them; a philosopher, worthy of the palmy
'times of ancient Greece; a man whom Carlyle and
'Berkely, whom you so uphold, would delight to honor;
· a man whom the worldlings of Boston hold in as much
'horror as the worldlings of ancient Athens did Socrates.
'They smile to hear their verdict confirmed from the
'other side of the Atlantic, by their censor, Harriet
'Martineau.

'I do not like that your book should be an abolition
'book. You might have borne your testimony as decid-
'edly as you pleased; but why leaven the whole book
'with it? This subject haunts us on almost every page.
'It *is* a great subject, but your book had other purposes
'to fulfil.

'I have thought it right to say all this to you, since I
'felt it. I have shrunk from the effort, for I fear that
'I must lose you. Not that I think all authors are like
'Gil Blas' archbishop. No; if your heart turns from
'me, I shall still love you, still think you noble. I know
'it must be so trying to fail of sympathy, at such a time,
'where we expect it. And, besides, I felt from the book
'that the sympathy between us is less general than I had
'supposed, it was so strong on several points. It is strong
'enough for me to love you ever, and I could no more
'have been happy in your friendship, if I had not spoken
'out now.'

SPIRITUAL LIFE.

'You question me as to the nature of the benefits
'conferred upon me by Mr. E.'s preaching. I answer,

that his influence has been more beneficial to me than
' that of any American, and that from him I first learned
' what is meant by an inward life.   Many other springs
' have since fed the stream of living waters, but he first
' opened the fountain.   That the " mind is its own place,"
' was a dead phrase to me, till he cast light upon my
' mind.   Several of his sermons stand apart in memory,
' like landmarks of my spiritual history.   It would take
' a volume to tell what this one influence did for me
' But perhaps I shall some time see that it was best for
' me to be forced to help myself.'

'Some remarks which I made last night trouble me,
' and I cannot fix my attention upon other things till I
' have qualified them.   I suffered myself to speak in too
' unmeasured terms, and my expressions were fitted to
' bring into discredit the religious instruction which has
' been given me, or which I have sought.

  'I do not think "all men are born for the purpose of
' " unfolding beautiful ideas;" for the vocation of many
' is evidently the culture of affections by deeds of kind-
' ness.   But I do think that the vocations of men and
' women differ, and that those who are forced to act out
' of their sphere are shorn of inward and outward
' brightness.

  'For myself, I wish to say, that, if I am in a mood of
' darkness and despondency, I nevertheless consider such
' a mood unworthy of a Christian, or indeed of any one
' who believes in the immortality of the soul.   No one,
' who had steady faith in this and in the goodness of
' God, could be otherwise than cheerful.   I reverence the
' serenity of a truly religious mind so much, that I think
' if I live, I may some time attain to it.

'Although I do not believe in a Special Providence
'regulating outward events, and could not reconcile such
'a belief with what I have seen of life, I do not the less
'believe in the paternal government of a Deity. That
'He should visit the souls of those who seek Him seems
'to me the nobler way to conceive of his influence.
'And if there were not some error in my way of seeking,
'I do not believe I should suffer from languor or dead-
'ness on spiritual subjects, at the time when I have most
'need to feel myself at home there. To find this error is
'my earnest wish; and perhaps I am now travelling to
'that end, though by a thorny road. It is a mortification
'to find so much yet to do; for at one time the scheme
'of things seemed so clear, that, with Cromwell, I might
'say, "I was once in grace." With my mind I prize
'high objects as much as then: it is my heart which is
'cold. And sometimes I fear that the necessity of urging
'them on those under my care dulls my sense of their
'beauty. It is so hard to prevent one's feelings from
'evaporating in words.'

'"The faint sickness of a wounded heart." How
'frequently do these words of Beckford recur to my
'mind! His prayer, imperfect as it is, says more to me
'than many a purer aspiration. It breathes such an
'experience of impassioned anguish. He had every-
'thing, — health, personal advantages, almost boundless
'wealth, genius, exquisite taste, culture; he could, in
'some way, express his whole being. Yet well-nigh he
'sank beneath the sickness of the wounded heart; and
'solitude, "country of the unhappy," was all he craved
'at last.

'Goethe, too, says he has known, in all his active,

'wise, and honored life, no four weeks of happiness.
'This teaches me on the other side; for, like Goethe, I
'have never given way to my feelings, but have lived
'active, thoughtful, seeking to be wise. Yet I have
'long days and weeks of heartache; and at those
'times, though I am busy every moment, and cultivate
'every pleasant feeling, and look always upwards to the
'pure ideal region, yet this ache is like a bodily wound,
'whose pain haunts even when it is not attended to, and
'disturbs the dreams of the patient who has fallen asleep
'from exhaustion.

'There is a German in Boston, who has a wound in
'his breast, received in battle long ago. It never troubles
'him, except when he sings, and then, if he gives out his
'voice with much expression, it opens, and cannot, for a
'long time, be stanched again. So with me: when I rise
'into one of those rapturous moods of thought, such as I
'had a day or two since, my wound opens again, and all
'I can do is to be patient, and let it take its own time to
'skin over. I see it will never do more. Some time ago
'I thought the barb was fairly out; but no, the frag-
'ments rankle there still, and will, while there is any
'earth attached to my spirit. Is it not because, in my
'pride, I held the mantle close, and let the weapon,
which some friendly physician might have extracted,
splinter in the wound?'

'*Sunday, July,* 1838. — I partook, for the first time,
of the Lord's Supper. I had often wished to do so,
but had not been able to find a clergyman, — from whom
I could be willing to receive it, — willing to admit me on
my own terms. Mr. H—— did so; and I shall ever
respect and value him, if only for the liberality he dis-

'played on this occasion. It was the Sunday after the
'death of his wife, a lady whom I truly honored, and
'should, probably, had we known one another longer,
'have also loved. She was the soul of truth and honor;
'her mind was strong, her reverence for the noble and
'beautiful fervent, her energy in promoting the best
'interests of those who came under her influence
'unusual. She was as full of wit and playfulness as
'of goodness. Her union with her husband was really
'one of mind and heart, of mutual respect and tenderness; likeness in unlikeness made it strong. I wished
'particularly to share in this rite on an occasion so suited
'to bring out its due significance.'

FAREWELL TO SUMMER.

'The Sun, the Moon, the Waters, and the Air,
'The hopeful, holy, terrible, and fair,
 'All that is ever speaking, never spoken,
 'Spells that are ever breaking, never broken,
'Have played upon my soul ; and every string
'Confessed the touch, which once could make it ring
 'Celestial notes. And still, though changed the tone,
 'Though damp and jarring fall the lyre hath known,
'It would, if fitly played, its deep notes wove
'Into one tissue of belief and love,
 'Yield melodies for angel audience meet,
 'And pæans fit Creative Power to greet.
'O injured lyre ! thy golden frame is marred,
'No garlands deck thee, no libations poured
 'Tell to the earth the triumphs of thy song ;
 'No princely halls echo thy strains along.
'But still the strings are there ; and, if they break,
'Even in death rare melody will make,
 'Might'st thou once more be tuned, and power be given
 'To tell in numbers all thou canst of heaven ! '

VISITS TO CONCORD.

BY R. W. EMERSON.

Je n'ai point rencontré, dans ma vie, de femme plus noble ; ayant autant de sympathie pour ses semblables, et dont l'esprit fut plus vivifiant. Je me suis tout de suite sentie attirée par elle. Quand je fis sa connoissance, j'ignorais que ce fut une femme remarquable.

IV.

VISITS TO CONCORD.

———

I BECAME acquainted with Margaret in 1835. Perhaps it was a year earlier that Henry Hedge, who had .ong been her friend, told me of her genius and studies, and loaned me her manuscript translation of Goethe's Tasso. I was afterwards still more interested in her, by the warm praises of Harriet Martineau, who had become acquainted with her at Cambridge, and who, finding Margaret's fancy for seeing me, took a generous interest in bringing us together. I remember, during a week in the winter of 1835–6, in which Miss Martineau was my guest, she returned again and again to the topic of Margaret's excelling genius and conversation, and enjoined it on me to seek her acquaintance; which I willingly promised. I am not sure that it was not in Miss Martineau's company, a little earlier, that I first saw her. And I find a memorandum, in her own journal, of a visit, made by my brother Charles and myself, to Miss Martineau, at Mrs. Farrar's. It was not, however, till the next July, after a little diplomatizing in billets by the ladies, that her first visit to our house was arranged, and she came to spend a fortnight with my wife. I still remember the first half-hour of Margaret's conversation. She was then twenty-six years old. She had a face and frame that would indicate fulness and tenacity of life. She was rather under the middle height; her complexion was fair, with strong fair hair. She was then, as always, carefully and becomingly dressed, and of ladylike self-possession. For the rest, her appearance had nothing prepossessing. Her extreme plainness, — a trick of incessantly opening and shutting her eyelids, — the nasal tone of her voice, — all repelled; and I said to myself, we shall never get far. It is to be said, that Margaret made a disagreeable first impression on most persons, including those who became afterwards her best friends, to such an extreme that they did not wish to be in the same room with her. This was partly the effect of her manners, which expressed an overweening sense of power, and slight esteem of others, and partly the prejudice of her fame. She had a dangerous reputation for satire, in addition to her great scholarship. The men thought she carried too many guns, and the women did not like one who despised them. I believe I fancied her too much interested in personal history; and her talk was a comedy in which dramatic justice was done to everybody's foibles. I remember that she made me laugh more than I liked; for I was, at that time, an eager scholar of ethics, and had tasted the sweets of solitude and stoicism, and I found something profane in the hours of amusing gossip into which she drew me, and, when I returned to my library, had much to think of the crackling of thorns under a pot. Margaret, who had stuffed me out as a philosopher, in her own fancy, was too intent on estab-lishing a good footing between us, to omit any art of winning. She studied my tastes, piqued and amused me, challenged frankness by frankness, and did not conceal the good opinion of me she brought with her, nor her wish to please. She was curious to know my opinions and experiences. Of course, it was impossible long to hold out against such urgent assault. She had an incredible variety of anecdotes, and the readiest wit to give an absurd turn to whatever passed; and the eyes, which were so plain at first, soon swam with fun and drolleries, and the very tides of joy and superabundant life.

This rumor was much spread abroad, that she was sneering, scoffing, critical, disdainful of humble people, and of all but the intellectual. I had heard it whenever she was named. It was a superficial judgment. Her satire was only the pastime and necessity of her talent, the play of superabundant animal spirits. And it will be seen, in the sequel, that her mind presently disclosed many moods and powers, in successive platforms or terraces, each above each, that quite effaced this first impression, in the opulence of the following pictures.

Let us hear what she has herself to say on the subject of tea-table-talk, in a letter to a young lady, to whom she was already much attached : —

'I am repelled by your account of your party. It is 'beneath you to amuse yourself with active satire, with 'what is vulgarly called quizzing. When such a person as —— chooses to throw himself in your way, I sympathize with your keen perception of his ridiculous points. But 'to laugh a whole evening at vulgar nondescripts, — is that 'an employment for one who was born passionately to 'love, to admire, to sustain truth ? This would be much

'more excusable in a chameleon like me. Yet, whatever
'may be the vulgar view of my character, I can truly
'say, I know not the hour in which I ever looked for the
'ridiculous. It has always been forced upon me, and is
'the accident of my existence. I would not want the
'sense of it when it comes, for that would show an
'obtuseness of mental organization; but, on peril of my
soul, I would not move an eyelash to look for it.'

When she came to Concord, she was already rich in
friends, rich in experiences, rich in culture. She was
well read in French, Italian, and German literature. She
had learned Latin and a little Greek. But her English
reading was incomplete; and, while she knew Molière,
and Rousseau, and any quantity of French letters,
memoirs, and novels, and was a dear student of Dante
and Petrarca, and knew German books more cordially
than any other person, she was little read in Shakspeare; and I believe I had the pleasure of making her
acquainted with Chaucer, with Ben Jonson, with Herbert, Chapman, Ford, Beaumont and Fletcher, with
Bacon, and Sir Thomas Browne. I was seven years
her senior, and had the habit of idle reading in old English books, and, though not much versed, yet quite
enough to give me the right to lead her. She fancied
that her sympathy and taste had led her to an exclusive
culture of southern European books.

She had large experiences. She had been a precocious
scholar at Dr. Park's school; good in mathematics and
in languages. Her father, whom she had recently lost,
had been proud of her, and petted her. She had drawn,
at Cambridge, numbers of lively young men about her.
She had had a circle of young women who were devoted

to her, and who described her as "a wonder of intellect, "who had yet no religion." She had drawn to her every superior young man or young woman she had met, and whole romances of life and love had been confided, counselled, thought, and lived through, in her cognizance and sympathy.

These histories are rapid, so that she had already beheld many times the youth, meridian, and old age of passion. She had, besides, selected, from so many, a few eminent companions, and already felt that she was not likely to see anything more beautiful than her beauties, anything more powerful and generous than her youths. She had found out her own secret by early comparison, and knew what power to draw confidence, what necessity to lead in every circle, belonged of right to her. Her powers were maturing, and nobler sentiments were subliming the first heats and rude experiments. She had outward calmness and dignity. She had come to the ambition to be filled with all nobleness.

Of the friends who surrounded her, at that period, it is neither easy to speak, nor not to speak. A life of Margaret is impossible without them, she mixed herself so inextricably with her company; and when this little book was first projected, it was proposed to entitle it "Margaret and her Friends," the subject persisting to offer itself in the plural number. But, on trial, that form proved impossible, and it only remained that the narrative, like a Greek tragedy, should suppose the chorus always on the stage, sympathizing and sympathized with by the queen of the scene.

Yet I remember these persons as a fair, commanding troop, every one of them adorned by some splendor of beauty, of grace, of talent, or of character, and comprising in their band persons who have since disclosed sterling worth and elevated aims in the conduct of life.

Three beautiful women, — either of whom would have been the fairest ornament of Papanti's Assemblies, but for the presence of the other, — were her friends. One of these early became, and long remained, nearly the central figure in Margaret's brilliant circle, attracting to herself, by her grace and her singular natural eloquence, every feeling of affection, hope, and pride.

Two others I recall, whose rich and cultivated voices in song were, — one a little earlier, the other a little later, — the joy of every house into which they came; and, indeed, Margaret's taste for music was amply gratified in the taste and science which several persons among her intimate friends possessed. She was successively intimate with two sisters, whose taste for music had been opened, by a fine and severe culture, to the knowledge and to the expression of all the wealth of the German masters.

I remember another, whom every muse inspired, skilful alike with the pencil and the pen, and by whom both were almost contemned for their inadequateness, in the height and scope of her aims. 'With her,' said Margaret, 'I can talk of anything. She is like me. She is able to 'look facts in the face. We enjoy the clearest, widest, 'most direct communication. She may be no happier 'than ——, but she will know her own mind too clearly 'to make any great mistake in conduct, and will learn a 'deep meaning from her days.'

'It is not in the way of tenderness that I love ——. 'I prize her always; and this is all the love some 'natures ever know. And I also feel that I may always 'expect she will be with me. I delight to picture to

'myself certain persons translated, illuminated. There
'are a few in whom I see occasionally the future being
'piercing, promising, — whom I can strip of all that masks
'their temporary relations, and elevate to their natural
'position. Sometimes I have not known these persons
'intimately, — oftener I have; for it is only in the deepest
'hours that this light is likely to break out. But some
'of those I have best befriended I cannot thus portray,
'and very few men I can. It does not depend at all
'on the beauty of their forms, at present; it is in the eye
'and the smile, that the hope shines through. I can see
'exactly how —— will look : not like this angel in the
'paper; she will not bring flowers, but a living coal, to
'the lips of the singer; her eyes will not burn as now
'with smothered fires, they will be ever deeper, and glow
'more intensely; her cheek will be smooth, but marble
'pale; her gestures nobly free, but few.'

Another was a lady who was devoted to landscape-
painting, and who enjoyed the distinction of being the
only pupil of Allston, and who, in her alliance with Margaret, gave as much honor as she received, by the security
of her spirit, and by the heroism of her devotion to her
friend. Her friends called her "the perpetual peace-
offering," and Margaret says of her, — 'She is here, and
'her neighborhood casts the mildness and purity too of
'the moonbeam on the else parti-colored scene.'

There was another lady, more late and reluctantly
entering Margaret's circle, with a mind as high, and
more mathematically exact, drawn by taste to Greek, as
Margaret to Italian genius, tempted to do homage to
Margaret's flowing expressive energy, but still more

inclined and secured to her side by the good sense and the heroism which Margaret disclosed, perhaps not a little by the sufferings which she addressed herself to alleviate, as long as Margaret lived. Margaret had a courage in her address which it was not easy to resist. She called all her friends by their Christian names. In their early intercourse I suppose this lady's billets were more punctiliously worded than Margaret liked; so she subscribed herself, in reply, 'Your affectionate "Miss Fuller."' When the difficulties were at length surmounted, and the conditions ascertained on which two admirable persons could live together, the best understanding grew up, and subsisted during her life. In her journal is a note : —

'Passed the morning in Sleepy Hollow, with ——. 'What fine, just distinctions she made! Worlds grew 'clearer as we talked. I grieve to see her fine frame 'subject to such rude discipline. But she truly said, '"I am not a failed experiment; for, in the bad hours, I '"do not forget what I thought in the better."'

None interested her more at that time, and for many years after, than a youth with whom she had been acquainted in Cambridge before he left the University, and the unfolding of whose powers she had watched with the warmest sympathy. He was an amateur, and, but for the exactions not to be resisted of an *American*, that is to say, of a commercial, career, — his acceptance of which she never ceased to regard as an apostasy, — himself a high artist. He was her companion, and, though much younger, her guide in the study of art. With him she examined, leaf by leaf, the designs of

Raphael, of Michel Angelo, of Da Vinci, of Guercino, the architecture of the Greeks, the books of Palladio, the Ruins, and Prisons of Piranesi; and long kept up a profuse correspondence on books and studies in which they had a mutual interest. And yet, as happened so often, these literary sympathies, though sincere, were only veils and occasions to beguile the time, so profound was her interest in the character and fortunes of her friend.

There was another youth, whom she found later, of invalid habit, which had infected in some degree the tone of his mind, but of a delicate and pervasive insight, and the highest appreciation for genius in letters, arts, and life. Margaret describes 'his complexion as clear 'in its pallor, and his eye steady.' His turn of mind, and his habits of life, had almost a monastic turn, — a jealousy of the common tendencies of literary men either to display or to philosophy. Margaret was struck with the singular fineness of his perceptions, and the pious tendency of his thoughts, and enjoyed with him his proud reception, not as from above, but almost on equal ground, of Homer and Æschylus, of Dante and Petrarch, of Montaigne, of Calderon, of Goethe. Margaret wished, also, to defend his privacy from the dangerous solicitations to premature authorship : —

'His mind should be approached close by one who 'needs its fragrance. All with him leads rather to 'glimpses and insights, than to broad, comprehensive 'views. Till he needs the public, the public does not 'need him. The lonely lamp, the niche, the dark cathe-'dral grove, befit him best. Let him shroud himself in 'the symbols of his native ritual, till he can issue forth 'on the wings of song.'

She was at this time, too, much drawn also to a man of poetic sensibility, and of much reading, — which he took the greatest pains to conceal, — studious of the art of poetry, but still more a poet in his conversation than in his poems, — who attracted Margaret by the flowing humor with which he fill°d the present hour, and the prodigality with which he forgot all the past.

'Unequal and uncertain,' she says, 'but in his good 'moods, of the best for a companion, absolutely aban-'doned to the revelations of the moment, without distrust 'or check of any kind, unlimited and delicate, abundant 'in thought, and free of motion, he enriches life, and fills 'the hour.'

'I wish I could retain ——'s talk last night. It was 'wonderful; it was about all the past experiences frozen 'down in the soul, and the impossibility of being pen-'etrated by anything. "Had I met you," said he, "when '"I was young! — but now nothing can penetrate." 'Absurd as was what he said, on one side, it was the 'finest poetic inspiration on the other, painting the cruel 'process of life, except where genius continually burns 'over the stubble fields.

'"Life," he said, "is continually eating us up." He said, "Mr. E. is quite wrong about books. He wants '"them all good; now I want many bad. Literature is '"not merely a collection of gems, but a great system of '"interpretation." He railed at me as artificial. "It don't '"strike me when you are alone with me," he says; "but '"it does when others are present. You don't follow out '"the fancy of the moment; you converse; you have '"treasured thoughts to tell; you are disciplined, — arti-'"ficial." I pleaded guilty, and observed that I supposed

' that it must be so with one of any continuity of thought,
' or earnestness of character. "As to that," says he,
' "I shall not like you the better for your excellence. I
' "don't know what is the matter. I feel strongly
' "attracted towards you; but there is a drawback in
' "my mind,—I don't know exactly what. You will
' "always be wanting to grow forward; now I like to
' "grow backward, too. You are too ideal. Ideal people
' "anticipate their lives; and they make themselves and
' "everybody around them restless, by always being
' "beforehand with themselves."

'I listened attentively; for what he said was excellent.
'Following up the humor of the moment, he arrests
'admirable thoughts on the wing. But I cannot but see
' that what they say of my or other obscure lives is true
' of every prophetic, of every tragic character. And then
'I like to have them make me look on that side, and
'reverence the lovely forms of nature, and the shifting
'moods, and the clinging instincts. But I must not let
'them disturb me. There is an only guide, the voice in
'the heart, that asks, "Was thy wish sincere? If so,
' "thou canst not stray from nature, nor be so perverted
' "but she will make thee true again." I must take my
'own path, and learn from them all, without being par-
'alyzed for the day. We need great energy, faith, and
'self-reliance to endure to-day. My age may not be the
'best, my position may be bad, my character ill-formed;
'but Thou, oh Spirit! hast no regard to aught but the
'seeking heart; and, if I try to walk upright, wilt guide
'me. What despair must he feel, who, after a whole
'life passed in trying to build up himself, resolves that it
' would have been far better if he had kept still as the
'clod of the valley, or yielded easily as the leaf to every

'breeze! A path has been appointed me. I have walked
'in it as steadily as I could. I am what I am; that
' which I am not, teach me in the others. I will ·bear the
'pain of imperfection, but not of doubt. E. must not
'shake me in my worldliness, nor —— in the fine
'motion that has given me what I have of life, nor this
'child of genius make me lay aside the armor, without
'which I had lain bleeding on the field long since; but,
'if they can keep closer to nature, and learn to interpret
'her as souls, also, let me learn from them what I
'have not.'

And, in connection with this conversation, she has
copied the following lines which this gentleman addressed
to her : —

" TO MARGARET.

" I mark beneath thy life the virtue shine
That deep within the star's eye opes its day;
I clutch the gorgeous thoughts thou throw'st away
From the profound unfathomable mine,
And with them this mean common hour do twine,
As glassy waters on the dry beach play.
And I were rich as night, them to combine
With my poor store, and warm me with thy ray.
From the fixed answer of those dateless eyes
I meet bold hints of spirit's mystery
As to what's past, and hungry prophecies
Of deeds to-day, and things which are to be;
Of lofty life that with the eagle flies,
And humble love that clasps humanity."

I have thus vaguely designated, among the numerous
group of her friends, only those who were much in her

company, in the early years of my acquaintance with her.

She wore this circle of friends, when I first knew her, as a necklace of diamonds about her neck. They were so much to each other, that Margaret seemed to represent them all, and, to know her, was to acquire a place with them. The confidences given her were thei. best, and she held them to them. She was an active inspiring companion and correspondent, and all the art, the thought, and the nobleness in New England, seemed, at that moment, related to her, and she to it. She was everywhere a welcome guest. The houses of her friends in town and country were open to her, and every hospitable attention eagerly offered. Her arrival was a holiday, and so was her abode. She stayed a few days, often a week, more seldom a month, and all tasks that could be suspended were put aside to catch the favorable hour, in walking, riding, or boating, to talk with this joyful guest, who brought wit, anecdotes, love-stories, tragedies, oracles with her, and, with her broad web of relations to so many fine friends, seemed like the queen of some parliament of love, who carried the key to all confidences, and to whom every question had been finally referred.

Persons were her game, specially, if marked by fortune, or character, or success; — to such was she sent. She addressed them with a hardihood, — almost a haughty assurance, — queen-like. Indeed, they fell in her way, where the access might have seemed difficult, by wonderful casualties; and the inveterate recluse, the coyest maid, the waywardest poet, made no resistance, but yielded at discretion, as if they had been waiting for her, all doors to this imperious dame. She disarmed the sus-

picion of recluse scholars by the absence of bookishness.
The ease with which she entered into conversation
made them forget all they had heard of her; and she
was infinitely less interested in literature than in life.
They saw she valued earnest persons, and Dante.
Petrarch, and Goethe, because they thought as she did,
and gratified her with high portraits, which she was
everywhere seeking. She drew her companions to surprising confessions. She was the wedding-guest, to
whom the long-pent story must be told; and they were
not less struck, on reflection, at the suddenness of the
friendship which had established, in one day, new and
permanent covenants. She extorted the secret of life,
which cannot be told without setting heart and mind
in a glow; and thus had the best of those she saw
Whatever romance, whatever virtue, whatever impressive experience, — this came to her; and she lived in a
superior circle; for they suppressed all their common-
place in her presence.

She was perfectly true to this confidence. She never
confounded relations, but kept a hundred fine threads
in her hand, without crossing or entangling any. An
entire intimacy, which seemed to make both sharers
of the whole horizon of each others' and of all truth,
did not yet make her false to any other friend; gave
no title to the history that an equal trust of another
friend had put in her keeping. In this reticence was
no prudery and no effort. For, so rich her mind, that she
never was tempted to treachery, by the desire of entertaining. The day was never long enough to exhaust her
opulent memory; and I, who knew her intimately for ten
years, — from July, 1836, till August, 1846, when she

sailed for Europe, — never saw her without surprise at
her new powers.

Of the conversations above alluded to, the substance
was whatever was suggested by her passionate wish for
equal companions, to the end of making life altogether
noble.   With the firmest tact she led the discourse
into the midst of their daily living and working,
recognizing the good-will and sincerity which each man
has in his aims, and treating so playfully and intellectually all the points, that 'one seemed to see his life
en beau, and was flattered by beholding what he had
found so tedious in its workday weeds, shining in glorious costume.   Each of his friends passed before him
in the new light; hope seemed to spring under his feet,
and life was worth living.   The auditor jumped for joy,
and thirsted for unlimited draughts.   What! is this the
dame, who, I heard, was sneering and critical? this the
blue-stocking, of whom I stood in terror and dislike?
this wondrous woman, full of counsel, full of tenderness,
before whom every mean thing is ashamed, and hides
itself; this new Corinne, more variously gifted, wise,
sportive, eloquent, who seems to have learned all languages, Heaven knows when or how, — I should think
she was born to them, — magnificent, prophetic, reading
my life at her will, and puzzling me with riddles like
this, 'Yours is an example of a destiny springing from
'character:' and, again, 'I see your destiny hovering
'before you, but it always escapes from you.'

The test of this eloquence was its range.   It told on
children, and on old people; on men of the world, and on
sainted maids.   She could hold them all by her honeyed
tongue.   A lady of the best eminence, whom Margaret

occasionally visited, in one of our cities of spindles, speaking one day of her neighbors, said, "I stand in a certain awe of the moneyed men, the manufacturers, and so on, knowing that they will have small interest in Plato, or in Biot; but I saw them approach Margaret, with perfect security, for she could give them bread that they could eat." Some persons are thrown off their balance when in society; others are thrown on to balance; the excitement of company, and the observation of other characters, correct their biases. Margaret always appeared to unexpected advantage in conversation with a large circle. She had more sanity than any other; whilst, in private, her vision was often through colored lenses.

Her talents were so various, and her conversation so rich and entertaining, that one might talk with her many times, by the parlor fire, before he discovered the strength which served as foundation to so much accomplishment and eloquence. But, concealed under flowers and music, was the broadest good sense, very well able to dispose of all this pile of native and foreign ornaments, and quite able to work without them. She could always rally on this, in every circumstance, and in every company, and find herself on a firm footing of equality with any party whatever, and make herself useful, and, if need be, formidable.

The old Anaximenes, seeking, I suppose, for a source sufficiently diffusive, said, that Mind must be *in the air*, which, when all men breathed, they were filled with one intelligence. And when men have larger measures of reason, as Æsop, Cervantes, Franklin, Scott, they gain in universality, or are no longer confined to a few associates, but are good company for all persons, — philosophers, women, men of fashion, tradesmen, and servants. Indeed, an older philosopher than Anaximenes, namely, language itself, had taught to distinguish superior or purer sense as *common* sense.

Margaret had, with certain limitations, or, must we say, *strictures*, these larger lungs, inhaling this universal element, and could speak to Jew and Greek, free and bond, to each in his own tongue. The Concord stage-coachman distinguished her by his respect, and the chambermaid was pretty sure to confide to her, on the second day, her homely romance.

I regret that it is not in my power to give any true report of Margaret's conversation. She soon became an established friend and frequent inmate of our house, and continued, thenceforward, for years, to come, once in three or four months, to spend a week or a fortnight with us. She adopted all the people and all the interests she found here. Your people shall be my people, and yonder darling boy I shall cherish as my own. Her ready sympathies endeared her to my wife and my mother, each of whom highly esteemed her good sense and sincerity. She suited each, and all. Yet, she was not a person to be suspected of complaisance, and her attachments, one might say, were chemical.

She had so many tasks of her own, that she was a very easy guest to entertain, as she could be left to herself, day after day, without apology. According to our usual habit, we seldom met in the forenoon. After dinner, we read something together, or walked, or rode. In the evening, she came to the library, and many and many a conversation was there held, whose details, if they could be preserved, would justify all encomiums. They interested me in every manner; — talent, memory,

wit, stern introspection, poetic play, religion, the finest
personal feeling, the aspects of the future, each followed
each in full activity, and left me, I remember, enriched
and sometimes astonished by the gifts of my guest.
Her topics were numerous, but the cardinal points
of poetry, love, and religion, were never far off. She
was a student of art, and, though untravelled, knew,
much· better than most persons who had been abroad,
the conventional reputation of each of the masters. She
was familiar with all the field of elegant criticism in literature. Among the problems of the day, these two
attracted her chiefly, Mythology and Demonology;
then, also, French Socialism, especially as it concerned
woman; the whole prolific family of reforms, and, of
course, the genius and career of each remarkable person.

She had other friends, in this town, beside those in
my house. A lady, already alluded to, lived in the village, who had known her longer than I, and whose prejudices Margaret had resolutely fought down, until she
converted her into the firmest and most efficient of
friends. In 1842, Nathaniel Hawthorne, already then
known to the world by his Twice-Told Tales, came to
live in Concord, in the "Old Manse," with his wife,
who was herself an artist. With these welcomed persons Margaret formed a strict and happy acquaintance. She liked their old house, and the taste which
had filled it with new articles of beautiful form, yet harmonized with the antique furniture left by the former
proprietors. She liked, too, the pleasing walks, and
rides, and boatings, which that neighborhood com·
manded.

In 1842, William Ellery Channing, whose wife was

her sister, built a house in Concord, and this circumstance made a new tie and another home for Margaret.

ARCANA.

It was soon evident that there was somewhat a little pagan about her; that she had some faith more or less distinct in a fate, and in a guardian genius; that her fancy, or her pride, had played with her religion. She had a taste for gems, ciphers, talismans, omens, coincidences, and birth-days. She had a special love for the planet Jupiter, and a belief that the month of September was inauspicious to her. She never forgot that her name, Margarita, signified a pearl. 'When I first met ' with the name Leila,' she said, 'I knew, from the very 'look and sound, it was mine; I knew that it meant 'night, — night, which brings out stars, as sorrow brings 'out truths.' Sortilege she valued. She tried *sortes voticæ*, and her hits were memorable. I think each new book which interested her, she was disposed to put to this test, and know if it had somewhat personal to say to her. As happens to such persons, these guesses were justified by the event. She chose carbuncle for her own stone, and when a dear friend was to give her a gem, this was the one selected. She valued what she had somewhere read, that carbuncles are male and female. The female casts out light, the male has his within himself. 'Mine,' she said, 'is the male.' And she was wont to put on her carbuncle, a bracelet, or some selected gem, to write letters to certain friends. One of her friends she coupled with the onyx, another in a decided way with the amethyst. She learned that the ancients esteemed this gem a talisman to dispel intoxication, to give good thoughts and understanding

'The Greek meaning is *antidote against drunkenness.*'
She characterized her friends by these stones, and wrote
to the last mentioned, the following lines: —

' TO ———.

' Slow wandering on a tangled way,
' To their lost child pure spirits say : —
' The diamond marshal thee by day,
' By night, the carbuncle defend,
' Heart's blood of a bosom friend.
　' On thy brow, the amethyst,
　' Violet of purest earth,
　' When by fullest sunlight kissed,
　' Best reveals its regal birth ;
' And when that haloed moment flies,
' Shall keep thee steadfast, chaste, and wise.'

Coincidences, good and bad, *contretemps*, seals, ciphers,
mottoes, omens, anniversaries, names, dreams, are all of a
certain importance to her.   Her letters are often dated on
some marked anniversary of her own, or of her correspondent's calendar.   She signalized saints' days, "All-
Souls," and "All-Saints," by poems, which had for her
a mystical value.   She remarked a preëstablished harmony of the names of her personal friends, as well as
of her historical favorites; that of Emanuel, for Swedenborg; and Rosencrantz, for the head of the Rosicru-
cians.   'If Christian Rosencrantz,' she said, 'is not a
'made name, the genius of the age interfered in the
'baptismal rite, as in the cases of the archangels of art,
'Michael and Raphael, and in giving the name of Eman-
'uel to the captain of the New Jerusalem.   *Sub rosa*
'*crux,* I think, is the true derivation, and not the chemical one, generation, corruption, &c.'   In this spirit, she

soon surrounded herself with a little mythology of her own. She had a series of anniversaries, which she kept. Her seal-ring of the flying Mercury had its legend. She chose the *Sistrum* for her emblem, and had it carefully drawn with a view to its being engraved on a gem. And I know not how many verses and legends came recommended to her by this symbolism. Her dreams, of course, partook of this symmetry. The same dream returns to her periodically, annually, and punctual to its night. One dream she marks in her journal as repeated for the fourth time : —

'In C., I at last distinctly recognized the figure of the
'early vision, whom I found after I had left A., who led
'me, on the bridge, towards the city, glittering in sunset,
'but, midway, the bridge went under water. I have
'often seen in her face that it was she, but refused to
'believe it.'

She valued, of course, the significance of flowers, and chose emblems for her friends from her garden.

' TO ————, WITH HEARTSEASE.

' Content, in purple lustre clad,
' Kingly serene, and golden glad,
' No demi-hues of sad contrition,
' No pallors of enforced submission; —
' Give me such content as this,
' And keep awhile the rosy bliss.'

DÆMONOLOGY.

This catching at straws of coincidence, where all is geometrical, seems the necessity of certain natures. It is true, that, in every good work, the particulars are right, and, that every spot of light on the ground, under the trees, is a perfect image of the sun. Yet, for astronomical purposes, an observatory is better than an orchard; and in a universe which is nothing but generations, or an unbroken suite of cause and effect, to infer Providence, because a man happens to find a shilling on the pavement just when he wants one to spend, is puerile, and much as if each of us should date his letters and notes of hand from his own birthday, instead of from Christ's or the king's reign, or the current Congress. These, to be sure, are also, at first, petty and private beginnings, but, by the world of men, clothed with a social and cosmical character.

It will be seen, however, that this propensity Margaret held with certain tenets of fate, which always swayed her, and which Goethe, who had found room and fine names for all this in his system, had encouraged; and, I may add, which her own experiences, early and late, seemed strangely to justify.

Some extracts, from her letters to different persons, will show how this matter lay in her mind.

'*December* 17, 1829. — The following instance of 'beautiful credulity, in Rousseau, has taken my mind 'greatly. This remote seeking for the decrees of fate, 'this feeling of a destiny, casting its shadows from the 'very morning of thought, is the most beautiful species 'of idealism in our day. 'T is finely manifested in 'Wallenstein, where the two common men sum up their 'superficial observations on the life and doings of Wal-'lenstein, and show that, not until this agitating crisis, 'have they caught any idea of the deep thoughts which

'shaped that hero, who has, without their feeling it
'moulded *their* existence.

'"Tasso," says Rousseau, "has predicted my misfor-
'"tunes. Have you remarked that Tasso has this
'"peculiarity, that you cannot take from his work a
'"single strophe, nor from any strophe a single line,
'"nor from any line a single word, without disarrang-
'"ing the whole poem? Very well! take away the
'"strophe I speak of, the stanza has no connection
'"with those that precede or follow it; it is absolutely
'"useless. *Tasso probably wrote it involuntarily, and*
'"*without comprehending it himself.*"

'As to the impossibility of taking from Tasso with-
'out disarranging the poem, &c., I dare say 'tis not one
'whit more justly said of his, than of any other narrative
'poem. *Mais, n' importe,* 'tis sufficient if Rousseau
'believed this. I found the stanza in question; admire
'its meaning beauty.

'I hope you have Italian enough to appreciate the sin-
'gular perfection in expression. If not, look to Fairfax's
'Jerusalem Delivered, Canto 12, Stanza 77; but Rous-
'seau says these lines have no connection with what goes
'before, or after; *they are preceded,* stanza 76, by these
'three lines, which he does not think fit to mention.'

  *   *   *   *   *

> " Misero mostro d'infelice amore ;
> Misero mostro a cui sol pena è degna
> Dell' immensa impietà, la vita indegna.'

> " Vivrò fra i miei tormenti e fra le cure,
> Mie giuste furie, forsennato errante.
> Paventerò l'ombre solinghe e scure,
> Che l'primo error mi recheranno avante :

E del sol che scoprì le mie sventure,
A schivo ed in orrore avrò il sembiante.
Temerò me medesmo ; e da me stesso
Sempre fuggendo, avrò me sempre appresso.''
LA GERUSALEMME LIBERATA, C. XII. 76, 77.

TO R. W. E.

'*Dec.* 12, 1843. — When Goethe received a letter from
'Zelter, with a handsome superscription, he said, "Lay
'"that aside; it is Zelter's true hand-writing. Every
'"man has a dæmon, who is busy to confuse and limit
'"his life. No way is the action of this power more
'"clearly shown, than in the hand-writing. On this
'"occasion, the evil influences have been evaded; the
'"mood, the hand, the pen and paper have conspired to
'"let our friend write truly himself."

'You may perceive, I quote from memory, as the sen-
'tences are anything but Goethean; but I think often of
'this little passage. With me, for weeks and months,
'the dæmon works his will. Nothing succeeds with me.
'I fall ill, or am otherwise interrupted. At these times,
'whether of frost, or sultry weather, I would gladly
'neither plant nor reap,— wait for the better times, which
'sometimes come, when I forget that sickness is ever
'possible ; when all interruptions are upborne like
'straws on the full stream of my life, and the words
'that accompany it are as much in harmony as sedges
'murmuring near the bank. Not all, yet not unlike.
'But it often happens, that something presents itself,
'and must be done, in the bad time; nothing presents
'itself in the good : so I, like the others, seem worse
'and poorer than I am.'

In another letter to an earlier friend, she expatiates a
little.

'As to the Dæmoniacal, I know not that I can say to
'you anything more precise than you find from Goethe
'There are no precise terms for such thoughts. The
'word *instinctive* indicates their existence. I intimated
'it in the little piece on the Drachenfels. It may be
'best understood, perhaps, by a symbol. As the sun
'shines from the serene heavens, dispelling noxious
'exhalations, and calling forth exquisite thoughts on the
'surface of earth in the shape of shrub or flower, so
'gnome-like works the fire within the hidden caverns
'and secret veins of earth, fashioning existences which
'have a longer share in time, perhaps, because they are
'not immortal in thought. Love, beauty, wisdom, good-
'ness are intelligent, but this power moves only to seize
'its prey. It is not necessarily either malignant or the
'reverse, but it has no scope beyond demonstrating its
'existence. When conscious, self-asserting, it becomes
'(as power working for its own sake, unwilling to
'acknowledge love for its superior, must) the devil.
'That is the legend of Lucifer, the star that would
'not own its centre. Yet, while it is unconscious, it is
'not devilish, only dæmoniac. In nature, we trace it in
'all volcanic workings, in a boding position of lights, in
'whispers of the wind, which has no pedigree; in
'deceitful invitations of the water, in the sullen rock,
'which never shall find a voice, and in the shapes of
'all those beings who go about seeking what they may
'devour. We speak of a mystery, a dread; we shud-
'der, but we approach still nearer, and a part of our
'nature listens, sometimes answers to this influence,
'which, if not indestructible, is at least indissolubly
'linked with the existence of matter.
   'In genius, and in character, it works, as you say

'instinctively; it refuses to be analyzed by the under-
'standing, and is most of all inaccessible to the person
'who possesses it. We can only say, I have it, he has
'it. You have seen it often in the eyes of those Italian
'faces you like. It is most obvious in the eye. As we
'look on such eyes, we think on the tiger, the serpent,
'beings who lurk, glide, fascinate, mysteriously control.
'For it is occult by its nature, and if it could meet you
'on the highway, and be familiarly known as an
'acquaintance, could not exist. The angels of light
'do not love, yet they do not insist on exterminating it.

'It has given rise to the fables of wizard, enchantress,
'and the like; these beings are scarcely good, yet not
'necessarily bad. Power tempts them. They draw
'their skills from the dead, because their being is
'coeval with that of matter, and matter is the mother
'of death.'

In later days, she allowed herself sometimes to
dwell sadly on the resistances which she called her
fate, and remarked, that 'all life that has been or could
'be natural to me, is invariably denied.'

She wrote long afterwards : —

'My days at Milan were not unmarked. I have
'known some happy hours, but they all lead to sorrow,
'and not only the cups of wine, but of milk, seem
'drugged with poison, for me. It does not seem to be
'my fault, this destiny. I do not court these things, —
'they come. I am a poor magnet, with power to be
'wounded by the bodies I attract.'

TEMPERAMENT.

I said that Margaret had a broad good sense, which brought her near to all people. I am to say that she had also a strong temperament, which is that counter force which makes individuality, by driving all the powers in the direction of the ruling thought or feeling, and, when it is allowed full sway, isolating them. These two tendencies were always invading each other, and now one and now the other carried the day. This alternation perplexes the biographer, as it did the observer. We contradict on the second page what we affirm on the first: and I remember how often I was compelled to correct my impressions of her character when living; for after I had settled it once for all that she wanted this or that perception, at our next interview she would say with emphasis the very word.

I think, in her case, there was something abnormal in those obscure habits and necessities which we denote by the word Temperament. In the first days of our acquaintance, I felt her to be a foreigner, — that, with her, one would always be sensible of some barrier, as if in making up a friendship with a cultivated Spaniard or Turk. She had a strong constitution, and of course its reäctions were strong; and this is the reason why in all her life she has so much to say of her *fate*. She was in jubilant spirits in the morning, and ended the day with nervous headache, whose spasms, my wife told me, produced total prostration. She had great energy of speech and action, and seemed formed for high emergencies.

Her life concentrated itself on certain happy days,

happy hours, happy moments. The rest was a void She had read that a man of letters must lose many days, to work well in one. Much more must a Sappho or a sibyl. The capacity of pleasure was balanced by the capacity of pain. 'If I had wist! —' she writes, 'I am a ' worse self-tormentor than Rousseau, and all my riches 'are fuel to the fire. My beautiful lore, like the tropic ' clime, hatches scorpions to sting me. There is a verse, ' which Annie of Lochroyan sings about her ring, that ' torments my memory, 't is so true of myself.'

When I found she lived at a rate so much faster than mine, and which was violent compared with mine, I foreboded rash and painful crises, and had a feeling as if a voice cried, *Stand from under!* — as if, a little further on, this destiny was threatened with jars and reverses, which no friendship could avert or console. This feeling partly wore off, on better acquaintance, but remained latent; and I had always an impression that her energy was too much a force of blood, and therefore never felt the security for her peace which belongs to more purely intellectual natures. She seemed more vulnerable. For the same reason, she remained inscrutable to me; her strength was not my strength, — her powers were a surprise. She passed into new states of great advance, but I understood these no better. It were long to tell her peculiarities. Her childhood was full of presentiments. She was then a somnambulist. She was subject to attacks of delirium, and, later, perceived that she had spectral illusions. When she was twelve, she had a determination of blood to the head. ' My parents,' she said, ' were much mortified to see the fineness of my complexion destroyed. My own vanity was for a time

'severely wounded; but I recovered, and made up my
'mind to be bright and ugly.'

She was all her lifetime the victim of disease and
pain. She read and wrote in bed, and believed that
she could understand anything better when she was
ill. Pain acted like a girdle, to give tension to her
powers. A lady, who was with her one day during a
terrible attack of nervous headache, which made Margaret totally helpless, assured me that Margaret was yet
in the finest vein of humor, and kept those who were
assisting her in a strange, painful excitement, between
laughing and crying, by perpetual brilliant sallies.
There were other peculiarities of habit and power.
When she turned her head on one side, she alleged she
had second sight, like St. Francis. These traits or
predispositions made her a willing listener to all the
uncertain science of mesmerism and its goblin brood,
which have been rife in recent years.

She had a feeling that she ought to have been a man,
and said of herself, 'A man's ambition with a woman's
'heart, is an evil lot.' In some verses which she wrote
'To the Moon,' occur these lines: —

> 'But if I steadfast gaze upon thy face,
> 'A human secret, like my own, I trace ;
> 'For, through the woman's smile looks the male eye.'

And she found something of true portraiture in a disagreeable novel of Balzac's, "*Le Livre Mystique*," in
which an equivocal figure exerts alternately a masculine
and a feminine influence on the characters of the plot.

Of all this nocturnal element in her nature she was
very conscious, and was disposed, of course, to give it

as fine names as it would carry, and to draw advantage
from it. 'Attica,' she said to a friend, 'is your prov-
'ince, Thessaly is mine: Attica produced the marble
'wonders of the great geniuses; but Thessaly is the
'land of magic.'

'I have a great share of Typhon to the Osiris, wild
'rush and leap, blind force for the sake of force.'

'Dante, thou didst not describe, in all thy apartments
'of Inferno, this tremendous repression of an existence
'half unfolded; this swoon as the soul was ready to be
'born.'

'Every year I live, I dislike routine more and more,
'though I see that society rests on that, and other false-
'hoods. The more I screw myself down to hours, the
'more I become expert at giving out thought and life
'in regulated rations, — the more I weary of this world,
'and long to move upon the wing, without props and
sedan chairs.'

TO R. W. E.

'*Dec.* 26, 1839. — If you could look into my mind
'just now, you would send far from you those who love
'and hate. I am on the Drachenfels, and cannot get
'off; it is one of my naughtiest moods. Last Sunday,
'I wrote a long letter, describing it in prose and verse,
'and I had twenty minds to send it you as a literary
'curiosity; then I thought, this might destroy relations,
'and I might not be able to be calm and chip marble
'with you any more, if I talked to you in magnetism
'and music; so I sealed and sent it in the due direction

'I remember you say, that forlorn seasons often turn out the most profitable. Perhaps I shall find it so. 'I have been reading Plato all the week, because I 'could not write. I hoped to be tuned up thereby. I 'perceive, with gladness, a keener insight in myself, 'day by day; yet, after all, could not make a good 'statement this morning on the subject of beauty.'

She had, indeed, a rude strength, which, if it could have been supported by an equal health, would have given her the efficiency of the strongest men. As it was, she had great power of work. The account of her reading in Groton is at a rate like Gibbon's, and, later, that of her writing, considered with the fact that writing was not grateful to her, is incredible. She often proposed to her friends, in the progress of intimacy, to write every day. 'I think less than a daily offering of 'thought and feeling would not content me, so much 'seems to pass unspoken.' In Italy, she tells Madame Arconati, that she has 'more than a hundred correspondents;" and it was her habit there to devote one day of every week to those distant friends. The facility with which she assumed stints of literary labor, which veteran feeders of the press would shrink from,— assumed and performed, — when her friends were to be served, I have often observed with wonder, and with fear, when I considered the near extremes of ill-health, and the manner in which her life heaped itself in high and happy moments, which were avenged by lassitude and pain.

'As each task comes,' she said, 'I borrow a readiness 'from its aspect, as I always do brightness from the face 'of a friend. Yet, as soon as the hour is past, I sink.

I think most of her friends will remember to have felt, at one time or another, some uneasiness, as if this athletic soul craved a larger atmosphere than it found ; as if she were ill-timed and mis-mated, and felt in herself a tide of life, which compared with the slow circulation of others as a torrent with a rill. She found no full expression of it but in music. Beethoven's Symphony was the only right thing the city of the Puritans had for her. Those to whom music has a representative value, affording them a stricter copy of their inward life than any other of the expressive arts, will, perhaps, enter into the spirit which dictated the following letter to her patron saint, on her return, one evening, from the Boston Academy of Music.

' TO BEETHOVEN.

'*Saturday Evening, 25th Nov.*, 1843.
' My only friend,

' How shall I thank thee for once more breaking the 'chains of my sorrowful slumber? My heart beats. I 'live again, for I feel that I am worthy audience for 'thee, and that my being would be reason enough for 'thine.

' Master, my eyes are always clear. I see that the 'universe is rich, if I am poor. . I see the insignificance 'of my sorrows. In my will, I am not a captive; in my 'intellect, not a slave. Is it then my fault that the palsy 'of my affections benumbs my whole life?

' I know that the curse is but for the time. I know 'what the eternal justice promises. But on this one 'sphere, it is sad. Thou didst say, thou hadst no 'friend but thy art. But that one is enough. I have

no art, in which to vent the swell of a soul as deep as
thine, Beethoven, and of a kindred frame. Thou wilt
not think me presumptuous in this saying, as another
might. I have always known that thou wouldst welcome and know me, as would no other who ever
'lived upon the earth since its first creation.

'Thou wouldst forgive me, master, that I have not
'been true to my eventual destiny, and therefore have
'suffered on every side "the pangs of despised love."
'Thou didst the same; but thou didst borrow from
'those errors the inspiration of thy genius. Why is it
'not thus with me? Is it because, as a woman, I am
'bound by a physical law, which prevents the soul from
'manifesting itself? Sometimes the moon seems mock-
'ingly to say so, — to say that I, too, shall not shine,
'unless I can find a sun. O, cold and barren moon,
'tell a different tale!

'But thou, oh blessed master! dost answer all my
'questions, and make it my privilege to be. Like a
'humble wife to the sage, or poet, it is my triumph that
'I can understand and cherish thee: like a mistress, I
'arm thee for the fight: like a young daughter, I ten-
'derly bind thy wounds. Thou art to me beyond com-
'pare, for thou art all I want. No heavenly sweetness
'of saint or martyr, no many-leaved Raphael, no golden
'Plato, is anything to me, compared with thee. The
'infinite Shakspeare, the stern Angelo, Dante, — bitter-
'sweet like thee, — are no longer seen in thy presence.
'And, beside these names, there are none that could
'vibrate in thy crystal sphere. Thou hast all of them,
'and that ample surge of life besides, that great winged
'being which they only dreamed of. There is none
'greater than Shakspeare; he, too, is a god: but his

'creations are successive; thy *fiat* comprehends them
'all.

' Last summer, I met thy mood in nature, on those
'wide impassioned plains flower and crag-bestrown.
' There, the tide of emotion had rolled over, and left the
'vision of its smiles and sobs, as I saw to-night from
' thee.

' If thou wouldst take me wholly to thyself——! I am
'lost in this world, where I sometimes meet angels, but
'of a different star from mine. Even so does thy spirit
'plead with all spirits. But thou dost triumph and bring
' them all in.

' Master, I have this summer envied the oriole which
'had even a swinging nest in the high bough. I have
'envied the least flower that came to seed, though that
' seed were strown to the wind. But I envy none when
'I am with thee.'

SELF-ESTEEM.

Margaret at first astonished and repelled us by a complacency that seemed the most assured since the days of
Scaliger. She spoke, in the quietest manner, of the girls
she had formed, the young men who owed everything
to her, the fine companions she had long ago exhausted
In the coolest way, she said to her friends, ' I now know
'all the people worth knowing in America, and I find no
'intellect comparable to my own.'   In vain, on one occasion, I professed my reverence for a youth of genius, and
my curiosity in his future, — ' O no, she was intimate
' with his mind,' and I 'spoiled him, by overrating him.'
Meantime, we knew that she neither had seen, nor
would see, his subtle superiorities.

I have heard, that from the beginning of her life, she
idealized herself as a sovereign. She told —— she early
saw herself to be intellectually superior to those around
her, and that for years she dwelt upon the idea, until
she believed that she was not her parents' child, but an
European princess confided to their care. She remembered, that, when a little girl, she was walking one day
under the apple trees with such an air and step, that her
father pointed her out to her sister, saying, *Incedit
regina*. And her letters sometimes convey these exult-
ations, as the following, which was written to a lady,
and which contained Margaret's translation of Goethe's
" Prometheus."

                        ' TO ——.

' 1838. — Which of us has not felt the questionings
' expressed in this bold fragment? Does it not seem,
' were we gods, or could steal their fire, we would make
' men not only happier, but free, — glorious? Yes, my
' life is strange; thine is strange. We are, we shall be,
' in this life, mutilated beings, but there is in my bosom a
' faith, that I shall see the reason; a glory, that I can
' endure to be so imperfect; and a feeling, ever elastic,
' that fate and time shall have the shame and the blame,
' if I am mutilated. I will do all I can, — and, if one
' cannot succeed, there is a beauty in martyrdom.

    ' Your letters are excellent. I did not mean to check
' your writing, only I thought that you might wish a
' confidence that I must anticipate with a protest. But
' I take my natural position always : and the more I see,
' the more I feel that it is regal. Without throne, sceptre,
' or guards, still a queen.'

It is certain that Margaret occasionally let slip, with all the innocence imaginable, some phrase betraying the presence of a rather mountainous ME, in a way to surprise those who knew her good sense. She could say, as if she were stating a scientific fact, in enumerating the merits of somebody, 'He appreciates *me*.' There was something of hereditary organization in this, and something of unfavorable circumstance in the fact, that she had in early life no companion, and few afterwards, in her finer studies; but there was also an ebullient sense of power, which she felt to be in her, which as yet had found no right channels. I remember she once said to me, what I heard as a mere statement of fact, and nowise as unbecoming, that 'no man gave 'such invitation to her mind as to tempt her to a full 'expression; that she felt a power to enrich her thought 'with such wealth and variety of embellishment as 'would, no·doubt, be tedious to such as she conversed 'with.'

Her impatience she expressed as she could. 'I feel 'within myself,' she said, 'an immense force, but I can- 'not bring it out. It may sound like a joke, but I do 'feel something corresponding to that tale of the Desti- 'nies falling in love with Hermes.'

In her journal, in the summer of 1844, she writes: — 'Mrs. Ware talked with me about education, — wilful 'education, — in which she is trying to get interested. I 'talk with a Goethean moderation on this subject, which 'rather surprises her and ——, who are nearer the 'entrance of the studio. I am really old on this subject. 'In near eight years' experience, I have learned as much 'as others would in eighty, from my great talent at 'explanation, tact in the use of means, and immediate

'and invariable power over the minds of my pupils.
' My wish has been, to purify my own conscience, when
' near them; give clear views of the aims of this life;
' show them where the magazines of knowledge lie; and
' leave the rest to themselves and the Spirit, who must
' teach and help them to self-impulse. I told Mrs. W. it
' was much if we did not injure them; if they were
' passing the time in a way that was *not bad*, so that
' good influences have a chance. Perhaps people in
' general must expect greater outward results, or they
' would feel no interest.'

Again: ' With the intellect I always have, always
' shall, overcome; but that is not the half of the work.
' The life, the life! O, my God! shall the life never be
' sweet ? '

I have inquired diligently of those who saw her often,
and in different companies, concerning her habitual tone,
and something like this is the report: — In conversation,
Margaret seldom, except as a special grace, admitted
others upon an equal ground with herself. She was
exceedingly tender, when she pleased to be, and most
cherishing in her influence; but to elicit this tenderness,
it was necessary to submit first to her personally. When
a person was overwhelmed by her, and answered not a
word, except, " Margaret, be merciful to me, a sinner,"
then her love and tenderness would come like a seraph's,
and often an acknowledgment that she had been too
harsh, and even a craving for pardon, with a humility,
— which, perhaps, she had caught from the other. But
her instinct was not humility, — that was always an
afterthought.

This arrogant tone of her conversation, if it came to
be the subject of comment, of course, she defended, and

with such broad good nature, and on grounds of simple truth, as were not easy to set aside. She quoted from Manzoni's *Carmagnola*, the lines : —

> " Tolga il ciel che alcuno
> Piu altamente di me pensi ch'io stesso."

"God forbid that any one should conceive more highly of me than I myself." Meantime, the tone of her journals is humble, tearful, religious, and rises easily into prayer.

I am obliged to an ingenious correspondent for the substance of the following account of this idiosyncrasy : —

Margaret was one of the few persons who looked upon life as an art, and every person not merely as an artist, but as a work of art. She looked upon herself as a living statue, which should always stand on a polished pedestal, with right accessories, and under the most fitting lights. She would have been glad to have everybody so live and act. She was annoyed when they did not, and when they did not regard her from the point of view which alone did justice to her. No one could be more lenient in her judgments of those whom she saw to be living in this light. Their faults were to be held as "the disproportions of the ungrown giant." But the faults of persons who were unjustified by this ideal, were odious. Unhappily, her constitutional self-esteem sometimes blinded the eyes that should have seen that an idea lay at the bottom of some lives which she did not quite so readily comprehend as beauty; that truth had other manifestations than those which engaged her natural sympathies; that sometimes the soul illuminated only the smallest arc — of a circle so large that it **was** lost in the clouds of another world.

This apology reminds me of a little speech once made to her, at his own house, by Dr. Channing, who held her in the highest regard: "Miss Fuller, when I consider that you are and have all that Miss —— has so long wished for, and that you scorn her, and that she still admires you, — I think her place in heaven will be very high."

But qualities of this kind can only be truly described by the impression they make on the bystander; and it is certain that her friends excused in her, because she had a right to it, a tone which they would have reckoned intolerable in any other. Many years since, one of her earliest and fastest friends quoted Spenser's sonnet as accurately descriptive of Margaret: —

> "Rudely thou wrongest my dear heart's desire,
> In finding fault with her too portly pride ;
> The thing which I do most in her admire
> Is of the world unworthy most envied.
> For, in those lofty looks is close implied
> Scorn of base things, disdain of foul dishonor,
> Threatening rash eyes which gaze on her so wide
> That loosely they ne dare to look upon her :
> Such pride is praise, such portliness is honor,
> That boldened innocence bears in her eyes ;
> And her fair countenance, like a goodly banner,
> Spreads in defiance of all enemies.
> Was never in this world aught worthy tried,
> Without a spark of some self-pleasing pride."

BOOKS.

She had been early remarked for her sense and sprightliness, and for her skill in school exercises. Now she had added wide reading, and of the books most grateful to her. She had read the Italian poets by herself, and from sympathy. I said, that, by the leading part she naturally took, she had identified herself with all the elegant culture in this country. Almost every person who had any distinction for wit, or art, or scholarship, was known to her; and she was familiar with the leading books and topics. There is a kind of undulation in the popularity of the great writers, even of the first rank. We have seen a recent importance given to Behmen and Swedenborg; and Shakspeare has unquestionably gained with the present generation. It is distinctive, too, of the taste of the period,— the new vogue given to the genius of Dante. An edition of Cary's translation, reprinted in Boston, many years ago, was rapidly sold; and, for the last twenty years, all studious youths and maidens have been reading the Inferno. Margaret had very early found her way to Dante, and from a certain native preference which she felt or fancied for the Italian genius. The following letter. though of a later date, relates to these studies:—

TO R. W. E.

'*December*, 1842.— When you were here, you seemed
' to think I might perhaps have done something on the
' *Vita Nuova;* and the next day I opened the book, and
' considered how I could do it. But you shall not expect
' that, either, for your present occasion. When I first
' mentioned it to you, it was only as a piece of Sunday
' work, which I thought of doing for you alone; and
' because it has never seemed to me you entered enough
' into the genius of the Italian to apprehend the mind,

'which has seemed so great to me, and a star unlike, if
'not higher than all the others in our sky. Else, I should
'have given you the original, rather than any version of
'mine. I intended to translate the poems, with which it
'is interspersed, into plain prose. Milnes and Longfellow
'have tried each their power at doing it in verse, and
'have done better, probably, than I could, yet not well.
'But this would not satisfy me for the public. Besides,
'the translating Dante is a piece of literary presumption,
'and challenges a criticism to which I am not sure that
'I am, as the Germans say, *gewachsen*. Italian, as well
'as German, I learned by myself, unassisted, except as
'to the pronunciation. I have never been brought into
'connection with minds trained to any severity in these
'kinds of elegant culture. I have used all the means
'within my reach, but my not going abroad is an
'insuperable defect in the technical part of my education.
'I was easily capable of attaining excellence, perhaps
'mastery, in the use of some implements. Now I know,
'at least, *what I do not know*, and I get along by never
'voluntarily going beyond my depth, and, when called
'on to do it, stating my incompetency. At moments
'when I feel tempted to regret that I could not follow out
'the plan I had marked for myself, and develop powers
'which are not usual here, I reflect, that if I had
'attained high finish and an easy range in these respects,
'I should not have been thrown back on my own
'resources, or known them as I do. But Lord Brougham
'should not translate Greek orations, nor a maid-of-all-
'work attempt such a piece of delicate handling as to
'translate the *Vita Nuova*.'

Here is a letter, without date, to another correspondent :

'To-day, on reading over some of the sonnets of Michel Angelo, I felt them more than usual. I know not
why I have not read them thus before, except that the
beauty was pointed out to me at first by another, instead
of my coming unexpectedly upon it of myself. All the
'great writers, all the persons who have been dear to
'me, I have found and chosen; they have not been pro-
'posed to me. My intimacy with them came upon me
'as natural eras, unexpected and thrice dear. Thus I
'have appreciated, but not been able to feel, Michel
'Angelo as a poet.

'It is a singular fact in my mental history, that, while
'I understand the principles and construction of language
'much better than formerly, I cannot read so well *les*
'*langues méridionales*. I suppose it is that I am less
'*méridionale* myself. I understand the genius of the
'north better than I did.'

Dante, Petrarca, Tasso, were her friends among the
old poets, — for to Ariosto she assigned a far lower place,
— Alfieri and Manzoni, among the new. But what was
of still more import to her education, she had read German books, and, for the three years before I knew her,
almost exclusively, — Lessing, Schiller, Richter, Tieck,
Novalis, and, above all, GOETHE. It was very obvious,
at the first intercourse with her, though her rich and
busy mind never reproduced undigested reading, that the
last writer, — food or poison, — the most powerful of all
mental reagents, — the pivotal mind in modern literature,
— for all before him are ancients, and all who have read
him are moderns, — that this mind had been her teacher,
and, of course, the place was filled, nor was there room
for any other. She had that symptom which appears in

all the students of Goethe,—an ill-dissembled contempt of all criticism on him which they hear from others, as if it were totally irrelevant; and they are themselves always preparing to say the right word, — a *prestige* which is allowed, of course, until they do speak : when they have delivered their volley, they pass, like their foregoers, to the rear..

The effect on Margaret was complete. She was perfectly timed to it. She found her moods met, her topics treated, the liberty of thought she loved, the same climate of mind. Of course, this book superseded all others, for the time, and tinged deeply all her thoughts. The religion, the science, the catholicism, the worship of art, the mysticism and dæmonology, and withal the clear recognition of moral distinctions as final and eternal, all charmed her; and Faust, and Tasso, and Mignon, and Makaria, and Iphigenia, became irresistible names. It was one of those agreeable historical coincidences, perhaps invariable, though not yet registered, the simultaneous appearance of a teacher and of pupils, between whom exists a strict affinity. Nowhere did Goethe find a braver, more intelligent, or more sympathetic reader. About the time I knew her, she was meditating a biography of Goethe, and did set herself to the task in 1837. She spent much time on it, and has left heaps of manuscripts, which are notes, transcripts, and studies in that direction. But she wanted leisure and health to finish it, amid the multitude of projected works with which her brain teemed. She used great discretion on this point, and made no promises. In 1839, she published her translation of Eckermann, a book which makes the basis of the translation of Eckermann since published in London, by Mr. Oxenford. In the Dial, in July, 1841, she wrote an article on Goethe, which is, on many accounts, her best paper.

CRITICISM.

Margaret was in the habit of sending to her correspondents, in lieu of letters, sheets of criticism on her recent readings. From such quite private folios, never intended for the press, and, indeed, containing here and there names and allusions, which it is now necessary to veil or suppress, I select the following notices, chiefly of French books. Most of these were addressed to me, but the three first to an earlier friend

'Reading Schiller's introduction to the Wars of the 'League, I have been led back to my•old friend, the 'Duke of Sully, and his charming king. He was a man, 'that Henri! How gay and graceful seems his unflinch-'ing frankness! He wore life as lightly as the feather 'in his cap. I have become much interested, too, in the 'two Guises, who had seemed to me mere intriguers, and 'not of so splendid abilities, when I was less able to 'appreciate the difficulties they daily and hourly com-'bated. I want to read some more books about them. 'Do you know whether I could get Matthieu, or de 'Thou, or the Memoirs of the House of Nevers?

'I do not think this is a respectable way of passing my 'summer, but I cannot help it.

'I never read any life of Molière. Are the facts very 'interesting? You see clearly in his writing what he 'was: a man not high, not poetic; but firm, wide, gen-'uine, whose clearsightedness only made him more noble. 'I love him well that he could see without showing those

'myriad mean faults of the social man, and yet make
'no nearer approach to misanthropy than his Alceste.
'These witty Frenchmen, Rabelais, Montaigne, Molière,
'are great as were their marshals and *preux chevaliers;*
'when the Frenchman tries to be poetical, he becomes
'theatrical, but he can be romantic, and also dignified,
'maugre shrugs and snuff-boxes.'

' *Thursday Evening.* — Although I have been much
'engaged these two days, I have read Spiridion twice.
'I could have wished to go through it the second time
'more at leisure, but as I am going away, I thought I
'would send it back, lest it should be wanted before my
'return.

'The development of the religious sentiment being
'the same as in Hélene, I at first missed the lyric
'effusion of that work, which seems to me more and
'more beautiful, as I think of it more. This, however,
'was a mere prejudice, of course, as the thought here is
'poured into a quite different mould, and I was not trou-
'bled by it on a second reading.

'Again, when I came to look at the work by itself, I
'thought the attempt too bold. A piece of character
'painting does not seem to be the place for a statement
'of these wide and high subjects. For here the philos-
'ophy is not merely implied in the poetry and religion,
'but assumes to show a face of its own. And, as none
'should meddle with these matters who are not in ear-
'nest, so, such will prefer to find the thought of a teacher
'or fellow-disciple expressed as directly and as bare of
ornament as possible.

'I was interested in De Wette's Theodor, and that
learned and (*on dit*) profound man seemed to me so

' to fail, that I did not finish the book, nor try whether 1
' could believe the novice should ever arrive at manly
' stature.

' I am not so clear as to the scope and bearing of this
' book, as of that.   I suppose if I were to read Lamen-
' nais, or L'Erminier, I should know what they all want
' or intend.   And if you meet with *Les paroles d'un
' Croyant*, I will beg you to get it for me, for 1 am more
' curious than' ever.   I had supposed the view taken
' by these persons in France, to be the same with that
' of Novalis and the German Catholics, in which I have
' been deeply interested.   But from this book, it would
' seem to approach the faith of some of my friends here,
' which has been styled Psychotheism.   And the gap in
' the theoretical fabric is the same as with them.   I read
' with unutterable interest the despair of Alexis in his
' Eclectic course, his return to the teachings of external
' nature, his new birth, and consequent appreciation of
' poetry and music.   But the question of Free Will, —
' how to reconcile its workings with necessity and com-
' pensation, — how to reconcile the life of the heart with
' that of the intellect, — how to listen to the whispering
' breeze of Spirit, while breasting, as a man should, the
' surges of the world, — these enigmas Sand and her
' friends seem to have solved no better than M. F. and
' her friends.

' The practical optimism is much the same as ours,
' except that there is more hope for the masses — soon.

' This work is written with great vigor, scarce any
' faltering on the wing.   The horrors are disgusting, as
' are those of every writer except Dante.   Even genius
' should content itself in dipping the pencil in cloud and
  mist.   The apparitions of Spiridion are managed with

great beauty. As in Hélene, as in Novalis, I recog-
'nized, with delight, the eye that gazed, the ear that
'listened, till the spectres came, as they do to the High-
'lander on his rocky couch, to the German peasant on
'his mountain. How different from the vulgar eye
'which looks, but never sees! Here the beautiful
'apparition advances from the solar ray, or returns
'to the fountain of light and truth, as it should, when
'eagle eyes are gazing.

'I am astonished at her insight into the life of thought.
'She must know it through some man. Women, under
'any circumstances, can scarce do more than dip the
'foot in this broad and deep river; they have not
'strength to contend with the current. Brave, if they
'do not delicately shrink from the cold water. No
'Sibyls have existed like those of Michel Angelo; those
'of Raphael are the true brides of a God. but not
'themselves divine. It is easy for women to be heroic
'in action, but when it comes to interrogating God, the
'universe, the soul, and, above all, trying to live above
'their own hearts, they dart down to their nests like
'so many larks, and, if they cannot find them, fret
'like the French Corinne. Goethe's Makaria was born
'of the stars. Mr. Flint's Platonic old lady a *lusus*
'*naturæ*, and the Dudevant has loved a philosopher.

'I suppose the view of the present state of Catholicism
'no way exaggerated. Alexis is no more persecuted
'than Abelard was, and is so, for the same reasons.
'From the examinations of the Italian convents in
'Leopold's time, it seems that the grossest materialism
'not only reigns, but is taught and professed in them.
'And Catholicism loads and infects as all dead forms
'do, however beautiful and noble during their lives.' * *

GEORGE SAND, AGAIN.

'1839. — When I first knew George Sand, I thought
'I found tried the experiment I wanted. I did not
'value Bettine so much; she had not pride enough
'for me; only now when I am sure of myself, would
'I pour out my soul at the feet of another. In the
'assured soul it is kingly prodigality; in one which
'cannot forbear, it is mere babyhood. I love *abandon*
'only when natures are capable of the extreme reverse.
'I knew Bettine would end in nothing, when I read her
'book. I knew she could not outlive her love.

'But in *Les Sept Cordes de la Lyre*, which I read first,
'I saw the knowledge of the passions, and of social
'institutions, with the celestial choice which rose above
'them. I loved Hélene, who could so well hear the ter-
'rene voices, yet keep her eye fixed on the stars. That
'would be my wish, also, to know all, then choose; I
'ever revered her, for I was not sure that I could have
'resisted the call of the Now, could have left the spirit,
'and gone to God. And, at a more ambitious age, I could
'not have refused the philosopher. But I hoped from
'her steadfastness, and I thought I heard the last tones
'of a purified life: — Gretchen, in the golden cloud, raised
'above all past delusions, worthy to redeem and upbear
'the wise man, who stumbled into the pit of error while
'searching for truth.

'Still, in *André* and in *Jacques*, I traced the same high
'morality of one who had tried the liberty of circumstance only to learn to appreciate the liberty of law,
to know that license is the foe of freedom. And,
though the sophistry of passion in these books disgusted
me, flowers of purest hue seemed to grow upon the

'dank and dirty ground I thought she had cast aside
'the slough of her past life, and began a new existence
'beneath the sun of a true Ideal.

'But here (in the *Lettres d'un Voyageur*) what do I
'see? An unfortunate bewailing her loneliness, bewailing
'her mistakes, writing for money! She has genius, and
'a manly grasp of mind, but not a manly heart! Will
'there never be a being to combine a man's mind and
'woman's heart, and who yet finds life too rich to weep
'over? Never?

'When I read in *Leone Lioni* the account of the jew-
'eller's daughter's life with her mother, passed in dress
'and in learning to be looked at when dressed, *avec un
'front impassible*, it reminded me exceedingly of ——,
'and her mother. What a heroine she would be for
'Sand! She has the same fearless softness with Juliet,
'and a sportive *naïveté*, a mixture of bird and kitten,
'unknown to the dupe of Lioni.

'If I were a man, and wished a wife, as many do,
'merely as an ornament, or silken toy, I would take
'—— as soon as any I know. Her fantastic, impas-
'sioned, and mutable nature would yield an inex-
'haustible amusement. She is capable of the most
'romantic actions; — wild as the falcon, and voluptuous
'as the tuberose, — yet she has not in her the elements
'of romance, like a deeper and less susceptible nature.
'My cold and reasoning E., with her one love lying,
'perhaps, never to be unfolded, beneath such sheaths
'of pride and reserve, would make a far better heroine.

'Both these characters are natural, while S. and **T.** are
'*naturally factitious*, because so imitative, and her mother
'differs from Juliet and her mother, by the impulse a single strong character gave them. Even at this distance

of time, there is a slight but perceptible taste of iron
'in the water.

'George Sand disappoints me, as almost all beings
'have, especially since I have been brought close to her
'person by the *Lettres d'un Voyageur*. Her remarks
'on Lavater seem really shallow, and hasty, *à la mode*
'*du genre feménin*. No self-ruling Aspasia she, but
'a frail woman mourning over a lot. Any peculiarity
'in her destiny seems accidental. She is forced to
'this and that, to earn her bread forsooth!

'Yet her style, — with what a deeply smouldering
'fire it burns! — not vehement, but intense, like Jean
'Jacques.'

ALFRED DE VIGNY.

'*Sept.*, 1839.

'"La harpe tremble encore, et la flûte soupire."

'Sometimes we doubt this, and think the music has
'finally ceased, so sultry still lies the air around us, or
'only disturbed by the fife and drum of talent, calling to
'the parade-ground of social life. The ——— grows dull.

'"Faith asks her daily bread,
And Fancy is no longer fed."

'So materialistic is the course of common life, that
'we *ask daily* new Messiahs from literature and art,
'to turn us from the Pharisaic observance of law, to
'the baptism of spirit. But stars arise upon our murky
'sky, and the flute *soupire* from the quarter where we
least expect it.

'*La jeune France!* I had not believed in this youth-
'ful pretender. I thought she had no pure blood in her
veins, no aristocratic features in her face, no natural
grace in her gait. I thought her an illegitimate

child of the generous, but extravagant youth of Ger-
'many. I thought she had been left at the foundling
'hospital, as not worth a parent's care, and that now,
'grown up, she was trying to prove at once her parent-
'age and her charms by certificates which might be
'headed, Innocent Adultery, Celestial Crime, &c.

    ' The slight acquaintance I had with Hugo, and com-
'pany, did not dispel these impressions. And I thought
'Chateaubriand (far too French for my taste also,)
'belonged to *l'ancien régime,* and that Béranger and
'Courier stood apart. Nodier, Paul de Kock, Sue, Jules
'Janin, I did not know, except through the absurd
'reports of English reviewers; Le Maistre and Lamen-
'nais, as little.

    ' But I have now got a peep at this galaxy. I begin to
'divine the meaning of St. Simonianism, Cousinism, and
'the movement which the same causes have produced in
'belles-lettres. I perceive that *la jeune France* is the
'legitimate, though far younger sister of Germany;
'taught by her, but not born of her, but of a common
'mother. I see, at least begin to see, what she has
'learned from England, and what the bloody rain of the
'revolution has done to fertilize her soil, naturally too
'light.

    ' Blessed be the early days when I sat at the feet of
'Rousseau, prophet sad and stately as any of Jewry!
'Every onward movement of the age, every downward
'step into the solemn depths of my own soul, recalls thy
'oracles, O Jean Jacques! But as these things only
'glimmer upon me at present, clouds of rose and amber,
'in the perspective of a long, dim woodland glade, which
'I must traverse if I would get a fair look at them from
'the hill-top, — as I cannot, to say sooth, get the works of

'these always working geniuses, but by slow degrees, in
'a country that has no need of them till her railroads
'and canals are finished,—I need not jot down my petty
'impressions of the movement writers. I wish to speak
'of one among them, aided, honored by them, but not
'of them. He is to *la jeune France* rather the herald of
'a tourney, or the master of ceremonies at a patriotic
'festival, than a warrior for her battles, or an advocate
'to win her cause.

   'The works of M. de Vigny having come in my way,
'I have read quite through this thick volume.

   'I read, a year since, in the London and Westminster,
'an admirable sketch of Armand Carrel. The writer
'speaks particularly of the use of which Carrel's expe-
'rience of practical life had been to him as an author;
'how it had tempered and sharpened the blade of his
'intellect to the Damascene perfection. It has been of
'like use to de Vigny, though not in equal degree.

   'De Vigny *passed*,— but for manly steadfastness, he
'would probably say *wasted*, — his best years in the army.
'He is now about forty; and we have in this book the
'flower of these best years. It is a night-blooming
'Cereus, for his days were passed in the duties of his
'profession. These duties, so tiresome and unprofitable
'in time of peace, were the ground in which the seed
'sprang up, which produced these many-leaved and calm
'night-flowers.

   'The first portion of this volume, *Servitude et Gran-*
'*deurs Militaires*, contains an account of the way in
'which he received his false tendency. Cherished on
'the "wounded knees" of his aged father, he listened
to tales of the great Frederic, whom the veteran had
'known personally. After an excellent sketch of the

king, he says: "I expatiate here, almost in spite of
"myself, because this was the first great man whose
'"portrait was thus drawn for me at home,—a portrait
'"after nature,—and because my admiration of him was
'"the first symptom of my useless love of arms,—the
'"first cause of one of the most complete delusions of
'"my life." This admiration for the great king remained
'so lively in his mind, that even Bonaparte in his ges-
'tures seemed to him, in later days, a plagiarist.

'At the military school, "the drum stifled the voices
'"of our masters, and the mysterious voices of books
'"seemed to us cold and pedantic. Tropes and loga-
'"rithms seemed to us only steps to mount to the star
'"of the Legion of Honor,—the fairest star of heaven
'"to us children.

'"No meditation could keep long in chains heads made
'"constantly giddy by the noise of cannon and bells for
'"the *Te Deum.* When one of our former comrades
'"returned to pay us a visit in uniform, and his arm in a
'"scarf, we blushed at our books, and threw them at the
'"heads of our teachers. Our teachers were always
'"reading us bulletins from the *grande armée,* and our
'"cries of *Vive l'Empereur* interrupted Tacitus and
'"Plato. Our preceptors resembled heralds of arms, our
'"study halls barracks, and our examinations reviews."

'Thus was he led into the army; and, he says, "It
'"was only very late, that I perceived that my services
'"were one long mistake, and that I had imported into
'"a life altogether active, a nature altogether contem-
'"plative."

'He entered the army at the time of Napoleon's fall,
'and, like others, wasted life in waiting for war. For
'these young persons could not believe that peace and

'calm were possible to France; could not believe that
'she could lead any life but one of conquest.

'As De Vigny was gradually undeceived, he says:
'" Loaded with an ennui which I did not dream of in a
'" life I had so ardently desired, it became a necessity to
'" me to detach myself by night from the vain and tire-
'" some tumult of military days. From these nights, in
'" which I enlarged in silence the knowledge I had
'" acquired from our public and tumultuous studies,
'" proceeded my poems and books. From these days,
'" there remain to me these recollections, whose chief
'" traits I here assemble around one idea. For, not
'" reckoning for the glory of arms, either on the present
'" or future, I sought it in the souvenirs of my comrades.
'" My own little adventures will not serve, except as
'" frame to those pictures of the military life, and of the
'" manners of our armies, all whose traits are by no
'" means known."

'And thus springs up, in the most natural manner,
'this little book on the army.

'It has the truth, the delicacy, and the healthiness of a
'production native to the soil; the merit of love-letters,
'journals, lyric poems, &c., written without any formal
'intention of turning life into a book, but because the
'writer could not help it. What, more than anything
'else, engaged the attention of De Vigny, was the false
'position of two beings towards a factitious society:
'the soldier, now that standing armies are the mode,
'and the poet, now that Olympic games or pastimes are
'not the mode. He has treated the first best, because
'with profounder *connoissance du fait*. For De Vigny is
not a poet; he has only an eye to perceive the existence
of these birds of heaven. But in few ways, except

'their own broken harp-tone's thrill, have their peculiar
'sorrows and difficulties been so well illustrated. The
'character of the soldier, with its virtues and faults, is
'portrayed with such delicacy, that to condense would
'ruin. The peculiar reserve, the habit of duty, the
'beauty of a character which cannot look forward, and
'need not look back, are given with distinguished finesse.

'Of the three stories which adorn this part of the book,
'*Le Cachet Rouge* is the loveliest, *La Canne au Jonc*
'the noblest. Never was anything more sweetly naïve
'than parts 'of *Le Cachet Rouge*. *La pauvre petite*
'*femme*, she was just such a person as my ——. And
'then the farewell injunctions, — *du pauvre petite maré*,
'— the nobleness and the coarseness of the poor captain.
'It is as original as beautiful, *c'est dire beaucoup*. In *La*
'*Canne au Jonc*, Collingwood, who embodies the high
'feeling of duty, is taken too raw out of a book, — his
'letters to his daughters. But the effect on the character
'of *le Capitaine Renaud*, and the unfolding of his interior
life, are done with the spiritual beauty of Manzoni.

'*Cinq-Mars* is a romance in the style of Walter Scott.
'It is well brought out, figures in good relief, lights well
'distributed, sentiment high, but nowhere exaggerated,
'knowledge exact, and the good and bad of human
'nature painted with that impartiality which becomes a
'man, and a man of the world. All right, no failure
'anywhere; also, no wonderful success, no genius, no
'magic. It is one of those works which I should con-
'sider only excusable as the amusement of leisure hours;
'and, though few could write it, chiefly valuable to the
'writer.

'Here he has arranged, as in a bouquet, what he knew,
— and a great deal it is, — of the time of Louis XIII.

'as he has of the Regency in "La Marechale d'Ancre,"
'—a much finer work, indeed one of the best-arranged
'and finished modern dramas.   The Leonora Galigai is
'better than anything I have seen in Victor Hugo, and
'as good as Schiller.   Stello is a bolder attempt.   It is
'the history of three poets,—Gilbert, André Chenier,
'Chatterton.   He has also written a drama called Chat-
'terton, inferior to the story here.   The "marvellous
'"boy" seems to have captivated his imagination mar-
'vellously.   In thought, these productions are worthless;
'for taste, beauty of sentiment, and power of description,
'remarkable.   His advocacy of the poets' cause is about
'as effective and well-planned as Don Quixote's tourney
'with the wind-mill.   How would you provide for the
'poet *bon homme* De Vigny?—from a joint-stock com-
'pany Poet's Fund, or how?

   'His translation of Othello, which I glanced at, is good
'for a Frenchman.

   'Among his poems, La Frégate, La Sérieuse, Madame
'de Soubise, and Dolorida, please me especially.   The
'last has an elegiac sweetness and finish, which are
'rare.   It also makes a perfect gem of a cabinet picture.
'Some have a fine strain of natural melody, and give
'you at once the key-note of the situation, as this:

> '"J'aime le son du cor le soir, au fond des bois,
>   Soit qu'il chante," &c.

And

> '" Qu'il est doux, qu'il est doux d'ecouter les histoires
>   Des histoires du temps passé
>   Quand les branches des arbres sont noires,
>   Quand la neige est essaisse, et charge un sol glacé,
>   Quand seul dans un ciel pâle un peuplier s'élance,
>   Quand sous le manteau blanc qui vient le 'e cacher

L'immobile corbeau sur l'arbre se balance
Comme la girouette au bout du long clocher."

'These poems generally are only interesting as the
'leisure hours of an interesting man.

'De Vigny writes in an excellent style; soft, fresh,
'deliberately graceful. Such a style is like fine manners;
you think of the words select, appropriate, rather than
'distinguished, or beautiful. De Vigny is a perfect gen-
'tleman; and his refinement is rather that of the gentle-
'man than that of the poets whom he is so full of. In
'character, he looks naturally at those things which
'interest the man of honor and the man of taste. But
'for literature, he would have known nothing about the
'poets. He should be the elegant and instructive com-
'panion of social, not the priest or the minstrel of solitary
'hours.

'Neither has he logic or grasp with his reasoning
'powers, though of this, also, he is ambitious. Observa-
'tion is his forte. To see, and to tell with grace, often
'with dignity and pathos, what he sees, is his proper
'vocation. Yet, where he fails, he has too much tact
'and modesty to be despised; and we cannot enough
'admire the absence of faults in a man whose ambition
'soared so much beyond his powers, and in an age and
'a country so full of false taste. He is never seduced
'into sentimentality, paradox, violent contrast, and, above
'all, never makes the mistake of confounding the horri-
'ble with the sublime. Above all, he never falls into the
'error, common to merely elegant minds, of painting
'leading minds " *en gigantesque.*" His Richelieu and
'his Bonaparte are treated with great calmness, and

' with dignified ease, almost as beautiful as majestic
' superiority.

' In this volume is contained all that is on record of
' the inner life of a man of forty years. How many
' suns, how many rains and dews, to produce a few buds
' and flowers, some sweet, but not rich fruit! We can-
' not help demanding of the man of talent that he should
' be like " the orange tree, that busy plant." But, as
' Landor says, " He who has any thoughts of any worth
' " can, and probably will, afford to let the greater part
' " lie fallow."

' I have not made a note upon De Vigny's notions of
' abnegation, which he repeats as often as Dr. Channing
' the same watch-word of self-sacrifice. It is that my
' views are not yet matured, and I can have no judg-
' ment on the point.'

BERANGER.

' *Sept.*, 1839. — I have lately been reading some of
' Béranger's *chansons*. The hour was not propitious.
' I was in a mood the very reverse of Roger Bontemps,
' and beset with circumstances the most unsuited to
' make me sympathize with the prayer —

> ' " Pardonnez la gaieté
> De ma philosophie ;"

' yet I am not quite insensible to their wit, high senti-
' ment, and spontaneous grace. A wit that sparkles all
' over the ocean of life, a sentiment that never puts the
' best foot forward, but prefers the tone of delicate
' humor, to the mouthings of tragedy ; a grace so aerial,
' that it nowhere requires the aid of a thought, for in

the light refrains of these productions, the meaning is
'felt as much as in the most pointed lines. Thus, in
'" Les Mirmidons," the refrain —

> '"Mirmidons, race féconde,
> Mirmidons
> Enfin nous commandons,
> Jupiter livre le monde,
> Aux mirmidons, aux mirmidons, (bis,)"

' The swarming of the insects about the dead lion is
'expressed as forcibly as in the most sarcastic passage
'of the chanson. In " La Faridondaine " every sound
'is a witticism, and levels to the ground a bevy of what
'Byron calls " garrison people."   " Halte là ! ou la sys-
'" tème des interpretations " is equally witty, though
'there the form seems to be as much in the saying,
'as in the comic melody of sound.

' In " Adieux à la Campagne," "Souvenirs du Peu-
'"ple," " La Déesse de la Liberté," " La Convoi
'"de David," a melancholy pathos breathes, which
'touches the heart the more that it is so unpretend-
'ing.   " Ce n'est plus Lisette," " Mon Habit," " L'In-
'"dépendant," "Vous vieillirez, O ma belle Maitresse," a
'gentle graceful sadness wins us. In " Le Dieu des
'" Bonnes Gens," " Les Etoiles qui filent," " Les Con-
'"seils de Lise," " Treize à Table," a noble dignity is
'admired, while such as " La Fortune " and " La Mé-
'" tempsycose " are inimitable in their childlike play-
'fulness.   " Ma Vocation " I have had and admired for
'many years.   He is of the pure ore, a darling fairy
'changling of great mother Nature ; the poet of the
'people, and, therefore, of all in the upper classes sufficiently intelligent and refined to appreciate the wit and

' sentiment of the people. But his wit is so truly French
in its lightness and sparkling, feathering vivacity, that
' one like me, accustomed to the bitterness of English
' tonics, suicidal November melancholy, and Byronic
' wrath of satire, cannot appreciate him at once. But
' when used to the gentler stimuli, we like them best,
' and we also would live awhile in the atmosphere of
' music and mirth, content if we have " bread for to-
' " day, and hope for to-morrow."

   ' There are fine lines in 'his " Cinq Mai ;" the sen-
' timent is as grand as Manzoni's, though not sustained
' by the same majestic sweep of diction, as, —

> ' " Ce rocher repousse l'espérance,
>   L'Aigle n'est plus dans le secret des dieux,
>   Il fatiguait la victoire à le suivre,
>   Elle était lasse : il ne l'attendit pas."

'And from "La Gérontocratie, ou les infiniment petits:"

> ' " Combien d'imperceptibles êtres,
>   De petits jésuites bilieux!
>   De milliers d'autres petits prêtres,
>   Lui portent de petits bons dieux."

' But wit, poet, man of honor, tailor's grandson and
' fairy's favorite, he must speak for himself, and the best
' that can be felt or thought of him cannot be said in
' the way of criticism. I will copy and keep a few of
' his songs. I should like to keep the whole collection
' by me, and take it up when my faith in human nature
' required the gentlest of fortifying draughts.

   ' How fine his answer to those who asked about the
' " de " before his name ! —

> ' " Je suis vilain,
>   Vilain, vilain," &c.

'" J' honore une race commune,
   Car, sensible, quoique malin,
   Je n'ai flatté que l'infortune."

'In a note to "Couplets on M. Laisney, *imprimeur à*
' "*Peronne*," he says: "It was in his printing-house
' "that I was put to prentice; not having been able to
' "learn orthography, he imparted to me the taste for
' "poetry, gave me lessons in versification, and corrected
' "my first essays." '

'Of Bonaparte, —

'" Un conquérant, dans sa fortune altière,
   Se fit un jeu des sceptres et des lois,
   Et de ses pieds on peut voir la poussière
   Empreinte encore sur le bandeau des rois."

'I admire, also, " Le Violon brisé," for its grace and
'sweetness. How fine Béranger on Waterloo! —

'" Its name shall never sadden verse of mine." '

TO R. W. E.

'*Niagara*, 1*st June*, 1843. — I send you a token, made
' by the hands of some Seneca Indian lady. If you use
' it for a watch-pocket, hang it, when you travel, at the
' head of your bed, and you may dream of Niagara. If
' you use it for a purse, you can put in it alms for poets
' and artists, and the subscription-money you receive for
' Mr. Carlyle's book. His book, as it happened, you
' gave me as a birthday gift, and you may take this as
' one to you; for, on yours, was W.'s birthday, J.'s wed-
' ding-day, and the day of ——'s death, and we set out
' on this journey. Perhaps there is something about it
' on the purse. The "number five which nature loves.'
is repeated on it.

'Carlyle's book I have, in some sense, read. It is
'witty, full of pictures, as usual. I would have gone
'through with it, if only for the sketch of Samson, and
'two or three bits of fun which happen to please me.
'No doubt it may be of use to rouse the unthinking to a
'sense of those great dangers and sorrows. But how
'open is he to his own assault. He rails himself out of
'breath at the short-sighted, and yet sees scarce a step
'before him. There is no valuable doctrine in his book,
'except the Goethean, *Do to-day the nearest duty.* Many
'are ready for that, could they but find the way. This
'he does not show. His proposed measures say noth-
'ing. Educate the people. That cannot be done by
'books, or voluntary effort, under these paralyzing cir-
'cumstances. Emigration! According to his own esti-
'mate of the increase of population, relief that way can
'have very slight effect. He ends as he began; as he did
'in Chartism. Everything is very bad. You are fools
'and hypocrites, or you would make it better. I cannot
'but sympathize with him about hero-worship; for I
'too, have had my fits of rage at the stupid irreverence
'of little minds, which also is made a parade of by the
'pedantic and the worldly. Yet it is a good sign. Democ-
'racy is the way to the new aristocracy, as irreligion to
'religion. By and by, if there are great men, they will
'not be brilliant exceptions, redeemers, but favorable
'samples of their kind.

'Mr. C.'s tone is no better than before. He is not
'loving, nor large; but he seems more healthy and
'gay.

'We have had bad weather here, bitterly cold. The
place is what I expected: it is too great and beautiful
'to agitate or surprise: it satisfies: it does not excite

' thought, but fully occupies. All is calm; even the rap-
' ids do not hurry, as we see them in smaller streams.
' The sound, the sight, fill the senses and the mind.

'At Buffalo, some ladies called on us, who extremely
' regretted they could not witness our emotions, on first
' seeing Niagara. " Many," they said, " burst into tears;
' " but with those of most sensibility, the hands become
' " cold as ice, and they would not mind if buckets of
' " cold water were thrown over them!" '

NATURE.

Margaret's love of beauty made her, of course, a
votary of nature, but rather for pleasurable excitement
than with a deep poetic feeling. Her imperfect vision
and her bad health were serious impediments to intimacy
with woods and rivers. She had never paid, — and it is
a little remarkable, — any attention to natural sciences.
She neither botanized, nor geologized, nor dissected. Still
she delighted in short country rambles, in the varieties
of landscape, in pastoral country, in mountain outlines,
and, above all, in the sea-shore. At Nantasket Beach,
and at Newport, she spent a month or two of many
successive summers. She paid homage to rocks, woods,
flowers, rivers, and the moon. She spent a good deal of
time out of doors, sitting, perhaps, with a book in some
sheltered recess commanding a landscape. She watched,
by day and by night, the skies and the earth, and believed
she knew all their expressions. She wrote in her journal,
or in her correspondence, a series of " moonlights," in
which she seriously attempts to describe the light and
scenery of successive nights of the summer moon. Or
course, her raptures must appear sickly and superficial

to an observer, who, with equal feeling, had better powers of observation.

Nothing is more rare than a talent to describe landscape, and, especially, skyscape, or cloudscape, although a vast number of letters, from correspondents between the ages of twenty and thirty, are filled with experiments in this kind. Margaret, in her turn, made many vain attempts, and, to a lover of nature, who knows that every day has new and inimitable lights and shades, one of these descriptions is as vapid as the raptures of a citizen arrived at his first meadow. Of course, he is charmed, but, of course, he cannot tell what he sees, or what pleases him. Yet Margaret often speaks with a certain tenderness and beauty of the impressions made upon her.

TO ———.

'*Fishkill*, 25 *Nov.*, 1844. — You would have been 'happy as I have been in the company of the mountains. 'They are companions both bold and calm. They 'exhilarate and they satisfy. To live, too, on the bank 'of the great river so long, has been the realization of a 'dream. Though I have been reading and thinking, yet 'this has been my life.'

'After they were all in bed,' she writes from the "Manse," in Concord, 'I went out, and walked till near 'twelve. The moonlight filled my heart. These embow- 'ering elms stood in solemn black, the praying monastics 'of this holy night; full of grace, in every sense; their 'life so full, so hushed; not a leaf stirred.'

'You say that nature does not keep her promise; but, 'surely, she satisfies us now and then for the time. 'The drama is always in progress, but here and there

she speaks out a sentence, full in its cadence, complete
' in its structure; it occupies, for the time, the sense and
' the thought. We have no care for promises. Will you
' say it is the superficialness of my life, that I have known
' hours with men and nature, that bore their proper fruit,
' — all present ate and were filled, and there were taken
' up of the fragments twelve baskets full? Is it because
' of the superficial mind, or the believing heart, that I can
' say this?'

'Only through emotion do we know thee, Nature! We
' lean upon thy breast, and feel its pulses vibrate to our
' own. That is knowledge, for that is love. Thought
' will never reach it.'

ART.

There are persons to whom a gallery is everywhere a
nome. In this country, the antique is known only by
plaster casts, and by drawings. The BOSTON ATHENÆUM,
— on whose sunny roof and beautiful chambers may
the benediction of centuries of students rest with mine!
— added to its library, in 1823, a small, but excellent
museum of the antique sculpture, in plaster; — the selection being dictated, it is said, by no less an adviser than
Canova. The Apollo, the Laocoon, the Venuses, Diana,
the head of the Phidian Jove, Bacchus, Antinous, the
Torso Hercules, the Discobolus, the Gladiator Borghese,
the Apollino, — all these, and more, the sumptuous gift
of Augustus Thorndike. It is much that one man should
have power to confer on so many, who never saw him, a
benefit so pure and enduring.

To these were soon added a heroic line of antique
23

busts, and, at last, by Horatio Greenough, the Night and Day of Michel Angelo. Here was old Greece and old Italy brought bodily to New England, and a verification given to all our dreams and readings. It was easy to collect, from the drawing-rooms of the city, a respectable picture-gallery for a summer exhibition. This was also done, and a new pleasure was invented for the studious, and a new home for the solitary. The Brimmer donation, in 1838, added a costly series of engravings chiefly of the French and Italian museums, and the drawings of Guercino, Salvator Rosa, and other masters. The separate chamber in which these collections were at first contained, made a favorite place of meeting for Margaret and a few of her friends, who were lovers of these works.

First led perhaps by Goethe, afterwards by the love she herself conceived for them, she read everything that related to Michel Angelo and Raphael. She read, pen in hand, Quatremère de Quincy's lives of those two painters, and I have her transcripts and commentary before me. She read Condivi, Vasari, Benvenuto Cellini, Duppa, Fuseli, and Von Waagen,— great and small. Every design of Michel, the four volumes of Raphael's designs, were in the rich portfolios of her most intimate friend. 'I have been very happy,' she writes, ' with ' four hundred and seventy designs of Raphael in my ' possession for a week.'

These fine entertainments were shared with many admirers, and, as I now remember them, certain months about the years 1839, 1840, seem colored with the genius of these Italians. Our walls were hung with prints of the Sistine frescoes; we were all petty collectors; and prints of Correggio and Guercino took the place, for the time, of epics and philosophy.

In the summer of 1839, Boston was still more rightfully adorned with the Allston Gallery; and the sculptures of our compatriots Greenough, and Crawford, and Powers, were brought hither. The following lines were addressed by Margaret to the Orpheus: —

'CRAWFORD'S ORPHEUS.

'Each Orpheus must to the abyss descend,
  'For only thus the poet can be wise, —
'Must make the sad Persephone his friend,
  'And buried love to second life arise ;
'Again his love must lose, through too much love,
  'Must lose his life by living life too true ;
'For what he sought below has passed above,
  'Already done is all that he would do ;
'Must tune all being with his single lyre ;
  'Must melt all rocks free from their primal pain ;
'Must search all nature with his one soul's fire ;
  'Must bind anew all forms in heavenly chain :
'If he already sees what he must do,
'Well may he shade his eyes from the far-shining view.'

Margaret's love of art, like that of most cultivated persons in this country, was not at all technical, but truly a sympathy with the artist, in the protest which his work pronounced on the deformity of our daily manners; her co-perception with him of the eloquence of form; her aspiration with him to a fairer life. As soon as her conversation ran into the mysteries of manipulation and artistic effect, it was less trustworthy. I remember that in the first times when I chanced to see pictures with her. I listened reverently to her opinions, and endeavored to see what she saw. But, on several occasions, finding myself unable to reach it, I came to suspect my guide, and to believe, at last, that her taste in works of art, though honest, was not on universal, but on idiosyncratic, grounds. As it has proved one of the most difficult problems of the practical astronomer to obtain an achromatic telescope, so an achromatic eye, one of the most needed, is also one of the rarest instruments of criticism.

She was very susceptible to pleasurable stimulus, took delight in details of form, color, and sound. Her fancy and imagination were easily stimulated to genial activity, and she erroneously thanked the artist for the pleasing emotions and thoughts that rose in her mind. So that, though capable of it, she did not always bring that highest tribunal to a work of art, namely, the calm presence of greatness, which only greatness in the object can satisfy. Yet the opinion was often well worth hearing on its own account, though it might be wide of the mark as criticism. Sometimes, too, she certainly brought to beautiful objects a fresh and appreciating love; and her written notes, especially on sculpture, I found always original and interesting. Here are some notes on the Athenæum Gallery of Sculpture, in August, 1840, which she sent me in manuscript : —

'Here are many objects worth study. There is Thor-
'waldsen's Byron. This is the truly beautiful, the ideal
'Byron. This head is quite free from the got-up, cari-
'catured air of disdain, which disfigures most likenesses
'of him, as it did himself in real life; yet sultry, stern,
'all-craving, all-commanding. Even the heavy style of
'the hair, too closely curled for grace, is favorable to the

'expression of concentrated life. While looking at this
'head, you learn to account for the grand failure in the
'scheme of his existence. The line of the cheek and chin
'are here, as usual, of unrivalled beauty.

'The bust of Napoleon is here also, and will naturally
'be named, in connection with that of Byron, since the one
'in letters, the other in arms, represented more fully than
'any other the tendency of their time; more than any
'other gave it a chance for reaction. There was another
'point of resemblance in the external being of the two,
'perfectly corresponding with that of the internal, a sense
'of which peculiarity drew on Byron some ridicule. I
'mean that it was the intention of nature, that neither
'should ever grow fat, but remain a Cassius in the com-
monwealth. And both these heads are taken while they
'were at an early age, and so thin as to be still beautiful.
'This head of Napoleon is of a stern beauty. A head
'must be of a style either very stern or very chaste, to
'make a deep impression on the beholder; there must be
'a great force of will and withholding of resources, giving
'a sense of depth below depth, which we call sternness;
'or else there must be that purity, flowing as from an
'inexhaustible fountain through every lineament, which
'drives far off or converts all baser natures. Napoleon's
'head is of the first description; it is stern, and not only
'so, but ruthless. Yet this ruthlessness excites no aver-
'sion; the artist has caught its true character, and given
'us here the Attila, the instrument of fate to serve a
'purpose not his own. While looking on it, came full to
mind the well-known lines, —

> '"Speak gently of his crimes:
> Who knows, Scourge of God, but in His eyes, those crimes
> Were virtues?"'

'His brows are tense and damp with the dews of
'thought. In that head you see the great future, careless
'of the black and white stones; and even when you turn
'to the voluptuous beauty of the mouth, the impression
'remains so strong, that Russia's snows, and mountains
'of the slain, seem the tragedy that must naturally follow
'the appearance of such an actor. You turn from him,
'feeling that he is a product not of the day, but of the
'ages, and that the ages must judge him.

'Near him is a head of Ennius, very intellectual; self-
'centred and self-fed; but wrung and gnawed by un-
'ceasing thoughts.

'Yet, even near the Ennius and Napoleon, our Amer-
'ican men look worthy to be perpetuated in marble or
'bronze, if it were only for their air of calm, unpretending
'sagacity. If the young American were to walk up an
'avenue lined with such effigies, he might not feel called
'to such greatness as the strong Roman wrinkles tell of,
'but he must feel that he could not live an idle life, and
'should nerve himself to lift an Atlas weight without
'repining or shrinking.

'The busts of Everett and Allston, though admirable
'as every-day likenesses, deserved a genius of a different
'order from Clevenger. Clevenger gives the man as he
'is at the moment, but does not show the possibilities of
'his existence. Even thus seen, the head of Mr. Everett
'brings back all the age of Pericles, so refined and classic
'is its beauty. The two busts of Mr. Webster, by Clev-
'enger and Powers, are the difference between prose, —
'healthy and energetic prose, indeed, but still prose, — and
'poetry. Clevenger's is such as we see Mr. Webster on
'any public occasion, when his genius is not called forth.
'No child could fail to recognize it in a moment. Pow-

ers' is not so good as a likeness, but has the higher
merit of being an ideal of the orator and statesman at a
great moment.   It is quite an American Jupiter in its
eagle calmness of conscious power.

'A marble copy of the beautiful Diana, not so spirited
'as the Athenæum cast.   S. C—— thought the difference
'was one of size.   This work may be seen at a glance;
'yet does not tire one after survey.   It has the freshness
'of the woods, and of morning dew. I admire those long
'lithe limbs, and that column of a throat.   The Diana
'is a woman's ideal of beauty; its elegance, its spirit, its
'graceful, peremptory air, are what we like in our own
'sex: the Venus is for men.   The sleeping Cleopatra
'cannot be looked at enough; always her sleep seems
'sweeter and more graceful, always more wonderful
'the drapery. A little Psyche, by a pupil of Bartolini,
'pleases us much thus far.   The forlorn sweetness
'with which she sits there, crouched down like a
'bruised butterfly, and the languid tenacity of her
'mood, are very touching.   The Mercury and Gany-
'mede with the Eagle, by Thorwaldsen, are still as
'fine as on first acquaintance. Thorwaldsen seems the
'grandest and simplest of modern sculptors. There is a
'breadth in his thought, a freedom in his design, we do
'not see elsewhere.

'A spaniel, by Gott, shows great talent, and knowledge
'of the animal.   The head is admirable; it is so full of
'playfulness and of doggish knowingness.'

I am tempted, by my recollection of the pleasure it
gave her, to insert here a little poem, addressed to Margaret by one of her friends, on the beautiful imaginative
picture in the gallery of 1840, called "The Dream."

" A youth, with gentle brow and tender cheek,
    Dreams in a place so silent, that no bird,
No rustle of the leaves his slumbers break ;
    Only soft tinkling from the stream is heard,
As in bright little waves it comes to greet
The beauteous One, and play upon his feet.

" On a low bank, beneath the thick shade thrown,
    Soft gleams over his brown hair are flitting,
His golden plumes, bending, all lovely shone ;
    It seemed an angel's home where he was sitting ,
Erect, beside, a silver lily grew,
And over all the shadow its sweet beauty threw.

" Dreams he of life ? O, then a noble maid
    Toward him floats, with eyes of starry light,
In richest robes all radiantly arrayed,
    To be his ladye and his dear delight.
Ah no ! the distance shows a winding stream ;
No lovely ladye moves, no starry eyes do gleam.

" Cold is the air, and cold the mountains blue ;
    The banks are brown, and men are lying there,
Meagre and old ; O, what have they to do
    With joyous visions of a youth so fair ?
He must not ever sleep as they are sleeping,
Onward through life he must be ever sweeping.

" Let the pale glimmering distance pass away;
    Why in the twilight art thou slumbering there ?
Wake, and come forth into triumphant day;
    Thy life and deeds must all be great and fair.
Canst thou not from the lily learn true glory,
Pure, lofty, lowly ? — such should be thy story.

" But no ! thou lovest the deep-eyéd Past,
    And thy heart clings to sweet remembrances ;
In dim cathedral aisles thou 'lt linger last,
    And fill thy mind with flitting fantasies.
But know, dear One, the world is rich to-day,
And the unceasing God gives glory forth alway."

I have said she was never weary of studying Michel
Angelo and Raphael; and here are some manuscript
"notes," which she sent me one day, containing a clear
expression of her feeling toward each of these masters,
after she had become tolerably familiar with their designs,
as far as prints could carry her : —

'On seeing such works as these of Michel Angelo, we
'feel the need of a genius scarcely inferior to his own,
'which should invent some word, or some music, adequate
'to express our feelings, and relieve us from the Titanic
'oppression.

'"Greatness," "majesty," "strength," — to these
'words we had before thought we attached their proper
'meaning. But now we repent that they ever passed our
'lips. Created anew by the genius of this man, we would
'create language anew, and give him a word of response
'worthy his sublime profession of faith. Could we not
'at least have reserved "godlike" for him? For never
'till now did we appreciate the primeval vigor of creation,
'the instant swiftness with which thought can pass to
'deed; never till now appreciate the passage, "Let
'"there be light, and there was light," which, be grateful,
'Michel! was clothed in human word before thee.

'One feels so repelled and humbled, on turning from
'Raphael to his contemporary, that I could have hated
'him as a Gentile Choragus might hate the prophet
'Samuel. Raphael took us to his very bosom, as if we
'had been fit for disciples, —

'"Parting with smiles the hair upon the brow,
And telling me none ever was preferred"

'This man waves his serpent wand over me, and beauty's
'self seems no better than a golden calf!

'I could not bear M. De Quincy for intimating that the
'archangel Michel could be jealous; yet I can easily see
'that he might have given cause, by undervaluing his
'divine contemporary. Raphael was so sensuous, so
'lovely and loving. All undulates to meet the eye, glides
'or floats upon the soul's horizon, as soft as is consist-
'ent with perfectly distinct and filled-out forms. The
'graceful Lionardo might see his pictures in moss; the
'beautiful Raphael on the cloud, or wave, or foliage;
'but thou, Michel, didst look straight upwards to the
'heaven, and grasp and bring thine down from the very
'sun of invention.

'How Raphael revels in the image! His life is all
'reproduced; nothing was abstract or conscious. Pan-
'theism, Polytheism, Greek god of Beauty, Apollo
'Musagetes,—what need of life beyond the divine work?
'"I paint," said he, "from an idea that comes into my
'"mind."

'But thou, Michel, didst not only feel but see the divine
'Ideal. Thine is the conscious monotheism of Jewry.
Like thy own Moses, even on the mount of celestial
'converse, thou didst ask thy God to show now his face,
'and didst write his words, not in the alphabet of flowers,
but on stone tables.

'It is, indeed, the two geniuses of Greece and Jewry,
'which are reproduced in these two men. Thauma-
'turgus nature saw fit to wait but a very few years
'before using these moulds again, in smaller space.
'Would you read the Bible aright? look at Michel; the
'Greek Mythology? look at Raphael. Would you know
how the sublime coëxists with the beautiful, or the

beautiful with the sublime? would you see power and
'truth regnant on the one side, with beauty and love
'harmonious and ministrant, but subordinate; or would
'you look at the other aspect of Deity?—study here.
'Would you open all the founts of marvel, admiration,
'and tenderness?—study both.

'One is not higher than the other; yet I am conscious
'of a slight rebuke from Michel, for having so poured
'out my soul at the feet of his brother angel. He seems
'to remind of Mr. E.'s view, and ask, "Why did you
'"not question whether there was not aught else? why
'"not reserve some inaccessible stronghold for me? why
'"did you unlock the floodgates of the mind to such
'"tides of emotion?" But there is no reality or per-
'manence in this; it is only a reminder that the feminine
'part of human nature must not be dominant.

'The prophets of Michel Angelo excite all my admira-
'tion at the man capable of giving to such a physique
'an expression which commands it. The soul is worthily
'lodged in these powerful frames; and she has the ease
'and dignity of one accustomed to command, and to
'command servants able to obey her hests. Who else
'could have so animated such forms, that they are im-
'posing, but never heavy? The strong man is made so
'majestic by his office, that you scarcely feel how strong
'he is. The wide folds of the drapery, the breadth of
'light and shade, are great as anything in

"the large utterance of the early gods."

'How they read,—these prophets and sibyls! Never
did the always-baffled, always reäspiring hope of the
'finite to compass the infinite find such expression, except
in the *sehnsucht* of music. They are buried in the

'volume. They cannot believe that it has not some-
'where been revealed, the word of enigma, the link
'between the human and divine, matter and spirit.
'Evidently, they hope to find it on the very next page
'I have always thought, that clearly enough did nature
'and the soul's own consciousness respond to the craving
'for immortality. I have thought it great weakness to
'need the voucher of a miracle, or of any of those direct
'interpositions of a divine power, which, in common par-
'lance, are alone styled revelation. When the revelations
'of nature seemed to me so clear, I had thought it was
'the weakness of the heart, or the dogmatism of the under-
'standing, which had such need of *a book*. But in these
'figures of Michel, the highest power seizes upon a scroll,
'hoping that some other mind may have dived to the
'depths of eternity for the desired pearl, and enable him,
'without delay, consciously to embrace the Everlasting
'Now.

'How fine the attendant intelligences! So youthful
'and fresh, yet so strong. Some merely docile and
'reverent, others eager for utterance before the thought
'be known, — so firm is the trust in its value, so great
'the desire for sympathy. Others so brilliant in the
'attention of the inquiring eye, so intelligent in every
'feature, that they seem to divine the whole, before they
'hear it.

'Zachariah is much the finer of the two prophets.

'Of the sibyls, the *Cumæa* would be disgusting, from
'her overpowering strength in the feminine form, if genius
'had not made her tremendous. Especially the bosom
'gives me a feeling of faintness and aversion I cannot
'express. The female breast looks made for the temple
'of sweet and chaste thoughts, while this is so formed

'as to remind you of the lioness in her lair, and suggest
'a word which I will not write.

'The *Delphica* is even beautiful, in Michel's fair, calm,
'noble style, like the mother and child asleep in the
'*Persica*, and *Night* in the casts I have just seen.

'The *Libica* is also more beautiful than grand. Her
'adjuncts are admirable. The elder figure, in the lowest
'pannel, — with what eyes of deep experience, and still
'unquenched enthusiasm, he sits meditating on the past!
'The figures at top are fiery with genius, especially the
'melancholy one, worthy to lift any weight, if he did
'but know how to set about it. As it is, all his strength
'may be wasted, yet he no whit the less noble.

'But the *Persica* is my favorite above all. She is the
'true sibyl. All the grandeur of that wasted frame
'comes from within. The life of thought has wasted
'the fresh juices of the body, and hardened the sere leaf
'of her cheek to parchment; every lineament is sharp,
'every tint tarnished; her face is seamed with wrinkles,
' — usually as repulsive on a woman's face as attractive
'on a man. We usually feel, on looking at a woman, as
'if Nature had given them their best dower, and Expe-
'rience could prove little better than a step-dame. But
'here, her high ambition and devotion to the life of
'thought gives her the masculine privilege of beauty in
'advancing years. Read on, hermitess of the world!
'what thou seekest is not there, yet thou dost not seek
'in vain.

'The adjuncts to this figure are worthy of it. On the
'right, below, those two divine sleepers, redeeming human
'nature, and infolding expectation in a robe of pearly
'sheen. Here is the sweetness of strength, — honey to
'the valiant; on the other side, its awfulness, — meat to

'the strong man. His sleep is more powerful than the
'waking of myriads of other men. What will he do
'when he has recruited his strength in this night's
'slumber? What wilt thou sing of it, wild-haired child
'of the lyre?

'I admire the heavy fall of the sleeper's luxuriant hair,
'which reminds one of the final shutting down of night
'upon a sullen twilight.

'The other figures, too, are full of augury, sad but
'life-like, in its poetry. On the shield, how perfectly is
'the expression of being struck home to the heart given!
'I wish I could have that shield, in some shape. Only
'a single blow was needed; the hand was sure, the
'breast shrinking, but unresisting. Die, child of my
'affection, child of my old age! Let the blood follow to
'the hilt, for it is the sword of the Lord!

'In looking again, this shield is on the *Libica*, and that
'of the *Persica* represents conquest, not sacrifice.

'Over all these figures broods the spirit of prophecy.
'You see their sternest deed is under the theocratic
'form. There is pride in action, but no selfism in these
'figures.

'When I first came to Michel, I clung to the beautiful
'Raphael, and feared his Druidical axe. But now, after
'the sibyls of Michel, it is unsafe to look at those of
'Raphael; for they seem weak, which is not so, only
'seems so, beside the sterner ideal.

'The beauty of composition here is great, and you feel
'that Michel's works are looked at fragment-wise in
'comparison. Here the eye glides along so naturally
'does so easily justice to each part.'

LETTERS.

I fear the remark already made on that susceptibility to details in art and nature which precluded the exercise of Margaret's sound catholic judgment, must be extended to more than her connoisseurship. She *had* a sound judgment, on which, in conversation, she could fall back, and anticipate and speak the best sense of the largest company. But, left to herself, and in her correspondence, she was much the victim of Lord Bacon's *idols of the cave,* or self-deceived by her own phantasms. I have looked over volumes of her letters to me and others. They are full of probity, talent, wit, friendship, charity, and high aspiration. They are tainted with a mysticism, which to me appears so much an affair of constitution, that it claims no more respect than the charity or patriotism of a man who has dined well, and feels better for it. One sometimes talks with a genial *bon vivant,* who looks as if the omelet and turtle have got into his eyes. In our noble Margaret, her personal feeling colors all her judgment of persons, of books, of pictures, and even of the laws of the world. This is easily felt in ordinary women, and a large deduction is civilly made on the spot by whosoever replies to their remark. But when the speaker has such brilliant talent and literature as Margaret, she gives so many fine names to these merely sensuous and subjective phantasms, that the hearer is long imposed upon, and thinks so precise and glittering nomenclature cannot be of mere *muscae volitantes,* phœnixes of the fancy, but must be of some real ornithology, hitherto unknown to him. This mere feeling exaggerates a host of trifles into a dazzling mythology. But when one goes to sift it, and find if there be a real meaning, it eludes search. Whole sheets of warm, florid writing are here, in which the eye is caught by "sapphire," "heliotrope," "dragon," "aloes," "Magna Dea," "limboes," "stars," and "purgatory," but can connect all this, or any part of it, with no universal experience.

In short, Margaret often loses herself in sentimentalism. That dangerous vertigo nature in her case adopted, and was to make respectable. As it sometimes happens that a grandiose style, like that of the Alexandrian Platonists, or like Macpherson's Ossian, is more stimulating to the imagination of nations, than the true Plato, or than the simple poet, so here was a head so creative of new colors, of wonderful gleams, — so iridescent, that it piqued curiosity, and stimulated thought, and communicated mental activity to all who approached her; though her perceptions were not to be compared to her fancy, and she made numerous mistakes. Her integrity was perfect, and she was led and followed by love, and was really bent on truth, but too indulgent to the meteors of her fancy.

FRIENDSHIP.

"Friends she must have, but in no one could find
A tally fitted to so large a mind."

It is certain that Margaret, though unattractive in person, and assuming in manners, so that the girls complained that "she put upon them," or, with her burly masculine existence, quite reduced them to satellites, yet inspired an enthusiastic attachment. I hear from one witness, as early as 1829, that "all the girls raved about Margaret Fuller," and the same powerful magnetism wrought, as she went on, from year to year, on all ingenuous natures. The loveliest and the highest endowed women were eager to lay their beauty, their grace, the hospitalities of sumptuous homes, and their costly gifts, at her feet. When I expressed, one day, many years afterwards, to a lady who knew her well, some surprise at the homage paid her by men in Italy, — offers of marriage having there been made her by distinguished parties, — she replied : " There is nothing extraordinary in it. Had she been a man, any one of those fine girls of sixteen, who surrounded her here, would have married her : they were all in love with her, she understood them so well." She had seen many persons, and had entire confidence in her own discrimination of characters. She saw and foresaw all in the first interview. She had certainly made her own selections with great precision, and had not been disappointed. When pressed for a reason, she replied, in one instance, 'I have no good reason to give for what I think of ——. 'It is a dæmoniacal intimation. Everybody at —— 'praised her, but their account of what she said gave 'me the same unfavorable feeling. This is the first 'instance in which I have not had faith, if you liked a 'person. Perhaps I am wrong now; perhaps, if I saw 'her, a look would give me a needed clue to her charac-'ter, and I should change my feeling. Yet I have never 'been mistaken in these intimations, as far as I recollect. 'I hope I am now.'

I am to add, that she gave herself to her friendships with an entireness not possible to any but a woman, with a depth possible to few women. Her friendships, as a girl with girls, as a woman with women, were not inmingled with passion, and had passages of romantic sacrifice and of ecstatic fusion, which I have heard with the ear, but could not trust my profane pen to report. There were, also, the ebbs and recoils from the other party, — the mortal unequal to converse with an immortal, — ingratitude, which was more truly incapacity, the collapse of overstrained affections and powers. At all events, it is clear that Margaret, later, grew more strict, and values herself with her friends on having the tie now "redeemed from all search after Eros." So much, however, of intellectual aim and activity mixed with her alliances, as to breathe a certain dignity and myrrh through them all. She and her friends are fellow-students with noblest moral aims. She is there for help and for counsel. 'Be to the best thou knowest ever 'true!' is her language to one. And that was the effect of her presence. Whoever conversed with her felt challenged by the strongest personal influence to a bold and generous life. To one she wrote, — 'Could a 'word from me avail you, I would say, that I have 'firm faith that nature cannot be false to her child, who 'has shown such an unalterable faith in her piety 'towards her.'

'These tones of my dear ——'s lyre are of the noblest. 'Will they sound purely through her experiences? Will 'the variations be faithful to the theme? Not always 'do those who most devoutly long for the Infinite, know 'best how to modulate their finite into a fair passage of 'the eternal Harmony.

'How many years was it the cry of my spirit, —

'"Give, give, ye mighty Gods!
Why do ye thus hold back?"—

'and, I suppose, all noble young persons think for the

time that they would have been more generous than
the Olympians. But when we have learned the high
lesson *to deserve*, — that boon of manhood, — we see
'they esteemed us too much, to give what we had not
'earned.'

The following passages from her journal and her letters are sufficiently descriptive, each in its way, of her
strong affections.

'At Mr. G.'s we looked over prints, the whole evening,
'in peace. Nothing fixed my attention so much as a
'large engraving of Madame Recamier in her boudoir.
'I have so often thought over the intimacy between her
'and Madame De Stael.

'It is so true that a woman may be in love with a
'woman, and a man with a man. I like to be sure of
'it, for it is the same love which angels feel, where —

'"Sie fragen nicht nach Mann und Weib."

'It is regulated by the same law as that of love
'between persons of different sexes; only it is purely
'intellectual and spiritual. Its law is the desire of the
'spirit to realize a whole, which makes it seek in another
'being what it finds not in itself. Thus the beautiful
'seek the strong, and the strong the beautiful; the
'mute seeks the eloquent, &c.; the butterfly settles
'always on the dark flower. Why did Socrates love
'Alcibiades? Why did Körner love Schneider? How
'natural is the love of Wallenstein for Max; that of De
'Stael for De Recamier; mine for ——. I loved ——
'for a time, with as much passion as I was then strong
'enough to feel. Her face was always gleaming before

'me; her voice was always echoing in my ear; all
'poetic thoughts clustered round the dear image. This
'love was a key which unlocked for me many a treasure
'which I still possess; it was the carbuncle which cast
 light into many of the darkest caverns of human
'nature. She loved me, too, though not so much,
'because her nature was "less high, less grave, less
'"large, less deep." But she loved more tenderly, less
'passionately. She loved me, for I well remember her
'suffering when she first could feel my faults, and knew
'one part of the exquisite veil rent away; how she
'wished to stay apart, and weep the whole day.

*   *   *   *   *

'I do not love her now with passion, but I still feel
'towards her as I can to no other woman. I thought
'of all this as I looked at Madame Recamier.'

TO R. W. E.

'*7th Feb.*, 1843. — I saw the letter of your new friend,
'and liked it much; only, at this distance, one could not
'be sure whether it was the nucleus or the train of a
'comet, that lightened afar. The dæmons are not busy
'enough at the births of most men. They do not give
'them individuality deep enough for truth to take root
'in. Such shallow natures cannot resist a strong head:
'its influence goes right through them. It is not stopped
'and fermented long enough. But I do not understand
'this hint of hesitation, because you have many friends
'already. We need not economize, we need not hoard
'these immortal treasures. Love and thought are not
'diminished by diffusion. In the widow's cruse is oil
'enough to furnish light for all the world.'

TO R. W. E.

'15th March, 1842. — It is to be hoped, my best one, that the experiences of life will yet correct your vocabulary, and that you will not always answer the burst of frank affection by the use of such a word as "flat-" tery."

'Thou knowest, O all-seeing Truth! whether that 'hour is base or unworthy thee, in which the heart 'turns tenderly towards some beloved object, whether 'stirred by an apprehension of its needs, or of its pres-'ent beauty, or of its great promise; when it would lay 'before it all the flowers of hope and love, would soothe 'its weariness as gently as might the sweet south, and '*flatter* it by as fond an outbreak of pride and devotion 'as is seen on the sunset clouds. Thou knowest 'whether these promptings, whether these longings, be 'not truer than intellectual scrutiny of the details of 'character; than cold distrust of the exaggerations even 'of heart. What we hope, what we think of those 'we love, is true, true as the fondest dream of love and 'friendship that ever shone upon the childish heart.

'The faithful shall yet meet a full-eyed love, ready as 'profound, that never needs turn the key on its retire-'ment, or arrest the stammering of an overweening 'trust.'

TO ———.

'I wish I could write you often, to bring before you 'the varied world-scene you cannot so well go out to 'unfold for yourself. But it was never permitted me, 'even where I wished it most. But the forest leaves fall 'unseen, and make a soil on which shall be reared the

'growths and fabrics of a nobler era.' This thought
'rounds off each day. Your letter was a little golden
'key to a whole volume of thoughts and feelings. I
'cannot make the one bright drop, like champagne in
'ice, but must pour a full gush, if I speak at all, and
'not think whether the water is clear either.'

With this great heart, and these attractions, it was
easy to add daily to the number of her friends. With
her practical talent, her counsel and energy, she was
pretty sure to find clients and sufferers enough, who
wished to be guided and supported. 'Others,' she
said, 'lean on this arm, which I have found so frail.
'Perhaps it is strong enough to have drawn a sword,
'but no better suited to be used as a *bolt*, than that of
'Lady Catharine Douglas, of loyal memory.' She could
not make a journey, or go to an evening party, without
meeting a new person, who wished presently to impart
his history to her. Very early, she had written to ——,
'My museum is so well furnished, that I grow lazy
'about collecting new specimens of human nature.'
She had soon enough examples of the historic development of rude intellect under the first rays of culture.
But, in a thousand individuals, the process is much the
same; and, like a professor too long pent in his college,
she rejoiced in encountering persons of untutored grace
and strength, and felt no wish to prolong the intercourse
when culture began to have its effect. I find in her
journal a characteristic note, on receiving a letter on
books and speculations, from one whom she had valued
for his heroic qualities in a life of adventure: —

'These letters of —— are beautiful, and moved me

' deeply. It looks like the birth of a soul. But I loved
' *thee,* fair, rich *earth,* — and all that is gone forever.
' This that comes now, we know in much farther stages.
' Yet there is silver sweet in the tone, generous nobility
' in the impulses.'

' Poor Tasso in the play offered his love and service
' too officiously to all. They all rejected it, and declared
' him mad, because he made statements too emphatic of
' his feelings. If I wanted only ideal figures to think
' about, there are those in literature I like better than any
' of your living ones. But I want far more. I want
' habitual intercourse, cheer, inspiration, tenderness. I
' want these for myself; I want to impart them. I have
' done as Timon did, for these last eight years. My early
' intercourses were more equal, because more natural.
' Since I took on me the vows of renunciation, I have
' acted like a prodigal. Like Timon, I have loved to give,
' perhaps not from beneficence, but from restless love.
' Now, like Fortunatus, I find my mistresses will not
' thank me for fires made of cinnamon; rather they run
' from too rich an odor. What shall I do? not curse,
' like him, (oh base!) nor dig my grave in the marge of
' the salt tide. Give an answer to my questions, dæmon!
  Give a rock for my feet, a bird of peaceful and sufficient
' song within my breast! I return to thee, my Father,
' from the husks that have been offered me. But I return
' as one who meant not to leave Thee.'

Of course, she made large demands on her companions,
and would soon come to sound their knowledge, and
guess pretty nearly the range of their thoughts. There
yet remained to command her constancy, what she valued

more, the quality and affection proper to each.   But she could rarely find natures sufficiently deep and magnetic. With her sleepless curiosity, her magnanimity, and her diamond-ring, like Annie of Lochroyan's, to exchange for gold or for pewter, she might be pardoned for her impatient questionings.   To me, she was uniformly generous; but neither did I escape.   Our moods were very different; and I remember, that, at the very time when I, slow and cold, had come fully to admire her genius, and was congratulating myself on the solid good understanding that subsisted between us, I was surprised with hearing it taxed by her with superficiality and halfness. She stigmatized our friendship as commercial.   It seemed, her magnanimity was not met, but I prized her only for the thoughts and pictures she brought me; — so many thoughts, so many facts yesterday, — so many to-day; — when there was an end of things to tell, the game was up: that, I did not know, as a friend should know, to prize a silence as much as a discourse, — and hence a forlorn feeling was inevitable; a poor counting of thoughts, and a taking the census of virtues, was the unjust reception so much love found.   On one occasion, her grief broke into words like these: 'The religious 'nature remained unknown to you, because it could not 'proclaim itself, but claimed to be divined.   The deepest 'soul that approached you was, in your eyes, nothing but 'a magic lantern, always bringing out pretty shows of 'life.'

But as I did not understand the discontent then, — of course, I cannot now.   It was a war of temperaments, and could not be reconciled by words; but, after each party had explained to the uttermost, it was necessary to fall back on those grounds of agreement which remained and leave the differences henceforward in respectful silence. The recital may still serve to show to sympa‑ thetic persons the true lines and enlargements of her genius. It is certain that this incongruity never inter‑ rupted for a moment the intercourse, such as it was, that existed between us.

I ought to add here, that certain mental changes brought new questions into conversation. In the summer of 1840, she passed into certain religious states, which did not impress me as quite healthy, or likely to be permanent; and I said, "I do not understand your tone; it seems exaggerated. You are one who can afford to speak and to hear the truth. Let us hold hard to the common‑ sense, and let us speak in the positive degree."

And I find, in later letters from her, sometimes playful, sometimes grave allusions to this explanation.

'Is —— there? Does water meet water? — no need 'of wine, sugar, spice, or even a *soupçon* of lemon to 'remind of a tropical climate? I fear me not. Yet, dear 'positives, believe me superlatively yours, MARGARET.'

The following letter seems to refer, under an Eastern guise, and with something of Eastern exaggeration of compliment too, to some such native sterilities in her cor‑ respondent: —

TO R. W. E.

'23*d Feb.*, 1840. — I am like some poor traveller of the 'desert, who saw, at early morning, a distant palm, and 'toiled all day to reach it. All day he toiled. The un‑ 'feeling sun shot pains into his temples; the burning air,

'filled with sand, checked his breath; he had no water,
'and no fountain sprung along his path. But his eye
'was bright with courage, for he said, "When I reach
'"the lonely palm, I will lie beneath its shade. I will
'"refresh myself with its fruit. Allah has reared it to
'"such a height, that it may encourage the wandering,
'"and bless and sustain the faint and weary." But
'when he reached it, alas! it had grown too high to shade
'the weary man at its foot. On it he saw no clustering
'dates, and its one draught of wine was far beyond his
'reach. He saw at once that it was so. A child, a bird,
'a monkey, might have climbed to reach it. A rude hand
'might have felled the whole tree; but the full-grown
'man, the weary man, the gentle-hearted, religious man,
'was no nearer to its nourishment for being close to the
'root; yet he had not force to drag himself further, and
'leave at once the aim of so many fond hopes, so many
'beautiful thoughts. So he lay down amid the inhos-
'pitable sands. The night dews pierced his exhausted
'frame; the hyena laughed, the lion roared, in the dis-
'tance; the stars smiled upon him satirically from their
'passionless peace; and he knew they were like the sun,
'as unfeeling, only more distant. He could not sleep for
'famine. With the dawn he arose. The palm stood as
'tall, as inaccessible, as ever; its leaves did not so
'much as rustle an answer to his farewell sigh. On
'and on he went, and came, at last, to a living spring.
'The spring was encircled by tender verdure, wild fruits
'ripened near, and the clear waters sparkled up to tempt
'his lip. The pilgrim rested, and refreshed himself, and
'looked back with less pain to the unsympathizing palm,
'which yet towered in the distance.

'But the wanderer had a mission to perform, which

'must have forced him to leave at last both palm and
'fountain. So on and on he went, saying to the palm,
'"Thou art for another;" and to the gentle waters, "I
'"will return."

'Not far distant was he when the sirocco came, and
'choked with sand the fountain, and uprooted the fruit-
'trees. When years have passed, the waters will have
'forced themselves up again to light, and a new oasis
'will await a new wanderer. Thou, Sohrab, wilt, ere
'that time, have left thy bones at Mecca. Yet the
'remembrance of the fountain cheers thee as a blessing;
'that of the palm haunts thee as a pang.

'So talks the soft spring gale of the Shah Nameh.
'Genuine Sanscrit I cannot write. My Persian and
'Arabic you love not. Why do I write thus to one who
'must ever regard the deepest tones of my nature as those
'of childish fancy or worldly discontent?'

PROBLEMS OF LIFE.

Already, too, at this time, each of the main problems
of human life had been closely scanned and interrogated
by her, and some of them had been much earlier settled.
A worshipper of beauty, why could not she also have
been beautiful? — of the most radiant sociality, why
should not she have been so placed, and so decorated, as
to have led the fairest and highest? In her journal is
a bitter sentence, whose meaning I cannot mistake:
'Of a disposition that requires the most refined, the most
'exalted tenderness, without charms to inspire it: — poor
'Mignon! fear not the transition through death; no
penal fires can have in store worse torments than thou
'art familiar with already.'

In the month of May, she writes: — 'When all things

' are blossoming, it seems so strange not to blossom too;
' that the quick thought within cannot remould its tene-
' ment. Man is the slowest aloes, and I am such a shabby
' plant, of such coarse tissue. I hate not to be beautiful,
' when all around is so.'

Again, after recording a visit to a family, whose taste
and culture, united to the most liberal use of wealth,
made the most agreeable of homes, she writes : ' Look-
' ing out on the wide view, I felt the blessings of my
' comparative freedom. I stand in no false relations.
' Who else is so happy? Here are these fair, unknowing
' children envying the depth of my mental life. They
' feel withdrawn by sweet duties from reality. Spirit ! I
' accept; teach me to prize and use whatsoever is given
' me.'

' At present,' she writes elsewhere, ' it skills not. I am
' able to take the superior view of life, and my place in
' it. But I know the deep yearnings of the heart and
' the bafflings of time will be felt again, and then I shall
' long for some dear hand to hold. But I shall never
' forget that my curse is nothing, compared with that of
' those who have entered into those relations, but not
' made them real; who only *seem* husbands, wives, and
' friends.'

' I remain fixed to be, without churlishness or coldness,
' as much alone as possible. It is best for me. I am not
' fitted to be loved, and it pains me to have close dealings
' with those who do not love, to whom my feelings are
' "strange." Kindness and esteem are very well. I am
' willing to receive and bestow them; but these alone are
' not worth feelings such as mine. And I wish I may

make no more mistakes, but keep chaste for mine own
'people.'

There is perhaps here, as in a passage of the same
journal quoted already, an allusion to a verse in the ballad of the Lass of Lochroyan : —

> " O yours was gude, and gude enough,
> But aye the best was mine ;
> For yours was o' the gude red gold,
> But mine o' the diamond fine."

'There is no hour of absolute beauty in all my past,
'though some have been made musical by heavenly
'hope, many dignified by intelligence. Long urged by
'the Furies, I rest again in the temple of Apollo. Celes-
'tial verities dawn constellated as thoughts in the heaven
'of my mind.

'But, driven from home to home, as a renouncer, I get
'the picture and the poetry of each. Keys of gold, silver,
'iron, and lead, are in my casket. No one loves me;
'but I love many a good deal, and see, more or less, into
'their eventual beauty. Meanwhile, I have no fetter on
'me, no engagement, and, as I look on others, — almost
'every other, — can I fail to feel this a great privilege?
'I have nowise tied my hands or feet; yet the varied
'calls on my sympathy have been such, that I hope not
'to be made partial, cold, or ignorant, by this isolation.
'I have no child; but now, as I look on these lovely
'children of a human birth, what low and neutralizing
'cares they bring with them to the mother! The chil-
'dren of the muse come quicker, and have not on them
the taint of earthly corruption.'

Practical questions in plenty the days and months

brought her to settle,—questions requiring all her wisdom, and sometimes more than all. None recurs with more frequency, at one period, in her journals, than the debate with herself, whether she shall make literature a profession. Shall it be woman, or shall it be artist?

WOMAN, OR ARTIST?

Margaret resolved, again and again, to devote herself no more to these disappointing forms of men and women, but to the children of the muse. 'The *dramatis per-* '*sonæ*,' she said, 'of my poems shall henceforth be 'chosen from the children of immortal Muse. I fix my 'affections no more on these frail forms.' But it was vain; she rushed back again to persons, with a woman's devotion.

Her pen was a non-conductor. She always took it up with some disdain, thinking it a kind of impiety to attempt to report a life so warm and cordial, and wrote on the fly-leaf of her journal, —

'"*Scrivo sol per sfogar' l'interno.*"'

'Since you went away,' she said, ' I have thought of 'many things I might have told you, but I could not 'bear to be eloquent and poetical. It is a mockery thus to 'play the artist with life, and dip the brush in one's own 'heart's blood. One would fain be no more artist, or 'philosopher, or lover, or critic, but a soul ever rushing 'forth in tides of genial life.'

'26 *Dec.*, 1842.— I have been reading the lives of Lord 'Herbert of Cherbury, and of Sir Kenelm Digby. These splendid, chivalrous, and thoughtful Englishmen are

'meat which my soul loveth, even as much as my Ital-
'ians. What I demand of men, — that they could act
'out all their thoughts, — these have. They are lives;
'— and of such I do not care if they had as many faults
'as there are days in the year, — there is the energy
'to redeem them. Do you not admire Lord Herbert's
'two poems on life, and the conjectures concerning celes-
'tial life? I keep reading them.'

' When I look at my papers, I feel as if I had never
'had a thought that was worthy the attention of any but
'myself; and 't is only when, on talking with people, I
'find I tell them what they did not know, that my con-
'fidence at all returns.'

'My verses, — I am ashamed when I think there is
'scarce a line of poetry in them, — all rhetorical and
'impassioned, as Goethe said of De Stael. However,
'such as they are, they have been overflowing drops
'from the somewhat bitter cup of my existence.'

'How can I ever write with this impatience of detail?
'I shall never be an artist; I have no patient love of
'execution; I am delighted with my sketch, but if I try
'to finish it, I am chilled. Never was there a great
'sculptor who did not love to chip the marble.'

'I have talent and knowledge enough to furnish a
'dwelling for friendship, but not enough to deck with
'golden gifts a Delphi for the world.'

'Then a woman of tact and brilliancy, like me, has an
'undue advantage in conversation with men. They are

'astonished at our instincts. They do not see where we
'got our knowledge; and, while they tramp on in their
'clumsy way, we wheel, and fly, and dart hither and
'thither, and seize with ready eye all the weak points,
'like Saladin in the desert. It is quite another thing
'when we come to write, and, without suggestion from
'another mind, to declare the positive amount of thought
'that is in us. Because we seemed to know all, they
'think we can tell all; and, finding we can tell so little,
'lose faith in their first opinion of us, *which, nathless,*
'*was true.*'

And again: 'These gentlemen are surprised that I
'write no better, because I talk so well. But I have
'served a long apprenticeship to the one, none to the
'other. I shall write better, but never, I think, so well
'as I talk; for then I feel inspired. The means are
'pleasant; my voice excites me, my pen never. I shall
'not be discouraged, nor take for final what they say, but
'sift from it the truth, and use it. I feel the strength to
'dispense with all illusions. I will stand steady, and
'rejoice in the severest probations.'

'What a vulgarity there seems in this writing for the
'multitude! We know not yet, have not made ourselves
'known to a single soul, and shall we address those still
'more unknown? Shall we multiply our connections,
'and thus make them still more superficial?
'I would go into the crowd, and meet men for the day,
'to help them for the day, but for that intercourse which
'most becomes us. Pericles, Anaxagoras, Aspasia,
'Cleone, is circle wide enough for me. I should think
'all the resources of my nature, and all the tribute it

'could enforce from external nature, none too much to
'furnish the banquet for this circle.

'But where to find fit, though few, representatives for
'all we value in humanity? Where obtain those golden
'keys to the secret treasure-chambers of the soul? No
'samples are perfect. We must look abroad into the
'wide circle, to seek a little here, and a little there, to
'make up our company. And is not the " prent book "
'a good beacon-light to tell where we wait the bark? —
'a reputation, the means of entering the Olympic game,
'where Pindar may perchance be encountered?

'So it seems the mind must reveal its secret; must
'reproduce. And I have no castle, and no natural circle,
· in which I might live, like the wise Makaria, observing
'my kindred the stars, and gradually enriching my
'archives. Makaria here must go abroad, or the stars
'would hide their light, and the archive remain a blank.

'For all the tides of life that flow within me, I am
'dumb and ineffectual, when it comes to casting my
'thought into a form. No old one suits me. If I could
'invent one, it seems to me the pleasure of creation would
'make it possible for me to write. What shall I do,
'dear friend? I want force to be either a genius or a
'character. One should be either private or public. I
' love best to be a woman; but womanhood is at present
'too straitly-bounded to give me scope. At hours, I live
' truly as a woman; at others, I should stifle; as, on the
' other hand, I should palsy, when I would play the
' artist.'

HEROISM.

These practical problems Margaret had to entertain
and to solve the best way she could. She says truly,

'there was none to take up her burden whilst she slept. But she was formed for action, and addressed herself quite simply to her part. She was a woman, an orphan, without beauty, without money; and these negatives will suggest what difficulties were to be surmounted where the tasks dictated by her talents required the good-will of "good society," in the town where she was to teach and write. But she was even-tempered and erect, and, if her journals are sometimes mournful, her mind was made up, her countenance beamed courage and cheerfulness around her. Of personal influence, speaking strictly,— an efflux, that is, purely of mind and character, excluding all effects of power, wealth, fashion, beauty, or literary fame,— she had an extraordinary degree; I think more than any person I have known. An interview with her was a joyful event. Worthy men and women, who had conversed with her, could not forget her, but worked bravely on in the remembrance that this heroic approver had recognized their aims. She spoke so earnestly, that the depth of the sentiment prevailed, and not the accidental expression, which might chance to be common. Thus I learned, the other day, that, in a copy of Mrs. Jameson's Italian Painters, against a passage describing Correggio as a true servant of God in his art, above sordid ambition, devoted to truth, "one of those superior beings of whom there are so few;" Margaret wrote on the margin, 'And yet all might be 'such.' The book lay long on the table of the owner, in Florence, and chanced to be read there by a young artist of much talent. "These words," said he, months afterwards, "struck out a new strength in me. They revived resolutions long fallen away, and made me set my face like a flint."

But Margaret's courage was thoroughly sweet in its temper. She accused herself in her youth of unamiable traits, but, in all the later years of her life, it is difficult to recall a moment of malevolence. The friends whom her strength of mind drew to her, her good heart held fast; and few persons were ever the objects of more persevering kindness. Many hundreds of her letters remain, and they are alive with proofs of generous friendship given and received.

Among her early friends, Mrs. Farrar, of Cambridge, appears to have discovered, at a critical moment in her career, the extraordinary promise of the young girl, and some false social position into which her pride and petulance, and the mistakes of others, had combined to bring her, and she set herself, with equal kindness and address, to make a second home for Margaret in her own house, and to put her on the best footing in the agreeable society of Cambridge. She busied herself, also, as she could, in removing all superficial blemishes from the gem. In a well-chosen travelling party, made up by Mrs. Farrar, and which turned out to be the beginning of much happiness by the friendships then formed, Margaret visited, in the summer of 1835, Newport, New York, and Trenton Falls; and, in the autumn, made the acquaintance, at Mrs. F.'s house, of Miss Martineau, whose friendship, at that moment, was an important stimulus to her mind.

Mrs. Farrar performed for her, thenceforward, all the offices of an almost maternal friendship. She admired her genius, and wished that all should admire it. She counselled and encouraged her, brought to her side the else unsuppliable aid of a matron and a lady, sheltered her in sickness, forwarded her plans with tenderness and constancy, to the last. I read all this in the tone of uniform gratitude and love with which this lady is mentioned in Margaret's letters. Friendships like this praise both parties; and the security with which people of a noble disposition approached Margaret, indicated the quality of her own infinite tenderness. A very intelligent woman applied to her what Stilling said of Goethe: "Her heart, which few knew, was as great as her mind, which all knew;" and added, that, "in character, Margaret was, of all she had beheld, the largest woman, and not a woman who wished to be a man." Another lady added, "She never disappointed you. To any one whose confidence she had once drawn out, she was thereafter faithful. She could talk of persons, and never gossip; for she had a fine instinct that kept her from any reality, and from any effect of treachery." I was still more struck with the remark that followed. "Her life, since she went abroad, is wholly unknown to me; but I have an unshaken trust that what Margaret did she can defend."

She was a right brave and heroic woman. She shrunk from no duty, because of feeble nerves. Although, after her father died, the disappointment of not going to Europe with Miss Martineau and Mrs. Farrar was extreme, and her mother and sister wished her to take her portion of the estate and go; and, on her refusal, entreated the interference of friends to overcome her objections; Margaret would not hear of it, and devoted herself to the education of her brothers and sisters, and then to the making a home for the family. She was exact and punctual in money matters, and maintained herself, and made her full contribution to the support of her family, by the reward of her labors as a teacher, and in her conversation classes. I have a letter from her at Jamaica Plain, dated November, 1840, which begins, —

'This day I write you from my own hired house, and 'am full of the dignity of citizenship. Really, it is 'almost happiness. I retain, indeed, some cares and ' responsibilities; but these will sit light as feathers, for I 'can take my own time for them. Can it be that this 'peace will be mine for five whole months? At any 'rate, five days have already been enjoyed.'

Here is another, written in the same year : —

'I do not wish to talk to you of my ill-health, 'except that I like you should know when it makes 'me do anything badly, since I wish you to excuse 'and esteem me. But let me say, once for all, in 'reply to your letter, that you are mistaken if you 'think I ever wantonly sacrifice my health. I have 'learned that we cannot injure ourselves without injur-'ing others; and besides, that we have no right; for 'ourselves are all we know of heaven. I do not try to 'domineer over myself. But, unless I were sure of 'dying, I cannot dispense with making some exertion, 'both for the present and the future. There is no mor-'tal, who, if I laid down my burden, would take care 'of it while I slept. Do not think me weakly disinter-'ested, or, indeed, disinterested at all.'

Every one of her friends knew assuredly that her sympathy and aid would not fail them when required. She went, from the most joyful of all bridals, to attend a near relative during a formidable surgical operation.

She was here to help others. As one of her friends
writes, ' She helped whoever knew her.' She adopted
the interests of humble persons, within her circle, with
heart-cheering warmth, and her ardor in the cause of
suffering and degraded women, at Sing-Sing, was as
irresistible as her love of books. She had, many years
afterwards, scope for the exercise of all her love and
devotion, in Italy, but she came to it as if it had been her
habit and her natural sphere. The friends who knew
her in that country, relate, with much surprise, that she,
who had all her lifetime drawn people by her wit, should
recommend herself so highly, in Italy, by her tenderness
and large affection. Yet the tenderness was only a face
of the wit ; as before, the wit was raised above all other
wit by the affection behind it. And, truly, there was
an ocean of tears always, in her atmosphere, ready to
fall.

There was, at New York, a poor adventurer, half
patriot, half author, a miserable man, always in such
depths of distress, with such squadrons of enemies,
that no charity could relieve, and no intervention save
him. He believed Europe banded for his destruction,
and America corrupted to connive at it. Margaret listened to these woes with such patience and mercy, that
she drew five hundred dollars, which had been invested
for her in a safe place, and put them in those hapless
hands, where, of course, the money was only the prey
of new rapacity, to be bewailed by new reproaches.
When one of her friends had occasion to allude to this,
long afterwards, she replied : —

' In answer to what you say of ——, I wish, indeed
' the little effort I made for him. had been wiselier

'applied. Yet these are not the things one regrets. It
'will not do to calculate too closely with the affectionate
'human impulse. We must consent to make many mis-
'takes, or we should move too slow to help our brothers
'much. I am sure you do not regret what you spent on
'Miani, and other worthless people. As things looked
'then, it would have been wrong not to have risked the
'loss.'

TRUTH.

But Margaret crowned all her talents and virtues with
a love of truth, and the power to speak it. In great and
in small matters, she was a woman of her word, and gave
those who conversed with her the unspeakable comfort
that flows from plain dealing. Her nature was frank
and transparent, and she had a right to say, as she says
in her journal : —

'I have the satisfaction of knowing, that, in my coun-
'sels, I have given myself no air of being better than
'I am.'

And again : —

'In the chamber of death, I prayed in very early
'years, "Give me truth; cheat me by no illusion." O,
'the granting of this prayer is sometimes terrible to me!
'I walk over the burning ploughshares, and they sear
'my feet. Yet nothing but truth will do; no love will
'serve that is not eternal, and as large as the universe;
'no philanthropy in executing whose behests I myself
'become unhealthy; no creative genius which bursts

'asunder my life, to leave it a poor black chrysalid
'behind.   And yet this last is too true of me.'

She describes a visit made in May, 1844, at the house
of some valued friends in West Roxbury, and adds:
'We had a long and deep conversation, happy in its
'candor.   Truth, truth, thou art the great preservative!
'Let free air into the mind, and the pestilence cannot
'lurk in any corner.'

And she uses the following language in an earnest
letter to another friend : —
  'My own entire sincerity, in every passage of life, gives
'me a right to expect that I shall be met by no unmean-
'ing phrases or attentions.'

  'Reading to-day a few lines of ——, I thought with
'refreshment of such lives as T.'s, and V.'s, and W.'s, so
'private and so true, where each line written is really the
'record of a thought or a feeling.   I hate poems which
'are a melancholy monument of culture for the sake of
'being cultivated, not of growing.'

Even in trifles, one might find with her the advantage
and the electricity of a little honesty.   I have had from
an eye-witness a note of a little scene that passed in
Boston, at the Academy of Music.   A party had gone
early, and taken an excellent place to hear one of Beethoven's symphonies.   Just behind them were soon
seated a young lady and two gentlemen, who made an
incessant buzzing, in spite of bitter looks cast on them
by the whole neighborhood, and destroyed all the musical comfort.   After all was over, Margaret leaned across

one seat, and catching the eye of this girl, who was pretty and well-dressed, said, in her blandest, gentlest voice, "May I speak with you one moment?" "Certainly," said the young lady, with a fluttered, pleased look, bending forward. "I only wish to say," said Margaret, "that I trust, that, in the whole course of your life, you will not suffer so great a degree of annoyance as you have inflicted on a large party of lovers of music this evening." This was said with the sweetest air, as if to a little child, and it was as good as a play to see the change of countenance which the young lady exhibited, who had no replication to make to so Christian a blessing.

On graver occasions, the same habit was only more stimulated; and I cannot remember certain passages which called it into play, without new regrets at the costly loss which our community sustains in the loss of this brave and eloquent soul.

People do not speak the truth, not for the want of not knowing and preferring it, but because they have not the organ to speak it adequately. It requires a clear sight, and, still more, a high spirit, to deal with falsehood in the decisive way. I have known several honest persons who valued truth as much as Peter and John, but, when they tried to speak it, *they* grew red and black in the face instead of Ananias, until, after a few attempts, they decided that aggressive truth was not their vocation, and confined themselves thenceforward to silent honesty, except on rare occasions, when either an extreme outrage, or a happier inspiration, loosened their tongue. But a soul is now and then incarnated, whom indulgent nature has not afflicted with any cramp or frost, but who can speak the right word at the right moment, qualify the selfish and hypocritical act with its real name, and

without any loss of serenity, hold up the offence to the
purest daylight. Such a truth-speaker is worth more
than the best police, and more than the laws or governors; for these do not always know their own side,
but will back the crime for want of this very truth-
speaker to expose them. That is the theory of the
newspaper, — to supersede official by intellectual influence. But, though the apostles establish the journal, it
usually happens that, by some strange oversight, Ananias
slips into the editor's chair. If, then, we could be provided with a fair proportion of truth-speakers, we could
very materially and usefully contract the legislative and
the executive functions. Still, the main sphere for this
nobleness is private society, where so many mischiefs go
unwhipped, being out of the cognizance of law, and
supposed to be nobody's business. And society is, at all
times, suffering for want of judges and headsmen, who
will mark and lop these malefactors.

Margaret suffered no vice to insult her presence, but
called the offender to instant account, when the law of
right or of beauty was violated. She needed not, of
course, to go out of her way to find the offender, and she
never did, but she had the courage and the skill to cut
heads off which were not worn with honor in her presence. Others might abet a crime by silence, if they
pleased; she chose to clear herself of all complicity, by
calling the act by its name.

It was curious to see the mysterious provocation which
the mere presence of insight exerts in its neighborhood.
Like moths about a lamp, her victims voluntarily came
to judgment: conscious persons, encumbered with egotism; vain persons, bent on concealing some mean vice;
arrogant reformers, with some halting of their own; the

compromisers, who wished to reconcile right and wrong;
— all came and held out their palms to the wise woman,
to read their fortunes, and they were truly told. Many
anecdotes have come to my ear, which show how useful the glare of her lamp proved in private circles, and
what dramatic situations it created. But these cannot
be told. The valor for dragging the accused spirits among
his acquaintance to the stake is not in the heart of the
present writer. The reader must be content to learn that
she knew how, without loss of temper, to speak with
unmistakable plainness to any party, when she felt that
the truth or the right was injured. For the same reason,
I omit one or two letters, most honorable both to her
mind and heart, in which she felt constrained to give the
frankest utterance to her displeasure. Yet I incline to
quote the testimony of one witness, which is so full and
so pointed, that I must give it as I find it.

"I have known her, by the severity of her truth, mow
down a crop of evil, like the angel of retribution itself,
and could not sufficiently admire her courage. A conversation she had with Mr. ——, just before he went to
Europe, was one of these things; and there was not a
particle of ill-will in it, but it was truth which she could
not help seeing and uttering, nor he refuse to accept.

"My friends told me of a similar verdict, pronounced
upon Mr. ——, at Paris, which they said was perfectly
tremendous. They themselves sat breathless; Mr. ——
was struck dumb; his eyes fixed on her with wonder
and amazement, yet gazing too with an attention which
seemed like fascination. When she had done, he still
looked to see if she was to say more, and when he found
she had really finished, he arose, took his hat, said
faintly, 'I thank you,' and left the room. He after-

wards said to Mr. ——, 'I never shall speak ill of her. She has done me good.' And this was the greater triumph, for this man had no theories of impersonality, and was the most egotistical and irritable of self-lovers, and was so unveracious, that one had to hope in charity that his organ for apprehending truth was deficient."

ECSTASY.

I have alluded to the fact, that, in the summer of 1840, Margaret underwent some change in the tone and the direction of her thoughts, to which she attributed a high importance. I remember, at an earlier period, when in earnest conversation with her, she seemed to have that height and daring, that I saw she was ready to do whatever she thought; and I observed that, with her literary riches, her invention and wit, her boundless fun and drollery, her light satire, and the most entertaining conversation in America, consisted a certain pathos of sentiment, and a march of character, threatening to arrive presently at the shores and plunge into the sea of Buddhism and mystical trances. The literature of asceticism and rapturous piety was familiar to her. The conversation of certain mystics, who had appeared in Boston about this time, had interested her, but in no commanding degree. But in this year, 1840, in which events occurred which combined great happiness and pain for her affections, she remained for some time in a sort of ecstatic solitude. She made many attempts to describe her frame of mind to me, but did not inspire me with confidence that she had now come to any experiences that were profound or permanent. She was vexed at the want of sympathy on my part, and I again felt that this craving for sympathy did not prove the inspiration. There was a certain restlessness and fever, which I did not like should deceive a soul which was capable of greatness. But jets of magnanimity were always natural to her; and her aspiring mind, eager for a higher and still a higher ground, made her gradually familiar with the range of the mystics, and, though never herself laid in the chamber called Peace, never quite authentically and originally speaking from the absolute or prophetic mount, yet she borrowed from her frequent visits to its precincts an occasional enthusiasm, which gave a religious dignity to her thought.

'I have plagues about me, but they don't touch me 'now. I thank nightly the benignant Spirit, for the un-'accustomed serenity in which it enfolds me.

'—— is very wretched; and once I could not have 'helped taking on me all his griefs, and through him the 'griefs of his class; but now I drink only the wormwood 'of the minute, and that has always equal parts,— a 'drop of sweet to a drop of bitter. But I shall never be 'callous, never unable to understand *home-sickness*. Am 'not I, too, one of the band who know not where to lay 'their heads? Am I wise enough to hear such things? 'Perhaps not; but happy enough, surely. For that 'Power which daily makes me understand the value of 'the little wheat amid the field of tares, and shows me 'how the kingdom of heaven is sown in the earth like a 'grain of mustard-seed, is good to me, and bids me call unhappiness happy.'

TO ——.

'*March*, 1842.— My inward life has been more rich

'and deep, and of more calm and musical flow than evei
'before. It seems to me that Heaven, whose course has
'ever been to cross-bias me, as Herbert said, is no niggard
'in its compensations. I have indeed been forced to take
'up old burdens, from which I thought I had learned what
'they could teach; the pen has been snatched from my
'hand just as I most longed to use it; I have been forced
'to dissipate, when I most wished to concentrate; to feel
'the hourly presence of others' mental wants, when, it
'seemed, I was just on the point of satisfying my own.
'But a new page is turned, and an era begun, from
'which I am not yet sufficiently remote to describe it as
'I would. I have lived a life, if only in the music I
'have heard, and one development seemed to follow
'another therein, as if bound together by destiny, and all
'things were done for me. All minds, all scenes, have
'ministered to me. Nature has seemed an ever-open
'secret; the Divine, a sheltering love; truth, an always-
'springing fountain; and my soul more alone, and less
'lonely, more hopeful, patient, · and, above all, more
'gentle and humble in its living. New minds have
'come to reveal themselves to me, though I do not wish
'it, for I feel myself inadequate to the ties already
'formed. I have not strength or time to meet the thoughts
'of those I love already. But these new have come
'with gifts too fair to be refused, and which have cheered
'my passive mind.'

'*June*, 1844. — Last night, in the boat, I could not
'help thinking, each has something, none has enough.
'I fear to want them all; and, through ages, if not
'forever, promises and beckons the life of reception,
'of renunciation. Passing every seven days from one

'region to the other, the maiden grows weary of *packing*
'*the trunk*, yet blesses Thee, O rich God!'

Her letters at this period betray a pathetic alternation
of feeling, between her aspiring for a rest in the absolute
Centre, and her necessity of a perfect sympathy with her
friends. She writes to one of them: —

'What I want, the word I crave, I do not expect
'to hear from the lips of man. I do not wish to be, I
'do not wish to have, a *mediator ;* yet I cannot help
'wishing, when I am with you, that some tones of the
'longed-for music could be vibrating in the air around
'us. But I will not be impatient again; for, though I
'am but as I am, I like not to feel the eyes I have loved
'averted.'

CONVERSATION.

I have separated and distributed as I could some of the
parts which blended in the rich composite energy which
Margaret exerted during the ten years over which my
occasional interviews with her were scattered. It remains
to say, that all these powers and accomplishments found
their best and only adequate channel in her conversation;
— a conversation which those who have heard it, unani-
mously, as far as I know, pronounced to be, in elegance,
in range, in flexibility, and adroit transition, in depth, in
cordiality, and in moral aim, altogether admirable; surprising and cheerful as a poem, and communicating its
own civility and elevation like a charm to all hearers.
She was here, among our anxious citizens, and frivolous
fashionists, as if sent to refine and polish her countrymen,

and announce a better day. She poured a stream of amber over the endless store of private anecdotes, of bosom histories, which her wonderful persuasion drew forth, and transfigured them into fine fables. Whilst she embellished the moment, her conversation had the merit of being solid and true. She put her whole character into it, and had the power to inspire. The companion was made a thinker, and went away quite other than he came. The circle of friends who sat with her were not allowed to remain spectators or players, but she converted them into heroes, if she could. The muse woke the muses, and the day grew bright and eventful. Of course, there must be, in a person of such sincerity, much variety of aspect, according to the character of her company. Only, in Margaret's case, there is almost an agreement in the testimony to an invariable power over the minds of all. I conversed lately with a gentleman who has vivid remembrances of his interviews with her in Boston, many years ago, who described her in these terms : — " No one ever came so near. Her mood applied itself to the mood of her companion, point to point, in the most limber, sinuous, vital way, and drew out the most extraordinary narratives; yet she had a light sort of laugh, when all was said, as if she thought she could live over that revelation. And this sufficient sympathy she had for all persons indifferently, — for lovers, for artists, and beautiful maids, and ambitious young statesmen, and for old aunts, and coach-travellers. Ah! she applied herself to the mood of her companion, as the sponge applies itself to water." The description tallies well enough with my observation. I remember she found, one day, at my house, her old friend Mr. ——, sitting with me. She looked at him attentively, and hardly seemed to know him. In the afternoon, he invited her to go with him to Cambridge. The next day she said to me, 'You fancy that you know ———. It is 'too absurd; you have never seen him. When I found 'him here, sitting like a statue, I was alarmed, and 'thought him ill. You sit with courteous, *un*confiding 'smile, and suppose him to be a mere man of talent. 'He is so with you. But the moment I was alone with 'him, he was another creature; his manner, so glassy 'and elaborate before, was full of soul, and the tones of 'his voice entirely different.' And I have no doubt that she saw expressions, heard tones, and received thoughts from her companions, which no one else ever saw or heard from the same parties, and that her praise of her friends, which seemed exaggerated, was her exact impression. We were all obliged to recall Margaret's testimony, when we found we were sad blockheads to other people.

I find among her letters many proofs of this power of disposing equally the hardest and the most sensitive people to open their hearts, on very short acquaintance. Any casual rencontre, in a walk, in a steamboat, at a concert, became the prelude to unwonted confidences.

1843.—'I believe I told you about one new man, a 'Philistine, at Brook Farm. He reproved me, as such 'people are wont, for my little faith. At the end of the 'first meeting in the hall, he seemed to me perfectly 'hampered in his old ways and technics, and I thought 'he would not open his mind to the views of others for 'years, if ever. After I wrote, we had a second meet-'ing, by request, on personal relations; at the end of 'which, he came to me, and expressed delight, and a

'feeling of new light and life, in terms whose modesty
'might have done honor to the wisest.'

'This afternoon we met Mr. —— in his wood; and
'he sat down and told us the story of his life, his court-
'ship, and painted the portraits of his father and mother
'with most amusing naïveté. He says: — "How do you
'"think I offered myself? I never had told Miss ——
'"that I loved her; never told her she was handsome;
'"and I went to her, and said, 'Miss ——, I've come to
'"offer myself; but first I'll give you my character.
'"I'm very poor; you'll have to work: I'm very
'"cross and irascible; you'll have everything to bear:
'"and I've liked many other pretty girls. Now what
'"do you say?' and she said, 'I'll have you:' and
'"she's been everything to me.

'"My mother was a Calvinist, very strict, but she was
'"always reading 'Abelard and Eloisa,' and crying over
'"it. At sixteen, I said to her: 'Mother, you've brought
'"me up well; you've kept me strict. Why don't I feel
'"that regeneration they talk of? why an't I one of
'"the elect?' And she talked to me about the potter
'"using his clay as he pleased; and I said: 'Mother, God
'"is not a potter: He's a perfect being; and he can't
'"treat the vessels he makes, anyhow, but with perfect
'"justice, or he's no God. So I'm no Calvinist.'"'

Here is a very different picture: —

'—— has infinite grace and shading in her character:
'a springing and tender fancy, a Madonna depth of
'meditative softness, and a purity which has been
'unstained, and keeps her dignified even in the most

'unfavorable circumstances. She was born for the love
'and ornament of life. I can scarcely forbear weeping
'sometimes, when I look on her, and think what happi-
'ness and beauty she might have conferred. She is as
'yet all unconscious of herself, and she rather dreads
'being with me, because I make her too conscious. She
'was on the point, at ——, of telling me all she knew
'of herself; but I saw she dreaded, while she wished,
'that I should give a local habitation and a name to what
'lay undefined, floating before her, the phantom of her
'destiny; or rather lead her to give it, for she always
'approaches a tragical clearness when talking with me.'

'—— has been to see us. But it serves not to know
'such a person, who perpetually defaces the high by
'such strange mingling with the low. It certainly is
'not pleasant to hear of God and Miss Biddeford in a
'breath. To me, this hasty attempt at skimming from
'the deeps of theosophy is as unpleasant as the rude
'vanity of reformers. Dear Beauty! where, where,
'amid these morasses and pine barrens, shall we make
'thee a temple? where find a Greek to guard it, — clear-
'eyed, deep-thoughted, and delicate enough to appreciate
'the relations and gradations which nature always ob-
'serves?'

An acute and illuminated woman, who, in this age
of indifferentism, holds on with both hands to the creed
of the Pilgrims, writes of Margaret, whom she saw but
once : — "She looked very sensible, but as if contending
with ill health and duties. She lay, all the day and
evening, on the sofa, and catechized me, who told my
literal traditions, like any old bobbin-woman."

I add the testimony of a man of letters, and most competent observer, who had, for a long time, opportunities of daily intercourse with her : —

"When I knew Margaret, I was so young, and perhaps too much disposed to meet people on my own ground, that I may not be able to do justice to her. Her nature was so large and receptive, so sympathetic with youth and genius, so aspiring, and withal so womanly in her understanding, that she made her companion think more of himself, and of a common life, than of herself. She was a companion as few others, if indeed any one, have been. Her heart was underneath her intellectualness, her mind was reverent, her spirit devout; a thinker without dryness; a scholar without pedantry. She could appreciate the finest thoughts, and knew the rich soil and large fields of beauty that made the little vase of otto. With her unusual wisdom and religious spirit, she seemed like the priestess of the youth, opening to him the fields of nature; but she was more than a priestess, a companion also. As I recall her image, I think she may have been too intellectual, and too conscious of intellectual relation, so that she was not sufficiently self-centred on her own personality; and hence something of a duality : but I may not be correct in this impression."

CONVERSATIONS IN BOSTON.

BY R. W. EMERSON.

"Do not scold me ; they are guests of my eyes. Do not frown, — they want no bread ; they are guests of my words."

TARTAR ECLOGUES

V.

CONVERSATIONS IN BOSTON.

In the year 1839, Margaret removed from Groton, and, with her mother and family, took a house at Jamaica Plain, five miles from Boston. In November of the next year the family removed to Cambridge, and rented a house there, near their old home. In 1841, Margaret took rooms for the winter in town, retaining still the house in Cambridge. And from the day of leaving Groton, until the autumn of 1844, when she removed to New York, she resided in Boston, or its immediate vicinity. Boston was her social centre. There were the libraries, galleries, and concerts which she loved; there were her pupils and her friends; and there were her tasks, and the openings of a new career.

I have vaguely designated some of the friends with whom she was on terms of intimacy at the time when I was first acquainted with her. But the range of her talents required an equal compass in her society; and she gradually added a multitude of names to the list. She knew already all the active minds at Cambridge; and has left a record of one good interview she had with

Allston. She now became intimate with Doctor Channing, and interested him to that point in some of her
studies, that, at his request, she undertook to render
some selections of German philosophy into English for
him. But I believe this attempt was soon abandoned.
She found a valuable friend in the late Miss Mary
Rotch, of New Bedford, a woman of great strength of
mind, connected with the Quakers not less by temperament than by birth, and possessing the best lights of that
once spiritual sect. At Newport, Margaret had made
the acquaintance of an elegant scholar, in Mr. Calvert,
of Maryland. In Providence, she had won, as by conquest, such a homage of attachment, from young and
old, that her arrival there, one day, on her return from
a visit to Bristol, was a kind of ovation. In Boston,
she knew people of every class, — merchants, politicians,
scholars, artists,' women, the migratory genius, and
the rooted capitalist, — and, amongst all, many excellent people, who were every day passing, by new
opportunities, conversations, and kind offices, into the
sacred circle of friends. The late Miss Susan Burley
had many points of attraction for her, not only in her
elegant studies, but also in the deep interest which that
lady took in securing the highest culture for women.
She was very well read, and, avoiding abstractions,
knew how to help herself with examples and facts. A
friendship that proved of great importance to the next
years was that established with Mr. George Ripley; an
accurate scholar, a man of character, and of eminent
powers of conversation, and already then deeply engaged
in plans of an expansive practical bearing, of which the
first fruit was the little community which flourished for
a few years at Brook Farm. Margaret presently became

connected with him in literary labors, and, as long as she remained in this vicinity, kept up her habits of intimacy with the colonists of Brook Farm. At West-Roxbury, too, she knew and prized the heroic heart, the learning and wit of Theodore Parker, whose literary aid was, subsequently, of the first importance to her. She had an acquaintance, for many years, — subject, no doubt, to alternations of sun and shade, — with Mr. Alcott. There was much antagonism in their habitual views, but each learned to respect the genius of the other. She had more sympathy with Mr. Alcott's English friend, Charles Lane, an ingenious mystic, and bold experimenter in practical reforms, whose dexterity and temper in debate she frankly admired, whilst his asceticism engaged her reverence. Neither could some marked difference of temperament remove her from the beneficent influences of Miss Elizabeth Peabody, who, by her constitutional hospitality to excellence, whether mental or moral, has made her modest abode for so many years the inevitable resort of studious feet, and a private theatre for the exposition of every question of letters, of philosophy, of ethics, and of art.

The events in Margaret's life, up to the year 1840, were few, and not of that dramatic interest which readers love. Of the few events of her bright and blameless years, how many are private, and must remain so. In reciting the story of an affectionate and passionate woman, the voice lowers itself to a whisper, and becomes inaudible. A woman in our society finds her safety and happiness in exclusions and privacies. She congratulates herself when she is not called to the market, to the courts, to the polls, to the stage, or to the orchestra. Only the most extraordinary genius can make the career of an artist secure and agreeable to her. Prescriptions almost invincible the female lecturer or professor of any science must encounter; and, except on points where the charities which are left to women as their legitimate province interpose against the ferocity of laws, with us a female politician is unknown. Perhaps this fact, which so dangerously narrows the career of a woman, accuses the tardiness of our civility, and many signs show that a revolution is already on foot.

Margaret had no love of notoriety, or taste for eccentricity, to goad her, and no weak fear of either. Willingly she was confined to the usual circles and methods of female talent. She had no false shame. Any task that called out her powers was good and desirable. She wished to live by her strength. She could converse, and teach, and write. She took private classes of pupils at her own house. She organized, with great success, a school for young ladies at Providence, and gave four hours a day to it, during two years. She translated Eckermann's Conversations with Goethe, and published in 1839. In 1841, she translated the Letters of Gunderode and Bettine, and published them as far as the sale warranted the work. In 1843, she made a tour to Lake Superior and to Michigan, and published an agreeable narrative of it, called "Summer on the Lakes."

Apparently a more pretending, but really also a private and friendly service, she edited the "Dial," a quarterly journal, for two years from its first publication in 1840. She was eagerly solicited to undertake the charge of this work, which, when it began, concentrated a good deal of hope and affection. It had its origin in a club of speculative students, who found the air in America getting a little close and stagnant; and the agitation had perhaps the fault of being too secondary or bookish in its origin, or caught not from primary instincts, but from English, and still more from German books. The journal was commenced with much hope, and liberal promises of many coöperators. But the workmen of sufficient culture for a poetical and philosophical magazine were too few; and, as the pages were filled by unpaid contributors, each of whom had, according to the usage and necessity of this country, some paying employment, the journal did not get his best work, but his second best. Its scattered writers had not digested their theories into a distinct dogma, still less into a practical measure which the public could grasp; and the magazine was so eclectic and miscellaneous, that each of its readers and writers valued only a small portion of it. For these reasons it never had a large circulation, and it was discontinued after four years. But the Dial betrayed, through all its juvenility, timidity, and conventional rubbish, some sparks of the true love and hope, and of the piety to spiritual law, which had moved its friends and founders, and it was received by its early subscribers with almost a religious welcome. Many years after it was brought to a close, Margaret was surprised in England by very warm testimony to its merits; and, in 1848, the writer of these pages found it holding the same affectionate place in many a private bookshelf in England and Scotland, which it had secured at home. Good or bad, it cost a good deal of precious labor from those who served it, and from Margaret most of all. As editor, she received a compensation for the first years, which was intended to be two hundred dollars *per annum*, but which, I fear, never reached even that amount.

But it made no difference to her exertion. She put so

much heart into it that she bravely undertook to open, in
the Dial, the subjects which most attracted her; and she
treated, in turn, Goethe, and Beethoven, the Rhine and
the Romaic Ballads, the Poems of John Sterling, and
several pieces of sentiment, with a spirit which spared
no labor; and, when the hard conditions of journalism held
her to an inevitable day, she submitted to jeopardizing a
long-cherished subject, by treating it in the crude and
forced article for the month. I remember, after she had
been compelled by ill health to relinquish the journal into
my hands, my grateful wonder at the facility with which
she assumed the preparation of laborious articles, that
might have daunted the most practised scribe.

But in book or journal she found a very imperfect
expression of herself, and it was the more vexatious,
because she was accustomed to the clearest and fullest.
When, therefore, she had to choose an employment that
should pay money, she consulted her own genius, as well
as the wishes of a multitude of friends, in opening a class
for conversation. In the autumn of 1839, she addressed
the following letter, intended for circulation, to Mrs.
George Ripley, in which her general design was stated: —

'My dear friend: — The advantages of a weekly
'meeting, for conversation, might be great enough to
'repay the trouble of attendance, if they consisted only
'in supplying a point of union to well-educated and
'thinking women, in a city which, with great preten-
'sions to mental refinement, boasts, at present, nothing
'of the kind, and where I have heard many, of mature
'age, wish for some such means of stimulus and cheer,
'and those younger, for a place where they could state
'their doubts and difficulties, with a hope of gaining

'aid from the experience or aspirations of others. And
'if my office were only to suggest topics, which would
'lead to conversation of a better order than is usual at
'social meetings, and to turn back the current when
'digressing into personalities or common-places, so that
'what is valuable in the experience of each might be
'brought to bear upon all, I should think the object not
'unworthy of the effort.

'But my ambition goes much further. It is to pass
'in review the departments of thought and knowl-
'edge, and endeavor to place them in due relation to
'one another in our minds. To systematize thought,
'and give a precision and clearness in which our sex
'are so deficient, chiefly, I think, because they have
'so few inducements to test and classify what they
'receive. To ascertain what pursuits are best suited to
'us, in our time and state of society, and how we may
'make best use of our means for building up the life of
'thought upon the life of action.

'Could a circle be assembled in earnest, desirous to
'answer the questions, — What were we born to do?
'and how shall we do it? — which so few ever propose
'to themselves till their best years are gone by, I should
'think the undertaking a noble one, and, if my resources
'should prove sufficient to make me its moving spring,
'I should be willing to give to it a large portion of
'those coming years, which will, as I hope, be my best.
'I look upon it with no blind enthusiasm, nor unlim-
'ited faith, but with a confidence that I have attained
'a distinct perception of means, which, if there are per-
'sons competent to direct them, can supply a great want,
'and promote really high objects. So far as I have tried
'them yet, hey have met with success so much beyond

'my hopes, that my faith will not easily be shaken, not
'my earnestness chilled. Should I, however, be disap-
'pointed in Boston, I could hardly hope that such a
'plan could be brought to bear on general society, in
'any other city of the United States. But I do not
'fear, if a good beginning can be made. I am confi-
'dent that twenty persons cannot be brought together
'from better motives than vanity or pedantry, to talk
'upon such subjects as we propose, without finding in
'themselves great deficiencies, which they will be very
'desirous to supply.

'Should the enterprise fail, it will be either from
'incompetence in me, or that sort of vanity in them
'which wears the garb of modesty. On the first of these
'points, I need not speak. I cannot be supposed to have
'felt so much the wants of others, without feeling my
'own still more deeply. And, from the depth of this
'feeling, and the earnestness it gave, such power as I
'have yet exerted has come. Of course, those who are
'inclined to meet me, feel a confidence in me, and
'should they be disappointed, I shall regret it not solely
'or most on my own account. I have not given my
'gauge without measuring my capacity to sustain defeat.
'For the other, I know it is very hard to lay aside the
'shelter of vague generalities, the art of coterie criticism,
'and the "delicate disdains" of *good society*, and fear-
'lessly meet the light, even though it flow from the sun
'of truth. Yet, as, without such generous courage,
'nothing of value can be learned or done, I hope to
'see many capable of it; willing that others should
'think their sayings crude, shallow, or tasteless, if, by
'such unpleasant means, they may attain real health

and vigor, which need no aid from rouge or candle-light, to brave the light of the world.

'Since I saw you, I have been told of persons who 'are desirous to join the class, "if only they need not '"talk." I am so sure that the success of the whole 'depends on conversation being general, that I do not ' wish any one to come, who does not intend, if possible, 'to take an active part. No one will be forced, but 'those who do not talk will not derive the same advan-'tages with those who openly state their impressions, 'and can consent to have it known that they learn by 'blundering, as is the destiny of man here below. And 'general silence, or side talks, would paralyze me. I 'should feel coarse and misplaced, were I to harangue 'over-much. In former instances, I have been able to 'make it easy and even pleasant, to twenty-five out of 'thirty, to bear their part, to question, to define, to state, 'and examine opinions. If I could not do as much now, 'I should consider myself as unsuccessful, and should 'withdraw. But I shall expect communication to be ' effected by degrees, and to do a great deal myself at 'the first meetings. My method has been to open a subject, — for instance, Poetry, as expressed in —

'External Nature;

'The life of man;

'Literature;

'The fine arts;

· or, The history of a nation to be studied in —

'Its religious and civil institutions

'Its literature and arts;

'The characters of its great men;

'and, after as good a general statement as I know 'how to make, select a branch of the subject, and lead

'others to give their thoughts upon it. When they have
'not been successful in verbal utterance of their thoughts,
'I have asked them to attempt it in writing. At the
'next meeting, I would read these "skarts of pen and
'"ink" aloud, and canvass their adequacy, without
'mentioning the names of the writers. I found this less
'necessary, as I proceeded, and my companions attained
'greater command both of thought and language; but
'for a time it was useful, and may be now. Great ad-
'vantage in point of discipline may be derived from even
'this limited use of the pen.

'I do not wish, at present, to pledge myself to any
'course of subjects. Generally, I may say, they will
'be such as literature and the arts present in endless
'profusion. Should a class be brought together, I should
'wish, first, to ascertain our common ground, and, in the
'course of a few meetings, should see whether it be prac-
'ticable to follow out the design in my mind, which, as
'yet, would look too grand on paper.

'Let us see whether there will be any organ, before
'noting down the music to which it may give breath.'

Accordingly, a class of ladies assembled at Miss Peabody's rooms, in West Street, on the 6th November,
1839. Twenty-five were present, and the circle com-
prised some of the most agreeable and intelligent
women to be found in Boston and its neighborhood.
The following brief report of this first day's meeting
remains: —

"Miss Fuller enlarged, in her introductory conversation, on the topics which she touched in her letter to
Mrs. Ripley.

'Women are now taught, at school, all that men are
'they run over, superficially, even *more* studies, without
'being really taught anything. When they come to the
'business of life, they find themselves inferior, and all
'their studies have not given them that practical good
'sense, and mother wisdom, and wit, which grew up
'with our grandmothers at the spinning-wheel. But,
'with this difference; men are called on, from a very
'early period, to reproduce all that they learn Their
'college exercises, their political duties, their professional
'studies, the first actions of life in any direction, call on
'them to put to use what they have learned. But
'women learn without any attempt to reproduce. Their
'only reproduction is for purposes of display.

'It is to supply this defect,' Miss Fuller said, 'that
'these conversations have been planned. She was not
'here to teach; but she had had some experience in the
'management of such a conversation as was now pro-
'posed; she meant to give her view on each subject, and
'provoke the thoughts of others.

'It would be best to take subjects on which we know
'words, and have vague impressions, and compel our-
'selves to define those words. We should have, proba-
'bly, mortifications to suffer; but we should be encour-
'aged by the rapid gain that comes from making a
'simple and earnest effort for expression.'

Miss Fuller had proposed the Grecian Mythology as
the subject of the first conversations, and now gave her
reasons for the choice. 'It is quite separated from all
'exciting local subjects. It is serious, without being sol-
'emn, and without excluding any mode of intellectual
'action; it is playful, as well as deep. It is sufficiently
'wide, for it is a complete expression of the cultivation

'of a nation. It is objective and tangible. It is, also
'generally known, and associated with all our ideas of
'the arts.

'It originated in the eye of the Greek. He lived
'out of doors: his climate was genial, his senses were
'adapted to it. He was vivacious and intellectual, and
'personified all he beheld. He *saw* the oreads, naiads,
'nereids. Their forms, as poets and painters give them,
'are the very lines of nature humanized, as the child's
'eye sees faces in the embers or in the clouds.

'Other forms of the mythology, as Jupiter, Juno,
'Apollo, are great instincts, or ideas, or facts of the
'internal constitution, separated and personified.'

After exhibiting their enviable mental health, and
rebutting the cavils of some of the speakers, — who
could not bear, in Christian times, by Christian ladies,
that heathen Greeks should be envied, — Miss Fuller
declared, 'that she had no desire to go back, and believed
'we have the elements of a deeper civilization; yet, the
'Christian was in its infancy; the Greek in its maturity;
'nor could she look on the expression of a great nation's
'intellect, as insignificant. These fables of the Gods
'were the result of the universal sentiments of religion,
'aspiration, intellectual action, of a people, whose politi-
'cal and æsthetic life had become immortal; and we
'must leave off despising, if we would begin to learn.' "

The reporter closes her account by saying: — "Miss
Fuller's thoughts were much illustrated, and all was
said with the most captivating address and grace, and
with beautiful modesty. The position in which she
placed herself with respect to the rest, was entirely lady-
like, and companionable. She told what she intended,

the earnest purpose with which she came, and, with great tact, indicated the indiscretions that might spoi the meeting."

Here is Margaret's own account of the first days.

'*25th Nov.*, 1839. — My class is prosperous. I was so 'fortunate as to rouse, at once, the tone of simple earnest-'ness, which can scarcely, when once awakened, cease to 'vibrate. All seem in a glow, and quite as receptive as I 'wish. They question and examine, yet follow leadings; 'and thoughts, not opinions, have ruled the hour every 'time. There are about twenty-five members, and every 'one, I believe, full of interest. The first time, ten took 'part in the conversation; the last, still more. Mrs '———— came out in a way that surprised me. She 'seems to have shaken off a wonderful number of films. 'She showed pure vision, sweet sincerity, and much tal-'ent. Mrs. ——— ——— keeps us in good order, and takes 'care that Christianity and morality are not forgotten. ' The first day's topic was, the genealogy of heaven and 'earth; then the Will, (Jupiter); the Understanding, '(Mercury): the second day's, the celestial inspiration 'of genius, perception and transmission of divine law, '(Apollo); the terrene inspiration, the impassioned aban-'donment of genius, (Bacchus). Of the thunderbolt, 'the caduceus, the ray, and the grape, having disposed 'as well as might be, we came to the wave, and the 'sea-shell it moulds to Beauty, and Love her parent 'and her child.

'I assure you, there is more Greek than Bostonian

'spoken at the meetings; and we may have pure honey
'of Hymettus to give you yet.'

To another friend she wrote : —

'The circle I meet interests me. So even devoutly
'thoughtful seems their spirit, that, from the very first,
'I took my proper place, and never had the feeling I
'dreaded, of display, of a paid Corinne. I feel as I
'would, truly a teacher and a guide. All are intelli-
'gent; five or six have talent. But I am never driven
'home for ammunition; never put to-any expense;
'never truly called out. What I have is always
'enough; though I feel how superficially I am treat-
'ing my subject.'

Here is an extract from the letter of a lady, who
joined the class, for the first time, at the eighth meeting, to her friend in New Haven : —

"Christmas made a holiday for Miss Fuller's class,
but it met on Saturday, at noon. As I sat there, my
heart overflowed with joy at the sight of the bright
circle, and I longed to have you by my side, for I know
not where to look for so much character, culture, and
so much love of truth and beauty, in any other circle of
women and girls. The names and faces would not
mean so much to you as to me, who have seen more
of the lives, of which they are the sign. Margaret,
beautifully dressed, (don't despise that, for it made a
fine picture,) presided with more dignity and grace than
I had thought possible. The subject was Beauty. Each
had written her definition, and Margaret began with

reading her own. This called forth questions, comments, and illustrations, on all sides. The style and manner, of course, in this age, are different, but the question, the high point from which it was considered, and the earnestness and simplicity of the discussion, as well as the gifts and graces of the speakers, gave it the charm of a Platonic dialogue. There was no pretension or pedantry in a word that was said. The tone of remark and question was simple as that of children in a school class; and, I believe, every one was gratified."

The conversations thus opened proceeded with spirit and success. Under the mythological forms, room was found for opening all the great questions, on which Margaret and her friends wished to converse. Prometheus was made the type of Pure Reason; Jupiter, of Will; Juno, the passive side of the same, or Obstinacy; Minerva, Intellectual Power, Practical Reason; Mercury, Executive Power, Understanding; Apollo was Genius, the Sun; Bacchus was Geniality, the Earth's answer. "Apollo and Bacchus were contrasted," says the reporter. " Margaret unfolded her idea of Bacchus. His whole life was triumph. Born from fire; a divine frenzy; the answer of the earth to the sun, — of the warmth of joy to the light of genius. He is beautiful, also; not severe in youthful beauty, like Apollo; but exuberant, — liable to excess. She spoke of the fables of his destroying Pentheus, &c., and suggested the interpretations. This Bacchus was found in Scripture. The Indian Bacchus is glowing; he is the genial apprehensive power; the glow of existence; mere joy."

Venus was Grecian womanhood, instinctive; Diana, chastity; Mars, Grecian manhood, instinctive. Venus made the name for a conversation on Beauty, which was extended through four meetings, as it brought in irresistibly the related topics of poetry, genius, and taste. Neptune was Circumstance; Pluto, the Abyss, the Undeveloped; Pan, the glow and sportiveness and music of Nature; Ceres, the productive power of Nature; Proserpine, the Phenomenon.

Under the head of Venus, in the fifth conversation, the story of Cupid and Psyche was told with fitting beauty, by Margaret; and many fine conjectural interpretations suggested from all parts of the room. The ninth conversation turned on the distinctive qualities of poetry, discriminating it from the other fine arts. Rhythm and Imagery, it was agreed, were distinctive. An episode to dancing, which the conversation took, led Miss Fuller to give the thought that lies at the bottom of different dances. Of her lively description the following record is preserved : —

'Gavottes, shawl dances, and all of that kind, are 'intended merely to exhibit the figure in as many atti- 'tudes as possible. They have no character, and say 'nothing, except, Look! how graceful I am!

'The minuet is conjugal; but the wedlock is chiv- 'alric. Even so would Amadis wind slow, stately, 'calm, through the mazes of life, with Oriana, when he 'had made obeisances enough to win her for a partner.

'English, German, Swiss, French, and Spanish 'dances all express the same things, though in very 'different ways. Love and its life are still the theme.

'In the English country dance, the pair who have 'chosen one another, submit decorously to the restraints 'of courtship and frequent separations, cross hands,

'four go round, down outside, in the most earnest,
'lively, complacent fashion. If they join hands to go
'down the middle, and exhibit their union to all spec-
'tators, they part almost as soon as meet, and disdain
'not to give hands right and left to the most indifferent
'persons, like marriage in its daily routine.

'In the Swiss, the man pursues, stamping with
'energy, marking the time by exulting flings, or snap-
'ping of the fingers, in delighted confidence of succeed-
'ing at last; but the maiden coyly, demurely, foots it
'round, yet never gets out of the way, intending to be
won.

'The German asks his *madchen* if she will, with
'him, for an hour forget the cares and common-places
'of life in a tumult of rapturous sympathy, and she
'smiles with Saxon modesty her *Ja*. He sustains her in
'his arms; the music begins. At first, in willing mazes
'they calmly imitate the planetary orbs, but the melodies
'flow quicker, their accordant hearts beat higher, and
'they whirl at last into giddy raptures, and dizzy evolu-
'tions, which steal from life its free-will and self-collec-
'tion, till nothing is left but mere sensation.

'The French couple are somewhat engaged with one
'another, but almost equally so with the world around
'them. They think it well to vary existence with plenty
'of coquetry and display. First, the graceful rever-
'ence to one another, then to their neighbors. Exhibit
'your grace in the *chassé*, — made apparently solely for
'the purpose of *déchasséing*, — then civil intimacy be-
'tween the ladies, in *la chaine*, then a decorous prom-
'enade of partners, then right and left with all the world,
and balance, &c. The quadrille also offers opportunity
'for talk. Looks and sympathetic motions are not

'enough for our Parisian friends, unless eked out by
'words.

'The impassioned bolero and fandango are the dances
'for me. They are not merely loving, but living; they
'express the sweet Southern ecstasy at the mere gift of
'existence. These persons are together, they live, they
'are beautiful; how can they say this in sufficiently
'plain terms? — I love, I live, I am beautiful! — I put
'on my festal dress to do honor to my happiness; I
'shake my castanets, that my hands, too, may be busy;
'I *felice, — felicissima!*'

This first series of conversations extended to thirteen,
the class meeting once a week at noon, and remaining
together for two hours. The class were happy, and the
interest increased. A new series of thirteen more weeks
followed, and the general subject of the new course was
"the Fine Arts." A few fragmentary notes only of these
hours have been shown me, but all those who bore any
part in them testify to their entire success. A very
competent witness has given me some interesting particulars : —

"Margaret used to come to the conversations very well
dressed, and, altogether, looked sumptuously. She began
them with an exordium, in which she gave her leading
views; and those exordiums were excellent, from the elevation of the tone, the ease and flow of discourse, and
from the tact with which they were kept aloof from any
excess, and from the gracefulness with which they were
brought down, at last, to a possible level for others to
follow. She made a pause, and invited the others to
come in. Of course, it was not easy for every one to
venture her remark, after an eloquent discourse and in

the presence of twenty superior women, who were all inspired. But whatever was said, Margaret knew how to seize the good meaning of it with hospitality, and to make the speaker feel glad, and not sorry, that she had spoken. She showed herself thereby fit to preside at such meetings, and imparted to the susceptible a wonderful reliance on her genius."

In her writing she was prone to spin her sentences without a sure guidance, and beyond the sympathy of her reader. But in discourse, she was quick, conscious of power, in perfect tune with her company, and would pause and turn the stream with grace and adroitness, and with so much spirit, that her face beamed, and the young people came away delighted, among other things, with "her beautiful looks." When she was intellectually excited, or in high animal spirits, as often happened, all deformity of features was dissolved in the power of the expression. So I interpret this repeated story of sumptuousness of dress, that this appearance, like her reported beauty, was simply an effect of a general impression of magnificence made by her genius, and mistakenly attributed to some external elegance; for I have been told by her most intimate friend, who knew every particular of her conduct at that time, that there was nothing of special expense or splendor in her toilette.

The effect of the winter's work was happiest. Margaret was made intimately known to many excellent persons.* In this company of matrons and maids, many tender spirits had been set in ferment. A new day had

---

* A friend has furnished me with the names of so many of the ladies as she recollects to have met, at one or another time, at these classes. Some of them were perhaps only occasional members. The list recalls how much talent, beauty, and worth were at that time constellated here : —

dawned for them; new thoughts had opened; the secret of life was shown, or, at least, that life had a secret. They could not forget what they had heard, and what they had been surprised into saying. A true refinement had begun to work in many who had been slaves to trifles. They went home thoughtful and happy, since the steady elevation of Margaret's aim had infused a certain unexpected greatness of tone into the conversation. It was, I believe, only an expression of the feeling of the class, the remark made, perhaps at the next year's course, by a lady of eminent powers, previously by no means partial to Margaret, and who expressed her frank admiration on leaving the house : — " I never heard, read of, or imagined a conversation at all equal to this we have now heard."

The strongest wishes were expressed, on all sides, that the conversations should be renewed at the beginning of the following winter. Margaret willingly consented; but, as I have already intimated, in the summer and autumn of 1840, she had retreated to some interior shrine, and believed that she came into life and society with some advantage from this devotion.

Of this feeling the new discussion bore evident traces.

Mrs. George Bancroft, Mrs. Barlow, Miss Burley, Mrs. L. M. Child, Miss Mary Channing, Miss Sarah Clarke, Mrs. E. P. Clark, Miss Dorr, Mrs. Edwards, Mrs. R. W. Emerson, Mrs. Farrar, Miss S. J. Gardiner, Mrs. R. W. Hooper, Mrs. S. Hooper, Miss Haliburton, Miss Howes, Miss E. Hoar, Miss Marianne Jackson, Mrs. T. Lee, Miss Littlehale, Mrs. E. G. Loring, Mrs. Mack, Mrs. Horace Mann, Mrs. Newcomb, Mrs. Theodore Parker, Miss E. P. Peabody, Miss S. Peabody, Mrs. S. Putnam, Mrs. Phillips, Mrs. Josiah Quincy, Miss B. Randall, Mrs. Samuel Ripley, Mrs. George Ripley, Mrs. George Russell, Miss Ida Russell, Mrs. Frank Shaw, Miss Anna B. Shaw, Miss Caroline Sturgis, Miss Tuckerman, Miss Maria White, Mrs. S. G. Ward, Miss Mary Ward, Mrs. W. Whiting.

Most of the last year's class returned, and new members gave in their names. The first meeting was holden on the twenty-second of November, 1840. By all accounts it was the best of all her days. I have again the notes, taken at the time, of the excellent lady at whose house it was held, to furnish the following sketch of the first and the following meetings. I preface these notes by an extract from a letter of Margaret.

TO W. H. C.

'*Sunday, Nov. 8th*, 1840. — On Wednesday I opened
' with my class. It was a noble meeting. I told them
' the great changes in my mind, and that I could not be
' sure they would be satisfied with me now, as they were
' when I was in deliberate possession of myself. I tried
' to convey the truth, and though I did not arrive at
' any full expression of it, they all, with glistening eyes,
' seemed melted into one love. Our relation is now per-
' fectly true, and I do not think they will ever interrupt
' me. —— sat beside me, all glowing; and the moment
' I had finished, she began to speak. She told me after-
' wards, she was all kindled, and none there could be
' strangers to her more. I was really delighted by the
' enthusiasm of Mrs. ——. I did not expect it. All
' her best self seemed called up, and she feels that these
' meetings will be her highest pleasure. ——, too, was
' most beautiful. I went home with Mrs. F., and had a
' long attack of nervous headache. She attended anx-
' iously on me, and asked if it would be so all winter.
' I said, if it were I did not care; and truly I feel just
' now such a separation from pain and illness, — such
' a consciousness of true life, while suffering most, —

'that pain has no effect but to steal some of my
' time.'

CONVERSATIONS ON THE FINE ARTS.

" Miss Fuller's fifth conversation was pretty much a
monologue of her own. The company collected proved
much larger than any of us had anticipated: a chosen
company, — several persons from homes out of town, at
considerable inconvenience; and, in one or two instances,
fresh from extreme experiences of joy and grief, — which
Margaret felt a very grateful tribute to her. She knew
no one came for experiment, but all in earnest love and
trust, and was moved by it quite to the heart, which
threw an indescribable charm of softness over her brilliancy. It is sometimes said, that women never are so
lovely and enchanting in the company of their own sex,
merely, but it requires the other to draw them out.
Certain it is that Margaret never appears, when I see
her, either so brilliant and deep in thought, or so desirous to please, or so modest, or so heart-touching, as in
this very party. Well, she began to say how gratifying it was to her to see so many come, because all
knew why they came, — that it was to learn from
each other and ourselves the highest ends of life, where
there could be no excitements and gratifications of personal ambition, &c. She spoke of herself, and said she
felt she had undergone changes in her own mind since
the last winter, as doubtless we all felt we had done;
that she was conscious of looking at all things less objec-
tively, — more from the law with which she identified
herself. This, she stated, was the natural progress of
our individual being, when we did not hinder its devel-

ɔpment, to advance from objects to law, from the circumference of being, where we found ourselves at our
birth, to the centre.

" This advance was enacted poesy. We could not, in
our individual lives, amid the disturbing influences of
other wills, which had as much right to their own action
as we to ours, enact poetry entirely ; the discordant, the
inferior, the prose, would intrude, but we should always
keep in mind that poetry of life was not something aside,
— a path that might or might not be trod, — it was the
only path of the true soul; and prose you may call the
deviation. We might not always be poetic in life, but
we might and should be poetic in our thought and intention. The fine arts were one compensation for the
necessary prose of life. The man who could not write
his thought of beauty in his life, — the materials of
whose life would not work up into poetry, — wrote it in
stone, drew it on canvas, breathed it in music, or built it
in lofty rhyme. In this statement, however, she guarded
her meaning, and said that to seek beauty was to miss
it often. We should only seek to live as harmoniously
with the great laws as our social and other duties permitted, and solace ourselves with poetry and the fine
arts."

I find a further record by the same friendly scribe,
which seems a second and enlarged account of the
introductory conversation, or else a sketch of the course
of thought which ran through several meetings, and
which very naturally repeated occasionally the same
thoughts. I give it as I find it : —

"She then recurred to the last year's conversations

and, first, the Grecian mythologies, which she looked at
as symbolical of a deeper intellectual and æsthetic life
than we were wont to esteem it, when looking at it from
a narrow religious point of view. We had merely
skimmed along the deeper study. She spoke of the
conversations on the different part played by Inspiration and Will in the works of man, and stated the
different views of inspiration, — how some had felt
it was merely perception; others apprehended it as
influx upon the soul from the soul-side of its being.
Then she spoke of the conversation upon poesy as the
ground of all the fine arts, and also of the true art of
life ; it being not merely truth, not merely good, but
the beauty which integrates both. On this poesy, she
dwelt long, aiming to show how life, — perfect life, —
could be the only perfect manifestation of it. Then she
spoke of the individual as surrounded, however, by
prose, — so we may here call the manifestation of the
temporary, in opposition to the eternal, always trenching
on it, and circumscribing and darkening. She spoke of
the acceptance of this limitation, but it should be called
by the right name, and always measured; and we
should inwardly cling to the truth that poesy was the
natural life of the soul; and never yield inwardly to the
common notion that poesy was a luxury, out of the
common track; but maintain in word and life that prose
carried the soul out of its track; and then, perhaps, it
would not injure us to walk in these by-paths, when
forced thither. She admitted that prose was the necessary human condition, and quickened our life indirectly
by necessitating a conscious demand on the source of
life. In reply to a remark I made, she very strongly
stated the difference between a poetic and a *dilettante*

life, and sympathized with the sensible people who were tired of hearing all the young ladies of Boston sighing like furnace after being beautiful. Beauty was something very different from prettiness, and a microscopic vision missed the grand whole. The fine arts were our compensation for not being able to live out our poesy, amid the conflicting and disturbing forces of this moral world in which we are. In sculpture, the heights to which our being comes are represented; and its nature is such as to allow us to leave out all that vulgarizes, — all that bridges over to the actual from the ideal. She dwelt long upon sculpture, which seems her favorite art. That was grand, when a man first thought to engrave his idea of man upon a stone, the most unyielding and material of materials, — the backbone of this phenomenal earth, — and, when he did not succeed, that he persevered; and so, at last, by repeated efforts, the Apollo came to be.

"But, no; music she thought the greatest of arts, — expressing what was most interior, — what was too fine to be put into any material grosser than air; conveying from soul to soul the most secret motions of feeling and thought. This was the only fine art which might be thought to be flourishing now. The others had had their day. This was advancing upon a higher intellectual ground.

"Of painting she spoke, but not so well. She seemed to think painting worked more by illusion than sculpture. It involved more prose, from its representing more objects. She said nothing adequate about *color*.

"She dwelt upon the histrionic art as the most complete, its organ being the most flexible and powerful.

"She then spoke of life, as the art, of which these all

were beautiful symbols; and said, in recurring to hei opinions expressed last winter, of Dante and Wordsworth, that she had taken another view, deeper, and more in accordance with some others which were then expressed. She acknowledged that Wordsworth had done more to make all men poetical, than perhaps any other; that he was the poet of reflection; that where he failed to poetize his subject, his simple faith intimated to the reader a poetry that he did not find in the book. She admitted that Dante's Narrative was instinct with the poetry concentrated often in single words. She uttered her old heresies about Milton, however, unmodified.

"I do not remember the transition to modern poetry and Milnes; but she read (very badly indeed) the Legendary Tale.

"We then had three conversations upon Sculpture, one of which was taken up very much in historical accounts of the sculpture of the ancients, in which color was added to form, and which seemed to prove that they were not, after all, sufficiently intellectual to be operated on by form exclusively. The question, of course, arose whether there was a modern sculpture, and why not. This led us to speak of the Greek sculpture as growing naturally out of their life and religion, and how alien it was to our life and to our religion. The Swiss lion, carved by Thorwaldsen 'ut of the side of a mountain rock, was described as a natural growth. Those who had seen it described it; and Mrs. —— spoke of it. She was also led to the story of ner acquaintance with Thorwaldsen, and drew tears from many eyes with her natural eloquence.

" Mrs. C. asked, if sculpture could express as well as painting the idea of immortality.

" Margaret thought the Greek art expressed immortality as much as Christian art, but did not throw it into the future, by preëminence. They expressed it in the present, by casting out of the mortal body every expression of infirmity and decay. The idealization of the human form makes a God. The fact that man can conceive and express this perfection of being, is as good a witness to immortality, as the look of aspiration in the countenance of a Magdalen.

" It is quite beyond the power of my memory to recall all the bright utterances of Margaret, in these conversations on Sculpture. It was a favorite subject with her. Then came two or three conversations on Painting, in which it seemed to be conceded that color expressed passion, whilst sculpture more severely expressed thought : yet painting did not exclude the expression of thought, or sculpture that of feeling, — witness Niobe, — but it must be an universal feeling, like the maternal sentiment.

" *March* 22, 1841. — The question of the day was, What is life ?

" Let us define, each in turn, our idea of living. Margaret did not believe we had, any of us, a distinct idea of life.

" A. S. thought so great a question ought to be given for a written definition. ' No,' said Margaret, ' that is of no ' use. When we go away to think of anything, we never ' do think. We all talk of life. We all have some thought ' now. Let us tell it. C——, what is life ? '

"C—— replied, — 'It is to laugh, or cry, according to our organization.'

"'Good,' said Margaret, 'but not grave enough. 'Come, what is life? I know what I think; I want 'you to find out what you think.'

"Miss P. replied, — 'Life is division from one's principle of life in order to a conscious reörganization. We are cut up by time and circumstance, in order to feel our reproduction of the eternal law.'

"Mrs. E., — 'We live by the will of God, and the object of life is to submit,' and went on into Calvinism.

"Then came up all the antagonisms of Fate and Freedom.

"Mrs. H. said, — 'God created us in order to have a perfect sympathy from us as free beings.'

"Mrs. A. B. said she thought the object of life was to attain absolute freedom. At this Margaret immediately and visibly kindled.

"C. S. said, — 'God creates from the fulness of life, and cannot but create; he created us to overflow, without being exhausted, because what he created, necessitated new creation. It is not to make us happy, but creation is his happiness and ours.'

"Margaret was then pressed to say what she considered life to be.

"Her answer was so full, clear, and concise, at once, that it cannot but be marred by being drawn through the scattering medium of my memory. But here are some fragments of her satisfying statement.

"She began with God as Spirit, Life, so full as to create and love eternally, yet capable of pause. Love and creativeness are dynamic forces, out of which we, individually, as creatures, go forth bearing his image, that is, having within our being the same dynamic forces, by which we also add constantly to the total sum of existence, and shaking off ignorance, and its effects, and by becoming more ourselves, *i. e.*, more divine; — destroying sin in its principle, we attain to absolute freedom, we return to God, conscious like himself, and, as his friends, giving, as well as receiving, felicity forevermore. In short, we become gods, and able to give the life which we now feel ourselves able only to receive.

"On Saturday morning, Mrs. L. E. and Mrs. E. H. were present, and begged Margaret to repeat the statement concerning life, with which she closed the last conversation. Margaret said she had forgotten every word she said. She must have been inspired by a good genius, to have so satisfied everybody, — but the good genius had left her. She would try, however, to say what she thought, and trusted it would resemble what she had said already. She then went into the matter, and, true enough, she did not use a single word she used before."

The fame of these conversations spread wide through all families and social circles of the ladies attending, and the golden report they gave, led to a proposal, that Margaret should undertake an evening class, of four or five lessons, to which gentlemen should also be admitted. This was put in effect, in the course of the winter, and I had myself the pleasure of assisting at one — the second — of these soirées. The subject was Mythology, and several gentlemen took part in it. Margaret spoke well, — she could not otherwise, — but I remember that she seemed encumbered, or interrupted, by the headiness or incapacity of the men, whom she had not had the advantage of training, and who fancied, no doubt, that, on such a question, they, too, must assert and dogmatize.

But, how well or ill they fared, may still be known; since the same true hand which reported for the Ladies' Class, drew up, at the time, the following note of the Evenings of Mythology. My distance from town, and engagements, prevented me from attending again. 1 was told that on the preceding and following evenings the success was more decisive.

" Margaret's plan, in these conversations, was a very noble one, and, had it been seconded, as she expected, they would have been splendid. She thought, that, by admitting gentlemen, who had access, by their classical education, to the whole historical part of the mythology, her own comparative deficiency, as she felt it, in this part of learning, would be made up; and that taking her stand on the works of art, which were the final development in Greece of these multifarious fables, the whole subject might be swept from zenith to nadir. But all that depended on others entirely failed. Mr. W. contributed some isolated facts, — told the etymology of names, and cited a few fables not so commonly known as most; but, even in the point of erudition, which Margaret did not profess, on the subject, she proved the best informed of the party, while no one brought an idea, except herself.

" Her general idea was, that, upon the Earth-worship and Sabæanism of earlier ages, the Grecian genius acted to humanize and idealize, but, still, with some regard to the original principle. What was a seed, or a root, merely, in the Egyptian mind, became a flower in Greece, — Isis, and Osiris, for instance, are reproduced in

Ceres and Proserpine, with some loss of generality, but with great gain of beauty; Hermes, in Mercury, with only more grace of form, though with great loss of grandeur; but the loss of grandeur was also an advance in philosophy, in this instance, the brain in the hand being the natural consequence of the application of Idea to practice, — the Hermes of the Egyptians.

"I do not feel that the class, by their apprehension of Margaret, do any justice to the scope and depth of her views. They come, — myself among the number, — I confess, — to be entertained; but she has a higher purpose. She, amid all her infirmities, studies and thinks with the seriousness of one upon oath, and there has not been a single conversation this winter, in either class, that had not in it the spirit which giveth life. Just in proportion to the importance of the subject, does she tax her mind, and say what is most important; while, of necessity, nothing is reported from the conversations but her brilliant sallies, her occasional paradoxes of form, and, sometimes, her impatient reacting upon dulness and frivolity. In particular points, I know, some excel her; in particular departments I sympathize more with some other persons; but, take her as a whole, she has the most to bestow on others by conversation of any person I have ever known. I cannot conceive of any species of vanity living in her presence. She distances all who talk with her.

"Mr. E. only served to display her powers. With his sturdy reiteration of his uncompromising idealism, his absolute denial of the fact of human nature, he gave her opportunity and excitement to unfold and illustrate her realism and acceptance of conditions. What is so noble is, that her realism is transparent with idea, — her human nature is the germ of a divine life. She proceeds in her search after the unity of things, the divine harmony, not by exclusion, as Mr. E. does, but by comprehension, — and so, no poorest, saddest spirit, but she will lead to hope and faith. I have thought, sometimes, that her acceptance of evil was *too great*, — that her theory of the good to be educed proved too much. But in a conversation I had with her yesterday, I understood her better than I had done. 'It might never be sin to us, at the moment,' she said, 'it must be an excess, on which conscience puts the restraint.' "

The classes thus formed were renewed in November of each year, until Margaret's removal to New York, in 1844. But the notes of my principal reporter fail me at this point. Afterwards, I have only a few sketches from a younger hand. In November, 1841, the class numbered from twenty-five to thirty members: the general subject is stated as " Ethics." And the influences on Woman seem to have been discussed under the topics of the Family, the School, the Church, Society, and Literature. In November, 1842, Margaret writes that the meetings have been unusually spirited, and congratulates herself on the part taken in them by Miss Burley, as 'a presence so positive as to be of great value to me.' The general subject I do not find. But particular topics were such as these: — " Is the ideal first or last ; divination or experience?" "Persons who never awake to life in this world." "Mistakes;" "Faith;" "Creeds;" " Woman;" " Dæmonology;" "Influence;" "Catholicism" (Roman) ; " The Ideal."

In the winter of 1843–4, the general subject was " Education." Culture, Ignorance, Vanity, Prudence,

Patience, and Health, appear to have been the titles of conversations, in which wide digressions, and much autobiographic illustration, with episodes on War, Bonaparte, Goethe, and Spinoza, were mingled. But the brief narrative may wind up with a note from Margaret on the last day.

'28*th April*, 1844. — It was the last day with my 'class. How noble has been my experience of such 'relations now for six years, and with so many and so 'various minds! Life is worth living, is it not?

'We had a most animated meeting. On bidding me 'good-bye, they all, and always, show so much good-will 'and love, that I feel I must really have become a friend 'to them. I was then loaded with beautiful gifts, accom-'panied with those little delicate poetic traits, of which 'I should delight to tell you, if we were near. Last 'came a beautiful bouquet, passion-flower, heliotrope, 'and soberer blooms. Then I went to take my repose 'on C——'s sofa, and we had a most serene afternoon ' together.'

APPENDIX.

APPENDIX.

A.

THOMAS FULLER AND HIS DESCENDANTS.

[From the New England Historical and Genealogical Register
for October, 1859.]

In 1638 THOMAS FULLER came over from England to
America, upon a tour of observation, intending, after he should
have gratified his curiosity by a survey of the wilderness world,
to return. While in Massachusetts, he listened to the preaching of Rev. Thomas Shepard, of Cambridge, who was then in
the midst of a splendid career of religious eloquence and effort,
the echo of which, after the lapse of two centuries, has scarcely
died away. Through his influence, Mr. Fuller was led to take
such an interest in the religion of the Puritan school, that the
land of liturgies and religious formulas, which he had left behind, became less attractive to him than the "forest aisles"
of America, where God might be freely worshipped. He has
himself left on record a metrical statement of the change in
his views which induced him to resolve to make his home in
Massachusetts. These verses were collected by the Rev.
Daniel Fuller of Gloucester from aged persons, who declare
that the author was urged, but in vain, to publish them. Now,
after the lapse of two centuries, we will favor the world with
a few of them, which will serve as a sample: —

332

APPENDIX.

"In thirty-eight I set my foot
On this New England shore;
My thoughts were then to stay one year,
And here remain no more.

But, by the preaching of God's word
By famous Shepard he,
In what a woful state I was,
I then began to see.

Christ cast his garments over me,
And all my sins did cover:
More precious to my soul was he
Than dearest friend or lover.

His pardoning mercy to my soul
All thought did far surmount;
The measure of his love to me
Was quite beyond account.

Ascended on his holy hill,
I saw the city clear,
And knew 'twas New Jerusalem,
I was to it so near.

I said, My mountain does stand strong,
And doubtless 'twill forever;
But soon God turned his face away,
And joy from me did sever.

Sometimes I am on mountains high,
Sometimes in valleys low: —
The state that man's in here below,
Doth ofttimes ebb and flow.

I heard the voice of God by man,
Yet sorrows held me fast;
But these my joys did far exceed;
God heard my cry at last.

Satan has flung his darts at me,
And thought the day to win;
Because he knew he had a friend
That always dwelt within.

But surely God will save my soul!
And, though you trouble have,
My children dear, who fear the Lord,
Your souls at death he'll save.

> All tears shall then be wiped away;
> And joys beyond compare,
> Where Jesus is and angels dwell,
> With every saint you'll share."

If these verses do not give evidence of the highest poetical culture and finish, they yet prove genuine Puritan blood, and hand down through the centuries the very laudable reason which induced Lieut. Thomas Fuller (so we find him styled in the probate proceedings on his will) to purchase and settle upon a large tract of land in New Salem, (afterwards Middleton;) and this land, we will say in passing, is still mainly owned and improved by his descendants. He built a house on it near a stream, about half a mile below Middleton Pond, and about the same distance west from Will's Hill. He did not reside continuously at Middleton; but for some years dwelt in Woburn, and was one of the first settlers and most active citizens of that town, as its records manifest. He died in the year 1698, bequeathing his remaining land to his youngest son, Jacob, having previously, in his lifetime, conveyed lands to his other children, by way of advancement. The last named (Jacob) was born in 1655, and continued to reside on the farm in Middleton till his death in 1731. He married Mary Bacon, and they had five children. His fifth child and second son was likewise named Jacob, who was born in 1700, and died October 17, 1767. He married Abigail Holton, and they had ten children — six sons and four daughters.

TIMOTHY FULLER, the sixth child and third son of the second Jacob Fuller, was born at Middleton, on the 18th of May, 1739. He entered Harvard University at the age of nineteen, and graduated in 1760. His name over that date may still be seen on the corner-stone of one of the college buildings. He applied himself to theology; and in March, 1767, received from the church and town of Princeton, Mass., a nearly unanimous invitation to become their pastor, having previously supplied their pulpit for two years. Here he was ordained the first minister of Princeton, 9th September, 1767. In 1770 he married Sarah Williams, daughter of Rev. Abraham Williams, of Sandwich, Mass. He was successful as a preacher, and his people were united in him till the war of the revolution broke out. He declared at the time, and ever afterwards, that he was friendly to the principles of the revolution, and anxiously desired that his country should be liberated from its dependence on the British crown; but he was naturally a very cautious man, and believed this result would be certain to come, if the country reserved itself for action till its strength was somewhat matured, and its resources in a better state of preparation. Resistance at the time he believed to be premature, and hazarding all by too precipitate action. Such views, however, were by no means congenial to the heated zeal of his townsmen. He first gave dissatisfaction by a discourse he preached to the " minute men," at the request of the town, choosing for his text 1 Kings xx. 11: " Let not him that girdeth on the harness boast himself as he that putteth it off." He was not a man to swerve from his own cool and deliberate views through the pressure of public opinion; and his persistence in them led to his dismissal, in 1776, from the pastorate by an ex parte council, his parish refusing to agree with him upon a mutual council. He removed soon after to Martha's Vineyard, and preached to the society in Chilmark till the war was ended. He then removed to Middleton, and brought a suit against the town of Princeton for his salary. His dismissal had been irregular, and the law of the case was in his favor; but the jury had too much sympathy with the motives that actuated the town to render a verdict in his behalf. It was supposed this result would be crushing to him, and that he would not be prepared to pay costs recovered by the town; and some were malignant enough to anticipate with pleasure the levy of the execution But they were disappointed; for, when the sheriff called upon him, he coolly counted out the amount of the execution in specie, which, in his habitual caution, he had carefully hoarded to meet this very exigency. He soon after returned to Prince-ton, where he applied himself to the careful education of his children, in connection with the cultivation of a large farm, which embraced within its bounds the Wachusett mountain.

None of his children attended any other than this family school; all were carefully taught, and several fitted for college at home. Those in the town who had been opposed to him, soon became reconciled, and even warmly attached. He was very active in town affairs, and represented Princeton in the convention which approved and adopted the present federal constitution. He himself, with his characteristic firmness, voted against the constitution, mainly on the ground of its recogni-tion of slavery; and he has left his reasons on record. In 1796, he removed to Merrimac, N. H., where he conti/ued to reside till his decease, on the morning of the 3d of July, 1805, at the age of sixty-seven, leaving a wife and ten chil-dren to mourn his loss. His wife deserves more than a pass-ing notice, as she must have had no small influence in mould-ing the character of the children. Her father, Rev. Abraham Williams, was a person of genuine piety, a warm patriot, and an ardent friend of the revolution. His letter accepting his call at Sandwich, which is still carefully preserved, breathes a pure Christian spirit; as also a subsequent communication, in which he kindly expresses a willingness to dispense with a portion of his salary to accommodate himself to the narrow means of his people. His will is likewise very characteris-tic. He emancipates his slaves, and requires his children to contribute to their support if they shall be destitute; and " deprives any child who may refuse to give bonds to perform this duty of his share of the estate, giving to such child in lieu thereof a new Bible of the cheapest sort, hoping that, by the blessing of Heaven, it may teach them to do justice and love mercy." He married Anna Buckminster, of Framingham, aunt of the distinguished clergyman, Rev. Joseph Buckminster, D. D., of Portsmouth, N. H., who was father of Rev. Joseph Stevens Buckminster, of Boston. Rev. Mr. Williams graduated from Harvard University in 1744, and died 12th of August, 1784, aged fifty-seven. His daughter Sarah, wife of Rev. Timothy Fuller, possessed a vigorous understanding and an honorable ambition, which she strove to infuse into her children. She died in 1822. Rev. Timothy Fuller left five daughters and five sons. The sons were Timothy, Abraham Williams, Henry Holton, William Williams, and Elisha; of these we shall speak more in detail.

TIMOTHY FULLER, the fourth child and eldest son, attained great distinction. The chief steps in his career may be thus summarily stated: He was born in Chilmark, Martha's Vineyard, 11th of July, 1778: graduated at Harvard University with the second honors in his class, 1801. He was a member of the Mass. Senate from 1813 to 1816; Representative in Congress from 1817 to 1825; Speaker of the Mass. House of Representatives in 1825; a member of the Executive Council in 1828; and died suddenly of Asiatic cholera, at his residence in Groton, Mass., October 1, 1835. In the narrow circumstances of his father, he was obliged to work his way through college, and be absent much in teaching; but such were his talent, industry, and scholarship, that it is believed he would have borne off the first honors had he not countenanced a rebellion of the students, caused by certain college rules regarded as oppressive. He was always an ardent advocate for freedom and the rights of man, and even while in college made himself marked as a Democratic Republican, in contradistinction to the Federalist party. After graduating, he taught in Leicester Academy, till he had acquired funds to complete his professional study of the law, which he did in the office of Hon. Levi Lincoln, of Worcester, and afterwards practised law in Boston. We copy the following description of the monument erected to his memory in Mount Auburn, which is taken from the Mount Auburn Memorial: —

"In the centre of the foreground, on Pyrola Path, is the chaste and beautiful marble sarcophagus, on which are inscribed the names of Hon. Timothy Fuller and two of his children, who departed life in infancy. This is a fitting memorial of a distinguished man. Mr. Fuller was a member of Congress from Massachusetts from 1817 to 1825, and was noted for reasoning power and eloquence. Among his marked speeches are his addresses upon the Seminole war, and in opposition to the Missouri Compromise, in 1820. Mr. Fuller was eminent among the Democratic Republicans of his time, and very influential in securing the election of John Quincy Adams to the presidency. His services as chairman of the Committee on Naval Affairs are not forgotten. Mr. Fuller had great distinction at the bar, and a large professional practice. He was untiring in his industry, grudged the hours nature demands for sleep, was a. fine classic scholar, and an extensive reader. These were traits in his character which won much public honor; but there were others — a strict integrity, a warmth of heart, and a liberal benevolence, endearing him to the humble and needy, and a tender and faithful attachment to his children and friends, which make his memory widely cherished. In the pressure of business, having to prepare many briefs by his evening fireside, he yet found time to instruct his daughter Margaret, to cultivate her rare intellect, and to incite her to a noble ambition. Having practised many years in Boston, with his residence in Cambridge, he in later years removed to Groton. Here, in his beautiful residence, he designed to write a history of his country, for which he had been long collecting materials, and to educate his younger children with the advantages of due physical development. Perhaps, too, in the afternoon of his life he was drawn, as many are, nearer the scenes of his childhood and youth, attracted towards the blue Wachusett and the range of New Hampshire hills. Here he died the 1st of October. 1835. Circumstances prevented his daughter Margaret from completing a memoir of him which she designed, and which, we believe, would have been a worthy record of a high-minded and distinguished man."

Mr. Fuller's published writings are, " An Oration delivered at Watertown, July 4, 1809 ; " " Address before the Massachusetts Peace Society, 1826 ; " " The Election for the Presidency considered, by a Citizen ; " Speeches on the Seminole War, Missouri Compromise, &c.

Hon. Timothy Fuller married Margaret Crane, daughter of Maj. Peter Crane, of Canton, Mass., May 28, 1809. She died Sabbath morning, July 31, 1859. A character like hers — so sweet and amiable, gifted, yet unpretending, with a rare intellect and ardent imagination, with warmth of sentiment and affectionate benignity of heart, together with tender susceptibilities and the love of a sympathetic nature for flowers and every beautiful type of the great Creator — is, indeed, one of the fairest ornaments of existence. Her life was one of habitual self-denial and devotion to duty in the various relations of her lot. We know not that she ever made an enemy ; and, on the contrary, we believe that she has drawn towards herself the heart of every one with whom she has come in contact. In youth she was possessed of great personal beauty, and was much admired in the Washington circles when her husband was in Congress. She had a rare conversational gift, aided by a lively fancy and a well-stored mind, which made her society much valued by the educated and the gifted. Above all, she was a sincere and devoted Christian.

MARGARET FULLER, the first child of this union, is well known to fame. After her father's death she was her mother's chief stay ; for, though of very little business experience, and with a natural aversion to financial affairs, she had a strength of mind and courageous firmness which stayed up her mother's hands when the staff on which she had leaned was stricken away. It had been the life-long desire of the daughter Margaret to go to Europe and complete her culture there, and arrangements with this view had been matured at her father's death. Her patrimony would have still sufficed for the destined tour ; but she must have left her mother sinking under a sense of helplessness, with young children to educate. Margaret, after a struggle between a long-cherished and darling project and her sense of duty, heroically resolved to give up her own brilliant hopes, and remain with her mother. She applied herself personally to the academic training of the children, who learned from her the rudiments of the classic languages and the first reading of some of its great authors. We extract from the " Mount Auburn Memorial " the following brief sketch of her and of the monument erected to her memory : —

" We have not yet mentioned the monument forming the chief attraction of the lot, and that by which so many feet are drawn thither : we allude, of course, to that commemorative of Madame Ossoli, her husband, and child. It contains a medallion likeness of Margaret Fuller Ossoli, a star, which was the signature to many of her literary contributions, and a sword, indicative of the Italian struggle, in which her husband fought, and where she herself ministered to the wounded, the whole surmounted by the cross, indicative of their Christian faith. It would certainly be foreign to our purpose, and quite inconsistent with the limits of this sheet, to attempt any sketch of her life. Nor is it necessary. She lives, and will, while life lasts, in the memory of a large circle of friends and admirers. Her journey in a foreign land, and what she did and suffered there, engaged the attention and sympathy of a large number of still living witnesses. Her melancholy death with her husband and child, returning home, just entering the haven of her native land, sent a thrill through this country, and caused tears to flow in other lands, and has not been, nor is to be, forgotten. The brightness of her genius, the nobleness and heroism of her life, are set forth in two volumes of Memoirs

from the pens of R. W. Emerson, Horace Greeley, W. H
Channing, J. F. Clarke, and other friends, which have been
widely circulated, and have presented the story of an extraordinary life. Her thougths, committed to paper by her own
eloquent and industrious pen, not only through the columns
of the New York Tribune, for a series of years, but in several literary works, still express her genius, and breathe her
noble aspirations. 'Woman in the Nineteenth Century,' 'At
Home and Abroad,' 'Art, Literature, and the Drama,' 'Life
without and Life within,' embalm much of the mind of Margaret Fuller; but her wonderful power of conversation lives in
memory alone. It is said that there has been no woman like her
in this respect since Madame de Stael; but while Margaret Fuller's conversation, in eloquence and effect, in sparkle and flow,
was fully equal to that of the gifted French woman, it had, su-
peradded, a merit which the latter could not claim. There is
hardly upon record one with her power to draw out others. She
not only talked surprisingly herself, but she made others do so.
While talking with her they seemed to make discoveries of
themselves, to wonder at their own thoughts, and to admire
the force and aspiration of their character — hitherto latent
to their own consciousness. She made those who conversed
with her forget to admire her in wondering at themselves.
As a friend, Margaret Fuller Ossoli is, and must be, tenderly and devoutly remembered by the very large and miscellaneous class who knew and loved her. What an assemblage they would make if gathered together! The rich and
the refined, the poor and the humble, the men and women of
genius struggling with destiny, and demanding audience for
new and noble thoughts; the poet, with his scorned and
broken lyre, to whose lays how few would stop and listen, and
still fewer echo in sympathy, — all these found in her a confidant to soothe their sorrows, and a friend to encourage and
point onward. She had a wonderful way of winning unsolicited confidence. All ran to her with their secrets; and she

was a storehouse of confidential disclosures. The servants about her, and all with whom she came in contact, found her a ready friend. There was but one thing needed to admit to the friendship of Margaret, and that was a pure purpose and a noble aim. Those who did not possess this instinctively shunned her. She had a penetrating eye to see through, and a power of satire to strip off, masks and pretences. She hated shams, hypocrisies, falsehoods, and outside show. Characters artificial and not genuine strove to keep at a safe distance from her; they dreaded the sting of her satire, the eagle look of her eye, and the eloquence of her tongue.

"Margaret Fuller Ossoli lived above the world, while she lived in it. She was one of those *exaltadas* who are described in her 'Woman in the Nineteenth Century;' which description has been thus thrown into a poetical dress: —

> " ' Who are these that move below,
> Often glancing as they go,
> With their homage-speaking eyes,
> Rapt looks upward to the skies?'
> Such *exalted ones* they name —
> Characters of heavenly frame,
> Walking on the pilgrim road,
> Living, moving still in God.
> 'Tell me why their eye intent
> Fastens on the firmament;
> Or where, in the gilded sky,
> Embers of the daylight die.'
> 'In this world another lies,
> Glorious as paradise;
> And their souls have eyes to see,
> Vision, undisclosed to thee.'
>
> 'Tell me why they oft appear
> Listening with attentive ear,
> While emotions seem to glance
> On the speaking countenance,
> Though no being breathes a word,
> Nor has aught the stillness stirred.'
> ' 'Tis because their ears have caught
> Hidden harmony of thought,

> Music high, and deep, and broad,
> Making melody to God !
> World of sight and world of sound,
> Close that clasp the earth around,
> These exalted ones discern,
> And with heavenly ardor burn.'

" We have not yet spoken of Margaret as the representative of woman. Nor can we, in these limits, allude to what she said, and what she strove to do, to vindicate the honor of her sex. We cannot close, however, without quoting the lines of the celebrated Walter Savage Landor. Her husband, the Marquis Ossoli, was captain of the Civic Guard during the Italian revolution, in 1848, and was not only a Roman noble, but, what is much higher, a noble Roman.

ON THE DEATH OF MARQUIS OSSOLI AND HIS WIFE, MARGARET FULLER.

> " Over his millions death has lawful power ;
> But over thee, brave Ossoli ! none — none !
> After a long struggle, in a fight
> Worthy of Italy to youth restored,
> Thou, far from home, art sunk beneath the surge
> Of the Atlantic; on its shore; in reach
> Of help; in trust of refuge; sunk with all
> Precious on earth to thee — a child, a wife!
> Proud as thou wert of her, America
> Is prouder, showing to her sons how high
> Swells woman's courage in a virtuous breast.
> She would not leave behind her those she loved:
> Such solitary safety might become
> Others — not her; not her who stood beside
> The pallet of the wounded, when the worst
> Of France and Perfidy assailed the walls
> Of unsuspicious Rome. Rest, glorious soul,
> Renowned for strength of genius, Margaret!
> Rest with the twain, too dear ! My words are few,
> And shortly none will hear my failing voice;
> But the same language with more full appeal
> Shall hail thee. Many are the sons of song
> Whom thou hast heard upon thy native plains,
> Worthy to sing of thee; the hour has come;
> Take we our seats, and let the dirge begin."

Of EUGENE FULLER, the second child, the following notice, taken from the annual obituary college record, by Joseph Palmer, M. D., published by the Boston Daily Advertiser, gives some account: —

" Eugene Fuller, the eldest son of Hon. Timothy and Margaret (Crane) Fuller, was born in Cambridge, Mass., May 14, 1815. After leaving college in 1834, he studied law, partly at the Dane Law School in Cambridge, and partly in the office of George Frederick Farley, Esq., of Groton, Mass. After his admission to the bar, he practised his profession two years in Charlestown, Mass. He afterwards went to New Orleans, and was connected with the public press of that city. He spent several summers there, and, some two or three years ago was affected by a sun-stroke, which resulted in a softening of the brain, and ultimately in a brain fever, which came very near proving fatal, and left him in a shattered condition. His friends hoping that medical treatment at the north might benefit him, he embarked, with an attendant, on board the Empire City for New York. When one day out, June 21, 1859, his attendant being prostrated with sea-sickness, Mr. Fuller was left alone, and was not afterwards seen He must have been lost overboard. The New Orleans Picayune of the 30th June, with which he was some time connected, says, ' His industry, reliability, and intelligence were equalled only by his invariably mild, correct, and gentlemanly demeanor, and he was liked and respected by all who knew him.' "

The second son of Hon. Timothy Fuller was WILLIAM HENRY FULLER. He applied himself to mercantile pursuits, first in New Orleans, afterwards in Cincinnati; and at present resides in Cambridge, Mass. He married Miss Frances Elizabeth Hastings, February 28, 1840.

The third* daughter was ELLEN KILSHAW FULLER, who married William E. Channing, author of several volumes of

---

* An older daughter, Julia Adelaide, died in childhood.

poetry. In the account of the Fuller lot in Mount Auburn, already quoted from, we have the following in reference to her : —

" Near by, on a simple and elegant monument, is inscribed ' Ellen Fuller Channing.' These words may mean little to a stranger, but they speak volumes to all who knew her, and are capable of loving and admiring an elevated and ideal character. Of great personal beauty, she was herself a poem. With a nature largely ideal, her whole life was a beautiful and poetic composition. In family love, in the refinement and elegances of domestic life, in the tender nurture and care of her children, she had a charm like music. The following lines, written by one who honored her, but faintly portray her to the mind : —

> ' Hers were the bright brow and the ringlet hair,
> The mind that ever dwelt i' the pure ideal;
> Herself a fairer figure of the real
> Than those the plastic fancy moulds of air.' "

REV. ARTHUR BUCKMINSTER FULLER,* the third son of Hon. Timothy Fuller, was born August 10, 1822. He was early instructed by his father and his sister, Margaret Fuller. At the age of twelve, he spent one year at Leicester Academy ; and, subsequently, studied with Mrs. Ripley, the wife of Rev. Samuel Ripley, of Waltham. In August, 1839, he entered college, at the age of seventeen, and graduated in 1843. During his college course he united with the church connected with the University. Immediately on graduation he purchased Belvidere Academy, in Belvidere, Boone Co., Illinois, which, assisted by a competent corps of instructors, he taught for the two subsequent years. During this time, Mr. Fuller occasionally preached, as a missionary, in Belvi-

---

* Rev. Mr. Fuller has collected most of the ancient records pertaining to the Fuller family. He has also in his possession an ancient chair, which tradition declares to have been brought from England to this country by the first Thomas Fuller, in 1638 ; and also a chair owned by Rev. Abraham Williams, of Sandwich.

dere and destitute places, and also to the established churches, having been interested in theological study during his senior year at college. He was a member of the Illinois Conference of Christian and Unitarian ministers, and by them licensed to preach. His first sermon was preached October, 1843, in Chicago, to the Unitarian church then under the charge of Rev. Joseph Harrington. In 1845 Mr. Fuller returned to New England; entered, one year in advance, the Cambridge Theological School, whence he graduated in August, 1847. After preaching three months at West Newton, to a society of which Hon. Horace Mann was a principal founder and a constant attendant, Mr. Fuller accepted a call to the pastorate of the Unitarian Society in Manchester, N. H., and was subsequently ordained, March 29, 1848. In September, 1852, Mr. Fuller received a call from the New North Church, on Hanover Street, in Boston, one of the most ancient churches in the city, being founded in 1714, and a church built that year on the spot where the present one now stands. This call Rev. Mr. Fuller refused, the relation between himself and the Manchester Society being a most happy one. The call was, however, renewed, and ultimately accepted, and Mr. Fuller was installed in Boston, June 1, 1853. Failing health, and the fact that the Protestant population was rapidly leaving the North End, induced Mr. Fuller to resign his city pastorate, and close his labors there July 31, 1859. He accepted at once, however, a call for a six months' charge of the Unitarian Church in Watertown, Mass., having preferred this temporary settlement to one of longer duration. In November, 1853, Mr. Fuller was chosen by the citizens of Ward 1, in Boston, a member of the School Committee, then a much smaller body than now, consisting of only twenty-four members. In January, 1854, Mr. Fuller was chosen by the Massachusetts House of Representatives chaplain of that body. In 1858 he was elected by the Massachusetts Senate their chaplain, both of which appointments he accepted, and dis

charged their duties.   In 1855 Rev. Mr. Fuller was selected
by the citizens of Groton, Mass., to deliver a bi-centennial
oration, it being the two hundredth anniversary of the settlement of that ancient town.   This oration was delivered October 31, 1855.   In 1857 Mr. Fuller was nominated, by the
republicans of Suffolk District No. 2, for the Massachusetts
Senate, but, with the other candidates of his party in that
district, failed of an election.   In 1858 Mr. Fuller was chosen
by the State Temperance Convention a member of the Executive Committee, and in the same year was elected a direct-
or of the Washingtonian Home, better known as the Home
for the Fallen.   Mr. Fuller's published writings are, " A Discourse in Vindication of Unitarianism from popular Charges
against it," Manchester, 1848; "Sabbath School Manual of
Christian Doctrines and Institutions," Boston, 1850; " A
Discourse occasioned by the Death of Hon. Richard Hazen
Ayer, delivered in the Unitarian Church, February 18, 1853 ; "
" An Historical Discourse, delivered in the New North Church,
October 1, 1854 ; " " A Discourse occasioned by the Death of
Miss Mercy Tufts, delivered in the Unitarian Church in
Quincy, Mass., January 24, 1858 ; " " Liberty versus Roman-
ism, or Romanism hostile to Civil and Religious Liberty, —
being two Discourses delivered in the New North Church, Bos-
ton," Boston, 1859.   Mr. Fuller has also edited four volumes
of his sister Margaret's works, and has prepared for the press
a complete and uniform edition of her works and memoirs.*

RICHARD FREDERICK FULLER was the fourth son.   He
graduated at Harvard University, 1844, studied law in Green-
field, Mass., afterwards a year at the Cambridge Law School,
and, having completed his studies in the office of his uncle,
Henry H. Fuller, Esq., in Boston, was admitted to the bar
on examination in open court, December, 1846, at the age of
twenty-two, and became, and continued for two years to be,

[* These volumes are now published simultaneously with these memoirs.
They are Woman in the Nineteenth Century, At Home and Abroad, Art,
Literature, and the Drama. and Life Without and Life Within. — ED.]

the law partner of his uncle ; and has subsequently practised law without a partner, in Boston. Having been fitted for college, at the age of sixteen he entered a store in Boston, at the solicitation of his family ; but mercantile life proving distasteful to him, he relinquished it at the end of one year. By severe application, he in six months made up for this lost year, at the same time keeping pace with the studies of the Sophomore class, and was admitted to college in the middle of the Sophomore year. He graduated the second or third scholar of his class.

This ends our account of those who have been noted in the family of Hon. Timothy Fuller. His brothers likewise attained distinction, and deserve now to be mentioned.

ABRAHAM WILLIAMS FULLER, the second son of Rev. Timothy Fuller, applied himself, on reaching manhood, to mercantile life. His strict application to business, his sagacity and integrity, speedily won the confidence of his employer, who, retiring from business about the time Abraham became of age, lent him an adequate capital, and set him up as his successor. The embargo, occurring at this time, caused a great rise in prices, and Abraham very soon acquired a large fortune. He at once relinquished mercantile business, and studied the law, and had an office in Boston till he died, April 6, 1847, unmarried, leaving a large property. A granite obelisk has been erected to his memory, near the tower, in Mount Auburn.

The third son was HENRY HOLTON FULLER, who graduated at Harvard College, 1811, the second scholar in his class, Edward Everett being the first, and was admitted to the Suffolk bar September 19, 1815. He went into partnership with his brother Timothy, and attained great distinction at the bar. He was a thorough and careful lawyer, a sound logician, and had a sparkling flow of wit and humor, which made him a great favorite with juries. When he could not answer arguments, he could almost always throw a grotesque coloring over them, and bring them into ridicule, possessing a vein of very cutting satire. He had a great run of business in court almost immediately; and at thirty years of age it was said that he had argued more cases than any lawyer of his age in Massachusetts. He himself remarked that he never was counsel in a case where the jury did not wish to give him the verdict, if they could find a fair way to do so. In conversation he was genial and sprightly, affable and pleasant to all about him, and a universal favorite with his juniors. He was several years a representative from Boston in the Massachusetts legislature, and very efficient in its debates and the transaction of the public business. At his death, September 15, 1852, the bench and bar joined in a public tribute of eulogy to his memory. A granite obelisk in Mount Auburn, near the tower, beside the monument of Abraham W. Fuller, is erected to his memory.

WILLIAM WILLIAMS FULLER likewise graduated at Harvard University, in 1813, and studied law. He practised several years in Hallowell, Me., afterwards in Lowell, Mass., and ultimately in Oregon, Ill. His mind was cool and deliberate, his judgment sound and reliable, and he obtained a very favorable reputation in his profession. He died at Oregon, Ill., 1849, leaving an infant child, who survived but a few months.

ELISHA FULLER, the youngest son, graduated at Harvard University, 1815, and studied law. He practised at Lowell, and afterwards at Worcester, Mass. He had a keenness of perception, a ready wit, and a sound knowledge of law, which won for him much success in practice. He was a person of remarkably buoyant temperament, and so cheerful and social a companion, that his advent was sure to banish gloom and low spirits, as sunshine dissipates the darkness. In person he closely resembled Henry, whose vivacity of discourse he also shared. Both were of rather small stature, with lively black eyes, and great sprightliness of manner. Elisha died the last of the five lawyers, 1855. Seldom, in one generation has a family numbered so many successful professional men as were the five brothers we have described.

B.

[From the Quarterly Journal.]

MEMORIAL OF MRS. MARGARET FULLER,

BY HER SON, RICHARD F. FULLER.

[The following interesting memoir of an excellent Christian woman was not prepared with any reference to being printed. It was written by one of her sons for the use of his children ; but, having had the privilege of reading it, I requested to be allowed to print it in the Quarterly Journal, and my request was granted. I think the readers of the Journal will be interested in this sketch. — EDITOR JOURNAL.]

MARGARET FULLER, the daughter of Major Peter Crane, was born in Canton, Mass., February 15, 1789. Her father, though an artisan of moderate circumstances, was quite scholarly for his day and condition in life, and possessed an original turn of mind, as well as marked independence of character. He left some disquisitions, preserved by his family, of no literary excellence, but indicative of a strong and untutored mind, coping with the intellectual problems of life, and feeling after truth by the unaided light of individual thought. He was noted for going on in his own course, with utter disregard of popularity, and of the view which others might take of his conduct. He served in the revolutionary war, and at one time, when there was no chaplain, performed the duties of that office for his regiment. Though belonging to no church, and entertaining, perhaps, rather crude views of his own in religious things, yet he had an influence over the minds of others, which induced his counsel and his prayers to be sought for in circumstances of distress. He died before I was born; but my grandmother lived till after I attained manhood. My father and mother often visited her at Canton, riding in a chaise, and carrying one of the children, sitting on a cricket at their feet; and my turn for these journeys came often. My father was an ardent lover of nature, which he doubly enjoyed in his escapes from the pressure of public and professional business; and his enjoyment of it, and the points of interest he called attention to, heightened my relish for this pure gratification. He drove slowly, and sang with my mother on the way. These journeys are ever memorable with me; and the visits were always celebrated in sacred song among the Canton kindred, which my father accompanied with the flute, enjoying music with almost passionate delight. Arriving at Canton, we were always joyously greeted by the bright and sunny face of my aged grandmother, who lived with a maiden aunt, and the uniformity of whose life was very agreeably varied by these visits, while my father never neglected to bring generous supplies for her rather meagre larder. She was a very pious woman, in the simplicity and devotion of the Baxter school, whose "Saint's Rest," as well as the works of Watts and Doddridge, were very familiar and precious to her, and formed, with her ever-diligently conned and well-worn Bible, almost the whole range of her literary acquirement. She was very fond of singing devotional hymns. Among others, I remember "China" was a great favorite, sung even with her last failing voice upon her death bed. As she sang it, the minor cadence and its reference to the grave rather affrighted and repelled my childish taste; but I have since been able to appreciate the sentiment which made it attractive. My grandmother had great sweetness of temper and a sunshine of disposition, which may have been received by my mother as an hereditary gift.

In childhood and youth, my mother was marked not only for rare bloom and personal beauty, but for an almost irrepressible gayety and buoyancy of temper. She was as full of the elasticity of life, and her heart as overflowing with the music of nature, as the early songsters of spring. She was above the medium height of woman, being in stature about five feet and nine or ten inches, and considerably taller than my father. She had blue eyes, a fair, white complexion, not liable to tan or freckle, and a rich bloom, like that of the peach, in her cheeks. This bloom was a very marked characteristic of her face, and one that she retained to quite mature life. It was transmitted to her daughter Ellen, and its rose has reappeared undiminished in the blooming cheeks of some of her grandchildren.

My mother had a very happy childhood. Her own temper, with its rare elasticity, was then, and ever through life, a fund of happiness for herself as well as others. As a child and maiden, she had a wild exuberance of spirits, regulated, however, by as strong a benevolence, and a tenderness of feeling and sympathy, which made her generally beloved. Her fondness for flowers was ever a passion with her, if so gentle and refined a sentiment may be thus denominated. I have heard her speak of her mother as one who, though sweet and loving, was determined not to spoil the child by sparing the rod, when occasion required its exercise, which, happily, was seldom. On one occasion, however, her mother had forbidden the children to eat certain grapes, and Margaret had yielded to the temptation of the luscious fruit, and despoiled the vine of some of its clusters. Her mother inquired of Abby, a younger daughter, if she had done it, and was answered, "No." On being further interrogated if she knew the offending party, Abby would not reply; and her mother attempted with the rod to compel her to answer. Abby bore it with heroic endurance, and continued mute, till Margaret, unable to endure the sight of this vicarious suffering, confessed the deed, and thereby transferred the rod to her own more deserving shoulders. Before she was out of her teens, she taught school in the district where she resided. One large boy presumed upon his familiar acquaintance and her well-known playfulness of dispo-

sition, which he could hardly believe it possible for her to lay
aside, and showed a disinclination to submit to her sceptre
in the school room. She displayed her characteristic energy
and courage, called the boy out upon the floor, and, ere he
could collect his forces for resistance, ferruled him soundly.
The dismayed youth quailed and submitted, and her authority
was afterwards unquestioned.

My mother has given some rather grotesque accounts of
riding to church on a pillion ; and of being sometimes taken
up behind a rustic cavalier, whose invitation she had unwill-
ingly accepted, to spare him the mortification of a refusal.
It was at church that my father first saw her, she happening,
through some chance, to be in Cambridge on the Sabbath.
He loved, and his love was returned. He soon led her to the
altar, a blooming girl of twenty, and ten years younger than
himself. Father was not blind to worldly advantages of
family and position ; and such were readily within the reach
of a rising young lawyer, whose talents had already become
favorably known. But it was well for him that he yielded
to a softer and a better sentiment. " His love for my
mother," says Margaret in her autobiographical sketch, " was
the green spot on which he stood apart from the common-
places of a mere bread-winning, bread-bestowing existence."
She adds, in describing her mother, " She was one of those
fair and flower-like natures which sometimes spring up even
beside the most dusty highways of life — a creature not to
be shaped into a merely useful instrument, but bound by one
law with the blue sky, the dew, and the frolic birds. Of all
persons whom I have known, she had in her most of the
angelic — of that spontaneous love for every living thing, for
man, and beast, and tree, which restores the golden age."
Not only was this union a blessing to father, but favorable to
the character of his children. Margaret used to say that we
derived our ideal sentiment mainly from our mother. And
certainly she had a good store of refined fancy and delicate

feeling, though coupled, as they but rarely are, with a ready hand and a willing mind for useful effort, graced by uninterrupted benignity and sweetness, and not marred by the moody and irritable temperament which are not unfrequently the blemish of an imaginative mind. None of her sons can fail to be grateful for sentiment, from whichever parent derived, since it is not only the most satisfactory evidence of a divine and immortal germ within, but affords that purer gratification of thought and fancy, which, better than any thing in life, deserves the name of pleasure, being a satisfaction to which memory can ever revert without self-reproach. It is true that such a temperament is apt to be more sensitive to the thorns in life's pathway; but, when religiously developed, which is its best and most congenial bias, it furnishes itself a corrective for its fault, and opens to the soul fountains of even heavenly consolation.

My mother's Cambridge years rather antedate my recollection; but in Groton her character and life are fresh in my memory. A picture of her is very prominent in my mind, as she stooped over her flower-bed, and toiled long sunny hours over its extensive border. Her unwearied labors in the heat attracted the admiration even of the hardy farmers. Her expression, as she knelt by the flower bed and bent her near-sighted gaze close to a plant, and, discovering some new unfolding promise of beauty, turned round to announce it with a child-like simplicity and a delighted smile, I think can never fade from the memories of her children. This image has often been renewed; and though latterly her hair, no less beautiful than before, has been gray, yet never thinned by years, her smile has gleamed ever with the same sunshiny, child-like triumph, her countenance never hardened or saddened by life's experience, nor her joy abated with the declining vigor of life. The flowers were ever new and ever young, and they kept her spirit still child-like in freshness of sentiment, simplicity of taste, and purity of soul, showing her ever guileless, single-hearted, and such as are of the kingdom of heaven.

My father's death was a dreadful stroke to my mother. It bowed her to the earth; but it did not break her spirit, and she rose again, leaning on the arm of her beloved Lord. My father had been a man of strength and of success, and on him she had entirely relied, never cognizant of the practical financial problems of life. His property was in unproductive real estate, and, with young children to be educated, it was necessary to change and straiten our style of living. The arithmetic of the business appalled my mother; she was as naturally inapt for it as the lilies that neither toil nor spin. But she was always remarkable for indefatigable industry; and she applied herself to the dairy, and the farm, and the economy of the table with heroic determination, while she was aided and encouraged by Margaret's firm and courageous, though far from financial or business-like, mind. She ever rose early, and her voice with the morning birds roused the rest of the household. Well do I remember the night of my father's death, when I was ten years of age. The solemn tones of the minister's voice in prayer, in the chamber of death, have not been — can never be — forgotten. Very soon after I was confined to my bed for a fortnight, with fever. Mother feared it might prove fatal. She never faltered; she was with me night and day. I remember well her voice as she called me her "dear lamb." Her soothing, gentle hand had no ornament but her simple wedding-ring of gold, without any stone, which she always wore, and which was buried with her. After my father's death she devoted every energy, with untiring self-sacrifice, to her children. Her economy in respect to herself was most rigorous. Her dress was as plain and simple as propriety would permit, and it was preserved with great care. She always persevered in this self-denial, wishing to husband what was hers for others. Her annual income from her share of the property was five or six hundred dollars, and she invariably saved about half of it, till the lot was purchased at Mount Auburn, which was obtained to commemorate the dear departed, and to testify her perennial remembrance. She contributed largely and principally toward its marble memorials, and adorned it with flowers, whose growth she assiduously fostered with her own hand. We think this was a great solace to her; and it evidently furnished her satisfaction, not merely to keep green and fresh holy memories, but to express in the language of flowers her never doubting Christian faith.

At Groton she was active in the efforts of the religious society to which she belonged. Indeed, from the time she united with the Unitarian Church in Cambridge, soon after her marriage, till her last sickness, and even during it, as far as possible, she was much and actively engaged in religious effort. Loving and full of charity towards those of every Christian name, she was herself an earnest and devoted Unitarian, through evil report and good report. She was among the first who formed the Lee Street Church and Society, in Cambridge; nor can her efforts in its behalf be soon forgotten. When her son, Rev. Arthur B. Fuller, was settled in Manchester, N. H., she was, with him, actively devoted to the interests of his society, and tenderly loved by all its members. When he left Manchester, to accept the call of the New North Church in Boston, she accompanied him, and there continued till her last sickness. Her sympathy for all, her teaching in the Sabbath school, her interest, always cordial and as laborious as her years would permit, in the benevolent organization of the society, and her Christian graces, which shone with so mild and lovely a light, won affection as well as respect from all who came in contact with her, no matter how variant their theological creed from her own.

Benevolence, of a sympathetic and hopeful cast, overflowed from the pure fountains of her Christian heart. The bad awoke in her much pity and little reproach. No one could desire a kinder judge than she to pass upon character or determine destiny. In the large charity of her soul, she hoped from the divine benignity a place for repentance would ever be preserved for all. She never spoke against others — dwelt much upon their virtues, gently and charitably upon their faults. She reproved her children if they spoke unfavorably of the absent, and always advocated their cause, and endeavored to excuse what was alleged against them. We sometimes held up the faults of others merely to notice the ingenuity with which she would seek for excuse, or strive to throw the veil of charity over them. I shall never forget her efforts by the bedside of a large, coarse man, a tenant of ours in Groton, who lived " without God and without hope in the world," until he took opium to end his wretched existence. Mother used every exertion to rescue him from death, and staid by him during the hours of fearful struggle between a powerful frame and the working of the poison. In the early part of it, before his mind entirely wandered, he said, " It will be all in vain; but you may try all means." The memory of this scene is in one view appalling, as representing a gross and sensual nature meeting the fearful fate itself had invoked; but, on the other hand, is beautiful as exhibiting one, like an angel, exerting every power to snatch him from his self-elected doom.

Mother's sympathy was sometimes taken advantage of to induce her to lend money which she could ill spare. One case in particular we used to jest a little about, of a man who induced her to lend him, on the plea that he " wanted to pay his debts, and become an honest man." We thought it would only change his creditor, and doubted if it would not make him a less honest man, not only by the pretext he used, but by his employing the money for other objects than that alleged. But in her readiness of sympathy she exhibited the charity that " believeth all things."

My mother's piety was as truly genuine as any I have ever

witnessed. It was meek and unpretending; it had a faith which buoyed her up in all the stormy passages of life, which drew the gleam of heaven down upon the earth, and sur-rounded her with its sanctifying light. Duty was her daily food — not a burden, nor an artificial action, but the spontaneous movement of her life. Self-sacrifice was as natural to her as self-gratification is to many others. When I say *natural*, I refer to that acquired nature which was the fruit of her Christian experience. She never attached any merit to self-sacrifice, nor regarded herself as having any claim to consideration with God or man founded on it. She took spiritual nourishment as regularly as physical. Prayer was habitual — a frequent, regular, and delightful exercise to her. God was her best friend. His book was read and re-read, to her last hours, with ever fresh satisfaction; it was not only inscribed on her memory, but written on the tables of her heart. The Psalms and the Gospel of John were, perhaps, especial favorites, though not to the disparagement of the rest. What I say of her Christian character may seem like extravagant eulogy to those who did not know her; but it will not to those who knew her well, (for whom this is especially written,) since her religion was not only sentimental and devotional, but lived out in all the little and large things of life, which ever showed her mindful of the things of others, and not of her own, and always denying herself and taking up the cross. What heightened it was her humility, she having no idea that she had any such grace of character, and the sunshiny cheerfulness with which she constantly bore the crosses of life, without the gloom or austerity which sometimes stamp the Christian self-conquest with something like servitude.

Early in the year 1839, our family moved to Jamaica Plain, a part of Roxbury, having succeeded in selling our Groton farm. My brother Arthur had, the autumn previous, gone to Waltham to complete his college preparatory studies, under the teaching of Mrs. Ripley. At Jamaica Plain, Margaret had two pupils from Providence in the house. I attended the school of Mr. S. M. Weld, in Jamaica Plain. I think mother had a good deal of rest here, now the cares and responsibilities, as well as the drudgery, of the farm were over. She had ever great enjoyment in Margaret's society. It was beautiful to see the relation between them — the noble, strong-minded, and courageous daughter sustaining and cheering the heart of that holy and loving parent. Our house in Jamaica Plain was elevated, with a fine view, near a brook, then called Willow Brook; and in the rear were rocks, at times almost covered with the wild columbine.

After I entered college, Margaret, to have me at home, as well as to be with my mother, took a house in Ellery Street, Cambridge. As I record this, memory seems to rush back upon me like a mighty wind, freighted with a mother's and sister's love. Here we resided till I graduated; and in the constant intercourse of my mother and sisters, I enjoyed a noble and elevating society, such as rarely can be expected this side of heaven. Not but there are many pure and noble natures, and often side by side; but they are not often fluent and expressive. Their souls rarely speak and flow forth from one to the other with benignant activity, as they might and should. We kept house in Cambridge till I graduated, in 1844. On my entering the Law School, we purchased the Prospect Street House, in Cambridge, and there resided till I went into the practice of my profession in Boston. This sojourn in Cambridge is marked in memory by the farewells we here took with Margaret on her departure for Europe. O, such a mother and sister! May life be so unselfish, noble, and aspiring that we may obtain admission into such companionship, when these years of fleeting change are passed away!

On my brother Arthur settling in Manchester, N. H., our mother went to live with him, and subsequently, after five years' residence there, removed with him to Boston, residing with him and her loving daughter-in-law * till the departure of the latter to " the better land," in 1856. During this mournful year, our pure and noble sister Ellen was also called to the higher divine life of heaven. Excepting these bereavements, these were sunny years for our mother. She was able to do much good in the parish, and she was the object of much attention. Mother had, for Margaret's sake, a particular sympathy for Italians. She would hear the poor man with his organ, and invariably give; which made the street of my brother's residence quite a common resort for these poor sons and daughters of the land of music. She also visited the suffering Italian women in their homes of penury, more, perhaps, than those of other poor, though she delighted to " lend to the Lord " by bestowing her widow's mite to the destitute of whatever kindred and nation.

We notice in the above narrative that mother had three different successive homes while father lived, and after his death five. But her flowers went with her every where; they were certain to spring up and bloom around her wherever she was. From first to last, as types of the Creator's infinite goodness, beauty, and perfection, she loved them with ardent and undiminished tenderness. Washington said his biography could not be written without the history of his country. Neither could mother's be expressively written without the history of flowers. Families and generations of plants adhered to her, year after year, like the tenantry of a feudal lord. When she left one residence, they accompanied her, or perhaps were set out in the hospitable garden of a friend till she acquired another home. There was a family of lilies, in particular, which adhered to her fortunes for a quarter of a century; and some of them she left in my garden. Mother felt much this frequent change of home. No longer, God be praised! is she tossed to and fro. She is

* Mrs. Elizabeth G. Fuller.

now in an eternal mansion — a home never to change — in the heavens. She is with her Saviour, her loved ones. Shortly before her death, when she could hardly articulate, she joined me in singing, —

> " There, at my Saviour's side,
> I shall be glorified —
>   Heaven is my home!
> There are the good and blest,
> Those I love most and best;
> There, too, I soon shall rest —
>   Heaven is my home."

Even later, she sang with Arthur, —

> " We are passing away, passing away!
> Let us hail the glad day."

Another favorite and oft-repeated hymn with her was that beautiful one by Montgomery, commencing, —

> " Forever with the Lord!
>   Amen, so let it be!
> Life from the dead is in that word —
>   'Tis immortality.
> Within this body pent,
>   Absent from thee I roam,
> Yet nightly pitch my moving tent
>   A day's march nearer home."

Mother had the truest delight in sacred music. When she taught our infant lips to pray, she also encouraged us to join her sweet voice in singing. She accompanied the tune with a gentle motion of one hand. Her love for tunes, like her affection for friends and flowers, was constant and unchanging. " Safely through another week," how often, from my first to my last recollection of her, did I hear her sing! " While with ceaseless course the sun," was another favorite. " Softly now the light of day," she sang constantly. " Brattle Street," " While thee I seek, protecting Power," she loved to sing, especially because Margaret sang it often on her home voyage. Tappan's beautiful hymn, "There is an hour of peaceful rest," she seemed to feel a rest in singing. She was not exclusive, but loved all beautiful hymns, and often bade me sing by the bedside in her last sickness.

In September, 1858, mother came to our house in Wayland to pass her last days. She was suffering from most painful disease, and a fatal result was inevitable. She was sick from that time, and confined to her bed seven months, till she left us on Sabbath morning, July 31, 1859, at half past eight o'clock. Such faith I never witnessed. She had a trust in her Saviour which took away every sad aspect from mortality. She rested in his love. Every day she pursued the even tenor of her Christian life, till she at last "fell asleep" as peacefully as an infant, so that the moment of departure was hardly distinguishable. She told Arthur, shortly before her decease, that she felt she had done with earth, and wanted to go home now. She was only solicitous lest her sickness should be a burden to others. She thanked even the hired nurse for what she did. She took the same *heavenly* interest in the world — that regard which those have for it who live above it — to the last. All that interested others, their plans, their hopes, their improvement, interested her to the very end of life. She suppressed groans and sighs of weariness, and rarely yielded to her pains any outward manifestation. She said she "believed God would give strength to a firm mind to bear whatever he imposed." Her sweetness, resignation, trust, and sympathy were such as to draw to her bedside young children, instead of frightening and repelling, as such scenes usually do. They loved to resort to her sick room. She sought to be useful after she could sit up no longer, by encouraging them in their studies; and as we had a family school, she had them study in her room. When she died, I felt that she had gone to be with Christ, which is far better. But such a spirit as hers enriched life, made it elevated and noble. To live was Christ, and to die was gain. Fitting

33

was it that on that calm and beautiful Sabbath morning her endless day, her glorious Sabbath, her peaceful rest should begin. Fitting that, as gently she had lived, she should as gently die.

> We watched her breathing through the night,
>   Her breathing soft and low,
> As in her breast the wave of life
>   Kept heaving to and fro.
>
>   .   .   .   .
>
> Our very hopes belied our fears,
>   Our fears our hopes belied ;
> We thought her dying when she slept,
>   And sleeping when she died."

C.

[The following poetical tributes, by Mrs. J. H. Hanaford, to the memory of Margaret, of our mother, and our noble and true-hearted brother Eugene, seem to me deserving of a place in this Appendix. No such tribute of affection and honor can fail to be grateful to those who cherish in holy remembrance the members of my family now so fast gathering on the eternal shores. In the closing part of " At Home and Abroad " I have collected other tributes to my sister, both in prose and verse, which the reader who desires can there find. — ED.]

THE ASCENDED SAINT.

[Suggested by the recent death of Mrs. Margaret Fuller, the honored mother of the late Margaret, Countess d' Ossoli.]

> Brightly the morning of the Sabbath dawned,
> And swiftly vanished all the stars of night;
> Like them to be unseen, but still shine on,
> A Christian spirit took its upward flight.
>
> Her years on earth were many, and those years
> All filled with usefulness and holy love;
> Sorrow had disciplined her soul for heaven,
> And trials fitted her for rest above.
>
> Shall we in sackcloth mourn when such depart —
> Freed spirits, like fair uncaged birds, to soar
> Far up and on toward wisdom infinite,
> 'Mid glories mortal minds may not explore ?
>
> O, no! we'll lift on high a triumph song;
> JUBILATE! all her griefs are o'er.
> Loved ones are left; but O! she greeteth now
> The loved and wept for who had gone before.
>
> Death hath removed each dark veil from her eye,
> And radiant spirits walk with her in white;
> No sea in heaven shrouds their beloved forms,
> No sorrow there, no weary, gloomy night.

Strike, strike your harps! sing loud, ye angel choir,
   And welcome gladly this companion new,
New in the courts of heaven, with youth renewed,
   But long ago, it may be, known to you.

The saint ascending to her own "sweet home"
   Claims from no sorrowing hearts a tear or sigh;
We mourn for those who tread earth's pathway still,
   But not for saints triumphant called to die.

Peace to the weary dust whose pain is o'er!
   Joy to the spirit whose long race is run!
God comfort those who wait the summons home,
   Hoping to meet her when their work is done!

EUGENE FULLER.

[Lines suggested by the recent death by drowning of Eugene Fuller
   Esq., brother of Margaret, Countess d' Ossoli.]

I knew him not; mine eye had never gazed
   Upon his thoughtful brow:
His name, so musical, I scarce had heard
   To recognize till now.

But neither years nor space will now erase
   From out my heart his name,
For with his sister's it will e'er be linked
   And share her deathless fame:

Since both have found, when homeward tending, rest
   Beneath the foamy wave,
Whereon no marble monument may stand
   To mark their watery grave.

O Sea! wert thou not satisfied to take
   The sister, good and wise,
And bear her with her loved ones to their home,
   Above the starry skies?

Why shouldst thou rend again those mourning hearts,
   O dark and treacherous Sea?
Why bid those hearts forevermore be sad,
   Ocean! at sight of thee?

Hush! gentle voices to my soul are calling,
  And, whispering, they tell —
" The Ocean is the Lord's; it doth His bidding.
  Repine not; all is well."

Beyond the confines of terrestrial regions
  There is a better shore;
God's love unfathomed, as the only sea,
  Flows round it evermore.

There parted friends shall meet, and Death's **dark wing** -
  Like sea-birds, screaming shrill —
Shall never flap above the drowning forms
  Of friends belovéd still.

God speed the dawning of that glorious day,
  When, sin-freed, we shall be
Where tears are wiped from every grief-dimmed **eye,**
  And where is no more sea.

MARGARET FULLER OSSOLI.

Friend of humanity! whose warm, true **heart**
  Throbbed ever to redeem a fallen race, —
Alas! that thou from earthly scenes shouldst **part,**
  Ere thou hadst reached in joy thy native place.

Thy noble husband, too, whose manly soul
  Longed for fair Freedom in *his* native land, —
Alas! that ocean's waves o'er him should roll,
  Ere he could view, in peace, Columbia's strand.

And that sweet "bud of promise," whose fair **bloom,**
  Evoked from out thy paradise of love,
Once made so fragrant thine Italian home,
  He, too, went with thee to the land above.

An undivided circle! nevermore
  Will tears of sad farewell your cheeks bedew;
For on that other, that celestial shore,
  Our God unites for aye pure hearts and **true.**

Margaret! thy name hath long been to my **soul**
  A talisman of influence pure and strong;
Though born a woman, born to have control
  O'er human hearts for virtue far and long.

33 *

Thy name shall be remembered when shall die
    The name of many a warrior of renown,
For thou on nobler fields gain'dst victory,
    And won from history a glorious crown.

O for the day when Italy shall know
    How to be truly free, in virtue strong! —
We wonder not that thou didst love her so —
    Home of the classics, and the land of song!

When dawns that day on fair Italia's shore,
    Thou shalt be well remembered by the free;
America and Europe evermore
    Shall, as the friend of Freedom, think of thee.

And happier thought! where souls, from every chain
    Made free, forever sing redeeming grace,
There shall thy loved ones hear thy voice again,
    And look with deepest joy upon thy face.

They who love man love God; and they who toil
    To break the chains from men and minds below,
Win, through the Lamb, a right to heaven's soil,
    Where boundless progress each glad soul may know.

God make me worthy, Margaret, to meet thee,
    And list to thy rich converse on the shore
Where holy love from heart to heart flows free,
    And weary spirits rest forevermore.

MEMOIRS

OF

MARGARET FULLER OSSOLI

BY

**R. W. EMERSON, W. H. CHANNING, AND
J. F. CLARKE**

𝔚𝔦𝔱𝔥 𝔞 𝔓𝔬𝔯𝔱𝔯𝔞𝔦𝔱 𝔞𝔫𝔡 𝔞𝔫 𝔄𝔭𝔭𝔢𝔫𝔡𝔦𝔵

Only a learned and a manly soul
  I purposed her, that should with even powers
The rock, the spindle, and the shears control
  Of Destiny, and spin her own free hours.
                      BEN JONSON.

Però che ogni diletto nostro e doglia
Sta in sì e nò saper, voler, potere ;
Adunque quel sol può, che col dovere
Ne trae la ragion fuor di sua soglia.

Adunque tu, lettor di queste note,
S' a te vuoi esser buono, e agli altri caro,
Vogli sempre poter quel che tu debbi.
                    LEONARDO DA VINCI.

VOL. II.

TABLE OF CONTENTS

FOR

VOLUME SECOND.

JAMAICA PLAIN.

BY W. H. CHANNING

" Quando
Lo raggio della grazia, onde s'accende
Verace amore, e che poi cresce amando,
Multiplicato in te tanto risplende,
Che ti conduce su per quella scala,
U' senza risalir nessun discende,
Qual ti negasse 'l vin della sua fiàla
Per la tua sete, in libertà non fòra,
Se non com' acqua ch' al mar non si cala.''
DANTE.

" Weite Welt und breites Leben,
Langer Jahre redlich Streben,
Stets geforscht und stets gegründet,
Nie geschlossen, oft geründet,
Aeltestes bewahrt mit Treue,
Freundlich aufgefasstes Neue,
Heitern Sinn und reine Zwecke :
Nun ! man kommt wohl eine Strecke.''
GOETHE.

"My purpose holds
To sail beyond the sunset, and the baths
Of all the western stars, until I die.
It may be that the gulfs will wash us down ;
It may be we shall touch the Happy Isles."

TENNYSON.

"Remember how august the heart is.   It contains the temple not only
of Love but of Conscience ; and a whisper is heard from the extremity of
one to the extremity of the other."

LANDOR

"If all the gentlest-hearted friends I knew
Concentred in one heart their gentleness,
That still grew gentler till its pulse was less
For life than pity,—I should yet be slow
To bring my own heart nakedly below
The palm of such a friend, that he should press
My false, ideal joy and fickle woe
Out to full light and knowledge."

ELIZABETH BARRETT

VI.

JAMAICA PLAIN.

I.

FIRST IMPRESSIONS.

IT was while Margaret was residing at Jamaica Plain, in the summer of 1839, that we first really met as friends, though for several years previous we had been upon terms of kindest mutual regard. And, as the best way of showing how her wonderful character opened upon me, the growth of our acquaintance shall be briefly traced.

The earliest recollection of Margaret is as a schoolmate of my sisters, in Boston. At that period she was considered a prodigy of talent and accomplishment; but a sad feeling prevailed, that she had been overtasked by her father, who wished to train her like a boy, and that she was paying the penalty for undue application, in nearsightedness, awkward manners, extravagant tendencies of thought, and a pedantic style of talk, that made her a butt for the ridicule of frivolous companions. Some seasons later, I call to mind seeing, at the "Commencements" and "Exhibitions" of Harvard University, a girl, plain in appearance, but of dashing air, who was invariably the centre of a listening group, and kept their merry interest alive by sparkles of wit and incessant small-talk. The bystanders called her familiarly, "Margaret," "Margaret Fuller;" for, though young, she was already noted for conversational gifts, and had the rare skill of attracting to her society, not spirited collegians only, but men mature in culture and of established reputation. It was impossible not to admire her fluency and fun; yet, though curiosity was piqued as to this entertaining personage, I never sought an introduction, but, on the contrary, rather shunned encounter with one so armed from head to foot in saucy sprightliness.

About 1830, however, we often met in the social circles of Cambridge, and I began to observe her more nearly. At first, her vivacity, decisive tone, downrightness, and contempt of conventional standards, continued to repel. She appeared too *intense* in expression, action, emphasis, to be pleasing, and wanting in that *retenue* which we associate with delicate dignity. Occasionally, also, words flashed from her of such scathing satire, that prudence counselled the keeping at safe distance from a body so surcharged with electricity. Then, again, there was an imperial — shall it be said imperious? — air, exacting deference to her judgments and loyalty to her behests, that prompted pride to retaliatory measures. She paid slight heed, moreover, to the trim palings of etiquette, but swept through the garden-beds and into the doorway of one's confidence so cavalierly, that a reserved person felt inclined to lock himself up in his sanctum. Finally, to the coolly-scanning eye, her friendships wore a look of such romantic exaggeration, that she seemed to walk enveloped in a shining fog of sentimentalism. In brief, it must candidly be confessed, that

I then suspected her of affecting the part of a Yankee Corinna.

But soon I was charmed, unaware, with the sagacity of her sallies, the profound thoughts carelessly dropped by her on transient topics, the breadth and richness of culture manifested in her allusions or quotations, her easy comprehension of new views, her just discrimination, and, above all, her *truthfulness.* "Truth at all cost," was plainly her ruling maxim. This it was that made her criticism so trenchant, her contempt of pretence so quick and stern, her speech so naked in frankness, her gaze so searching, her whole attitude so alert. Her estimates of men, books, manners, events, art, duty, destiny, were moulded after a grand ideal; and she was a severe judge from the very loftiness of her standard. Her stately deportment, border though it might on arrogance, but expressed high-heartedness. Her independence, even if haughty and rash, was the natural action of a self-centred will, that waited only fit occasion to prove itself heroic. Her earnestness to read the hidden history of others was the gauge of her own emotion. The enthusiasm that made her speech so affluent, when measured by the average scale, was the unconscious overflow of a poetic temperament. And the ardor of her friends' affection proved the faithfulness of her love. Thus gradually the mist melted away, till I caught a glimpse of her real self. We were one evening talking of American literature, — she contrasting its boyish crudity, half boastful, half timid, with the tempered, manly equipoise of thorough-bred European writers, and I asserting that in its mingled practicality and aspiration might be read bright auguries; when, betrayed by sympathy, she laid bare her secret hope of what Woman might be and do, as an author, in our Republic. The sketch was an outline only, and dashed off with a few swift strokes, but therein appeared her own portrait, and we were strangers no more.

It was through the medium of others, however, that at this time I best learned to appreciate Margaret's nobleness of nature and principle. My most intimate friend in the Theological School, James Freeman Clarke, was her constant companion in exploring the rich gardens of German literature; and from his descriptions I formed a vivid image of her industry, comprehensiveness, buoyancy, patience, and came to honor her intelligent interest in high problems of science, her aspirations after spiritual greatness, her fine æsthetic taste, her religiousness. By power to quicken other minds, she showed how living was her own. Yet more near were we brought by common attraction toward a youthful visitor in our circle, the untouched freshness of whose beauty was but the transparent garb of a serene, confiding, and harmonious soul, and whose polished grace, at once modest and naïve, sportive and sweet, fulfilled the charm of innate goodness of heart. Susceptible in temperament, anticipating with ardent fancy the lot of a lovely and refined woman, and morbidly exaggerating her own slight personal defects, Margaret seemed to long, as it were, to transfuse with her force this nymph-like form, and to fill her to glowing with her own lyric fire. No drop of envy tainted the sisterly love, with which she sought by genial sympathy thus to live in another's experience, to be her guardian-angel, to shield her from contact with the unworthy, to rouse each generous impulse, to invigorate thought by truth incarnate in beauty, and with unfelt ministry to weave bright threads in her web of fate.

Thus more and more Margaret became an object of
respectful interest, in whose honor, magnanimity and
strength I learned implicitly to trust.

Separation, however, hindered our growing acquaintance, as we both left Cambridge, and, with the exception
of a few chance meetings in Boston and a ramble or
two in the glens and on the beaches of Rhode Island, held
no further intercourse till the summer of 1839, when,
as has been already said, the friendship, long before
rooted, grew up and leafed and bloomed.

I I.

A CLUE.

I HAVE no hope of conveying to readers my sense of
the beauty of our relation, as it lies in the past with
brightness falling on it from Margaret's risen spirit. It
would be like printing a chapter of autobiography, to
describe what is so grateful in memory, its influence
upon one's self. And much of her inner life, as confidentially disclosed, could not be represented without
betraying a sacred trust. All that can be done is to
open the outer courts, and give a clue for loving hearts
to follow. To such these few sentences may serve as a
guide.

'When I feel, as I do this morning, the poem of exist-
'ence, I am repaid for all trial. The bitterness of
'wounded affection, the disgust at unworthy care, the
'aching sense of how far deeds are transcended by our
'lowest aspirations, pass away as I lean on the bosom
'of Nature, and inhale new life from her breath. Could
'but love, like knowledge, be its own reward!'

'Oftentimes I have found in those of my own sex more 'gentleness, grace, and purity, than in myself; but seldom 'the heroism which I feel within my own breast. I 'blame not those who think the heart cannot bleed be-'cause it is so strong; but little they dream of what lies 'concealed beneath the determined courage. Yet mine 'has been the Spartan sternness, smiling while it hides 'the wound. I long rather for the Christian spirit, which 'even on the cross prays, "Father, forgive them," and 'rises above fortitude to heavenly satisfaction.'

'Remember that only through aspirations, which some-'times make me what is called unreasonable, have I been 'enabled to vanquish unpropitious circumstances, and 'save my soul alive.'

'All the good I have ever done has been by calling on 'every nature for its highest. I will admit that some-'times I have been wanting in gentleness, but never in 'tenderness, nor in noble faith.'

'The heart which hopes and dares is also accessible 'to terror, and this falls upon it like a thunderbolt. It 'can never defend itself at the moment, it is so surprised. 'There is no defence but to strive for an equable temper 'of courageous submission, of obedient energy, that shall 'make assault less easy to the foe.

'*This* is the dart within the heart, as well as I can tell 'it: — At moments, the music of the universe, which 'daily I am upheld by hearing, seems to stop. I fall 'like a bird when the sun is eclipsed, not looking for 'such darkness. The sense of my individual law — 'that lamp of life — flickers. I am repelled in what is

'most natural to me. I feel as, when a suffering child,
'I would go and lie with my face to the ground, to sob
'away my little life.'

'In early years, when, though so frank as to the
'thoughts of the mind, I put no heart confidence in
'any human being, my refuge was in my journal. I
'have burned those records of my youth, with its bitter
'tears, and struggles, and aspirations. Those aspira-
'tions were high, and have gained only broader founda-
'tions and wider reach. But the leaves had done their
'work. For years to write there, instead of speaking,
'had enabled me to soothe myself; and the Spirit was
'often my friend, when I sought no other. Once again
'I am willing to take up the cross of loneliness. Re-
'solves are idle, but the anguish of my soul has been
'deep. It will not be easy to profane life by rhetoric.'

'I woke thinking of the monks of La Trappe; — how
'could they bear their silence? When the game of life
'was lost for me, in youthful anguish I knew well the
'desire for that vow; but if I had taken it, my heart
'would have burned out my physical existence long ago.'

'Save me from plunging into the depths to learn the
'worst, or from being led astray by the winged joys of
'childish feeling. I pray for truth in proportion as there
'is strength to receive.'

'My law is incapable of a charter. I pass all bounds,
'and cannot do otherwise. Those whom it seems to me
I am to meet again in the Ages, I meet, soul to soul,
'now. I have no knowledge of any circumstances ex-
'cept the degree of affinity.'

' I feel that my impatient nature needs the dark days.
'I would learn the art of limitation, without compro-
'mise, and act out my faith with a delicate fidelity.
' When loneliness becomes too oppressive, I feel Him
'drawing me nearer, to be soothed by the smile of an
' All-Intelligent Love. He will not permit the freedom
' essential to growth to be checked. If I can give myself
' up to Him, I shall not be too proud, too impetuous,
'neither too timid, and fearful of a wound or cloud.'

III.

TRANSCENDENTALISM.

THE summer of 1839 saw the full dawn of the Transcendental movement in New England. The rise of this
enthusiasm was as mysterious as that of any form of
revival; and only they who were of the faith could
comprehend how bright was this morning-time of a
new hope. Transcendentalism was an assertion of the
inalienable integrity of man, of the immanence of Divinity in instinct. In part, it was a reaction against
Puritan Orthodoxy; in part, an effect of renewed study
of the ancients, of Oriental Pantheists, of Plato and the
Alexandrians, of Plutarch's Morals, Seneca and Epictetus; in part, the natural product of the culture of the
place and time. On the somewhat stunted stock of
Unitarianism, — whose characteristic dogma was trust in
individual reason as correlative to Supreme Wisdom, —
had been grafted German Idealism, as taught by masters
of most various schools, — by Kant and Jacobi, Fichte

and Novalis, Schelling and Hegel, Schleiermacher and
De Wette, by Madame de Stael, Cousin, Coleridge, and
Carlyle; and the result was a vague yet exalting conception of the godlike nature of the human spirit.
Transcendentalism, as viewed by its disciples, was a
pilgrimage from the idolatrous world of creeds and
rituals to the temple of the Living God in the soul. It
was a putting to silence of tradition and formulas, that
the Sacred Oracle might be heard through intuitions of
the single-eyed and pure-hearted. Amidst materialists,
zealots, and sceptics, the Transcendentalist believed in
perpetual inspiration, the miraculous power of will, and
a birthright to universal good. He sought to hold communion face to face with the unnameable Spirit of his
spirit, and gave himself up to the embrace of nature's
beautiful joy, as a babe seeks the breast of a mother.
To him the curse seemed past; and love was without
fear. "All mine is thine" sounded forth to him in
ceaseless benediction, from flowers and stars, through the
poetry, art, heroism of all ages, in the aspirations of his
own genius, and the budding promise of the time. His
work was to be faithful, as all saints, sages, and lovers
of man had been, to Truth, as the very Word of God. His
maxims were, — "Trust, dare and be; infinite good is
ready for your asking; seek and find. All that your
fellows can claim or need is that you should become, in
fact, your highest self; fulfil, then, your ideal." Hence,
among the strong, withdrawal to private study and contemplation, that they might be "alone with the Alone;"
solemn yet glad devotedness to the Divine leadings in the
inmost will; calm concentration of thought to wait for
and receive wisdom; dignified independence, stern yet
sweet, of fashion and public opinion; honest originality

of speech and conduct, exempt alike from apology or dictation, from servility or scorn. Hence, too, among the weak, whimsies, affectation, rude disregard of proprieties, slothful neglect of common duties, surrender to the claims of natural appetite, self-indulgence, self-absorption. and self-idolatry.

By their very posture of mind, as seekers of the new, the Transcendentalists were critics and "come-outers" from the old. Neither the church, the state, the college, society, nor even reform associations, had a hold upon their hearts. The past might be well enough for those who, without make-belief, could yet put faith in common dogmas and usages; but for them the matin-bells of a new day were chiming, and the herald-trump of freedom was heard upon the mountains. Hence, leaving ecclesi-astical organizations, political parties, and familiar circles, which to them were brown with drought, they sought in covert nooks, of friendship for running waters, and fruit from the tree of life. The journal, the letter, became of greater worth than the printed page; for they felt that systematic results were not yet to be looked for, and that in sallies of conjecture, glimpses and flights of ecstasy, the "Newness" lifted her veil to her votaries. Thus, by mere attraction of affinity, grew together the brotherhood of the "Like-minded," as they were pleas-antly nicknamed by outsiders, and by themselves, on the ground that no two were of the same opinion. The only password of membership to this association, which had no compact, records, or officers, was a hopeful and liberal spirit; and its chance conventions were determined merely by the desire of the caller for a "talk," or by the arrival of some guest from a distance with a budget of pre-sumptive novelties. Its "symposium" was a pic-nic, whereto each brought of his gains, as he felt prompted, a bunch of wild grapes from the woods, or bread-corn from his threshing-floor. The tone of the assemblies was cordial welcome for every one's peculiarity; and scholars, farmers, mechanics, merchants, married women, and maidens, met there on a level of courteous respect. The only guest not tolerated was intolerance; though strict justice might add, that these "Illuminati' were as unconscious of their special cant as smoker. are of the perfume of their weed, and that a professed declaration of universal independence turned,out in practice to be rather oligarchic.

Of the class of persons most frequently found at these meetings Margaret has left the following sketch : —

'"I am not mad, most noble Festus," was Paul s
'rejoinder, as he turned upon his vulgar censor with the
'grace of a courtier, the dignity of a prophet, and the
'mildness of a saint. But many there are, who, adher-
'ing to the faith of the soul with that unusual earnestness
'which the world calls "mad," can answer their critics
'only by the eloquence of their characters and lives.
'Now, the other day, while visiting a person whose highest
'merit, so far as I know, is to save his pennies, I was
'astounded by hearing him allude to some of most
'approved worth among us, thus : "You know *we* con
'"sider *those men* insane."
'What this meant, I could not at first well guess, so completely was my scale of character turned topsy-turvy. But revolving the subject afterward, I perceived that WE was the multiple of Festus, and THOSE MEN of Paul. All the circumstances seemed the same as in 'that Syrian hall; for the persons in question were they

' who cared more for doing good than for fortune and
' success, — more for the one risen from the dead than for
' fleshly life, — more for the Being in whom we live and
' move than for King Agrippa.

'Among this band of candidates for the mad-house, I
found the young poet who valued insight of nature's
' beauty, and the power of chanting to his fellow-men a
heavenly music, above the prospect of fortune, political
' power, or a standing in fashionable society. At the
' division of the goods of this earth, he was wandering
'like Schiller's poet. But the difference between Amer-
' ican and German regulations would seem to be, that in
' Germany the poet, when not "with Jove," is left at
' peace on earth; while here he is, by a self-constituted
' police, declared "mad."

'Another of this band was the young girl who, early
' taking a solemn view of the duties of life, found it
' difficult to serve an apprenticeship to its follies. She
' could not turn her sweetness into "manner," nor culti-
' vate love of approbation at the expense of virginity of
' heart. In so called society she found no outlet for her
' truest, fairest self, and so preferred to live with external
' nature, a few friends, her pencil, instrument, and books.
' She, they say, is "mad."

'And he, the enthusiast for reform, who gives away
' fortune, standing in the world, peace, and only not life
' because bigotry is now afraid to exact the pound of
' flesh as well as the ducats, — he, whose heart beats high
' with hopes for the welfare of his race, is "mad."

'And he, the philosopher, who does not tie down his
speculation to the banner of the day, but lets the wings
of his thought upbear him where they will, as if they
were stronger and surer than the balloon let off for the

' amusement of the populace, — he must be " mad." Off
' with him to the moon ! that paradise of noble fools, who
' had visions of possibilities too grand and lovely for this
' sober earth.

' And ye, friends, and lovers, who see, through all the
' films of human nature, in those you love, a divine energy,
' worthy of creatures who have their being in very God,
' ye, too, are " mad " to think they can walk in the dust,
' and yet shake it from their feet when they come upon
' the green. These are no winged Mercuries, no silver-
' sandalled Madonnas. Listen to " the world's " truth
' and soberness, and we will show you that your heart
' would be as well placed in a hospital, as in these air-
' born palaces.

' And thou, priest, seek thy God among the people, and
' not in the shrine. The light need not penetrate thine
' own soul. Thou canst catch the true inspiration from
' the eyes of thy auditors. Not the Soul of the World,
' not the ever-flowing voice of nature, but the articulate
' accents of practical utility, should find thy ear ever
' ready. Keep always among men, and consider what
' they like; for in the silence of thine own breast will be
' heard the voices that make men " mad." Why shouldst
' thou judge of the consciousness of others by thine own ?
' May not thine own soul have been made morbid, by
' retiring too much within ? If Jesus of Nazareth had
' not fasted and prayed so much alone, the devil could
' never have tempted him; if he had observed the public
' mind more patiently and carefully, he would have
: waited till the time was ripe, and the minds of men
prepared for what he had to say. He would thus have
escaped the ignominious death, which so prematurely
cut short his " usefulness." Jewry would thus, gently

'soberly, and without disturbance, have been led to a
'better course.

  '"Children of this generation!"—ye Festuses and
'Agrippas!—ye are wiser, we grant, than "the children
'"of light;" yet we advise you to commend to a higher
'tribunal those whom much learning, or much love, has
'made "mad." For if they stay here, almost will they
'persuade even you!'

Amidst these meetings of the Transcendentalists it
was, that, after years of separation, I again found Margaret. Of this body she was member by grace of nature.
Her romantic freshness of heart, her craving for the
truth, her self-trust, had prepared her from childhood to
be a pioneer in prairie-land; and her discipline in German schools had given definite form and tendency to her
idealism. Her critical yet aspiring intellect filled her
with longing for germs of positive affirmation in place
of the chaff of thrice-sifted negation; while her æsthetic
instinct responded in accord to the praise of Beauty as
the beloved heir of Good and Truth, whose right it is to
reign. On the other hand, strong common-sense saved
her from becoming visionary, while she was too well-
read as a scholar to be caught by conceits, and had been
too sternly tried by sorrow to fall into fanciful effeminacy.
It was a pleasing surprise to see how this friend of
earlier days was acknowledged as a peer of the realm, in
this new world of thought. Men,—her superiors in
years, fame and social position,—treated her more with
the frankness due from equal to equal, than the half-
condescending deference with which scholars are wont
to adapt themselves to women. They did not talk down
o her standard, nor translate their dialect into popular

phrase, but trusted to her power of interpretation. It was evident that they prized her verdict, respected her criticism, feared her rebuke, and looked to her as an umpire. Very observable was it, also, how, in side-talks with her, they became confidential, seemed to glow and brighten into their best mood, and poured out in full measure what they but scantily hinted in the circle at large.

IV.

GENIUS.

It was quite a study to watch the phases througn which Margaret passed, in one of these assemblies. There was something in the air and step with which she chose her place in the company, betokening an instinctive sense, that, in intellect, she was of blood royal and needed to ask no favors. And then she slowly gathered her attention to take in the significance of the scene. Near-sighted and habitually using an eye-glass, she rapidly scanned the forms and faces, pausing intently where the expression of particular heads or groups suggested thought, and ending her survey with some apt home-thrust to her next neighbors, as if to establish full *rapport*, and so to become a medium for the circulating life. Only when thus in magnetic relations with all present, by a clear impress of their state and place, did she seem prepared to rise to a higher stage of communion. Then she listened, with ear finely vibrating to every tone, with all capacities responsive in sympathy, with a swift and ductile power of appreciation, that made her feel to the quick the varying moods of different speakers, and yet the while

with coolest self-possession. Now and then a slight
smile, flickering over her countenance, as lightning plays
on the surface of a cloud, marked the inward process
whereby she was harmonizing in equilibrium opposing
thoughts. And, as occasion offered, a felicitous quota-
tion, pungent apothegm, or symbolic epithet, dropped
unawares in undertone, showed how swiftly scattered
rays were brought in her mind to a focus.

When her turn came, by a graceful transition she
resumed the subject where preceding speakers had
left it, and, briefly summing up their results, proceeded to unfold her own view. Her opening was
deliberate, like the progress of some massive force gaining its momentum; but as she felt her way, and moving in a congenial element, the sweep of her speech
became grand. The style of her eloquence was senten-
tious, free from prettiness, direct, vigorous, charged with
vitality. Articulateness, just emphasis and varied accent,
brought out most delicate shades and brilliant points of
meaning, while a rhythmical collocation of words gave a
finished form to every thought. She was affluent in
historic illustration and literary allusion, as well as in
novel hints. She knew how to concentrate into racy
phrases the essential truth gathered from wide research,
and distilled with patient toil; and by skilful treatment
she could make green again the wastes of common-
place. Her statements, however rapid, showed breadth
of comprehension, ready memory, impartial judgment,
nice analysis of differences, power of penetrating through
surfaces to realities, fixed regard to central laws and
habitual communion with the Life of life. Critics,
indeed, might have been tempted to sneer at a certain
oracular grandiloquence, that bore away her soberness

ın moments of elation; though even the most captious must presently have smiled at the humor of her descriptive touches, her dexterous exposure of folly and pretension, the swift stroke of her bright wit, her shrewd discernment, promptitude, and presence of mind. The reverential, too, might have been pained at the sternness wherewith popular men, measures, and established customs, were tried and found guilty, at her tribunal; but even while blaming her aspirations as rash, revolutionary and impractical, no honest conservative could fail to recognize the sincerity of her aim. And every deep observer of character would have found the explanation of what seemed vehement or too high-strung, in the longing of a spirited woman to break every trammel that checked her growth or fettered her movement.

In conversations like these, one saw that the richness of Margaret's genius resulted from a rare combination of opposite qualities. To her might have been well applied the words first used as describing George Sand: "Thou large-brained Woman, and large-hearted Man." She blended in closest union and swift interplay feminine receptiveness with masculine energy. She was at once impressible and creative, impulsive and deliberate, pliant in sympathy yet firmly self-centred, confidingly responsive while commanding in originality. By the vivid intensity of her conceptions, she brought out in those around their own consciousness, and, by the glowing vigor of her intellect, roused into action their torpid powers. On the other hand, she reproduced a truth, whose germ had just been imbibed from others, moulded after her own image and quickened by her own life, with marvellous rapidity. And

the presence of congenial minds so stimulated the prolific power of her imagination, that she was herself
astonished at the fresh beauty of her new-born
thoughts. 'There is a mortifying sense,' she writes,
'of having played the Mirabeau after a talk with a
'circle of intelligent persons. They come with a store
'of acquired knowledge and reflection, on the subject
'in debate, about which I may know little, and have
'reflected less; yet, by mere apprehensiveness and
'prompt intuition, I may appear their superior. Spon-
'taneously I appropriate all their material, and turn it to
'my own ends, as if it was my inheritance from a long
'train of ancestors. Rays of truth flash out at the
'moment, and they are startled by the light thrown
'over their familiar domain. Still they are gainers,
'for I give them new impulse, and they go on their
'way rejoicing in the bright glimpses they have caught.
'I should despise myself, if I purposely appeared thus
'brilliant, but I am inspired as by a power higher than
'my own.' All friends will bear witness to the strict fidelity of this sketch. There were seasons when she seemed
borne irresistibly on to the verge of prophecy, and fully
embodied one's notion of a sibyl.

Admirable as Margaret appeared in public, I was yet
more affected by this peculiar mingling of impressibility
and power to influence, when brought within her private sphere. I know not how otherwise to describe her
subtle charm, than by saying that she was at once a
clairvoyante and a magnetizer. She read another's
bosom-secret, and she imparted of her own force. She
interpreted the cipher in the talisman of one's destiny,
that he had tried in vain to spell alone; by sympathy she
brought out the invisible characters traced by experi-

ence on his heart; and in the mirror of her conscience he might see the image of his very self, as dwarfed in actual appearance, or developed after the divine ideal. Her. sincerity was terrible. In her frank exposure no foible was spared, though by her very reproof she roused dormant courage and self-confidence. And so unerring seemed her insight, that her companion felt as if standing bare before a disembodied spirit, and communicated without reserve thoughts and emotions, which, even to himself, he had scarcely named.

This penetration it was that caused Margaret to be so dreaded, in general society, by superficial observers. They, who came nigh enough to test the quality of her spirit, could not but perceive how impersonal was her justice; but, contrasted with the dead flat of conventional tolerance, her candor certainly looked rugged and sharp. The frivolous were annoyed at her contempt of their childishness, the ostentatious piqued at her insensibility to their show, and the decent scared lest they should be stripped of their shams; partisans were vexed by her spurning their leaders; and professional sneerers, — civil in public to those whom in private they slandered, — could not pardon the severe truth whereby she drew the sting from their spite. Indeed, how could so undisguised a censor but shock the prejudices of the moderate, and wound the sensibilities of the diffident; how but enrage the worshippers of new demigods in literature, art and fashion, whose pet shrines she demolished; how but cut to the quick, alike by silence or by speech, the self-love of the vain, whose claims she ignored? So gratuitous, indeed, appeared her hypercriticism, that I could not refrain from remonstrance, and to one of my appeals she thus replied: 'If a horror for

'the mania of little great men, so prevalent in this coun-
'try, — if aversion to the sentimental exaggerations to
' which so many minds are prone, — if finding that most
'men praise, as well as blame, too readily, and that
'overpraise desecrates the lips and makes the breath
'unworthy to blow the coal of devotion, — if rejection of
'the ——s and ——s, from a sense that the priestess
'must reserve her pæans for Apollo, — if untiring effort
'to form my mind to justice and revere only the super-
'latively good, that my praise might be praise; if this be
'to offend, then have I offended.'

V

THE DIAL.

SEVERAL talks among the Transcendentalists, during
the autumn of 1839, turned upon the propriety of estab-
lishing an organ for the expression of freer views than
the conservative journals were ready to welcome. The
result was the publication of the "Dial," the first number of which appeared early in the summer of 1840,
under the editorship of Margaret, aided by R. W. Emerson and George Ripley. How moderate were her
own hopes, in regard to this enterprise, is clearly enough
shown by passages from her correspondence.

'*Jamaica Plain,* 22*d March,* 1840. * * * I have a
'great deal written, but, as I read it over, scarce a word
'seems pertinent to the place or time. When I meet
'people, it is easy to adapt myself to them; but when I
'write, it is into another world, — not a better one, perhaps, but one with very dissimilar habits of thought to

'tnis wnerein I am domesticated. How much those of
'us, who have been formed by the European mind,
'nave to unlearn, and lay aside, if we would act here!
'I would fain do something worthily that belonged to the
'country where I was born, but most times I fear it may
'not be.

'What others can do, — whether all that has been
'said is the mere restlessness of discontent, or there are
'thoughts really struggling for utterance,—will be tested
'now. A perfectly free organ is to be offered for the
'expressio* of individual thought and character. There
'are no party measures to be carried, no particular stand-
'ard to be set up. A fair, calm tone, a recognition of
'universal principles, will, I hope, pervade the essays in
'every form. I trust there will be a spirit neither of
'dogmatism nor of compromise, and that this journal
'will aim, not at leading public opinion, but at stimulat-
'ing each man to judge for himself, and to think more
'deeply and more nobly, by letting him see how some
'minds are kept alive by a wise self-trust. We must not
'be sanguine as to the amount of talent which will be
'brought to bear on this publication. All concerned are
'rather indifferent, and there is no great promise for the
'present. We cannot show high culture, and I doubt
'about vigorous thought. But we shall manifest free
'action as far as it goes, and a high aim. It were much
'if a periodical could be kept open, not to accomplish
'any outward object, but merely to afford an avenue for
'what of liberal and calm thought might be originated
'among us, by the wants of individual minds.' * *

'*April* 19, 1840. — Things go on pretty well, but doubt-
'less people will be disappointed, for they seem to be look-

'ing for the Gospel of Transcendentalism. It may prove
'as Jouffroy says it was with the successive French min-
'istries : "The public wants something positive, and
'"seeing that such and such persons are excellent at
'"fault-finding, it raises them to be rulers, when, lo!
'"they have no noble and full Yea, to match their
'"shrill and bold Nay, and so are pulled down again."
'Mr. Emerson knows best what he wants; but he has
'already said it in various ways. Yet, this experiment
'is well worth trying; hearts beat so high, they must
'be full of something, and here is a way to breathe it
'out quite freely. It is for dear New England that I
'want this review. For myself, if I had wished to write
'a few pages now and then, there were ways and means
'enough of disposing of them. But in truth I have not
'much to say; for since I have had leisure to look at
·myself, I find that, so far from being an original genius,
'I have not yet learned to think to any depth, and that
'the utmost I have done in life has been to form my
'character to a certain consistency, cultivate my tastes,
'and learn to tell the truth with a little better grace
'than I did at first. For this the world will not care
'much, so I shall hazard a few critical remarks only, or
'an unpretending chalk sketch now and then, till I have
'learned to do something. There will be beautiful poe-
'sies; about prose we know not yet so well. We shall
'be the means of publishing the little Charles Emerson
'left as a mark of his noble course, and, though it lies
'in fragments, all who read will be gainers.'

'1840. — Since the Revolution, there has been little,
'in the circumstances of this country, to call out the
'higher sentiments. The effect of continued prosperity

'is the same on nations as on individuals, — it ɛaves the
'nobler faculties undeveloped. The need of bringing
' out the physical resources of a vast extent of country
' the commercial and political fever incident to our insti-
' tutions, tend to fix the eyes of men on what is local
' and temporary, on the external advantages of their
' condition. The superficial diffusion of knowledge,
' unless attended by a correspondent deepening of its
' sources, is likely to vulgarize rather than to raise the
' thought of a nation, depriving them of another sort of
' education through sentiments of reverence, and lead-
' ing the multitude to believe themselves capable of judg-
' ing what they but dimly discern. They see a wide
' surface, and forget the difference between seeing and
' knowing. In this hasty way of thinking and living
' they traverse so much ground that they forget that
' not the sleeping railroad passenger, but the botanist,
' the geologist, the poet, really see the country, and that,
' to the former, "a miss is as good as a mile." In a word,
' the tendency of circumstances has been to make our
' people superficial, irreverent, and more anxious to get a
' living than to live mentally and morally. This ten-
' dency is no way balanced by the slight literary culture
' common here, which is mostly English, and consists in
' a careless reading of publications of the day, having
' the same utilitarian tendency with our own proceed-
' ings. The infrequency of acquaintance with any of
' the great fathers of English lore marks this state of
' things.

' New England is now old enough, — some there
' have leisure enough, — to look at all this; and the
' consequence is a violent reäction, in a small minority,
' against a mode of culture that rears such fruits

' They see that political freedom does not necessarily
' produce liberality of mind, nor freedom in church
' institutions — vital religion ; and, seeing that these
' changes cannot be wrought from without inwards, they
' are trying to quicken the soul, that they may work
' from within outwards. Disgusted with the vulgarity
' of a commercial aristocracy, they become radicals; dis-
' gusted with the materialistic working of "rational" reli-
- gion, they become mystics. They quarrel with all that
' is, because it is not spiritual enough. They would, per-
' haps, be patient if they thought this the mere sensual-
' ity of childhood in our nation, which it might outgrow;
: but they think that they see the evil widening, deepen-
' ing, — not only debasing the life, but corrupting the
' thought of our people, and they feel that if they know
' not well what should be done, yet that the duty of
' every good man is to utter a protest against what is
' done amiss.

' Is this protest undiscriminating? are these opinions
' crude? do these proceedings threaten to sap the bul-
' warks on which men at present depend? I confess
' it all, yet I see in these men promise of a better wis-
' dom than in their opponents. Their hope for man is
' grounded on his destiny as an immortal soul, and not as
' a mere comfort-loving inhabitant of earth, or as a sub-
' scriber to the social contract. It was not meant that
' the soul should cultivate the earth, but that the earth
' should educate and maintain the soul. Man is not
' made for society, but society is made for man. No
' institution can be good which does not tend to improve
' the individual. In these principles I have confidence
' so profound, that I am not afraid to trust those whc
  hold them, despite their partial views, imperfectly

'developed characters, and frequent want of practical
'sagacity. I believe, if they have opportunity to state
'and discuss their opinions, they will gradually sift them,
'ascertain their grounds and aims with clearness, and do
'the work this country needs. I hope for them as for
'"the leaven that is hidden in the bushel of meal, till
'"all be leavened." The leaven is not good by itself,
'neither is the meal; let them combine, and we shall yet
'have bread.

'Utopia it is impossible to build up. At least, my
'hopes for our race on this one planet are more limited
'than those of most of my friends. I accept the limita-
'tions of human nature, and believe a wise acknowledg-
'ment of them one of the best conditions of progress.
'Yet every noble scheme, every poetic manifestation,
'prophesies to man his eventual destiny. And were not
'man ever more sanguine than facts at the moment
'justify, he would remain torpid, or be sunk in sensuality.
'It is on this ground that I sympathize with what is
'called the "Transcendental party," and that I feel
'their aim to be the true one. They acknowledge in the
'nature of man an arbiter for his deeds, — a standard
'transcending sense and time, — and are, in my view,
'the true utilitarians. They are but at the beginning of
'their course, and will, I hope, learn how to make use
'of the past, as well as to aspire for the future, and to
'be true in the present moment.

'My position as a woman, and the many private
'duties which have filled my life, have prevented my
'thinking deeply on several of the great subjects which
'these friends have at heart. I suppose, if ever I become
'capable of judging, I shall differ from most of them on
important points. But I am not afraid to trust any who

'are true, and in intent noble, with their own course
'nor to aid in enabling them to express their thoughts,
'whether I coincide with them or not.

'On the subject of Christianity, my mind is clear. If
'Divine, it will stand the test of any comparison. I
'believe the reason it has so imperfectly answered to the
'aspirations of its Founder is, that men have received it
'on external grounds. I believe that a religion, thus
'received, may give the life an external decorum, but will
'never open the fountains of holiness in the soul.

'One often thinks of Hamlet as the true represen-
'tative of idealism in its excess. Yet if, in his short
'life, man be liable to some excess, should we not rather
'prefer to have the will palsied like Hamlet, by a deep-
'searching tendency and desire for poetic perfection,
'than to have it enlightened by worldly sagacity, as in
'the case of Julius Cæsar, or made intense by pride alone,
'as in that of Coriolanus?

'After all, I believe it is absurd to attempt to speak on
'these subjects within the limits of a letter. I will try
'to say what I mean in print some day. Yet one word
'as to "the material," in man. Is it not the object of all
'philosophy, as well as of religion and poetry, to prevent
'its prevalence? Must not those who see most truly be
'ever making statements of the truth to combat this
'sluggishness, or worldliness? What else are sages,
'poets, preachers, born to do? Men go an undulating
'course, — sometimes on the hill, sometimes in the valley.
'But he only is in the right who in the valley forgets
'not the hill-prospect, and knows in darkness that the
'sun will rise again. That is the real life which is sub-
'ordinated to, not merged in, the ideal; he is only wise
'who can bring the lowest act of his life into sympathy

'with its highest thought. And this I take to be the one 'only aim of our pilgrimage here. I agree with those 'who think that no true philosophy will try to ignore or 'annihilate the material part of man, but will rather seek 'to put it in its place, as servant and minister to the 'soul.'

V I.

THE WOMAN.

In 1839 I had met Margaret upon the plane of intellect. In the summer of 1840, on my return from the West, she was to be revealed in a new aspect.

It was a radiant and refreshing morning, when I entered the parlor of her pleasant house, standing upon a slope beyond Jamaica Plain to the south. She was absent at the moment, and there was opportunity to look from the windows on a cheerful prospect, over orchards and meadows, to the wooded hills and the western sky. Presently Margaret appeared, bearing in her hand a vase of flowers, which she had been gathering in the garden. After exchange of greetings, her first words were of the flowers, each of which was symbolic to her of emotion, and associated with the memory of some friend. I remember her references only to the Daphne Odora, the Provence Rose, the sweet-scented Verbena, and the Heliotrope; the latter being her chosen emblem, true bride of the sun that it is.

From flowers she passed to engravings hanging round the room. 'Here,' said she, 'are Dante and Beatrice.

'"Approach, and know that I am Beatrice.
'"The power of ancient love was strong within me." '

'She is beautiful enough, is not she, for that highei
'moment? But Dante! Yet who could paint a Dante,
'— and Dante in heaven? They give but his shadow,
'as he walked in the forest-maze of earth. Then here
'is the Madonna del Pesce; not divine, like the Foligno,
'not deeply maternal, like the Seggiola, not the beätified
'"Mother of God" of the Dresden gallery, but graceful,
'and "not too bright and good for human nature's daily
'"food." And here is Raphael himself, the young seer
'of beauty, with eyes softly contemplative, yet lit with
'central fires,' &c.

There were gems, too, and medallions and seals, to be
examined, each enigmatical, and each blended by remem-
t,ances with some fair hour of her past life.

Talk on art led the way to Greece and the Greeks,
whose mythology Margaret was studying afresh. She
had been culling the blooms of that poetic land, and
could not but offer me leaves from her garland. She
spoke of the statue of Minerva-Polias, cut roughly from
an olive-tree, yet cherished as the heaven-descended
image of the most sacred shrine, to which was due the
Panathenaic festival. 'The less ideal perfection in the
'figure, the greater the reverence of the adorer. Was
'not this because spiritual imagination makes light of
'results, and needs only a germ whence to unfold Olym-
'pic splendors?'

She spoke of the wooden column left standing from
the ruins of the first temple to Juno, amidst the marble
walls of the magnificent fane erected in its place: —
'This is a most beautiful type, is not it, of the manner
in which life's earliest experiences become glorified by
our perfecting destiny?'

'In the temple of Love and the Graces, one Grace bore

' a rose, a second a branch of myrtle, a third dice; — who
' can read that riddle ?'

' " Better is it," said Appollonius, " on entering a small
' " shrine to find there a statue of gold and ivory, than in
' " a large temple to behold only a coarse figure of terra
' " cotta." How often, after leaving with disgust the
' so-called great affairs of men, do we find traces of
' angels' visits in quiet scenes of home.

' The Hours and the Graces appear as ornaments on
' all thrones and shrines, except those of Vulcan and
' Pluto. Alas for us, when we become so sunk in utili-
' tarian toil as to be blind to the beauty with which even
' common cares are daily wreathed !'

And so on and on, with myth and allusion.

Next, Margaret spoke of the friends whose generosity
had provided the decorations on her walls, and the
illustrated books for her table, — friends who were fellow-
students in art, history, or science, — friends whose very
life she shared. Her heart seemed full to overflow with
sympathy for their joys and sorrows, their special trials
and struggles, their peculiar tendencies of character and
respective relations. The existence of each was to her
a sacred process, whose developments she watched with
awe, and whose leadings she reverently sought to aid.
She had scores of pretty anecdotes to tell, sweet bowers
of sentiment to open, significant lessons of experience to
interpret, and scraps of journals or letters to read aloud,
as the speediest means of introducing me to her chosen
circle. There was a fascinating spell in her piquant
descriptions, and a genial glow of sympathy animated
to characteristic movement the figures, who in varying
pantomime replaced one another on the theatre of her
fancy. Frost-bound New England melted into a dream·

ιand of romance beneath the spice-breeze of her Eastern narrative. Sticklers for propriety might have found fault at the freedom with which she confided her friends' histories to one who was a comparative stranger to them; but I could not but note how conscientiousness reined in her sensibilities and curbed their career, as they reached the due bounds of privacy. She did but realize one's conception of the transparent truthfulness that will per-vade advanced societies of the future, where the very atmosphere shall be honorable faith.

Nearer and nearer Margaret was approaching a secret throned in her heart that day; and the preceding transi-tions were but a prelude of her orchestra before the en-trance of the festal group. Unconsciously she made these preparations for paying worthy honors to a high senti-ment. She had lately heard of the betrothal of two of her best-loved friends; and she wished to communicate the graceful story in a way that should do justice to the facts and to her own feelings. It was by a spontaneous impulse of her genius, and with no voluntary foreshaping, that she had grouped the previous tales; but no drama could have been more artistically constructed than the steps whereby she led me onward to the denouement; and the look, tone, words, with which she told it, were fluent with melody as the song of an improvisatrice.

Scarcely had she finished, when, offering some light refreshment, — as it was now past noon, — she proposed a walk in the open air. She led the way to Bussey's wood, her favorite retreat during the past year, where she had thought and read, or talked with intimate friends. We climbed the rocky path, resting a moment or two at every pretty point, till, reaching a moss-cushioned ledge near the summit, she seated herself. For a time she was

silent, entranced in delighted communion with the
exquisite hue of the sky, seen through interlacing boughs
and trembling leaves, and the play of shine and shadow
over the wide landscape. But soon, arousing from her
reverie, she took up the thread of the morning's talk.
My part was to listen; for I was absorbed in contem-
plating this, to me, quite novel form of character. It
has been seen how my early distaste for Margaret's
society was gradually changed to admiration. Like all
her friends, I had passed through an avenue of sphinxes
before reaching the temple. But now it appeared that
thus far I had never been admitted to the adytum.

As, leaning on one arm, she poured out her stream
of thought, turning now and then her eyes full upon me,
to see whether I caught her meaning, there was leisure
to study her thoroughly. Her temperament was pre-
dominantly what the physiologists would call nervous-
sanguine; and the gray eye, rich brown hair and light
complexion, with the muscular and well-developed frame,
bespoke delicacy balanced by vigor. Here was a sensitive yet powerful being, fit at once for rapture or sustained effort, intensely active, prompt for adventure, firm
for trial. She certainly had not beauty; yet the high
arched dome of the head, the changeful expressiveness
of every feature, and her whole air of mingled dignity
and impulse, gave her a commanding charm. Especially
characteristic were two physical traits. The first was
a contraction of the eyelids almost to a point, — a trick
caught from near-sightedness, — and then a sudden
dilation, till the iris seemed to emit flashes; — an effect,
no doubt, dependent on her highly-magnetized condition.
The second was a singular pliancy of the vertebræ and
muscles of the neck, enabling her by a mere movement

to denote each varying emotion; in moments of tenderness, or pensive feeling, its curves were swan-like in
grace, but when she was scornful or indignant it con-
tracted, and made swift turns like that of a bird of prey.
Finally, in the animation, yet *abandon* of Margaret's
attitude and look, were rarely blended the fiery force of
northern, and the soft languor of southern races.

Meantime, as I was thus, through her physiognomy,
tracing the outlines of her spiritual form, she was narrating
chapters from the book of experience. How superficially,
heretofore, had I known her! We had met chiefly as
scholars. But now I saw before me one whose whole
life had been a poem, — of boundless aspiration and hope
almost wild in its daring, — of indomitable effort amidst
poignant disappointment, — of widest range, yet persistent
unity. Yes! here was a poet in deed, a true worshipper
of Apollo, who had steadfastly striven to brighten and
make glad existence, to harmonize all jarring and discordant strings, to fuse most hard conditions and cast
them in a symmetric mould, to piece fragmentary fortunes into a mosaic symbol of heavenly order. Here
was one, fond as a child of joy, eager as a native of the
tropics for swift transition from luxurious rest to passionate excitement, prodigal to pour her mingled force of
will, thought, sentiment, into the life of the moment,
all radiant with imagination, longing for communion
with artists of every age in their inspired hours, fitted by
genius and culture to mingle as an equal in the most
refined circles of Europe, and yet her youth and early
womanhood had passed away amid the very decent, yet
drudging, descendants of the prim Puritans. Trained
among those who could have discerned her peculiar
power, and early fed with the fruits of beauty for which

her spirit pined, she would have developed into one of
the finest lyrists, romancers and critics, that the modern
literary world has seen.   This she knew; and this tan-
talization of her fate she keenly felt.

But the tragedy of Margaret's history was deeper yet.
Behind the poet was the woman, — the fond and relying,
the heroic and disinterested woman.   The very glow of
her poetic enthusiasm was but an outflush of trustful
affection; the very restlessness of her intellect was the
confession that her heart had found no home.   A "book-
worm," "a dilettante," "a pedant," I had heard her
sneeringly called; but now it was evident that her seeming
insensibility was virgin pride, and her absorption in study
the natural vent of emotions, which had met no object
worthy of life-long attachment.   At once, many of her
peculiarities became intelligible.   Fitfulness, unlooked-for
changes of mood, misconceptions of words and actions,
substitution of fancy for fact, — which had annoyed me
during the previous season, as inconsistent in a person
of such capacious judgment and sustained self-govern-
ment, — were now referred to the morbid influence
of affections pent up to prey upon themselves.   And,
what was still more interesting, the clue was given to a
singular credulousness, by which, in spite of her unusual
penetration, Margaret might be led away blindfold.   As
this revelation of her ardent nature burst upon me, and
as, rapidly recalling the past, I saw how faithful she had
kept to her high purposes, — how patient, gentle, and
thoughtful for others, how active in self-improvement
and usefulness, how wisely dignified she had been,— I
could not but bow to her in reverence.

We walked back to the house amid a rosy sunset, and
it was with no surprise that I heard her complain of an

agonizing nervous headache, which compelled her at once to retire, and call for assistance. As for myself, while going homeward, I reflected with astonishment on the unflagging spiritual energy with which, for hour after hour, she had swept over lands and seas of thought, and, as my own excitement cooled, I became conscious of exhaustion, as if a week's life had been concentrated in a day.

The interview, thus hastily sketched, may serve as a fair type of our usual intercourse. Always I found her open-eyed to beauty, fresh for wonder, with wings poised for flight, and fanning the coming breeze of inspiration. Always she seemed to see before her, —

> " A shape all light, which with one hand did fling
> Dew on the earth, as if she were the dawn,
> And the invisible rain did ever sing
> À silver music on the mossy lawn."

Yet more and more distinctly did I catch a plaintive tone of sorrow in her thought and speech, like the wail of an Æolian harp heard at intervals from some upper window. She had never met one who could love her as she could love; and in the orange-grove of her affections the white, perfumed blossoms and golden fruit wasted away unclaimed. Through the mask of slight personal defects and ungraceful manners, of superficial hauteur and egotism, and occasional extravagance of sentiment, no equal had recognized the rare beauty of her spirit. She was yet alone.

Among her papers remains this pathetic petition : —

'I am weary of thinking. I suffer great fatigue from 'living. Oh God, take me! take me wholly! Thou

knowest that I love none but Thee. All this beautiful
' poesy of my being lies in Thee. Deeply I feel it. I ask
' nothing. Each desire, each passionate feeling, is on the
' surface only; inmostly Thou keepest me strong and
' pure. Yet always to be thus going out into moments,
' into nature, and love, and thought! Father, I am
' weary! Reassume me for a while, I pray Thee. Oh
' let me rest awhile in Thee, Thou only Love! In the
' depth of my prayer I suffer much. Take me only
' awhile. No fellow-being will receive me. I cannot
' pause; they will not detain me by their love. Take
' me awhile, and again I will go forth on a renewed ser-
' vice. It is not that I repine, my Father, but I sink
' from want of rest, and none will shelter me. Thou
' knowest it all. Bathe me in the living waters of Thy
' Love.'

VII

THE FRIEND.

YET, conscious as she was of an unfulfilled destiny,
and of an undeveloped being, Margaret was no pining
sentimentalist. The gums oozing from wounded boughs
she burned as incense in her oratory; but in outward
relations she was munificent with sympathy. 'Let me
' be, Theodora, a bearer of heavenly gifts to my fel-
' lows,' is written in her journals, and her life fulfilled
the aspiration. The more one observed her, the more
surprising appeared the variety, earnestness, and constancy of her friendships. Far and wide reached her
wires of communication, and incessant was the inter

change of messages of good-will. She was never so preoccupied and absorbed as to deny a claimant for her affectionate interest; she never turned her visitors back upon themselves, mortified and vexed at being misunderstood. With delicate justice she appreciated the special form, force, tendency of utterly dissimilar characters; and her heart responded to every appeal alike of humblest suffering or loftiest endeavor. In the plain, yet eloquent phrase of the backwoodsman, " the string of her door-latch was always out," and every wayfarer was free to share the shelter of her roof, or a seat beside her hearth-stone. Or, rather, it might be said, in symbol of her wealth of spirit, her palace, with its galleries of art, its libraries and festal-halls, welcomed all guests who could enjoy and use them.

She was, indeed, The Friend. This was her vocation. She bore at her girdle a golden key to unlock all caskets of confidence. Into whatever home she entered she brought a benediction of truth, justice, tolerance, and honor; and to every one who sought her to confess, or seek counsel, she spoke the needed word of stern yet benignant wisdom. To how many was the forming of her acquaintance an era of renovation, of awakening from sloth, indulgence or despair, to heroic mastery of fate, of inward serenity and strength, of new-birth to real self-hood, of catholic sympathies, of energy consecrated to the Supreme Good. Thus writes to her one who stands among the foremost in his own department : " What I am I owe, in large measure, to the stimulus you imparted. You roused my heart with high hopes; you raised my aims from paltry and vain pursuits to those which tasked and fed the soul; you inspired me with a great ambition, and made me see the worth and

meaning of life; you awakened in me confidence in my
own powers, showed me my special and distinct ability,
and quickened my individual consciousness by intelligent sympathy with tendencies and feelings which I but
half understood; you gave me to myself. This is a
most benign influence to exercise, and for it, above all
other benefits, gratitude is due. Therefore have you
an inexhaustible bank of gratitude to draw from. Bless
God that he has allotted to you such a ministry."

The following extracts from her letters will show how
profusely Margaret poured out her treasures upon her
friends; but they reveal, too, the painful processes of
alchemy whereby she transmuted her lead into gold.

'Your idea of friendship apparently does not include
'intellectual intimacy, as mine does, but consists of
'mutual esteem and spiritual encouragement. This is
'the thought represented, on antique gems and bas-
'reliefs, of the meeting between God and Goddess, I
'find; for they rather offer one another the full flower
'of being, than grow together. As in the figures before
'me, Jupiter, king of Gods and men, meets Juno, the
'sister and queen, not as a chivalric suppliant, but as a
'stately claimant; and she, crowned, pure, majestic,
'holds the veil aside to reveal herself to her august
'spouse.'

'How variously friendship is represented in literature!
'Sometimes the two friends kindle beacons from afar to
'apprize one another that they are constant, vigilant,
'and each content in his several home. Sometimes, two
pilgrims, they go different routes in service of the same

'saint, and remember one another as they give alms,
'learn wisdom, or pray in shrines along the road.
'Sometimes, two knights, they bid farewell with mailed
'hand of truth and honor all unstained, as they ride
'forth on their chosen path to test the spirit of high
'emprise, and free the world from wrong, — to meet
'again for unexpected succor in the hour of peril, or
'in joyful surprise to share a frugal banquet on the
'plat of greensward opening from forest glades.   Some-
'times, proprietors of two neighboring estates, they have
'interviews in the evening to communicate their exper-
'iments and plans, or to study together the stars from
'an observatory; if either is engaged he simply declares
'it; they share enjoyments cordially; they exchange
'praise or blame frankly; in citizen-like good-fellow-
'ship they impart their gains.

   'All these views of friendship are noble and beauti-
'ful, yet they are not enough for our manifold nature.
'Friends should be our incentives to Right, yet not only
'our guiding, but our prophetic stars.   To love by sight
'is much, to love by faith is more; together they make
'up the entire love, without which heart, mind, and
'soul cannot be alike satisfied.   Friends should love
'not merely for the absolute worth of each to the
'other, but on account of a mutual fitness of char-
'acter.   They are not merely one another's priests or
'gods, but ministering angels, exercising in their part
'the same function as the Great Soul does in the whole,
'— of seeing the perfect through the imperfect, nay,
'creating it there.   Why am I to love my friend the
'less for any obstruction in his life?   Is not that the very
'time for me to love most tenderly, when I must see his
'life in despite of seeming?   When he shows it to me I

'can only admire; I do not give myself, I am taken cap-
'tive.

  'But how shall I express my meaning? Perhaps I
'can do so from the tales of chivalry, where I find what
'corresponds far more thoroughly with my nature, than
'in these stoical statements. The friend of Amadis
'expects to hear prodigies of valor of the absent Preux,
'but if he be mutilated in one of his first battles, shall
'he be mistrusted by the brother of his soul, more than
'if he had been tested in a hundred? If Britomart
'finds Artegall bound in the enchanter's spell, can
'she doubt therefore him whom she has seen in the
'magic glass? A Britomart does battle in his cause,
'and frees him from the evil power, while a dame
'of less nobleness might sit and watch the enchanted
'sleep, weeping night and day, or spur on her white
'palfrey to find some one more helpful than herself.
'These friends in chivalry are always faithful through
'the dark hours to the bright. The Douglas motto,
'"tender and true," seems to me most worthy of the
'strongest breast. To borrow again from Spencer, I
'am entirely satisfied with the fate of the three brothers.
'I could not die while there was yet life in my brother's
'breast. I would return from the shades and nerve him
'with twofold life for the fight. I could do it, for our
'hearts beat with one blood. Do you not see the truth
'and happiness of this waiting tenderness? The verse —

> '"Have I a lover
> Who is noble and free,
> I would he were nobler
> Than to love me," —

does not come home to my heart, though *this* does:

'" I could not love thee, sweet, so much,
  Loved I not honor more." '

* * * ' *October* 10*th*, 1840. — I felt singular pleasure
in seeing you quote Hood's lines on " Melancholy."
'I thought nobody knew and loved his serious poems
'except myself, and two or three others, to whom I
'imparted them.* Do you like, also, the ode to Au-
'tumn, and —

'" Sigh on, sad heart, for love's eclipse " ?

' It was a beautiful time when I first read these poems.
'I was staying in Hallowell, Maine, and could find no
'books that I liked, except Hood's poems. You know
'how the town is built, like a terraced garden on the
'river's bank ; I used to go every afternoon to the
'granite quarry which crowns these terraces, and read
'till the sunset came casting its last glory on the oppo-
'site bank. They were such afternoons as those in
September and October, clear, soft, and radiant. Nature held nothing back. 'T is many years since, and
'I have never again seen the Kennebec, but remember
'it as a stream of noble character. It was the first river
'I ever sailed up, realizing all which that emblem dis-
'closes of life. Greater still would the charm have
'been to sail downward along an unknown stream,
'seeking not a home, but a ship upon the ocean.'

' *Newbury*, *Oct.* 18, 1840. — It rained, and the day
was pale and sorrowful, the thick-fallen leaves even

---

* This was some years before their reprint in this country, it should be
noticed.

'shrouded the river. We went out in the boat, and sat
' under the bridge. The pallid silence, the constant fall
' of the rain and leaves, were most soothing, life had
' been for many weeks so crowded with thought and
' feeling, pain and pleasure, rapture and care. Nature
' seemed gently to fold us in her matron's mantle. On
' such days the fall of the leaf does not bring sadness, —
' only meditation. Earth seemed to loose the record of
' past summer hours from her permanent life, as lightly,
' and spontaneously, as the great genius casts behind
' him a literature, — the Odyssey he has outgrown. In
' the evening the rain ceased, the west wind came,
' and we went out in the boat again for some hours;
' indeed, we staid till the last clouds passed from the
' moon. Then we climbed the hill to see the full light
' in solemn sweetness over fields, and trees, and river.

' I never enjoyed anything more in its way than the
' three days alone with ——— in her boat, upon the lit-
' tle river. Not without reason was it that Goethe lim-
' its the days of intercourse to *three*, in the Wanderjahre.
' If you have lived so long in uninterrupted communion
' with any noble being, and with nature, a remembrance
' of man's limitations seems to call on Polycrates to
' cast forth his ring. She seemed the very genius of
' the scene, so calm, so lofty, and so secluded. I never
' saw any place that seemed to me so much like home.
' The beauty, though so great, is so unobtrusive.

' As we glided along the river, I could frame my com-
' munity far more naturally and rationally than ———.
' A few friends should settle upon the banks of a stream
' like this, planting their homesteads. Some should be
' farmers, some woodmen, others bakers, millers, &c.
By land, they should carry to one another the commod

'ities; on the river they should meet for society. At
' sunset many, of course, would be out in their boats,
' but they would love the hour too much ever to disturb
' one another. I saw the spot where we should discuss
' the high mysteries that Milton speaks of. Also, I saw
' the spot where I would invite select friends to live
' through the noon of night, in silent communion.
' When we wished to have merely playful chat, or
' talk on politics or social reform, we would gather in
' the mill, and arrange those affairs while grinding the
' corn. What a happy place for children to grow up in !
' Would it not suit little —— to go to school to the cardi-
'nal flowers in her boat, beneath the great oak-tree ? I
' think she would learn more than in a phalanx of juve
'nile florists. But, truly, why has such a thing never
' been ? One of these valleys so immediately suggests
' an image of the fair company that might fill it, and
' live so easily, so naturally, so wisely. Can we not
' people the banks of some such affectionate little stream ?
' I distrust ambitious plans, such as Phalansterian organ-
' izations !

' —— is quite bent on trying his experiment. I hope
' he may succeed ; but as they were talking the other
' evening, I thought of the river, and all the pretty
' symbols the tide-mill presents, and felt if I could
' at all adjust the economics to the more simple pro-
' cedure, I would far rather be the miller, hoping to
' attract by natural affinity some congenial baker, " und
' " so weiter." However, one thing seems sure, that
' many persons will soon, somehow, somewhere, throw
' off a part, at least, of these terrible weights of the
' social contract, and see if they cannot lie more at
' ease in the lap of Nature. I do not feel the same

'interest in these plans, as if I had a firmer hold on life,
'but I listen with much pleasure to the good sugges-
'tions.'

*   *   *   *   *

'*Oct.* 19*th*, 1840. ———— was here. Generally I go
'out of the room when he comes, for his great excita-
'bility makes me nervous, and his fondness for detail is
'wearisome. But to-night I was too much fatigued to
'do anything else, and did not like to leave mother; so
'I lay on the sofa while she talked with him.

'My mind often wandered, yet ever and anon, as I lis-
'tened again to him, I was struck with admiration at the
'compensations of Nature. Here is a man, isolated from
'his kind beyond any I know, of an ambitious temper
'and without an object, of tender affections and without
'a love or a friend. I don't suppose any mortal, unless
'it be his aged mother, cares more for him than we do,
'— scarce any value him so much. The disease, which
'has left him, in the eyes of men, a scathed and blighted
'tree, has driven him back to Nature, and she has not
'refused him sympathy. I was surprised by the refine-
'ment of his observations on the animals, his pets.
'He has carried his intercourse with them to a degree
'of perfection we rarely attain with our human friends.
'There is no misunderstanding between him and his
'dogs and birds; and how rich has been the acquaint-
'ance in suggestion! Then the flowers! I liked to
'hear him, for he recorded all their pretty ways, — not
'like a botanist, but a lover. His interview with the
'Magnolia of Lake Pontchartrain was most romantic.
'And what he said of the Yuca seems to me so pretty,
'that I will write it down, though somewhat more con-
cisely than he told it : —

'"I had kept these plants of the Yuca Filamentosa
'" six or seven years, though they had never bloomed.
'"I knew nothing of them, and had no notion of what
'"feelings they would excite. Last June I found in
"bud the one which had the most favorable expos-
'"ure. A week or two after, another, which was more
'"in the shade, put out flower-buds; and I thought I
'"should be able to watch them, one after the other;
'"but, no! the one which was most favored waited for
'"the other, and both flowered together at the full of
'"the moon. This struck me as very singular, but as
'"soon as I saw the flower by moonlight I under-
'"stood it. This flower is made for the moon, as
'"the Heliotrope is for the sun, and refuses other influ-
'"ences or to display her beauty in any other light.

'"The first night I saw it in flower, I was con-
'"scious of a peculiar delight, I may even say rapture.
'"Many white flowers are far more beautiful by day;
'"the lily, for instance, with its firm, thick leaf, needs
'"the broadest light to manifest its purity. But these
'"transparent leaves of greenish white, which look dull
'"in the day, are melted by the moon to glistening sil-
'"ver. And not only does the plant not appear in its
'"destined hue by day, but the flower, though, as bell-
'"shaped, it cannot quite close again after having once
'"expanded, yet presses its petals together as closely
'"as it can, hangs down its little blossoms, and its tall
'"stalk seems at noon to have reared itself only to
'"betray a shabby insignificance. Thus, too, with the
'"leaves, which have burst asunder suddenly like the
'"fan-palm to make way for the stalk, — their edges
'"in the day time look ragged and unfinished, as if
'"nature had left them in a hurry for some more

'"pleasing task. On the day after the evening when
'"I had thought it so beautiful, I could not conceive
'"how I had made such a mistake.

'" But the second evening I went out into the garden
'"again. In clearest moonlight stood my flower, more
'"beautiful than ever. The stalk pierced the air like a
'"spear, all the little bells had erected themselves around
'"it in most graceful array, with petals more transpa-
'"rent than silver, and of softer light than the diamond.
'"Their edges were clearly, but not sharply defined.
'"They seemed to have been made by the moon's
'"rays. The leaves, which had looked ragged by day,
'"now seemed fringed by most delicate gossamer, and
'"the plant might claim with pride its distinctive epi-
'"thet of Filamentosa. I looked at it till my feelings
'"became so strong that I longed to share it. The
'"thought which filled my mind was that here we
'"saw the type of pure feminine beauty in the moon's
'"own flower. I have since had further opportunity
'"of watching the Yuca, and verified these observa-
'"tions, that she will not flower till the full moon, and
'"chooses to hide her beauty from the eye of day."

'Might not this be made into a true poem, if written
'out merely as history of the plant, and no observer
'introduced? How finely it harmonizes with all legends
'of Isis, Diana, &c.! It is what I tried to say in the
'sonnet, —

'Woman's heaven,
'Where palest lights a silvery sheen diffuse.

'In tracing these correspondences, one really does
take hold of a Truth, of a Divine Thought.' * *

'*October* 25*th*, 1840. — This week I have not read any
'book, nor once walked in the woods and fields. I meant
'to give its days to setting outward things in order,
'and its evenings to writing. But, I know not how it is,
'I can never simplify my life; always so many ties, so
'many claims! However, soon the winter winds will
'chant matins and vespers, which may make my house
'a cell, and in a snowy veil enfold me for my prayer.
'If I cannot dedicate myself this time, I will not expect
'it again. Surely it should be! These Carnival masks
'have crowded on me long enough, and Lent must be at
'hand. * *

'—— and —— have been writing me letters, to answer
'which required all the time and thought I could give
'for a day or two. ——'s were of joyful recognition,
'and so beautiful I would give much to show them to
'you. ——'s have singularly affected me. They are
'noble, wise, of most unfriendly friendliness. I don't
'know why it is, I always seem to myself to have gone
'so much further with a friend than I really have. Just
'as at Newport I thought —— met me, when he did not,
'and sang a joyful song which found no echo, so here
'—— asks me questions which I thought had been
'answered in the first days of our acquaintance, and
'coldly enumerates all the charming qualities which make
'it impossible for him to part with me! He scolds me.
'though in the sweetest and solemnest way. I will not
'quote his words, though their beauty tempts me, for
'they do not apply, they do not touch ME.

'Why is it that the religion of my nature is so much
'hidden from my peers? why do they question me, who
'never question them? why persist to regard as a
'meteor an orb of assured hope? Can no soul know

'me wholly? shall I never know the deep delight of
'gratitude to any but the All-Knowing? I shall wait for
'—— very peaceably, in reverent love as ever; but I
'cannot see why he should not have the pleasure of
'knowing now a friend, who has been "so tender and
' " true." '

'—— was here, and spent twenty-four hours in telling
'me a tale of deepest tragedy. Its sad changes should
'be written out in Godwin's best manner: such are the
'themes he loved, as did also Rousseau. Through all
'the dark shadows shone a pure white ray, one high,
'spiritual character, a man, too, and of advanced age.
'I begin to respect men more, — I mean actual men.
'What men may be, I know; but the men of to-day have
'seemed to me of such coarse fibre, or else such poor
'wan shadows'

'—— had scarcely gone, when —— came and wished
'to spend a few hours with me. I was totally exhausted,
'but I lay down, and she sat beside me, and poured out
'all her noble feelings and bright fancies. There was
'little light in the room, and she gleamed like a cloud

—— ' " of pearl and opal,"

'and reminded me more than ever of

—— ' " the light-haired Lombardess
Singing a song of her own native land,"

'to the dying Correggio, beside the fountain.

'I am astonished to see how much Bettine's book is to
'all these people. This shows how little courage they
'have had to live out themselves. She really brings
'them a revelation. The men wish they had been loved
 by Bettine; the girls wish to write down the thoughts

'that come, and see if just such a book does not grow
'up. ——, however, was one of the few who do not
'over estimate her; she truly thought Bettine only pub-
'lishes what many burn. Would not genius be common
'as light, if men trusted their higher selves?'

'I heard in town that —— is a father, and has gone
'to see his child. This news made me more grave even
'than such news usually does; I suppose because I have
'known the growth of his character so intimately. I
'called to mind a letter he had written me of what we
'had expected of our fathers. The ideal father, the pro-
'foundly wise, provident, divinely tender and benign, he
'is indeed the God of the human heart. How solemn
'this moment of being called to prepare the way, to
'*make way* for another generation! What fulfilment
'does it claim in the character of a man, that he should
'be worthy to be a father! — what purity of motive,
'what dignity, what knowledge! When I recollect how
'deep the anguish, how deeper still the want, with which
'I walked alone in hours of childish passion, and called
'for a Father, often saying the word a hundred times, till
'stifled by sobs, how great seems the duty that name
'imposes! Were but the harmony preserved through-
'out! Could the child keep learning his earthly, as he
'does his heavenly Father, from all best experience of
'life, till at last it were the climax: "I am the Father.
'" Have ye seen me? — ye have seen the Father." But
'how many sons have we to make one father? Surely,
'to spirits, not only purified but perfected, this must
'appear the climax of earthly being, — a wise and worthy
'parentage. Here I always sympathize with Mr. Alcott.
He views the relation truly.'

'*Dec.* 3, 1840. —— bids me regard her "as a sick
"child;" and the words recall some of the sweetest hours
of existence.   My brother Edward was born on my
'birth-day, and they said he should be my child.   But
'he sickened and died just as the bud of his existence
'showed its first bright hues.   He was some weeks
'wasting away, and I took care of him always half the
'night.   He was a beautiful child, and became very dear
'to me then.   Still in lonely woods the upturned violets
'show me the pleading softness of his large blue eyes, in
'those hours when I would have given worlds to prevent
'his suffering, and could not.   I used to carry him about
'in my arms for hours; it soothed him, and I loved to
'feel his gentle weight of helpless purity upon my heart,
'while night listened around.   At last, when death came,
'and the soul took wing like an overtasked bird from his
'sweet form, I felt what I feel now.   Might I free ——,
'as that angel freed him!

'In daily life I could never hope to be an unfailing
'fountain of energy and bounteous love.   My health is
'frail; my earthly life is shrunk to a scanty rill; I am
'little better than an aspiration, which the ages will
'reward, by empowering me to incessant acts of vigorous
'beauty.   But now it is well with me to be with those
'who do not suffer overmuch to have me suffer.   It is
'best for me to serve where I can better bear to fall short.
'I could visit —— more nobly than in daily life, through
'the soul of our souls.   When she named me her Priestess,
'that name made me perfectly happy.   Long has been
'my consecration; may I not meet those I hold dear at
'the altar?   How would I pile up the votive offerings,
'and crowd the fires with incense!   Life might be full

'and fair; for, in my own way, I could live for my
' friends.' * *

' *Dec. 8th*, 1840. — My book of amusement has been
' the Evenings of St. Petersburg. I do not find the
' praises bestowed on it at all exaggerated. Yet De
' Maistre is too logical for me. I only catch a thought
' here and there along the page. There is a grandeur
' even in the subtlety of his mind. He walks with a step
' so still, that, but for his dignity, it would be stealthy,
' yet with brow erect and wide, eye grave and deep. He
' is a man such as I have never known before.' * *

' I went to see Mrs. Wood in the Somnambula. Nothing
' could spoil this opera, which expresses an ecstasy, a
' trance of feeling, better than anything I ever heard. I
' have loved every melody in it for years, and it was
' happiness to listen to the exquisite modulations as they
' flowed out of one another, endless ripples on a river
' deep, wide and strewed with blossoms. I never have
' known any one more to be loved than Bellini. No
' wonder the Italians make pilgrimages to his grave. In
' him thought and feeling flow always in one tide; he
' never divides himself. He is as melancholy as he is
' sweet; yet his melancholy is not impassioned, but purely
' tender.'

' *Dec.* 15, 1840. — I have not time to write out as I
' should this sweet story of Melissa, but here is the out-
' line : —
' More than four years ago she received an injury,
' which caused her great pain in the spine, and went to
' the next country town to get medical advice. She
' stopped at the house of a poor blacksmith, an acquaint-

'ance only, and has never since been able to be moved.
' Her mother and sister come by turns to take care of her.
' She cannot help herself in any way, but is as completely
' dependent as an infant. The blacksmith and his wife
' gave her the best room in their house, have ever since
' ministered to her as to a child of their own, and, when
' people pity them for having to bear such a burthen,
' they say, "It is none, but a blessing."

' Melissa suffers all the time, and great pain. She
' cannot amuse or employ herself in any way, and all
' these years has been as dependent on others for new
' thoughts, as for daily cares. Yet her mind has deep-
' ened, and her character refined, under those stern
' teachers, Pain and Gratitude, till she has become the
' patron saint of the village, and the muse of the village
' school-mistress. She has a peculiar aversion to egotism,
' and could not bear to have her mother enlarge upon her
' sufferings.

' "Perhaps it will pain the lady to hear that," said the
' mild, religious sufferer, who had borne all without a
' complaint.

' "Whom the Lord loveth he chasteneth." The poor
' are the generous; the injured, the patient and loving.

' All that —— said of this girl was in perfect harmony
' with what De Maistre says of the saint of St. Peters-
' burg, who, almost devoured by cancer, when asked,
' "Quelle est la premiere grace que vous demanderez a
' "Dieu, ma chére enfant, lorsque vous serez devant
' "lui?" she replied, "Je lui demanderai pour mes
' "bienfaiteurs la grace de l'aimer autant que je l'aime."

' When they were lamenting for her, "Je ne suis pas,
' "dit elle, aussi malheureuse que vous le croyez; Dieu
' "me fait la grace de ne penser, qu'a lui." * *

'Next of Edith.   Tall, gaunt, hard-favored was this
'candidate for the American calendar; but Bonifacia
'might be her name.   From her earliest years she had
'valued all she knew, only as she was to teach it again.
'Her highest ambition was to be the school-mistress; her
'recreation to dress the little ragged things, and take care
'of them out of school hours.   She had some taste for
'nursing the grown-up, but this was quite subordinate to
'her care of the buds of the forest.   Pure, perfectly benefi-
'cent, lived Edith, and never thought of any thing or
'person, but for its own sake.   When she had attained
'midway the hill of life, she happened to be boarding in
'the house with a young farmer, who was lost in admira-
'tion of her lore.   How he wished he, too, could read!
"What, can't you read?   O, let me teach you!" — "You
"never can; I was too thick-skulled to learn even at
"school.   I am sure I never could now."   But Edith
was not to be daunted by any fancies of incapacity, and
set to work with utmost zeal to teach this great grown
·man the primer.   She succeeded, and won his heart
'thereby.   He wished to requite the raising him from the
'night of ignorance, as Howard and Nicholas Poussin
'did the kind ones who raised them from the night of the
'tomb, by the gift of his hand.   Edith consented, on
'condition that she might still keep school.   So he had
'his sister come to "keep things straight."   Edith and
'he go out in the morning, — he to his field, she to her
'school, and meet again at eventide, to talk, and plan,
'and, I hope, to read also.
   'The first use Edith made of her accession of property,
'through her wedded estate, was to give away all she
'thought superfluous to a poor family she had long pitied,
'and to invite a poor sick woman to her "spare cham-

' "ber." Notwithstanding a course like this, her husband
'has grown rich, and proves that the pattern of the wid-
'ow's cruse was not lost in Jewry.

'Edith has become the Natalia of the village, as is
'Melissa its "Schöne Seele." '

'*Dec.* 22, 1840. — "Community" seems dwindling to
'a point, and I fancy the best use of the plan, as pro-
'jected thus far, will prove the good talks it has caused
'here, upon principles. I feel and find great want of
'wisdom in myself and the others. We are not ripe to
'reconstruct society yet. O Christopher Columbus! how
'art thou to be admired, when we see how other men
'go to work with their lesser enterprises! —— knows
'deepest what he wants, but not well how to get it.
'—— has a better perception of means, and less insight
'as to principles; but this movement has done him a
'world of good. All should say, however, that they
'consider this plan as a mere experiment, and are willing
'to fail. I tell them that they are not ready till they can
'say that. —— says he can bear to be treated unjustly
'by all concerned, — which is much. He is too sanguine
'as it appears to me, but his aim is worthy, and, with
'his courage and clear intellect, his experiment will not,
'at least to him, be a failure.'

'*Feb.* 19, 1841. — Have I never yet seen so much as
'*one* of my spiritual family? The other night they sat
'round me, so many who have thought they loved, or
'who begin to love me. I felt myself kindling the same
'fire in all their souls. I looked on each, and no eye
'repelled me. Yet there was no warmth for me on all
'those altars. Their natures seemed deep, yet there was

'not one from which I could draw the living fountain. I
'could only cheat the hour with them, prize, admire, and
'pity. It was sad; yet who would have seen sadness
'in me? * *

'Once I was almost all intellect; now I am almost all
'feeling. Nature vindicates her rights, and I feel all
'Italy glowing beneath the Saxon crust. This cannot
'last long; I shall burn to ashes if all this smoulders
'here much longer. I must die if I do not burst forth in
'genius or heroism.

'I meant to have translated the best passages of "Die
'"Gunderode,"—which I prefer to Bettine's correspond-
'ence with Goethe. The two girls are equal natures,
'and both in earnest. Goethe made a puppet-show, for
'his private entertainment, of Bettine's life, and we won-
'der she did not feel he was not worthy of her homage.
'Gunderode is to me dear and admirable, Bettine only
'interesting. Gunderode is of religious grace, Bettine
'the fulness of instinctive impulse; Gunderode is the
'ideal, Bettine nature; Gunderode throws herself into the
'river because the world is all too narrow, Bettine lives
'and follows out every freakish fancy, till the enchanting
'child degenerates into an eccentric and undignified old
'woman. There is a medium somewhere. Philip Sid-
'ney found it; others had it found for them by fate.'

'*March* 29, 1841. — * * Others have looked at society
'with far deeper consideration than I. I have felt so
'unrelated to this sphere, that it has not been hard for
'me to be true. Also, I do not believe in Society. I feel
'that every man must struggle with these enormous ills.
'in some way, in every age; in that of Moses, or Plato,
'or Angelo, as in our own. So it has not moved me

'much to see my time so corrupt, but it would if I were
'in a false position.

'—— went out to his farm yesterday, full of cheer, as
'one who doeth a deed with sincere good will. He has
'shown a steadfastness and earnestness of purpose most
'grateful to behold. I do not know what their scheme
'will ripen to; at present it does not deeply engage my
'hopes. It is thus far only a little better way than others.
'I doubt if they will get free from all they deprecate in
'society.'

'*Paradise Farm, Newport, July*, 1841.— Here are no
'deep forests, no stern mountains, nor narrow, sacred
'valleys; but the little white farm-house looks down
'from its gentle slope on the boundless sea, and beneath
'the moon, beyond the glistening corn-fields, is heard the
'endless surge. All around the house is most gentle and
'friendly, with many common flowers, that seem to have
'planted themselves, and the domestic honey-suckle
'carefully trained over the little window. Around are
'all the common farm-house sounds, — the poultry mak-
'ing a pleasant recitative between the carols of singing
'birds; even geese and turkeys are not inharmonious
'when modulated by the diapasons of the beach. The
'orchard of very old apple-trees, whose twisted forms
'tell of the glorious winds that have here held revelry,
'protects a little homely garden, such as gives to me an
'indescribable refreshment, where the undivided vege-
'table plots and flourishing young fruit-trees, mingling
'carelessly, seem as if man had dropt the seeds just
where he wanted the plants, and they had sprung up
'at once. The family, too, look, at first glance, well-
'suited to the place, — homely, kindly, unoppressed. of

'honest pride and mutual love, not unworthy to look out
'upon the far-shining sea.

  * * 'Many, many sweet little things would I tell you,
'only they are so very little. I feel just now as if I could
'live and die here. I am out in the open air all the time,
'except about two hours in the early morning. And now
'the moon is fairly gone late in the evening. While she
'was here, we staid out, too. Everything seems sweet
'here, so homely, so kindly; the old people chatting so
'contentedly, the young men and girls laughing together
'in the fields, — not vulgarly, but in the true kinsfolk way,
'— little children singing in the house and beneath the
'berry-bushes. The never-ceasing break of the surf is a
'continual symphony, calming the spirits which this
'delicious air might else exalt too much. Everything on
'the beach becomes a picture; the casting the seine, the
'ploughing the deep for seaweed. This, when they do
'it with horses, is prettiest of all; but when you see the
'oxen in the surf, you lose all faith in the story of Europa,
'as the gay waves tumble in on their lazy sides. The
'bull would be a fine object on the shore, but not, not in
'the water. Nothing short of a dolphin will do! Late
'to-night, from the highest Paradise rocks, seeing ——
'wandering, and the horsemen careering on the beach,
'so spectrally passing into nature, amid the pale, brood-
'ing twilight, I almost thought myself in the land of
'souls!

  'But in the morning it is life, all cordial and common.
'This half-fisherman, half-farmer life seems very favor-
'able to manliness. I like to talk with the fishermen;
'they are not boorish, not limited, but keen-eyed, and of
'a certain rude gentleness. Two or three days ago I
'saw the sweetest picture. There is a very tall rock,

'one of the natural pulpits, at one end of the beach.
'As I approached, I beheld a young fisherman with his
'little girl; he had nestled her into a hollow of the rock,
·and was standing before her, with his arms round her,
'and looking up in her face. Never was anything so
'pretty. I stood and stared, country fashion; and pres-
'ently he scrambled up to the very top with her in his
·arms. She screamed a little as they went, but when
'they were fairly up on the crest of the rock, she
'chuckled, and stretched her tiny hand over his neck, to
'go still further. Yet, when she found he did not wish
'it, she leaned against his shoulder, and he sat, feeling
'himself in the child like that exquisite Madonna, and
'looking out over the great sea. Surely, the "kindred
' "points of heaven and home" were known in his breast,
' whatever guise they might assume.

  'The sea is not always lovely and bounteous, though
'generally, since we have been here, she has beamed her
'bluest. The night of the full moon we staid out on the
'far rocks. The afternoon was fair; the sun set nobly,
'wrapped in a violet mantle, which he left to the moon,
'in parting. She not only rose red, lowering, and of im-
'patient attitude, but kept hiding her head all the evening
'with an angry, struggling movement. —— said,
' "This is not Dian;" and I replied, "No; now we see
' "the Hecate." But the damp, cold wind came sobbing,
'and the waves began wailing, too, till I was seized with
'a feeling of terror, such as I never had before, even in
'the darkest, and most treacherous, rustling wood. The
'moon seemed sternly to give me up to the dæmons of
'the rock, and the waves to mourn a tragic chorus, till
·I felt their cold grasp. I suffered so much, that I feared
'we should never get home without some fatal catas-

'trophe.   Never was I more relieved than when, as we
'came up the hill, the moon suddenly shone forth.   It
'was ten o'clock, and here every human sound is hushed,
'and lamp put out at that hour.   How tenderly the
'grapes and tall corn-ears glistened and nodded ! and the
'trees stretched out their friendly arms, and the scent of
'every humblest herb was like a word of love.   The
'waves, also, at that moment put on a silvery gleam,
'and looked most soft and regretful.   That was a real
'voice from nature.'

'*February*, 1842. — I am deeply sad at the loss of little
'Waldo, from whom I hoped more than from almost any
'living being.   I cannot yet reconcile myself to the
'thought that the sun shines upon the grave of the
beautiful blue-eyed boy, and I shall see him no more.
'Five years he was an angel to us, and I know not
'that any person was ever more the theme of thought to
'me.   As I walk the streets they swarm with apparently
'worthless lives, and the question will rise, why he, why
'just he, who "bore within himself the golden future,"
'must be torn away?   His father will meet him again;
'but to me he seems lost, and yet that is weakness.   I
'*must* meet that which he represented, since I so truly
'loved it.   He was the only child I ever saw, that I
'sometimes wished I could have called mine.
'I loved him more than any child I ever knew, as he
'was of nature more fair and noble.   You would be
'surprised to know how dear he was to my imagination.
'I saw him but little, and it was well; for it is unwise
'to bind the heart where there is no claim.   But it is all
'gone, and is another of the lessons brought by each
year, that we are to expect suggestions only, and not

fulfilments, from each form of beauty, and to regard
' them merely as Angels of The Beauty.'

' *June*, 1842.— Why must children be with perfect
' people, any more than people wait to be perfect to be
' friends? The secret is,— is it not?— for parents to feel
' and be willing their children should know that they are
' but little older than themselves; only a class above, and
' able to give them some help in learning their lesson.
' Then parent and child keep growing together, in the
' same house. Let them blunder as we blundered. God
' is patient for us; why should not we be for them? As-
' piration teaches always, and God leads, by inches. A
' perfect being would hurt a child no less than an im-
' perfect.'

' It always makes my annoyances seem light, to be
' riding about to visit these fine houses. Not that I am
' intolerant towards the rich, but I cannot help feeling at
' such times how much characters require the discipline
' of difficult circumstances. To say nothing of the need
' the soul has of a peace and courage that cannot be dis-
' turbed, even as to the intellect, how can one be sure of
' not sitting down in the midst of indulgence to pamper
' tastes alone, and how easy to cheat one's self with the
' fancy that a little easy reading or writing is quite work.
' I am safer; I do not sleep on roses. I smile to myself,
' when with these friends, at their care of me. I let
them do as they will, for I know it will not last long
enough to spoil me.'

' I take great pleasure in talking with Aunt Mary.*

* Miss Rotch, of New Bedford.

'Her strong and simple nature checks not, falters not.
'Her experience is entirely unlike mine, as, indeed, is
'that of most others whom I know. No rapture, no
'subtle process, no slow fermentation in the unknown
'depths, but a rill struck out from the rock, clear and cool
'in all its course, the still, small voice. She says the
'guide of her life has shown itself rather as a restraining,
'than an impelling principle. I like her life, too, as far
'as I see it; it is dignified and true.'

'*Cambridge, July*, 1842.— A letter at Providence
'would have been like manna in the wilderness. I came
'into the very midst of the fuss,* and, tedious as it was at
'the time, I am glad to have seen it. I shall in future be
'able to believe real, what I have read with a dim disbelief
'of such times and tendencies. There is, indeed, little
'good, little cheer, in what I have seen : a city full of
'grown-up people as wild, as mischief-seeking, as full of
'prejudice, careless slander, and exaggeration, as a herd
'of boys in the play-ground of the worst boarding-school.
'Women whom I have seen, as the domestic cat, gentle,
'graceful, cajoling, suddenly showing the disposition, if
'not the force, of the tigress. I thought I appreciated the
'monstrous growths of rumor before, but I never did.
'The Latin poet, though used to a court, has faintly
'described what I saw and heard often, in going the
'length of a street. It is astonishing what force, purity
'and wisdom it requires for a human being to keep clear
'of falsehoods. These absurdities, of course, are linked
'with good qualities, with energy of feeling, and with
'a love of morality, though narrowed and vulgarized by

* The Dorr rebellion.

'the absence of the intelligence which should enlighten.
'I had the good discipline of trying to make allowance
'for those making none, to be charitable to their want of
'charity, and cool without being cold. But I don't know
' when I have felt such an aversion to my environment,
'and prayed so earnestly day by day, — "O, Eternal;
'"purge from my inmost heart this hot haste about
'"ephemeral trifles," and "keep back thy servant from
'"presumptuous sins; let them not have dominion over
'"me."

'What a change from the almost vestal quiet of
'"Aunt Mary's" life, to all this open-windowed, open-
'eyed screaming of "poltroon," "nefarious plan,"
'"entire depravity," &c. &c.'.

'*July*, 1842. *Boston.* — I have been entertaining the
'girls here with my old experiences at Groton. They
'have been very fresh in my mind this week. Had I
'but been as wise in such matters then as now, how
'easy and fair I might have made the whole! Too late,
'too late to live, but not too late to think! And as that
'maxim of the wise Oriental teaches, "the Acts of this
'"life shall be the Fate of the next."'

* * * 'I would have my friends tender of me, not
'because I am frail, but because I am capable of
'strength; — patient, because they see in me a principle
'that must, at last, harmonize all the exuberance of
'my character. I did not well understand what you
'felt, but I am willing to admit that what you said of
'my "over-great impetuosity" is just. You will, per-
'haps, feel it more and more. It may at times hide my
'better self. When it does, speak, I entreat, as harshly
as you feel. Let me be always sure I know the worst

'I believe you will be thus just, thus true, for we are 'both servants of Truth.'

'*August*, 1842. *Cambridge.* — Few have eyes for the 'pretty little features of a scene. In this, men are not 'so good as boys. Artists are always thus young; poets are; but the pilgrim does not lay aside his belt of steel, 'nor the merchant his pack, to worship the flowers on 'the fountain's brink. I feel, like Herbert, the weight 'of "business to be done," but the bird-like particle 'would skim and sing at these sweet places. It seems 'strange to leave them; and that we do so, while so 'fitted to live deeply in them, shows that beauty is the 'end but not the means.

'I have just been reading the new poems of Tenny- 'son. Much has he thought, much suffered, since the 'first ecstasy of so fine an organization clothed all the 'world with rosy light. He has not suffered himself to 'become a mere intellectual voluptuary, nor the songster 'of fancy and passion, but has earnestly revolved the 'problems of life, and his conclusions are calmly noble. 'In these later verses is a still, deep sweetness; how 'different from the intoxicating, sensuous melody of his 'earlier cadence! I have loved him much this time, and 'taken him to heart as a brother. One of his themes has 'long been my favorite, — the last expedition of Ulysses, '— and his, like mine, is the Ulysses of the Odyssey, 'with his deep romance of wisdom, and not the world- 'ling of the Iliad. How finely marked his slight descrip- 'tion of himself and of Telemachus. In Dora, Locksley 'Hall, the Two Voices, Morte D'Arthur, I find my own 'life, much of it, written truly out.'

'*Concord, August* 25, 1842. — Beneath this roof of peace, beneficence, and intellectual activity, I find just the alternation of repose and satisfying pleasure that I need. * * *

'Do not find fault with the hermits and scholars. The true text is: —

> '"Mine own Telemachus
> He does his work — I mine."

All do the work, whether they will or no; but he is "mine own Telemachus" who does it in the spirit of religion, never believing that the last results can be 'arrested in any one measure or set of measures, listen-'ing always to the voice of the Spirit, — and who does 'this more than ——?

'After the first excitement of intimacy with him, — 'when I was made so happy by his high tendency, 'absolute purity, the freedom and infinite graces of an 'intellect cultivated much beyond any I had known, — 'came with me the questioning season. I was greatly 'disappointed in my relation to him. I was, indeed, 'always called on to be worthy, — this benefit was sure 'in our friendship. But I found no intelligence of my 'best self; far less was it revealed to me in new modes; 'for not only did he seem to want the living faith which 'enables one to discharge this holiest office of a friend, 'but he absolutely distrusted me in every region of my 'life with which he was unacquainted. The same trait 'I detected in his relations with others. He had faith 'in the Universal, but not in the Individual Man; he 'met men, not as a brother, but as a critic. Philosophy appeared to chill instead of exalting the poet.

'But now I am better acquainted with him. His

' "accept " is true; the "I shall learn," with which he
' answers every accusation, is no less true.   No one can
' feel his limitations, in fact, more than he, though he
' always speaks confidently from his present knowledge
' as all he has yet, and never qualifies or explains.
' He feels himself "shut up in a crystal cell," from
' which only "a great love or a great task could release
' "me," and hardly expects either from what remains in
' this life.   But I already see so well how these limita-
' tions have fitted him for his peculiar work, that I can
' no longer quarrel with them; while from his eyes looks
' out the angel that must sooner or later break every
' chain.   Leave him in his cell affirming absolute truth;
' protesting against humanity, if so he appears to do;
' the calm observer of the courses of things.   Surely,
' "he keeps true to his thought, which is the great
' "matter."   He has already paid his debt to his time;
' how much more he will give we cannot know; but
' already I feel how invaluable is a cool mind, like his,
' amid the warring elements around us.   As I look at
' him more by his own law, I understand him better;
' and as I understand him better, differences melt away.
' My inmost heart blesses the fate that gave me birth in
' the same clime and time, and that has drawn me into
' such a close bond with him as, it is my hopeful faith,
' will never be broken, but from sphere to sphere ever
' more hallowed. * * *

' What did you mean by saying I had imbibed much
' of his way of thought? I do indeed feel his life steal-
' ing gradually into mine; and I sometimes think that
' my work would have been more simple, and my
' unfolding to a temporal activity more rapid and easy,
' if we had never met. But when I look forward to

'eternal growth, I am always aware that I am far
'larger and deeper for him. His influence has been to
'me that of lofty assurance and sweet serenity. He
'says, I come to him as the European to the Hindoo,
'or the gay Trouvére to the Puritan in his steeple hat.
'Of course this implies that our meeting is partial. I
'present to him the many forms of nature and solicit
'with music; he melts them all into spirit and reproves
'performance with prayer. When I am with God alone,
'I adore in silence. With nature I am filled and grow
'only. With most men I bring words of now past life,
'and do actions suggested by the wants of their natures
'rather than my own. But he stops me from doing
'anything, and makes me think.'

'*October*, 1842. * * To me, individually, Dr. Chan-
'ning's kindness was great; his trust and esteem were
'steady, though limited, and I owe him a large debt of
'gratitude.

'His private character was gentle, simple, and perfectly
'harmonious, though somewhat rigid and restricted in
'its operations. It was easy to love, and a happiness to
'know him, though never, I think, a source of the highest
'social pleasure to be with him. His department was
'ethics; and as a literary companion, he did not throw
'himself heartily into the works of creative genius, but
'looked, wherever he read, for a moral. In criticism he
'was deficient in "individuality," if by that the phrenol-
'ogists mean the power of seizing on the peculiar mean-
'ings of special forms. I have heard it said, that, under
changed conditions, he might have been a poet. He
'had, indeed, the poetic sense of a creative spirit working everywhere. Man and nature were living to him ·

'and though he did not yield to sentiment in particulars
'he did in universals. But his mind was not recreative,
' or even representative.

'He was deeply interesting to me as having so true a
'respect for woman. This feeling in him was not chiv-
'alrous; it was not the sentiment of an artist; it was
'not the affectionateness of the common son of Adam,
'who knows that only her presence can mitigate his
'loneliness; but it was a religious reverence. To him
'she was a soul with an immortal destiny. Nor was
'there at the bottom of his heart one grain of masculine
'assumption. He did not wish that Man should protect
'her, but that God should protect her and teach her the
'meaning of her lot.

'In his public relations he is to be regarded not only
'as a check upon the evil tendencies of his era, but yet
'more as a prophet of a better age already dawning as
'he leaves us. In his later days he filled yet another
'office of taking the middle ground between parties.
'Here he was a fairer figure than ever before. His
'morning prayer was, "Give me more light; keep my
'"soul open to the light;" and it was answered. He
'steered his middle course with sails spotless and untorn.
'He was preserved in a wonderful degree from the
'prejudices of his own past, the passions of the present,
'and the exaggerations of those who look forward to
'the future. In the writings where, after long and
'patient survey, he sums up the evidence on both sides,
'and stands umpire, with the judicial authority of a
'pure intent, a steadfast patience, and a long experience,
'the mild wisdom of age is beautifully tempered by the
'ingenuous sweetness of youth. These pieces resemble
'charges to a jury; they have always been heard with

affectionate deference, if not with assent, and have
exerted a purifying influence.' * *

'*November*, 1842. — When souls meet direct and all
' secret thoughts are laid open, we shall need no forbear-
' ance, no prevention, no care-taking of any kind. Love
' will be pure light, and each action simple, — too simple
' to be noble. But there will not be always so much
' to pardon in ourselves and others. Yesterday we
' had at my class a conversation on Faith. Deeply
' true things were said and felt. But to-day the virtue
' has gone out of me; I have accepted all, and yet there
' will come these hours of weariness,—weariness of human
' nature in myself and others. " Could ye not watch one
' " hour?" Not one faithfully through! * * To speak
' with open heart and " tongue affectionate and true," —
' to enjoy real repose and the consciousness of a thorough
' mutual understanding in the presence of friends when
' we do meet, is what is needed. That being granted, I
' do believe I should not wish any surrender of time or
' thought from a human being. But I have always a
' sense that I cannot meet or be met *in haste ;* as ——
' said he could not look at the works of art in a chance
' half-hour, so cannot I thus rudely and hastily turn
' over the leaves of any mind. In peace, in stillness
' that permits the soul to flow, beneath the open sky, I
' would see those I love.'

VIII.

SOCIALISM.

IN the preceding extracts will have been noticed frequent reference to the Association Movement, which, during the winter of 1840–41, was beginning to appear simultaneously at several points in New England. In Boston and its vicinity several friends, for whose characters Margaret felt the highest honor, and with many of whose views, theoretic and practical, she accorded, were earnestly considering the possibility of making such industrial, social, and educational arrangements, as would simplify economies, combine leisure for study with healthful and honest toil, avert unjust collisions of caste, equalize refinements, awaken generous affections, diffuse courtesy, and sweeten and sanctify life as a whole. Chief among these was the Rev. George Ripley who, convinced by his experience in a faithful ministry that the need was urgent for a thorough application of the professed principles of Fraternity to actual relations, was about staking his all of fortune, reputation, position, and influence, in an attempt to organize a joint-stock community at Brook Farm. How Margaret was inclined to regard this movement has been already indicated. While at heart sympathizing with the heroism that prompted it, in judgment she considered it premature. But true to her noble self, though regretting the seemingly gratuitous sacrifice of her friends, she gave them without stint the cheer of her encouragement and the light of her counsel. She visited them often; entering genially into their trials and pleasures, and missing no chance to drop good seed in every furrow upturned by the ploughshare or softened by the rain. In the secluded yet intensely animated circle of these co-workers I frequently met her during several succeeding years, and rejoice to bear testimony to the justice, magnanimity, wisdom, patience, and many-sided goodwill, that governed her every thought and deed. The feelings with which she watched the progress of this experiment are thus exhibited in her journals: —

'My hopes might lead to Association, too, — an asso-'ciation, if not of efforts, yet of destinies. In such an 'one I live with several already, feeling that each one, 'by acting out his own, casts light upon a mutual 'destiny, and illustrates the thought of a master mind. 'It is a constellation, not a phalanx, to which I would 'belong.'

'Why bind oneself to a central or any doctrine? 'How much nobler stands a man entirely unpledged, 'unbound! Association may be the great experiment 'of the age, still it is only an experiment. It is not 'worth while to lay such stress on it; let us try it, 'induce others to try it, — that is enough.'

'It is amusing to see how the solitary characters tend 'to outwardness, — to association, — while the social 'and sympathetic ones emphasize the value of solitude, '— of concentration, — so that we hear from each the 'word which, from his structure, we least expect.'

'On Friday I came to Brook Farm. The first day or 'two here is desolate. You seem to belong to nobody,

'— to have a right to speak to nobody; but very soon
'you learn to take care of yourself, and then the freedom
'of the place is delightful.

'It is fine to see how thoroughly Mr. and Mrs. R. act
'out, in their own persons, what they intend.

'All Saturday I was off in the woods.   In the evening
'we had a general conversation, opened by me, upon
'Education, in its largest sense, and on what we can do
'for ourselves and others.   I took my usual ground:
'The aim is perfection; patience the road.   The present
'object is to give ourselves and others a tolerable chance.
'Let us not be too ambitious in our hopes as to immediate
'results.   Our lives should be considered as a tendency,
'an approximation only.   Parents and teachers expect
'to do too much.   They are not legislators, but only
'interpreters to the next generation.   Soon, very soon,
'does the parent become merely the elder brother of his
'child; — a little wiser, it is to be hoped. ——— dif-
'fered from me as to some things I said about the gra-
'dations of experience, — that "to be brought prematurely
'"near perfect beings would chill and discourage."   He
'thought it would cheer and console.   He spoke well, —
'with a youthful nobleness.   ——— said "that the most
'"perfect person would be the most impersonal"— philo-
'sophical bull that, I trow — "and, consequently, would
'"impede us least from God."   Mr. R. spoke admirably
'on the nature of loyalty.   The people showed a good
'deal of the *sans-culotte* tendency in their manners, —
'throwing themselves on the floor, yawning, and going
'out when they had heard enough.   Yet, as the majority
'differ from me, to begin with, — that being the reason
'this subject was chosen, — they showed, on the whole,
more respect and interest than I had expected.   As I

'am accustomed to deference, however, and need it for
'the boldness and animation which my part requires, I
'did not speak with as much force as usual. Still, I
'should like to have to face all this; it would have the
'same good effects that the Athenian assemblies had on
'the minds obliged to encounter them.

'Sunday. A glorious day; — the woods full of per-
'fume. I was out all the morning. In the afternoon,
'Mrs. R. and I had a talk. I said my position would
'be too uncertain here, as I could not work. ———
'said: — "They would all like to work for a person of
'"genius. They would not like to have this service
'"claimed from them, but would like to render it of
'"their own accord." "Yes," I told her; "but where
'"would be my repose, when they were always to be
'"judging whether I was worth it or not. It would be
'"the same position the clergyman is in, or the wander-
'"ing beggar with his harp. Each day you must prove
'"yourself anew. You are not in immediate relations
'"with material things."

'We talked of the principles of the community. I
'said I had not a right to come, because all the confi-
'dence in it I had was as an *experiment* worth trying,
'and that it was a part of the great wave of inspired
'thought. ——— declared they none of them had
'confidence beyond this; but they seem to me to have.
'Then I said, "that though I entirely agreed about the
'"dignity of labor, and had always wished for the pres-
'"ent change, yet I did not agree with the principle of
'"paying for services by time;* neither did I believe in
'"the hope of excluding evil, for that was a growth of

---

* This was a transitional arrangement only.

' " nature, and one condition of the development of
' " good." We had valuable discussion on these points.

' All Monday morning in the woods again. Afternoon,
' out with the drawing party; I felt the evils of want
' of conventional refinement, in the impudence with which
' one of the girls treated me. She has since thought of
' it with regret, I notice; and, by every day's observa-
' tion of me, will see that she ought not to have done it.'

' In the evening, a husking in the barn. Men, women,
· and children, all engaged. It was a most picturesque
' scene, only not quite light enough to bring it out fully.
' I staid and helped about half an hour, then took a long
' walk beneath the stars.'

' Wednesday. I have been too much absorbed to-day
' by others, and it has made me almost sick. Mrs. ———
· came to see me, and we had an excellent talk, which
' occupied nearly all the morning. Then Mrs. ———
' wanted to see me, but after a few minutes I found I
' could not bear it, and lay down to rest. Then
' ——— came. Poor man; — his feelings and work
' are wearing on him. He looks really ill now. Then
' ——— and I went to walk in the woods. I was deeply
' interested in all she told me. If I were to write down
' all she and four other married women have confided to
' me, these three days past, it would make a cento, on one
' subject, in five parts. Certainly there should be some
' great design in my life; its attractions are so inva-
' riable.'

' In the evening, a conversation on Impulse. The
' reason for choosing this subject is the great tendency

'here to advocate spontaneousness, at the expense of
'reflection. It was a much better conversation than the
'one before. None yawned, for none came, this time,
'from mere curiosity. There were about thirty-five
'present, which is a large enough circle. Many engaged
'in the talk. I defended nature, as I always do; — the
'spirit ascending through, not superseding, nature. But
'in the scale of Sense, Intellect, Spirit, I advocated to-
'night the claims of Intellect, because those present
'were rather disposed to postpone them. On the nature
'of Beauty we had good talk. ——— spoke well. She
'seemed in a much more reverent humor than the other
'night, and enjoyed the large plans of the universe
'which were unrolled. ———, seated on the floor, with
the light falling from behind on his long gold locks,
'made, with sweet, serene aspect, and composed tones,
'a good exposé of his way of viewing things.'

'Saturday. Well, good-by, Brook Farm. I know
'more about this place than I did when I came; but the
'only way to be qualified for a judge of such an experi-
'ment would be to become an active, though unimpas-
'sioned, associate in trying it. Some good things are
'proven, and as for individuals, they are gainers. Has
'not ——— vied, in her deeds of love, with "my Cid," and
'the holy Ottilia? That girl who was so rude to me stood
'waiting, with a timid air, to bid me good-by. Truly,
'the soft answer turneth away wrath.

'I have found myself here in the amusing position of
'a conservative. Even so is it with Mr. R. There are
'too many young people in proportion to the others. I
heard myself saying, with a grave air, "Play out the

' "play, gentles." Thus, from generation to generation,
'rises and falls the wave.'

Again, a year afterward, she writes: —

'Here I have passed a very pleasant week. The
'tone of the society is much sweeter than when I was
'here a year ago. There is a pervading spirit of mutual
'tolerance and gentleness, with great sincerity. There
'is no longer a passion for grotesque freaks of liberty,
'but a disposition, rather, to study and enjoy the liberty
'of law. The great development of mind and character
'observable in several instances, persuades me that this
'state of things affords a fine studio for the soul-sculptor.
'To a casual observer it may seem as if there was not
'enough of character here to interest, because there are
'no figures sufficiently distinguished to be worth paint-
'ing for the crowd; but there is enough of individuality
'in free play to yield instruction; and one might have,
'from a few months' residence here, enough of the
'human drama to feed thought for a long time.'

Thus much for Margaret's impressions of Brook
Farm and its inmates. What influence she in turn
exerted on those she met there, may be seen from the
following affectionate tribute, offered by one of the
young girls alluded to in the journal: —

"Would that I might aid, even slightly, in doing
justice to the noble-hearted woman whose departure we
must all mourn. But I feel myself wholly powerless to
do so; and after I explain what my relation to her was,

you will understand how this can be, without holding me indolent or unsympathetic.

"When I first met Miss Fuller, I had already cut from my moorings, and was sailing on the broad sea of experience, conscious that I possessed unusual powers of endurance, and that I should meet with sufficient to test their strength. She made no offer of guidance, and once or twice, in the succeeding year, alluded to the fact that she 'had never helped me.' This was in a particular sense, of course, for she helped all who knew her. She was interested in my rough history, but could not be intimate, in any just sense, with a soul so unbalanced, so inharmonious as mine then was. For my part, I reverenced her. She was to me the embodiment of wisdom and tenderness. I heard her converse, and, in the rich and varied intonations of her voice, I recognized a being to whom every shade of sentiment was familiar. She knew, if not by experience then by no questionable intuition, how to interpret the inner life of every man and woman; and, by interpreting, she could soothe and strengthen. To her, psychology was an open book. When she came to Brook Farm, it was my delight to wait on one so worthy of all service, — to arrange her late breakfast in some remnants of ancient China, and to save her, if it might be, some little fatigue or annoyance, during each day. After a while she seemed to lose sight of my more prominent and disagreeable peculiarities, and treated me with affectionate regard."

Being a confirmed Socialist, I often had occasion to discuss with Margaret the problems involved in the "Combined Order" of life; and though unmoved by her scepticism, I could not but admire the sagacity, foresight, comprehensiveness, and catholic sympathy with which she surveyed this complicated subject. Her objections, to be sure, were of the usual kind, and turned mainly upon two points, — the difficulty of so allying labor and capital as to secure the hoped-for coöperation, and the danger of merging the individual in the mass to such degree as to paralyze energy, heroism, and genius; but these objections were urged in a way that brought out her originality and generous hopes. There was nothing abject, timid, or conventional in her doubts. The end sought she prized; but the means she questioned. Though pleased in listening to sanguine visions of the future, she was slow to credit that an organization by "Groups and Series" would yield due incentive for personal development, while ensuring equilibrium through exact and universal justice. She felt, too, that Society was not a machine to be put together and set in motion, but a living body, whose breath must be Divine inspiration, and whose healthful growth is only hindered by forcing. Finally, while longing as earnestly as any Socialist for "Liberty and Law made one in living union," and assured in faith that an era was coming of "Attractive Industry" and "Harmony," she was still for herself. inclined to seek sovereign independence in comparative isolation. Indeed, at this period, Margaret was in spirit and in thought preeminently a Transcendentalist.

IX.

CREDO.

IN regard to Transcendentalism again, there was reason to rejoice in having found a friend, so firm to keep

ıeı own ground, while so liberal to comprehend another's stand-point, as was Margaret. She knew, noı
only theoretically, but practically, how endless are the
ⅾiversities of human character and of Divine discipline,
and she reverenced fellow-spirits too sincerely ever to
wish to waıp them to her will, or to repress their normal
development. She was stern but in one claim, that each
should be faithful to apparent leadings of the Truth ;
and could avow widest differences of conviction without feeling that love was thereby chilled, or the hand
withheld from cordial aid. Especially did she render
service by enabling one, — through her blended insight,
candor, and clearness of understanding,—to see in bright
reflection his own mental state.

It would be doing injustice to a person like Margaret, always more enthusiastic than philosophical, to
attribute to her anything like a system of theology ; for,
hopeful, reverent, aspiring, and free from scepticism, she
felt too profoundly the vastness of the universe and of
destiny ever to presume that with her span rule she
ⅽould measure the Infinite. Yet the tendency of her
ⅼhoughts can readily be traced in the following passages
ⅰrom note-books and letters : —

'When others say to me, and not without apparent
'ground, that "the Outward Church is a folly which
'"keeps men from enjoying the communion of the
'"Church Invisible, and that in the desire to be helped
'"by, and to help others, men lose sight of the only
'"sufficient help, which they might find by faithful
"solitary intentness of spirit," I answer it is true, and
the present deadness and emptiness summon us to turn
our thoughts in that direction. Being now without

'any positive form of religion, any unattractive sym-
'bols, or mysterious rites, we are in the less danger of
'stopping at surfaces, of accepting a mediator instead
'of the Father, a sacrament instead of the Holy Ghost.
'And when I see how little there is to impede and bewil-
'der us, I cannot but accept, — should it be for many
'years, — the forlornness, the want of fit expression, the
'darkness as to what is to be expressed, even that char-
'acterize our time.

'But I do not, therefore, as some of our friends do,
'believe that it will always be so, and that the church
'is tottering to its grave, never to rise again. The
'church was the growth of human nature, and it is so
'still. It is but one result of the impulse which makes
'two friends clasp one another's hands, look into one
'another's eyes at sight of beauty, or the utterance of
'a feeling of piety. So soon as the Spirit has mourned
'and sought, and waited long enough to open new
'depths, and has found something to express, there
'will again be a Cultus, a Church. The very people,
'who say that none is needed, make one at once. They
'talk with, they write to one another. They listen to
'music, they sustain themselves with the poets; they
'like that one voice should tell the thoughts of sev-
'eral minds, one gesture proclaim that the same life is
'at the same moment in many breasts.

'I am myself most happy in my lonely Sundays, and
'do not feel the need of any social worship, as I have
'not for several years, which I have passed in the same
'way. Sunday is to me priceless as a day of peace and
'solitary reflection. To all who will, it may be true
'that, as Herbert says : —

" Sundays the pillars are
On which Heaven's palace arched lies;
The other days fill up the space
And hollow room with vanities;"

' and yet in no wise " vanities," when filtered by the
' Sunday crucible. After much troubling of the waters
' of my life, a radiant thought of the meaning and
' beauty of earthly existence will descend like a heal-
' ing angel. The stillness permits me to hear a pure
' tone from the One in All. But often I am not alone.
' The many now, whose hearts, panting for truth and
' love, have been made known to me, whose lives flow
' in the same direction as mine, and are enlightened
' by the same star, are with me. I am in church, the
' church invisible, undefiled by inadequate expression.
' Our communion is perfect; it is that of a common
' aspiration; and where two or three are gathered
' together in one region, whether in the flesh or the
' spirit, He will grant their request. Other communion
' would be a happiness, — to break together the bread of
' mutual thought, to drink the wine of loving life, — but
' it is not necessary.

' Yet I cannot but feel that the crowd of men whose
' pursuits are not intellectual, who are not brought by
' their daily walk into converse with sages and poets,
' who win their bread from an earth whose mysteries
' are not open to them, whose worldly intercourse is
' more likely to stifle than to encourage the sparks of
' love and faith in their breasts, need on that day
' quickening more than repose. The church is now
' rather a lecture-room than a place of worship; it
should be a school for mutual instruction. I must
rejoice when any one, who lays spiritual things to

' heart, feels the call rather to mingle with men, than tc
' retire and seek by himself.

'You speak of men going up to worship by "house-
' "holds," &c. Were the actual family the intellectual
'family, this might be; but as social life now is, how
'can it? Do we not constantly see the child, born in
'the flesh to one father, choose in the spirit another?
'No doubt this is wrong, since the sign does not stand
'for the thing signified, but it is one feature of the time.
'How will it end? Can families worship together till
'it does end?'

'I have let myself be cheated out of my Sunday, by
'going to hear Mr. ——. As he began by reading the
'first chapter of Isaiah, and the fourth of John's Epistle,
'I made mental comments with pure delight. "Bring
'"no more vain oblations." "Every one that loveth is
'"born of God, and knoweth God." "We know that
'"we dwell in Him, and He in us, because he hath
'"given us of the Spirit." Then pealed the organ, full
'of solemn assurance. But straightway uprose the
'preacher to deny mysteries, to deny the second birth,
'to deny influx, and to renounce the sovereign gift of
'insight, for the sake of what he deemed a "*rational*"
'exercise of will. As he spoke I could not choose but
'deny him all through, and could scarce refrain from
'rising to expound, in the light of my own faith, the
'words of those wiser Jews which had been read. Was
'it not a sin to exchange friendly greeting as we parted,
'and yet tell him no word of what was in my mind?

'Still I saw why he looked at things as he did. The
'old religionists did talk about "grace, conversion," and
the like, technically, without striving to enter into the

' idea, till they quite lost sight of it. Undervaluing the
· intellect, they became slaves of a sect, instead of organs
' of the Spirit. This Unitarianism has had its place.
' There was a time for asserting " the dignity of human
' " nature," and for explaining total depravity into tem-
' porary inadequacy, — a time to say that the truths of
' *essence*, if simplified at all in statement from their infinite
' variety of existence, should be spoken of as One, rather
than Three, though that number, if they would only
let it reproduce itself simply, is of highest significance.
Yet the time seems now to have come for reinterpreting
the old dogmas. For one I would now preach the
Holy Ghost as zealously as they have been preaching
Man, and faith instead of the understanding, and mysticism instead &c. But why go on? It certainly is
by no means useless to preach. In my experience of
the divine gifts of solitude, I had forgotten what might
be done in this other way. That crowd of upturned
faces, with their look of unintelligent complacency!
Give tears and groans, rather, if there be a mixture of
physical excitement and bigotry. Mr. —— is heard
because, though he has not entered into the secret of
piety, he wishes to be heard, and with a good purpose,
— can make a forcible statement, and kindle himself
with his own thoughts. How many persons must
there be who cannot worship alone, since they are
content with so little! Can none wake the spark that
' will melt them, till they take beautiful forms? Were
' one to come now, who could purge us with fire, how
' would these masses glow and be clarified!

' Mr. —— made a good suggestion: — "Such things
' " could not be said in the open air." Let men preach
' for the open air, and speak now thunder and light-

'ning, now dew and rustling leaves. Yet must the
'preacher have the thought of his day before he can
'be its voice. None have it yet; but some of our friends,
'perhaps, are nearer than the religious world at large,
'because neither ready to dogmatize, as if they had
'got it, nor content to stop short with mere impressions
'and presumptuous hopes. I feel that a great truth is
'coming. Sometimes it seems as if we should have it
'among us in a day. Many steps of the Temple have
'been ascended, steps of purest alabaster, and of shin-
'ing jasper, also of rough-brick, and slippery moss-
'grown stone. We shall reach what we long for, since
'we trust and do not fear, for our God knows not fear,
'only reverence, and his plan is All in All.'

'Who can expect to utter an absolutely pure and clear
'tone on these high subjects? Our earthly atmósphere
'is too gròss to permit it. Yet, a severe statement has
'rather an undue charm for me, as I have a nature of
'great emotion, which loves free abandonment. I am
'ready to welcome a descending Moses, come to turn all
'men from idolatries. For my priests have been very
'generally of the Pagan greatness, revering nature and
'seeking excellence, but in the path of progress, not of
'renunciation. The lyric inspirations of the poet come
'very differently on the ear from the "still, small voice."
'They are, in fact, all one revelation; but one must be
'at the centre to interpret it. To that centre I have
'again and again been drawn, but my large natural
'life has been, as yet, but partially transfused with spir-
'itual consciousness. I shun a premature narrowness,
'and bide my time. But I am drawn to look at
'natures who take a different way, because they seem

' to complete my being for me. They, too, tolerate me
' in my many phases for the same reason, probably. It
' pleased me to see, in one of the figures by which the
' Gnostics illustrated the progress of man, that Severity
' corresponded to Magnificence.'

'In my quiet retreat, I read Xenophon, and became
' more acquainted with his Socrates. I had before
' known only the Socrates of Plato, one much more
' to my mind. Socrates conformed to the Greek Church,
' and it is evident with a sincere reverence, because it
' was the growth of the *national* mind. He thought
' best to stand on its platform, and to illustrate, though
' with keen truth, by received forms. This was his
' right way, as his influence was naturally private, for
' individuals who could in some degree respond to the
' teachings of his dæmon ; he knew the multitude
' would not understand him. But it was the other
' way that Jesus took, preaching in the fields, and pluck-
' ing ears of corn on the Sabbath.'

'Is it my defect of spiritual experience, that while
' that weight of sagacity, which is the iron to the dart
' of genius, is needful to satisfy me, the undertone of
' another and a deeper knowledge does not please, does
' not command me ? Even in Handel's Messiah, I am
' half incredulous, half impatient, when the sadness of
' the second part comes to check, before it interprets, the
' promise of the first ; and the strain, " Was ever sorrow
' " like to his sorrow," is not for me, as I have been, as
' I am. Yet Handel was worthy to speak of Christ.
' The great chorus, " Since by man came death, by man
" came also the resurrection of the dead ; for as in

' " Adam all die, even so in Christ shall all be made
' " alive," if understood in the large sense of every man
' his own Saviour, and Jesus only representative of the
' way all must walk to accomplish our destiny, is indeed
' a worthy gospel.'

' Ever since —— told me how his feelings had
' changed towards Jesus, I have wished much to
' write some sort of a Credo, out of my present state,
' but have had no time till last night. I have not sat-
' isfied myself in the least, and have written very has-
' tily, yet, though not full enough to be true, this
' statement is nowhere false to me.

* * * ' Whatever has been permitted by the law of
' being, must be for good, and only in time not good.
' We trust, and are led forward by experience. Light
' gives experience of outward life, faith of inward life,
' and then we discern, however faintly, the necessary
' harmony of the two. The moment we have broken
' through an obstruction, not accidentally, but by the
' aid of faith, we begin to interpret the Universe, and to
' apprehend why evil is permitted. Evil is obstruction ;
' Good is accomplishment.

' It would seem that the Divine Being designs through
' man to express distinctly what the other forms of
' nature only intimate, and that wherever man remains
' imbedded in nature, whether from sensuality, or
' because he is not yet awakened to consciousness, the
' purpose of the whole remains unfulfilled. Hence our
' displeasure when Man is not in a sense above Nature.
' Yet, when he is not so closely bound with all other
' manifestations, as duly to express their Spirit, we are
' also displeased. He must be at once the highest form of

'Nature, and conscious of the meaning she has been
'striving successively to unfold through those below
'him. Centuries pass; whole races of men are expended
'in the effort to produce one that shall realize this Ideal,
'and publish Spirit in the human form. Here and there
'is a degree of success. Life enough is lived through a
'man, to justify the great difficulties attendant on the
'existence of mankind. And then throughout all realms
'of thought vibrates the affirmation, "This is my
'" beloved Son, in whom I am well pleased."

'I do not mean to lay an undue stress upon the posi-
'tion and office of man, merely because I am of his race,
'and understand best the scope of his destiny. The
'history of the earth, the motions of the heavenly
'bodies, suggest already modes of being higher than
'ours, and which fulfil more deeply the office of inter-
'pretation. But I do suppose man's life to be the rivet
'in one series of the great chain, and that all higher
'existences are analogous to his. Music suggests their
'mode of being, and, when carried up on its strong
'wings, we foresee how the next step in the soul's
'ascension shall interpret man to the universe, as
'he now interprets those forms beneath himself. * *

'The law of Spirit is identical, whether displaying
'itself as genius, or as piety, but its modes of expression
'are distinct dialects. All souls desire to become the
'fathers of souls, as citizens, legislators, poets, artists,
'sages, saints; and, so far as they are true to the law of
'their incorruptible essence, they are all Anointed, all
'Emanuel, all Messiah; but they are all brutes and
'devils so far as subjected to the law of corruptible existence. * *

'As wherever there is a tendency a form is gradually

'evolved, as its Type, — so is it the law of each class
'and order of human thoughts to produce a form which
'shall be the visible representation of its aim and striv-
'ings, and stand before it as its King. This effort to pro-
'duce a kingly type it was, that clothed itself with
'power as Brahma or Osiris, that gave laws as Confu-
'cius or Moses, that embodied music and eloquence in
'the Apollo. This it was that incarnated itself, at one
'time as Plato, at another as Michel Angelo, at another
'as Luther, &c. Ever seeking, it has produced Ideal
'after Ideal of the beauty, into which mankind is capa-
'ble of being developed; and one of the highest, in some
'respects the very highest, of these kingly types, was
'the life of Jesus of Nazareth.

'Few believe more in his history than myself, and it
'is very dear to me. I believe, in my own way, in the
'long preparation of ages for his coming, and the truth
'of prophecy that announced him. I see a necessity, in
'the character of Jesus, why Abraham should have
'been the founder of his nation, Moses its lawgiver,
'and David its king and poet. I believe in the gen-
'esis of the patriarchs, as given in the Old Testament.
'I believe in the prophets, — that they foreknew not
'only what their nation longed for, but what the devel-
'opment of universal Man requires, — a Redeemer, an
'Atoner, a Lamb of God, taking away the sins of the
'world. I believe that Jesus came when the time was
'ripe, and that he was peculiarly a messenger and Son
'of God. I have nothing to say in denial of the story
'of his birth; whatever the actual circumstances were,
'he was born of a Virgin, and the tale expresses a truth
'of the soul. I have no objection to the miracles, except
'where they do not happen to please one's feelings.

'Why should not a spirit, so consecrate and intent,
'develop new laws, and make matter plastic? I
'can imagine him walking the waves, without any
'violation of my usual habits of thought. He could not
'remain in the tomb, they say; certainly not, — death is
'impossible to such a being. He remained upon earth;
'most true, and all who have met him since on the
'way, have felt their hearts burn within them. He
'ascended to heaven; surely, how could it be other-
'wise? * *

'Would I could express with some depth what I feel
'as to religion in my very soul; it would be a clear note
'of calm assurance. But for the present this must suf-
'fice with regard to Christ. I am grateful here, as
'everywhere, when Spirit bears fruit in fulness; it attests
'the justice of aspiration, it kindles faith, it rebukes
'sloth, it enlightens resolve. But so does a beautiful
'infant. Christ's life is only one modification of the
'universal harmony. I will not loathe sects, persuasions,
'systems, though I cannot abide in them one moment,
'for I see that by most men they are still needed. To
'them their banners, their tents; let them be Fire-wor-
'shippers, Platonists, Christians; let them live in the
'shadow of past revelations. But, oh, Father of our
'souls, the One, let me seek Thee! I would seek Thee
'in these forms, and in proportion as they reveal Thee,
'they teach me to go beyond themselves. I would learn
'from them all, looking only to Thee! But let me set
'no limits from the past, to my own soul, or to any
'soul.

'Ages may not produce one worthy to loose the shoes
'of the Prophet of Nazareth; yet there will surely be
'another manifestation of that Word which was in

'the beginning.   And all future manifestations will
'come, like Christianity, "not to destroy the law and
' " the prophets, but to fulfil."   The very greatness of
' this manifestation demands a greater.   As an Abraham
'called for a Moses, and a Moses for a David, so does
' Christ for another Ideal.   We want a life more com-
'plete and various than that of Christ.   We have had a
' Messiah to teach and reconcile; let us now have a Man
' to live out all the symbolical forms of human life, with
' the calm beauty of a Greek God, with the deep con-
'sciousness of a Moses, with the holy love and purity
' of Jesus.'

X.

SELF-SOVEREIGNTY.

To one studying the signs of the times, it was quite
instructive to watch the moods of a mind so sensitive as
Margaret's; for her delicate meter indicated in advance
each coming change in the air-currents of thought. But
I was chiefly interested in the processes whereby she
was gaining harmony and unity. The more one studied
her, the more plainly he saw that her peculiar power
was the result of fresh, fervent, exhaustless, and indomitable affections. The emotive force in her, indeed, was
immense in volume, and most various in tendency; and
it was wonderful to observe the outward equability of
one inwardly so impassioned.

This was, in fact, the first problem to be solved in
gaining real knowledge of her commanding character:
" How did a person, by constitution so impetuous, become
so habitually serene?" In temperament Margaret seemed

a Bacchante,* prompt for wild excitement, and fearless to tread by night the mountain forest, with song and dance of delirious mirth; yet constantly she wore the laurel in token of purification, and, with water from fresh fountains, cleansed the statue of Minerva. Stagnancy and torpor were intolerable to her free and elastic impulses; a brilliant fancy threw over each place and incident Arcadian splendor; and eager desire, with energetic purposes, filled her with the consciousness of large latent life; and yet the lower instincts were duly subordinated to the higher, and dignified self-control ordered her deportment. Somehow, according to the doctrine of the wise Jacob Boehme, the fierce, hungry fire had met in embrace the meek, cool water, and was bringing to birth the pleasant light-flame of love. The transformation, though not perfected, was fairly begun.

Partly I could see how this change had been wrought. Ill health, pain, disappointment, care, had tamed her spirits. A wide range through the romantic literature of ancient and modern times had exalted while expending her passions. In the world of imagination, she had discharged the stormful energy which would have been destructive in actual life. And in thought she had bound herself to the mast while sailing past the Sirens. Through sympathy, also, from childhood, with the tragi-comedy

---

* This sentence was written before I was aware that Margaret, as will be seen hereafter, had used the same symbol to describe Madame Sand. The first impulse, of course, when I discovered this coincidence, was to strike out the above passage ; yet, on second thought, I have retained it, as indicating an actual resemblance between these two grand women. In Margaret, however, the benediction of their noble-hearted sister, Elizabeth Barrett, had already been fulfilled ; for she to " woman's claim " had ever joined " the angel-grace

" Of a pure genius sanctified from blame."

of many lives around her, she had gained experience of
the laws and limitations of providential order.   Gradually, too, she had risen to higher planes of hope, whence
opened wider prospects of destiny and duty.   More than
all, by that attraction of opposites which a strong will is
most apt to feel, she had sought, as chosen companions,
persons of scrupulous reserve, of modest coolness, and
severe elevation of view.   Finally, she had been taught,
by a discipline specially fitted to her dispositions, to trust
the leadings of the Divine Spirit.   The result was, that
at this period Margaret had become a Mystic.   Her
prisoned emotions found the freedom they pined for in
contemplation of nature's exquisite harmonies,— in poetic
regards of the glory that enspheres human existence,
when seen as a whole from beyond the clouds, — and
above all in exultant consciousness of life ever influent
from the All-Living.

A few passages from her papers will best illustrate this
proneness to rapture.

'My tendency is, I presume, rather to a great natural
'than to a deep religious life.   But though others may
'be more conscientious and delicate, few have so steady
'a faith in Divine Love.   I may be arrogant and
'impetuous, but I am never harsh and morbid.   May
'there not be a mediation, rather than a conflict, between
'piety and genius?   Greek and Jew, Italian and Saxon,
'are surely but leaves on one stem, at last.'

'I am in danger of giving myself up to experiences
'till they so steep me in ideal passion that the desired
'goal is forgotten in the rich present.   Yet I think I am
'learning how to use life more wisely.'

'Forgive me, beautiful ones, who earlier learned the
'harmony of your beings, — with whom eye, voice, and
'hand are already true to the soul! Forgive me still
'some "lispings and stammerings of the passionate age."
'Teach me, — me, also, — to utter my pæan in its full
'sweetness. These long lines are radii from one centre;
'aid me to fill the circumference. Then each moment,
'each act, shall be true. The pupil has found the car-
'buncle,* but knows not yet how to use it day by day.
'But "though his companions wondered at the pupil,
'"the master loved him." He loves me, my friends.
'Do ye trust me. Wash the tears and black stains
'from the records of my life by the benignity of a true
'glance; make each discord harmony, by striking again
'the key-note; forget the imperfect interviews, burn the
'imperfect letters, till at last the full song bursts forth,
'the key-stone is given from heaven to the arch, the past
'is all pardoned and atoned for, and we live forever in
'the Now.' * *

'Henceforth I hope I shall not write letters thus full
'of childish feeling; for in feeling I am indeed a child,
'and the least of children. Soon I must return into the
'Intellect, for *there*, in sight, at least, I am a man, and
'could write the words very calmly and in steadfast
'flow. But, lately, the intellect has been so subordinated
'to the soul, that I am not free to enter the Basilikon,
'and plead and hear till I am called. But let me not
'stay too long in this Sicilian valley, gathering my
'flowers, for "night cometh."'

'The other evening, while hearing the Creation, in

---

* Novalis.

'the music of "There shoots the healing plant," I felt
'what I would ever feel for suffering souls. Some-
'where in nature is the Moly, the Nepenthe, desired from
'the earliest ages of mankind. No wonder the music
'dwelt so exultingly on the passage : —

'"In native worth and honor clad."

'Yes; even so would I ever see man. I will wait, and
'never despair, through all the dull years.'

'I am "too fiery." Even so. Ceres put her foster
'child in the fire because she loved him. If they thought
'so before, will they not far more now? Yet I wish to
'be seen as I am, and would lose all rather than soften
'away anything. Let my friends be patient and gentle,
'and teach me to be so. I never promised any one
'patience or gentleness, for those beautiful traits are not
'natural to me; but I would learn them. Can I not?'

'Of all the books, and men, and women, that have
'touched me these weeks past, what has most entered
'my soul is the music I have heard, — the masterly
'expression from that violin; the triumph of the
'orchestra, after the exploits on the piano; Braham, in
'his best efforts, when he kept true to the dignity of
'art; the Messiah, which has been given on two succes-
'sive Sundays, and the last time in a way that deeply
'expressed its divine life; but above all, Beethoven's
'seventh symphony. What majesty! what depth!
'what tearful sweetness! what victory! This was
'truly a fire upon an altar. There are a succession
'of soaring passages, near the end of the third move-

'ment, which touch me most deeply. Though soar-
'ing, they hold on with a stress which almost breaks
'the chains of matter to the hearer. O, how refreshing,
'after polemics and philosophy, to soar thus on strong
'wings! Yes, Father, I will wander in dark ways
'with the crowd, since thou seest best for me to be tied
'down. But only in thy free ether do I know myself.
'When I read Beethoven's life, I said, "I will never
'"repine." When I heard this symphony, I said, "I
'"will triumph."'

'To-day I have finished the life of Raphael, by Quatre-
'mere de Quincy, which has so long engaged me. It
'scarce goes deeper than a *catalogue raisonnée*, but is
'very complete in its way. I could make all that
'splendid era alive to me, and inhale the full flower of
'the Sanzio. Easily one soars to worship these angels
'of Genius. To venerate the Saints you must well nigh
'be one.
'I went out upon the lonely rock which commands so
'delicious a panoramic view. A very mild breeze had
'sprung up after the extreme heat. A sunset of the
'melting kind was succeeded by a perfectly clear moon-
'rise. Here I sat, and thought of Raphael. I was
'drawn high up in the heaven of beauty, and the mists
'were dried from the white plumes of contemplation.'
'Only by emotion do we know thee, Nature. To
'lean upon thy heart, and feel its pulses vibrate to
'our own; — that is knowledge, for that is love, the
'love of infinite beauty, of infinite love. Thought will
'never make us be born again.
'My fault is that I think I feel *too much*. O that my
'friends would teach me that "simple art of not too

' ·" much ! " How can I expect them to bear the cease-
' less eloquence of my nature ? '

'Often it has seemed that I have come near enough to
' the limits to see what they are. But suddenly arises
' afar the Fata Morgana, and tells of new Sicilies, of
' their flowery valleys and fields of golden grain. Then,
' as I would draw near, my little bark is shattered on
' the rock, and I am left on the cold wave. Yet with
' my island in sight I do not sink.'

'I look not fairly to myself, at the present moment.
' If noble growths are always slow, others may ripen far
' worthier fruit than is permitted to my tropical heats
' and tornadoes. Let me clasp the cross on my breast,
' as I have done a thousand times before.'

' Let me but gather from the earth one full-grown fragrant flower ;
' Within my bosom let it bloom through its one blooming hour ;
' Within my bosom let it die, and to its latest breath
' My own shall answer, " Having lived, I shrink not now from death."
' It is this niggard halfness that turns my heart to stone ;
' 'T is the cup seen, not tasted, that makes the infant moan.
' For once let me press firm my lips upon the moment's brow,
' For once let me distinctly feel I am all happy now,
' And bliss shall seal a blessing upon that moment's brow.'

'I was in a state of celestial happiness, which lasted
' a great while. For months I was all radiant with
' faith, and love, and life. I began to be myself. Night
' and day were equally beautiful, and the lowest and
' highest equally holy. Before, it had seemed as if the
' Divine only gleamed upon me; but then it poured into
' and through me a tide of light. I have passed down
' from the rosy mountain, now; but I do not forget its

'pure air, nor how the storms looked as they rolled
'beneath my feet. I have received my assurance, and
'if the shadows should lie upon me for a century, they
'could never make me forgetful of the true hour.
'Patiently I bide my time.'

The last passage describes a peculiar illumination, to
which Margaret often referred as the period when her
earthly being culminated, and when, in the noon-tide of
loving enthusiasm, she felt wholly at one with God,
with Man, and the Universe. It was ever after, to her,
an earnest that she was of the Elect. In a letter to one
of her confidential female friends, she thus fondly looks
back to this experience on the mount of transfiguration: —

'You know how, when the leadings of my life found
'their interpretation, I longed to share my joy with those
'I prized most; for I felt that if they could but under-
'stand the past we should meet entirely. They received
'me, some more, some less, according to the degree of
'intimacy between our natures. But now I have done
'with the past, and again move forward. The path
'looks more difficult, but I am better able to bear its
'trials. We shall have much communion, even if not
'in the deepest places. I feel no need of isolation, but
'only of temperance in thought and speech, that the
'essence may not evaporate in words, but grow plente-
'ous within. The Life will give me to my own. I am
'not yet so worthy to love as some others are, because
'my manifold nature is not yet harmonized enough to
'be faithful, and I begin to see how much it was the
'want of a pure music in me that has made the good

'doubt me. Yet have I been true to the best light I
'had, and if I am so now much will be given.

'During my last weeks of solitude I was very happy,
'and all that had troubled me became clearer. The
'angel was not weary of waiting for Gunhilde, till she
'had unravelled her mesh of thought, and seeds of
'mercy, of purification, were planted in the breast.
'Whatever the past has been, I feel that I have always
'been reading on and on, and that the Soul of all souls
'has been patient in love to mine. New assurances
'were given me, that if I would be faithful and humble,
'there was no experience that would not tell its heavenly
'errand. If shadows have fallen, already they give way
'to a fairer if more tempered light; and for the present
'I am so happy that the spirit kneels.

'Life is richly worth living, with its continual revela-
'tions of mighty woe, yet infinite hope; and I take it to
'my breast. Amid these scenes of beauty, all that is
'little, foreign, unworthy, vanishes like a dream. So
'shall it be some time amidst the Everlasting Beauty
'when true joy shall begin and never cease.'

Filled thus as Margaret was with ecstasy, she was yet
more than willing, — even glad, — to bear her share in the
universal sorrow. Well she knew that pain must be proportioned to the fineness and fervor of her organization;
that the very keenness of her sensibility exposed her to
constant disappointment or disgust; that no friend, however faithful, could meet the demands of desires so eager,
of sympathies so absorbing. Contrasted with her radiant
visions, how dreary looked actual existence; how gall-
ing was the friction of petty hindrances; how heavy
the yoke of drudging care! Even success seemed failure,

when measured by her conscious aim; and experience
had brought out to consciousness excesses and defects,
which humbled pride while shaming self-confidence.
But suffering as she did with all the intensity of so
passionate a nature, Margaret still welcomed the searching discipline. 'It is only when Persephone returns from
'lower earth that she weds Dyonysos, and passes from
'central sadness into glowing joy,' she writes. And
again: 'I have no belief in beautiful lives; we are born
'to be mutilated; and the blood must flow till in every
'vein its place is supplied by the Divine ichor.' And
she reiterates: 'The method of Providence with me is
'evidently that of "cross-biassing," as Herbert hath it.'
In a word, to her own conscience and to intimate friends
she avowed, without reserve, that there was in her
'much rude matter that needed to be spiritualized.'
Comment would but weaken the pathos of the following passages, in which so plainly appears a once wilful
temper striving, with child-like faith, to obey: —

'I have been a chosen one; the lesson of renuncia-
'tion was early, fully taught, and the heart of stone
'quite broken through. The Great Spirit wished to
'leave me no refuge but itself. Convictions have been
'given, enough to guide me many years if I am stead-
'fast. How deeply, how gratefully I feel this blessing,
'as the fabric of others' hopes are shivering round me.
'Peace will not always flow thus softly in my life; but,
'O, our Father! how many hours has He consecrated
'to Himself. How often has the Spirit chosen the
'time, when no ray came from without, to descend
'upon the orphan life!'

'A humbler, tenderer spirit! Yes, I long for it. But
'how to gain it? I see no way but prayerfully to bend
'myself to meet the hour. Let friends be patient with
'me, and pardon some faint-heartedness. The buds
'will shiver in the cold air when the sheaths drop. It
'will not be so long. The word "Patience" has been
'spoken; it shall be my talisman. A nobler courage
'will be given, with gentleness and humility. My con-
'viction is clear that all my troubles are needed, and
'that one who has had so much light thrown upon the
'path, has no excuse for faltering steps.'

'Could we command enthusiasm; had we an interest
'with the gods which would light up those sacred fires
'at will, we should be even seraphic in our influences.
'But life, if not a complete waste of wearisome hours,
'must be checkered with them; and I find that just
'those very times, when I feel all glowing and radiant
'in the happiness of receiving and giving out again the
'divine fluid, are preludes to hours of languor, weari-
'ness, and paltry doubt, born of —

> '"The secret soul's mistrust
> To find her fair ethereal wings
> Weighed down by vile, degraded dust."

'To this, all who have chosen or been chosen to a life
'of thought must submit. Yet I rejoice in my heritage.
'Should I venture to complain? Perhaps, if I were to
'reckon up the hours of bodily pain, those passed in
'society with which I could not coalesce, those of
'ineffectual endeavor to penetrate the secrets of nature
'and of art, or, worse still, to reproduce the beautiful in
'some way for myself, I should find they far outnum-

'bered those of delightful sensation, of full and soothing
'thought, of gratified tastes and affections, and of proud
'hope. Yet these last, if few, how lovely, how rich in
'presage! None, who have known them, can in their
'worst estate fail to hope that they may be again upborne
'to higher, purer blue.'

'As I was steeped in the divine tenth book of the
'Republic, came ——'s letter, in which he so insultingly
'retracts his engagements. I finished the book obsti-
'nately, but could get little good of it; then went to ask
'comfort of the descending sun in the woods and fields.
'What a comment it was on the disparity between my
'pursuits and my situation to receive such a letter while
'reading that book! However, I will not let life's mean
'perplexities blur from my eye the page of Plato; nor,
'if natural tears must be dropt, murmur at a lot, which,
'with all its bitterness, has given time and opportunity
'to cherish an even passionate love for Truth and
'Beauty.'

'Black Friday it has been, and my heart is well nigh
'wearied out. Shall I never be able to act and live with
'persons of views high as my own? or, at least, with
'some steadiness of feeling for me to calculate upon?
'Ah, me! what woes within and without; what assaults
'of folly; what mean distresses; and, oh, what wounds
'from cherished hands! Were ye the persons who should
'stab thus? Had I, too, the Roman right to fold my
'robe about me decently, and breathe the last sigh! The
'last! Horrible, indeed, should sobs, deep as these, be
'drawn to all eternity. But no; life could not hold out
'for more than one lease of sorrow. This anguish

'however, will be wearied out, as I know by experience,
'alas! of how many such hours.'

'I am reminded to-day of the autumn hours at
'Jamaica Plain, where, after arranging everything for
'others that they wanted of me, I found myself, at
'last, alone in my still home, where everything, for
'once, reflected my feelings. It was so still, the air
'seemed full of spirits. How happy I was! with what
'sweet and solemn happiness! All things had tended to
'a crisis in me, and I was in a higher state, mentally
'and spiritually, than I ever was before or shall be
'again, till death shall introduce me to a new sphere. I
'purposed to spend the winter in study and self-collec-
'tion, and to write constantly. I thought I should thus
'be induced to embody in beautiful forms all that lay in
'my mind, and that life would ripen into genius. But
'a very little while these fair hopes bloomed; and, since
'I was checked then, I do never expect to blossom forth
'on earth, and all postponements come naturally. At
'that time it seemed as if angels left me. Yet, now, I
'think they still are near. Renunciation appears to be
'entire, and I quite content; yet, probably, 't is no such
'thing, and that work is to be done over and over
'again.'

'Do you believe our prayers avail for one another?
'and that happiness is good for the soul? Pray, then,
'for me, that I may have a little peace, — some green
'and flowery spot, 'mid which my thoughts may rest;
'yet not upon fallacy, but only upon something genuine.
'I am deeply homesick, yet where is that home? If
'not on earth, why should we look to heaven? I would

'tain truly live wherever I must abide, and bear with
'full energy on my lot, whatever it is. He, who alone
'knoweth, will affirm that I have tried to work whole-
'hearted from an earnest faith. Yet my hand is often
'languid, and my heart is slow. I would be gone; but
'whither? I know not; if I cannot make this spot of
'ground yield the corn and roses, famine must be my lot
'forever and ever, surely.'

'I remember how at a similar time of perplexity,
'when there were none to counsel, hardly one to sym-
'pathize, and when the conflicting wishes of so many
'whom I loved pressed the aching heart on every side,
'after months of groping and fruitless thought, the
'merest trifle precipitated the whole mass; all became
'clear as crystal, and I saw of what use the tedious
'preparation had been, by the deep content I felt in the
'result.'

'Beethoven! Tasso! It is well to think of you!
'What sufferings from baseness, from coldness! How
'rare and momentary were the flashes of joy, of confi-
'dence and tenderness, in these noblest lives! Yet
'could not their genius be repressed. The Eternal
'Justice lives. O, Father, teach the spirit the meaning
'of sorrow, and light up the generous fires of love and
'hope and faith, without which I cannot live!'

'What signifies it that Thou dost always give me to
'drink more deeply of the inner fountains? And why
'do I seek a reason for these repulsions and strange
'arrangements of my mortal lot, when I always gain
from them a deeper love for all men, and a deeper trust

'in Thee? Wonderful are thy ways! But lead me
'the darkest and the coldest as Thou wilt.'

'Please, good Genius of my life, to make me very
'patient, resolute, gentle, while no less ardent; and after
'having tried me well, please present, at the end of
'some thousand years or so, a sphere of congenial and
'consecutive labors; of heart-felt, heart-filling wishes
'carried out into life on the instant; of aims obviously,
'inevitably proportioned to my highest nature. Sometime, in God's good time, let me live as swift and
'earnest as a flash of the eye. Meanwhile, let me
'gather force slowly, and drift along lazily, like yonder
'cloud, and be content to end in a few tears at last.'

'To-night I lay on the sofa, and saw how the flame
'shot up from beneath, through the mass of coal that
'had been piled above. It shot up in wild beautiful jets,
'and then unexpectedly sank again, and all was black,
'unsightly and forlorn. And thus, I thought, is it with
'my life at present. Yet if the fire beneath persists
'and conquers, that black dead mass will become all
'radiant, life-giving, fit for the altar or the domestic
'hearth. Yes, and it shall be so.'

'My tendency at present is to the deepest privacy.
'Where can I hide till I am given to myself? Yet I
'love the others more and more. When they are with
'me I must give them the best from my scrip. I see
'their infirmities, and would fain heal them, forgetful
'of my own! But am I left one moment alone, then, a
'poor wandering pilgrim, but no saint, I would seek the
'shrine, and would therein die to the world. Then if

'from the poor relics some miracles might be wrought,
'that should be for my fellows. Yet some of the saints
'were able to work in their generation, for they had
'renounced all!'

'Forget, if you can, all of petulant or overstrained
'that may have displeased you in me, and commend me
'in your prayers to my best self. When, in the solitude
'of the spirit, comes upon you some air from the dis-
'tance, a breath of aspiration, of faith, of pure tender-
'ness, then believe that the Power which has guided
'me so faithfully, emboldens my thoughts to frame a
'prayer for you.'

'Beneath all pain inflicted by Nature, be not only
'serene, but more; let it avail thee in prayer. Put up,
'at the moment of greatest suffering, a prayer; not for
'thy own escape, but for the enfranchisement of some
'being dear to thee, and the Sovereign Spirit will accept
'thy ransom.'

'Strive, strive, my soul, to be innocent; yes! benefi-
'cent. Does any man wound thee? not only forgive,
'but work into thy thought intelligence of the kind of
'pain, that thou mayest never inflict it on another spirit.
'Then its work is done; it will never search thy whole
'nature again. O, love much, and be forgiven!'

'No! we cannot leave society while one clod remains
'unpervaded by divine life. We cannot live and grow
'in consecrated earth, alone. Let us rather learn to
'stand up like the Holy Father, and with extended
arms bless the whole world.'

'It will be happiness indeed, if, on passing this first
'stage, we are permitted, in some degree, to alleviate the
'ills of those we love, — to lead them on a little way; to
'aid them when they call. Often it seems to me, it
'would be sweet to feel that I had certainly conferred
'one benefit. All my poor little schemes for others are
'apparently blighted, and now, as ever, I am referred to
'the Secular year for the interpretation of my moments.'

In one of Margaret's manuscripts is found this beautiful symbol: — ' There is a species of Cactus, from whose
' outer bark, if torn by an ignorant person, there exudes
'a poisonous liquid; but the natives, who know the
'plant, strike to the core, and there find a sweet, refresh-
'ing juice, that renews their strength.' Surely the preceding extracts prove that she was learning how to draw
life-giving virtue from the very heart of evil. No superficial experience of sorrow embittered her with angry
despair; but through profound acceptance, she sought to
imbibe, from every ill, peace, purity and gentleness.

The two fiery trials through which she had been
made to pass, and through which she was yet to pass
again and again, — obstruction to the development of
her genius, and loneliness of heart, — were the very furnace needed to burn the dross from her gold, till it could
fitly image the Heavenly Refiner. By inherited traits,
and indiscreet treatment, self-love had early become so
excessive that only severest discipline could transmute
it to disinterestedness. Pity for her own misfortunes
had, indeed, taught her to curb her youthful scorn for
mediocrity, and filled her with considerateness and delicate sensibility. Constant experience, too, of the won-

derful modes whereby her fate was shaped by overruling
mercy, had chastened her love of personal sway, and
her passion for a commanding career; and Margaret
could humble herself, — did often humble herself, —
with an all-resigning contrition, that was ·most touching
to witness in one naturally so haughty. Of this the following letter to a valued friend gives illustration : —

'I ought, I know, to have laid aside my own cares
'and griefs, been on the alert for intelligence that would
·gratify you, and written letters such as would have been
'of use and given pleasure to my wise, tender, ever
'faithful friend. But no; I first intruded on your happi-
'ness with my sorrowful epistles, and then, because you
'did not seem to understand my position, with sullen
'petulance I resolved to write no more. Nay, worse; I
'tried to harden my heart against you, and felt, "If you
'"cannot be all, you shall be nothing."

'It was a bad omen that I lost the locket you gave
'me, which I had constantly worn. Had that been
'daily before my eyes, to remind me of all your worth,
'— of the generosity with which you, a ripe and wise
·character, received me to the privileges of equal friend-
'ship; of the sincerity with which you reproved and the
'love with which you pardoned my faults; of how much
'you taught me, and bore with from me, — it would
'have softened the flint of my heart, and I should have
'relaxed from my isolation.

'How shall I apologize for feelings which I now
'recognize as having been so cold, so bitter and unjust?
'I can only say I have suffered greatly, till the tone of
'my spirits seems destroyed. Since I have been at
'leisure to realize how very ill I have been, under what

' constant pain and many annoyances I have kept myself
' upright, and how, if I have not done my work, I have
' learned my lesson to the end, I should be inclined to
' excuse myself for every fault, except this neglect and
' ingratitude against friends. Yet, if you can forgive, I
' will try to forgive myself, and I do think I shall never
' so deeply sin again.'

Yet, though thus frank to own to herself and to her
peers her errors, Margaret cherished a trust in her powers,
a confidence in her destiny, and an ideal of her being,
place and influence, so lofty as to be extravagant. In
the morning-hour and mountain-air of aspiration, her
shadow moved before her, of gigantic size, upon the
snow-white vapor.

In accordance with her earnest charge, ' Be true as
' Truth to me,' I could not but expose this propensity to
self-delusion; and her answer is her best explanation and
defence : — ' I protest against your applying to me, even
' in your most transient thought, such an epithet as
' "determined exaggeration." Exaggeration, if you
' will; but not determined. No; I would have all open
' to the light, and would let my boughs be pruned, when
' they grow rank and unfruitful, even if I felt the knife
' to the quick of my being. Very fain would I have a
' rational modesty, without self-distrust; and may the
' knowledge of my failures leaven my soul, and check
' its intemperance. If you saw me wholly, you would
' not, I think, feel as you do; for you would recognize
' the force, that regulates my life and tempers the ardor
' with an eventual calmness. You would see, too, that
' the more I take my flight in poetical enthusiasm, the
' stronger materials I bring back for my nest. Certainly

I am nowise yet an angel; but neither am I an utterly
weak woman, and far less a cold intellect. God is
rarely afar off. Exquisite nature is all around. Life
'affords vicissitudes enough to try the energies of the
'human will. I can pray, I can act, I can learn, I can
'constantly immerse myself in the Divine Beauty. But
'I also need to love my fellow-men, and to meet the
'responsive glance of my spiritual kindred.'

Again, she says:—'I like to hear you express your
'sense of my defects. The word "arrogance" does
'not, indeed, appear to me to be just; probably because
'I do not understand what you mean. But in due
'time I doubtless shall; for so repeatedly have you
'used it, that it must stand for something real in my
'large and rich, yet irregular and unclarified nature.
'But though I like to hear you, as I say, and think
'somehow your reproof does me good, by myself, I
'return to my native bias, and feel as if there was
'plenty of room in the universe for my faults, and as if
'I could not spend time in thinking of them, when so
'many things interest me more. I have no defiance or
'coldness, however, as to these spiritual facts which I
'do not know; but I must follow my own law, and bide
'my time, even if, like Œdipus, I should return a crimi-
'nal, blind and outcast, to ask aid from the gods. Such
'possibilities, I confess, give me great awe; for I have
'more sense than most, of the tragic depths that may
'open suddenly in the life. Yet, believing in God,
'anguish cannot be despair, nor guilt perdition. I feel
'sure that I have never wilfully chosen, and that my
'life has been docile to such truth as was shown it. In
'an environment like mine, what may have seemed too
lofty or ambitious in my character was absolutely

'needed to keep the heart from breaking and enthusiasm
'from extinction.'

Such Egoism as this, though lacking the angel grace
of unconsciousness, has a stoical grandeur that commands respect. Indeed, in all that Margaret spoke,
wrote, or did, no cynic could detect the taint of meanness. Her elation came not from opium fumes of
vanity, inhaled in close chambers of conceit, but from
the stimulus of sunshine, fresh breezes, and swift movement upon the winged steed of poesy. Her existence
was bright with romantic interest to herself. There
was an amplitude and elevation in her aim, which were
worthy, as she felt, of human honor and of heavenly
aid; and she was buoyed up by a courageous good-will,
amidst all evils, that she knew would have been recognized as heroic in the chivalric times, when "every
morning brought a noble chance." Neither was her
self-regard of an engrossing temper. On the contrary,
the sense of personal dignity taught her the worth of the
lowliest human being, and her intense desire for harmonious conditions quickened a boundless compassion
for the squalid, downcast, and drudging multitude. She
aspired to live in majestic fulness of benignant and joyful activity, leaving a track of light with every footstep;
and, like the radiant Iduna, bearing to man the golden
apples of immortality, she would have made each meeting with her fellows rich with some boon that should
never fade, but brighten in bloom forever.

This characteristic self-esteem determined the quality
of Margaret's influence, which was singularly penetrating, and most beneficent where most deeply and
continuously felt. Chance acquaintance with her, like
a breath from the tropics, might have prematurely burst

the buds of feeling in sensitive hearts, leaving after blight and barrenness. Natures, small in compass and of fragile substance, might have been distorted and shattered by attempts to mould themselves on her grand model. And in her seeming unchartered impulses, — whose latent law was honorable integrity, — eccentric spirits might have found encouragement for capricious license. Her morbid subjectivity, too, might, by contagion, have affected others with undue self-consciousness. And, finally, even intimate friends might have been tempted, by her flattering love, to exaggerate their own importance, until they recognized that her regard for them was but one niche in a Pantheon at whose every shrine she offered incense. But these ill effects were superficial accidents. The peculiarity of her power was to make all who were in concert with her feel the miracle of existence. She lived herself with such concentrated force in the moments, that she was always effulgent with thought and affection, — with conscience, courage, resource, decision, a penetrating and forecasting wisdom. Hence, to associates, her presence seemed to touch even common scenes and drudging cares with splendor, as when, through the scud of a rain-storm, sunbeams break from serene blue openings, crowning familiar things with sudden glory. By manifold sympathies, yet central unity, she seemed in herself to be a goodly company, and her words and deeds imparted the virtue of a collective life. So tender was her affection, that, like a guardian genius, she made her friends' souls her own, and identified herself with their fortunes: and yet, so pure and high withal was her justice, that, in her recognition of their past success and present claims, there came a summons for fresh endeavor after the perfect. The very thought of her roused manliness to emulate the vigorous freedom, with which one was assured, that wherever placed she was that instant acting; and the mere mention of her name was an inspiration of magnanimity, and faithfulness, and truth.

> ' " Sincere has been their striving ; great their love,"

'is a sufficient apology for any life,' wrote Margaret; and how preëminently were these words descriptive of herself. Hers was indeed

> " The equal temper of heroic hearts,
> Made weak by time and fate, but strong in will,
> To strive, to seek, to find, and not to yield."

This indomitable aspiration found utterance in the following verses, on

'SUB ROSA CRUX.

> • In times of old, as we are told,
>   ' When men more childlike at the feet
>   ' Of Jesus sat than now,
> ' A chivalry was known, more bold
> ' Than ours, and yet of stricter vow,
>   ' And worship more complete.
>
> ' Knights of the Rosy Cross ! they bore
> ' Its weight within the breast, but wore
>   ' Without the sign, in glistening ruby bright.
> ' The gall and vinegar they drank alone,
> ' But to the world at large would only own
>   ' The wine of faith, sparkling with rosy light.
>
> ' They knew the secret of the sacred oil,
>   ' Which, poured upon the prophet's head,

' Could keep him wise and pure for aye,
' Apart from all that might distract or soil ,
' With this their lamps they fed,
' Which burn in their sepulchral shrines,
    ' Unfading night and day.

' The pass-word now is lost
' To that initiation full and free ;
    ' Daily we pay the cost
' Of our slow schooling for divine degree.
    ' We know no means to feed an undying lamp,
    ' Our lights go out in every wind and damp.

' We wear the cross of Ebony and Gold,
' Upon a dark back-ground a form of light,
    ' A heavenly hope within a bosom cold,
A starry promise in a frequent night ;
    ' And oft the dying lamp must trim again,
    ' For we are conscious, thoughtful, striving men

' Yet be we faithful to this present trust,
' Clasp to a heart resigned this faithful Must ;
        ' Though deepest dark our efforts should enfold,
        ' Unwearied mine to find the vein of gold ;
' Forget not oft to waft the prayer on high ; —
' The rosy dawn again shall fill the sky.

' And by that lovely light all truth revealed, —
' The cherished forms, which sad distrust concealed,
        ' Transfigured, yet the same, will round us stand,
        ' The kindred angels of a faithful band ;
' Ruby and ebon cross then cast aside,
' No lamp more needed, for the night has died.

' " Be to the best thou knowest ever true,"
    ' Is all the creed.
' Then be thy talisman of rosy hue,
    ' Or fenced with thorns, that wearing, thou must bleed.
' Or, gentle pledge of love's prophetic view,
    ' The faithful steps it will securely lead.

'Happy are all who reach that distant shore,
    'And bathe in heavenly day ;
'Happiest are those who high the banner bore,
    'To marshal others on the way,
'Or waited for them, fainting and way-worn,
    'By burthens overborne.'

NEW YORK.

JOURNALS, LETTERS, &c.

"How much, preventing God, how much I owe
　To the defences thou hast round me set !
Example, Custom, Fear, Occasion slow, —
　These scorned bondsmen were my parapet.
　I dare not peep over this parapet,
To gauge with glance the roaring gulf below,
The depths of sin to which I had descended,
Had not these me against myself defended."

"Di te, finor, chiesto non hai severa
　Ragione a tè ; di sua virtù non cade
Sospetto in cor conscio a se stesso."
　　　　　　　　　　　ALFIERI.

"He that lacks time to mourn, lacks time to mend ;
Eternity mourns that.　'T is an ill cure
For life's worst ills, to have no time to feel them.
Where sorrow 's held intrusive, and turned out,
There wisdom will not enter, nor true power,
Nor aught that dignifies humanity."
　　　　　　　　　　　TAYLOR.

" That time of year thou may'st in me behold,
    When yellow leaves, or none, or few do hang
Upon those boughs which shake against the cold,
    Bare ruined choirs, where late the sweet birds sang.
In me thou seest the twilight of such day,
    As after sunset fadeth in the west ;
Which by and by black night doth take away, —
    Death's second self, that seals up all in rest.
In me thou seest the glowing of such fire,
    That on the ashes of his youth doth lie ;
As the death-bed whereon it must expire,
    Consumed with that which it was nourished by '
                        SHAKSPEARE.   [Sonnet lxxiii.]

" Aber zufrieden mit stillerem Ruhme,
    Brechen die Frauen des Augenblick's Blume,
    Nähren sie sorgsam mit liebendem Fleiss,
    Freier in ihrem gebundenen Wirken,
    Reicher als er in des Wissens Bezirken
    Und in der Dichtung unendlichem Kreiz."
                        SCHILLER.

" Not like to like, but like in difference ;
    Yet in the long years liker must they grow, —
    The man be more of woman, she of man ;
    He gain in sweetness and in moral height,
    Nor lose the wrestling thews that throw the world .
    She mental breadth, nor fail in childward care .
    More as the double-natured poet each ;
    Till at the last she set herself to man,
    Like perfect music unto noble words."
                        TENNYSON.

VII.

NEW YORK.

———

LEAVING HOME.

INCESSANT exertion in teaching and writing, added to pecuniary anxieties and domestic cares, had so exhausted Margaret's energy, in 1844, that she felt a craving for fresh interests, and resolved to seek an entire change of scene amid freer fields of action.

'The tax on my mind is such,' she writes, 'and I am 'so unwell, that I can scarcely keep up the spring of my 'spirits, and sometimes fear that I cannot go through 'with the engagements of the winter. But I have never 'stopped yet in fulfilling what I have undertaken, and 'hope I shall not be compelled to now. How farcical 'seems the preparation needed to gain a few moments' 'life; yet just so the plant works all the year round for 'a few days' flower.'

But in brighter mood she says, again: — 'I congratu-'late myself that I persisted, against every persuasion, 'in doing all I could last winter; for now I am and shall 'be free from debt, and I look on the position of debtor 'with a dread worthy of some respectable Dutch burgo-'master. My little plans for others, too, have suc-'ceeded; our small household is well arranged, and all 'goes smoothly as a wheel turns round. Mother, more-'over, has learned not to be over-anxious when I suffer,

'so that I am not obliged to suppress my feelings when
'it is best to yield to them. Thus, having more calm-
'ness, I feel often that a sweet serenity is breathed
'through every trifling duty. I am truly grateful for
'being enabled to fulfil obligations which to some might
'seem humble, but which to me are sacred.'

And in mid-summer comes this pleasant picture : —
'Every day, I rose and attended to the many little calls
'which are always on me, and which have been more
'of late. Then, about eleven, I would sit down to write,
'at my window, close to which is the apple-tree, lately
'full of blossoms, and now of yellow birds. Opposite me
'was Del Sarto's Madonna; behind me Silenus, holding
'in his arms the infant Pan. I felt very content with
'my pen, my daily bouquet, and my yellow birds.
'About five I would go out and walk till dark; then
'would arrive my proofs, like crabbed old guardians,
'coming to tea every night. So passed each day. The
'23d of May, my birth-day, about one o'clock, I wrote
'the last line of my little book ;* then I went to Mount
'Auburn, and walked gently among the graves.'

As the brothers had now left college, and had entered
or were entering upon professional and commercial life,
while the sister was married, and the mother felt calls
to visit in turn her scattered children, it was determined
to break up the "Home." 'As a family,' Margaret
writes, 'we are henceforth to be parted. But though
'for months I had been preparing for this separation, the
'last moments were very sad. Such tears are childish
'tears, I know, and belie a deeper wisdom. It is foolish

* Summer on the Lakes.

'in me to be so anxious about my family. As I went
'along, it seemed as if all I did was for God's sake; but
' if it had been, could I now thus fear? My relations to
'them are altogether fair, so far as they go. As to their
'being no more to me than others of my kind, there is
'surely a mystic thrill betwixt children of one mother,
'which can never cease to be felt till the soul is quite born
'anew. The earthly family is the scaffold whereby we
'build the spiritual one. The glimpses we here obtain of
'what such relations should be are to me an earnest that
'the family is of Divine Order, and not a mere school of
'preparation. And in the state of perfect being which
'we call Heaven, I am assured that family ties will
'attain to that glorified beauty of harmonious adapta-
'tion, which stellar groups in the pure blue typify.'

Margaret's admirable fidelity, as daughter and sister,
— amidst her incessant literary pursuits, and her far-
reaching friendships, — can be justly appreciated by
those only who were in her confidence; but from the
following slight sketches generous hearts can readily
infer what was the quality of her home-affections.

' Mother writes from Canton that my dear old grand-
'mother is dead. I regret that you never saw her. She
' was a picture of primitive piety, as she sat holding the
' "Saint's Rest" in her hand, with her bowed, trembling
' figure, and her emphatic nods, and her sweet blue eyes.
'They were bright to the last, though she was ninety.
'It is a great loss to mother, who felt a large place
'warmed in her heart by the fond and grateful love of
' this aged parent.'

' We cannot be sufficiently grateful for our mother, —

'so fair a blossom of the white amaranth; truly t) us a
'mother in this, that we can venerate her piety. Our
'relations to her have known no jar. Nothing vulgar
'has sullied them; and in this respect life has been truly
'domesticated. Indeed, when I compare my lot with
'others, it seems to have had a more than usual likeness
'to home; for relations have been as noble as sincerity
'could make them, and there has been a frequent breath
'of refined affection, with its sweet courtesies. Mother
'thanks God in her prayers for "all the acts of mutual
'"love which have been permitted;" and looking back,
'I see that these have really been many. I do not
'recognize this, as the days pass, for to my desires life
'would be such a flower-chain of symbols, that what is
'done seems very scanty, and the thread shows too much.

'She has just brought me a little bouquet. Her
'flowers have suffered greatly by my neglect, when I
'would be engrossed by other things in her absences.
'But, not to be disgusted or deterred, whenever she can
'glean one pretty enough, she brings it to me. Here is
'the bouquet, — a very delicate rose, with its half-blown
'bud, heliotrope, geranium, lady-pea, heart's-ease; all
'sweet-scented flowers! Moved by their beauty, I
'wrote a short note, to which this is the reply. Just
'like herself!*

'"I should not love my flowers if they did not put
'"forth all the strength they have, in gratitude for your
'"preserving care, last winter, and your wasted feelings

---

* The editor must offer as excuse for printing, without permission
asked, this note, found carefully preserved among Margaret's papers,
that he knew no other way of so truly indicating the relation between
mother and daughter. This lily is eloquent of the valley where it grew.

                                                      W. H. C.

' " over the unavoidable effects of the frost, that came so
' " unexpectedly to nip their budding beauties. I ap-
' " preciate all you have done, knowing at what cost
' " any plant must be nourished by one who sows in
" fields more precious than those opened, in early life,
' " to my culture. One must have grown up with flow-
' " ers, and found joy and sweetness in them, amidst
' " disagreeable occupations, to take delight in their
' " whole existence as I do. They have long had power
' " to bring me into harmony with the Creator, and to
' " soothe almost any irritation. Therefore I under-
' " stand your love for these beautiful things, and it
" ' gives me real pleasure to procure them for you.

' " You have done everything that the most affection-
' " ate and loving daughter could, under all circum-
' " stances. My faith in your generous desire to increase
' " my happiness is founded on the knowledge I have
' " gained of your disposition, through your whole life.
' " I should ask your sympathy and aid, whenever it
' " could be available, knowing that you would give it
' " first to me. Waste no thought on neglected duties.
' " I know of none. Let us pursue our appointed paths,
' " aiding each other in rough places; and if I live to
' " need the being led by the hand, I always feel that
' " you will perform this office wisely and tenderly.
' " We shall ever have perfect peace between us. Yours,
' " in all love." '

Margaret adds : — ' It has been, and still is, hard for me
' to give up the thought of serenity, and freedom from
' toil and care, for mother, in the evening of a day which
' has been all one work of disinterested love. But I am
' now confident that she will learn from every trial its

'lesson; and if I cannot be her protector, I can be at
'least her counsellor and soother.'

From the less private parts of Margaret's correspondence with the younger members of the family, some
passages may be selected, as attesting her quick and
penetrating sympathy, her strict truth, and influential
wisdom. They may be fitly prefaced by these few but
emphatic words from a letter of one of her brothers : —

"I was much impressed, during my childhood, at
Groton, with an incident that first disclosed to me the
tenderness of Margaret's character. I had always
viewed her as a being of different nature from myself,
to whose altitudes of intellectual life I had no thought
of ascending. She had been absent during the winter,
and on her return asked me for some account of my experiences. Supposing that she could not enter into such
insignificant details, I was not frank or warm in my
confidence, though I gave no reason for my reserve; and
the matter had passed from my mind, when our mother
told me that Margaret had shed tears, because I seemed
to heed so little her sisterly sympathy. 'Tears from
one so learned,' thought I, 'for the sake of one so
inferior!' Afterwards, my heart opened to her, as to
no earthly friend.

"The characteristic trait of Margaret, to which all
her talents and acquirements were subordinate, was
sympathy, — universal sympathy. She had that large
intelligence and magnanimity which enabled her to
comprehend the struggles and triumphs of every form
of character. Loving all about her, whether rich or
poor, rude or cultivated, as equally formed after a

Divine Original, with an equal birth-right of immortal growth, she regarded rather their aspirations than their accomplishments. And this was the source of her marvellous influence. Those who had never thought of their own destiny, nor put faith in their own faculties, found in her society not so much a display of her gifts, as surprising discoveries of their own. She revealed to them the truth, that all can be noble by fidelity to the highest self. She appreciated, with delicate tenderness, each one's peculiar trials, and, while never attempting to make the unhappy feel that their miseries were unreal, she pointed out the compensations of their lot, and taught them how to live above misfortune. She had consolation and advice for every one in trouble, and wrote long letters to many friends, at the expense not only of precious time, but of physical pain.

"When now, with the experience of a man, I look back upon her wise guardianship over our childhood, her indefatigable labors for our education, her constant supervision in our family affairs, her minute instructions as to the management of multifarious details, her painful conscientiousness in every duty; and then reflect on her native inaptitude and even disgust for practical affairs, on her sacrifice, — in the very flower of her genius, — of her favorite pursuits, on her incessant drudgery and waste of health, on her patient bearing of burdens, and courageous conflict with difficult circumstances, her character stands before me as heroic."

It was to this brother that Margaret wrote as follows: —

'It is a great pleasure to me to give you this book

'both that I have a brother whom I think worthy to
'value it, and that I can give him something worthy to
'be valued more and more through all his life.   What-
·ever height we may attain in knowledge, whatever
'facility in the expression of thoughts, will only enable
'us to do more justice to what is drawn from so deep a
·source of faith and intellect, and arrayed, oftentimes,
'in the fairest hues of nature.   Yet it may not be well
'for a young mind to dwell too near one tuned to so
'high a pitch as this writer, lest, by trying to come into
'concord with him, the natural tones be overstrained,
'and the strings weakened by untimely pressure.   Do
'not attempt, therefore, to read this book through, but
'keep it with you, and when the spirit is fresh and ear-
'nest turn to it.   It is full of the tide-marks of great
'thoughts, but these can be understood by one only who
'has gained, by experience, some knowledge of these
'tides.   The ancient sages knew how to greet a brother
'who had consecrated his life to thought, and was never
'disturbed from his purpose by a lower aim.   But it
'is only to those perfected in purity that Pythagoras can
·show a golden thigh.

     'One word as to your late readings.   They came in a
·timely way to admonish you, amidst mere disciplines,
·as to the future uses of such disciplines.   But systems
·of philosophy are mere pictures to him, who has not
'yet learned how to systematize.   From an inward
'opening of your nature these knowledges must begin
·to be evolved, ere you can apprehend aught beyond
·their beauty, as revealed in the mind of another.
·Study in a reverent and patient spirit, blessing the day
'that leads you the least step onward.   Do not ride
'hobbies.   Do not hasten to conclusions.   Be not coldly

' sceptical towards any thinker, neither credulous of his
' views. A man, whose mind is full of error, may give
' us the genial sense of truth, as a tropical sun, while it
' rears crocodiles, yet ripens the wine of the palm-tree.

' To turn again to my Ancients: while they believed
' in self-reliance with a force little known in our day,
' they dreaded no pains of initiation, but fitted them-
' selves for intelligent recognition of the truths on which
' our being is based, by slow gradations of travel, study,
' speech, silence, bravery, and patience. That so it may
' be with you, dear ——, hopes your sister and friend.'

A few extracts from family letters written at different
times, and under various conditions, may be added.

' I read with great interest the papers you left with
' me. The picture and the emotions suggested are
' genuine. The youthful figure, no doubt, stands por-
' tress at the gate of Infinite Beauty; yet I would say to
' one I loved as I do you, do not waste these emotions,
' nor the occasions which excite them. There is danger
' of prodigality, — of lavishing the best treasures of the
' breast on objects that cannot be the permanent ones.
' It is true, that whatever thought is awakened in the
' mind becomes truly ours; but it is a great happiness to
' owe these influences to a cause so proportioned to our
' strength as to grow with it. I say this merely because
' I fear that the virginity of heart which I believe
' essential to feeling a real love, in all its force and
' purity, may be endangered by too careless excursions
' into the realms of fancy.'

' It is told us, we should pray, " lead us not into temp-

' " tation ;" and I agree.   Yet I think it cannot be, that,
' with a good disposition, and the means you have had
' to form your mind and discern a higher standard, your
' conduct or happiness can be so dependent on circum-
' stances, as you seem to think.   I never advised your
' taking a course which would blunt your finer powers
' and I do not believe that winning the means of pecu-
' niary independence need do so.   I have not found that
' it does, in my own case, placed at much greater disad-
' vantage than you are.   I have never considered, either,
' that there was any misfortune in your lot.   Health,
' good abilities, and a well-placed youth, form a union
' of advantages possessed by few, and which leaves you
' little excuse for fault or failure.   And so to your bet-
' ter genius and the instruction of the One Wise, I com-
' mend you.'

' It gave me great pleasure to get your last letter, for
' these little impromptu effusions are the genuine letters.
' I rejoice that man and nature seem harmonious to
' you, and that the heart beats in unison with the
' voices of Spring.   May all that is manly, sincere,
' and pure, in your wishes, be realized !   Obliged to
' live myself without the sanctuary of the central rela-
' tions, yet feeling I must still not despair, nor fail to
' profit by the precious gifts of life, while " leaning
' " upon our Father's hand," I still rejoice, if any one
' can, in the true temper, and with well-founded hopes,
' secure a greater completeness of earthly existence
' This fortune is as likely to be yours, as any one's
' I know.   It seems to me dangerous, however, to med-
' dle with the future. I never lay my hand on it to
' grasp it with impunity.'

' Of late I have often thought of you with strong
' yearnings of affection and desire to see you. It would
' seem to me, also, that I had not devoted myself to you
' enough, if I were not conscious that by any more atten-
' tion to the absent than I have paid, I should have
' missed the needed instructions from the present. And
' I feel that any bond of true value will endure necessary
' neglect.'

' There is almost too much of bitter mixed in the cup
' of life. You say religion is a mere sentiment with you,
' and that if you are disappointed in your first, your
' very first hopes and plans, you do not know whether
' you shall be able to act well. I do not myself see
' how a reflecting soul can endure the passage through
' life, except by confidence in a Power that must at last
' order all things right, and the resolution that it shall
' not be our own fault if we are not happy, — that we
' will resolutely deserve to be happy. There are many
' bright glimpses in life, many still hours; much worthy
' toil, some deep and noble joys; but, then, there are
' so many, and such long, intervals, when we are kept
' from all we want, and must perish but for such
' thoughts.'

' You need not fear, dear ——, my doing anything
' to chill you. I am only too glad of the pure happi-
' ness you so sweetly describe. I well understand what
' you say of its invigorating you for every enterprise.
' I was always sure it would be so with me, —.that
' resigned, I could do well, but happy I could do excel-
' lently. Happiness must, with the well-born, expand

' the generous affections towards all men, and invigorate
' one to deserve what the gods have given.'

   Margaret's charities and courtesies were not limited to
her kindred. She fell, at once, into agreeable relations
with her domestics, became their confidant, teacher, and
helper, studied their characters, consulted their convenience, warned them of their dangers or weaknesses, and
rejoiced to gratify their worthy tastes ; and, in return,
no lady could receive, from servants, more punctual or
hearty attendance. She knew how to command and
how to persuade, and her sympathy was perfect. They
felt the power of her mind, her hardy directness, prompt
judgment, decision and fertility of resource, and liked to
aid one who knew so well her own wants. ' Around
' my path,' she writes, ' how much humble love contin-
' ually flows. These every-day and lowly friends never
' forget my wishes, never censure my whims, make no
' demands on me, and load me with gifts and uncom-
' plaining service. Though sometimes forgetful of their
' claims, I try to make it up when we do meet, and I
' trust give little pain as I pass along this world.'
   Even in extreme cases of debasement she found
more to admire than to contemn, and won the confidence of the fallen by manifesting her real respect.
" There was in my family," writes a friend, " a very
handsome young girl, who had been vicious in her
habits, and so enamored of one of her lovers, that when
he deserted her, she attempted to drown herself. She
was rescued, and some good people were eager to reform
her life. While she was engaged in housework for us,
Margaret saw her, and one day asked —— if she could
not help her —— replied : ' No ! for should I begin to

talk with her, I should show my consciousness of her history so much as to be painful.' Margaret was very indignant at this weakness. Said she, ' This girl is ' taken away, you know, from all her objects of interest, ' and must feel her life vacant and dreary. Her mind ' should be employed; she should be made to feel her ' powers.' It was plain that if Margaret had been near her, she would have devoted herself at once to her education and reëstablishment."

About the time of breaking up their home, Margaret thus expressed, to one of her brothers, her hopes and plans. ' You wish, dear ——, that I was not obliged to ' toil and spin, but could live, for a while, like the lilies. ' I wish so, too, for life has fatigued me, my strength is ' little, and the present state of my mind demands repose ' and refreshment, that it may ripen some fruit worthy ' of the long and deep experiences through which I ' have passed. I do not regret that I have shared the ' labors and cares of the suffering million, and have ' acquired a feeling sense of the conditions under which ' the Divine has appointed the development of the human. ' Yet, if our family affairs could now be so arranged, · that I might be tolerably tranquil for the next six or ' eight years, I should go out of life better satisfied with ' the page I have turned in it, than I shall if I must ' still toil on. A noble career is yet before me, if I can ' be unimpeded by cares. I have given almost all my ' young energies to personal relations; but, at present, I ' feel inclined to impel the general stream of thought. ' Let my nearest friends also wish that I should now ' take share in more public life.'

THE HIGHLANDS.

Seeking thus, at once, expansion and rest in new employments, Margaret determined, in the autumn of 1844,
to accept a liberal offer of Messrs. Greeley and McEl-
rath, to become a constant contributor to the New York
Tribune. But before entering upon her new duties, she
found relaxation, for a few weeks, amid the grand scenery of the Hudson. In October, she writes from Fishkill Landing : — ' Can I find words to tell you how I
' enjoy being here, encircled by the majestic beauty of
' these mountains ? I felt regret, indeed, in bidding fare-
' well to Boston, so many marks of affection were shown
' me at the last, and so many friendships, true if imper-
' fect, were left behind. But now I am glad to feel
' enfranchized in the society of Nature. I have a well-
' ordered, quiet house to dwell in, with nobody's humors
' to consult but my own. From my windows I see over
' the tops of variegated trees the river, with its purple
' heights beyond, and a few moments' walk brings me to
' the lovely shore, where sails are gliding continually by,
' and the huge steamers sweep past with echoing tread,
' and a train of waves, whose rush relieves the monotone
' of the ripples. In the country behind us are mountain-
' paths, and lonely glens, with gurgling streams, and
' many-voiced water-falls. And over all are spread the
' gorgeous hues of autumn.'
And again : — ' " From the brain of the purple moun-
' " tain " flows forth cheer to my somewhat weary mind
' I feel refreshed amid these bolder shapes of nature.
' Mere gentle and winning landscapes are not enough.
' How I wish my birth had been cast among the sources
' of the streams, where the voice of hidden torrents is

'heard by night, and the eagle soars, and the thun-
'der resounds in prolonged peals, and wide blue shad-
'ows fall like brooding wings across the valleys! Amid
'such scenes, I expand and feel at home. All the fine
'days I spend among the mountain passes, along the
'mountain brooks, or beside the stately river. I enjoy
'just the tranquil happiness I need in communion with
'this fair grandeur.'

And, again : — 'The boldness, sweetness, and variety
'here, are just what I like. I could pass the autumn
'in watching the exquisite changes of light and shade
'on the heights across the river. How idle to pretend
'that one could live and write as well amid fallow flat
'fields! This majesty, this calm splendor, could not but
'exhilarate the mind, and make it nobly free and plas-
'tic.'

These few weeks among the Highlands, — spent mostly
in the open air, under October's golden sunshine, the
slumberous softness of the Indian summer, or the brilliant, breezy skies of November, — were an important
era for Margaret. She had —

> " lost the dream of Doing
> And the other dream of Done;
> The first spring in the pursuing,
> The first pride in the Begun,
> First recoil from incompleteness in the face of what is won."

But she was striving, also, to use her own words, ' to
' be patient to the very depths of the heart, to expect no
' hasty realizations, not to make her own plan her law
' of life, but to learn the law and plan of God.' She

adds, however : — ' What heaven it must be to have the
' happy sense of accomplishing something, and to feel
' the glow of action without exhausted weariness! Surely
' the race would have worn itself out by corrosion, if
' men in all ages had suffered, as we now do, from the
' consciousness of an unattained Ideal.'

Extracts from journals will best reveal her state of
mind.

  ' I have a dim consciousness of what the terrible expe-
' riences must be by which the free poetic element is har-
' monized with the spirit of religion. In their essence
and their end these are one, but rarely in actual exis-
' tence. I would keep what was pure and noble in my
' old native freedom, with that consciousness of falling
' below the best convictions which now binds me to the
' basest of mankind, and find some new truth that shall
' reconcile and unite them. Once it seemed to me, that
' my heart was so capable of goodness, my mind of clear-
' ness, that all should acknowledge and claim me as a
' friend. But now I see that these impulses were pro-
' phetic of a yet distant period. The " intensity " of
' passion, which so often unfits me for life, or, rather, for
' *life here*, is to be moderated, not into dulness or lan-
' guor, but a gentler, steadier energy.'

' The stateliest, strongest vessel must sometimes be
' brought into port to refit. If she will not submit to
' be fastened to the dock, stripped of her rigging, and
' scrutinized by unwashed artificers, she may spring
' a leak when riding most proudly on the subject wave.
' Norway fir nor English oak can resist forever the
' insidious assaults of the seemingly conquered ocean.

The man who clears the barnacles from the keel is 'more essential than he who hoists the pennant on the 'lofty mast.'

'A week of more suffering than I have had for a long 'time, — from Sunday to Sunday, — headache night and 'day! And not only there has been no respite, but it 'has been fixed in one spot — between the eyebrows! — 'what does that promise? — till it grew real torture. 'Then it has been depressing to be able to do so little, 'when there was so much I had at heart to do. It 'seems that the black and white guardians, depicted 'on the Etrurian monuments, and in many a legend, are 'always fighting for my life. Whenever I have any 'cherished purpose, either outward obstacles swarm 'around, which the hand that would be drawing beau-'tiful lines must be always busy in brushing away, or 'comes this great vulture, and fastens his iron talons 'on the brain.

'But at such times the soul rises up, like some fair 'child in whom sleep has been mistaken for death, a 'living flower in the dark tomb. He casts aside his 'shrouds and bands, rosy and fresh from the long 'trance, undismayed, not seeing how to get out, yet 'sure there is a way.

'I think the black jailer laughs now, hoping that 'while I want to show that Woman can have the free, 'full action of intellect, he will prove in my own self that she has not physical force to bear it. Indeed, I am too poor an example, and do wish I was bodily strong and fair. Yet, I will not be turned from the deeper convictions.'

'Driven from home to home, as a Renouncer, I gain
'the poetry of each. Keys of gold, silver, iron, lead, are
'in my casket. Though no one loves me as I would be
'loved, I yet love many well enough to see into their
'eventual beauty. Meanwhile, I have no fetters, and
'when one perceives how others are bound in false
'relations, this surely should be regarded as a privi-
'lege. And so varied have been my sympathies, that
'this isolation will not, I trust, make me cold, ignorant,
'nor partial. My history presents much superficial, tem-
'porary tragedy. The Woman in me kneels and weeps
'in tender rapture; the Man in me rushes forth, but
'only to be baffled. Yet the time will come, when,
'from the union of this tragic king and queen, shall be
'born a radiant sovereign self.'

'I have quite a desire to try my powers in a narrative
'poem; but my head teems with plans, of which there
'will be time for very few only to take form. Milton,
'it is said, made for himself a list of a hundred subjects
'for dramas, and the recorder of the fact seems to think
'this many. I think it very few, so filled is life with
'innumerable themes.'

'*Sunday Evening.* — I have employed some hours of
'the day, with great satisfaction, in copying the Poet's
'Dreams from the Pentameron of Landor. I do not
'often have time for such slow, pleasing labor. I have
'thus imprinted the words in my mind, so that they will
'often recur in their original beauty.

'I have added three sonnets of Petrarca, all written
'after the death of Laura. They are among his noblest,
'all pertinent to the subject, and giving three aspects of

'that one mood. The last lines of the last sonnet are a
'fit motto for Boccaccio's dream.

'In copying both together, I find the prose of the
'Englishman worthy of the verse of the Italian. It is
'a happiness to see such marble beauty in the halls of
'a contemporary.

'How fine it is to see the terms "onesto," "gentile,"
'used in their original sense and force.

> 'Soft, solemn day!
> 'Where earth and heaven together seem to meet,
> 'I have been blest to greet
> 'From human thought a kindred sway;
> 'In thought these stood
> 'So near the simple Good,
> 'That what we nobleness and honor call,
> 'They viewed as honesty, the common dower of all.'

Margaret was reading, in these weeks, the Four Books
of Confucius, the Desatir, some of Taylor's translations
from the Greek, a work on Scandinavian Mythology,
Mœhler's Symbolism, Fourier's Noveau Monde Indus-
triel, and Landor's Pentameron, — but she says, in her
journal, 'No book is good enough to read in the open
'air, among these mountains; even the best seem partial,
'civic, limiting, instead of being, as man's voice should
'be, a tone higher than nature's.'

And again: — 'This morning came ——'s letter,
'announcing Sterling's death: —

> '"Weep for Dedalus all that is fairest."

'The news was very sad: Sterling did so earnestly wish
'to do a man's work, and had done so small a portion
'of his own. This made me feel how fast my years are
'flitting by, and nothing done. Yet these few beautiful

'days of leisure I cannot resolve to give at all to work
'I want absolute rest, to let the mind lie fallow, to keep
'my whole nature open to the influx of truth.'

At this very time, however, she was longing to write
with full freedom and power. 'Formerly,' she says,
'the pen did not seem to me an instrument capable of
'expressing the spirit of a life like mine. An enchanter's
'mirror, on which, with a word, could be made to rise
'all apparitions of the universe, grouped in new rela-
'tions; a magic ring, that could transport the wearer,
'himself invisible, into each region of grandeur or
'beauty; a divining-rod, to tell where lie the secret
'fountains of refreshment; a wand, to invoke elemental
'spirits; — only such as these seemed fit to embody one's
'thought with sufficient swiftness and force. In earlier
'years I aspired to wield the sceptre or the lyre; for I
'loved with wise design and irresistible command to
'mould many to one purpose, and it seemed all that man
'could desire to breathe in music and speak in words,
'the harmonies of the universe. But the golden lyre
'was not given to my hand, and I am but the prophecy
'of a poet. Let me use, then, the slow pen. I will
'make no formal vow to the long-scorned Muse; I
'assume no garland; I dare not even dedicate myself as
'a novice; I can promise neither patience nor energy; —
'but I will court excellence, so far as an humble heart
'and open eye can merit it, and, if I may gradually grow
'to some degree of worthiness in this mode of expression,
'I shall be grateful.'

WOMAN.

It was on "Woman in the Nineteenth Century" that

Margaret was now testing her power as a writer. 'I
'have finished the pamphlet,' she writes; 'though the
'last day it kept spinning out beneath my hand. After
'taking a long walk, early one most exhilarating morn-
'ing, I sat down to work, and did not give it the last
'stroke till near nine in the evening. Then I felt a
'delightful glow, as if I had put a good deal of my true
'life in it, and as if, should I go away now, the measure
'of my foot-print would be left on the earth.'

A few extracts from her manuscripts upon this subject
may be of interest, as indicating the spirit and aim with
which she wrote : —

'To those of us who hate emphasis and exaggeration,
'who believe that whatever is good of its kind is good,
'who shrink from love of excitement and love of sway,
'who, while ready for duties of many kinds, dislike
'pledges and bonds to any, — this talk about " Woman's
'"Sphere," " Woman's Mission," and all such phrases
'as mark the present consciousness of an impending
'transition from old conventions to greater freedom, are
'most repulsive. And it demands some valor to lift one's
'head amidst the shower of public squibs, private sneers,
'anger, scorn, derision, called out by the demand that
'women should be put on a par with their brethren,
'legally and politically; that they should hold property
'not by permission but by right, and that they should
'take an active part in all great movements. But
'though, with Mignon, we are prompted to characterize
'heaven as the place where

'" Sie fragen nicht nach Mann nie Weib,"

'yet it is plain that we must face this agitation; and
' beyond the dull clouds overhead hangs in the horizon
' Venus, as morning-star, no less fair, though of more
' melting beauty, than the glorious Jupiter, who shares
' with her the watch.'

' The full, free expression of feeling must be rare, for
' this book of Bettina Brentano's to produce such an
' effect.   Men who have lived in the society of women
' all their days, seem never before to have dreamed of
' their nature; they are filled with wonderment and
' delight at these revelations, and because they see the
' woman, fancy her a genius.   But in truth her inspiration
' is nowise extraordinary; and I have letters from various
' friends, lying unnoticed in my portfolio, which are quite
' as beautiful.   For one, I think that these veins of gold
' should pass in secret through the earth, inaccessible to
' all who will not take the trouble to mine for them.   I
' do not like Bettina for publishing her heart, and am
' ready to repeat to her Serlo's reproof to Aurelia.'

' How terrible must be the tragedy of a woman who
' awakes to find that she has given herself wholly to a
' person for whom she is not eternally fitted!   I cannot
' look on marriage as on the other experiments of life :
' it is the one grand type that should be kept forever
' sacred.   There are two kinds of love experienced by
' high and rich souls.   The first seeks, according to
' Plato's myth, another half, as being not entire in itself,
' but needing a kindred nature to unlock its secret cham-
' bers of emotion, and to act with quickening influence
' on all its powers, by full harmony of senses, affections,
' intellect, will; the second is purely ideal, beholding in

'its object divine perfection, and delighting in it only in
'degree as it symbolizes the essential good. But why
'is not this love steadily directed to the Central Spirit,
'since in no form, however suggestive in beauty, can
'God be fully revealed ? Love's delusion is owing to
'one of man's most godlike qualities, — the earnestness
'with which he would concentrate his whole being, and
'thus experience the Now of the I Am. Yet the noblest
'are not long deluded; they love really the Infinite Beauty,
'though they may still keep before them a human form,
'as the Isis, who promises hereafter a seat at the golden
'tables. How high is Michel Angelo's love, for instance,
'compared with Petrarch's ! Petrarch longs, languishes;
'and it is only after the death of Laura that his muse
'puts on celestial plumage. But Michel always soars;
'his love is a stairway to the heavens.'

'Might not we women do something in regard to this
'Texas Annexation project? I have never felt that I
'had any call to take part in public affairs before; but
'this is a great moral question, and we have an obvious
'right to express our convictions. I should like to con-
'vene meetings of the women everywhere, and take our
'stand.'

'Had Christendom but been true to its standard, while
'accommodating its modes of operation to the calls of
'successive times, woman would now have not only
'equal *power* with man, — for of that omnipotent nature
'will never permit her to be defrauded, — but a *chartered*
'power, too fully recognized to be abused. Indeed, all
that is wanting is, that man should prove his own
'freedom by making her free. Let him abandon con-

' ventional restriction, as a vestige of that Oriental bar-
' barity which confined woman to a seraglio. Let him
' trust her entirely, and give her every privilege already
' acquired for himself, — elective franchise, tenure of
' property, liberty to speak in public assemblies, &c.

' Nature has pointed out her ordinary sphere by the
' circumstances of her physical existence. She cannot
' wander far. If here and there the gods send their
' missives through women, as through men, let them
' speak without remonstrance. In no age have men
' been able wholly to hinder them. A Deborah must
' always be a spiritual mother in Israel; a Corinna may
' be excluded from the Olympic games, yet all men will
' hear her song, and a Pindar sit at her feet. It is man's
' fault that there ever were Aspasias and Ninons. These
' exquisite forms were intended for the shrines of virtue.

' Neither need men fear to lose their domestic deities.
' Woman is born for love, and it is impossible to turn her
' from seeking it. Men should deserve her love as an
' inheritance, rather than seize and guard it like a prey.
' Were they noble, they would strive rather not to be
' loved too much, and to turn her from idolatry to the
' true, the only Love. Then, children of one Father,
' they could not err, nor misconceive one another.

' Society is now so complex, that it is no longer pos-
' sible to educate woman merely as woman; the tasks
' which come to her hand are so various, and so large a
' proportion of women are thrown entirely upon their
' own resources. I admit that this is not their state of
' perfect development; but it seems as if heaven, having
' so long issued its edict in poetry and religion, without
' securing intelligent obedience, now commanded the

'world in prose, to take a high and rational view. The
'lesson reads to me thus : —

'Sex, like rank, wealth, beauty, or talent, is but an
'accident of birth. As you would not educate a soul to
'be an aristocrat, so do not to be a woman. A genera
'regard to her usual sphere is dictated in the economy of
'nature. You need never enforce these provisions rigor-
'ously. Achilles had long plied the distaff as a princess,
'yet, at first sight of a sword, he seized it. So with
'woman, one hour of love would teach her more of her
'proper relations, than all your formulas and conventions.
'Express your views, men, of what you *seek* in woman :
'thus best do you give them laws. Learn, women, what
'you should *demand* of men : thus only can they become
'themselves. Turn both from the contemplation of what
'i. merely phenomenal in your existence, to your per-
'manent life as souls. Man, do not prescribe how the
'Divine shall display itself in woman. Woman, do not
'expect to see all of God in man. Fellow-pilgrims and
'helpmeets are ye, Apollo and Diana, twins of one
'heavenly birth, both beneficent, and both armed. Man,
 fear not to yield to woman's hand both the quiver and
'the lyre; for if her urn be filled with light, she will use
'both to the glory of God. There is but one doctrine for
'ye both, and that is the doctrine of the SOUL.'

Thus, in communion with the serene loveliness ot
mother-earth, and inspired with memories of Isis and
Ceres, of Minerva and Freia, and all the commanding
forms beneath which earlier ages symbolized their sense
of the Divine Spirit in woman, Margaret cherished
visions of the future, and responded with full heart to
the poet's prophecy : —

" Then comes the statelier Eden back to men;
   Then reign the world's great bridals, chaste and calm;
   Then springs the crowning race of human-kind.''

It was but after the usual order of our discordant life,
— where Purgatory lies so nigh to Paradise, — that she
should thence be summoned to pass a Sunday with the
prisoners at Sing-Sing. This was the period when, in
fulfilment of the sagacious and humane counsels of
Judge Edmonds, a system of kind discipline, combined
with education, was in practice at that penitentiary, and
when the female department was under the matronly
charge of Mrs. E. W. Farnum, aided by Mrs. Johnson,
Miss Bruce, and other ladies, who all united sisterly
sympathy with energetic firmness. Margaret thus describes her impressions : —

' We arrived on Saturday evening, in such resplendent
' moonlight, that we might have mistaken the prison for
' a palace, had we not known but too well what those
' massive walls contained.

' Sunday morning we attended service in the chapel
' of the male convicts. They listened with earnest
' attention, and many were moved to tears. I never felt
' such sympathy with an audience as when, at the words
' " Men and brethren," that sea of faces, marked with
' the scars of every ill, were upturned, and the shell of
' brutality burst apart at the touch of love. I knew that
' at least heavenly truth would not be kept out by self-
' complacence and dependence on good appearances.

' After twelve at noon, all are confined in their cells,
' that the keepers may have rest from their weekly
' fatigue. But I was allowed to have some of the women
' out to talk with, and the interview was very pleasant.

They showed the natural aptitude of the sex for refine-
' ment. These women were among the so-called worst,
' and all from the lowest haunts of vice. Yet nothing
' could have been more decorous than their conduct,
' while it was also frank ; and they showed a sensibility
' and sense of propriety, which would not have disgraced
' any society. All passed, indeed, much as in one of my
' Boston classes. I told them I was writing about Wo-
' man ; and, as my path had been a favored one, I wanted
' to gain information from those who had been tempted
' and afflicted. They seemed to reply in the same spirit
' in which I asked. Several, however, expressed a wish
' to see me alone, as they could then say *all*, which they
' could not bear to before one another. I shall go there
' again, and take time for this. It is very gratifying to
' see the influence these few months of gentle and intel-
' ligent treatment have had upon these women ; indeed,
' it is wonderful.'

So much were her sympathies awakened by this visit,
that she rejoiced in the opportunity, soon after offered,
of passing Christmas with these outcasts, and gladly
consented to address the women in their chapel. "There
was," says one present, "a most touching tenderness,
blended with dignity, in her air and tone, as, seated in
the desk, she looked round upon her fallen sisters, and
begun : 'To me the pleasant office has been given, of
' wishing you a happy Christmas.' A simultaneous
movement of obeisance rippled over the audience, with
a murmured 'Thank you ;' and a smile was spread
upon those sad countenances, like sunrise sparkling on
a pool." A few words from this discourse, — which was
extemporaneous, but of which she afterward made an

imperfect record, — will show the temper in which she
spoke: —

'I have passed other Christmas days happily, but
'never felt as now, how fitting it is that this festival
'should come among the snows and chills of winter;
'for, to many of you, I trust, it is the birth-day of a
'higher life, when the sun of good-will is beginning to
'return, and the evergreen of hope gives promise of the
'eternal year. * * *

'Some. months ago, we were told of the riot, the
'license, and defying spirit which made this place so
'wretched, and the conduct of some now here was such
'that the world said: — "Women once lost are far
'"worse than abandoned men, and cannot be restored."
'But, no! It is not so! I know my sex better. It is
'because women have so much feeling, and such a
'rooted respect for purity, that they seem so shameless
'and insolent, when they feel that they have erred and
'that others think ill of them. They know that even
'the worst of men would like to see women pure as
'angels, and when they meet man's look of scorn, the
'desperate passion that rises is a perverted pride, which
'might have been their guardian angel. Might have
'been! Rather let me say, which may be; for the
'great improvement so rapidly wrought here gives us
'all warm hopes. * * *

'Be not in haste to leave these walls. Yesterday,
'one of you, who was praised, replied, that "if she did
'"well she hoped that efforts would be made to have her
'"pardoned." I can feel the monotony and dreariness
'of your confinement, but I entreat you to believe that
'for many of you it would be the greatest misfortune to

be taken from here too soon. You know, better than I can, the temptations that await you in the world; and 'you must now perceive how dark is the gulf of sin 'and sorrow, towards which they would hurry you. ' Here, you have friends indeed; friends to your better 'selves; able and ready to help you. Born of unfortu- 'nate marriages, inheriting dangerous inclinations, neg- ' lected in childhood, with bad habits and bad associates, ' as certainly must be the case with some of you, how 'terrible will be the struggle when you leave this ' shelter! O, be sure that you are fitted to triumph ' over evil, before you again expose yourselves to it! ' And, instead of wasting your time and strength in vain ' wishes, use this opportunity to prepare yourselves for ' a better course of life, when you are set free. * * *

' When I was here before, I was grieved by hearing ' several of you say, "I will tell you what you wish to ' " know, if I can be alone with you; but not before ' " the other prisoners; for, if they know my past faults, ' " they will taunt me with them." O, never do that! ' To taunt the fallen is the part of a fiend. And you! ' you were meant by Heaven to become angels of sym- ' pathy and love. It says in the Scripture : " Their ' " angels do always behold in heaven the face of my ' " Father." So was it with you in your childhood; ' so is it now. Your angels stand forever there to inter- ' cede for you; and to you they call to be gentle and ' good. Nothing can so grieve and discourage those ' heavenly friends as when you mock the suffering. It ' was one of the highest praises of Jesus, " The bruised ' reed he will not break." Remember that, and never insult, where you cannot aid, a companion. * * *

' Let me warn you earnestly against acting insincerely,

' and appearing to wish to do right for the sake of appro-
' bation.   I know you must prize the good opinion of
' your friendly protectors; but do not buy it at the cost
' of truth.   Try to be, not to seem.   Only so far as you
' earnestly wish to do right for the sake of right, can
' you gain a principle that will sustain you hereafter;
' and that is what we.wish, not fair appearances now.
' A career can never be happy that begins with false-
' hood.   Be inwardly, outwardly true; then you will
' never be weakened or hardened by the consciousness
' of playing a part; and if, hereafter, the unfeeling or
' thoughtless give you pain, or take the dreadful risk
' of pushing back a soul emerging from darkness, you
' will feel the strong support of a good conscience. * * *
    ' And never be discouraged; never despond; never
' say, "It is too late."   Fear not, even if you relapse
' again and again.   Many of you have much to contend
' with.   Some may be so faulty, by temperament or
' habit, that they can never on this earth lead a wholly
' fair and harmonious life, however much they strive.
' Yet do what you can.   If in one act, — for one day, —
' you can do right, let that live like a point of light in
' your memory; for if you have done well once you can
' again.   If you fall, do not lie grovelling; but rise upon
' your feet once more, and struggle bravely on.   And
' if aroused conscience makes you suffer keenly, have
' patience to bear it.   God will not let you suffer more
' than you need to fit you for his grace.   At the very
' moment of your utmost pain, persist to seek his aid,
' and it will be given abundantly.   Cultivate this spirit
' of prayer.   I do not mean agitation and excitement,
' but a deep desire for truth, purity, and goodness, and

' you will daily learn how near He is to every one of
' us.'

These fragments, from a hasty report transcribed
when the impressions of the hour had grown faint, give
but a shadow of the broad good sense, hearty fellow-
feeling, and pathetic hopefulness, which made so effective her truly womanly appeal.

This intercourse with the most unfortunate of her
sex, and a desire to learn more of the causes of their
degradation, and of the means of restoring them, led
Margaret, immediately on reaching New York, to visit
the various benevolent institutions, and especially the
prisons on Blackwell's Island. And it was while walking among the beds of the lazar-house, — mis-called
"hospital," — which then, to the disgrace of the city,
was the cess-pool of its social filth, that an incident
occurred, as touching as it was surprising to herself. A
woman was pointed out who bore a very bad character,
as hardened, sulky, and impenetrable. She was in bad
health and rapidly failing. Margaret requested to be
left alone with her; and to her question, ' Are you
' willing to die ? ' the woman answered, " Yes;" adding,
with her usual bitterness, "not on religious grounds,
though." 'That is well, — to understand yourself,' was
Margaret's rejoinder. She then began to talk with her
about her health, and her few comforts, until the conversation deepened in interest. At length, as Margaret
rose to go, she said: ' Is there not anything I can do
' for you ? ' The woman replied : " I should be glad if
you will pray with me."

The condition of these wretched beings was brought
the more home to her heart, as the buildings were directly

in sight from Mr. Greeley's house, at Turtle Bay, where
Margaret, on her arrival, went to reside. 'Seven
' hundred females,' she writes, ' are now confined in
' the Penitentiary opposite this point. We can pass
' over in a boat in a few minutes. I mean to visit, talk,
' and read with them. I have always felt great interest
' in those women who are trampled in the mud tc
' gratify the brute appetites of men, and wished that I
' might be brought naturally into contact with them.
' Now I am.'

THE TRIBUNE AND HORACE GREELEY.

It was early in December of 1844 that Margaret took
up her abode with Mr. and Mrs. Greeley, in a spacious
old wooden mansion, somewhat ruinous, but delightfully
situated on the East River, which she thus describes : —

' This place is, to me, entirely charming; it is so com-
' pletely in the country, and all around is so bold and
' free. It is two miles or more from the thickly settled
' parts of New York, but omnibuses and cars give me
' constant access to the city, and, while I can readily see
' what and whom I will, I can command time and retire-
' ment. Stopping on the Haarlem road, you enter a
' lane nearly a quarter of a mile long, and going by a
' small brook and pond that locks in the place, and
' ascending a slightly rising ground, get sight of the
' house, which, old-fashioned and of mellow tint, fronts
' on a flower-garden filled with shrubs, large vines, and
' trim box borders. On both sides of the house are
' beautiful trees, standing fair, full-grown, and clear.
' Passing through a wide hall, you come out upon a

'piazza, stretching the whole length of the house,
' where one can walk in all weathers; and thence by a
' step or two, on a lawn, with picturesque masses of
' rocks, shrubs and trees, overlooking the East River.
' Gravel paths lead, by several turns, down the steep
' bank to the water's edge, where round the rocky point
' a small bay curves, in which boats are lying. And,
' owing to the currents, and the set of the tide, the
' sails glide sidelong, seeming to greet the house as they
' sweep by. The beauty here, seen by moonlight, is
' truly transporting. I enjoy it greatly, and the *genius*
' *loci* receives me as to a home.'

Here Margaret remained for a year and more, writing
regularly for the Tribune. And how high an estimate
this prolonged and near acquaintance led her to form
for its Editor, will appear from a few passages in her
letters : —

' Mr. Greeley is a man of genuine excellence, honor-
' able, benevolent, and of an uncorrupted disposition.
' He is sagacious, and, in his way, of even great abil-
' ities. In modes of life and manner he is a man of the
' people, and of the American people.' And again : —
' Mr. Greeley is in many ways very interesting for me to
' know. He teaches me things, which my own influ-
' ence on those, who have hitherto approached me, has
' prevented me from learning. In our business and
' friendly relations, we are on terms of solid good-will
' and mutual respect. With the exception of my own
' mother, I think him the most disinterestedly generous
' person I have ever known.' And later she writes : —
' You have heard that the Tribune Office was burned

' to the ground. For a day I thought it must make a
' difference, but it has served only to increase my admi-
' ration for Mr. Greeley's smiling courage. He has
' really a strong character.'

On the other side, Mr. Greeley thus records his recollections of his friend : —

"My first acquaintance with Margaret Fuller was
made through the pages of 'The Dial.' The lofty
range and rare ability of that work, and its un-Ameri-
can richness of culture and ripeness of thought, naturally filled the 'fit audience, though few,' with a high
estimate of those who were known as its conductors
and principal writers. Yet I do not now remember
that any article, which strongly impressed me, was
recognized as from the pen of its female editor, prior to
the appearance of 'The Great Lawsuit,' afterwards
matured into the volume more distinctively, yet not
quite accurately, entitled ' Woman in the Nineteenth
Century.' I think this can hardly have failed to make
a deep impression on the mind of every thoughtful
reader, as the production of an original, vigorous, and
earnest mind. 'Summer on the Lakes,' which appeared
some time after that essay, though before its expansion
into a book, struck me as less ambitious in its aim, but
more graceful and delicate in its execution ; and as one
of the clearest and most graphic delineations, ever given,
of the Great Lakes, of the Prairies, and of the receding
barbarism, and the rapidly advancing, but rude, repulsive semi-civilization, which were contending with most
unequal forces for the possession of those rich lands. I
still consider 'Summer on the Lakes' unequalled,

especially in its pictures of the Prairies and of the sun-
nier aspects of Pioneer life.

"Yet, it was the suggestion of Mrs. Greeley, — who
had spent some weeks of successive seasons in or near
Boston, and who had there made the personal acquaintance of Miss Fuller, and formed a very high estimate
and warm attachment for her, — that induced me, in
the autumn of 1844, to offer her terms, which were
accepted, for her assistance in the literary department of
the Tribune. A home in my family was included in the
stipulation. I was myself barely acquainted with her,
when she thus came to reside with us, and I did not
fully appreciate her nobler qualities for some months
afterward. Though we were members of the same
household, we scarcely met save at breakfast; and my
time and thoughts were absorbed in duties and cares,
which left me little leisure or inclination for the ameni-
ties of social intercourse. Fortune seemed to delight in
placing us two in relations of friendly antagonism, — or
rather, to develop all possible contrasts in our ideas and
social habits. She was naturally inclined to luxury
and a good appearance before the world. My pride, if
I had any, delighted in bare walls and rugged fare
She was addicted to strong tea and coffee, both which I
rejected and contemned, even in the most homœo-
pathic dilutions; while, my general health being sound,
and hers sadly impaired, I could not fail to find in her
dietetic habits the causes of her almost habitual illness;
and once, while we were still barely acquainted, when
she came to the breakfast-table with a very severe
headache, I was tempted to attribute it to her strong
potations of the Chinese leaf the night before. She told
me quite frankly that she ' declined being lectured on

'the food or beverage she saw fit to take;' which was but reasonable in one who had arrived at her maturity of intellect and fixedness of habits. So the subject was thenceforth tacitly avoided between us; but, though words were suppressed, looks and involuntary gestures could not so well be; and an utter divergency of views on this and kindred themes created a perceptible distance between us.

"Her earlier contributions to the Tribune were not her best, and I did not at first prize her aid so highly as I afterwards learned to do. She wrote always freshly, vigorously, but not always clearly; for her full and intimate acquaintance with continental literature, especially German, seemed to have marred her felicity and readiness of expression in her mother tongue. While I never met another woman who conversed more freely or lucidly, the attempt to commit her thoughts to paper seemed to induce a singular embarrassment and hesitation. She could write only when in the vein; and this needed often to be waited for through several days, while the occasion sometimes required an immediate utterance. The new book must be reviewed before other journals had thoroughly dissected and discussed it else the ablest critique would command no general attention, and perhaps be, by the greater number, unread. That the writer should wait the flow of inspiration, or at least the recurrence of elasticity of spirits and relative health of body, will not seem unreasonable to the general reader; but to the inveterate hack-horse of the daily .press, accustomed to write at any time, on any subject, and with a rapidity limited only by the physi cal ability to form the requisite pen-strokes, the notion of waiting for a brighter day, or a happier frame of

mind, appears fantastic and absurd. He would as soon
think of waiting for a change in the moon. Hence,
while I realized that her contributions evinced rare
intellectual wealth and force, I did not value them as I
should have done had they been written more fluently
and promptly. They often seemed to make their appearance 'a day after the fair.'

"One other point of tacit antagonism between us
may as well be noted. Margaret was always a most
earnest, devoted champion of the Emancipation of
Women, from their past and present condition of inferi-
ority, to an independence on Men. She demanded for
them the fullest recognition of Social and Political
Equality with the rougher sex; the freest access to all
stations, professions, employments, which are open to
any. To this demand I heartily acceded. It seemed
to me, however, that her clear perceptions of abstract
right were often overborne, in practice, by the influence
of education and habit; that while she demanded absolute equality for Woman, she exacted a deference and
courtesy from men to women, *as* women, which was
entirely inconsistent with that requirement. In my
view, the equalizing theory can be enforced only by
ignoring the habitual discrimination of men and women,
as forming separate *classes*, and regarding all alike as
simply *persons*, — as human beings. So long as a lady
shall deem herself in need of some gentleman's arm to
conduct her properly out of a dining or ball-room, — so
long as she shall consider it dangerous or unbecoming to
walk half a mile alone by night, — I cannot see how
the 'Woman's Rights' theory is ever to be anything
more than a logically defensible abstraction. In this
view Margaret did not at all concur, and the diversity

was the incitement to much perfectly good-natured, but
nevertheless sharpish sparring between us. Whenever
she said or did anything implying the usual demand of
Woman on the courtesy and protection of Manhood, I
was apt, before complying, to look her in the face and
exclaim with marked emphasis, — quoting from her
'Woman in the Nineteenth Century,' — 'LET THEM BE
SEA-CAPTAINS IF THEY WILL!' Of course, this was given
and received as raillery, but it did not tend to ripen
our intimacy or quicken my esteem into admiration.
Though no unkind word ever passed between us, nor
any approach to one, yet we two dwelt for months
under the same roof, as scarcely more than acquaintances, meeting once a day at a common board, and
having certain business relations with each other.
Personally, I regarded her rather as my wife's cherished
friend than as my own, possessing many lofty qualities
and some prominent weaknesses, and a good deal
spoiled by the unmeasured flattery of her little circle
of inordinate admirers. For myself, burning no incense
on any human shrine, I half-consciously resolved to
'keep my eye-beam clear,' and escape the fascination
which she seemed to exert over the eminent and cultivated persons, mainly women, who came to our out-of-
the-way dwelling to visit her, and who seemed generally to regard her with 'a strangely Oriental adoration.

"But as time wore on, and I became inevitably better
and better acquainted with her, I found myself drawn,
almost irresistibly, into the general current. I found
that her faults and weaknesses were all superficial and
obvious to the most casual, if undazzled, observer.
They rather dwindled than expanded upon a fuller
knowledge; or rather, took on new and brighter aspects

in the light of her radiant and lofty soul. I learned to know her as a most fearless and unselfish champion of Truth and Human Good at all hazards, ready to be their standard-bearer through danger and obloquy, and, if need be, their martyr. I think few have more keenly appreciated the material goods of life, — Rank, Riches, Power, Luxury, Enjoyment; but I know none who would have more cheerfully surrendered them all, if the well-being of our Race could thereby have been promoted. I have never met another in whom the inspiring hope of Immortality was so-strengthened into profoundest conviction. She did not *believe* in our future and unending existence, — she *knew* it, and lived ever in the broad glare of its morning twilight. With a limited income and liberal wants, she was yet generous beyond the bounds of reason. Had the gold of California been all her own, she would have disbursed nine tenths of it in eager and well-directed efforts to stay, or at least diminish, the flood of human misery. And it is but fair to state, that the liberality she evinced was fully paralleled by the liberality she experienced at the hands of others. Had she needed thousands, and made her wants known, she had friends who would have cheerfully supplied her. I think few persons, in their pecuniary dealings, have experienced and evinced more of the better qualities of human nature than Margaret Fuller. She seemed to inspire those who approached her with that generosity which was a part of her nature.

"Of her writings I do not purpose to speak critically. I think most of her contributions to the Tribune, while she remained with us, were characterized by a directness, terseness, and practicality, which are wanting in

some of her earlier productions. Good judges have
confirmed my own opinion, that, while her essays in the
Dial are more elaborate and ambitious, her reviews in
the Tribune are far better adapted to win the favor and
sway the judgment of the great majority of readers.
But, one characteristic of her writings I feel bound to
commend, — their absolute truthfulness. She never
asked how this would sound, nor whether that would
do, nor what would be the effect of saying anything;
but simply, 'Is it the truth? Is it such as the public
should know?' And if her judgment answered, 'Yes,'
she uttered it; no matter what turmoil it might excite,
nor what odium it might draw down on her own head.
Perfect conscientiousness was an unfailing characteristic
of her literary efforts. Even the severest of her critiques,
— that on Longfellow's Poems, — for which an impulse
in personal pique has been alleged, I happen with certainty to know had no such origin. When I first
handed her the book to review, she excused herself,
assigning the wide divergence of her views of Poetry
from those of the author and his school, as her reason.
She thus induced me to attempt the task of reviewing it
myself. But day after day sped by, and I could find
no hour that was not absolutely required for the performance of some duty that *would not* be put off, nor
turned over to another. At length I carried the book
back to her in utter despair of ever finding an hour in
which even to look through it; and, at my renewed and
earnest request, she reluctantly undertook its discussion.
The statement of these facts is but an act of justice to
her memory.

"Profoundly religious, — though her creed was, at
once, very broad and very short, with a genuine love

for inferiors in social position, whom she was habitually
studying, by her counsel and teachings, to elevate and
improve,— she won the confidence and affection of those
who attracted her, by unbounded sympathy and trust.
She probably- knew the cherished secrets of more hearts
than any one else, because she freely imparted her own.
With a full share both of intellectual and of family
pride, she preëminently recognized and responded to the
essential brotherhood of all human kind, and needed but
to know that a fellow-being required her counsel or
assistance, to render her, not merely willing, but eager
to impart it.   Loving ease, luxury, and the world's good
opinion, she stood ready to renounce them all, at the
call of pity or of duty.   I think no one, not radically
averse to the whole system of domestic servitude, would
have treated servants, of whatever class, with such
uniform and thoughtful consideration, — a regard which
wholly merged their factitious condition in their antece-
dent and permanent humanity.   I think few servants
ever lived weeks with her, who were not dignified and
lastingly benefited by her influence and· her counsels.
They might be at first repelled, by what seemed her too
stately manner and exacting disposition, but they soon
learned to esteem and love her.

"I have known few women, and scarcely another
maiden, who had the heart and the courage to speak
with such frank compassion, in mixed circles, of the most
degraded and outcast portion of the sex.   The contemplation of their treatment, especially by the guilty
authors of their ruin, moved her to a calm and mournful
indignation, which she did not attempt to suppress nor
control.   Others were willing to pity and deplore; Margaret was more inclined to vindicate and to redeem.

She did not hesitate to avow that on meeting some of these abused, unhappy sisters, she had been surprised to find them scarcely fallen morally below the ordinary standard of Womanhood, — realizing and loathing their debasement; anxious to escape it; and only repelled by the sad consciousness that for them sympathy and society remained only so long as they should persist in the ways of pollution. Those who have read her 'Woman,' may remember some daring comparisons therein suggested between these Pariahs of society and large classes of their respectable sisters; and that was no fitful expression, — no sudden outbreak, — but impelled by her most deliberate convictions. I think, if she had been born to large fortune, a house of refuge for all female outcasts desiring to return to the ways of Virtue, would have been one of her most cherished and first realized conceptions.

" Her love of children was one of her most prominent characteristics. The pleasure she enjoyed in their society was fully counterpoised by that she imparted. To them she was never lofty, nor reserved, nor mystical; for no one had ever a more perfect faculty for entering into their sports, their feelings, their enjoyments. She could narrate almost any story in language level to their capacities, and in a manner calculated to bring out their hearty and often boisterously expressed delight. She possessed marvellous powers of observation and imitation or mimicry; and, had she been attracted to the stage, would have been the first actress America has produced, whether in tragedy or comedy. Her faculty of mimicking was not needed to commend her to the hearts of children, but it had its effect in increasing the fascinations of her genial nature and heartfelt joy in their society. To amuse and instruct them was an achievement for which she would readily forego any personal object; and her intuitive perception of the toys, games, stories, rhymes, &c., best adapted to arrest and enchain their attention, was unsurpassed. Between her and my only child, then living, who was eight months old when she came to us, and something over two years when she sailed for Europe, tendrils of affection gradually intertwined themselves, which I trust Death has not severed, but rather multiplied and strengthened. She became his teacher, playmate, and monitor; and he requited her with a prodigality of love and admiration.

"I shall not soon forget their meeting in my office, after some weeks' separation, just before she left us forever. His mother had brought him in from the country and left him asleep on my sofa, while she was absent making purchases, and he had rolled off and hurt himself in the fall, waking with the shock in a phrensy of anger, just before Margaret, hearing of his arrival, rushed into the office to find him. I was vainly attempting to soothe him as she entered; but he was running from one end to the other of the office, crying passionately, and refusing to be pacified. She hastened to him, in perfect confidence that her endearments would calm the current of his feelings, — that the sound of her well-remembered voice would banish all thought of his pain, — and that another moment would see him restored to gentleness; but, half-wakened, he did not heed her, and probably did not even realize who it was that caught him repeatedly in her arms and tenderly insisted that he should restrain himself. At last she desisted in despair; and, with the bitter tears streaming down her face, observed : — 'Pickie, many friends have treated me unkindly, but no one had ever the power to cut me to the heart, as you have!' Being thus let alone, he soon came to himself, and their mutual delight in the meeting was rather heightened by the momentary estrangement.

"They had one more meeting; their last on earth! 'Aunty Margaret' was to embark for Europe on a certain day, and 'Pickie' was brought into the city to bid her farewell. They met this time also at my office, and together we thence repaired to the ferry-boat, on which she was returning to her residence in Brooklyn to complete her preparations for the voyage. There they took a tender and affecting leave of each other. But soon his mother called at the office, on her way to the departing ship, and we were easily persuaded to accompany her thither, and say farewell once more, to the manifest satisfaction of both Margaret and the youngest of her devoted friends. Thus they parted, never to meet again in time. She sent him messages and presents repeatedly from Europe; and he, when somewhat older, dictated a letter in return, which was joyfully received and acknowledged. When the mother of our great-souled friend spent some days with us nearly two years afterward, 'Pickie' talked to her often and lovingly of 'Aunty Margaret,' proposing that they two should 'take a boat and go over and see her,'— for, to his infantile conception, the low coast of Long Island, visible just across the East River, was that Europe to which she had sailed, and where she was unaccountably detained so long. Alas! a far longer and more adventurous journey was required to reünite those loving souls! The 12th of July, 1849, saw him stricken down, from health

to death, by the relentless cholera; and my letter, announcing that calamity, drew from her a burst of passionate sorrow, such as hardly any bereavement but the
loss of a very near relative could have impelled.   Another year had just ended, when a calamity, equally sudden, bereft a wide circle of her likewise, with her husband
and infant son.   Little did I fear, when I bade her a
confident Good-by, on the deck of her outward-bound
ship, that the sea would close over her earthly remains,
ere we should meet again; far less that the light of my
eyes and the cynosure of my hopes, who then bade her
a tenderer and sadder farewell, would precede her on
the dim pathway to that 'Father's house,' whence
is no returning!   Ah, well!   God is above all, and
gracious alike in what he conceals and what he dis-
closes; — benignant and bounteous, as well when he
reclaims as when he bestows.   In a few years, at
farthest, our loved and lost ones will welcome us to their
home."

Favorably as Mr. Greeley speaks of Margaret's articles
in the Tribune, it is yet true that she never brought her
full power to bear upon them; partly because she was
too much exhausted by previous over-work, partly because it hindered her free action to aim at popular effect.
Her own estimate of them is thus expressed: — 'I go on
'very moderately, for my strength is not great, and I
'am connected with one who is anxious that I should
'not overtask it.   Body and mind, I have long required
'rest and mere amusement, and now obey Nature as
'much as I can.   If she pleases to restore me to an ener-
'getic state, she will by-and-by; if not, I can only hope
'this world will not turn me out of doors too abruptly

'I value my present position very much, as enabling me
'to speak effectually some right words to a large circle;
'and, while I can do so, am content.' Again she says
— 'I am pleased with your sympathy about the Trib-
'une, for I do not find much among my old friends.
'They think I ought to produce something excellent,
'while I am satisfied to aid in the great work of popular
'education. I never regarded literature merely as a col-
'lection of exquisite products, but rather as a means of
'mutual interpretation. Feeling that many are reached
'and in some degree helped, the thoughts of every day
'seem worth noting, though in a form that does not
'inspire me.' The most valuable of her contributions,
according to her own judgment, were the Criticisms on
Contemporary Authors in Europe and America. A few
of these were revised in the spring of 1846, and, in connection with some of her best articles selected from the
Dial, Western Messenger, American Monthly, &c., appeared in two volumes of Wiley and Putnam's Library
of American Books, under the title of PAPERS ON ART AND
LITERATURE.

SOCIETY.

Heralded by her reputation as a scholar, writer, and
talker, and brought continually before the public by her
articles in the Tribune, Margaret found a circle of
acquaintance opening before her, as wide, various, and
rich, as time and inclination permitted her to know.
Persons sought her in her country retreat, attracted
alike by idle curiosity, desire for aid, and respectful
sympathy. She visited freely in several interesting
families in New York and Brooklyn; occasionally ac-

cepted invitations to evening parties, and often met, at
the somewhat celebrated *soirées* of Miss Lynch, the
assembled authors, artists, critics, wits, and *dilettanti*
of New York. As was inevitable, also, for one of such
powerful magnetic influence, liberal soul and broad
judgment, she once again became, as elsewhere she had
been, a confidant and counsellor of the tempted and
troubled; and her geniality, lively conversation, and
ever fresh love, gave her a home in many hearts. But
the subdued tone of her spirits at this period led her
to prefer seclusion.

Of her own social habits she writes: — 'It is not well
'to keep entirely apart from the stream of common life;
'so, though I never go out when busy, nor keep late
'hours, I find it pleasanter and better to enter somewhat
'into society. I thus meet with many entertaining ac-
'quaintance, and some friends. I can never, indeed,
'expect, in America, or in this world, to form relations
'with nobler persons than I have already known; nor
'can I put my heart into these new ties as into the old
'ones, though probably it would still respond to com-
'manding excellence. But my present circle satisfies
'my wants. As to what is called "good society," I am
'wholly indifferent. I know several women, whom I
'like very much, and yet more men. I hear good
'music, which answers my social desires better than
'any other intercourse can; and I love four or five inter-
'esting children, in whom I always find more genuine
'sympathy than in their elders.'

Of the impression produced by Margaret on those who
were but slightly acquainted with her, some notion may
be formed from the following sketch: — "In general
society, she commanded respect rather than admiration

All persons were curious to see her, and in full rooms her fine head and spiritual expression at once marked her out from the crowd; but the most were repelled by what seemed conceit, pedantry, and a harsh spirit of criticism, while, on her part, she appeared to regard those around her as frivolous, superficial, and conventional. Indeed, I must frankly confess, that we did not meet in pleasant relations, except now and then, when the lifting of a veil, as it were, revealed for a moment the true life of each. Yet I was fond of looking at her from a distance, and defending her when silly people were inclined to cavil at her want of feminine graces. Then I would say, ' I would like to be an artist now, that I might paint, not the care-worn countenance and the uneasy air of one seemingly out of harmony with the scene about her, but the soul that sometimes looks out from under those large lids. Michel Angelo would ·have made her a Sibyl.' I remember I was surprised to find her height no greater; for her writings had always given me an impression of magnitude. Thus I studied though I avoided her, admitting, the while, proudly and joyously, that she was a woman to reverence. A trifling incident, however, gave me the key to much in her character, of which, before, I had not dreamed. It was one evening, after a Valentine party, where Frances Osgood, Margaret Fuller, and other literary ladies, had attracted some attention, that, as we were in the dressing-room preparing to go home, I heard Margaret sigh deeply. Surprised and moved, I said, ' Why?' — 'Alone, as usual,' was her pathetic answer, followed by a few sweet, womanly remarks, touching as they were beautiful. Often, after, I found myself recalling her look and tone, with tears in my eyes; for before I had regarded her as a being cold, and abstracted, if not scornful."

Cold, abstracted, and scornful! About this very time it was that Margaret wrote in her journal: — 'Father, 'let me not injure my fellows during this period of re-'pression. I feel that when we meet my tones are not 'so sweet as I would have them. O, let me not wound! 'I, who know so well how wounds can burn and ache, 'should not inflict them. Let my touch be light and 'gentle. Let me keep myself uninvaded, but let me not 'fail to be kind and tender, when need is. Yet I would 'not assume an overstrained poetic magnanimity. Help 'me to do just right, and no more. O, make truth pro-'found and simple in me!' Again: — 'The heart bleeds, '— faith almost gives way, — to see man's seventy 'years of chrysalis. Is it not too long? Enthusiasm 'must struggle fiercely to burn clear amid these fogs. In 'what little, low, dark cells of care and prejudice, with-'out one soaring thought or melodious fancy, do poor 'mortals — well-intentioned enough, and with religious 'aspiration too — forever creep. And yet the sun sets 'to-day as gloriously bright as ever it did on the temples 'of Athens, and the evening star rises as heavenly pure 'as it rose on the eye of Dante. O, Father! help me to 'free my fellows from the conventional bonds whereby 'their sight is holden. By purity and freedom let me 'teach them justice.' And yet again: — 'There comes 'a consciousness that I have no real hold on life, — no 'real, permanent connection with any soul. I seem a 'wandering Intelligence, driven from spot to spot, that I 'may learn all secrets, and fulfil a circle of knowledge. This thought envelopes me as a cold atmosphere. I

' do not see how I shall go through this destiny.　I can
' if it is mine; but I do not feel that I can.'

Casual observers mistook Margaret's lofty idealism
for personal pride; but thus speaks one who really knew
her : — " You come like one of the great powers of
nature, harmonizing with all beauty of the soul or of
the earth.　You cannot be discordant with anything
that is true and deep.　I thank God for the noble privilege of being recognized by so large, tender, and radiant
a soul as thine."

EUROPE.

LETTERS

"I go to prove my soul.
ı see my way, as birds their trackless way
In some time, God's good time, I shall arrive
He guides me and the bird.   In his good time!

BROWNING.

ˢ¹ One, who, if he be called upon to face
   Some awful moment, to which Heaven has joined
   Great issues, good or bad for human kind,
   Is happy as a lover, and attired
   With sudden brightness, like a man inspired;
   And, through the heat of conflict, keeps the law
   In calmness made, and sees what he foresaw."

WORDSWORTH.

"Italia! Italia! O tu cui feo la sorte
    Dono infelice di bellezza, ond' hai
    Funesta dote d' infiniti guai,
    Che in fronte scritti per gran doglia porte.
 Deh, fossi tu men bella, ò almen più forte!"

FILICAJA.

"Oh . not to guess it at the first .
But I did guess it, — that is, I divined,
Felt by an instinct how it was; — why else
Should I pronounce you free from all that heap
Of sins, which had been irredeemable?
I felt they were not yours."

BROWNING

"Nests there are many of this very year,
Many the nests are, which the winds shall shake,
    The rains run through and other birds beat down
Yours, O Aspasia! rests against the temple
    Of heavenly love, and, thence inviolate,
It shall not fall this winter, nor the next."

LANDOR.

"Lift up your heart upon the knees of God,
Losing yourself, your smallness and your darkness
In His great light, who fills and moves the world,
Who hath alone the quiet of perfect motion."

STERLING,

VIII.

EUROPE.

———

[IT has been judged best to let Margaret herself tell the story of her travels. In the spring of 1846, her valued friends, Marcus Spring and lady, of New York, had decided to make a tour in Europe, with their son, and they invited Miss Fuller to accompany them. An arrangement was soon made on such terms as she could accept, and the party sailed from Boston in the "Cambria," on the first of August. The following narrative is made up of letters addressed by her to various correspondents. Some extracts, describing distinguished persons whom she saw, have been borrowed from her letters to the New York Tribune.]

TO MRS. MARGARET FULLER.

Liverpool, Aug. 16, 1846.

My dear Mother: —

The last two days at sea passed well enough, as a number of agreeable persons were introduced to me, and there were several whom I knew before. I enjoyed nothing on the sea; the excessively bracing air so affected

me that I could not bear to look at it. The sight of
land delighted me. The tall crags, with their breakers
and circling sea-birds; then the green fields, how glad!
We had a very fine day to come ashore, and made the
shortest passage ever known. The stewardess said,
"Any one who complained this time tempted the
Almighty." I did not complain, but I could hardly
have borne another day. I had no appetite; but am
now making up for all deficiencies, and feel already a
renovation beginning from the voyage; and, still more,
from freedom and entire change of scene.

We came here Wednesday, at noon; next day we went
to Manchester; the following day to Chester; returning
here Saturday evening.

On Sunday we went to hear James Martineau; were
introduced to him, and other leading persons. The next
day and evening I passed in the society of very pleasant
people, who have made every exertion to give me the
means of seeing and learning; but they have used up
all my strength.

LONDON.

TO C. S.

As soon as I reached England, I found how right we
were in supposing there was elsewhere a greater range
of interesting character among the men, than with us.
I do not find, indeed, any so valuable as three or four
among the most marked we have known; but many
that are strongly individual, and have a fund of hidden
life.

In Westmoreland, I knew, and have since been seeing in London, a man, such as would interest you
a good deal; Mr. Atkinson. He is sometimes called the

"prince of the English mesmerisers;" and he has the fine instinctive nature you may suppose from that. He is a man of about thirty; in the fulness of his powers; tall, and finely formed, with a head for Leonardo to paint; mild and composed, but powerful and sagacious; he does not think, but perceives and acts. He is intimate with artists, having studied architecture himself as a profession; but has some fortune on which he lives. Sometimes stationary and acting in the affairs of other men; sometimes wandering about the world and learning; he seems bound by no tie, yet looks as if he had relatives in every place.

I saw, also, a man, — an artist, — severe and antique in his spirit; he seemed burdened by the sorrows of aspiration; yet very calm, as secure in the justice of fate. What he does is bad, but full of a great desire. His name is David Scott. I saw another, — a pupil of De la Roche, — very handsome, and full of a voluptuous enjoyment of nature: him I liked a little in a different way.

By far the most beauteous person I have seen is Joseph Mazzini. If you ever see Saunders' "People's Journal," you can read articles by him that will give you some notion of his mind, especially one on his friends, headed "Italian Martyrs." He is one in whom holiness has purified, but somewhat dwarfed the man.

Our visit to Mr. Wordsworth was fortunate. He is seventy-six; but his is a florid, fair old age. He walked with us to all his haunts about the house. Its situation is beautiful, and the "Rydalian Laurels" are magnificent. Still, I saw abodes among the hills that I should have preferred for Wordsworth; more wild and

still more romantic. The fresh and lovely Rydal
Mount seems merely the retirement of a gentleman,
rather than the haunt of a poet. He showed his
benignity of disposition in several little things, especially
in his attentions to a young boy we had with us. This
boy had left the circus, exhibiting its feats of horseman-
ship, in Ambleside, "for that day only," at his own
desire to see Wordsworth; and I feared he would be
dissatisfied, as I know I should have been at his age,
if, when called to see a poet, I had found no Apollo
flaming with youthful glory, laurel-crowned, and lyre in
hand; but, instead, a reverend old man clothed in black,
and walking with cautious step along the level garden-
path. However, he was not disappointed; and Wordsworth, in his turn, seemed to feel and prize a congenial
nature in this child.

Taking us into the house, he showed us the picture
of his sister, repeating with much expression some lines
of hers, and those so famous of his about her, beginning
"Five years," &c.; also, his own picture, by Inman, of
whom he spoke with esteem. I had asked to see a
picture in that room, which has been described in one
of the finest of his later poems. A hundred times had I
wished to see this picture, yet when seen was not disappointed by it. The light was unfavorable, but it had a
light of its own, —

> " whose mild gleam
> Of beauty never ceases to enrich
> The common light."

Mr. Wordsworth is fond of the hollyhock; a par-
tiality scarcely deserved by the flower, but which marks

the simplicity of his tastes. He had made a long avenue of them, of all colors, from the crimson brown to
rose, straw-color, and white, and pleased himself with
having made proselytes to a liking for them, among his
neighbors.

I never have seen such magnificent fuchsias as at
Ambleside, and there was one to be seen in every cot-
tage-yard. They are no longer here under the shelter
of the green-house, as with us, and as they used to be
in England. The plant, from its grace and finished
elegance, being a great favorite of mine, I should like to
see it as frequently and of as luxuriant growth at home,
and asked their mode of culture, which I here mark
down for the benefit of all who may be interested.
Make a bed of bog-earth and sand ; put down slips of
the fuchsia, and give them a great deal of water; this
is all they need. People leave them out here in winter,
but perhaps they would not bear the cold of our Jan-
uaries.

Mr. Wordsworth spoke with more liberality than we
expected of the recent measures about the Corn-laws,
saying that "the principle was certainly right, though
whether existing interests had been as carefully attended to as was right, he was not prepared to say,"
&c. His neighbors were pleased to hear of his speaking
thus mildly, and hailed it as a sign that he was opening
his mind to more light on these subjects. They lament
that his habits of seclusion keep him ignorant of
the real wants of England and the world. Living in this
region, which is cultivated by small proprietors, where
there is little poverty, vice, or misery, he hears not the
voice which cries so loudly from other parts of England,
and will not be stilled by sweet, poetic suasion, or

philosophy, for it is the cry of men in the jaws of destruction.

It was pleasant to find the reverence inspired by this great and pure mind warmest near home. Our land-lady, in heaping praises upon him, added, constantly, "and Mrs. Wordsworth, too." "Do the people here," said I, "value Mr. Wordsworth most because he is a celebrated writer?" "Truly, madam," said she, "I think it is because he is so kind a neighbor."

"True to the kindred points of Heaven and Home."

EDINBURGH. — DE QUINCEY.

At Edinburgh we were in the wrong season, and many persons we most wished to see were absent. We had, however, the good fortune to find Dr. Andrew Combe, who received us with great kindness. I was impressed with great and affectionate respect, by the benign and even temper of his mind, his extensive and accurate knowledge, accompanied by a large and intelligent liberality. Of our country he spoke very wisely and hopefully.

I had the satisfaction, not easily attainable now, of seeing De Quincey for some hours, and in the mood of conversation. As one belonging to the Wordsworth and Coleridge constellation (he, too, is now seventy years of age), the thoughts and knowledge of Mr. De Quincey lie in the past, and oftentimes he spoke of matters now become trite to one of a later culture. But to all that fell from his lips, his eloquence, subtle and forcible as the wind, full and gently falling as the evening dew, lent a peculiar charm. He is an admirable narrator; not rapid, but gliding along like a rivulet through a green meadow, giving and taking a thousand little beauties not absolutely required to give his story due relief, but each, in itself, a separate boon.

I admired, too, his urbanity; so opposite to the rapid, slang, Vivian-Greyish style, current in the literary conversation of the day. "Sixty years since," men had time to do things better and more gracefully.

CHALMERS.

With Dr. Chalmers we passed a couple of hours. He is old now, but still full of vigor and fire. We had an opportunity of hearing a fine burst of indignant eloquence from him. "I shall blush to my very bones," said he, " if the *Chaarrch*," (sound these two *rrs* with as much burr as possible, and you will get an idea of his mode of pronouncing that unweariable word,) "if the Chaarrch yield to the storm." He alluded to the outcry now raised by the Abolitionists against the Free Church, whose motto is, "Send back the money;" *i. e.*, the money taken from the American slaveholders. Dr. C felt, that if they did not yield from conviction, they must not to assault. His manner in speaking of this gave me a hint of the nature of his eloquence. He seldom preaches now.

A Scottish gentleman told me the following story : — Burns, still only in the dawn of his celebrity, was invited to dine with one of the neighboring so-called gentry, unhappily quite void of true gentle blood. On arriving, he found his plate set in the servants' room. After dinner, he was invited into a room where guests were assembled, and, a chair being placed for him at the lower end of the board, a glass of wine was offered, and he was requested to sing one of his songs for the entertainment of the company.. He drank off the wine, and thundered forth in reply his grand song " For a' that and a' that," and having finished his prophecy and prayer, nature's nobleman left his churlish entertainers to hide their heads in the home they had disgraced.

A NIGHT ON BEN LOMOND.

At Inversnaid, we took a boat to go down Loch Lomond, to the little inn of Rowardennan, from which the ascent is made of Ben Lomond. We found a day of ten thousand, for our purpose; but, unhappily, a large party had come with the sun, and engaged all the horses, so that if we went, it must be on foot. This was something of an enterprise for me, as the ascent is four miles, and toward the summit quite fatiguing. However, in the pride of newly-gained health and strength, I was ready, and set forth with Mr. S. alone. We took no guide, and the people of the house did not advise us to take one, as they ought.

On reaching the peak, the sight was one of beauty and grandeur such as imagination never painted. You see around you no plain ground, but on every side constellations, or groups of hills, exquisitely dressed in the soft purple of the heather, amid which gleam the lakes, like eyes that tell the secrets of the earth, and drink in those of the heavens. Peak beyond peak caught from the shifting light all the colors of the prism, and, on the furthest, angel companies seemed hovering in glorious white robes.

About four o'clock we began our descent. Near the

summit, the traces of the path are not distinct, and I said to Mr. S., after a while, that we had lost it. He said he thought that was of no consequence; we could find our way down. I said I thought it was, as the ground was full of springs that were bridged over in the path way. He accordingly went to look for it, and I stood still, because I was so tired I did not like to waste any labor.

Soon he called to me that he had found it, and I followed in the direction where he seemed to be. But I mistook, overshot it, and saw him no more. In about ten minutes I became alarmed, and called him many times. It seems, he on his side shouted also, but the brow of some hill was between us, and we neither saw nor heard one another. I then thought I would make the best of my way down, and I should find him when I arrived. But, in doing so, I found the justice of my apprehension about the springs, so soon as I got to the foot of the hills; for I would sink up to my knees in bog, and must go up the hills again, seeking better crossing places. Thus I lost much time. Nevertheless, in the twilight, I saw, at last, the lake, and the inn of Rowardennan on its shore.

Between me and it, lay, direct, a high heathery hill, which I afterwards found is called "The Tongue," because hemmed in on three sides by a water-course. It looked as if, could I only get to the bottom of that, I should be on comparatively level ground. I then attempted to descend in the water-course, but, finding that impracticable, climbed on the hill again, and let myself down by the heather, for it was very steep, and full of deep holes. With great fatigue, I got to the bottom, but when I was about to cross the water-course there, I felt afraid, it looked so deep in the dim twilight. I got down as far as I could by the root of a tree, and threw down a stone. It sounded very hollow, and I was afraid to jump. The shepherds told me afterwards, if I had, I should probably have killed myself, it was so deep, and the bed of the torrent full of sharp stones.

I then tried to ascend the hill again, for there was no other way to get off it; but soon sank down utterly exhausted. When able to get up again, and look about me, it was completely dark. I saw, far below me, a light, that looked about as big as a pin's head, that I knew to be from the inn at Rowardennan, but heard no sound except the rush of the waterfall, and the sighing of the night wind.

For the first few minutes after I perceived I had come to my night's lodging, such as it was, the circumstance looked appalling. I was very lightly clad, my feet and dress were very wet, I had only a little shawl to throw round me, and the cold autumn wind had already come, and the night mist was to fall on me, all fevered and exhausted as I was. I thought I should not live through the night, or, if I did, I must be an invalid henceforward. I could not even keep myself warm by walking, for, now it was dark, it would be too dangerous to stir. My only chance, however, lay in motion, and my only help in myself; and so convinced was I of this, that I did keep in motion the whole of that long night, imprisoned as I was on such a little perch of that great mountain.

For about two hours, I saw the stars, and very cheery and companionable they looked; but then the mist fell, and I saw nothing more, except such apparitions as visited Ossian, on the hill-side, when he went out by night, and struck the bosky shield, and called to him the spirits of the heroes, and the white-armed maids, with

their blue eyes of grief. To me, too, came those visionary shapes. Floating slowly and gracefully, their white
robes would unfurl from the great body of mist in which
they had been engaged, and come upon me with a kiss
pervasively cold as that of death. Then the moon rose.
I could not see her, but her silver light filled the mist.
Now I knew it was two o'clock, and that, having
weathered out so much of the night, I might the rest;
and the hours hardly seemed long to me more.

It may give an idea of the extent of the mountain,
that, though I called, every now and then, with all my
force, in case by chance some aid might be near, and
though no less than twenty men, with their dogs, were
looking for me, I never heard a sound, except the rush
of the waterfall and the sighing of the night wind, and
once or twice the startling of the grouse in the heather.
It was sublime indeed, — a never-to-be-forgotten presentation of stern, serene realities. At last came the signs
of day, — the gradual clearing and breaking up; some
faint sounds from I know not what; the little flies, too,
arose from their bed amid the purple heather, and bit
me. Truly they were very welcome to do so. But
what was my disappointment to find the mist so thick,
that I could see neither lake nor inn, nor anything to
guide me. I had to go by guess, and, as it happened,
my Yankee method served me well. I ascended the
hill, crossed the torrent, in the waterfall, first drinking
some of the water, which was as good at that time as
ambrosia. I crossed in that place, because the waterfall
made steps, as it were, to the next hill. To be sure,
they were covered with water, but I was already entirely wet with the mist, so that it did not matter. I
kept on scrambling, as it happened, in the right direc-

tion, till, about seven, some of the shepherds found me. The moment they came, all my feverish strength departed, and they carried me home, where my arrival relieved my friends of distress far greater than I had undergone; for I had my grand solitude, my Ossianic visions, and the pleasure of sustaining myself; while they had only doubt, amounting to anguish, and a fruitless search through the night.

Entirely contrary to my forebodings, I only suffered for this a few days, and was able to take a parting look at my prison, as I went down the lake, with feelings of complacency. It was a majestic-looking hill, that Tongue, with the deep ravines on either side, and the richest robe of heather I have anywhere seen.

Mr. S. gave all the men who were looking for me a dinner in the barn, and he and Mrs. S. ministered to them; and they talked of Burns, — really the national writer, and known by them, apparently, as none other is, — and of hair-breadth 'scapes by flood and fell. Afterwards they were all brought up to see me, and it was gratifying to note the good breeding and good feeling with which they deported themselves. Indeed, this adventure created quite an intimate feeling between us and the people there. I had been much pleased before, in attending one of their dances, at the genuine independence and politeness of their conduct. They were willing to dance their Highland flings and strathspeys, for our amusement, and did it as naturally and as freely as they would have offered the stranger the best chair.

I have mentioned with satisfaction seeing some persons who illustrated the past dynasty in the progress of
thought here : Wordsworth, Dr. Chalmers, De Quincey,
Andrew Combe. With a still higher pleasure, because
to one of my own sex, whom I have honored almost
above any, I went to pay my court to Joanna Baillie.
I found on her brow, not, indeed, a coronal of gold,
but a serenity and strength undimmed and unbroken
by the weight of more. than fourscore years, or by the
scanty appreciation which her thoughts have received.
We found her in her little calm retreat, at Hampstead,
surrounded by marks of love and reverence from distinguished and excellent friends. Near her was the
sister, older than herself, yet still sprightly and full of
active kindness, whose character and their mutual relations she has, in one of her last poems, indicated with
such a happy mixture of sagacity, humor, and tender
pathos, and with so absolute a truth of outline.

Mary and William Howitt are the main support of the
People's Journal. I saw them several times at their
cheerful and elegant home. In Mary Howitt, I found
the same engaging traits of character we are led to
expect from her books for children. At their house, I
became acquainted with Dr. Southwood Smith, the well-
known philanthropist. He is at present engaged in the
construction of good tenements, calculated to improve
the condition of the working people.

TO R. W. E.

Paris, Nov. 16, 1846. — I meant to write on my arrival in London, six weeks ago; but as it was not wnat
is technically called "the season," I thought I had best
send all my letters of introduction at once, ·that I might
glean what few good people I could.   But more than I
expected were in town.   These introduced others, and in
three days I was engaged in such a crowd of acquaintance, that I had hardly time to dress, and none to sleep,
during all the weeks I was in London.

I enjoyed the time extremely.   I find myself much in
my element in European society.   It does not, indeed,
come up to my ideal, but so many of the encumbrances
are cleared away that used to weary me in America,
that I can enjoy a freer play of faculty, and feel, if not
like a bird in the air, at least as easy as a fish in water.

In Edinburgh, I met Dr. Brown.   He is still quite a
young man, but with a high ambition, and, I should
think, commensurate powers.   But all is yet in the bud
with him.   He has a friend, David Scott, a painter, full
of imagination, and very earnest in his views of art.   I
had some pleasant hours with them, and the last night
which they and I passed with De Quincey, a real grand
conversazione, quite in the Landor style, which lasted,
in full harmony, some hours.

CARLYLE.

Of the people I saw in London, you will wish me to
speak first of the Carlyles.   Mr. C. came to see me at
once, and appointed an evening to be passed at their
house.   That first time, I was delighted with him.   He

was in a very sweet humor, — full of wit and pathos, without being overbearing or oppressive. I was quite carried away with the rich flow of his discourse; and the hearty, noble earnestness of his personal being brought back the charm which once was upon his writing, before I wearied of it. I admired his Scotch, his way of singing his great full sentences, so that each one was like the stanza of a narrative ballad. He let me talk, now and then, enough to free my lungs and change my position, so that I did not get tired. That evening, he talked of the present state of things in England, giving light, witty sketches of the men of the day, fanatics and others, and some sweet, homely stories he told of things he had known of the Scotch peasantry. Of you he spoke with hearty kindness; and he told, with beautiful feeling, a story of some poor farmer, or artisan, in the country, who on Sunday lays aside the cark and care of that dirty English world, and sits reading the Essays, and looking upon the sea.

I left him that night, intending to go out very often to their house. I assure you there never was anything so witty as Carlyle's description of —— ——. It was enough to kill one with laughing. I, on my side, contributed a story to his fund of anecdote on this subject, and it was fully appreciated. Carlyle is worth a thousand of you for that; — he is not ashamed to laugh, when he is amused, but goes on in a cordial human fashion.

The second time, Mr. C. had a dinner-party, at which was a witty, French, flippant sort of man, author of a History of Philosophy, and now writing a Life of Goethe, a task for which he must be as unfit as irreligion and sparkling shallowness can make him. But he told stories admirably, and was allowed sometimes to inter-

VOL. II.

rupt Carlyle a little, of which one was glad, for, that night, he was in his more acrid mood; and, though much more brilliant than on the former evening, grew wearisome to me, who disclaimed and rejected almost everything he said.

For a couple of hours, he was talking about poetry, and the whole harangue was one eloquent proclamation of the defects in his own mind. Tennyson wrote in verse because the schoolmasters had taught him that it was great to do so, and had thus, unfortunately, been turned from the true path for a man. Burns had, in like manner, been turned from his vocation. Shakspeare had not had the good sense to see that it would have been better to write straight on in prose; — and such nonsense, which, though amusing enough at first, he ran to death after a while. The most amusing part is always when he comes back to some refrain, as in the French Revolution of the *sea-green*. In this instance, it was Petrarch and *Laura*, the last word pronounced with his ineffable sarcasm of drawl. Although he said this over fifty times, I could not ever help laughing when *Laura* would come,—Carlyle running his chin out, when he spoke it, and his eyes glancing till they looked like the eyes and beak of a bird of prey. Poor Laura! Lucky for her that her poet had already got her safely canonized beyond the reach of this Teufelsdrockh vulture.

The worst of hearing Carlyle is that you cannot interrupt him. I understand the habit and power of haranguing have increased very much upon him, so that you are a perfect prisoner when he has once got hold of you. To interrupt him is a physical impossibility. If you get a chance to remonstrate for a moment, he raises his voice and bears you down. True, he does you no injustice, and, with his admirable penetration, sees the disclaimer in your mind, so that you are not morally delinquent; but it is not pleasant to be unable to utter it. The latter part of the evening, however, he paid us for this, by a series of sketches, in his finest style of railing and raillery, of modern French literature, not one of them, perhaps, perfectly just, but all drawn with the finest, boldest strokes, and, from his point of view, masterly. All were depreciating, except that of Béranger. Of him he spoke with perfect justice, because with hearty sympathy.

I had, afterward, some talk with Mrs. C., whom hitherto I had only *seen*, for who can speak while her husband is there? I like her very much; — she is full of grace, sweetness, and talent. Her eyes are sad and charming. * * *

After this, they went to stay at Lord Ashburton's, and I only saw them once more, when they came to pass an evening with us. Unluckily, Mazzini was with us, whose society, when he was there alone, I enjoyed more than any. He is a beauteous and pure music; also, he is a dear friend of Mrs. C.; but his being there gave the conversation a turn to "progress" and ideal subjects, and C. was fluent in invectives on all our "rose-water imbecilities." We all felt distant from him, and Mazzini, after some vain efforts to remonstrate, became very sad. Mrs. C. said to me, "These are but opinions to Carlyle; but to Mazzini, who has given his all, and helped bring his friends to the scaffold, in pursuit of such subjects, it is a matter of life and death."

All Carlyle's talk, that evening, was a defence of mere force, — success the test of right; — if people would not behave well, put collars round their necks; — find a

hero, and let them be his slaves, &c.   It was very
Titanic, and anti-celestial. I wish the last evening had
been more melodious. However, I bid Carlyle farewell
with feelings of the warmest friendship and admiration.
We cannot feel otherwise to a great and noble nature,
whether it harmonize with our own or not.   I never
appreciated the work he has done for his age till I saw
England. I could not. You must stand in the shadow
of that mountain of shams, to know how hard it is to
cast light across it.

Honor to Carlyle! *Hoch!* Although in the wine
with which we drink this health, I, for one, must mingle
the despised "rose-water."

And now, having to your eye shown the defects of
my own mind, in the sketch of another, I will pass on
more lowly, — more willing to be imperfect, — since
Fate permits such noble creatures, after all, to be only
this or that. It is much if one is not only a crow or
magpie; — Carlyle is only a lion. Some time we may,
all in full, be intelligent and humanly fair.

CARLYLE, AGAIN.

Paris, Dec., 1846. — Accustomed to the infinite wit
and exuberant richness of his writings, his talk is still
an amazement and a splendor scarcely to be faced with
steady eyes. He does not converse; — only harangues.
It is the usual misfortune of such marked men, —happily
not one invariable or inevitable, — that they cannot
allow other minds room to breathe, and show themselves
in their atmosphere, and thus miss the refreshment and
instruction which the greatest never cease to need from
the experience of the humblest. Carlyle allows no one

a chance, but bears down all opposition, not only by his wit and onset of words, resistless in their sharpness as so many bayonets, but by actual physical superiority, — raising his voice, and rushing on his opponent with a torrent of sound. This is not in the least from unwillingness to allow freedom to others. On the contrary, no man would more enjoy a manly resistance to his thought. But it is the habit of a mind accustomed to follow out its own impulse, as the hawk its prey, and which knows not how to stop in the chase. Carlyle, indeed, is arrogant and overbearing; but in his arrogance there is no littleness, — no self-love. It is the heroic arrogance of some old Scandinavian conqueror; — it is his nature, and the untamable energy that has given him power to crush the dragons. You do not love him, perhaps, nor revere; and perhaps, also, he would only laugh at you if you did; but you like him heartily, and like to see him the powerful smith, the Siegfried, melting all the old iron in his furnace till it glows to a sunset red, and burns you, if you senselessly go too near. He seems, to me, quite isolated, — lonely as the desert, — yet never was a man more fitted to prize a man, could he find one to match his mood. He finds them, but only in the past. He sings, rather than talks. He pours upon you a kind of satirical, heroical, critical poem, with regular cadences, and generally, near the beginning hits upon some singular epithet, which serves as a *refrain* when his song is full, or with which, as with a knitting needle, he catches up the stitches, if he has chanced, now and then, to let fall a row. For the higher kinds of poetry he has no sense, and his talk on that subject is delightfully and gorgeously absurd. He sometimes stops a minute to laugh at it himself, then begins anew with

fresh vigor; for all the spirits he is driving before him
seem to him as Fata Morgana, ugly masks, in fact, if
he can but make them turn about; but he laughs that
they seem to others such dainty Ariels. His talk, like
his books, is full of pictures; his critical strokes masterly.
Allow for his point of view, and his survey is admirable.
He is a large subject. I cannot speak more or wiselier
of him now, nor needs it; — his works are true, to blame
and praise him, — the Siegfried of England, — great and
powerful, if not quite invulnerable, and of a might rather
to destroy evil, than legislate for good.

Of Dr. Wilkinson I saw a good deal, and found him a
substantial person, — a sane, strong, and well-exer-
cised mind, — but in the last degree unpoetical in its
structure. He is very simple, natural, and good; excellent to see, though one cannot go far with him; and he
would be worth more in writing, if he could get time to
write, than in personal intercourse. He may yet find
time; — he is scarcely more than thirty. Dr. W. wished
to introduce me to Mr. Clissold, but I had not time; shall
find it, if in London again. Tennyson was not in town.

Browning has just married Miss Barrett, and gone to
Italy. I may meet them there. Bailey is helping his
father with a newspaper! His wife and child (Philip
Festus by name) came to see me. I am to make them
a visit on my return. Marston I saw several times, and
found him full of talent. That is all I want to say at
present; — he is a delicate nature, that can only be
known in its own way and time. I went to see his
"Patrician's Daughter." It is an admirable play for
the stage. At the house of W. J. Fox, I saw first himself, an eloquent man, of great practical ability, then
Cooper, (of the "Purgatory of Suicides,") and others.

My poor selection of miscellanies has been courteously greeted in the London journals. Openings were made for me to write, had I but leisure ; it is for that I look to a second stay in London, since several topics came before me on which I wished to write and publish *there*.

I became acquainted with a gentleman who is intimate with all the English artists, especially Stanfield and Turner, but was only able to go to his house once, at this time. Pictures I found but little time for, yet enough to feel what they are now to be to me. I was only at the Dulwich and National Galleries and Hampton Court. Also, have seen the Vandykes, at Warwick ; but all the precious private collections I was obliged to leave untouched, except one of Turner's, to which I gave a day. For the British Museum, I had only one day, which I spent in the Greek and Egyptian Rooms, unable even to look at the vast collections of drawings, &c. But if I live there a few months, I shall go often. O, were life but longer, and my strength greater! Ever I am bewildered by the riches of existence, had I but more time to open the oysters, and get out the pearls. Yet some are mine, if only for a necklace or rosary.

PARIS.

TO HER MOTHER.

Paris, Dec. 26, 1846. — In Paris I have been obliged to give a great deal of time to French, in order to gain the power of speaking, without which I might as usefully be in a well as here. That has prevented my doing nearly as much as I would. Could I remain six months in this great focus of civilized life, the time would be all too short for my desires and needs.

My Essay on American Literature has been translated into French, and published in "La Revue Indépendante," one of the leading journals of Paris; only, with that delight at manufacturing names for which the French are proverbial, they put, instead of *Margaret*, *Elizabeth*. Write to ——, that aunt Elizabeth has appeared unexpectedly before the French public! She will not enjoy her honors long, as a future number, which is to contain a notice of "Woman in the Nineteenth Century," will rectify the mistake.

I have been asked, also, to remain in correspondence with La Revue Indépendante, after my return to the United States, which will be very pleasant and advantageous to me.

I have some French acquaintance, and begin to take pleasure in them, now that we can hold intercourse more easily. Among others, a Madame Pauline Roland I find an interesting woman. She is an intimate friend of Béranger and of Pierre Leroux.

We occupy a charming suite of apartments, Hotel Rougement, Boulevard Poissonière. It is a new hotel, and has not the arched gateways and gloomy court-yard of the old mansions. My room, though small, is very pretty, with the thick, flowered carpet and marble slabs; the French clock, with Cupid, of course, over the fireplace, in which burns a bright little wood fire; the canopy bedstead, and inevitable large mirror; the curtains, too, are thick and rich, the closet, &c., excellent, the attendance good. But for all this, one pays dear. We do not find that one can live *pleasantly* at Paris for little money; and we prefer to economize by a briefer stay, if at all.

TO E. H.

Paris, Jan. 18, 1847, and *Naples, March* 17, 1847.— You wished to hear of George Sand, or, as they say in Paris, "Madame Sand." I find that all we had heard of her was true in the outline; I had supposed it might be exaggerated. She had every reason to leave her husband,— a stupid, brutal man, who insulted and neglected her. He afterwards gave up their child to her for a sum of money. But the love for which she left him lasted not well, and she has had a series of lovers, and I am told has one now, with whom she lives on the footing of combined means, independent friendship! But she takes rank in society like a man, for the weight of her thoughts, and has just given her daughter in marriage. Her son is a grown-up young man, an artist. Many women visit her, and esteem it an honor. Even an American here, and with the feelings of our country on such subjects, Mrs. ——, thinks of her with high esteem. She has broken with La Mennais, of whom she was once a disciple.

I observed to Dr. François, who is an intimate of hers, and loves and admires her, that it did not seem a good sign that she breaks with her friends. He said it was not so with her early friends; that she has chosen to buy a chateau in the region where she passed her childhood, and that the people there love and have always loved her dearly. She is now at the chateau, and, I begin to fear, will not come to town before I go.

VOL. II.

Since I came, I have read two charming stories recently written by her. Another longer one she has just sold to *La Presse* for fifteen thousand francs. She does not receive nearly as much for her writings as Balzac, Dumas, or Sue. She has a much greater influence than they, but a less circulation.

She stays at the chateau, because the poor peopl there were suffering so much, and she could help them. She has subscribed *twenty thousand francs* for their relief, in the scarcity of the winter. It is a great deal to earn by one's pen: a novel of several volumes sold for only fifteen thousand francs, as I mentioned before. * * *

At last, however, she came; and I went to see her at her house, Place d'Orleans. I found it a handsome modern residence. She had not answered my letter, written about a week before, and I felt a little anxious lest she should not receive me; for she is too much the mark of impertinent curiosity, as well as too busy, to be easily accessible to strangers. I am by no means timid, but I have suffered, for the first time in France, some of the torments of *mauvaise honte*, enough to see what they must be to many.

It is the custom to go and call on those to whom you bring letters, and push yourself upon their notice; thus you must go quite ignorant whether they are disposed to be cordial. My name is always murdered by the foreign servants who announce me. I speak very bad French; only lately have I had sufficient command of it to infuse some of my natural spirit in my discourse. This has been a great trial to me, who am eloquent and free in my own tongue, to be forced to feel my thoughts struggling in vain for utterance.

The servant who admitted me was in the picturesque costume of a peasant, and, as Madame Sand afterward told me, her god-daughter, whom she had brought from her province. She announced me as "*Madame Salere*," and returned into the ante-room to tell me, "*Madame says she does not know you.*" I began to think I was doomed to a rebuff, among the crowd who deserve it. However, to make assurance sure, I said, "Ask if she has not received a letter from me." As I spoke, Madame S. opened the door, and stood looking at me an instant. Our eyes met. I never shall forget her look at that moment. The doorway made a frame for her figure; she is large, but well-formed. She was dressed in a robe of dark violet silk, with a black mantle on her shoulders, her beautiful hair dressed with the greatest taste, her whole appearance and attitude, in its simple and lady-like dignity, presenting an almost ludicrous contrast to the vulgar caricature idea of George Sand. Her face is a very little like the portraits, but much finer; the upper part of the forehead and eyes are beautiful, the lower, strong and masculine, expressive of a hardy temperament and strong passions, but not in the least coarse; the complexion olive, and the air of the whole head Spanish, (as, indeed, she was born at Madrid, and is only on one side of French blood.) All these details I saw at a glance; but what fixed my attention was the expression of *goodness*, nobleness, and power, that pervaded the whole, — the truly human heart and nature that shone in the eyes. As our eyes met, she said, "*C'est vous*," and held out her hand. I took it, and went into her little study; we sat down a moment, then I said, "*Il me fait de bien de vous voir*," and I am sure I said it with my whole heart, for it made me very happy to see such a woman, so large and s′ developed a character, and everything that *is* good in it so *really* good. I loved, shall always love her.

She looked away, and said, *"Ah! vous m'avez écrit une lettre charmante."* This was all the preliminary of our talk, which then went on as if we had always known one another. She told me, before I went away, that she was going that very day to write to me; that when the servant announced me she did not recognize the name, but after a minute it struck her that it might be *La dame Americaine*, as the foreigners very commonly call me, for they find my name hard to remember. She was very much pressed for time, as she was then preparing copy for the printer, and, having just returned, there were many applications to see her, but she wanted me to stay then, saying, "It is better to throw things aside, and seize the present moment." I staid a good part of the day, and was very glad afterwards, for I did not see her again uninterrupted. Another day I was there, and saw her in her circle. Her daughter and another lady were present, and a number of gentlemen. Her position there was of an intellectual woman and good friend, — the same as my own in the circle of my acquaintance as distinguished from my intimates. Her daughter is just about to be married. It is said, there is no congeniality between her and her mother; but for her son she seems to have much love, and he loves and admires her extremely. I understand he has a good and free character, without conspicuous talent.

Her way of talking is just like her writing, — lively, picturesque, with an undertone of deep feeling, and the same skill in striking the nail on the head every now and then with a blow.

We did not talk at all of personal or private matters. I saw, as one sees in her writings, the want of an independent, interior life, but I did not feel it as a fault, there is so much in her of her kind. I heartily enjoyed the sense of so rich, so prolific, so ardent a genius. I liked the woman in her, too, very much; I never liked a woman better.

For the rest I do not care to write about it much, for I cannot, in the room and time I have to spend, express my thoughts as I would; but as near as I can express the sum total, it is this. S—— and others who admire her, are anxious to make a fancy picture of her, and represent her as a Helena (in the Seven Chords of the Lyre); all whose mistakes are the fault of the present state of society. But to me the truth seems to be this. She has that purity in her soul, for she knows well how to love and prize its beauty; but she herself is quite another sort of person. She needs no defence, but only to be understood, for she has bravely acted out her nature, and always with good intentions. She might have loved one man permanently, if she could have found one contemporary with her who could interest and command her throughout her range; but there was hardly a possibility of that, for such a person. Thus she has naturally changed the objects of her affection, and several times. Also, there may have been something of the Bacchante in her life, and of the love of night and storm, and the free raptures amid which roamed on the mountain-tops the followers of Cybele, the great goddess, the great mother. But she was never coarse, never gross, and I am sure her generous heart has not failed to draw some rich drops from every kind of wine-press. When she has done with an intimacy, she likes to break it off suddenly, and this has happened often, both with men and women. Many calumnies upon her are traceable to this cause.

I forgot to mention, that, while talking, she *does* smoke all the time her little cigarette. This is now a common practice among ladies abroad, but I believe originated with her.

For the rest, she holds her place in the literary and social world of France like a man, and seems full of energy and courage in it. I suppose she has suffered much, but she has also enjoyed and done much, and her expression is one of calmness and happiness. I was sorry to see her *exploitant* her talent so carelessly. She does too much, and this cannot last forever; but " Teverino " and the " Mare au Diable," which she has lately published, are as original, as masterly in truth, and as free in invention, as anything she has done.

Afterwards I saw Chopin, not with her, although he lives with her, and has for the last twelve years. I went to see him in his room with one of his friends. He is always ill, and as frail as a snow-drop, but an exquisite genius. He played to me, and I liked his talking scarcely less. Madame S. loved Liszt before him; she has thus been intimate with the two opposite sides of the musical world. Mickiewicz says, " Chopin talks with spirit, and gives us the Ariel view of the universe. Liszt is the eloquent *tribune* to the world of men, a little vulgar and showy certainly, but I like the tribune best." It is said here, that Madame S. has long had only a friendship for Chopin, who, perhaps, on his side prefers to be a lover, and a jealous lover; but she does not leave him, because he needs her care so much, when sick and suffering. About all this, I do not know; you cannot know much about anything in France, except what you see with your two eyes. Lying is ingrained in "*la grande nation*," as they so plainly show no less in literature than life.

RACHEL.

In France the theatre is living; you see something really good, and good throughout. Not one touch of that stage-strut and vulgar bombast of tone, which the English actor fancies indispensable to scenic illusion, is tolerated here. For the first time in my life, I saw something represented in a style uniformly good, and should have found sufficient proof, if I had needed any, that all men will prefer what is good to what is bad, if only a fair opportunity for choice be allowed. When I came here, my first thought was to go and see Mademoiselle Rachel. I was sure that in her I should find a true genius. I went to see her seven, or eight times, always in parts that required great force of soul, and purity of taste, even to conceive them, and only once had reason to find fault with her. On one single occasion, I saw her violate the harmony of the character, to produce effect at a particular moment; but, almost invariably, I found her a true artist, worthy Greece, and worthy at many moments to have her conceptions immortalized in marble.

Her range even in high tragedy is limited. She can only express the darker passions, and grief in its mos desolate aspects. Nature has not gifted her with those softer and more flowery attributes, that lend to pathos its utmost tenderness. She does not melt to tears, or calm or elevate the heart by the presence of that tragic beauty that needs all the assaults of fate to make it show its immortal sweetness. Her noblest aspect is when sometimes she expresses truth in some severe shape, and rises, simple and austere, above the mixed elements around her. On the dark side, she is very great in hatred and revenge. I admired her more in Phèdre than in any other part in which I saw her; the guilty love inspired by the hatred of a goddess was expressed, in all its symptoms, with a force and terrible naturalness, that almost suffocated the beholder. After she had taken the poison, the exhaustion and paralysis of the system, — the sad, cold, calm submission to Fate, — were still more grand.

I had heard so much about the power of her eye in one fixed look, and the expression she could concentrate in a single word, that the utmost results could only satisfy my expectations. It is, indeed, something magnificent to see the dark cloud give out such sparks, each one fit to deal a separate death; but it was not that I admired most in her. It was the grandeur, truth, and depth of her conception of each part, and the sustained purity with which she represented it.

The French language from her lips is a divine dialect; it is stripped of its national and personal peculiarities, and becomes what any language must, moulded by such a genius, the pure music of the heart and soul. I never could remember her tone in speaking any word; it was too perfect; you had received the thought quite direct Yet, had I never heard her speak a word, my mind would be filled by her attitudes. Nothing more graceful can be conceived, nor could the genius of sculpture surpass her management of the antique drapery.

She has no beauty, except in the intellectual severity

of her outline, and she bears marks of race, that will grow stronger every year, and make her ugly at last. Still it will be a *grandiose*, gypsy, or rather Sibylline ugliness, well adapted to the expression of some tragic parts. Only it seems as if she could not live long; she expends force enough upon a part to furnish out a dozen common lives.

TO R. W. E.

Paris, Jan. 18, 1847.—I can hardly tell you what a fever consumes me, from sense of the brevity of my time and opportunity. Here I cannot sleep at night, because I have been able to do so little in the day. Constantly I try to calm my mind into content with small achievements, but it is difficult. You will say, it is not so mightily worth knowing, after all, this picture and natural history of Europe. Very true; but I am so constituted that it pains me to come away, having touched only the glass over the picture.

I am assiduous daily at the Academy lectures, picture galleries, Chamber of Deputies, — last week, at the court and court ball. So far as my previous preparation enabled me, I get something from all these brilliant shows,—thoughts, images, fresh impulse. But I need, to initiate me into various little secrets of the place and time,—necessary for me to look at things to my satisfaction,—some friend, such as I do not find here. My steps have not been fortunate in Paris, as they were in England. No doubt, the person exists here, whose aid I want; indeed, I feel that it is so; but we do not meet, and the time draws near for me to depart.

French people I find slippery, as they do not know

exactly what to make of me, the rather as I have not the command of their language. *I* see *them*, their brilliancy, grace, and variety, the thousand slight refinements of their speech and manner, but cannot meet them in their way. My French teacher says, I speak and act like an Italian, and I hope, in Italy, I shall find myself more at home.

I had, the other day, the luck to be introduced to Béranger, who is the only person beside George Sand I cared very particularly to see here. I went to call on La Mennais, to whom I had a letter. I found him in a little study; his secretary was writing in a large room through which I passed. With him was a somewhat citizen-looking, but vivacious elderly man, whom I was, at first, sorry to see, having wished for half an hour's undisturbed visit to the Apostle of Democracy. But those feelings were quickly displaced by joy, when he named to me the great national lyrist of France, the great Béranger. I had not expected to see him at all, for he is not to be seen in any show place; he lives in the hearts of the people, and needs no homage from their eyes. I was very happy, in that little study, in the presence of these two men, whose influence has been so real and so great. Béranger has been much to me, — his wit, his pathos, and exquisite lyric grace. I have not received influence from La Mennais, but I see well what he has been, and is, to Europe.

TO LA MENNAIS.

Monsieur : —

As my visit to you was cut short before I was quite satisfied, it was my intention to seek you again immediately; although I felt some scruples at occupying your valuable time, when I express myself so imperfectly in your language. But I have been almost constantly ill since, and now am not sure of finding time to pay you my respects before leaving Paris for Italy. In case this should be impossible, I take the liberty to write, and to present you two little volumes of mine. It is only as a tribute of respect. I regret that they do not contain some pieces of mine which might be more interesting to you, as illustrative of the state of affairs in our country. Some such will find their place in subsequent numbers. These, I hope, you will, if you do not read them, accept kindly as a salutation from our hemisphere. Many there delight to know you as a great apostle of the ideas which are to be our life, if Heaven intends us a great and permanent life. I count myself happy in having seen you, and in finding with you Béranger, the genuine poet, the genuine man of France. I have felt all the enchantment of the lyre of Béranger; have paid my warmest homage to the truth and wisdom adorned with such charms, such wit and pathos. It was a great pleasure to see himself. If your leisure permits, Monsieur, I will ask a few lines in reply. I should like to keep some words from your hand, in case I should not look upon you more here below; and am always, with gratitude for the light you have shed on so many darkened spirits,

Yours, most respectfully,

MARGARET FULLER.

Paris, Jan., 1847. — I missed hearing M. Guizot, (I am sorry for it,) in his speech on the Montpensier marriage. I saw the little Duchess, the innocent or ignorant topic of all this disturbance, when presented at court. She went round the circle on the arm of the queen. Though only fourteen, she looks twenty, but has something fresh, engaging, and girlish about her.

I attended not only at the presentation, but at the ball given at the Tuileries directly after. These are fine shows, as the suite of apartments is very handsome, brilliantly lighted, — the French ladies surpassing all others in the art of dress; indeed, it gave me much pleasure to see them. Certainly there are many ugly ones; but they are so well dressed, and have such an air of graceful vivacity, that the general effect was of a flower-garden. As often happens, several American women were among the most distinguished for positive beauty; one from Philadelphia, who is by many persons considered the prettiest ornament of the dress circle at the Italian opera, was especially marked by the attention of the king. However, these ladies, even if here a long time, do not attain the air and manner of French women. The magnetic fluid that envelops them is less brilliant and exhilarating in its attractions.

Among the crowd wandered Leverrier, in the costume of Academician, looking as if he had lost, not found, his planet. French *savants* are more generally men of the world, and even men of fashion, than those of other climates; but, in his case, he seemed not to find it easy to exchange the music of the spheres for the music of fiddles.

Speaking of Leverrier leads to another of my disappointments. I went to the Sorbonne to hear him lecture, not dreaming that the old pedantic and theological character of those halls was strictly kept up in these days of light. An old guardian of the inner temple seeing me approach, had his speech all ready, and, manning the entrance, said, with a disdainful air, before we had time to utter a word, "Monsieur may enter if he pleases, but madame must remain here" (*i. e.*, in the court-yard). After some exclamations of surprise, I found an alternative in the Hotel de Clugny, where I passed an hour very delightfully, while waiting for my companion.

I was more fortunate in hearing Arago, and he justified all my expectations. Clear, rapid, full, and equal, his discourse is worthy its celebrity, and I felt repaid for the four hours one is obliged to spend in going, in waiting, and in hearing, for the lecture begins at half past one, and you must be there before twelve to get a seat, so constant and animated is his popularity.

I was present on one good occasion, at the Academy,— the day that M. Rémusat was received there, in the place of Royer Collard. I looked down, from one of the tribunes, upon the flower of the celebrities of France; that is to say, of the celebrities which are authentic, *comme il faut*. Among them were many marked faces, many fine heads; but, in reading the works of poets, we always fancy them about the age of Apollo himself, and I found with pain some of my favorites quite old, and very unlike the company on Parnassus, as represented by Raphael. Some, however, were venerable, even noble to behold.

The poorer classes have suffered from hunger this winter. All signs of this are kept out of sight in Paris. A pamphlet called "The Voice of Famine," stating facts, though in a tone of vulgar and exaggerated declamation, was suppressed as soon as published. While Louis Philippe lives, the gases may not burst up

to flame, but the need of radical measures of reform is
strongly felt in France; and the time will come, before
long, when such will be imperatively demanded.

FOURIER.

The doctrines of Fourier are making progress, and
wherever they spread, the necessity of some practical
application of the precepts of Christ, in lieu of the
mummeries of a worn-out ritual, cannot fail to be felt.
The more I see of the terrible ills which infest the body
politic of Europe, the more indignation I feel at the selfishness or stupidity of those in my own country who
oppose an examination of these subjects, — such as is
animated by the hope of prevention.   Educated in an
age of gross materialism, Fourier is tainted by its faults;
in attempts to reörganize society, he commits the error
of making soul the result of health of body, instead of
body the clothing of soul; but his heart was that of a
genuine lover of his kind, of a philanthropist in the
sense of Jesus; his views are large and noble; his life
was one of devout study on these subjects, and I should
pity the person who, after the briefest sojourn in Manchester and Lyons, the most superficial acquaintance
with the population of London and Paris, could seek
to hinder a study of his thoughts, or be wanting in
reverence for his purposes.

ROUSSEAU.

To the actually so-called Chamber of Deputies, I was
indebted for a sight of the manuscripts of Rousseau
treasured in their library.   I saw them and touch ed

them, — those manuscripts just as he has celebrated them, written on the fine white paper, tied with ribbon. Yellow and faded age has made them, yet at their touch I seemed to feel the fire of youth, immortally glowing, more and more expansive, with which his soul has pervaded this century. He was the precursor of all we most prize. True, his blood was mixed with madness, and the course of his actual life made some *detours* through villanous places; but his spirit was intimate with the fundamental truths of human nature, and fraught with prophecy. There is none who has given birth to more life for this age; his gifts are yet untold; they are too present with us; but he who thinks really must often think with Rousseau, and learn him ever more and more. Such is the method of genius, — to ripen fruit for the crowd by those rays of whose heat they complain.

TO R. W. E.

Naples, March 15, 1847. — Mickiewicz, the Polish poet, first introduced the Essays to acquaintance in Paris. I did not meet him anywhere, and, as I heard a great deal of him which charmed me, I sent him your poems, and asked him to come and see me. He came, and I found in him the man I had long wished to see, with the intellect and passions in due proportion for a full and healthy human being, with a soul constantly inspiring. Unhappily, it was a very short time before I came away. How much time had I wasted on others which I might have given to this real and important relation.

After hearing music from Chopin and Neukomm, I quitted Paris on the 25th February, and came, *via*

Chalons, Lyons, Avignon, (where I waded through melting snow to Laura's tomb,) Arles, to Marseilles; thence, by steamer, to Genoa, Leghorn, and Pisa. Seen through a cutting wind, the marble palaces, the gardens, the magnificent water-view of Genoa, failed to charm. Only at Naples have I found *my* Italy. Between Leghorn and Naples, our boat was run into by another, and we only just escaped being drowned.

ROME.

Rome, May, 1847. — Of the fragments of the great time, I have now seen nearly all that are treasured up here. I have as yet nothing of consequence to say of them. Others have often given good hints as to how they *look*. As to what they *are*, it can only be known by approximating to the state of soul out of which they grew. They are many and precious; yet is there not so much of high excellence as I looked for. They wil' not float the heart on a boundless sea of feeling, like the starry night on our Western Prairies. Yet I love much to see the galleries of marbles, even where there are not many separately admirable, amid the cypresses and ilexes of Roman villas; and a picture that is good at all, looks best in one of these old palaces. I have heard owls hoot in the Colosseum by moonlight, and they spoke more to the purpose than I ever heard any other voice on that subject. I have seen all the pomps of Holy Week in St. Peter's, and found them less imposing than an habitual acquaintance with the church itself, with processions of monks and nuns stealing in, now and then, or the swell of vespers from some side chapel. The ceremonies of the church have been numerous and splendid, during our stay, and they borrow unusual interest from the love and expectation inspired by the present pontiff. He is a man of noble and good aspect, who has set his heart on doing something solid for the benefit of man. A week or two ago, the Cardinal Secretary published a circular, inviting the departments to measures which would give the people a sort of representative council. Nothing could seem more limited than this improvement, but it was a great measure for Rome. At night, the Corso was illuminated, and many thousands passed through it in a torch-bearing procession, on their way to the Quirinal, to thank the Pope, upbearing a banner on which the edict was printed.

TO W. H. C.

Rome, May 7, 1847. — I write not to you about these countries, of the famous people I see, of magnificent shows and places. All these things are only to me• an illuminated margin on the text of my inward life. Earlier, they would have been more. Art is not important to me now. I like only what little I find that is transcendantly good, and even with that feel very familiar and calm. I take interest in the state of the people, their manners, the state of the race in them. I see the future dawning; it is in important aspects Fourier's future. But I like no Fourierites; they are terribly wearisome here in Europe; the tide of things does not wash through them as violently as with us, and they have time to run in the tread-mill of system. Still, they serve this great future which I shall not live to see I must be born again.

VOL. II.

Florence, June 20, 1847. — I have just come hithei from Rome. Every minute, day and night, there is something to be seen or done at Rome, which we cannot bear to lose. We lived on the Corso, and all night long, after the weather became fine, there was conversation or music before my window. I never seemed really to sleep while there, and now, at Florence, where there is less to excite, and I live in a more quiet quarter, I feel as if I needed to sleep all the time, and cannot rest as I ought, there is so much to do.

I now speak French fluently, though not correctly, yet well enough to make my thoughts avail in the cultivated society here, where it is much spoken. But to know the common people, and to feel truly in Italy, I ought to speak and understand the spoken Italian well, and I am now cultivating this sedulously. If I remain, I shall have, for many reasons, advantages for observation and enjoyment, such as are seldom permitted to a foreigner.

I forgot to mention one little thing rather interesting. At the *Miserere* of the Sistine chapel, I sat beside Goethe's favorite daughter-in-law, Ottilia, to whom I was introduced by Mrs. Jameson.

Florence, July 1, 1847. — I do not wish to go through Germany in a hurried way, and am equally unsatisfied to fly through Italy; and shall, therefore, leaving my companions in Switzerland, take a servant to accompany me, and return hither, and hence to Rome for the autumn, perhaps the winter. I should always suffer the pain of Tantalus thinking of Rome, if I could not see it more thoroughly than I have as yet even begun to; for it was all *outside* the two months, just finding out where objects were. I had only just begun to know them, when I was obliged to leave. The prospect of returning presents many charms, but it leaves me alone in the midst of a strange land.

I find myself happily situated here, in many respects. The Marchioness Arconati Visconti, to whom I brought a letter from a friend of hers in France, has been good to me as a sister, and introduced me to many interesting acquaintance. The sculptors, Powers and Greenough, I have seen much and well. Other acquaintance I possess, less known to fame, but not less attractive.

Florence is not like Rome. At first, I could not bear the change; yet, for the study of the fine arts, it is a still richer place. Worlds of thought have risen in my mind; some time you will have light from all.

Milan, Aug. 9, 1847. — Passing from Florence, I came to Bologna. A woman should love Bologna, for there has the intellect of woman been cherished. In their Certosa, they proudly show the monument to Matilda Tambreni, late Greek professor there. In their anatomical hall, is the bust of a woman, professor of anatomy. In art, they have had Properzia di Rossi, Elisabetta Sirani, Lavinia Fontana, and delight to give their works a conspicuous place. In other cities, the men alone have their Casino dei Nobili, where they give balls and conversazioni. Here, women have one, and are the soul

of society.   In Milan, also, I see, in the Ambrosian
Library, the bust of a female mathematician.

Lago di Garda, Aug. 1, 1847. — Do not let what I
have written disturb you as to my health.   I have
rested now, and am as well as usual.   This advantage
I derive from being alone, that, if I feel the need of it, I
can stop.

I left Venice four days ago; have seen well Vicenza,
Verona, Mantua, and am reposing, for two nights and a
day, in this tranquil room which overlooks the beautiful
Lake of Garda.   The air is sweet and pure, and I hear
no noise except the waves breaking on the shore.

I think of you a great deal, especially when there are
flowers.   Florence was all flowers.   I have many mag-
nolias and jasmines.   I always wish you could see them.
The other day, on the island of San Lazaro, at the
Armenian Convent, where Lord Byron used to go, I
thought of you, seeing the garden full of immense
oleanders in full bloom.   One sees them everywhere at
Venice.

TO HER TRAVELLING COMPANIONS AFTER PARTING.

Milan, Aug. 9, 1847. — I remained at Venice near a
week after your departure, to get strong and tranquil
again.   Saw all the pictures, if not enough, yet pretty
well.   My journey here was very profitable.   Vicenza,
Verona, Mantua, I saw really well, and much there is
to see.   Certainly I had learned more than ever in any
previous ten days of my existence and have formed an

idea of what is needed for the study of art in these regions. But, at Brescia, I was taken ill with fever. I cannot tell you how much I was alarmed when it seemed to me it was affecting my head. I had no medicine; nothing could I do except abstain entirely from food, and drink cold water. The second day, I had a bed made in a carriage, and came on here. I am now pretty well, only very weak.

TO R. W. E.

Milan, Aug. 10, 1847. — Since writing you from Florence, I have passed the mountains; two full, rich days at Bologna; one at Ravenna; more than a fort night at Venice, intoxicated with the place, and with Venetian art, only to be really felt and known in its birth-place. I have passed some hours at Vicenza, seeing mainly the Palladian structures; a day at Verona,— a week had been better; seen Mantua, with great delight; several days in Lago di Garda, — truly happy days there; then, to Brescia, where I saw the Titians, the exquisite Raphael, the Scavi, and the Brescian Hills. I could charm you by pictures, had I time.

To-day, for the first time, I have seen Manzoni. Manzoni has spiritual efficacy in his looks; his eyes glow still with delicate tenderness, as when he first saw Lucia, or felt them fill at the image of Father Cristoforo. His manners are very engaging, frank, expansive; every word betokens the habitual elevation of his thoughts; and (what you care for so much) he says distinct, good things; but you must not expect me to note them down. He lives in the house of his fathers, in the simplest manner. He has taken the liberty to

marry a new wife for his own pleasure and companionship, and the people around him do not 'like it, because
she does not, to their fancy, make a good pendant to
him. But I liked her very well, and saw why he married her. They asked me to return often, if I pleased,
and I mean to go once or twice, for Manzoni seems to
like to talk with me.

Rome, Oct., 1847. — Leaving Milan, I went on the
Lago Maggiore, and afterward into Switzerland. Of
this tour I shall not speak here; it was a little romance
by itself.

Returning from Switzerland, I passed a fortnight on
the Lake of Como, and afterward visited Lugano.
There is no exaggeration in the enthusiastic feeling
with which artists and poets have viewed these Italian
lakes. The "*Titan*" of Richter, the "*Wanderjahre*"
of Goethe, the Elena of Taylor, the pictures of Turner,
had not prepared me for the visions of beauty that daily
entranced the eyes and heart in those regions. To our
country, Nature has been most bounteous, but we have
nothing in the same class that can compare with these
lakes, as seen under the Italian heaven. As to those
persons who have pretended to discover that the effects
of light and atmosphere were no finer than they found
in our own lake scenery, I can only say that they must
be exceedingly obtuse in organization, — a defect not
uncommon among Americans.

Nature seems to have labored to express her full heart
in as many ways as possible, when she made these
lakes, moulded and planted their shores. Lago Maggiore
is grandiose, resplendent in its beauty; the view of the
Alps gives a sort of lyric exaltation to the scene. Lago

di Garda is so soft and fair on one side, — the ruins of
ancient palaces rise softly with the beauties of that
shore; but at the other end, amid the Tyrol, it is so
sublime, so calm, so concentrated in its meaning!
Como cannot be better described in generals than in the
words of Taylor : —

"Softly sublime, profusely fair"

Lugano is more savage, more free in its beauty. I
was on it in a high gale; there was little danger, just
enough to exhilarate; its waters wild, and clouds blowing across its peaks. I like the boatmen on these
lakes; they have strong and prompt character; of
simple features, they are more honest and manly than
Italian men are found in the thoroughfares; their talk
is not so witty as that of the Venetian gondoliers,
but picturesque, and what the French call *incisive*.
Very touching were some of their histories, as they
told them to me, while pausing sometimes on the
lake. Grossi gives a true picture of such a man in
his family relations; the story may be found in "Marco
Visconti."

On this lake, I met Lady Franklin, wife of the
celebrated navigator. She has been in the United
States, and showed equal penetration and candor in
remarks on what she had seen there. She gave me
interesting particulars as to the state of things in Van
Diemen's Land, where she passed seven years, when
her husband was in authority there.

TO C. S.

Lake of Como, Aug. 22, 1847. — Rome was much poisoned to me. But, after a time, its genius triumphed, and I became absorbed in its proper life. Again I suffered from parting, and have since resolved to return, and pass at least a part of the winter there. People may write and prate as they please of Rome, they cannot convey thus a portion of its spirit. The whole heart must be yielded up to it. It is something really transcendent, both spirit and body. Those last glorious nights, in which I wandered about amid the old walls and columns, or sat by the fountains in the Piazza del' Popolo, or by the river, were worth an age of pain, — only one hates pain in Italy.

Tuscany I did not like as well. It is a great place to study the history of character and art. Indeed, there I did really begin to study, as well as gaze and feel. But I did not like it. Florence is more in its spirit like Boston, than like an Italian city. I knew a good many Italians, but they were busy and intellectual, not like those I had known before. But Florence is full of really good, great pictures. There first I saw some of the great masters. Andrea del Sarto, in particular, one sees only there, and he is worth much. His wife, whom he always paints, and for whom he was so infatuated, has some bad qualities, and in what is good a certain wild nature or *diablerie.*

Bologna is truly an Italian city, one in which I should like to live; full of hidden things, and its wonders of art are very grand. The Caracci and their friends had vast force; **not** much depth, but enough force to occupy one a good while, — and Domenichino, when good at all, is very great.

Venice was a dream of enchantment; *there* was no disappointment. Art and life are one. There is one glow of joy, one deep shade of passionate melancholy; Giorgione, as a man, I care more for now than any of the artists, though he had no ideas.

In the first week, floating about in a gondola, I seemed to find myself again.

I was not always alone in Venice, but have come through the fertile plains of Lombardy, seen the lakes Garda and Maggiore, and a part of Switzerland, alone, except for occasional episodes of companionship, sometimes romantic enough.

In Milan I stayed a while, and knew some radicals, young, and interested in ideas. Here, on the lake, I have fallen into contact with some of the higher society, — duchesses, marquises, and the like. My friend here is Madame Arconati, Marchioness Visconti. I have formed connection with a fair and brilliant Polish lady, born Princess Radzivill. It is rather pleasant to come a little on the traces of these famous histories; also, both these ladies take pleasure in telling me of spheres so unlike mine, and do it well.

The life here on the lake is precisely what we once imagined as being so pleasant. These people have charming villas and gardens on the lake, adorned with fine works of art. They go to see one another in boats. You can be all the time in a boat, if you like; if you want more excitement, or wild flowers, you climb the mountains. I have been here for some time, and shall stay a week longer. I have found soft repose here.

Now, I am to return to Rome, seeing many things **by** the way.

Florence, Sept. 25, 1847.— I hope not to want a further remittance for a long time.   I shall not, if I can settle myself at Rome so as to avoid spoliation.   That is very difficult in this country.   I have suffered from it already. The haste, the fatigue, the frequent illness in travelling, have tormented me.   At Rome I shall settle myself for five months, and make arrangements to the best of my judgment, and with counsel of experienced friends, and have some hope of economy while there; but am not sure, as much more vigilance than I can promise is needed against the treachery of servants and the cunning of landlords.

You are disappointed by my letter from Rome.   But 1 did not feel equal then to speaking of the things of Rome, and shall not, till better acquaintance has steadied my mind.   It is a matter of conscience with me not to make use of crude impressions, and what they call here "coffee-house intelligence," as travellers generally do.   I prefer skimming over the surface of things, till I feel solidly ready to write.

Milan I left with great regret, and hope to return.   I knew there a circle of the aspiring youth, such as I have not in any other city.   I formed many friendships, and learned a great deal.   One of the young men, Guerrieri by name, (and of the famous Gonzaga family,) I really love.   He has a noble soul, the quietest sensibility, and a brilliant and ardent, though not a great, mind.   He is eight-and-twenty.   After studying medicine for the culture, he has taken law as his profession.   His mind and that of Hicks, an artist of our country now here, a little younger, are two that would interest you greatly. Guerrieri speaks no English; I speak French now as fluently as English, but incorrectly. To make use of it, I ought to have learned it earlier.

Arriving here, Mr. Mozier, an American, who from a prosperous merchant has turned sculptor, come hither to live, and promises much excellence in his profession, urged me so much to his house, that I came. At first, I was ill from fatigue, and staid several days in bed; but his wife took tender care of me, and the quiet of their house and regular simple diet have restored me. As soon as I have seen a few things here, I shall go to Rome. On my way, I stopped at Parma, — saw the works of Correggio and Parmegiano. I have now seen what Italy contains most important of the great past; I begin to hope for her also a great future, — the signs have improved so much since I came. I am most fortunate to be here at this time.

Interrupted, as always. How happy I should be if my abode at Rome would allow some chance for tranquil and continuous effort. But I dare not hope much, from the difficulty of making any domestic arrangements that can be relied on. The fruit of the moment is so precious, that I must not complain. I learn much; but to do anything with what I learn is, under such circumstances, impossible. Besides, I am in great need of repose; I am almost inert from fatigue of body and spirit.

TO E. H.

Florence, Sept., 1847. — I cannot even begin to speak of the magnificent scenes of nature, nor the works of art, that

have raised and filled my mind since I wrote from Naples. Now I begin to be in Italy! but I wish to drink
deep of this cup before I speak my enamored words.
Enough to say, Italy receives me as a long-lost child,
and I feel myself at home here, and if I ever tell anything about it, you will hear something real and domestic.

Among strangers I wish most to speak to you of my
friend the Marchioness A. Visconti, a Milanese. She is a
specimen of the really high-bred lady, such as I have
not known. Without any physical beauty, the grace
and harmony of her manners produce all the impression
of beauty. She has also a mind strong, clear, precise,
and much cultivated. She has a modest nobleness that
you would dearly love. She is intimate with many of
the first men. She seems to love me much, and to wish
I should have whatever is hers. I take great pleasure
in her friendship.

TO R. W. E.

Rome, Oct. 28, 1847. — I am happily settled for the
winter, quite by myself, in a neat, tranquil apartment in
the Corso, where I see all the motions of Rome, — in a
house of loving Italians, who treat me well, and do not
interrupt me, except for service. I live alone, eat alone,
walk alone, and enjoy unspeakably the stillness, after all
the rush and excitement of the past year.

I shall make no acquaintance from whom I do not
hope a good deal, as my time will be like pure gold to
me this winter; and, just for happiness, Rome itself is
sufficient.

To-day is the last of the October feasts of the Trasteverini. I have been, this afternoon, to see them dancing.

This morning I was out, with half Rome, to see the Civic Guard manœuvring in that great field near the tomb of Cecilia Metella, which is full of ruins. The effect was noble, as the band played the Bolognese march, and six thousand Romans passed in battle array amid these fragments of the great time.

TO R. F. F

Rome, Oct. 29, 1847.— I am trying to economize, — anxious to keep the Roman expenses for six months within the limits of four hundred dollars. Rome is not as cheap a place as Florence, but then I would not give a pin to live in Florence.

We have just had glorious times with the October feasts, when all the Roman people were out. I am now truly happy here, quiet and familiar; no longer a staring, sight-seeing stranger, riding about finely dressed in a coach to see muses and sibyls. I see these forms now in the natural manner, and am contented.

Keep free from false ties; they are the curse of life. I find myself so happy here, alone and free.

TO M. S.

Rome, Oct. 1847.— I arrived in Rome again nearly a fortnight ago, and all mean things were forgotten in the joy that rushed over me like a flood. Now I saw the true Rome. I came with no false expectations, and I came to live in tranquil companionship, not in the restless impertinence of sight-seeing, so much more painful here than anywhere else.

I had made a good visit to Vicenza; a truly Italiar

town, with much to see and study. But all other places
faded away, now that I again saw St. Peter's, and heard
the music of the fountains.

The Italian autumn is not as beautiful as I expected,
neither in the vintage of Tuscany nor here. The
country is really sere and brown; but the weather is
fine, and these October feasts are charming. Two days
I have been at the Villa Borghese. There are races, bal-
loons, and, above all, the private gardens open, and good
music on the little lake.

TO ———.

Rome, morning of the 17*th Nov.,* 1847.— It seems great
folly to send the enclosed letter. I have written it in my
nightly fever. All day I dissipate my thoughts on outward beauty. I have many thoughts, happiest moments,
but as yet I do not have even this part in a congenial
way. I go about in a coach with several people; but
English and Americans are not at home here. Since I
have experienced the different atmosphere of the European mind, and been allied with it, nay, mingled in the
bonds of love, I suffer more than ever from that which
is peculiarly American or English. I should like to
cease from hearing the language for a time. Perhaps
I should return to it; but at present I am in a state of
unnatural divorce from what I was most allied to.

There is a Polish countess here, who likes me much.
She has been very handsome, still is, in the style of the
full-blown rose. She is a widow, very rich, one of the
emancipated women, naturally vivacious, and with talent. This woman *envies me ;* she says, " How happy
you are; so free, so serene, so attractive, so self-pos-

sessed!" I say not a word, but I do not look on myself as particularly enviable. A little money would have made me much more so; a little money would have enabled me to come here long ago, and find those that belong to me, or at least try my experiments; then my health would never have sunk, nor the best years of my life been wasted in useless friction. Had I money now, — could I only remain, take a faithful servant, and live alone, and still see those I love when it is best, that would suit me. It seems to me, very soon I shall be calmed, and begin to enjoy.

TO HER MOTHER.

Rome, Dec. 16, 1847. — My life at Rome is thus far all I hoped. I have not been so well since I was a child, nor so happy ever, as during the last six weeks. I wrote you about my home; it continues good, perfectly clean, food wholesome, service exact. For all this I pay, but not immoderately. I think the sum total of my expenses here, for six months, will not exceed four hundred and fifty dollars.

My *marchesa*, of whom I rent my rooms, is the greatest liar I ever knew, and the most interested, heartless creature. But she thinks it for her interest to please me, as she sees I have a good many persons who value me; and I have been able, without offending her, to make it understood that I do not wish her society. Thus I remain undisturbed.

Every Monday evening, I receive my acquaintance. I give no refreshment, but only light the saloon, and decorate it with fresh flowers, of which I have plenty still. How I wish *you* could see them!

Among the frequent guests are known to you Mr. and Mrs. Cranch, Mr. and Mrs. Story. Mr. S. has finally given up law, for the artist's life. His plans are not matured, but he passes the winter at Rome.

On other evenings, I do not receive company, unless by appointment. I spend them chiefly in writing or study. I have now around me the books I need to know Italy and Rome. I study with delight, now that I can verify everything. The days are invariably fine, and each day I am out from eleven till five, exploring some new object of interest, often at a great distance.

TO R. W. E.

Rome, Dec. 20, 1847. — Nothing less than two or three years, free from care and forced labor, would heal all my hurts, and renew my life-blood at its source. Since Destiny will not grant me that, I hope she will not leave me long in the world, for I am tired of keeping myself up in the water without corks, and without strength to swim. I should like to go to sleep, and be born again into a state where my young life should not be prematurely taxed.

Italy has been glorious to me, and there have been hours in which I received the full benefit of the vision. In Rome, I have known some blessed, quiet days, when I could yield myself to be soothed and instructed by the great thoughts and memories of the place. But those days are swiftly passing. Soon I must begin to exert myself, for there is this incubus of the future, and none to help me, if I am not prudent to face it. So ridiculous, too, this mortal coil, — such small things!

I find how true was the lure that always drew me

towards Europe. It was no false instinct that said I might here find an atmosphere to develop me in ways I need. Had I only come ten years earlier! Now my life must be a failure, so much strength has been wasted on abstractions, which only came because I grew not in the right soil. However, it is a less failure than with most others, and not worth thinking twice about. Heaven has room enough, and good chances in store, and I can live a great deal in the years that remain.

TO R. W. E.

Rome, Dec. 20, 1847. — I don't know whether you take an interest in the present state of things in Italy, but you would if you were here. It is a fine time to see the people. As to the Pope, it is as difficult here as elsewhere to put new wine into old bottles, and there is something false as well as ludicrous in the spectacle of the people first driving their princes to do a little justice, and then *evviva*-ing them at such a rate. This does not apply to the Pope; he is a real great heart, a generous man. The love for him is genuine, and I like to be within its influence. It was his heart that gave the impulse, and this people has shown, to the shame of English and other prejudice, how unspoiled they were at the core, how open, nay, how wondrous swift to answer a generous appeal!

They are also gaining some education by the present freedom of the press and of discussion. I should like to write a letter for England, giving my view of the present position of things here.

Rome, October 18, 1847.— In the spring, when I came to Rome, the people were in the intoxication of joy at the first serious measures of reform taken by the Pope. I saw with pleasure their childlike joy and trust. Still doubts were always present whether this joy was not premature. From the people themselves the help must come, and not from the princes. Rome, to resume her glory, must cease to be an ecclesiastical capital. Whilst I sympathized with the warm love of the people, the adulation of leading writers, who were willing to take all from the prince of the Church as a gift and a bounty, instead of steadily implying that it was the right of the people, was very repulsive to me. Passing into Tuscany, I found the liberty of the press just established. The Grand Duke, a well-intentioned, though dull, man, had dared to declare himself an Italian prince. I arrived in Florence too late for the great fête of the 12th September, in honor of the grant of the National Guard, but the day was made memorable by the most generous feeling on all sides. Some days before were passed by reconciling all strifes, composing all differences between cities, districts, and individuals. On that day they all embraced in sign of this; exchanged banners as a token that they would fight for one another.

AMERICANS IN ITALY.

The Americans took their share in this occasion, and Greenough, — one of the few Americans who, living in Italy, takes the pains to know whether it is alive or dead, who penetrates beyond the cheats of tradesmen and the cunning of a mob corrupted by centuries of slavery, to know the real mind, the vital blood of Italy, — took a leading part. I am sorry to say that a large portion of my countrymen here take the same slothful and prejudiced view as the English, and, after many years' sojourn, betray entire ignorance of Italian literature and Italian life beyond what is attainable in a month's passage through the thoroughfares. However, they did show, this time, a becoming spirit, and erected the American Eagle where its cry ought to be heard from afar. Crawford, here in Rome, has had the just feeling to join the Guard, and it is a real sacrifice for an artist to spend time on the exercises; but it well becomes the sculptor of Orpheus. In reference to what I have said of many Americans in Italy, I will only add that they talk about the corrupt and degenerate state of Italy as they do about that of our slaves at home. They come ready trained to that mode of reasoning which affirms, that, because men are degraded by bad institutions, they are not fit for better.

I will only add some words upon the happy augury I draw from the wise docility of the people. With what readiness they listened to wise counsel and the hopes of the Pope that they would give no advantage to his enemies at a time when they were so fevered by the knowledge that conspiracy was at work in their midst! That was a time of trial. On all these occasions of popular excitement their conduct is like music, in such order, and with such union of the melody of feeling with discretion where to stop; but what is wonderful is that they acted in the same manner on that difficult occasion. The influence of the Pope here is without bounds; he can always calm the crowd at once. But in Tuscany, where they have no such one idol, they listened in the same way on a very trying occasion. The first announcement of the regulation for the Tuscan National Guard terribly disappointed the people. They felt that the Grand Duke, after suffering them to demonstrate such trust and joy on this feast of the 12th, did not really trust, on his side; that he meant to limit them all he could; they felt baffled, cheated; hence young men in anger tore down at once the symbols of satisfaction and respect; but the leading men went among the people, begged them to be calm, and wait till a deputation had seen the Grand Duke. The people listened at once to men who, they were sure, had at heart their best good — waited; the Grand Duke became convinced, and all ended without disturbance. If the people continue to act thus, their hopes cannot be baffled.

The American in Europe would fain encourage the hearts of these long-oppressed nations, now daring to hope for a new era, by reciting triumphant testimony from the experience of his own country. But we must stammer and blush when we speak of many things. I take pride here, that I may really say the liberty of the press works well, and that checks and balances naturally evolve from it, which suffice to its government. I may say, that the minds of our people are alert, and that talent has a free chance to rise. It is much. But dare I say, that political ambition is not as darkly sullied as in other countries? Dare I say, that men of most influence in political life are those who represent most virtue, or even intellectual power? Can I say, our social laws are generally better, or show a nobler insight into the wants of man and woman? I do indeed say what I believe, that voluntary association for improvement in these particulars will be the grand means for my nation to grow, and give a nobler harmony to the coming age. Then there is this cancer of slavery, and this wicked war that has grown out of it. How dare I speak of these things here? I listen to the same arguments against the emancipation of Italy, that are used against the emancipation of our blacks; the same arguments in favor of the spoliation of Poland, as for the conquest of Mexico.

How it pleases me here to think of the Abolitionists! I could never endure to be with them at home; they were so tedious, often so narrow, always so rabid and exaggerated in their tone. But, after all, they had a high motive, something eternal in their desire and life; and, if it was not the only thing worth thinking of, it was really something worth living and dying for, to free a great nation from such a blot, such a plague. God strengthen them, and make them wise to achieve their purpose!

I please myself, too, with remembering some ardent souls among the American youth, who, I trust, will yet expand and help to give soul to the huge, over-fed, too-hastily-grown-up body. May they be constant! "Were man but constant, he were perfect." It is to the youth that Hope addresses itself. But I dare not expect too much of them. I am not very old; yet of those who, in life's morning, I saw touched by the light of a high hope, many have seceded. Some have become voluptuaries; some mere family men, who think it is quite life enough to win bread for half a dozen people, and treat them decently; others are lost through indolence and vacillation. Yet some remain constant.

"I have witnessed many a shipwreck, yet still beat noble hearts.'
VOL. II.

Rome, January, 1848. — As one becomes domesticated here, ancient and modern Rome, at first so jumbled together, begin to separate. You see where objects and limits anciently were. When this happens, one feels first truly at ease in Rome. Then the old kings, the consuls, the tribunes, the emperors, the warriors of eagle sight and remorseless beak, return for us, and the toga-clad procession finds room to sweep across the scene; the seven hills tower, the innumerable temples glitter, and the Via Sacra swarms with triumphal life once more.

Rome, Jan. 12, 1848. — In Rome, here, the new Council is inaugurated, and the elections have given tolerable satisfaction. Twenty-four carriages had been lent by the princes and nobles, at the request of the city, to convey the councillors. Each deputy was followed by his target and banner. In the evening, there was a ball given at the Argentine. Lord Minto was there, Prince Corsini, now senator, the Torlonias, in uniform of the Civic Guard, Princess Torlonia, in a sash of their colors given her by the Civic Guard, which she waved in answer to their greetings. But the beautiful show of the evening was the *Trasteverini* dancing the *Saltarello* in their most beautiful costume. I saw them thus to much greater advantage than ever before. Several were nobly handsome, and danced admirably. The *saltarello* enchants me; in this is really the Italian wine, the Italian sun.

The Pope, in receiving the councillors, made a speech, intimating that he meant only to improve, not to *reform*, and should keep things safe locked with the keys of St Peter.

I was happy the first two months of my stay here, seeing all the great things at my leisure. But now, after a month of continuous rain, Rome is no more Rome. The atmosphere is far worse than that of Paris. It is impossible to walk in the thick mud. The ruins, and other great objects, always solemn, appear terribly gloomy, steeped in black rain and cloud; and my apartment, in a street of high houses, is dark all day. The bad weather may continue all this month and all next. If I could use the time for work, I should not care; but this climate makes me so ill, I can do but little.

TO C. S.

Rome, Jan. 12, 1848. — My time in Lombardy and Switzerland was a series of beautiful pictures, dramatic episodes, not without some original life in myself. When I wrote to you from Como, I had a peaceful season. I floated on the lake with my graceful Polish countess, hearing her stories of heroic sorrow ; or I walked in the delicious gardens of the villas, with many another summer friend. Red banners floated, children sang and shouted, the lakes of Venus and Diana glittered in the sun. The pretty girls of Bellaggio, with their coral necklaces, brought flowers to the " American countess," and " hoped she would be as happy as she deserved." Whether this cautious wish is fulfilled, I know not, but certainly I left all the glitter of life behind at Como.

My days at Milan were not unmarked. I have known some happy hours, but they all lead to sorrow ; and not only the cups of wine, but of milk, seem drugged with poison for me. It does not *seem* to be my fault, this

Destiny; I do not court these things, — they come. I am a poor magnet, with power to be wounded by the bodies I attract.

Leaving Milan, I had a brilliant day in Parma. I had not known Correggio before; he deserves all his fame. I stood in the parlor of the Abbess, the person for whom all was done, and Paradise seemed opened by the nymph, upon her car of light, and the divine children peeping through the vines. Sweet soul of love! I should weary of you, too; but it was glorious that day.

I had another good day, too, crossing the Apennines. The young crescent moon rose in orange twilight, just as I reached the highest peak. I was alone on foot; I heard no sound; I prayed.

At Florence, I was very ill. For three weeks, my life hung upon a thread. The effect of the Italian climate on my health is not favorable. I feel as if I had received a great injury. I am tired and woe-worn; often, in the bed, I wish I could weep my life away. However, they brought me gruel, I took it, and after a while rose up again. In the time of the vintage, I went alone to Sienna. This is a real untouched Italian place. This excursion, and the grapes, restored me at that time.

When I arrived in Rome, I was at first intoxicated to be here. The weather was beautiful, and many circumstances combined to place me in a kind of passive, childlike well-being. That is all over now, and, with this year, I enter upon a sphere of my destiny so difficult, that I, at present, see no way out, except through the gate of death. It is useless to write of it; you are at a distance and cannot help me; — whether accident or angel will, I have no intimation. I have no reason to hope I shall not reap what I have sown, and do not. Yet how I shall endure it I cannot guess; it is all a dark, sad enigma. The beautiful forms of art charm no more, and a love, in which there is all fondness, but no help, flatters in vain. I am all alone; nobody around me sees any of this. My numerous friendly acquaintances are troubled if they see me ill, and who so affectionate and kind as Mr. and Mrs. S.?

TO MADAME ARCONATI.

Rome, Jan. 14, 1848. — What black and foolish calumnies are these on Mazzini! It is as much for his interest as his honor to let things take their course, at present. To expect anything else, is to suppose him base. And on what act of his life dares any one found such an insinuation? I do not wonder that you were annoyed at his manner of addressing the Pope; but to me it seems that he speaks as he should, — near God and beyond the tomb; not from power to power, but from soul to soul, without regard to temporal dignities. It must be admitted that the etiquette, Most Holy Father, &c., jars with this.

TO R. W. E.

Rome, March 14, 1848. — Mickiewicz is with me here, and will remain some time; it was he I wanted to see, more than any other person, in going back to Paris, and I have him much better here. France itself I should like to see, but remain undecided, on account of my health which has suffered so much, this winter, that I must make it the first object in moving for the summer. One

VOL. II.

physician thinks it will of itself revive, when once the rains have passed, which have now lasted from 16th December to this day. At present, I am not able to leave the fire, or exert myself at all.

In all the descriptions of the Roman Carnival, the fact has been omitted of daily rain. I felt, indeed, ashamed to perceive it, when no one else seemed to, whilst the open windows caused me convulsive cough and head-ache. The carriages, with their cargoes of happy women dressed in their ball dresses and costumes, drove up and down, even in the pouring rain. The two hand-some *contadine*, who serve me, took off their woollen gowns, and sat five hours at a time, in the street, in white cambric dresses, and straw hats turned up with roses. I never saw anything like the merry good-humor of these people. I should always be ashamed to com-plain of anything here. But I had always looked forward to the Roman Carnival as a time when I could play too; and it even surpassed my expectations, with its exuberant gayety and innocent frolic, but I was un-able to take much part. The others threw flowers all day, and went to masked balls all night; but I went out only once, in a carriage, and was more exhausted with the storm of flowers and sweet looks than I could be by a storm of hail. I went to the German Artists' ball where were some pretty costumes, and beautiful music; and to the Italian masked ball, where interest lies in intrigue.

I have scarcely gone to the galleries, damp and cold as tombs; or to the mouldy old splendor of churches, where, by the way, they are just wailing over the theft of St.

Andrew's head, for the sake of the jewels. It is quite a new era for this population to plunder the churches; but hey are suffering terribly, and Pio's municipality does, as et, nothing.

Rome, March 29, 1848.—I have been engrossed, stunned almost, by the public events that have succeeded one another with such rapidity and grandeur. It is a time such as I always dreamed of, and for long secretly hoped to see. I rejoice to be in Europe at this time, and shall return possessed of a great history. Perhaps I shall be called to act. At present, I know not where to go, what to do. War is everywhere. I cannot leave Rome, and the men of Rome are marching out every day into Lombardy. The citadel of Milan is in the hands of my friends, Guerriere, &c., but there may be need to spill much blood yet in Italy. France and Germany are not in such a state that I can go there now. A glorious flame burns higher and higher in the heart of the nations.

The rain was constant through the Roman winter, falling in torrents from 16th December to 19th March. Now the Italian heavens wear again their deep blue, the sun is glorious, the melancholy lustres are stealing again over the Campagna, and hundreds of larks sing unwearied above its ruins. Nature seems in sympathy with the great events that are transpiring. How much has happened since I wrote! — the resistance of Sicily, and the revolution of Naples; now the fall cf

Louis Philippe; and Metternich is crushed in Austria. I saw the Austrian arms dragged through the streets here, and burned in the Piazza del Popolo. The Italians embraced one another, and cried, *miracolo, Providenza!* the Tribune Ciceronachio fed the flame with fagots; Adam Mickiewicz, the great poet of Poland, long exiled from his country, looked on; while Polish women brought little pieces that had been scattered in the street, and threw into the flames. When the double-headed eagle was pulled down from the lofty portal of the Palazzo di Venezia, the people placed there, in its stead, one of white and gold, inscribed with the name, ALTA ITALIA; and instantly the news followed, that Milan, Venice, Modena, and Parma, were driving out their tyrants. These news were received in Rome with indescribable rapture. Men danced, and women wept with joy along the street. The youths rushed to enrol themselves in regiments to go to the frontier. In the Colosseum, their names were received.

Rome, April 1, 1848. — Yesterday, on returning from Ostia, I find the official news, that the Viceroy Ranieri has capitulated at Verona; that Italy is free, independent, and one. I trust this will prove no April foolery. It seems too good, too speedy a realization of hope.

Rome, April 30, 1848. — It is a time such as I always dreamed of; and that fire burns in the hearts of men around me which can keep me warm. Have I something to do here? or am I only to cheer on the warriors, and after write the history of their deeds? The first is all I have done yet, but many have blessed me

ROME. **237**

for my sympathy, and blest me by the action it impelled.

My private fortunes are dark and tangled; my strength
to govern them (perhaps that I am enervated by this
climate) much diminished. I have thrown myself on
God, and perhaps he will make my temporal state very
tragical. I am more of a child than ever, and hate
suffering more than ever, but suppose I shall live with it,
if it must come.

I did not get your letter, about having the rosary blessed
for ———, before I left Rome, and now, I suppose, she
would not wish it, as none can now attach any value to
the blessing of Pius IX. Those who loved him can no
longer defend him. It has become obvious, that those
first acts of his in the papacy were merely the result of
a kindly, good-natured temperament; that he had not
thought to understand their bearing, nor force to abide
by it. He seems quite destitute of moral courage. He
is not resolute either on the wrong or right side. First,
he abandoned the liberal party; then, yielding to the
will of the people, and uniting, in appearance, with a
liberal ministry, he let the cardinals betray it, and defeat
the hopes of Italy. He cried peace, peace! but had not a
word of blame for the sanguinary acts of the King of
Naples, a word of sympathy for the victims of Lombardy. Seizing the moment of dejection in the nation,
he put in this retrograde ministry; sanctioned their acts,
daily more impudent; let them neutralize the constitution he himself had given; and when the people slew his
minister, and assaulted him in his own palace, he yielded
anew; he dared not die, or even run the slight risk, —
for only by accident could he have perished. His person as a Pope is still respected, though his character as

a man is despised. All the people compare him with Pius VII. saying to the French, "Slay me if you will; I *cannot* yield," and feel the difference.

I was on Monte Cavallo yesterday. The common people were staring at the broken windows and burnt door of the palace where they have so often gone to receive a blessing, the children playing, "*Sedia Papale. Morte ai Cardinali, e morte al Papa!*"

The men of straw are going down in Italy everywhere; the real men rising into power. Montanelli, Guerazzi, Mazzini, are real men; their influence is of character. Had we only been born a little later! Mazzini has returned from his seventeen years' exile, "to see what he foresaw." He has a mind far in advance of his times, and yet Mazzini sees not all.

Rome, May 7, 1848. — Good and loving hearts will be unprepared, and for a time must suffer much from the final dereliction of Pius IX. to the cause of freedom. After the revolution opened in Lombardy, the troops of the line were sent thither; the volunteers rushed to accompany them, the priests preached the war as a crusade, the Pope blessed the banners. The report that the Austrians had taken and hung as a brigand one of the Roman Civic Guard, — a well-known artist engaged in the war of Lombardy, — roused the people; and they went to the Pope, to demand that he should declare war against the Austrians. The Pope summoned a consistory, and then declared in his speech that he had only intended local reforms; that he regretted the misuse that had been made of his name; and wound up by lamenting the war as offensive to the spirit of religion. A momentary stupefaction, followed by a passion of indignation, in which the words *traitor* and *imbecile* were heard, received this astounding speech. The Pope was besieged with deputations, and, after two days' struggle, was obliged to place the power in the hands of persons most opposed to him, and nominally acquiesce in their proceedings.

TO R. W. E. (*in London*).

Rome, May 19, 1848. — I should like to return with you, but I have much to do and learn in Europe yet. I am deeply interested in this public drama, and wish to see it *played out.* Methinks I have *my part* therein, either as actor or historian.

I cannot marvel at your readiness to close the book of European society. The shifting scenes entertain poorly. The flux of thought and feeling leaves some fertilizing soil; but for me, few indeed are the persons I should wish to see again; nor do I care to push the inquiry further. The simplest and most retired life would now please me, only I would not like to be confined to it, in case I grew weary, and now and then craved variety, for exhilaration. I want some scenes of natural beauty, and, imperfect as love is, I want human beings to love, as I suffocate without. For intellectual stimulus, books would mainly supply it, when wanted.

Why did you not try to be in Paris at the opening of the Assembly? There were elements worth scanning.

TO R. F. F.

Rome, May 20, 1848. — My health is much revived by the spring here, as gloriously beautiful as the winter was dreary. We know nothing of spring in our country. Here the soft and brilliant weather is unbroken, except now and then by a copious shower, which keeps everything fresh. The trees, the flowers, the bird-songs are in perfection. I have enjoyed greatly my walks in the villas, where the grounds are of three or four miles in extent, and like free nature in the wood-glades and still paths; while they have an added charm in the music of their many fountains, and the soft gleam, here and there, of sarcophagus or pillar.

I have been a few days at Albano, and explored its beautiful environs alone, to much greater advantage than I could last year, in the carriage with my friends.

I went, also, to Frascati and Ostia, with an English family, who had a good carriage, and were kindly, intelligent people, who could not disturb the Roman landscape.

Now I am going into the country, where I can live very cheaply, even keeping a servant of my own, without which guard I should not venture alone into the unknown and wilder regions.

I have been so disconcerted by my Roman winter, that I dare not plan decisively again. The enervating breath of Rome paralyzes my body, but I know and love her. The expression, "City of the Soul," designates her, and her alone.

TO MADAME ARCONATI.

Rome, May 27, 1848. — This is my last day at Rome. I have been passing several days at Subiaco and Tivoli, and return again to the country to-morrow. These scenes of natural beauty have filled my heart, and increased, if possible, my desire that the people who have this rich inheritance may no longer be deprived of its benefits by bad institutions.

The people of Subiaco are poor, though very industrious, and cultivating every inch of ground, with even English care and neatness; — so ignorant and uncultivated, while so finely and strongly made by Nature. May God grant now, to this people, what they need!

An illumination took place last night, in honor of the "Illustrious Gioberti." He is received here with great triumph, his carriage followed with shouts of "*Viva Gioberti, morte ai Jesuiti!*" which must be pain to the many Jesuits, who, it is said, still linger here in disguise. His triumphs are shared by Mamiani and Orioli, self-trumpeted celebrities, self-constituted rulers of the Roman states, — men of straw, to my mind, whom the fire already kindled will burn into a handful of ashes.

I sit in my obscure corner, and watch the progress of events. It is the position that pleases me best, and, I believe, the most favorable one. Everything confirms me in my radicalism; and, without any desire to hasten matters, indeed with surprise to see them rush so like a torrent, I seem to see them all tending to realize my own hopes.

My health and spirits now much restored, I am beginning to set down some of my impressions. I am going into the mountains, hoping there to find pure, strengthening air, and tranquillity for so many days as to allow me to do something.

TO R. F. F———.

Rieti, July 1, 1848. — Italy is as beautiful as even I hoped, and I should wish to stay here several years, if I had a moderate fixed income. One wants but little money here, and can have with it many of the noblest enjoyments. I should have been very glad if fate would allow me a few years of congenial life, at the end of not a few of struggle and suffering. But I do not hope it; my fate will be the same to the close, — beautiful gifts shown, and then withdrawn, or offered on conditions that make acceptance impossible.

TO MADAME ARCONATI.

Corpus Domini, June 22, 1848. — I write such a great number of letters, having not less than a hundred correspondents, that it seems, every day, as if I had just written to each. There is no one, surely, this side of the salt sea, with whom I wish more to keep up the interchange of thought than with you.

I believe, if you could know my heart as God knows it, and see the causes that regulate my conduct, you would always love me. But already, in absence, I have lost, for the present, some of those who were dear to me, by failure of letters, or false report. After sorrowing much about a falsehood told me of a dearest friend, I found his letter at Torlonia's, which had been there ten months, and, duly received, would have made all right. There is something fatal in my destiny about correspondence.

But I will say no more of this; only the loss of that letter to you, at such an unfortunate time, — just when I most wished to seem the loving and grateful friend I was, — made me fear it might be my destiny to lose you too. But if any cross event shall do me this ill turn on faith, we shall meet again in that clear state of intelligence which men call heaven.

I see by the journals that you have not lost Montanelli. That noble mind is still spared to Italy. The Pope's heart is incapable of treason; but he has fallen short of the office fate assigned him.

I am no bigoted Republican, yet I think that form of government will eventually pervade the civilized world. Italy may not be ripe for it yet, but I doubt if she finds peace earlier; and this hasty annexation of Lombardy to the crown of Sardinia seems, to me, as well as I can judge, an act unworthy and unwise. Base, indeed, the monarch, if it was needed, and weak no less than base; for he was already too far engaged in the Italian cause to retire with honor or wisdom.

I am here, in a lonely mountain home, writing the narrative of my European experience. To this I devote great part of the day. Three or four hours I pass in the open air, on donkey or on foot. When I have exhausted this spot, perhaps I shall try another. Apply as I may it will take three months, at least, to finish my book It grows upon me.

TO R. W. E.

Rieti, July 11, 1848. — Once I had resolution to face my difficulties myself, and try to give only what was pleasant to others; but now that my courage has fairly given way, and the fatigue of life is beyond my strength, I do not prize myself, or expect others to prize me.

Some years ago, I thought you very unjust, because you did not lend full faith to my spiritual experiences; but I see you were quite right. I thought I had tasted

of the true elixir, and that the want of daily bread, or
the pangs of imprisonment, would never make me a com-
plaining beggar. A widow, I expected still to have the
cruse full for others. Those were glorious hours, and
angels certainly visited me; but there must have been
too much earth, — too much taint of weakness and folly,
so that baptism did not suffice. I know now those same
things, but at present they are words, not living spells.

I hear, at this moment, the clock of the Church del
Purgatorio telling noon in this mountain solitude. Snow
yet lingers on these mountain-tops, after forty days of
hottest sunshine, last night broken by a few clouds, pref-
atory to a thunder storm this morning. It has been so
hot here, that even the peasant in the field says, *"Non
porro piu resistere,"* and slumbers in the shade, rather
than the sun. I love to see their patriarchal ways of
guarding the sheep and tilling the fields. They are a
simple race. Remote from the corruptions of foreign
travel, they do not ask for money, but smile upon and
bless me as I pass, — for the Italians love me; they say
I am so *" simpatica."* I never see any English or Americans, and now think wholly in Italian; only the surgeon
who bled me, the other day, was proud to speak a little
French, which he had learned at Tunis! The ignorance
of this people is amusing. I am to them a divine visit-
ant, — an instructive Ceres, — telling them wonderful
tales of foreign customs, and even legends of the lives of
their own saints. They are people whom I could love
and live with. Bread and grapes among them would
suffice me.

TO HER MOTHER.

Rome, Nov. 16, 1848.— * * * Of other circumstances which complicate my position I cannot write. Were you here, I would confide in you fully, and have more than once, in the silence of the night, recited to you those most strange and romantic chapters in the story of my sad life. At one time when I thought I might die, I empowered a person, who has given me, as far as possible to him, the aid and sympathy of a brother, to communicate them to you, on his return to the United States. But now I think we shall meet again, and I am sure you will always love your daughter, and will know gladly that in all events she has tried to aid and striven never to injure her fellows. In earlier days, I dreamed of doing and being much, but now am content with the Magdalen to rest my plea hereon, " *She has loved much.*"

You, loved mother, keep me informed, as you have, of important facts, *especially* the *worst.* The thought of you, the knowledge of your angelic nature, is always one of my greatest supports. Happy those who have such a mother! Myriad instances of selfishness and corruption of heart cannot destroy the confidence in human nature.

I am again in Rome, situated for the first time entirely to my mind. I have but one room, but large; and everything about the bed so gracefully and adroitly disposed that it makes a beautiful parlor, and of course I pay much less. I have the sun all day, and an excellent chimney. It is very high and has pure air, and the most beautiful view all around imaginable. Add, that l am with the dearest, delightful old couple one can imagine, quick, prompt, and kind, sensible and contented. Having no children, they like to regard me and the Prussian sculptor, my neighbor, as such; yet are too delicate and too busy ever to intrude. In the attic, dwells a priest, who insists on making my fire when Antonia is away. To be sure, he pays himself for his trouble, by asking a great many questions. The stories below are occupied by a frightful Russian princess with moustaches, and a footman who ties her bonnet for her; and a fat English lady, with a fine carriage, who gives all her money to the church, and has made for the house a terrace of flowers that would delight you. Antonia has her flowers in a humble balcony, her birds, and an immense black cat; always addressed by both husband and wife as " Amoretto," (little love!)

The house looks out on the Piazza Barberini, and I see both that palace and the Pope's. The scene to-day has been one of terrible interest. The poor, weak Pope has fallen more and more under the dominion of the cardinals, till at last all truth was hidden from his ʾyes. He had suffered the minister, Rossi, to go on, tightening the reins, and, because the people preserved a sullen silence, he thought they would bear it. Yesterday, the Chamber of Deputies, illegally prorogued, was opened anew. Rossi, after two or three most unpopular measures, had the imprudence to call the troops of the line to defend him, instead of the National Guard. On the 14th, the Pope had invested him with the privileges of a Roman citizen: (he had renounced his country when an exile, and returned to it as ambassador of Louis Philippe.) This position he enjoyed but one day. Yesterday, as he descended from his carriage, to enter the Chamber, the crowd howled and hissed; then pushed him, and, as he turned his head in consequence, a sure hand stabbed him in the back. He said no word, but died almost instantly in the arms of a cardinal. The act was undoubtedly the result of the combination of many, from the dexterity with which it was accomplished, and the silence which ensued. Those who had not abetted beforehand seemed entirely to approve when done. The troops of the line, on whom he had relied, remained at their posts, and looked coolly on. In the evening, they walked the streets with the people, singing, "Happy the hand which rids the world of a tyrant!" Had Rossi lived to enter the Chamber, he would have seen the most terrible and imposing mark of denunciation known in the history of nations, — the whole house, without a single exception, seated on the benches of opposition. The news of his death was received by the deputies with the same cold silence as by the people. For me, I never thought to have heard of a violent death with satisfaction, but this act affected me as one of terrible justice.

To-day, all the troops and the people united and went to the Quirinal to demand a change of measures. They found the Swiss Guard drawn out, and the Pope dared not show himself. They attempted to force the door of his palace, to enter his presence, and the guard fired. I saw a man borne by wounded. The drum beat to call out the National Guard. The carriage of Prince Barberini has returned with its frightened inmates and liveried retinue, and they have suddenly barred up the court-yard gate. Antonia, seeing it, observes, "Thank Heaven, we are poor, we have nothing to fear!" This is the echo of a sentiment which will soon be universa in Europe.

Never feel any apprehensions for my safety from such causes. There are those who will protect me, if necessary, and, besides, I am on the conquering side. These events have, to me, the deepest interest. These days are what I always longed for, — were I only free from private care! But, when the best and noblest want bread to give to the cause of liberty, I can just not demand *that* of them; their blood they would give me.

You cannot conceive the enchantment of this place. So much I suffered here last January and February, I thought myself a little weaned; but, returning, my heart swelled even to tears with the cry of the poet: —

"O, Rome, *my* country, city of the soul!"

Those have not lived who have not seen Rome. Warned, however, by the last winter, I dared not rent my lodgings for the year. I hope I am acclimated. I have been through what is called the grape-cure, much more charming, certainly, than the water-cure. At present I am very well; but, alas! because I have gone to bed early, and done very little. I do not know if I can maintain any labor. As to my life, I think that it is not the will of Heaven it should terminate very soon. I have had another strange escape. I had taken passage in the diligence to come to Rome; two rivers were to be passed, — the Turano and the Tiber, — but passed by good bridges, and a road excellent when not broken unexpectedly by torrents from the mountains. The diligence sets out between three and four in the morning, long before light. The director sent me word that

the Marchioness Crispoldi had taken for herself and
family a coach extraordinary, which would start two
hours later, and that I could have a place in that, if
I liked; so I accepted. The weather had been beautiful, but, on the eve of the day fixed for my departure,
the wind rose, and the rain fell in torrents. I observed
that the river which passed my window was much
swollen, and rushed with great violence. In the night, I
heard its voice still stronger, and felt glad I had not to
set out in the dark. I rose with twilight, and was
expecting my carriage, and wondering at its delay,
when I heard, that the great diligence, several miles
below, had been seized by a torrent; the horses were
up to their necks in water, before any one dreamed of
the danger. The postilion called on all the saints, and
threw himself into the water. The door of the diligence
could not be opened, and the passengers forced themselves, one after another, into the cold water, — dark
too. Had I been there I had fared ill; a pair of strong
men were ill after it, though all escaped with life.

For several days, there was no going to Rome; but, at
last, we set forth in two great diligences, with all the
horses of the route. For many miles, the mountains
and ravines were covered with snow; I seemed to have
returned to my own country and climate. Few miles
passed, before the conductor injured his leg under the
wheel, and I had the pain of seeing him suffer all the
way, while "Blood of Jesus," "Souls of Purgatory,"
was the mildest beginning of an answer to the jeers of
the postilions upon his paleness. We stopped at a miserable osteria, in whose cellar we found a magnificent
remain of Cyclopean architecture, — as indeed in Italy
one is paid at every step, for discomfort or danger, by

some precious subject of thought. We proceeded very slowly, and reached just at night a solitary little inn, which marks the site of the ancient home of the Sabine virgins, snatched away to become the mothers of Rome. We were there saluted with the news that the Tiber, also, had overflowed its banks, and it was very doubtful if we could pass. But what else to do? There were no accommodations in the house for thirty people, or even for three, and to sleep in the carriages, in that wet air of the marshes, was a more certain danger than to attempt the passage. So we set forth; the moon, almost at the full, smiling sadly on the ancient grandeurs, then half draped in mist, then drawing over her face a thin white veil. As we approached the Tiber, the towers and domes of Rome could be seen, like a cloud lying low on the horizon. The road and the meadows, alike under water, lay between us and it, one sheet of silver. The horses entered; they behaved nobly; we proceeded, every moment uncertain if the water would not become deep; but the scene was beautiful, and I enjoyed it highly. I have never yet felt afraid when really in the presence of danger, though sometimes in its apprehension.

At last we entered the gate; the diligence stopping to be examined, I walked to the gate of Villa Ludovisi, and saw its rich shrubberies of myrtle, and its statues so pale and eloquent in the moonlight.

Is it not cruel that I cannot earn six hundred dollars a year, living here? I could live on that well, now I know Italy. Where I have been, this summer, a great basket of grapes sells for one cent! — delicious salad, enough for three or four persons, one cent, — a pair of chickens, fifteen cents. Foreigners cannot live so, but

I could, now that I speak the language fluently, and know the price of everything. Everybody loves, and wants to serve me, and I cannot earn this pitiful sum to learn and do what I want.

Of course, I wish to see America again; but in my own time, when I am ready, and not to weep over hopes destroyed and projects unfulfilled.

My dear friend, Madame Arconati, has shown me generous love; — a *contadina*, whom I have known this summer, hardly less. Every Sunday, she came in her holiday dress, — beautiful corset of red silk richly embroidered, rich petticoat, nice shoes and stockings, and handsome coral necklace, on one arm an immense basket of grapes, in the other a pair of live chickens, to be eaten by me for her sake, ("*per amore mio*,") and wanted no present, no reward; it was, as she said, "for the honor and pleasure of her acquaintance." The old father of the family never met me but he took off his hat, and said, "Madame, it is to me a *consolation* to see you." Are there not sweet flowers of affection in life, glorious moments, great thoughts? — why must they be so dearly paid for?

Many Americans have shown me great and thoughtful kindness, and none more so than W. S—— and his wife. They are now in Florence, but may return. I do not know whether I shall stay here or not; shall be guided much by the state of my health.

All is quieted now in Rome. Late at night the Pope had to yield, but not till the door of his palace was half burnt, and his confessor killed. This man, Parma, provoked his fate by firing on the people from a window It seems the Pope never gave order to fire; his guard acted from a sudden impulse of their own. The new ministry chosen are little inclined to accept. It is almost impossible for any one to act, unless the Pope is stripped of his temporal power, and the hour for that is not yet quite ripe; though they talk more and more of proclaiming the Republic, and even of calling my friend Mazzini.

If I came home at this moment, I should feel as if forced to leave my own house, my own people, and the hour which I had always longed for. If I do come in this way, all I can promise is to plague other people as little as possible. My own plans and desires will be postponed to another world.

Do not feel anxious about me. Some higher power leads me through strange, dark, thorny paths, broken at times by glades opening down into prospects of sunny beauty, into which I am not permitted to enter. If God disposes for us, it is not for nothing. This I can say, my heart is in some respects better, it is kinder and more humble. Also, my mental acquisitions have certainly been great, however inadequate to my desires.

TO M. S.

Rome, Nov. 23, 1848. — Mazzini has stood alone in Italy, on a sunny height, far above the stature of other men. He has fought a great fight against folly, compromise, and treason; steadfast in his convictions, and of almost miraculous energy to sustain them, is he. He has foes; and at this moment, while he heads the insurrection in the Valtellina, the Roman people murmur his name, and long to call him here.

How often rings in my ear the consolatory word of Körner, after many struggles, many undeceptions, "Though the million suffer shipwreck, yet noble hearts survive!"

I grieve to say, the good-natured Pio has shown himself utterly derelict, alike without resolution to abide by
the good or the ill. He is now abandoned and despised
by both parties. The people do not trust his word, for
they know he shrinks from the danger, and shuts the
door to pray quietly in his closet, whilst he knows the
cardinals are misusing his name to violate his pledges.
The cardinals, chased from Rome, talk of electing an
anti-Pope; because, when there was danger, he has
always yielded to the people, and they say he has over-
stepped his prerogative, and broken his papal oath. No
one abuses him, for it is felt that in a more private station he would have acted a kindly part; but he has
failed of so high a vocation, and balked so noble a hope,
that no one respects him either. Who would have
believed, a year ago, that the people would assail his
palace? I was on Monte Cavallo yesterday, and saw
the broken windows, the burnt doors, the walls marked
by shot, just beneath the loggia, on which we have seen
him giving the benediction. But this would never have
happened, if his guard had not fired first on the people.
It is true it was without his order, but, under a different
man, the Swiss would never have dared to incur such a
responsibility.

Our old acquaintance, Sterbini, has risen to the ministry. He has a certain influence, from his consistency
and independence, but has little talent.

Of me you wish to know; but there is little I can
tell you at this distance. I have had happy hours,
learned much, suffered much, and outward things have
not gone fortunately with me. I have had glorious
hopes, but they are overclouded now, and the future
looks darker than ever, indeed, quite impossible to my

steps. I have no hope, unless that God will show me
some way I do not know of now; but I do not wish to
trouble you with more of this.

TO W. S.

Rome, Dec. 9, 1848. — As to Florence itself, I do not
like it, with the exception of the galleries and churches,
and Michel Angelo's marbles. I do not like it, for the
reason you *do*, because it seems like home. It seems
a kind of Boston to me, — the same good and the same
ill; I have had enough of both. But I have so many
dear friends in Boston, that I must always wish to
go there sometimes; and there are so many precious
objects of study in Florence, that a stay of several
months could not fail to be full of interest. Still, the
spring must be the time to be in Florence; there are so
many charming spots to visit in the environs, much
nearer than those you go to in Rome, within scope of
an afternoon's drive. I saw them only when parched
with sun and covered with dust. In the spring they
must be very beautiful.

December, 1848. — I felt much what you wrote, "*if it
were well with my heart.*" How seldom it is that a mortal is permitted to enjoy a paradisaical scene, unhaunted
by some painful vision from the past or the future! With
me, too, dark clouds of care and sorrow have sometimes
blotted out the sunshine. I have not lost from my side
an only sister, but have been severed from some visions
still so dear, they looked almost like hopes. The future
seems too difficult for me. I have been as happy as I
could, and I feel that this summer, as last, had I been

with my country folks, the picture of Italy would not have been so lively to me. Now I have been quite off the beaten track of travel, have seen, thought, spoken, dreamed only what is Italian. I have learned much, received many strong and clear impressions. While among the mountains, I was for a good while quite alone, except for occasional chat with the contadine, who wanted to know if Pius IX. was not *un gran carbonaro!* — a reputation which he surely ought to have forfeited by this time. About me they were disturbed : " *E sempre sola soletta,*" they said, " *eh perche?* "

Later, I made one of those accidental acquaintances, such as I have spoken of to you in my life of Lombardy, which may be called romantic : two brothers, elderly men, the last of a very noble family, formerly lords of many castles, still of more than one; both unmarried, men of great polish and culture. None of the consequences ensued that would in romances : they did not any way adopt me, nor give me a casket of diamonds, nor any of their pictures, among which were originals by several of the greatest masters, nor their rich cabinets, nor miniatures on agate, nor carving in wood and ivory. They only showed me their things, and their family archives of more than a hundred volumes, (containing most interesting documents about Poland, where four of their ancestors were nuncios,) manuscript letters from Tasso, and the like. With comments on these, and legendary lore enough to furnish Cooper or Walter Scott with a thousand romances, they enriched me; unhappily, I shall never have the strength or talent to make due use of it. I was sorry to leave them, for now I have recrossed the frontier into the Roman States. I will not tell you where, — I know not that I shall ever tell where, — these months have been passed. The great Goethe hid thus in Italy; "Then," said he, "I did indeed feel alone, — when no formeɪ friend could form an *idea* where I was." Why should not —— and I enjoy this fantastic luxury of *incognito* also, when we can so much more easily?

I will not name the place, but I will describe it. The rooms are spacious and airy; the loggia of the sleeping room is rude, but it overhangs a lovely little river, with its hedge of willows. Opposite is a large and rich vine-yard; on one side a ruined tower, on the other an old casino, with its avenues of cypress, give human interest to the scene. A cleft amid the mountains full of light leads on the eye to a soft blue peak, very distant. At night the young moon trembles in the river, and its soft murmur soothes me to sleep; it needs, for I have had lately a bad attack upon the nerves, and been obliged to stop writing for the present. I think I shall stay here some time, though I suppose there are such sweet places all over Italy, if one only looks for one's self. Poor, beautiful Italy! how she has been injured of late! It is dreadful to see the incapacity and meanness of those to whom she had confided the care of her redemption.

I have thus far passed this past month of fine weather most delightfully in revisiting my haunts of the autumn before. Then, too, I was uncommonly well and strong; it was the golden period of my Roman life. The expe-rience what long confinement may be expected after, from the winter rains, has decided me *never* to make my hay when the sun shines: *i. e.*, to give no fine day to books and pens.

The places of interest I am nearest now are villas Albani and Ludovisi, and Santa Agnese, St. Lorenzo, and the vineyards near Porta Maggiore. I have passed

one day in a visit to Torre dei Schiavi and the neighborhood, and another on Monte Mario, both Rome and the
Campagna-day golden in the mellowest lustre of the
Italian sun. * * * But to you I may tell, that I always
go with Ossoli, the most congenial companion I ever
had for jaunts of this kind. We go out in the morning,
carrying the roast chestnuts from Rome; the bread and
wine are found in some lonely little osteria; and so we
dine; and reach Rome again, just in time to see it, from
a little distance, gilded by the sunset.

This moon having been so clear, and the air so warm,
we have visited, on successive evenings, all the places
we fancied: Monte Cavallo, now so lonely and abandoned, — no lights there but moon and stars, — Trinità
de' Monti, Santa Maria Maggiore, and the Forum. So
now, if the rain must come, or I be driven from Rome,
I have all the images fair and fresh in my mind.

About public events, why remain ignorant? Take a
daily paper in the house. The Italian press has recovered from the effervescence of childish spirits; — you can
now approximate to the truth from its reports. There
are many good papers now in Italy. Whatever represents the Montanelli ministry is best for you. That
gives the lead now. I see good articles copied from the
"Alba."

TO MADAME ARCONATI.

Rome, Feb. 5, 1849. — I am so delighted to get your
letter, that I must answer on the instant. I try with all
my force to march straight onwards, — to answer the
claims of the day; to act out my feeling as seems right
at the time, and not heed the consequences; — but in

my affections I am tender and weak; where I have really loved, a barrier, a break, causes me ˜great suffering.   I read in your letter that I am still dear to you as you to me.   I always felt, that if we had passed more time together, — if the intimacy, for which there was ground in the inner nature, had become consolidated, — no after differences of opinion or conduct could have destroyed, though they might interrupt its pleasure. But it was of few days' standing, — our interviews much interrupted.   I felt as if I knew you much better than you could me, because I had occasion to see you amid your various and habitual relations.   I was afraid you might change, or become indifferent; now I hope not.

True, I have written, shall write, about the affairs of Italy, what you will much dislike, if ever you see it.   I have done, may do, many things that would be very unpleasing to you; yet there *is* a congeniality, I dare to say, pure, and strong, and good, at the bottom of the heart, far, far deeper than these differences, that would always, on a real meeting, keep us friends. For me, I could never have but one feeling towards you.

Now, for the first time, I enjoy a full communion with the spirit of Rome.   Last winter, I had here many friends; now all are dispersed, and sometimes I long to exchange thoughts with a friendly circle; but generally I am better content to live thus: — the impression made by all the records of genius around is more unbroken; I begin to be very familiar with them.   The sun shines always, when last winter it never shone.   I feel strong; I can go everywhere on foot.   I pass whole days abroad sometimes I take a book, but seldom read it : — why should I, when every stone talks?

In spring, I shall go often out of town. I have read " La Rome Souterraine" of Didier, and it makes me wish to see Ardea and Nettuno. Ostia is the only one of those desolate sites that I know yet. I study sometimes Niebuhr, and other books about Rome, but not to any great profit.

In the circle of my friends, two have fallen. One a person of great wisdom, strength, and calmness. She was ever to me a most tender friend, and one whose sympathy I highly valued. Like you by nature and education conservative, she was through thought liberal. With no exuberance or passionate impulsiveness herself, she knew how to allow for these in others. The other was a woman of my years, of the most precious gifts in heart and genius. She had also beauty and fortune. She died at last of weariness and intellectual inanition. She never, to any of us, her friends, hinted her sufferings. But they were obvious in her poems, which, with great dignity, expressed a resolute but most mournful resignation.

TO R. F. F.

Rome, Feb. 23, 1849. — It is something if one can get free foot-hold on the earth, so as not to be jostled out of hearing the music, if there should be any spirits in the air to make such.

For my part, I have led rather too lonely a life of late. Before, it seemed as if too many voices of men startled away the inspirations; but having now lived eight months much alone, I doubt that good has come of it and think to return, and go with others for a little. I have realized in these last days the thought of Goethe,— "He who would in loneliness live, ah! he is soon alone. Each one loves, each one lives, and leaves him to his pain." I went away and hid, all summer. Not content with that, I said, on returning to Rome, I must be busy and receive people little. They have taken me at my word, and hardly one comes to see me. Now, if I want play and prattle, I shall have to run after them. It is fair enough that we all, in turn, should be made to feel our need of one another.

Never was such a winter as this. Ten weeks now of unbroken sunshine and the mildest breezes. Of course, its price is to be paid. The spring, usually divine here, with luxuriant foliage and multitudinous roses, will be all scorched and dusty. There is fear, too, of want of food for the poor Roman state.

I pass my days in writing, walking, occasional visits to the galleries. I read little, except the newspapers; these take up an hour or two of the day. I own, my thoughts are quite fixed on the daily bulletin of men and things. I expect to write the history, but because it is so much in my heart. If you were here, I rather think you would be impassive, like the two most esteemed Americans I see. They do not believe in the sentimental nations. Hungarians, Poles, Italians, are too demonstrative for them, too fiery, too impressible. They like better the loyal, slow-moving Germans; even the Russian, with his dog's nose and gentlemanly servility, pleases them better than *my* people. There is an antagonism of race.

Rome, June 6, 1849. — The help I needed was external, practical. I knew myself all the difficulties and pains of my position; they were beyond present relief; from sympathy I could struggle with them, but had not life enough left, afterwards, to be a companion of any worth. To be with persons generous and refined, who would not pain; who would sometimes lend a helping hand across the ditches of this strange insidious marsh, was all I could have now, and this you gave.

On Sunday, from our loggia, I witnessed a terrible, a real battle. It began at four in the morning; it lasted to the last gleam of light. The musket-fire was almost unintermitted; the roll of the cannon, especially from St. Angelo, most majestic. As all passed at Porta San Pancrazio and Villa Pamfili, I saw the smoke of every discharge, the flash of the bayonets; with a glass could see the men. Both French and Italians fought with the most obstinate valor. The French could not use their heavy cannon, being always driven away by the legions Garibaldi and ———, when trying to find positions for them. The loss on our side is about three hundred killed and wounded; theirs must be much greater. In one casino have been found seventy dead bodies of theirs. I find the wounded men at the hospital in a transport of indignation. The French soldiers fought so furiously, that they think them false as their general, and cannot endure the remembrance of their visits, during the armistice, and talk of brotherhood. You will have heard how all went: — how Lesseps, after appearing here fifteen days as *plenipotentiary*, signed a treaty not dishonorable to Rome; then Oudinot refused to ratify it, saying, *the plenipotentiary had surpassed his powers:* Lesseps runs back to Paris, and Oudinot attacks: — an affair alike infamous for the French from beginning to end. The cannonade on one side has continued day and night, (being full moon,) till this morning; they seeking to advance or take other positions, the Romans firing on them. The French throw rockets into the town; one burst in the court-yard of the hospital, just as I arrived there yesterday, agitating the poor sufferers very much; they said they did not want to die like mice in a trap.

TO M. S.

Rome, March 9, 1849. — Last night, Mazzini came to see me. You will have heard how he was called to Italy, and received at Leghorn like a prince, as he is; unhappily, in fact, the only one, the only great Italian. It is expected, that, if the republic lasts, he will be President. He has been made a Roman citizen, and elected to the Assembly; the labels bearing, in giant letters, "*Giuseppe Mazzini, cittadino Romano*," are yet up all over Rome. He entered by night, on foot, to avoid demonstrations, no doubt, and enjoy the quiet of his own thoughts, at so great a moment. The people went under his windows the next night, and called him out to speak; but I did not know about it. Last night, I heard a ring; then somebody speak my name; the voice struck upon me at once. He looks more divine than ever, after all his new, strange sufferings. He asked after all of you. He stayed two hours, and we talked, though rapidly, of everything. He hopes to come often, but the crisis is tremendous, and all will come on him; since, if any one can save Italy from her foes, inward and outward, it will be he. But he is very doubtful whether this be possible; the foes are too many, too strong, too subtle. Yet Heaven helps sometimes. I only grieve I cannot aid him; freely would I give my life to aid him, only bargaining for a quick death. I don't like slow torture. I fear that it is in reserve for him, to survive defeat. True, he can never be utterly defeated; but to see Italy bleeding, prostrate once more, will be very dreadful for him.

He has sent me tickets, twice, to hear him speak in the Assembly. It was a fine, commanding voice. But, when he finished, he looked very exhausted and melancholy. He looks as if the great battle he had fought had been too much for his strength, and that he was only sustained by the fire of the soul.

All this I write to you, because you said, when I was suffering at leaving Mazzini,— "You will meet him in heaven." This I believe will be, despite all my faults.

[In April, 1849, Margaret was appointed, by the "Roman Commission for the succor of the wounded," to the charge of the hospital of the *Fate-Bene Fratelli;* the Princess Belgioioso having charge of the one already opened. The following is a copy of the original letter from the Princess, which is written in English, announcing the appointment.]

Comitato di Soccorso Pei Feriti,
April 30, 1849.

Dear Miss Fuller: —

You are named Regolatrice of the Hospital of the *Fate-Bene Fratelli.* Go there at twelve, if the alarm bell has not rung before. When you arrive there, you will receive all the women coming for the wounded, and give them your directions, so that you are sure to have a certain number of them night and day.

May God help us.

CHRISTINE TRIVULZE,

of Belgioioso.

Miss Fuller, Piazza Barberini, No. 60.

TO R. W. E.

Rome, June 10, 1849. — I received your letter amid the round of cannonade and musketry. It was a terrible battle fought here from the first till the last light of day. I could see all its progress from my balcony. The Italians fought like lions. It is a truly heroic spirit that animates them. They make a stand here for honor and their rights, with little ground for hope that they can resist, now they are betrayed by France.

Since the 30th April, I go almost daily to the hospitals, and, though I have suffered, — for I had no idea before, how terrible gunshot-wounds and wound-fever are, — yet I have taken pleasure, and great pleasure, in being with the men; there is scarcely one who is not moved by a noble spirit. Many, especially among the Lombards, are the flower of the Italian youth. When they begin to get better, I carry them books and flowers; they read, and we talk.

The palace of the Pope, on the Quirinal, is now used for convalescents. In those beautiful gardens, I walk with them, — one with his sling, another with his crutch. The gardener plays off all his water-works for the defenders of the country, and gathers flowers for me, their friend.

A day or two since, we sat in the Pope's little pavilion, where he used to give private audience. The sun was going gloriously down over Monte Mario, where gleamed the white tents of the French light-horse among the trees. The cannonade was heard at intervals. Two bright-eyed boys sat at our feet, and gathered up eagerly every word said by the heroes of the day. It was a beautiful hour, stolen from the midst of ruin and sorrow; and tales were told as full of grace and pathos as in the gardens of Boccaccio, only in a very different spirit, — with noble hope for man, with reverence for woman.

The young ladies of the family, very young girls, were filled with enthusiasm for the suffering, wounded patriots, and they wished to go to the hospital to give their services. Excepting the three superintendents, none but married ladies were permitted to serve there, but their services were accepted. Their governess then wished to go too, and, as she could speak several languages, she was admitted to the rooms of the wounded soldiers, to interpret for them, as the nurses knew nothing but Italian, and many of these poor men were suffering, because they could not make their wishes known. Some are French, some German, and many Poles. Indeed, I am afraid it is too true that there were comparatively but few Romans among them. This young lady passed several nights there.

Should I never return, — and sometimes I despair of doing so, it seems so far off, so difficult, I am caught in such a net of ties here, — if ever you know of my life here, I think you will only wonder at the constancy with which I have sustained myself; the degree of profit to which, amid great difficulties, I have put the time, at least in the way of observation. Meanwhile, love me all you can; let me feel, that, amid the fearful agitations of the world, there are pure hands, with healthful, even pulse, stretched out toward me, if I claim their grasp.

I feel profoundly for Mazzini; at moments I am tempted to say, "Cursed with every granted prayer," — so cunning is the dæmon. He is become the inspiring soul of his people. He saw Rome, to which all his hopes through life tended, for the first time as a Roman citizen, and to become in a few days its ruler. He has animated, he sustains her to a glorious effort, which, if it fails, this time, will not in the age. His country will be free. Yet to me it would be so dreadful to cause all this bloodshed, to dig the graves of such martyrs.

Then Rome is being destroyed; her glorious oaks; her villas, haunts of sacred beauty, that seemed the possession of the world forever, — the villa of Raphael, the villa of Albani, home of Winkelmann, and the best expression of the ideal of modern Rome, and so many other sanctuaries of beauty, — all must perish, lest a foe should level his musket from their shelter. *I* could not, could not!

I know not, dear friend, whether I ever shall get home across that great ocean, but here in Rome I shall no longer wish to live. O, Rome, *my* country! could I imagine that the triumph of what I held dear was to heap such desolation on thy head!

Speaking of the republic, you say, do not I wish Italy had a great man? Mazzini is a great man. In mind, **a** great poetic statesman; in heart, a lover; in action, decisive and full of resource as Cæsar. Dearly I love Mazzini. He came in, just as I had finished the first letter to you. His soft, radiant look makes melancholy music in my soul; it consecrates my present life, that, like the Magdalen, I may, at the important hour, shed all the consecrated ointment on his head. There is one, Mazzini, who understands thee well; who knew thee no less when an object of popular fear, than now of idolatry; and who, if the pen be not held too feebly, will help posterity to know thee too.

TO W. H. C.

Rome, July 8, 1849. — I do not yet find myself tranquil and recruited from the painful excitements of these last days. But, amid the ruined hopes of Rome, the shameful oppressions she is beginning to suffer, amid these noble, bleeding martyrs, my brothers, I cannot fix my thoughts on anything else.

I write that you may assure mother of my safety, which in the last days began to be seriously imperilled. Say, that as soon as I can find means of conveyance, without an expense too enormous, I shall go again into the mountains. There I shall find pure, bracing air, and I hope stillness, for a time. Say, she need feel no anxiety, if she do not hear from me for some time. I may feel indisposed to write, as I do now; my heart is too full.

Private hopes of mine are fallen with the hopes of Italy. I have played for a new stake, and lost it. Life looks too difficult. But for the present I shall try to wave all thought of self and renew my strength.

After the attempt at revolution in France failed, could

I have influenced Mazzini, I should have prayed him to capitulate, and yet I feel that no honorable terms can be made with such a foe, and that the only way is *never* to yield; but the sound of the musketry, the sense that men were perishing in a hopeless contest, had become too terrible for my nerves. I did not see Mazzini, the last two weeks of the republic. When the French entered, he walked about the streets, to see how the people bore themselves, and then went to the house of a friend. In the upper chamber of a poor house, with his life-long friends, — the Modenas, — I found him. Modena, who abandoned not only what other men hold dear, — home, fortune, peace, — but also endured, without the power of using the prime of his great artist-talent, a ten years' exile in a foreign land; his wife every way worthy of him, — such a woman as I am not.

Mazzini had suffered millions more than I could; he had borne his fearful responsibility; he had let his dearest friends perish; he had passed all these nights without sleep; in two short months, he had grown old; all the vital juices seemed exhausted; his eyes were all blood-shot; his skin orange; flesh he had none; his hair was mixed with white; his hand was painful to the touch; but he had never flinched, never quailed; had protested in the last hour against surrender; sweet and calm, but full of a more fiery purpose than ever; in him I revered the hero, and owned myself not of that mould.

You say truly, I shall come home humbler. God grant it may be entirely humble! In future, while more than ever deeply penetrated with principles, and the need of the martyr spirit to sustain them, I will ever own that there are few worthy, and that I am one of the least.

A silken glove might be as good a gauntlet as one of steel, but I, infirm of mood, turn sick even now as I think of the past.

July, 1849. — I cannot tell you what I endured in leaving Rome; abandoning the wounded soldiers; knowing that there is no provision made for them, when they rise from the beds where they have been thrown by a noble courage, where they have suffered with a noble patience. Some of the poorer men, who rise bereft even of the right arm, — one having lost both the right arm and the right leg, — I could have provided for with a small sum. Could I have sold my hair, or blood from my arm, I would have done it. Had any of the rich Americans remained in Rome, they would have given it to me; they helped nobly at first, in the service of the hospitals, when there was far less need; but they had all gone. What would I have given that I could have spoken to one of the Lawrences, or the Phillipses; they could and would have saved the misery. These poor men are left helpless in the power of a mean and vindictive foe. You felt so oppressed in the slave-states; imagine what I felt at seeing all the noblest youth, all the genius of this dear land, again enslaved.

TO W. H. C.

Rieti, Aug. 28, 1849. — You say, you are glad I have had this great opportunity for carrying out my principles. Would it were so! I found myself inferior in courage and fortitude to the occasion. I knew not how

VOL. II.

to bear the havoc and anguish incident to the struggle for these principles. I rejoiced that it lay not with me to cut down the trees, to destroy the Elysian gardens, for the defence of Rome; I do not know that I could have done it. And the sight of these far nobler growths, the beautiful young men, mown down in their stately prime, became too much for me. I forget the great ideas, to sympathize with the poor mothers, who had nursed their precious forms, only to see them all lopped and gashed. You say, I sustained them; often have they sustained my courage: one, kissing the pieces of bone that were so painfully extracted from his arm, hanging them round his neck to be worn as the true relics of to-day; mementoes that he also had done and borne something for his country and the hopes of humanity. One fair young man, who is made a cripple for life, clasped my hand as he saw me crying over the spasms I could not relieve, and faintly cried, " Viva l'Italia." " Think only, *cara bona donna*," said a poor wounded soldier, " that I can always wear my uniform on *festas*, just as it is now, with the holes where the balls went through, for a memory." " God is good; God knows," they often said to me, when I had not a word to cheer them.

THE WIFE AND MOTHER.*

Beneath the ruins of the Roman Republic, how many private fortunes were buried! and among these victims was Margaret. In that catastrophe, were swallowed up hopes sacredly cherished by her through weary months, at the risk of all she most prized.

* The first part of this chapter is edited by R. W. E. ; the remainder by W. H. C.

Soon after the entrance of the French, she wrote thus, to the resident Envoy of the United States:

My dear Mr. Cass, — I beg you to come and see me, and give me your counsel, and, if need be, your aid, to get away from Rome. From what I hear this morning, I fear we may be once more shut up here; and I shall die, to be again separated from what I hold most dear. There are, as yet, no horses on the way we want to go, or we should post immediately.

You may feel, like me, sad, in these last moments, to leave this injured Rome. So many noble hearts I abandon here, whose woes I have known! I feel, if I could not aid, I might soothe. But for my child, I would not go, till some men, now sick, know whether they shall live or die.

Her child! Where was he? In RIETI, — at the foot of the Umbrian Apennines, — a day's journey to the north-east of Rome. Thither Margaret escaped with her husband, and thence she wrote the following letter:

Dearest Mother, — I received your letter a few hours before leaving Rome. Like all of yours, it refreshed me, and gave me as much satisfaction as anything could, at that sad time. Its spirit is of eternity, and befits an epoch when wickedness and perfidy so impudently triumph, and the best blood of the generous and honorable is poured out like water, seemingly in vain.

I cannot tell you what I suffered to abandon the wounded to the care of their mean foes; to see the young men, that were faithful to their vows, hunted from their homes, — hunted like wild beasts; denied a refuge in every civilized land. Many of those I loved are sunk to the bottom of the sea, by Austrian cannon, or will be shot. Others are in penury, grief, and exile. May God give due recompense for all that has been endured!

My mind still agitated, and my spirits worn out, I have not felt like writing to any one. Yet the magnificent summer does not smile quite in vain for me. Much exercise in the open air, living much on milk and fruit, have recruited my health, and I am regaining the habit of sleep, which a month of nightly cannonade in Rome had destroyed.

Receiving, a few days since, a packet of letters from America, I opened them with more feeling of hope and good cheer, than for a long time past. The first words that met my eye were these, in the hand of Mr. Greeley: — "Ah, Margaret, the world grows dark with us! You grieve, for Rome is fallen; — I mourn, for Pickie is dead."

I have shed rivers of tears over the inexpressibly affecting letter thus begun. One would think I might have become familiar enough with images of death and destruction; yet somehow the image of Pickie's little dancing figure, lying, stiff and stark, between his parents, has made me weep more than all else. There was little hope he could do justice to himself, or lead a happy life in so perplexed a world; but never was a character of richer capacity, — never a more charming child. To me he was most dear, and would always have been so. Had he become stained with earthly faults, I could never have forgotten what he was when fresh from the soul's home, and what he was to me when my soul pined for sympathy, pure and unalloyed.

The three children I have seen who were fairest in my eyes, and gave most promise of the future, were Waldo, Pickie, Hermann Clarke; — all nipped in the bud. Endless thoughts has this given me, and a resolve to seek the realization of all hopes and plans elsewhere, which resolve will weigh with me as much as it can weigh before the silver cord is finally loosed. Till then, Earth, our mother, always finds strange, unexpected ways to draw us back to her bosom, — to make us seek anew a nutriment which has never failed to cause us frequent sickness.

This brings me to the main object of my present letter, — a piece of intelligence about myself, which I had hoped I might be able to communicate in such a way as to give you *pleasure*. That I cannot, — after suffering much in silence with that hope, — is like the rest of my earthly destiny.

The first moment, it may cause you a pang to know that your eldest child might long ago have been addressed by another name than yours, and has a little son a year old.

But, beloved mother, do not feel this long. I do assure you, that it was only great love for you that kept me silent. I have abstained a hundred times, when your sympathy, your counsel, would have been most precious, from a wish not to harass you with anxiety. Even now I would abstain, but it has become necessary, on account of the child, for us to live publicly and permanently together; and we have no hope, in the present state of Italian affairs, that we can do it at any better advantage, for several years, than now.

My husband is a Roman, of a noble but now impoverished house. His mother died when he was an infant, his father is dead since we met, leaving some property, but encumbered with debts, and in the present state of Rome hardly available, except by living there. He has three older brothers, all provided for in the Papal service; — one as Secretary of the Privy Chamber, the other two as members of the Guard Noble. A similar career would have been opened to him, but he embraced liberal principles, and, with the fall of the Republic, has lost all, as well as the favor of his family, who all sided with the Pope. Meanwhile, having been an officer in the Republican service, it was best for him to leave Rome. He has taken what little money he had, and we plan to live in Florence for the winter. If he or I can get the means, we shall come together to the United States, in the summer; — earlier we could not, on account of the child.

He is not in any respect such a person as people in general would expect to find with me. He had no instructor except an old priest, who entirely neglected his education; and of all that is contained in books he is absolutely ignorant, and he has no enthusiasm of character. On the other hand, he has excellent practical sense; has been a judicious observer of all that passed before his eyes; has a nice sense of duty, which, in its unfailing, minute activity, may put most enthusiasts to shame; a very sweet temper, and great native refinement. His love for me has been unswerving and most tender. I have never suffered a pain that he could relieve. His devotion, when I am ill, is to be compared only with yours. His delicacy in trifles, his sweet domestic graces, remind me of E——. In him I have found a home, and one that interferes with no tie. Amid many ills and cares, we have had much joy together, in the sympathy with natural beauty, — with our child, — with all that is innocent and sweet.

I do not know whether he will always love me so well, for I am the elder, and the difference will become, in a few years, more perceptible than now. But life is so uncertain, and it is so necessary to take good things with their limitations, that I have not thought it worth while to calculate too curiously.

However my other friends may feel, I am sure that *you* will love him very much, and that he will love you no less. Could we all live together, on a moderate income, you would find peace with us. Heaven grant, that, on returning, I may gain means to effect this object. He, of course, can do nothing, while we are in the United States, but perhaps I can; and now that my health is better, I shall be able to exert myself, if sure that my child is watched by those who love him, and who are good and pure.

What shall I say of my child? All might seem hyperbole, even to my dearest mother. In him I find satisfaction, for the first time, to the deep wants of my heart. Yet, thinking of those other sweet ones fled, I must look upon him as a treasure only lent. He is a fair child, with blue eyes and light hair; very affectionate, graceful, and sportive. He was baptized, in the Roman Catholic Church, by the name of Angelo Eugene Philip, for his father, grandfather, and my brother. He inherits the title of marquis.

Write the name of my child in your Bible, ANGELO OSSOLI, *born September* 5, 1848. God grant he may live, to see you, and may prove worthy of your love!

More I do not feel strength to say. You can hardly guess how all attempt to express something about the great struggles and experiences of my European life enfeebles me. When I get home, — if ever I do, — it will be told without this fatigue and excitement. I trust there will be a little repose, before entering anew on this wearisome conflict.

I had addressed you twice, — once under the impression that I should not survive the birth of my child; again during the siege of Rome, the father and I being both in danger. I took Mrs. Story, and, when she left Rome, Mr. Cass, into my confidence. Both were kind as sister and brother. Amid much pain and struggle, sweet is the memory of the generous love I received from William and Emelyn Story, and their uncle. They helped me gently through a most difficult period. Mr. Cass, also, who did not know me at all, has done everything possible for me.

A letter to her sister fills out these portraits of her husband and child.

About Ossoli * I do not like to say much, as he is an exceedingly delicate person. He is not precisely reserved, but it is not natural to him to talk about the objects of strong affection. I am sure he would not try to describe me to his sister, but would rather she would take her own impression of me; and, as much as possible, I wish to do the same by him. I presume that, to many of my friends, he will be nothing, and they will not understand that I should have life in common with

* Giovanni Angelo Ossoli.

him. But I do not think he will care; — he has not the slightest tinge of self-love. He has, throughout our intercourse, been used to my having many such ties. He has no wish to be anything to persons with whom he does not feel spontaneously bound, and when I am occupied, is happy in himself. But some of my friends and my family, who will see him in the details of practical life, cannot fail to prize the purity and simple strength of his character; and, should he continue to love me as he has done, his companionship will be an inestimable blessing to me. I say *if*, because all human affections are frail, and I have experienced too great revulsions in my own, not to know it. Yet I feel great confidence in the permanence of his love. It has been unblemished so far, under many trials; especially as I have been more desponding and unreasonable, in many ways, than I ever was before, and more so, I hope, than I ever shall be again. But at all such times, he never had a thought except to sustain and cheer me. He is capable of the sacred love, — the love passing that of woman. He showed it to his father, to Rome, to me. Now he loves his child in the same way. I think he will be an excellent father, though he could not speculate about it, nor, indeed, about anything.

Our meeting was singular, — fateful, I may say. Very soon he offered me his hand through life, but I never dreamed I should take it. I loved him, and felt very unhappy to leave him; but the connection seemed so every way unfit, I did not hesitate a moment. He, however, thought I should return to him, as I did. I acted upon a strong impulse, and could not analyze at all what passed in my mind. I neither rejoice nor grieve; — for bad or for good, I acted out my character

Had I never connected myself with ary one, my path was clear; now it is all hid; but, in that case, my development must have been partial. As to marriage, I think the intercourse of heart and mind may be fully enjoyed without entering into this partnership of daily life. Still, I do not find it burdensome. The friction that I have seen mar so much the domestic happiness of others does not occur with us, or, at least, has not occurred. Then, there is the pleasure of always being at hand to help one another.

Still, the great novelty, the immense gain, to me, is my relation with my child. I thought the mother's heart lived in me before, but it did not; — I knew nothing about it. Yet, before his birth, I dreaded it. I thought I should not survive; but if I did, and my child did, was I not cruel to bring another into this terrible world? I could not, at that time, get any other view. When he was born, that deep melancholy changed at once into rapture; but it did not last long. Then came the prudential motherhood. I grew a coward, a caretaker, not only for the morrow, but, impiously faithless, for twenty or thirty years ahead. It seemed very wicked to have brought the little tender thing into the midst of cares and perplexities we had not feared in the least for ourselves. I imagined everything; — he was to be in danger of every enormity the Croats were then committing upon the infants of Lombardy; — the house would be burned over his head; but, if he escaped, how were we to get money to buy his bibs and primers? Then his father was to be killed in the fighting, and I to die of my cough, &c. &c.

During the siege of Rome, I could not see my little boy. What I endured at that time, in various ways not many would survive. In the burning sun, I went every day, to wait, in the crowd, for letters about him. Often they did not come. I saw blood that had streamed on the wall where Ossoli was. I have a piece of a bomb that burst close to him. I sought solace in tending the suffering men; but when I beheld the beautiful fair young men bleeding to death, or mutilated for life, I felt the woe of all the mothers who had nursed each to that full flower, to see them thus cut down. I felt the *consolation*, too, — for those youths died worthily. I was a Mater Dolorosa, and I remembered that she who helped Angelino into the world came from the sign of the Mater Dolorosa. I thought, even if he lives, if he comes into the world at this great troubled time, terrible with perplexed duties, it may be to die thus at twenty years, one of a glorious hecatomb, indeed, but still a sacrifice. It seemed then I was willing he should die.

Angelino's birth-place is thus sketched:

My baby saw mountains when he first looked forward into the world. RIETI, — not only an old classic town of Italy, but one founded by what are now called the Aborigines, — is a hive of very ancient dwellings with red brown roofs, a citadel and several towers. It is in a plain, twelve miles in diameter one way, not much less the other, and entirely encircled with mountains of the noblest form. Casinos and hermitages gleam here and there on their lower slopes. This plain is almost the richest in Italy, and full of vineyards. Rieti is near the foot of the hills on one side, and the rapid Velino makes almost the circuit of its walls, on its way to Terni. I had my apartment shut out from the family, on the bank of this river, and saw the mountains, as I lay on my restless couch. There was a piazza, too, or, as they call it here, a loggia, which hung over the river, where I walked most of the night, for I could not sleep at all in those months. In the wild autumn storms, the stream became a roaring torrent, constantly lit up by lightning flashes, and the sound of its rush was very sublime. I see it yet, as it swept away on its dark green current the heaps of burning straw which the children let down from the bridge. Opposite my window was a vineyard, whose white and purple clusters were my food for three months. It was pretty to watch the vintage, — the asses and wagons loaded with this wealth of amber and rubies, — the naked boys, singing in the trees on which the vines are trained, as they cut the grapes, — the nut-brown maids and matrons, in their red corsets and white head-clothes, receiving them below, while the babies and little children were frolicking in the grass.

In Rieti, the ancient Umbrians were married thus. In presence of friends, the man and maid received together the gifts of fire and water; the bridegroom then conducted to his house the bride. At the door, he gave her the keys, and, entering, threw behind him nuts, as a sign that he renounced all the frivolities of boyhood.

I intend to write all that relates to the birth of Angelino, in a little book, which I shall, I hope, show you sometime. I have begun it, and then stopped ; — it seemed to me he would die. If he lives, I shall finish it, before the details are at all faded in my mind. Rieti is a place where I should have liked to have him born, and where I should like to have him now, — but that the people are so wicked. They are the most ferocious and mercenary population of Italy. I did not know this, when I went there, and merely expected to be solitary and quiet among poor people. But they looked on the "Marchioness" as an ignorant *Inglese*, and they fancy all *Inglesi* have wealth untold. Me they were bent on plundering in every way. They made me suffer terribly in the first days.

THE PRIVATE MARRIAGE.

The high-minded friend, spoken of with such grateful affection by Margaret, in her letter to her mother, thus gracefully narrates the romance of her marriage; and the narrative is a noble proof of the heroic disinterestedness with which, amidst her own engrossing trials, Margaret devoted herself to others. Mrs. Story writes as follows: —

"During the month of November, 1847, we arrived in Rome, purposing to spend the winter there. At that time, Margaret was living in the house of the Marchesa ———, in the Corso, *Ultimo Piano*. Her rooms were pleasant and cheerful, with a certain air of elegance and refinement, but they had not a sunny exposure, that all-essential requisite for health, during the damp Roman winter. Margaret suffered from ill health this winter, and she afterwards attributed it mainly to the fact, that she had not the sun. As soon as she heard of our arrival, she stretched forth a friendly, cordial hand, and greeted us most warmly. She gave us great assistance in our search for convenient lodgings, and we were soon happily established near her. Our intercourse was henceforth most frequent and intimate, and knew no cloud nor coldness. Daily we were much with her, and daily we felt more sensible of the worth and value of our friend. To me she seemed so unlike what I had thought her to be in America, that I continually said, 'How have I misjudged you, — you are not at all such a person as I took you to be.' To this she replied, 'I am not the same person, but in many respects another; — my life has new channels now, and how thankful I am that I have been able to come out into larger interests,— but, partly, you did not know me at home in the true light.' It was true, that I had not known her much personally, when in Boston; but through her friends, who were mine also, I had learned to think of her as a person on intellectual stilts, with a large share of arrogance, and little sweetness of temper. How unlike to this was she now! — so delicate, so simple, confiding, and affectionate; with a true womanly heart and soul, sensitive and generous, and, what was to me a still greater surprise, possessed of so broad a charity, that she could cover with its mantle the faults and defects of all about her.

" We soon became acquainted with the young Marquis Ossoli, and met him frequently at Margaret's rooms. He appeared to be of a reserved and gentle nature, with quiet, gentleman-like manners, and there was something melancholy in the expression of his face, which made one desire to know more of him. In figure, he was tall, and of slender frame, with dark hair and eyes; we judged that he was about thirty years of age, possibly younger. Margaret spoke of him most frankly, and soon told us the history of her first acquaintance with him, which, as nearly as I can recall, was as follows: —

"She went to hear vespers, the evening of 'Holy Thursday,' soon after her first coming to Rome, in the spring of 1847, at St. Peter's. She proposed to her companions that some place in the church should be designated, wheie, after the services, they should meet, — she being inclined, as was her custom always in St. Peter's, to wander alone among the different chapels. When, at length, she saw that the crowd was dispersing, she returned to the place assigned, but could not find her party. In some perplexity, she walked about, with her glass carefully examining each group. Presently, a young man of gentlemanly address came up to her, and begged, if she were seeking any one, that he might be permitted to assist her; and together they continued the search through all parts of the church. At last, it became evident, beyond a doubt, that her party could no longer be there, and, as it was then quite late, the crowd all gone, they went out into the piazza to find a carriage, in which she might go home. In the piazza, in front of St. Peter's, generally may be found many carriages; but, owing to the delay they had made, there were then none, and Margaret was compelled to walk, with her stranger friend, the long distance between the Vatican and the Corso. At this time, she had little command of the language for conversational purposes, and their words were few, though enough to create in each a desire for further knowledge and acquaintance. At her door, they parted, and Margaret, finding her friends already at home, related the adventure."

This chance meeting at vesper service in St. Peter's prepared the way for many interviews; and it was before Margaret's departure for Venice, Milan, and Como, that Ossoli first offered her his hand, and was refused. Mrs. Story continues: —

"After her return to Rome, they met again, and he became her constant visitor; and as, in those days, Margaret watched with intense interest the tide of

political events, his mind was also turned in the direc
tion of liberty and better government. Whether Ossoli,
unassisted, would have been able to emancipate himself from the influence of his family and early education, both eminently conservative and narrow, may be
a question ; but that he did throw off the shackles,
and espouse the cause of Roman liberty with warm
zeal, is most certain.   Margaret had known Mazzini in
London, had partaken of his schemes for the future of
his country, and was taking every pains to inform herself in regard to the action of all parties, with a view to
write a history of the period.   Ossoli brought her every
intelligence that might be of interest to her, and busied
himself in learning the views of both parties, that she
might be able to judge the matter impartially.

"Here I may say, that, in the estimation of most of
those who were in Italy at this time, the loss of Margaret's history and notes is a great and irreparable one.
No one could have possessed so many avenues of direct
information from both sides.   While she was the friend
and correspondent of Mazzini, and knew the springs of
action of his party; through her husband s family and
connections, she knew the other view; so that, whatever
might be the value of her deductions, her facts could
not have been other than of highest worth.   Together,
Margaret and Ossoli went to the meetings of either side;
and to her he carried all the flying reports of the day,
such as he had heard in the café, or through his friends.

"In a short time, we went to Naples, and Margaret, in
the course of a few months, to Aquila and Rieti.   Meanwhile, we heard from her often by letter, and wrote to
urge her to join us in our villa at Sorrento.   During
this summer, she wrote constantly upon her history of

.he Italian movement, for which she had collected materials through the past winter. We did not again meet, until the following spring, March, 1849, when we went from Florence back to Rome. Once more we were with her, then, in most familiar every-day intercourse, and as at this time a change of government had taken place, — the Pope having gone to Molo di Gaeta, — we watched with her the great movements of the day. Ossoli was now actively interested on the liberal side; he was holding the office of captain in the *Guardia Civica*, and enthusiastically looking forward to the success of the new measures.

"During the spring of 1849, Mazzini came to Rome. He went at once to see Margaret, and at her rooms met Ossoli. After this interview with Mazzini, it was quite evident that they had lost something of the faith and hopeful certainty with which they had regarded the issue, for Mazzini had discovered the want of singleness of purpose in the leaders of the Provisional Government. Still zealously Margaret and Ossoli aided in everything the progress of events; and when it was certain that the French had landed forces at Civita Vecchia, and would attack Rome, Ossoli took station with his men on the walls of the Vatican gardens, where he remained faithfully to the end of the attack. Margaret had, at the same time, the entire charge of one of the hospitals, and was the assistant of the Princess Belgioioso, in charge of '*dei Pellegrini*,' where, during the first day, they received seventy wounded men, French and Romans.

"Night and day, Margaret was occupied, and, with the princess, so ordered and disposed the hospitals, that their conduct was truly admirable. All the work was skilfully divided, so that there was no confusion or hurry,

and, from the chaotic condition in which these places had
been left by the priests, — who previously had charge of
them, — they brought them to a state of perfect regular-
ity and discipline. Of money they had very little, and
they were obliged to give their time and thoughts, in its
place. From the Americans in Rome, they raised
a subscription for the aid of the wounded of either
party; but, besides this, they had scarcely any means
to use. I have walked through the wards with Margaret, and seen how comforting was her presence to
the poor suffering men. 'How long will the Signora
stay?' 'When will the Signora come again?' they
eagerly asked. For each one's peculiar tastes she had a
care: to one she carried books; to another she told the
news of the day; and listened to another's oft-repeated
tale of wrongs, as the best sympathy she could give.
They raised themselves up on their elbows, to get the
last glimpse of her as she was going away. There were
some of the sturdy fellows of Garibaldi's Legion there,
and to them she listened, as they spoke with delight of
their chief, of his courage and skill; for he seemed to
have won the hearts of his men in a remarkable manner.

"One incident I may as well narrate in this connection.
It happened, that, some time before the coming of the
French, while Margaret was travelling quite by herself,
on her return from a visit to her child, who was out at
nurse in the country, she rested for an hour or two at
a little wayside *osteria*. While there, she was startled
by the *padrone*, who, with great alarm, rushed into the
room, and said, 'We are quite lost! here is the Legion
Garibaldi! These men always pillage, and, if we do
not give all up to them without pay, they will kill us.'
Margaret looked out upon the road, and saw that it was

quite true, that the legion was coming thither with all
speed.   For a moment, she said, she felt uncomfortably;
for such was the exaggerated account of the conduct of
the men, that she thought it quite possible that they
would take her horses, and so leave her without the
means of proceeding on her journey.   On they came,
and she determined to offer them a lunch at her own
expense; having faith that gentleness and courtesy was
the best protection from injury.   Accordingly, as soon as
they arrived, and rushed boisterously into the *osteria*,
she rose, and said to the *padrone*, 'Give these good
men wine and bread on my account; for, after their ride,
they must need refreshment.'   Immediately, the noise
and confusion subsided; with respectful bows to her,
they seated themselves and partook of the lunch, giving
her an account of their journey.   When she was ready to
go, and her *vettura* was at the door, they waited upon
her, took down the steps, and assisted her with much
gentleness and respectfulness of manner, and she drove
off, wondering how men with such natures could have
the reputation they had.   And, so far as we could gather,
except in this instance, their conduct was of a most
disorderly kind.

"Again, on another occasion, she showed how great
was her power over rude men.   This was when two
contadini at Rieti, being in a violent quarrel, had rushed
upon each other with knives.   Margaret was called by
the women bystanders, as the Signora who could most
influence them to peace.   She went directly up to the
men, whose rage was truly awful to behold, and, stepping
between them, commanded them to separate.   They
parted, but with such a look of deadly revenge, that
Margaret felt her work was but half accomplished.   Sh

therefore sought them out separately, and talked with each, urging forgiveness; it was long, however, before she could see any change of purpose, and only by repeated conversations was it, that she brought about her desire, and saw them meet as friends. After this, her reputation as peace-maker was great, and the women in the neighborhood came to her with long tales of trouble, urging her intervention. I have never known anything more extraordinary than this influence of hers over the passion and violence of the Italian character. Repeated instances come to my mind, when a look from her has had more power to quiet excitement, than any arguments and reasonings that could be brought to bear upon the subject. Something quite superior and apart from them, the people thought her, and yet knew her as the gentle and considerate judge of their vices.

"I may also mention here, that Margaret's charities, according to her means, were larger than those of any other whom I ever knew. At one time, in Rome, while she lived upon the simplest, slenderest fare, spending only some ten or twelve cents a day for her dinner, she lent, unsolicited, her last fifty dollars to an artist, who was then in need. That it would ever be returned to her, she did not know; but the doubt did not restrain the hand from giving. In this instance, it was soon repaid her; but her charities were not always towards the most deserving. Repeated instances of the false pretences, under which demands for charity are made, were known to her after she had given to unworthy objects; but no experience of this sort ever checked her kindly impulse to give, and being once deceived taught her no lesson of distrust. She ever listened with ready ear to all who came to her in any form of distress. Indeed, to use the language of another friend, 'the prevalent impress.on at Rome, among all who knew her, was, that she was a mild saint and a ministering angel.'

"I have, in order to bring in these instances of her influence on those about her, deviated from my track. We return to the life she led in Rome during the attack of the French, and her charge of the hospitals, where she spent daily some seven or eight hours, and, often, the entire night. Her feeble frame was a good deal shaken by so uncommon a demand upon her strength, while, at the same time, the anxiety of her mind was intense. I well remember how exhausted and weary she was; how pale and agitated she returned to us after her day's and night's watching; how eagerly she asked for news of Ossoli, and how seldom we had any to give her, for he was unable to send her a word for two or three days at a time. Letters from the country there were few or none, as the communication between Rieti and Rome was cut off.

"After one such day, she called me to her bedside, and said that I must consent, for her sake, to keep the SECRET she was about to confide. Then she told me of her marriage; where her child was, and where he was born; and gave me certain papers and parchment documents which I was to keep; and, in the event of her and her husband's death, I was to take the boy to her mother in America, and confide him to her care, and that of her friend, Mrs. —— ——.

"The papers thus given me, I had perfect liberty to read; but after she had told me her story, I desired no confirmation of this fact, beyond what her words had given. One or two of the papers she opened, and we together read them. One was written on parchment, in

Latin, and was a certificate, given by the priest who married them, saying that Angelo Eugene Ossoli was the legal heir of whatever title and fortune should come to his father. To this was affixed his seal, with those of the other witnesses, and the Ossoli crest was drawn in full upon the paper. There was also a book, in which Margaret had written the history of her acquaintance and marriage with Ossoli, and of the birth of her child. In giving that to me, she said, 'If I do not survive to tell this myself to my family, this book will be to them invaluable. Therefore keep it for them. If I live, it will be of no use, for my word will be all that they will ask.' I took the papers, and locked them up. Never feeling any desire to look into them, I never did; and as she gave them to me, I returned them to her, when I left Rome for Switzerland.

"After this, she often spoke to me of the necessity there had been, and still existed, for her keeping her marriage a secret. At the time, I argued in favor of her making it public, but subsequent events have shown me the wisdom of her decision. The *explanation* she gave me of the secret marriage was this:

"They were married in December, soon after, — as I think, though I am not positive, — the death of the old Marquis Ossoli. The estate he had left was undivided, and the two brothers, attached to the Papal household, were to be the executors. This patrimony was not large, but, when fairly divided, would bring to each a little property, — an income sufficient, with economy, for life in Rome. Every one knows, that law is subject to ecclesiastical influence in Rome, and that marriage with a Protestant would be destructive to all prospects of favorable administration. And beside being of another religious faith, there was, in this case, the additional crime of having married a liberal, — one who had publicly interested herself in radical views. Taking the two facts together, there was good reason to suppose, that, if the marriage were known, Ossoli must be a beggar, and a banished man, under the then existing government; while, by waiting a little, there was a chance, — a fair one, too, — of an honorable post under the new government, whose formation every one was anticipating. Leaving Rome, too, at that time, was deserting the field wherein they might hope to work much good, and where they felt that they were needed. Ossoli's brothers had long before begun to look jealously upon him. Knowing his acquaintance with Margaret, they feared the influence she might exert over his mind in favor of liberal sentiments, and had not hesitated to threaten him with the Papal displeasure. Ossoli's education had been such, that it certainly argues an uncommon elevation of character, that he remained so firm and single in his political views, and was so indifferent to the pecuniary advantages which his former position offered, since, during many years, the Ossoli family had been high in favor and in office, in Rome, and the same vista opened for his own future, had he chosen to follow their lead. The Pope left for Molo di Gaeta, and then came a suspension of all legal procedure, so that the estate was never divided, before we left Italy, and I do not know that it has ever been.

"Ossoli had the feeling, that, while his own sister and family could not be informed of his marriage, no others should know of it; and from day to day they hoped on for the favorable change which should enable them to declare it. Their child was born; and, for his sake, in order to defend him, as Margaret said, from the stings of poverty, they were patient waiters for the restored law of the land. Margaret felt that she would, at any cost to herself, gladly secure for her child a condition above want; and, although it was a severe trial, — as her letters to us attest, — she resolved to wait, and hope, and keep her secret. At the time when she took me into her confidence, she was so full of anxiety and dread of some shock, from which she might not recover, that it was absolutely necessary to make it known to some friend. She was living with us at the time, and she gave it to me. Most sacredly, but timidly, did I keep her secret; for, all the while, I was tormented with a desire to be of active service to her, and I was incapacitated from any action by the position in which I was placed.

"Ossoli's post was one of considerable danger, he being in one of the most exposed places; and, as Margaret saw his wounded and dying comrades, she felt that another shot might take him from her, or bring him to her care in the hospital. Eagerly she watched the carts, as they came up with their suffering loads, dreading that her worst fears might be confirmed. No argument of ours could persuade Ossoli to leave his post to take food or rest. Sometimes we went to him, and carried a concealed basket of provisions, but he shared it with so many of his fellows, that his own portion must have been almost nothing. Haggard, worn, and pale, he walked over the Vatican grounds with us, pointing out, now here, now there, where some poor fellow's blood sprinkled the wall; Margaret was with us, and for a few moments they could have an anxious talk about their child.

"To get to the child, or to send to him, was quite impossible, and for days they were in complete ignorance about him. At length, a letter came: and in it the nurse declared that unless they should immediately send her, in advance-payment, a certain sum of money, she would altogether abandon Angelo. It seemed, at first, impossible to forward the money, the road was so insecure, and the bearer of any parcel was so likely to be seized by one party or the other, and to be treated as a spy. But finally, after much consideration, the sum was sent to the address of a physician, who had been charged with the care of the child. I think it did reach its destination, and for a while answered the purpose of keeping the wretched woman faithful to her charge."

AQUILA AND RIETI.

Extracts from Margaret's and Ossoli's letters will guide us more into the heart of this home-tragedy, so sanctified with holy hope, sweet love, and patient heroism. They shall be introduced by a passage from a journal written many years before.

"My Child! O, Father, give me a bud on my tree of life, so scathed by the lightning and bound by the frost! Surely a being born wholly of my being, would not let me lie so still and cold in lonely sadness. This is a new sorrow; for always, before, I have wanted a superior or equal, but now it seems that only the feeling of a parent for a child could exhaust the richness of one's soul. All powerful Nature, how dost thou lead me into thy heart and rebuke every factitious feeling, every thought of pride, which has severed me from the Universe! How did I aspire to be a pure flame, ever pointing upward on the altar! But these thoughts of consecration, though true to the time, are false to the whole.   There needs no consecration to the wise heart, for all is pervaded by One Spirit, and the Soul of all existence is the Holy of Holies.   I thought ages would pass, before I had this parent feeling, and then, that the desire would rise from my fulness of being.   But now it springs up in my poverty and sadness.   I am well aware that I ought not to be so happy.   I do not deserve to be well beloved in any way, far less as the mother by her child.   I am too rough and blurred an image of the Creator, to become a bestower of life.   Yet, if I refuse to be anything else than my highest self, the true beauty will finally glow out in fulness."

At what cost, were bought the blessings so long pined for !   Early in the summer of 1848, Margaret left Rome for Aquila, a small, old town, once a baronial residence, perched among the mountains of Abruzzi.   She thus sketches her retreat : —

"I am in the midst of a theatre of glorious, snow-crowned mountains, whose pedestals are garlanded with the olive and mulberry, and along whose sides run bridle-paths, fringed with almond groves and vineyards. The valleys are yellow with saffron flowers; the grain fields enamelled with the brilliant blue corn-flower and red poppy.   They are of intoxicating beauty, and like nothing in America.   The old genius of Europe has so mellowed even the marbles here, that one cannot have the feeling of holy virgin loneliness, as in the New World.   The spirits of the dead crowd me in most solitary p'aces.   Here and there, gleam churches or shrines. The little town, much ruined, lies on the slope of a hill, with the houses of the barons gone to decay, and unused churches, over whose arched portals are faded frescoes, with the open belfry, and stone wheel-windows, always so beautiful. Sweet little paths lead away through the fields to convents, — one of Passionists, another of Capuchins; and the draped figures of the monks, pacing up and down the hills, look very peaceful. In the churches still open, are pictures, not by great masters, but of quiet, domestic style, which please me much, especially one of the Virgin offering her breast to the child Jesus. There is often sweet music in these churches; they are dressed with fresh flowers, and the incense is not oppressive, so freely sweeps through them the mountain breeze."

Here Margaret remained but a month, while Ossoli was kept fast by his guard duties in Rome. "*Addio, tutto caro*," she writes; "I shall receive you with the greatest joy, when you can come. If it were only possible to be nearer to you! for, except the good air and the security, this place does not please me." And again: — "How much I long to be near you! You write nothing of yourself, and this makes me anxious and sad. Dear and good! I pray for thee often, now that it is all I can do for thee. We must hope that Destiny will at last grow weary of persecuting. Ever thy affectionate." Meantime Ossoli writes: — " Why do you not send me tidings of yourself, every post-day? since the post leaves Aquila three times a week. I send you journals or letters every time the post leaves Rome. You should do the same. Take courage, and thus you will make me happier also; and you can think how sad I must feel in not being near you, dearest, to care for al your wants."

By the middle of July, Margaret could bear her loneliness no longer, and, passing the mountains, advanced
to Rieti, within the frontier of the Papal States.   Here
Ossoli could sometimes visit her on a Sunday, by
travelling in the night from Rome.   "Do not fail to
come," writes Margaret.   "I shall have your coffee
warm.   You will arrive early, and I can see the diligence pass the bridge from my window."   But now
threatened a new trial, terrible under the circumstances,
yet met with the loving heroism that characterized all
her conduct.   The civic guard was ordered to prepare
for marching to Bologna.   Under date of August 17th,
Ossoli writes : — "*Mia Cara!*   How deplorable is my
state !   I have suffered a most severe struggle.   If your
condition were other than it is, I could resolve more
easily; but, in the present moment, I cannot leave you !
Ah, how cruel is Destiny !   I understand well how
much you would sacrifice yourself for me, and am
deeply grateful; but I cannot yet decide."   Margaret is
alone, without a single friend, and not only among
strangers, but surrounded by people so avaricious, cunning, and unscrupulous, that she has to be constantly
on the watch to avoid being fleeced; she is very poor,
and has no confidant, even in Rome, to consult with;
she is ill, and fears death in the near crisis; yet thus,
with true Roman greatness, she counsels her husband : —
"It seems, indeed, a marvel how all things go contrary
to us !   That, just at this moment, you should be called
upon to go away.   But do what is for your honor.   If
honor requires it, go.   I will try to sustain myself.   I
leave it to your judgment when to come, — if, indeed,
you can ever come again !   At least, we have had some
hours of peace together, if now it is all over.   Adieu

.ove; I embrace thee always, and pray for thy welfare. Most affectionately, adieu."

From this trial, however, she was spared. Pio Nono hesitated to send the civic guard to the north of Italy. Then Margaret writes: — "On our own account, love, I shall be most grateful, if you are not obliged to go. But how unworthy, in the Pope! He seems now a man without a heart. And that traitor, Charles Albert! He will bear the curse of all future ages. Can you learn particulars from Milan? I feel sad for our poor friends there; how much they must suffer! * * * I shall be much more tranquil to have you at my side, for it would be sad to die alone, without the touch of one dear hand. Still, I repeat what I said in my last: if duty prevents you from coming, I will endeavor to take care of myself." Again, two days later, she says: — "I feel, love, a profound sympathy with you, but am not able to give perfectly wise counsel. It seems to me, indeed, the worst possible moment to take up arms, except in the cause of duty, of honor; for, with the Pope so cold, and his ministers so undecided, nothing can be well or successfully done. If it is possible for you to wait for two or three weeks, the public state will be determined, — as will also mine, — and you can judge more calmly. Otherwise, it seems to me that I ought to say nothing. Only, if you go, come here first. I must see you once more. Adieu, dear. Our misfortunes are many and unlooked for. Not often does destiny demand a greater price for some happy moments. Yet never do I repent of our affection; and for thee, if not for me, I hope that life has still some good in store. Once again, adieu! May God give thee counsel and help, since they are not in the power of thy affectionate Margherita."

On the 5th of September, Ossoli was "at her side," and together, with glad and grateful hearts, they welcomed their boy; though the father was compelled to return the next day to Rome. Even then, however, a new chapter of sorrows was opening. By indiscreet treatment, Margaret was thrown into violent fever, and became unable to nurse her child. Her waiting maid, also, proved so treacherous, that she was forced to dismiss her, and wished "never to set eyes on her more;" and the family, with whom she was living, displayed most detestable meanness. Thus helpless, ill, and solitary, she could not even now enjoy the mother's privilege. Yet she writes cheerfully: — "My present nurse is a very good one, and I feel relieved. We must have courage; but it is a great care, alone and ignorant, to guard an infant in its first days of life. He is very pretty for his age; and, without knowing what name I intended giving him, the people in the house call him *Angiolino*, because he is so lovely." Again: — "He is so dear! It seems to me, among all disasters and difficulties, that if he lives and is well, he will become a treasure for us two, that will compensate us for everything." And yet again: — "This —— is faithless, like the rest. Spite of all his promises, he will not bring the matter to inoculate Nino, though, all about us, persons are dying with small-pox. I cannot sleep by night, and I weep by day, I am so disgusted; but you are too far off to help me. The baby is more beautiful every hour. He is worth all the trouble he causes me, — poor child that I am, — alone here, and abused by everybody."

Yet new struggles, new sorrows! Ossoli writes: —

'Our affairs must be managed with the utmost caution
imaginable, since my thought would be to keep the
baby out of Rome for the sake of greater secrecy, if
only we can find a good nurse who will take care of
him like a mother." To which Margaret replies: —
"He is always so charming, how can I ever, ever leave
him! I wake in the night, — I look at him. I think:
Ah, it is impossible! He is so beautiful and good, I
could die for him!" Once more: — "In seeking rooms,
do not pledge me to remain in Rome, for it seems to
me, often, I cannot stay long without seeing the boy.
He is so dear, and life seems so uncertain. It is necessary that I should be in Rome a month, at least, to write,
and also to be near you. But I must be free to return
here, if I feel too anxious and suffering for him. O,
love! how difficult is life! But thou art good! If it
were only possible to make thee happy!" And, finally,
"Signora speaks very highly of ——, the nurse of
Angelo, and says that her aunt is an excellent woman,
and that the brothers are all good. Her conduct pleases
me well. This consoles me a little, in the prospect of
leaving my child, if that is necessary."

So, early in November, Ossoli came for her, and they
returned together. In December, however, Margaret
passed a week more with her darling, making two
fatiguing and perilous journeys, as snows had fallen on
the mountains, and the streams were much swollen by
the rains. And then, from the combined motives of
being near her husband, watching and taking part in
the impending struggle of liberalism, earning support by
her pen, preparing her book, and avoiding suspicion, she
remained for three months in Rome. "How many
nights I have passed," she writes, "entirely in contriv-

ing possible means, by which, through resolution and effort on my part, that one sacrifice could be avoided. But it was impossible. I could not take the nurse from her family; I could not remove Angelo, without immense difficulty and risk. It is singular, how everything has worked to give me more and more sorrow. Could I but have remained in peace, cherishing the messenger dove, I should have asked no more, but should have felt overpaid for all the pains and bafflings of my sad and broken life." In March, she flies back to Rieti, and finds "our treasure in the best of health, and plump, though small. When first I took him in my arms, he made no sound, but leaned his head against my bosom, and kept it there, as if he would say, How could you leave me? They told me, that all the day of my departure he would not be comforted, always looking toward the door. He has been a strangely precocious infant, I think, through sympathy with me, for I worked very hard before his birth, with the hope that all my spirit might be incarnated in him. In that regard, it may have been good for him to be with these more instinctively joyous natures. I see that he is more serene, is less sensitive, than when with me, and sleeps better. The most solid happiness I have known has been when he has gone to sleep in my arms. What cruel sacrifices have I made to guard my secret for the present, and to have the mode of disclosure at my own option! It will, indeed, be just like all the rest, if these sacrifices are made in vain."

At Rieti, Margaret rested till the middle of April, when, returning once more to Rome, she was, as we have seen, shut up within the beleagured city.

The siege ended, the anxious mother was free to seek her child once more, in his nest among the mountains. Her fears had been but too prophetic. "Though the physician sent me reässuring letters," she writes, "I yet often seemed to hear Angelino calling to me amid the roar of the cannon, and always his tone was of crying. And when I came, I found mine own fast waning to the tomb! His nurse, lovely and innocent as she appeared, had betrayed him, for lack of a few *scudi!* He was worn to a skeleton; his sweet, childish grace all gone! Everything I had endured seemed light to what I felt when I saw him too weak to smile, or lift his wasted little hand. Now, by incessant care, we have brought him back, — who knows if that be a deed of love? — into this hard world once more. But I could not let him go, unless I went with him; and I do hope that the cruel law of my life will, at least, not oblige us to be separated. When I saw his first returning smile, — that poor, wan, feeble smile! — and more than four weeks we watched him night and day, before we saw it, — new resolution dawned in my heart. I resolved to live, day by day, hour by hour, for his dear sake. So, if he is only treasure lent, — if he too must go, as sweet Waldo, Pickie, Hermann, did, — as all *my* children do! — I shall at least have these days and hours with him."

How intolerable was this last blow to one stretched so long on the rack, is plain from Margaret's letters. "I shall never again," she writes, "be perfectly, be religiously generous, so terribly do I need for myself the love I have given to other sufferers. When you read this, I hope your heart will be happy; for I still like to know that others are happy, — it consoles me." Again her agony wrung from her these bitter words, — the bitterest she ever uttered, — words of transient madness, yet most characteristic : — " Oh God ! help me, is all my cry. Yet I have little faith in the Paternal love I need, so ruthless or so negligent seems the government of this earth.   I feel calm, yet sternly, towards Fate.   This last plot against me has been so cruelly, cunningly wrought, that I shall never acquiesce.   I submit, because useless resistance is degrading, but I demand an explanation.   I see that it is probable I shall never receive one, while I live here, and suppose I can bear the rest of the suspense, since I have comprehended all its difficulties in the first moments.   Meanwhile, I live day by day, though no on manna."   But now comes a sweeter, gentler strain : — " I have been the object of great love from the noble and the humble; I have felt it towards both.   Yet I am *tired out*, — tired of thinking and hoping, — tired of seeing men err and bleed.   I take interest in some plans, — Socialism for instance, — but the interest is shallow as the plans.   These are needed, are even good; but man will still blunder and weep, as he has done for so many thousand years.   Coward and footsore, gladly would I creep into some green recess, where I might see a few not unfriendly faces, and where not more wretches should come than I could relieve.   Yes! I am weary, and faith soars and sings no more.   Nothing good of me is left except at the bottom of the heart, a melting tenderness : — ' She loves much.' "

CALM AFTER STORM.

Morning rainbows usher in tempests, and certainly youth's romantic visions had prefigured a stormy day of life for Margaret.   But there was yet to be a serene and glowing hour before the sun went down. Angel grew strong and lively once more; rest and peace restored her elasticity of spirit, and extracts from various letters will show in what tranquil blessedness, the autumn and winter glided by. After a few weeks' residence at Rieti, the happy three journeyed on, by way of Perugia, to Florence, where they arrived at the end of September. Thence, Margaret writes: —

It was so pleasant at Perugia! The pure mountain air is such perfect elixir, the walks are so beautiful on every side, and there is so much to excite generous and consoling feelings! I think the works of the Umbrian school are never well seen except in their home; — they suffer by comparison with works more rich in coloring, more genial, more full of common life. The depth and tenderness of their expression is lost on an observer stimulated to a point out of their range. Now, I can prize them. We went every morning to some church rich in pictures, returning at noon for breakfast. After breakfast, we went into the country, or to sit and read under the trees near San Pietro. Thus I read Nicolo di' Lapi, a book unenlivened by a spark of genius, but interesting, to me, as illustrative of Florence.

Our little boy gained strength rapidly there; — every day he was able to go out with us more. He is now full of life and gayety. We hope he will live, and grow into a stout man yet.

Our journey here was delightful; — it is the first time I have seen Tuscany when the purple grape hangs garlanded from tree to tree. We were in the early days of the vintage: the fields were animated by men and women, some of the latter with such pretty little bare

feet, and shy, soft eyes, under the round straw hat!
They were beginning to cut the vines, but had not done
enough to spoil any of the beauty.

Here, too, I feel better pleased than ever before. Florence seems so cheerful and busy, after ruined Rome, I
feel as if I could forget the disasters of the day, for a
while, in looking on the treasures she inherits.

    *   *   *   *   *

To-day we have been out in the country, and found
a little chapel, full of *contadine*, their lovers waiting
outside the door. They looked charming in their black
veils, — the straw hat hanging on the arm, — with shy,
glancing eyes, and cheeks pinched rosy by the cold;
for it is cold here as in New England. On foot, we
have explored a great part of the environs; and till now
I had no conception of their beauty. When here before,
I took only the regular drives, as prescribed for all lady
and gentlemen travellers. This evening we returned by
a path that led to the banks of the Arno. The Duomo,
with the snowy mountains, were glorious in the rosy tint
and haze, just before sunset. What a difference it makes
to come home to a child! — how it fills up all the gaps
of life, just in the way that is most consoling, most refreshing! Formerly, I used to feel sad at that hour; the
day had not been nobly spent, I had not done my duty
to myself and others, and I felt so lonely! Now I never
feel lonely; for, even if my little boy dies, our souls will
remain eternally united. And I feel *infinite* hope for
him, — hope that he will serve God and man more loy-
ally than I have done; and, seeing how full he is of life,
— how much he can afford to throw away, — I feel the
inexhaustibleness of nature, and console myself for my
own incapacities.

Florence, Oct. 14, 1849. — Weary in spirit, with the deep disappointments of the last year, I wish to dwell little on these things for the moment, but seek some consolation in the affections. My little boy is quite well now, and I often am happy in seeing how joyous and full of activity he seems. Ossoli, too, feels happier here. The future is full of difficulties for us, but, having settled our plans for the present, we shall set it aside while we may. "Sufficient for the day is the evil thereof;" and if the good be not always sufficient, in our case it is; so let us say grace to our dinner of herbs.

Florence, Nov. 7. — Dearest Mother, — Of all your endless acts and words of love, never was any so dear to me as your last letter; — so generous, so sweet, so holy! What on earth is so precious as a mother's love; and who has a mother like mine!

I was thinking of you and my father, all that first day of October, wishing to write, only there was much to disturb me that day, as the police were threatening to send us away. It is only since I have had my own child that I have known how much I always failed to do what I might have done for the happiness of you both; only since I have seen so much of men and their trials, that I have learned to prize my father as he deserved; only since I have had a heart daily and hourly testifying to me its love, that I have understood, too late, what it was for you to be deprived of it. It seems to me as if I had never sympathized with you as I ought, or tried to embellish and sustain your life, as far as is possible, after such an irreparable wound.

It will be sad for me to leave Italy, uncertain of return. Yet when I think of you, beloved mother; of brothers and sisters, and many friends, I wish to come. Ossoli is perfectly willing. He leaves in Rome a sister, whom he dearly loves. His aunt is dying now. He will go among strangers; but to him, as to all the young Italians, America seems the land of liberty. He hopes, too, that a new revolution will favor return, after a number of years, and that then he may find really a home in Italy. All this is dark; — we can judge only for the present moment. The decision will rest with me, and I shall wait till the last moment, as I always do, that I may have all the reasons before me.

I thought, to-day, ah, if she could only be with us now! But who knows how long this interval of peace will last? I have learned to prize such, as the halcyon prelude to the storm. It is now about a fortnight, since the police gave us leave to stay, and we feel safe in our little apartment. We have no servant except the nurse, with occasional aid from the porter's wife, and now live comfortably so, tormented by no one, helping ourselves. In the evenings, we have a little fire now; — the baby sits on his stool between us. He makes me think how I sat on mine, in the chaise, between you and father. He is exceedingly fond of flowers; — he has been enchanted, this evening, by this splendid Gardenia, and these many crimson flowers that were given me at Villa Correggi, where a friend took us in his carriage. It was a luxury, this ride, as we have entirely renounced the use of a carriage for ourselves. How enchanted you would have been with that villa! It seems now as if, with the certainty of a very limited income, we could be so happy! But I suppose, if we had it, one of us would die, or the baby. Do not you die, my beloved mother; — let us together have some halcyon moments, again, with God, with nature, with sweet childhood, with the remembrance of pure trust and good intent; away from perfidy and care, and the blight of noble designs.

Ossoli wishes you were here, almost as much as I. When there is anything really lovely and tranquil, he often says, " Would not *'La Madre'* like that?" He wept when he heard your letter. I never saw him weep at any other time, except when his father died, and when the French entered Rome. He has, I think, even a more holy feeling about a mother, from having lost his own, when very small. It has been a life-long want with him. He often shows me a little scar on his face, made by a jealous dog, when his mother was caressing him as an infant. He prizes that blemish much.

Florence, December 1, 1849. — I do not know what to write about the baby, he changes so much, — has so many characters. He is like me in that, for his father's character is simple and uniform, though not monotonous, any more than are the flowers of spring flowers of the valley. Angelino is now in the most perfect rosy health, — a very gay, impetuous, ardent, but sweet-tempered child. He seems to me to have nothing in common with his first babyhood, with its ecstatic smiles, its exquisite sensitiveness, and a distinction in the gesture and attitudes that struck everybody. His temperament is apparently changed by taking the milk of these robust women. He is now come to quite a knowing age, — fifteen months.

In the morning, as soon as dressed, he signs to come into our room; then draws our curtain with his little dimpled hand, kisses me rather violently, pats my face, laughs, crows, shows his teeth, blows like the

bellows, stretches himself, and says "*bravo.*" Then,
having shown off all his accomplishments, he expects,
as a reward, to be tied in his chair, and have his play-
things. These engage him busily, but still he calls to
us to sing and drum, to enliven the scene. Sometimes
he summons me to kiss his hand, and laughs very much
at this. Enchanting is that baby-laugh, all dimples and
glitter, — so strangely arch and innocent! Then I wash
and dress him. That is his great time. He makes it
last as long as he can, insisting to dress and wash me
the while, kicking, throwing the water about, and full
of all manner of tricks, such as, I think, girls never
dream of. Then comes his walk; — we have beautiful
walks here for him, protected by fine trees, always warm
in mid-winter. The bands are playing in the distance,
and children of all ages are moving about, and sitting
with their nurses. His walk and sleep give me about
three hours in the middle of the day.

I feel so refreshed by his young life, and Ossoli dif-
fuses such a power and sweetness over every day, that I
cannot endure to think yet of our future. Too much
have we suffered already, trying to command it. I
do not feel force to make any effort yet. I suppose
that very soon now I must do something, and hope I
shall feel able when the time comes. My constitution
seems making an effort to rally, by dint of much sleep.
I had slept so little, for a year and a half, and, after the
birth of the child, I had such anxiety and anguish when
separated from him, that I was consumed as by nightly
fever. The last two months at Rome would have
destroyed almost any woman. Then, when I went to
him, he was so ill, and I was constantly up with him at
night, carrying him about. Now, for two months, we

have been tranquil. We have resolved to enjoy being together as much as we can, in this brief interval, — perhaps all we shall ever know of peace. It is very sad we have no money, we could be so quietly happy a while. I rejoice in all Ossoli did; but the results, in this our earthly state, are disastrous, especially as my strength is now so impaired. This much I hope, in life or death, to be no more separated from Angelino.

Last winter, I made the most vehement efforts at least to redeem the time, hoping thus good for the future. But, of at least two volumes written at that time, no line seems of any worth. I had suffered much constraint, — much that was uncongenial, harassing, even torturing, before; but this kind of pain found me unprepared; — the position of a mother separated from her only child is too frightfully unnatural.

* * * * *

The Christmas holidays interest me now, through my child, as they never did for myself. I like to go out to watch the young generation who will be his contemporaries. On Monday, we went to the *Cascine.* After we had taken the drive, we sat down on a stone seat in the sunny walk, to see the people pass; — the Grand Duke and his children; the elegant Austrian officers, who will be driven out of Italy when Angelino is a man; Princess Demidoff; Harry Lorrequer; an absurd brood of fops; many lovely children; many little frisking dogs, with their bells, &c. The sun shone brightly on the Arno; a barque moved gently by; all seemed good to the baby. He laid himself back in my arms, smiling, singing to himself, and dancing his feet. I hope he will retain some trace in his mind of the perpetual exhilarating picture of Italy. It cannot but be important in its influence.

while yet a child, to walk in these stately gardens, full of sculpture, and hear the untiring music of the fountains.

Christmas-eve we went to the Annunziata, for midnight mass. Though the service is not splendid here as in Rome, we yet enjoyed it; — sitting in one of the side chapels, at the foot of a monument, watching the rich crowds steal gently by, every eye gleaming, every gesture softened by the influence of the pealing choir, and the hundred silver lamps swinging their full light, in honor of the abused Emanuel.

But far finest was it to pass through the Duomo. No one was there. Only the altars were lit up, and the priests, who were singing, could not be seen by the faint light. The vast solemnity of the interior is thus really felt. The hour was worthy of Brunelleschi. I hope he walked there so. The Duomo is more divine than St. Peter's, and worthy of genius pure and unbroken. St. Peter's is, like Rome, a mixture of sublimest heaven with corruptest earth. I adore the Duomo, though no place can now be to me like St. Peter's, where has been passed the splendidest part of my life. My feeling was always perfectly regal, on entering the piazza of St. Peter's. No spot on earth is worthier the sunlight; — on none does it fall so fondly.

*   *   *   *   *

You ask me, how I employ myself here. I have been much engaged in writing out my impressions, which will be of worth so far as correct. I am anxious only to do historical justice to facts and persons; but there will not, so far as I am aware, be much thought, for I believe I have scarce expressed what lies deepest in my mind. I take no pains, but let the good genius guide my pen.

I did long to lead a simple, natural life, *at home*, learning of my child, and writing only when imperatively
urged by the need of utterance; but when we were
forced to give up the hope of subsisting on a narrow independence, without tie to the public, we gave up the
peculiar beauty of our lives, and I strive no more. I
only hope to make good terms with the publishers.

Then, I have been occupied somewhat in reading
Louis Blanc's Ten Years, Lamartine's Girondists, and
other books of that class, which throw light on recent
transactions.

I go into society, too, somewhat, and see several delightful persons, in an intimate way. The Americans
meet twice a week, at the house of Messrs. Mozier and
Chapman, and I am often present, on account of the
friendly interest of those resident here. With our friends,
the Greenoughs, I have twice gone to the opera. Then
I see the Brownings often, and love and admire them
both, more and more, as I know them better. Mr.
Browning enriches every hour I pass with him, and is a
most cordial, true, and noble man. One of my most
highly prized Italian friends, also, Marchioness Arconati
Visconti, of Milan, is passing the winter here, and I see
her almost every day.

*   *   *   *   *

My love for Ossoli is most pure and tender, nor has
any one, except my mother or little children, loved me so
genuinely as he does. To some, I have been obliged to
make myself known; others have loved me with a mixture of fancy and enthusiasm, excited by my talent at
embellishing life. But Ossoli loves me from simple
affinity; — he loves to be with me, and to serve and
soothe me   Life will probably be a severe struggle, but

I hope I shall be able to live through all that is before
us, and not neglect my child or his father. He has suffered enough since we met; — it has ploughed furrows
in his life. He has done all he could, and cannot blame
himself. Our outward destiny looks dark, but we must
brave it as we can. I trust we shall always feel mutual
tenderness, and Ossoli has a simple, childlike piety, that
will make it easier for him.

MARGARET AND HER PEERS.

Pure and peaceful as was the joy of Margaret's Florence winter, it was ensured and perfected by the fidelity
of friends, who hedged around with honor the garden of
her home. She had been called to pass through a most
trying ordeal, and the verdict of her peers was heightened
esteem and love. With what dignified gratitude she
accepted this well-earned proof of confidence, will appear
from the following extracts.

TO MRS. E. S.

Thus far, my friends have received news that must
have been an unpleasant surprise to them, in a way that,
á moi, does them great honor. None have shown littleness or displeasure, at being denied my confidence while
they were giving their own. Many have expressed the
warmest sympathy, and only one has shown a disposition to transgress the limit I myself had marked, and to
ask questions. With her, I think, this was because she
was annoyed by what people said, and wished to be able
to answer them. I replied to her, that I had communicated already all I intended, and should not go into

detail; — that when unkind things were said about me, she should let them pass. Will you, dear E——, do the same? I am sure your affection for me will prompt you to add, that you feel confident whatever I have done has been in a good spirit, and not contrary to *my* ideas of right. For the rest, you will not admit for me, — as I do not for myself, — the rights of the social inquisition of the United States to know all the details of my affairs. If my mother is content; if Ossoli and I are content; if our child, when grown up, shall be content; that is enough. You and I know enough of the United States to be sure that many persons there will blame whatever is peculiar. The lower-minded persons, everywhere, are sure to think that whatever is mysterious must be bad. But I think there will remain for me a sufficient number of friends to keep my heart warm, and to help me earn my bread; — that is all that is of any consequence. Ossoli seems to me more lovely and good every day; our darling child is well now, and every day more gay and playful. For his sake I shall have courage; and hope some good angel will show us the way out of our external difficulties.

TO W. W. S.

It was like you to receive with such kindness the news of my marriage. A less generous person would have been displeased, that, when we had been drawn so together, — when we had talked so freely, and you had shown towards me such sweet friendship, — I had not told you. Often did I long to do so, but I had, for reasons that seemed important, made a law to myself to keep this secret as rigidly as possible, up to a certain

.

moment. That moment came. Its decisions were not
such as I had hoped; but it left me, at least, without
that painful burden, which I trust never to bear again
Nature keeps so many secrets, that I had supposed the
moral writers exaggerated the dangers and plagues of
keeping them; but they cannot exaggerate. All that
can be said about mine is, that I at least acted out, with,
to me, tragic thoroughness, "The wonder, a woman
keeps a secret." As to my not telling *you*, I can merely
say, that I was keeping the information from my family
and dearest friends at home; and, had you remained near
me a very little later, you would have been the very first
person to whom I should have spoken, as you would
have been the first, on this side of the water, to whom I
should have written, had I known where to address you.
Yet I hardly hoped for your sympathy, dear W——.
I am very glad if I have it. May brotherly love ever be
returned unto you, in like measure. Ossoli desires his
love and respect to be testified to you both.

TO THE MARCHIONESS VISCONTI ARCONATI.

Reading a book called "The Last Days of the Republic in Rome," I see that my letter, giving my impressions of that period, may well have seemed to you
strangely partial. If we can meet as once we did, and
compare notes in the same spirit of candor, while making
mutual allowance for our different points of view, your
testimony and opinions would be invaluable to me. But
will you have patience with my democracy, — my revolutionary spirit? Believe that in thought I am more
radical than ever. The heart of Margaret you know, — it
is always the same. Mazzini is immortally dear to me

— a thousand times dearer for all the trial I saw made of him in Rome; — dearer for all he suffered. Many of his brave friends perished there. We who, less worthy, survive, would fain make up for the loss, by our increased devotion to him, the purest, the most disinterested of patriots, the most affectionate of brothers. You will not love me less that I am true to him.

Then, again, how will it affect you to know that I have united my destiny with that of an obscure young man, — younger than myself; a person of no intellectual culture, and in whom, in short, you will see no reason for my choosing; yet more, that this union is of long standing; that we have with us our child, of a year old, and that it is only lately I acquainted my family with the fact?

If you decide to meet with me as before, and wish to say something about the matter to your friends, it will be true to declare that there have been pecuniary reasons for this concealment. But *to you*, in confidence, I add, this is only half the truth; and I cannot explain, or satisfy my dear friend further. I should wish to meet her independent of all relations, but, as we live in the midst of "society," she would have to inquire for me now as Margaret Ossoli. That being done, I should like to say nothing more on the subject.

However you may feel about all this, dear Madame Arconati, you will always be the same in my eyes. I earnestly wish you may not feel estranged; but, if you do, I would prefer that you should act upon it. Let us meet as friends, or not at all. In all events, I remain ever yours, MARGARET.

TO THE MARCHIONESS VISCONTI ARCONATI.

My loved friend, — I read your letter with greatest content. I did not know but that there might seem something offensively strange in the circumstances I mentioned to you. Goethe says, "There is nothing men pardon so little as singular conduct, for which no reason is given;" and, remembering this, I have been a little surprised at the even increased warmth of interest with which the little American society of Florence has received me, with the unexpected accessories of husband and child, — asking no questions, and seemingly satisfied to find me thus accompanied. With you, indeed, I thought it would be so, because you are above the world; only, as you have always walked in the beaten path, though with noble port, and feet undefiled, I thought you might not like your friends to be running about in these blind alleys. It glads my heart, indeed, that you do not care for this, and that we may meet in love.

You speak of our children. Ah! dear friend, I do, indeed, feel we shall have deep sympathy there. I do not believe mine will be a brilliant child, and, indeed, I see nothing peculiar about him. Yet he is to me a source of ineffable joys, — far purer, deeper, than anything I ever felt before, — like what Nature had sometimes given, but more intimate, more sweet. He loves me very much; his little heart clings to mine. I trust, if he lives, to sow there no seeds which are not good, to be always growing better for his sake. Ossoli, too, will be a good father. He has very little of what is called intellectual development, but unspoiled instincts, affections pure and constant, and a quiet sense of duty, which, to me, — who have seen much of the great faults in characters of enthusiasm and genius, — seems of highest value.

When you write by post, please direct "Marchesa Ossoli," as all the letters come to that address. I did not explain myself on that point. The fact is, it looks to me silly for a radical like me to be carrying a title; and yet, while Ossoli is in his native land, it seems disjoining myself from him, not to bear it. It is a sort of thing that does not naturally belong to me, and, unsustained by fortune, is but a *souvenir* even for Ossoli. Yet it has appeared to me, that for him to drop an inherited title would be, in some sort, to acquiesce in his brothers' disclaiming him, and to abandon a right he may passively wish to maintain for his child. How does it seem to you? I am not very clear about it. If Ossoli should drop the title, it would be a suitable moment to do so on becoming an inhabitant of Republican America.

TO MRS. C. T.

What you say of the meddling curiosity of people repels me, it is so different here. When I made my appearance with a husband and a child of a year old, nobody did the least act to annoy me. All were most cordial; none asked or implied questions. Yet there were not a few who might justly have complained, that, when they were confiding to me all their affairs, and doing much to serve me, I had observed absolute silence to them. Others might, for more than one reason, be displeased at the choice I made. All have acted in the kindliest and most refined manner. An Italian lady, with whom I was intimate, — who might be qualified in the Court Journal, as one of the highest rank, sustained by the most scrupulous decorum,— when I wrote, "Dear friend, I am married; I have a child. There are particulars, as to my reasons for keeping this secret, I do not wish to tell. This is rather an odd affair; will it make any difference in our relations?" — answered, "What difference can it make, except that I shall love you more, now that we can sympathize as mothers?" Her first visit here was to me; she adopted at once Ossoli and the child to her love.

—— wrote me that —— was a little hurt, at first, that I did not tell him, even in the trying days of Rome, but left him to hear it, as he unluckily did, at the *table d'hôte* in Venice; but his second and prevailing thought was regret that he had not known it, so as to soothe and aid me, — to visit Ossoli at his post, — to go to the child in the country. Wholly in that spirit was the fine letter he wrote me, one of my treasures. The little American society have been most cordial and attentive; one lady, who has been most intimate with me, dropped a tear over the difficulties before me, but she said, "Since you have seen fit to take the step, all your friends have to do, now, is to make it as easy for you as they can."

TO MRS. E. S.

I am glad to have people favorably impressed, because I feel lazy and weak, unequal to the trouble of friction, or the pain of conquest. Still, I feel a good deal of contempt for those so easily disconcerted or reässured. I was not a child; I had lived in the midst of that New England society, in a way that entitled me to esteem, and a favorable interpretation, where there was doubt about my motives or actions. I pity those who are inclined to think ill, when they might as well have inclined the other way. However, let them go; there are many in the world who stand the test, enough to keep us from shivering to death. I am, on the whole, fortunate in friends whom I can truly esteem, and in whom I know the kernel and substance of their being too well to be misled by seemings.

TO MRS. C. T.

I had a letter from my mother, last summer, speaking of the fact, that she had never been present at the marriage of one of her children. A pang of remorse came as I read it, and I thought, if Angelino dies,* I will not give her the pain of knowing that I have kept this secret from her; — she shall hear of this connection, as if it were something new. When I found he would live, I wrote to her and others. It half killed me to write those few letters, and yet, I know, many are wondering that I did not write more, and more particularly. My mother received my communication in the highest spirit. She said, she was sure a first object with me had been, now and always, to save her pain. She blessed us. She rejoiced that she should not die feeling there was no one left to love me with the devotion she thought I needed. She expressed no regret at our poverty, but offered her feeble means. Her letter was a noble crown to her life of disinterested, purifying love.

* This was when Margaret found Nino so ill at Rieti.

FLORENCE.

The following notes respecting Margaret's residence in Florence were furnished to the editors by Mr. W. H. Hurlbut.

I passed about six weeks in the city of Florence, during the months of March and April, 1850. During the whole of that time Madame Ossoli was residing in a house at the corner of the Via della Misericordia and the Piazza Santa Maria Novella. This house is one of those large, well built modern houses that show strangely in the streets of the stately Tuscan city. But if her rooms were less characteristically Italian, they were the more comfortable, and, though small, had a quiet, home-like air. Her windows opened upon a fine view of the beautiful Piazza; for such was their position, that while the card-board façade of the church of Sta. Maria Novella could only be seen at an angle, the exquisite Campanile rose fair and full against the sky. She enjoyed this most graceful tower very much, and, I think, preferred it even to Giotto's noble work. Its quiet religious grace was grateful to her spirit, which seemed to be yearning for peace from the cares that had so vexed and heated the world about her for a year past.

I saw her frequently at these rooms, where, surrounded by her books and papers, she used to devote her mornings to her literary labors. Once or twice I called in the morning, and found her quite immersed in manuscripts and journals. Her evenings were passed usually in the society of her friends, at her own rooms, or at theirs. With the pleasant circle of Americans, then living in Florence, she was on the best terms, and though she seemed always to bring with her her own most intimate society, and never to be quite free from the company of busy thoughts, and the cares to which her life had introduced her, she was always cheerful, and her remarkable powers of conversation subserved on all occasions the kindliest purposes of good-will in social intercourse.

The friends with whom she seemed to be on the terms of most sympathy, were an Italian lady, the Marchesa Arconati Visconti,* — the exquisite sweetness of whose voice interpreted, even to those who knew her only as a transient acquaintance, the harmony of her nature, — and some English residents in Florence, among whom I need only name Mr. and Mrs. Browning, to satisfy the most anxious friends of Madame Ossoli that the last months of her Italian life were cheered by all the light that communion with gifted and noble natures could afford.

The Marchesa Arconati used to persuade Madame Ossoli to occasional excursions with her into the environs of Florence, and she passed some days of the beautiful spring weather at the villa of that lady.

Her delight in nature seemed to be a source of great comfort and strength to her. I shall not easily forget the account she gave me, on the evening of one delicious Sunday in April, of a walk which she had taken with her husband in the afternoon of that day, to the hill of San Miniato. The amethystine beauty of the Apen-

---

* Just before I left Florence, Madame Ossoli showed me a small marble figure of a child, playing among flowers or vine leaves, which she said, was a portrait of the child of Madame Arconati, presented to her by that lady. I mention this circumstance, because I have understood that a figure answering this description was recovered from the wreck of the Elizabeth.

nines, — the cypress trees that sentinel the way up to the ancient and deserted church, — the church itself, standing high and lonely on its hill, begirt with the vine-clad, crumbling walls of Michel Angelo, — the repose of the dome-crowned city in the vale below, — seemed to have wrought their impression with peculiar force upon her mind that afternoon. On their way home, they had entered the conventual church that stands half way up the hill, just as the vesper service was beginning, and she spoke of the simple spirit of devotion that filled the place, and of the gentle wonder with which, to use her own words, the "peasant women turned their glances, the soft dark glances of the Tuscan peasant's eyes," upon the strangers, with a singular enthusiasm. She was in the habit of taking such walks with her husband, and she never returned from one of them, I believe, without some new impression of beauty and of lasting truth. While her judgment, intense in its sincerity, tested, like an *aqua regia*, the value of all facts that came within her notice, her sympathies seemed, by an instinctive and unerring action, to transmute all her experiences instantly into permanent treasures.

The economy of the house in which she lived afforded me occasions for observing the decisive power, both of control and of consolation, which she could exert over others. Her maid, — an impetuous girl of Rieti, a town which rivals Tivoli as a hot-bed of homicide, — was constantly involved in disputes with a young Jewess, who occupied the floor above Madame Ossoli. On one occasion, this Jewess offered the maid a deliberate and unprovoked insult. The girl of Rieti, snatching up a knife, ran up stairs to revenge herself after her national fashion. The porter's little daughter followed her,

and, running into Madame Ossoli's rooms, besought
her interference. Madame Ossoli reached the apartment
of the Jewess, just in time to interpose between that
beetle-browed lady and her infuriated assailant. Those
who know the insane license of spirit which distin-
guishes the Roman mountaineers, will understand that
this was a position of no slight hazard. The Jewess
aggravated the danger of the offence by the obstinate
maliciousness of her aspect and words. Such, however,
was Madame Ossoli's entire self-possession and forbear-
ance, that she was able to hold her ground, and to
remonstrate with this difficult pair of antagonists so
effectually, as to bring the maid to penitent tears, and
the Jewess to a confession of her injustice, and a
promise of future good behavior.

The porter of the house, who lived in a dark cavern-
ous hole on the first floor, was slowly dying of a con-
sumption, the sufferings of which were imbittered by
the chill dampness of his abode. His hollow voice and
hacking cough, however, could not veil the grateful
accent with which he uttered any allusion to Madame
Ossoli. He was so close a prisoner to his narrow,
windowless chamber, that when I inquired for Madame
Ossoli he was often obliged to call his little daughter,
before he could tell me whether Madame was at home,
or not; and he always tempered the official uniformity
of the question with some word of tenderness. Indeed,
he rarely pronounced her name; sufficiently indicating to
the child whom it was that I was seeking, by the affectionate epithet he used, "*Lita! e la cara Signora in casa?*"

The composure and force of Madame Ossoli's character would, indeed, have given her a strong influence for
good over any person with whom she was brought into

contact ; but this influence must have been even extraordinary over the impulsive and ill-disciplined children
of passion and of sorrow, among whom she was thrown
in Italy.

Her husband related to me once, with a most reverent enthusiasm, some stories of the good she had done.
in Rieti, during her residence there. The Spanish troops
were quartered in that town, and the dissipated habits
of the officers, as well as the excesses of the soldiery,
kept the place in a constant irritation. Though overwhelmed with cares and anxieties, Madame Ossoli found
time and collectedness of mind enough to interest herself in the distresses of the towns-people, and to pour
the soothing oil of a wise sympathy upon their wounded
and indignant feelings. On one occasion, as the Marchese told me, she undoubtedly saved the lives of a
family in Rieti, by inducing them to pass over in silence
an insult offered to one of them by an intoxicated Spanish soldier, — and, on another, she interfered between
two brothers, maddened by passion, and threatening to
stain the family hearth with the guilt of fratricide.*

---

* The circumstances of this story, perhaps, deserve to be recorded.
The brothers were two young men, the sons and the chief supports of
Madame Ossoli's landlord at Rieti. They were both married, — the
younger one to a beautiful girl, who had brought him no dowry, and
who, in the opinion of her husband's family, had not shown a proper
disposition to bear her share of the domestic burdens and duties. The
bickerings and disputes which resulted from this state of affairs, on one
unlucky day, took the form of an open and violent quarrel. The younger
son, who was absent from home when the conflict began, returned to find
it at its height, and was received by his wife with passionate tears,
and by his relations with sharp recriminations. His brother, especially,
took it upon himself to upbraid him, in the name of all his family, for
bringing into their home-circle such a firebrand of discord. Charges and
counter charges followed in rapid succession, and hasty words soon led to

Such incidents, and the calm tenor of Madame Ossoli's confident hopes, — the assured faith and unshaken bravery, with which she met and turned aside the complicated troubles, rising sometimes into absolute perils, of their last year in Italy, — seemed to have inspired her husband with a feeling of respect for her, amounting to reverence This feeling, modifying the manifest tenderness with which he hung upon her every word and look, and sought to anticipate her simplest wishes, was luminously visible in the air and manner of his affectionate devotion to her.

The frank and simple recognition of his wife's singular nobleness, which he always displayed, was the best evidence that his own nature was of a fine and noble strain. And those who knew him best, are, I believe, unanimous in testifying that his character did in no respect belie the evidence borne by his manly and truthful countenance, to its warmth and its sincerity. He

blows. From blows the appeal to the knife was swiftly made, and when Madame Ossoli, attracted by the unusual clamor, entered upon the scene of action, she found that blood had been already drawn, and that the younger brother was only restrained from following up the first assault by the united force of all the females, who hung about him, while the older brother, grasping a heavy billet of wood, and pale with rage, stood awaiting his antagonist. Passing through the group of weeping and terrified women, Madame Ossoli made her way up to the younger brother and, laying her hand upon his shoulder, asked him to put down his weapon and listen to her. It was in vain that he attempted to ignore her presence. Before the spell of her calm, firm, well-known voice, his fury melted away. She spoke to him again, and besought him to show himself a man, and to master his foolish and wicked rage. With a sudden impulse, he flung his knife upon the ground, turned to Madame Ossoli, clasped and kissed her hand, and then running towards his brother, the two met in a fraternal embrace, which brought the threatened tragedy to a joyful termination.

seemed quite absorbed in his wife and child. I cannot
remember ever to have found Madame Ossoli alone, on
those evenings when she remained at home. Her husband was always with her. The picture of their room
rises clearly on my memory. A small square room,
sparingly, yet sufficiently furnished, with polished floor
and frescoed ceiling, — and, drawn up closely before the
cheerful fire, an oval table, on which stood a monkish
lamp of brass, with depending chains that support quaint
classic cups for the olive oil. There, seated beside his
wife, I was sure to find the Marchese, reading from
some patriotic book, and dressed in the dark brown,
red-corded coat of the Guardia Civica, which it was
his melancholy pleasure to wear at home. So long
as the conversation could be carried on in Italian, he
used to remain, though he rarely joined in it to any
considerable degree; but if a number of English and
American visitors came in, he used to take his leave and
go to the Café d'Italia, being very unwilling, as Madame Ossoli told me, to impose any seeming restraint, by
his presence, upon her friends, with whom he was unable to converse. For the same reason, he rarely remained
with her at the houses of her English or American
friends, though he always accompanied her thither, and
returned to escort her home.

I conversed with him so little that I can hardly venture to make any remarks on the impression which I
received from his conversation, with regard to the character of his mind. Notwithstanding his general reserve
and curtness of speech, on two or three occasions he
showed himself to possess quite a quick and vivid fancy,
and even a certain share of humor. I have heard him
tell stories remarkably well. One tale, especially, which

related to a dream he had in early life, about a treasure concealed in his father's house, which was thrice repeated, and made so strong an impression on his mind as to induce him to batter a certain panel in the library almost to pieces, in vain, but which received something like a confirmation from the fact, that a Roman attorney, who rented that and other rooms from the family, after his father's death, grew suddenly and unaccountably rich, — I remember as being told with great felicity and vivacity of expression.

His recollections of the trouble and the dangers through which he had passed with his wife seemed to be overpoweringly painful. On one occasion, he began to tell me a story of their stay in the mountains : He had gone out to walk, and had unconsciously crossed the Neapolitan frontier. Suddenly meeting with a party of the Neapolitan *gendarmerie*, he was called to account for his trespass, and being unable to produce any papers testifying to his loyalty, or the legality of his existence, he was carried off, despite his protestations, and lodged for the night in a miserable guard-house, whence he was taken, next morning, to the head-quarters of the officer commanding in the neighborhood. Here, matters might have gone badly with him, but for the accident that he had upon his person a business letter directed to himself as the Marchese Ossoli. A certain abbé, the regimental chaplain, having once spent some time in Rome, recognized the name as that of an officer in the Pope's Guardia Nobile,* whereupon, the Neapolitan officers not only ordered him to be released, but sent him back, with

---

* It will be understood, that this officer was the Marchese's older brother, who still adheres to the Papal cause.

many apologies, in a carriage, and under an armed escort, to the Roman territory. When he reached this part of his story, and came to his meeting with Madame Ossoli, the remembrance of her terrible distress during the period of his detention so overcame him, that he was quite unable to go on.

Towards their child he manifested an overflowing tenderness, and most affectionate care.

Notwithstanding the intense contempt and hatred which Signore Ossoli, in common with all the Italian liberals, cherished towards the ecclesiastical body, he seemed to be a very devout Catholic. He used to attend regularly the vesper service, in some of the older and quieter churches of Florence; and, though I presume Madame Ossoli never accepted in any degree the Roman Catholic forms of faith, she frequently accompanied him on these occasions. And I know that she enjoyed the devotional influences of the church ritual, as performed in the cathedral, and at Santa Croce, especially during the Easter-week.

Though condemned by her somewhat uncertain position at Florence,* as well as by the state of things in Tuscany at that time, to a comparative inaction, Madame Ossoli never seemed to lose in the least the warmth of her interest in the affairs of Italy, nor did she bate one jot of heart or hope for the future of that country. She was much depressed, however, I think, by the apparent apathy and prostration of the Liberals in Tuscany; and the presence of the Austrian troops in Florence was as painful and annoying to her, as it could have been to any Florentine patriot. When it was understood that

---

* She believed herself to be, and I suppose really was, under the surveillance of the police during her residence in Florence.

Prince Lichtenstein had requested the Grand Duke to order a general illumination in honor of the anniversary of the battle of Novara, Madame Ossoli, I recollect, was more moved, than I remember on any other occasion to have seen her. And she used to speak very regretfully of the change which had come over the spirit of Florence, since her former residence there. Then all was gayety and hope. Bodies of artisans, gathering recruits as they passed along, used to form themselves into choral bands, as they returned from their work at the close of the day, and filled the air with the chants of liberty. Now, all was a sombre and desolate silence.

Her own various cares so occupied Madame Ossoli that she seemed to be very much withdrawn from the world of art. During the whole time of my stay in Florence, I do not think she once visited either of the Grand Ducal Galleries, and the only studio in which she seemed to feel any very strong interest, was that of Mademoiselle Favand, a lady whose independence of character, self-reliance, and courageous genius, could hardly have failed to attract her congenial sympathies.

But among all my remembrances of Madame Ossoli, there are none more beautiful or more enduring than those which recall to me another person, a young stranger, alone and in feeble health, who found, in her society, her sympathy, and her counsels, a constant atmosphere of comfort and of peace. Every morning, wild-flowers, freshly gathered, were laid upon her table by the grateful hands of this young man; every evening, beside her seat in her little room, his mild, pure face was to be seen, bright with a quiet happiness, that must have bound his heart by no weak ties to her with whose fate his own was so closely to be linked.

And the recollection of such benign and holy influences breathed upon the human hearts of those who
came within her sphere, will not, I trust, be valueless to
those friends, in whose love her memory is enshrined with
more immortal honors than the world can give or take
away.

HOMEWARD.

BY W. H. CHANNING.

Last, having thus revealed all I could love
And having received all love bestowed on it,
I would die : so preserving through my course
God full on me, as I was full on men :
And He would grant my prayer — " I have gone through
All loveliness of life ; make more for me,
If not for men, — or take me to Thyself,
Eternal, Infinite Love ! "

BROWNING.

Till another open for me
In God's Eden-land unknown,
With an angel at the doorway,
White with gazing at His Throne ;
And a saint's voice in the palm-trees, singing, — "ALL IS LOST, and *won*.'

ELIZABETH BARRETT.

Là ne venimmo : e lo scaglión **primaio**
  Biánco marmo éra sì pulito e terso,
  Ch 'io mi specchiava in esso, qual io **paie.**
Era 'l secondo tinto, più che pérso,
  D'una petrína rúvida ed arsiccia,
  Crepata per lo lungo e per traverso.
Lo terzo, che di sopra s'ammassiccia,
  Pórfido mi parea sì fiammegiánte,
  Come sangue che fuor di vena spiccia.
Sopra questa teneva ambo le piante
  L' angel di Dio, sedendo in su la sóglia,
  Che mi sembiava pietra di diamante.
Per li tre gradi su di buona voglia
  Mi trasse 'l duca mio, dicendo, chiédi
  Umilmente che 'l serráme scioglia.

DANTE.

Che luce è questa, e qual nuova beltate?
  Dicean tra lor ; perch' abito sì adorno
  Dal mondo errante a quest 'alto soggiorno
  Non salì mai in tutta questa etàte.
Ella contenta aver cangiato albergo,
  Si paragona pur coi più perfetti.

PETRARCA.

IX.

HOMEWARD.

SPRING-TIME.

SPRING, bright prophet of God's eternal youth, herald
forever eloquent of heaven's undying joy, has once more
wrought its miracle of resurrection on the vineyards and
olive-groves of Tuscany, and touched with gently-
wakening fingers the myrtle and the orange in the
gardens of Florence. The Apennines have put aside
their snowy winding-sheet, and their untroubled faces
salute with rosy gleams of promise the new day, while
flowers smile upward to the serene sky amid the grass
and grain fields, and fruit is swelling beneath the blossoms along the plains of Arno. "The Italian spring,"
writes Margaret, "is as good as Paradise. Days come
of glorious sunshine and gently-flowing airs, that expand
the heart and uplift the whole nature. The birds are
twittering their first notes of love; the ground is enamelled with anemones, cowslips, and crocuses; every
old wall and ruin puts on its festoon and garland; and
the heavens stoop daily nearer, till the earth is folded in
an embrace of ight and her every pulse beats music."

"This world is indeed a sad place, despite its sunshine, birds, and crocuses. But I never felt as happy as now, when I always find the glad eyes of my little boy to welcome me. I feel the tie between him and me so real and deep-rooted, that even death shall not part us. So sweet is this unimpassioned love; it knows no dark reäctions, it does not idealize, and cannot be daunted by the faults of its object. Nothing but a child can take the worst bitterness out of life, and break the spell of loneliness. I shall not be alone in other worlds, whenever Eternity may call me."

And now her face is turned homeward. "I am homesick," she had written years before, "but where is that HOME?"

OMENS.

"My heart is very tired, — my strength is low, —
My hands are full of blossoms plucked before,
Held dead within them till myself shall die."

ELIZABETH BARRETT.

Many motives drew Margaret to her native land: heart-weariness at the reäction in Europe; desire of publishing to best advantage the book whereby she hoped at once to do justice to great principles and brave men, and to earn bread for her dear ones and herself; and, above all, yearning to be again among her family and earliest associates. "I go back," she writes, "prepared for difficulties; but it will be a consolation to be with my mother, brothers, sister, and old friends, and I find it imperatively necessary to be in the United States, for a while at least, to make such arrangements with the printers as may free me from immediate care. I did think, at one time, of coming alone with Angelino, and then writing for Ossoli to come later, or returning to Italy; knowing that it will be painful for him to go, and that there he must have many lonely hours. But he is separated from his old employments and natural companions, while no career is open for him at present. Then, I would not take his child away for several months; for his heart is fixed upon him as fervently as mine. And, again, it would not only be very strange and sad to be so long without his love and care, but I should be continually solicitous about his welfare. Ossoli, indeed, cannot but feel solitary at first, and I am much more anxious about his happiness than my own. Still, he will have our boy, and the love of my family, especially of my mother, to cheer him, and quiet communings with nature give him pleasure so simple and profound, that I hope he will make a new life for himself, in our unknown country, till changes favor our return to his own. I trust, that we shall find the means to come together, and to remain together."

Considerations of economy determined them, spite of many misgivings, to take passage in a merchantman from Leghorn. "I am suffering," she writes, "as never before, from the horrors of indecision. Happy the fowls of the air, who do not have to think so much about their arrangements! The barque *Elizabeth* will take us, and is said to be an uncommonly good vessel, nearly new, and well kept. We may be two months at sea, but to go by way of France would more than double the expense. Yet, now that I am on the point of deciding to come in her, people daily dissuade me, saying that I have no conception of what a voyage of sixty or seventy days will be in point of fatigue and suffering; that the

insecurity, compared with packet-ships or steamers, is
great; that the cabin, being on deck, will be terribly
exposed, in case of a gale, &c., &c. I am well aware of
the proneness of volunteer counsellors to frighten and
excite one, and have generally disregarded them. But
this time I feel a trembling solicitude on account of my
child, and am doubtful, harassed, almost ill." And
again, under date of April 21, she says: "I had intended,
if I went by way of France, to take the packet-ship
'*Argo*,' from Havre; and I had requested Mrs. —— to
procure and forward to me some of my effects left at
Paris, in charge of Miss F——, when, taking up *Galig-
nani*, my eye fell on these words: 'Died, 4th of April,
Miss F——;' and, turning the page, I read, 'The wreck
of the *Argo*,' — a somewhat singular combination!
There were notices, also, of the loss of the fine English
steamer *Adelaide*, and of the American packet *John
Skiddy*. Safety is not to be secured, then, by the wisest
foresight. I shall embark more composedly in our
merchant-ship, praying fervently, indeed, that it may
not be my lot to lose my boy at sea, either by unsolaced
illness, or amid the howling waves; or, if so, that Ossoli,
Angelo, and I may go together, and that the anguish
may be brief."

Their state-rooms were taken, their trunks packed,
their preparations finished, they were just leaving Florence, when letters came, which, had they reached her a
week earlier, would probably have induced them to
remain in Italy. But Margaret had already by letter
appointed a rendezvous for the scattered members of her
family in July; and she would not break her engagements with the commander of the barque. It was destined that they were to sail, — to sail in the *Elizabeth*, to

sail then. And, even in the hour of parting, clouds, whose tops were golden in the sunshine, whose base was gloomy on the waters, beckoned them onward. "Beware of the sea," had been a singular prophecy, given to Ossoli when a boy, by a fortune-teller, and this was the first ship he had ever set his foot on. More than ordinary apprehensions of risk, too, hovered before Margaret. "I am absurdly fearful," she writes, "and various omens have combined to give me a dark feeling. I am become indeed a miserable coward, for the sake of Angelino. I fear heat and cold, fear the voyage, fear biting poverty. I hope I shall not be forced to be as brave for him, as I have been for myself, and that, if I succeed to rear him, he will be neither a weak nor a bad man. But I love him too much! In case of mishap, however, I shall perish with my husband and my child, and we may be transferred to some happier state." And again: "I feel perfectly willing to stay my threescore years and ten, if it be thought I need so much tuition from this planet; but it seems to me that my future upon earth will soon close. It may be terribly trying, but it will not be so very long, now. God will transplant the root, if he wills to rear it into fruit-bearing." And, finally: "I have a vague expectation of some crisis, — I know not what. But it has long seemed, that, in the year 1850, I should stand on a plateau in the ascent of life, where I should be allowed to pause for a while, and take more clear and commanding views than ever before. Yet my life proceeds as regularly as the fates of a Greek tragedy, and I can but accept the pages as they turn." * *

These were her parting words: —

"*Florence, May* 14, 1850. — I will believe, I shall be

welcome with my treasures, — my husband and child.
For me, I long so much to see you! Should anything
hinder our meeting upon earth, think of your daughter,
as one who always wished, at least, to do her duty, and
who always cherished you, according as her mind opened
to discover excellence.

"Give dear love, too, to my brothers; and first to my
eldest, faithful friend! Eugene;* a sister's love to Ellen;
love to my kind and good aunts, and to my dear cousin.
E., — God bless them!

"I hope we shall be able to pass some time together
yet, in this world. But, if God decrees otherwise, —
here and HEREAFTER, — my dearest mother,

"Your loving child, MARGARET."

THE VOYAGE.†

The seventeenth of May, the day of sailing, came, and
the *Elizabeth* lay waiting for her company. Yet, even
then, dark presentiments so overshadowed Margaret, that
she passed one anxious hour more in hesitation, before
she could resolve to go on board. But Captain Hasty
was so fine a model of the New England seaman, strong-
minded, prompt, calm, decided, courteous; Mrs. Hasty
was so refined, gentle, and hospitable; both had already
formed so warm an attachment for the little family, in
their few interviews at Florence and Leghorn; Celeste
Paolini, a young Italian girl, who had engaged to render
kindly services to Angelino, was so lady-like and pleasing; their only other fellow-passenger, Mr. Horace Sum-

---

* See Appendix C, at end of Vol. I.—A. B. F.

† The following account is as accurate, even in minute details, as conversation with several of the survivors enabled me to make it.—W. H. C.

ner, of Boston, was so obliging and agreeab.e a friend;
and the good ship herself looked so trim, substantial, and
cheery, that it seemed weak and wrong to turn back.
They embarked; and, for the first few days, all went
prosperously, till fear was forgotten. Soft breezes sweep
them tranquilly over the smooth bosom of the Mediterra-
nean; Angelino sits among his heaps of toys, or listens
to the seraphine, or leans his head with fondling hands
upon the white goat, who is now to be his foster-parent,
or in the captain's arms moves to and fro, gazing curiously at spars and rigging, or watches with delight the
swelling canvass; while, under the constant stars, above
the unresting sea, Margaret and Ossoli pace the deck of
their small ocean-home, and think of storms left behind,
— perhaps of coming tempests.

But now Captain Hasty fell ill with fever, could
hardly drag himself from his state-room to give necessary
orders, and lay upon the bed or sofa, in fast-increased
distress, though glad to bid Nino good-day, to kiss his
cheek, and pat his hand. Still, the strong man grew
weaker, till he could no longer draw from beneath the
pillow his daily friend, the Bible, though his mind was
yet clear to follow his wife's voice, as she read aloud the
morning and evening chapter. But alas for the brave,
stout seaman! alas for the young wife, on almost her
first voyage! alas for crew! alas for company! alas for
the friends of Margaret! The fever proved to be con-
fluent small-pox, in the most malignant form. The good
commander had received his release from earthly duty.
The *Elizabeth* must lose her guardian. With calm confidence, he met his fate, and, at eight o'clock on Sunday
morning, June 3d, he breathed his last. At midnight,
the *Elizabeth* had anchored off Gibraltar; but the

authorities refused permission for any one to land, and directed that the burial should be made at sea. As the news spread through the port, the ships dropped their flags half-mast, and at sunset, towed by the boat of a neighboring frigate, the crew of the *Elizabeth* bore the body of their late chief, wrapped in the flag of his nation, to its rest in deep water. Golden twilight flooded the western sky, and shadows of high-piled clouds lay purple on the broad Atlantic. In that calm, summer sunset funeral, what eye foresaw the morning of horror, of which it was the sad forerunner?

At Gibraltar, they were detained a week by adverse winds, but, on the 9th of June, set sail again. The second day after, Angelino sickened with the dreadful malady, and soon became so ill, that his life was despaired of. His eyes were closed, his head and face swollen out of shape, his body covered with eruption. Though inexperienced in the disease, the parents wisely treated their boy with cooling drinks, and wet applications to the skin; under their incessant care, the fever abated, and, to their unspeakable joy, he rapidly recovered. Sobered and saddened, they could again hope, and enjoy the beauty of the calm sky and sea. Once more Nino laughs, as he splashes in his morning bath, and playfully prolongs the meal, which the careful father has prepared with his own hand, or, if he has been angered, rests his head upon his mother's breast, while his palm is pressed against her cheek, as, bending down, she sings to him; once more, he sits among his toys, or fondles and plays with the white-haired goat, or walks up and down in the arms of the steward, who has a boy of just his age, at home, now waiting to embrace him; or among the sailors, with whom he is a universal favorite, prattles in baby dialect as he tries to imitate their cry, to work the pumps, and pull the ropes. Ossoli and Sumner, meanwhile, exchange alternate lessons in Italian and English. And Margaret, among her papers, gives the last touches to her book on Italy, or with words of hope and love comforts like a mother the heart-broken widow. Slowly, yet peacefully, pass the long summer days, the mellow moonlit nights; slowly, and with even flight, the good Elizabeth, under gentle airs from the tropics, bears them safely onward. Four thousand miles of ocean lie behind; they are nearly home.

THE WRECK.

" There are blind ways provided, the foredone
Heart-weary player in this pageant world
Drops out by, letting the main masque defile
By the conspicuous portal : — I am through,
Just through."   BROWNING.

On Thursday, July 18th, at noon, the Elizabeth was off the Jersey coast, somewhere between Cape May and Barnegat; and, as the weather was thick, with a fresh breeze blowing from the east of south, the officer in command, desirous to secure a good offing, stood east-north-east. His purpose was, when daylight showed the highlands of Neversink, to take a pilot, and run before the wind past Sandy Hook. So confident, indeed, was he of safety, that he promised his passengers to land them early in the morning at New York. With this hope, their trunks were packed, the preparations made to greet their friends, the last good-night was spoken, and with grateful hearts Margaret and Ossoli put Nino to rest, for the last time, as they thought, on ship-board, — for the last time, as it was to be, on earth!

By nine o'clock, the breeze rose to a gale, which every hour increased in violence, till at midnight it became a hurricane. Yet, as the Elizabeth was new and strong, and as the commander, trusting to an occasional cast of the lead, assured them that they were not nearing the Jersey coast, — which alone he dreaded, — the passengers remained in their state-rooms, and caught such uneasy sleep as the howling storm and tossing ship permitted. Utterly unconscious, they were, even then, amidst perils, whence only by promptest energy was it possible to escape. Though under close-reefed sails, their vessel was making way far more swiftly than any one on board had dreamed of; and for hours, with the combined force of currents and the tempest, had been driving headlong towards the sand-bars of Long Island. About four o'clock, on Friday morning, July 19th, she struck, — first draggingly, then hard and harder,—on Fire Island beach.

The main and mizzen masts were at once cut away; but the heavy marble in her hold had broken through her bottom, and she bilged. Her bow held fast, her stern swung round, she careened inland, her broadside was bared to the shock of the billows, and the waves made a clear breach over her with every swell. The doom of the poor Elizabeth was sealed now, and no human power could save her. She lay at the mercy of the maddened ocean.

At the first jar, the passengers, knowing but too well its fatal import, sprang from their berths. Then came the cry of "Cut away," followed by the crash of falling timbers, and the thunder of the seas, as they broke across the deck. In a moment more, the cabin skylight was dashed in pieces by the breakers, and the spray, pouring down like a cataract, put out the lights, while the cabin door was wrenched from its fastenings, and the waves swept in and out. One scream, one only, was heard from Margaret's state-room; and Sumner and Mrs. Hasty, meeting in the cabin, clasped hands, with these few but touching words : " We must die." " Let us die calmly, then." "I hope so, Mrs. Hasty." It was in the gray dusk, and amid the awful tumult, that the companions in misfortune met. The side of the cabin to the leeward had already settled under water ; and furniture, trunks, and fragments of the skylight were floating to and fro ; while the inclined position of the floor made it difficult to stand ; and every sea, as it broke over the bulwarks, splashed in through the open roof. The windward cabin-walls, however, still yielded partial shelter, and against it, seated side by side, half leaning backwards, with feet braced upon the long table, they awaited what next should come. At first, Nino, alarmed at the uproar, the darkness, and the rushing water, while shivering with the wet, cried passionately ; but soon his mother, wrapping him in such garments as were at hand and folding him to her bosom, sang him to sleep. Celeste too was in an agony of terror, till Ossoli, with soothing words and a long and fervent prayer, restored her to self-control and trust. Then calmly they rested, side by side, exchanging kindly partings and sending messages to friends, if any should survive to be their bearer. Meanwhile, the boats having been swamped or carried away, and the carpenter's tools washed overboard, the crew had retreated to the top-gallant forecastle ; but, as the passengers saw and heard nothing of them, they supposed that the officers and crew had deserted the ship, and that they were left alone.   Thus passed three hours.

At length, about seven, as there were signs that the cabin would soon break up, and any death seemed preferable to that of being crushed among the ruins, Mrs. Hasty made her way to the door, and, looking out at intervals between the seas as they swept across the vessel amidships, saw some one standing by the foremast. His face was toward the shore.   She screamed and beckoned, but her voice was lost amid the roar of the wind and breakers, and her gestures were unnoticed. Soon, however, Davis, the mate, through the door of the forecastle caught sight of her, and, at once comprehending the danger, summoned the men to go to the rescue. At first none dared to risk with him the perilous attempt; but, cool and resolute, he set forth by himself, and now holding to the bulwarks, now stooping as the waves combed over, he succeeded in reaching the cabin.   Two sailors, emboldened by his example, followed.   Preparations were instantly made to conduct the passengers to the forecastle, which, as being more strongly built and lying further up the sands, was the least exposed part of the ship.   Mrs. Hasty volunteered to go the first.   With one hand clasped by Davis, while with the other each grasped the rail, they started, a sailor moving close behind.   But hardly had they taken three steps, when a sea broke loose her hold, and swept her into the hatchway.   "Let me go," she cried, "your life is important to all on board."   But cheerily, and with a smile,* he answered, "Not quite yet;" and, seizing in his teeth her long hair, as it floated past him, he caught with both

---

* Mrs. Hasty's own words while describing the incident.

nands at some near support, and, aided by the seaman,
set her once again upon her feet. A few moments more
of struggle brought them safely through. In turn, each
of the passengers was helped thus laboriously across the
deck, though, as the broken rail and cordage had at one
place fallen in the way, the passage was dangerous and
difficult in the extreme. Angelino was borne in a
canvas bag, slung round the neck of a sailor. Within
the forecastle, which was comparatively dry and sheltered, they now seated themselves, and, wrapped in the
loose overcoats of the seamen, regained some warmth.
Three times more, however, the mate made his way to
the cabin; once, to save her late husband's watch, for
Mrs. Hasty; again for some doubloons, money-drafts, and
rings in Margaret's desk; and, finally, to procure a bottle
of wine and a drum of figs for their refreshment. It was
after his last return, that Margaret said to Mrs. Hasty,
"There still remains what, if I live, will be of more
value to me than anything," referring, probably, to her
manuscript on Italy; but it seemed too selfish to ask
their brave preserver to run the risk again.

There was opportunity now to learn their situation,
and to discuss the chances of escape. At the distance of
only a few hundred yards, appeared the shore, — a lonely
waste of sand-hills, so far as could be seen through the
spray and driving rain. But men had been early observed, gazing at the wreck, and, later, a wagon had been
drawn upon the beach. There was no sign of a life-
boat, however, or of any attempt at rescue; and, about
nine o'clock, it was determined that some one should
try to land by swimming, and, if possible, get help
Though it seemed almost sure death to trust one's self
to the surf, a sailor, with a life-preserver, jumped over-

board, and, notwithstanding a current drifting him to leeward, was seen to reach the shore. A second, with the aid of a spar, followed in safety; and Sumner, encouraged by their success, sprang over also; but, either struck by some piece of the wreck, or unable to combat with the waves, he sank. Another hour or more passed by; but though persons were busy gathering into carts whatever spoil was stranded, no life-boat yet appeared; and, after much deliberation, the plan was proposed, — and, as it was then understood, agreed to, — that the passengers should attempt to land, each seated upon a plank, and grasping handles of rope, while a sailor swam behind. Here, too, Mrs. Hasty was the first to venture, under the guard of Davis. Once and again, during their passage, the plank was rolled wholly over, and once and again was righted, with its bearer, by the dauntless steersman; and when, at length, tossed by the surf upon the sands, the half-drowned woman still holding, as in a death-struggle, to the ropes, was about to be swept back by the undertow, he caught her in his arms, and, with the assistance of a bystander, placed her high upon the beach. Thus twice in one day had he perilled his own life to save that of the widow of his captain, and even over that dismal tragedy his devotedness casts one gleam of light.

Now came Margaret's turn. But she steadily refused to be separated from Ossoli and Angelo. On a raft with them, she would have boldly encountered the surf, but alone she would not go. Probably, she had appeared to assent to the plan for escaping upon planks, with the view of inducing Mrs. Hasty to trust herself to the care of the best man on board; very possibly, also, she had never learned the result of their attempt, as, seated within the forecastle, she could not see the beach. She knew, too, that if a life-boat could be sent, Davis was one who would neglect no effort to expedite its coming. While she was yet declining all persuasions, word was given from the deck, that the life-boat had finally appeared. For a moment, the news lighted up again the flickering fire of hope. They might yet be saved, — be saved together! Alas! to the experienced eyes of the sailors it too soon became evident that there was no attempt to launch or man her. The last chance of aid from shore, then, was gone utterly. They must rely on their own strength, or perish. And if ever they were to escape, the time had come; for, at noon, the storm had somewhat lulled; but already the tide had turned, and it was plain that the wreck could not hold together through another flood. In this emergency, the commanding officer, who until now had remained at his post, once more appealed to Margaret to try to escape, — urging that the ship would inevitably break up soon; that it was mere suicide to remain longer; that he did not feel free to sacrifice the lives of the crew, or to throw away his own; finally, that he would himself take Angelo, and that sailors should go with Celeste, Ossoli, and herself. But, as before, Margaret decisively declared that she would not be parted from her husband or her child. The order was then given to "save themselves," and all but four of the crew jumped over, several of whom, together with the commander, reached shore alive, though severely bruised and wounded by the drifting fragments. There is a sad consolation in believing that, if Margaret judged it to be impossible that the *three* should escape, she in all probability was right. It required a most rare combination of courage, promptness,

and persistency, to do what Davis had done for **Mrs.**
Hasty. We may not conjecture the crowd of thoughts
which influenced the lovers, the parents, in this awful
crisis; but doubtless one wish was ever uppermost, —
that, God willing, the last hour might come for ALL, if it
must come for *one*.

It was now past three o'clock, and as, with the rising
tide, the gale swelled once more to its former violence,
the remnants of the barque fast yielded to the resistless
waves. The cabin went by the board, the after-parts
broke up, and the stern settled out of sight. Soon, too,
the forecastle was filled with water, and the helpless
little band were driven to the deck, where they clustered
round the foremast. Presently, even this frail support
was loosened from the hull, and rose and fell with every
billow. It was plain to all that the final moment drew
swiftly nigh. Of the four seamen who still stood by the
passengers, three were as efficient as any among the
crew of the Elizabeth. These were the steward, carpenter, and cook. The fourth was an old sailor, who,
broken down by hardships and sickness, was going home
to die. These men were once again persuading Margaret, Ossoli and Celeste to try the planks, which they
held ready in the lee of the ship, and the steward, by
whom Nino was so much beloved, had just taken the
little fellow in his arms, with the pledge that he would
save him or die, when a sea struck the forecastle, and
the foremast fell, carrying with it the deck, and all upon
it. The steward and Angelino were washed upon the
beach, both dead, though warm, some twenty minutes
after. The cook and carpenter were thrown far upon
the foremast, and saved themselves by swimming.
Celeste and Ossoli caught for a moment by the rigging,

but the next wave swallowed them up. Margaret sank at once. When last seen, she had been seated at the foot of the foremast, still clad in her white night-dress, with her hair fallen loose upon her shoulders. It was over, — that twelve hours' communion, face to face, with Death! It was over! and the prayer was granted, "that Ossoli, Angelo, and I, may go together, and that the anguish may be brief!"

*   *   *   *   *   *

A passage from the journal of a friend of Margaret, whom the news of the wreck drew at once to the scene, shall close this mournful story : —

"The hull of the Elizabeth, with the foremast still bound to it by cordage, lies so near the shore, that it seems as if a dozen oar-strokes would carry a boat along-side. And as one looks at it glittering in the sunshine, and rocking gently in the swell, it is hard to feel recon-ciled to our loss. Seven resolute men might have saved every soul on board. I know how different was the prospect on that awful morning, when the most violent gale that had visited our coast for years, drove the bil-lows up to the very foot of the sand-hills, and when the sea in foaming torrents swept across the beach into the bay behind. Yet I cannot but reluctantly declare my judgment, that this terrible tragedy is to be attributed, so far as human agency is looked at, to our wretched system, or *no-system*, of life-boats. The life-boat at Fire Island light-house, three miles distant only, was not brought to the beach till between twelve and one o'clock, more than eight hours after the Elizabeth was stranded, and more than six hours after the wreck could easily have been seen. When the life-boat did finally

come, the beachmen could not be persuaded to launch
or man her. And even the mortar, by which a rope
could and should have been thrown on board, was not
once fired. A single lesson like this might certainly
suffice to teach the government, insurance companies,
and humane societies, the urgent need, that to every
life-boat should be attached ORGANIZED CREWS, stimulated
to do their work faithfully, by ample pay for actual service, generous salvage-fees for cargoes and persons, and
a pension to surviving friends where life is lost. * * *

" No trace has yet been found of Margaret's manuscript on Italy, though the denials of the wreckers as to
having seen it, are not in the least to be depended on.
For, greedy after richer spoil, they might well have
overlooked a mass of written paper; and, even had they
kept it, they would be slow to give up what would so
clearly prove their participation in the heartless robbery,
that is now exciting such universal horror and indignation. Possibly it was washed away before reaching the
shore, as several of the trunks, it is said, were open and
empty, when thrown upon the beach. But it is sad to
think, that very possibly the brutal hands of pirates
may have tossed to the winds, or scattered on the sands,
pages so rich with experience and life. The only papers
of value saved, were the love-letters of Margaret and
Ossoli.*

" It is a touching coincidence, that the only one of
Margaret's treasures which reached the shore, was the
lifeless form of Angelino. When the body, stripped of
every rag by the waves, was rescued from the surf, a
sailor took it reverently in his arms, and, wrapping it in

* The letters from which extracts were quoted in the previous chapter.

his neckcloth, bore it to the nearest house. There when washed, and dressed. in a child's frock, found in Margaret's trunk, it was laid upon a bed; and as the rescued seamen gathered round their late playfellow and pet, there were few dry eyes in the circle. Several of them mourned for Nino, as if he had been their own; and even the callous wreckers were softened, for the moment, by a sight so full of pathetic beauty. The next day, borne upon their shoulders in a chest, which one of the sailors gave for a coffin, it was buried in a hollow among the sand heaps. As I stood beside the lonely little mound, it seemed that never was seen a more affecting type of orphanage. Around, wiry and stiff, were scanty spires of beach-grass; near by, dwarf-cedars, blown flat by wintry winds, stood like grim guardians; only at the grave-head a stunted wild-rose, wilted and scraggy, was struggling for existence. Thoughts came of the desolate childhood of many a little one in this hard world; and there was joy in the assurance, that Angelo was neither motherless nor fatherless, and that Margaret and her husband were not childless in that New World, which so suddenly they had entered together.

"To-morrow, Margaret's mother, sister, and brothers will remove Nino's body to New England."

*   *   *   *   *

Was this, then, thy welcome home? A howling hurricane, the pitiless sea, wreck on a sand-bar, an idle life-boat, beach-pirates, and not one friend! In those twelve hours of agony, did the last scene appear but as the fitting close for a life of storms, where no safe haven was ever in reach; where thy richest treasures were so often stranded; where even the dearest and nearest seemed always too far off, or just too late, to help.

Ah, no! not so. The clouds were gloomy on the waters, truly; but their tops were golden in the sun. It was in the Father's House that welcome awaited thee.

> " Glory to God ! to God ! he saith,
> Knowledge by suffering entereth,
> And Life is perfected by Death."